THE PAPERS OF ULYSSES S. GRANT

THE PAPERS OF

ULYSSES S. GRANT

Volume 17: January 1 – September 30, 1867

Edited by John Y. Simon

ASSOCIATE EDITOR
David L. Wilson

ASSISTANT EDITOR
J. Thomas Murphy

EDITORIAL ASSISTANT
Sue E. Dotson

SOUTHERN ILLINOIS UNIVERSITY PRESS

CARBONDALE AND EDWARDSVILLE

Library of Congress Cataloging in Publication Data (Revised)

Grant, Ulysses Simpson, Pres. U.S., 1822–1885.
   The papers of Ulysses S. Grant.

   Prepared under the auspices of the Ulysses S. Grant Association.
   Bibliographical footnotes.
   CONTENTS: v. 1. 1837–1861—v. 2. April–September 1861.
—v. 3. October 1, 1861–January 7, 1862.—v. 4. January 8–March 31,
1862.—v. 5. April 1–August 31, 1862.—v. 6. September 1–Decem-
ber 8, 1862.—v. 7. December 9, 1862–March 31, 1863.—v. 8.
April 1–July 6, 1863.—v. 9. July 7–December 31, 1863.—v. 10.
January 1–May 31, 1864.—v. 11. June 1–August 15, 1864.—v. 12.
August 16–November 15, 1864.—v. 13. November 16, 1864–Feb-
ruary 20, 1865.—v. 14. February 21–April 30, 1865.—v. 15. May 1–
December 31, 1865.—v. 16. 1866.—v. 17. January 1–September 30,
1867.
   1. Grant, Ulysses Simpson, Pres. U.S., 1822–1885. 2. United
States—History—Civil War, 1861–1865—Campaigns and battles
—Sources. 3. United States—Politics and government—1869–1877
—Sources. 4. Presidents—United States—Biography. 5. Generals—
United States—Biography. I. Simon, John Y., ed. II. Wilson, David
L. 1943—. III. Ulysses S. Grant Association.
E660.G756   1967   973.8'2'0924   67–10725
ISBN 0–8093–1692–7 (v. 17)

To Sara Dunlap Jackson

Contents

Introduction

AS THE STRUGGLE between Congress and President Andrew Johnson over Reconstruction policy intensified in 1867, General Ulysses S. Grant grew increasingly uncomfortable in his position as general in chief. Within the administration, Secretary of War Edwin M. Stanton, Grant's immediate superior, favored congressional policies; within the army, presidential policies threatened the safety of troops in the South, white as well as black. Attempts by unreconstructed Southerners to regain political control led to recurrent disorder and violence, outbursts that triggered more indignation at army headquarters than in the White House.

In March, Congress took control through a series of measures, all involving Grant. The Reconstruction Act divided the ten unreconstructed states of the former Confederacy into five military districts, governed by officers directed to conduct elections for constitutional conventions and to supervise the process of creating new fundamental law under which new state governments would emerge that acknowledged the results of the war through ratifying the Fourteenth Amendment and implementing black suffrage. Essentially, Congress intended to turn the clock back two years to eliminate Johnson's Reconstruction policy.

To further Reconstruction goals, Congress required that all military orders pass through Grant, who could neither be removed nor reassigned; otherwise, military government might augment the powers of the commander in chief. Finally, Congress, through the Tenure of

Office Act, limited presidential power to remove cabinet officers, a measure designed to protect Stanton.

As a result, Congress enormously increased Grant's responsibilities by adding civil to military duties. To bypass Johnson, the five district commanders had considerable independence in implementing and enforcing the Reconstruction Act, although all looked to Grant for guidance. Thus Grant was thrown into the process of interpreting legislation and deciding matters of voter eligibility and election procedure. He could expect little assistance from the president or the attorney general. "I feel the same obligation," wrote Grant, "to stand at my post that I did whilst there were rebel armies in the field to contend with."

After Congress began a long adjournment in late July, Johnson challenged the constitutionality of the Tenure of Office Act by suspending Stanton and appointing Grant secretary of war *ad interim*. Johnson thought that he had the right case because he had inherited Stanton from a preceding administration rather than appointing him, and Stanton himself believed that the law was unconstitutional and, furthermore, did not apply to him. Johnson counted on Grant's great personal popularity to soften objections to Stanton's departure. Grant had no special fondness for Stanton, disliked vindictive as well as conservative approaches to Reconstruction, but wanted to avoid involvement with Johnson's policy. To refuse to serve, however, would imperil officers enforcing the law. Johnson had already indicated a desire to remove Major General Philip H. Sheridan, commanding the district embracing Louisiana and Texas. Aware that by entering the War Department he would shore up Johnson's popularity, Grant did so anyway, believing that the alternatives were worse. Almost as soon as Grant entered the cabinet, Johnson removed Sheridan.

Serving in the cabinet, however, changed relatively little in Grant's life. As general in chief, he continued to command officers in the South as well as those on the frontier. Holding two offices, he received more mail, although that directed to the secretary of war received less attention. It was less urgent than military matters, and, unlike Johnson, Grant believed that he held the War Department on only a temporary basis. Letters he signed as secretary of war *ad interim*, even when accompanied by the drafts prepared by War Department personnel, appear in this volume and the next. By signing these letters, Grant assumed responsibility and made them a part of his documentary record.

Much Grant correspondence in 1867 involved his St. Louis County farm, acreage purchased from his wife's family and designed as a retreat from the pressures of Washington. He never got near it all year. He vacationed, instead, at Long Branch, N.J., a seashore resort from which he could more speedily return to Washington. Comfortably settled there, he wrote that he was "nearly ready to desert." Instead, of course, he returned to increasingly onerous duties.

We are indebted to Sara Dunlap Jackson for assistance in searching the National Archives; to Harriet F. Simon for proofreading; and to Jacqueline Moore and Michael Smith, graduate students at Southern Illinois University, for research assistance.

Financial support for the period during which this volume was prepared came from Southern Illinois University, the National Endowment for the Humanities, and the National Historical Publications and Records Commission.

JOHN Y. SIMON

January 31, 1990

Editorial Procedure

1. *Editorial Insertions*

A. Words or letters in roman type within brackets represent editorial reconstruction of parts of manuscripts torn, mutilated, or illegible.

B. [. . .] or [— — —] within brackets represent lost material which cannot be reconstructed. The number of dots represents the approximate number of lost letters; dashes represent lost words.

C. Words in *italic* type within brackets represent material such as dates which were not part of the original manuscript.

D. Other material crossed out is indicated by ~~cancelled~~ type.

E. Material raised in manuscript, as "4th," has been brought in line, as "4th."

2. *Symbols Used to Describe Manuscripts*

AD	Autograph Document
ADS	Autograph Document Signed
ADf	Autograph Draft
ADfS	Autograph Draft Signed
AES	Autograph Endorsement Signed
AL	Autograph Letter
ALS	Autograph Letter Signed
ANS	Autograph Note Signed

D	Document
DS	Document Signed
Df	Draft
DfS	Draft Signed
ES	Endorsement Signed
LS	Letter Signed

3. Military Terms and Abbreviations

Act.	Acting
Adjt.	Adjutant
AG	Adjutant General
AGO	Adjutant General's Office
Art.	Artillery
Asst.	Assistant
Bvt.	Brevet
Brig.	Brigadier
Capt.	Captain
Cav.	Cavalry
Col.	Colonel
Co.	Company
C.S.A.	Confederate States of America
Dept.	Department
Div.	Division
Gen.	General
Hd. Qrs.	Headquarters
Inf.	Infantry
Lt.	Lieutenant
Maj.	Major
Q. M.	Quartermaster
Regt.	Regiment or regimental
Sgt.	Sergeant
USMA	United States Military Academy, West Point, N.Y.
Vols.	Volunteers

4. Short Titles and Abbreviations

ABPC	*American Book-Prices Current* (New York, 1895–)

CG	*Congressional Globe* Numbers following represent the Congress, session, and page.
J. G. Cramer	Jesse Grant Cramer, ed., *Letters of Ulysses S. Grant to his Father and his Youngest Sister, 1857–78* (New York and London, 1912)
DAB	*Dictionary of American Biography* (New York, 1928–36)
Garland	Hamlin Garland, *Ulysses S. Grant: His Life and Character* (New York, 1898)
HED	*House Executive Documents*
HMD	*House Miscellaneous Documents*
HRC	*House Reports of Committees* Numbers following *HED, HMD,* or *HRC* represent the number of the Congress, the session, and the document.
Ill. AG Report	J. N. Reece, ed., *Report of the Adjutant General of the State of Illinois* (Springfield, 1900)
Johnson, Papers	LeRoy P. Graf and Ralph W. Haskins, eds., *The Papers of Andrew Johnson* (Knoxville, 1967–)
Lewis	Lloyd Lewis, *Captain Sam Grant* (Boston, 1950)
Lincoln, Works	Roy P. Basler, Marion Dolores Pratt, and Lloyd A. Dunlap, eds., *The Collected Works of Abraham Lincoln* (New Brunswick, 1953–55)
Memoirs	*Personal Memoirs of U. S. Grant* (New York, 1885–86)
O.R.	*The War of the Rebellion: A Compilation of the Official Records of the Union and Confederate Armies* (Washington, 1880–1901)
O.R. (Navy)	*Official Records of the Union and Confederate Navies in the War of the Rebellion* (Washington, 1894–1927) Roman numerals following *O.R.* or *O.R.* (Navy) represent the series and the volume.
PUSG	John Y. Simon, ed., *The Papers of Ulysses S. Grant* (Carbondale and Edwardsville, 1967–)
Richardson	Albert D. Richardson, *A Personal History of Ulysses S. Grant* (Hartford, Conn., 1868)
SED	*Senate Executive Documents*
SMD	*Senate Miscellaneous Documents*
SRC	*Senate Reports of Committees* Numbers following

SED, SMD, or SRC represent the number of the Congress, the session, and the document.

USGA Newsletter   *Ulysses S. Grant Association Newsletter*

Young   John Russell Young, *Around the World with General Grant* (New York, 1879)

5. Location Symbols

CLU   University of California at Los Angeles, Los Angeles, Calif.

CoHi   Colorado State Historical Society, Denver, Colo.

CSmH   Henry E. Huntington Library, San Marino, Calif.

CSt   Stanford University, Stanford, Calif.

CtY   Yale University, New Haven, Conn.

CU-B   Bancroft Library, University of California, Berkeley, Calif.

DLC   Library of Congress, Washington, D.C. Numbers following DLC-USG represent the series and volume of military records in the USG papers.

DNA   National Archives, Washington, D.C. Additional numbers identify record groups.

IaHA   Iowa State Department of History and Archives, Des Moines, Iowa.

I-ar   Illinois State Archives, Springfield, Ill.

IC   Chicago Public Library, Chicago, Ill.

ICarbS   Southern Illinois University, Carbondale, Ill.

ICHi   Chicago Historical Society, Chicago, Ill.

ICN   Newberry Library, Chicago, Ill.

ICU   University of Chicago, Chicago, Ill.

IHi   Illinois State Historical Library, Springfield, Ill.

In   Indiana State Library, Indianapolis, Ind.

InFtwL   Lincoln National Life Foundation, Fort Wayne, Ind.

InHi   Indiana Historical Society, Indianapolis, Ind.

InNd   University of Notre Dame, Notre Dame, Ind.

InU   Indiana University, Bloomington, Ind.

KHi   Kansas State Historical Society, Topeka, Kan.

MdAN   United States Naval Academy Museum, Annapolis, Md.

MeB	Bowdoin College, Brunswick, Me.
MH	Harvard University, Cambridge, Mass.
MHi	Massachusetts Historical Society, Boston, Mass.
MiD	Detroit Public Library, Detroit, Mich.
MiU-C	William L. Clements Library, University of Michigan, Ann Arbor, Mich.
MoSHi	Missouri Historical Society, St. Louis, Mo.
NHi	New-York Historical Society, New York, N.Y.
NIC	Cornell University, Ithaca, N.Y.
NjP	Princeton University, Princeton, N.J.
NjR	Rutgers University, New Brunswick, N.J.
NN	New York Public Library, New York, N.Y.
NNP	Pierpont Morgan Library, New York, N.Y.
NRU	University of Rochester, Rochester, N.Y.
OClWHi	Western Reserve Historical Society, Cleveland, Ohio.
OFH	Rutherford B. Hayes Library, Fremont, Ohio.
OHi	Ohio Historical Society, Columbus, Ohio.
OrHi	Oregon Historical Society, Portland, Ore.
PCarlA	U.S. Army Military History Institute, Carlisle Barracks, Pa.
PHi	Historical Society of Pennsylvania, Philadelphia, Pa.
PPRF	Rosenbach Foundation, Philadelphia, Pa.
RPB	Brown University, Providence, R.I.
TxHR	Rice University, Houston, Tex.
USG 3	Maj. Gen. Ulysses S. Grant 3rd, Clinton, N.Y.
USMA	United States Military Academy Library, West Point, N.Y.
ViHi	Virginia Historical Society, Richmond, Va.
ViU	University of Virginia, Charlottesville, Va.
WHi	State Historical Society of Wisconsin, Madison, Wis.
Wy-Ar	Wyoming State Archives and Historical Department, Cheyenne, Wyo.
WyU	University of Wyoming, Laramie, Wyo.

Chronology

JAN. 4.   At a cabinet meeting, USG agreed with President Andrew Johnson's decision to veto a D.C. suffrage bill that enfranchised blacks and disfranchised disloyal men.

JAN. 14.   USG inquired about the investigation of the military disaster at Fort Phil Kearny, Dakota Territory.

JAN. 15.   USG commented favorably on a proposal of Lieutenant General William T. Sherman to keep Indians north of the Platte River, south of the Arkansas River.

JAN. 29.   USG recommended the imposition of martial law in Tex.

FEB. 1.   USG renewed his recommendation that the Bureau of Indian Affairs be transferred from the Dept. of the Interior to the War Dept.

FEB. 8.   USG reported violations of the Civil Rights Act in the South.

FEB. 8.   USG attended a meeting of the trustees of the Peabody Education Fund.

MAR. 2.   By the Tenure of Office Act, Congress limited Johnson's power to remove civilian officials, seeking to protect Secretary of War Edwin M. Stanton. Legislation of the same day required that military orders be issued by USG as gen. in chief, and protected him from removal or reassignment.

MAR. 2.   Congress passed legislation, later known as the First Reconstruction Act, dividing ten former C.S.A. states (excluding Tenn.) into five military districts commanded by officers directed to call conventions to write new constitutions.

MAR. 4.   Congress passed the First Reconstruction Act over Johnson's veto. USG considered the veto message "ridiculous."

Mar. 11.   After consultation with Johnson, USG appointed commanders for the military districts: First (Va.), Bvt. Maj. Gen. John M. Schofield; Second (N.C. and S.C.), Maj. Gen. Daniel E. Sickles; Third (Ala., Ga., and Fla.), Maj. Gen. George H. Thomas; Fourth (Ark. and Miss.), Bvt. Maj. Gen. Edward O. C. Ord; Fifth (La. and Tex.), Maj. Gen. Philip H. Sheridan.

Mar. 15.   When Thomas objected to this new assignment, USG left him in command of the Dept. of the Cumberland and assigned Bvt. Maj. Gen. John Pope to command the Third Military District. On April 1, Pope assumed command at Montgomery, Ala.

Mar. 19.   In New York City, USG attended a meeting of the Peabody trustees.

Mar. 23.   Second Reconstruction Act extended power of military governors to supervise state election processes.

Mar. 24.   USG wrote a friend that he had "given up the idea of going to Mo. this spring."

April 5.   USG cautioned Sheridan about removing government officials lest he himself be removed. On the same day, however, USG wrote that Sheridan "makes no mistakes."

April 27.   USG's forty-fifth birthday.

April 29.   USG returned from a "very pleasant week" in Philadelphia.

April 29.   USG expressed good wishes for reestablishment of the College of William and Mary.

May 29.   USG made plans to take possession of Alaska.

June 7.   USG commented on Sheridan's removal of Governor J. Madison Wells of La.

June 17.   USG presented diplomas to graduates at West Point.

June 19.   Execution of the Emperor Maximilian marked the final chapter of the French occupation of Mexico.

June 20.   USG arrived at Gettysburg and toured the battlefield the next morning.

June 26.   USG testified briefly at the trial of John H. Surratt, charged as a conspirator in the assassination of President Abraham Lincoln.

July 11.   USG at West Point.

July 18.   USG testified before the Judiciary Committee, U.S. House of Representatives, then considering the impeachment of Johnson. USG testified again on July 20.

JULY 19. Third Reconstruction Act affirmed the independence of military district commanders from executive control.

JULY 20. USG left Washington for New York City, on his way to Long Branch, N.J.

JULY 22. Stanton ordered USG to Nashville, Thomas to Memphis, to prevent anticipated violence at elections. On July 23, USG responded that he saw "no need" to go to Nashville.

JULY 25. USG recommended that Sherman, Maj. Gen. Winfield S. Hancock, and Bvt. Maj. Gen. Alfred H. Terry represent the army among the commissioners negotiating with Indians.

AUG. 1. USG urged Johnson not to remove Stanton.

AUG. 5. Johnson asked Stanton to resign, and Stanton refused.

AUG. 11. USG visited Stanton at home to inform him that he would be suspended the next day.

AUG. 12. Johnson suspended Stanton from office and appointed USG secretary of war *ad interim*.

AUG. 12. USG made further plans for the transfer of Alaska.

AUG. 17. In response to Johnson's orders, USG assigned Thomas to command the Fifth Military District, Sheridan to command the Dept. of the Mo., and Hancock to command the Dept. of the Cumberland.

AUG. 21. USG sent nurses to New Orleans in response to a yellow fever epidemic.

AUG. 26. Johnson issued orders replacing Sickles in command of the Second Military District with Bvt. Maj. Gen. Edward R. S. Canby, who assumed command on Sept. 5.

AUG. 26. Johnson ordered Sheridan removed from the Fifth Military District. Hancock replaced him because Thomas's health prevented him from taking the assignment.

SEPT. 13. USG recommended against reopening the case of Fitz John Porter.

SEPT. 16. With Hancock's arrival in New Orleans delayed by the yellow fever epidemic, Bvt. Maj. Gen. Joseph A. Mower assumed temporary command of the Fifth Military District.

The Papers of Ulysses S. Grant
January 1–September 30, 1867

To Henry Stanbery

———

Washington, D. C. Jan. 4th *1867*.

DEAR SIR:

Col. R. W. Healy,[1] who served with credit in the Union Army during the rebellion, has since become a resident of Ala. He is now an applicant for the office of United States Marshal for the Middle District of that state.

It has not been my habit to recommend any one for Civil appointments; but as Col. Healy has been a Union soldier and comes recommended for an important Civil Office, in a state lately in rebellion, by the bar of that state, and also by officers of the Army doing duty there, I venture to depat from the rule which I had established and to add my recommendation to the others for his appointment.

I hope Col. Healy may receive the appointment of United States Marshal for the Middle District of Ala. and that he may prove a valuable officer.

> I have the honor to be,
> with great respect,
> your obt. svt.
> U. S. GRANT
> General,

To HON. HENRY STANBERRY,
ATTY. GN. OF THE U. STATES,

ALS (incomplete facsimile), Sotheby Parke-Bernet, Sale No. 5379, Oct. 31, 1985, no. 75; (incomplete facsimile) Paul C. Richards, Catalogue 202 [1985], no. 271.

1. Robert W. Healy was promoted to col., 58th Ill., as of Oct. 3, 1865, and mustered out as of April 1, 1866. He was confirmed as U.S. marshal, southern district of Ala., on Feb. 23, 1867.

To Charles W. Ford

Washington, D. C. Jan. 4th *1867.*

DEAR FORD:

Enclosed I send you the deed for property which I bought from J. C. Dent and which is not yet recorded. Will you do me the favor to notify Dent that you have it and want the stamps put on it so that it can be recorded. I paid John Dent before I saw the deed $24.500 00 supposing that still more would be due him. On looking at the deed after I got home however I find there is but 280¼ acres instead of about 338 as I had supposed. I have written to John Dent to pay to you the balance, or difference, between the amount paid and the amount due him. If he says nothing about it please show him this letter. I have entered the amount due him at $80 pr. acre which is $5.00 more than I agreed to give him.

When I sent you a check to pay Benton I could not think of his initials to save my life although I knew them as well as I did yours. This is rather a poor apology to make to a person who befriends you as Benton did me, but it is the fact. Please assure him that I fully appreciate it and will endeavor to prove it some day.

Yours Truly
U. S. GRANT

ALS, USG 3.

To Edwin M. Stanton

Headqrs. AUS. Jan 7. 1867.

Respy. forwarded to the Secretary of War—with the request that these papers be submitted to the Attorney General for information as to what is necessary to secure the release of Mr A. B. Morey[1] from indictment and bail

The facts of the case are as follows, Private A B. Morey, 124th Ills., Vol. Infy. was detailed for detective duty in Nov. 1862 by my order and remained in such duty until July 1865. During this time and in accordance with my instructions in such cases, he took from a citizen, 2 tents, believed to be the property of the United States and turned them over to the Provost Marshal.

He now stands indicted, and is under bail in the sum of ($3.000) three thousand dollars to appear for trial before the Civil Courts of Vicksburg, Miss, for stealing these tents. Having simply executed my instructions, in my opinion, Mr Morey is not responsible to the Civil Courts, and should be released from bail and indictment.

U S. GRANT, General.

Copy, DNA, RG 108, Register of Letters Received. *HED*, 39-2-40, p. 3. On Jan. 7, 1867, USG wrote to Secretary of War Edwin M. Stanton. "Will you please forward the enclosed papers to the Atty. Gn. without delay? Morey, the sufferer from the action of Mississippi Courts, is now in the City awaiting action in his case." ALS, DLC-Edwin M. Stanton. On Jan. 17, Attorney Gen. Henry Stanbery wrote to Stanton. ". . . The papers accompanying your letter contain copies of the orders under which Morey acted, and are sufficient for his defence in the State Court, or to authorize the removal of the case into the Circuit Court, and for his defence in that Court. I would, therefore, advise that instructions be sent to the officer in command at Vicksburg to furnish for the use of Morey the documents or orders under which he acted, and to see that his case is properly defended. . . ." LS, DNA, RG 107, Letters Received from Bureaus. *HED*, 39-2-40, p. 4.

On April 7, 1866, Amos B. Morey wrote a letter received at USG's hd. qrs. complaining that military authorities had not protected him from indictment by a civil court. DNA, RG 108, Register of Letters Received. On April 19, Maj. George K. Leet endorsed this letter. "Respectfully referred to M G. T. J. Wood, Comdg Dept. Mississippi who will enfore the provisions of G. O. No 3. applicable to this case." Copy, *ibid*. On April 16, George W. Brownell wrote a letter received at USG's hd. qrs. "Reports himself as one of firm, viz: Graham, Beatty & co. gov't. lessees of plantation, known as the 'Marble Place,' on the Big Black Riv., which, during the war they were obliged to abandon—and now, are much inconvenienced by Mr. Marble's civil suits for rent, &c. Enclose Gen. T. J. Woods letter to Counsel of Mr. Brownell, showing the Genls disposition somewhat loose in enforcing Gen. order No. 3. Hdqrs. AUS." *Ibid*. On April 24, Leet endorsed this letter. "Respy. referred to M G. T. J Wood, Comdg. Dept. Mississippi, who is directed to see that G. O. No. 3. is strictly and rigidly enforced in all proper cases." Copy, *ibid*. On May 9, Maj. Gen. Thomas J. Wood, Vicksburg, wrote to Leet at length concerning both cases and defending his enforcement of General Orders No. 3, concluding: ". . . But so soon as the necessary proof and information were submitted, a special order was published in each case addressed to the proper civil officers to dismiss the suits against Messrs Morey and Brownell—In this connection I beg to call the attention of the Commanding General to my telegraphic despatches to him of the 3rd and 5th inst and his replies of the 4th and 8th inst—I feel the imputation of looseness in enforcing General Orders No 3 all the more keenly, and esteem it the more endorsed, from the fact that in a term of service, now in the twenty-first year of its continuance, this is the first instance in which I have been supposed to be loose or slack in rendering a sacred and rigid compliance to the orders of my lawful Military Superiors—" LS, *ibid.*, Letters Received. On May 19, Leet wrote to Wood. "I am directed by Lieut General Grant to acknowledge the receipt of your communication of the 9th inst. relative to endorsements from these Headquarters on the papers of Morey & Brownell, and in reply to say that it is eminently satisfactory, and that in making the endorsements referred to there was no thought of charging you with remissness of duty." Copies, DLC-USG, V, 47, 109; DNA, RG 108, Letters Sent.

On June 23, U.S. Representative Elihu B. Washburne wrote to Brig. Gen. John A. Rawlins. "Here are some papers in that Capt. Green matter. It would seem that the Court treated Wood's order with Contempt and went on and tried the Case and put Green through. It looks rather singular that Wood should have permitted this." ALS, *ibid.*, Letters Received. Washburne enclosed a letter of June 16 from William B. Green, Galena, to USG. "Myself G. W Brownell and Others leased from the Gen. Government in 1864 a plantation on the Big Black in the rear of Vicksburg state of Miss. for the purpose of raising a crop of cotton, Owing to the withdrawal of the troops from the Big Black we were compelled after partially cultivating the crop to abandon it, managing to only get three Bales of cotton after an expenditure of some $10,000 As soon as the courts were reinstated E. G. Marble the owner of the Plantation commenced an action against me *individually* for rent or use of farm. I had supposed the case would be dismissed under Military Order No 3, but for some reason the order has not been enforced, and a judgment has been obtained against me, and I have just receivd the Enclosed despatch saying that the court will not grant an appeal of the case to the U. S. Court. I am loth to believe I am living under a Government which will allow such injustice to be done to any of its citizens, and hope that something will be done to relieve me . . . To give you some idea of the state of things at Vicksburg I give you an extract from a letter of Mr. Brownel ~~here~~, to his brother here as to the way our counsel there spoke in regard to the case previous to meeting of the court, We were compelled to employ a southren lawyer there being no other there 'He (the lawyer) did not intend to plead order No 3, ~~he~~—he would not plead it because the military did not intend to enforce it, did not know why, but was satisfied it was so, would not plead it also from the fact that if he did, and it failed, it would kill him, and injure the Military.' " ALS, *ibid.* On June 22, Leet endorsed a copy of this letter to Wood for report. AES, *ibid.*, RG 109, Union Provost Marshals' File of Papers Relating to Individual Civilians. On July 2, Wood wrote to Leet at length defending himself and enclosing a letter from Green's attorney. ". . . From this letter it will be seen 1st that Mr Green's letter of the 16th ult, is, in all its essential statements, a tissue of misstatements from begining to end, 2nd that it is untrue that Genl Orders No 3 were not pleaded in this case in bar of trial—3rd that it is untrue that an appeal, under the provisions of the act of Congress, of April 11th 1866, has been denied to Mr Green; but on the contrary the case has been carried to the United States District Court for this State. 4th That it is not true that a judgement has been rendered, against Mr Green. I furthermore add my opinion to that of Mr Burdell [*Burwell*] that no decision against Mr Green will ever be rendered—. . . . I know not who the lawyer may be referred to in the letter of Mr Brownell, an extract from which is given in Mr Green's letter to Lieut Genl Grant—I am well assured that Mr Burdell is not the lawyer. But this I will remark: that I most respectfully, yet most earnestly, request that the loose and unresponsible statements of nameless lawyers be not received as an exponent of my administration of this Military department—. . . I forward herewith a copy of my letter of May 9th connected with this very case, to which I received a reply from the Lieut General, that my explanation was *eminently* satisfactory." ALS, *ibid.*, RG 108, Letters Received.

On Oct. 6, Duff Green, U.S. marshal, southern district of Miss., Vicksburg, wrote to USG. "Mr. A B. Morey, the bearer of this, stands charged by the civil authorities here of having forcibly taken from a Jew here two camp tents during the occupation of this place by the United States forces. Mr. Morey I knew to be a detective under the employment of Colonel Waddell, then provost marshal, and I have every reason to believe acted under the orders of Colonel Waddell in the matter. I have never known or heard of his giving any one any unnecessary trouble, or annoying any citizen unnecessarily in the pursuance of his official duties. I think he is being prosecuted without a just cause, and he ought to be relieved. His case has been on hand for some months, subjecting him to much inconvenience and cost. I ask, if it is consistent with your views, that you will take such steps as you think most expedient to have him relieved as early as possible." *HED*, 39-2-40, pp. 2–3.

1. Morey enlisted as private, 124th Ill., on Aug. 6, 1862, at Aurora, Ill., and was mustered out on Aug. 15, 1865. On Nov. 27, 1862, Col. William S. Hillyer had issued a pass. "Private Amos B. Morey, of company E, one hundred and twenty-fourth Illinois volunteers, has permission to pass through all the camps of this command at all hours, day and night, on special service, till further orders; and he will be permitted to come to these headquarters at his pleasure. The commanding officer of his company will release him from duty at any time he may request, until further orders." *Ibid.*, p. 2. On July 22, 1863, USG, Vicksburg, had issued a permit. "A. B. Morey is authorized to collect, bale & ship to the north all the rags within the limits of the Rebel Fortifications—for this purpose he is authorized to employ—to be paid by himself for their services—any unemployed negroes—particularly negro women & children" Copies (2), DNA, RG 108, Letters Received. On July 3, 1865, 12:40 P.M., USG telegraphed to Maj. Gen. Peter J. Osterhaus. "Release A. B. Morey from prison and send any charges there may be against him here. He was in the emply of Treasury Agt. Montrose." ALS (telegram sent), *ibid.*, RG 107, Telegrams Collected (Bound); telegram sent, *ibid.*; copies, *ibid.*, RG 108, Letters Sent; DLC-USG, V, 46, 109. On Aug. 3, Maj. Gen. Henry W. Slocum, Vicksburg, forwarded papers relating to Morey's case. Copies, DNA, RG 108, Letters Received. Among other things, it had been charged that Morey "did sell or cause to be sold as rags a lot of wall, common, & Sibley tents, to the number of about one hundred, military property of the United States & did appropriate the proceeds to his own use. This at Vicksburg, Miss., during the year 1863." Copies (2), *ibid.* On May 11, 1864, Slocum had ordered Morey returned to his regt. after learning that he maintained a "negro show" and "Beer Saloon." Morey had also been jailed for several weeks

in the fall of 1864 for abusing his position as military detective. Maj. Gen.
Napoleon J. T. Dana then ordered Morey back to his regt., but somehow he
remained a detective until July 25, 1865. *Ibid.*

To Maj. Gen. George H. Thomas

Washington, D. C. Jan. 7th *1867*.

GENERAL:

A large amount of Northern Capital has been invested in de-
veloping the Gold Mines of Northern Georgia. On account of the
class of people living in that section of the state great sensitiveness
is felt for the safety both of life and property there. As we occupy
the state with United States troops, and as there is more Capital
invested in the section of the state refered to than in any other, and
again, as the whole Nation is more interested in the success of their
enterprise than in any other in the state confined to the same extent
of territory, I think it advisable to occupy the Gold regions of
Ga. Buncomb County, with two companies of Infantry. The old
United States Mint at Dahlonega can be made available as quarters. With a few huts such as the men can put up quickly I think
three companies may be made comfortable. I wish you to send a
Field officer with the companies you send to Dahlonega, and one
whose discretion and judgement you can rely on. The object of
sending these troops to Buncomb County Ga. is to give security to
life and property and to encourage capital to go there for the developement of the Mines.

Please send these troops without delay.

Very respectfully
your obt. svt.
U. S. GRANT
General,

To MAJ GN. G. H. THOMAS,
COMD.G DEPT. OF THE TENN.
LOUISVILLE KY.

ALS, DNA, RG 393, Dept. of the Tenn., Unbound Materials, Letters Received. On Jan. 10, 1867, Maj. Gen. George H. Thomas wrote to USG. "I have the honor to acknowledge the receipt of your letter of the 7th inst. regarding the stationing of troops at Dohlanega, Ga., and to report that Genl. Ruger has been ordered to detach two companies of his regiment, to garrison Dohlanega, in accordance with your wishes." Copy, *ibid.*, Letters Sent. See *PUSG*, 16, 392–94.

On Dec. 13, 1866, Thomas had written a letter received at USG's hd. qrs. concerning placement of troops in his command. DNA, RG 108, Register of Letters Received. On Jan. 8, 1867, Thomas wrote to USG. "In re-districting the Department, one difficulty occurs to me, which I failed to mention in my communication of the 13th December last, and that is this:—Bvt. Maj. Gen. Chas R. Woods, Lieut. Col. 33rd Infantry, is on duty according to his Brevet rank by virtue of S. O. No 258 W. D. A. G. O, Washington May 31st 1866. This Regiment will be stationed in the District of Chattanooga, and the colonel is present with it. Is it intended that General Woods shall remain thus on duty?" Copy, *ibid.*, RG 393, Dept. of the Tenn., Letters Sent. On Jan. 10, Thomas wrote to USG. "Before issuing the order re-districting the Department of the Tennessee I have the honor to request that I may be informed whether it is intended to retain the following named officers on duty in this Department, and according to their highest grade, lineal and brevet. . . ." Copy, *ibid.* On Jan. 16, Maj. George K. Leet endorsed this letter. "Respy. returned to MG. Geo. H. Thomas, USA. Commanding Dept. of the Tennessee. MG. Wager Swayne will be retained for the present with his volunteer rank. Genl. Thomas is authorized to retain BMG. Chas. R. Woods and BMG. Jeff. C. Davis [unt]il March 1st. '67. at which time they will be relieved and ordered to join [t]heir respective regiments. The Genl in Chief has recommended that Genl Davis be assigned to duty according to his brevet rank, and that Genl. Tillson be mustered out of service. Except the above cases, the assignment of officers to the command of districts will be according to lineal rank." Copy, *ibid.*, RG 108, Register of Letters Received. On the same day, USG wrote to Secretary of War Edwin M. Stanton. "I have the honor to recommend the muster out, at his own request, of Brevet Major General Davis Tillson, US Vols.; also that Brevet Major General Jeff C. Davis, Commanding District of Kentucky, be assigned to duty according to his brevet rank." LS, *ibid.*, RG 94, ACP, 1900 1873.

On Jan. 11, USG telegraphed to Thomas. "If Gn. Wood is not yet relieved from the Command of Mississippi suspend the order relieving him until March." ALS (telegram sent), *ibid.*, RG 107, Telegrams Collected (Bound); telegram sent (on Jan. 12, 9:00 A.M.), *ibid.*; copies, *ibid.*, RG 108, Telegrams Sent; (dated Jan. 12) *ibid.*, RG 393, Dept. of the Cumberland, Telegrams Received; DLC-USG, V, 56. On Jan. 12, Thomas telegraphed to USG. "General T. J Wood was relieved from Command of Dist of Miss on December eleventh (11) eighteen Sixty Six (1866)." Telegram received (at 4:30 P.M.), DNA, RG 107, Telegrams Collected (Bound); (at 2:36 P.M.) *ibid.*, RG 108, Telegrams Received; copies (one sent by mail), *ibid.*, Letters Received; *ibid.*, RG 393, Dept. of the Cumberland, Telegrams Sent; DLC-USG, V, 55.

On Jan. 17, noon, USG telegraphed to Thomas. "Come to Washington as soon as you can make it convenient. Direct Gn. T. J. Wood to come also." ALS (telegram sent), DNA, RG 107, Telegrams Collected (Bound); telegram sent, *ibid.*; copies, *ibid.*, RG 108, Telegrams Sent; *ibid.*, RG 393, Dept. of the Cumberland, Telegrams Received; DLC-USG, V, 56. On Jan. 18, Thomas telegraphed to USG. "Telegram of 17th inst recd Will start tomorrow if I can cross the River. Cannot cross today" Telegram received (at 4:00 P.M.), DNA, RG 107, Telegrams Collected (Bound); *ibid.*, RG 108, Telegrams Received; copies, *ibid.*, RG 393, Dept. of the Cumberland, Telegrams Sent; DLC-USG, V, 55.

To Joseph Casey

Washington D. C.
Jan 11th 1867.

DEAR JUDGE.

This will introduce to you Mrs Kearney, the widow of an old Army Officer who served his Country faithfully through a long life. At his death he left his widow, and orphans, property near this City, which was occupied, and destroyed, by Union Troops during the rebellion, for which she has received no compensation.

Her claim is entirely just in my opinion and I have advised her that she will probably have to go before your Court to recover it. Will you be kind enough to see Mrs Kearney whom I have known for many years, and if consistent with your duties, advise her as to the course she should take. I have not advised her to go to a Claim Agent or other Atty, because it seems to me they rather complicate claims and the fact of them having them in charge is rather calculated to cast suspicion upon their validity.

With great respect
your obt. svt.
U. S. GRANT.
General.

TO CHIEF JUSTICE CASEY.
U S. COURT OF CLAIMS.

Copies, Blair Lee Papers, NjP; DLC-John Sherman. On Feb. 5, 1867, Judge Joseph Casey, U.S. Court of Claims, wrote to USG. "Your letter of the 11th ult. introducing Mrs Kearney, and asking me to advise her in reference to her claim against the United States, has just been placed in my hands by that Lady. Congress by the Act 1st July, 1864, has deprived our Court of jurisdiction in cases of this kind. Nor have they authorized any other Department or tribunal to adjudicate and allow them. At present. Congress alone can give relief. I have therefore taken the liberty, of enclosing a copy of your letter, to the Committee of Claims, in each House, and have asked them, if deemed advisable, to pass a special Act for her relief. There are a great number of Claims, of loyal people in the insurrectionary States, which cannot now be considered at all, but which appeal strongly to the justice of the nation, for recognition and payment. Regretting that it is not in my power to do more, to further and promote your kind wishes towards this very deserving Lady—. . ." Copy, *ibid.* For the claim of Louisa Kearney, widow of Lt. Col. James Kearney, see *SRC*, 41-2-259; *ibid.*, 45-3-559.

To Robert C. Schenck

WASHINGTON, D. C., January 12th, 1867.
HON. R. C. SCHENCK, *Chairman of Military Committee of the House of Representatives.*

GENERAL:—A bill passed Congress authorizing the Secretary of War, to purchase from Dr. A. Dunbar, for the use of Government, his secret for treating the horse's foot. No specific amount to be paid for this secret was mentioned in this bill, nor the manner of communicating it to Army Farriers. The Dr. now wants paid to him $100,000, to be used in establishing a school in the city of New York, to teach his art to all who wish to take tuitions, and, as I understand, to teach all Farriers in Government service, free.

I wish to abstain from making direct recommendations for appropriations that can be avoided, and will therefore only speak of what I think of the merits of Dr. Dunbar's discovery.

Being naturally fond of the horse, I have examined into this matter closely. I am satisfied that most of the lameness heretofore supposed to exist in the joints, shoulder, hip, or back, exists in the feet, and that Dr. Dunbar has discovered the remedy.

I believe the average time of the usefulness of the horse, particularly when subjected to hard use, will be increased one half by an intelligent application of his treatment. I have seen instances where many valuable horses have been unserviceable for years, and by the application of Dr. Dunbar's treatment have been fully restored in a few weeks. There is nothing in this treatment that cannot be learned by any blacksmith in a short time, nor is there anything in it that does not strike any one examining it, as being something that ought to have been known before. The wonder is, that so simple a remedy for most common defects, in so useful an animal as the horse, was not cotemporaneous with his usefulness.

I think Dr. Dunbar has in his possession a secret with which this whole country would be much benefited, by having it diffused until every Farrier should become acquainted with it.

Dr. Dunbar can show strong letters from parties in New York, who have tried his remedy, strongly recommending it.

Very respectfully, your obedient servant,

U. S. GRANT,

General.

Alexander Dunbar, *A Treatise on the Diseases Incident to the Horse*, . . . (Wilmington, Del., 1871), pp. 146–47. On July 19, 1866, USG had written to U.S. Representative Robert C. Schenck of Ohio. "Dr. Alexander Dunbar has asked me for a letter addressed to your committee, expressing my views in relation to the advantages of his system of treating the horse's foot, and the benefits that would be derived by its introduction into the army. I have examined the system, and also had the views of persons who have tried it, they say with great success, in horses of great value. There is no doubt in my mind but what it possesses great merit, and would save to the service immensely, in dollars, and in additional efficiency, if it could be succesfully introduced. On this point I would say that I do not see how it is to be successfully introduced, except Dr. Dunbar should be required to give his time exclusively to teaching Farriers in the army, such at least as might be sent to him, or he to them, and they, in turn, to become teachers. One year is the least time I should think necessary to accomplish this end." *Ibid.*, p. 145. See *PUSG*, 16, 54–58.

On Oct. 12, 1867, Bvt. Brig. Gen. Richard S. Satterlee, chief medical purveyor, New York City, wrote to USG. "The subject of veterinary surgery, as applicable to the cavalry, artillery, and other horses in the army service, has long occupied my attention. Efforts were long ago made to procure educated veterinary surgeons for our cavalry, but without success, on account of want of educated men. Just before the breaking out of the late rebellion, a charter for a veterinary college was obtained from the State of New York, and a building erected, under what was thought favorable auspices, mainly by the persevering exertions of Dr. Busteed, [now the president of the faculty of the revived veterinary college]. I had watched with great interest what was then being done, and had, in consultation with the superintendent, made up my mind to recommend to the government the plan which I now propose to you, when from want of character and necessary knowledge in the man who had the management of the institution, it failed, and the property was converted to other uses. Doctor Busteed however, much to his credit, continued his efforts; until now they have a lecture room, containing ample seats for a respectable audience, and a very creditable museum of anatomical specimens, together with dissecting room, and a stable hospital where they propose to receive horses for treatment, and with a competent corps of professors they are now prepared to enter upon the work of instruction. They also promise to open a free *clinique*, when it is believed many will bring their sick horses for advice. . . ." LS (brackets in original), DNA, RG 94, Letters Received, 1012S 1867. On Oct. 19, Bvt. Maj. Gen. Edward D. Townsend endorsed this letter. "Reply asking if Dr Dunbar is connected with the College, and asking how the expense would be defrayed, and what the terms would be. Say if Dr Dunbar is of the Faculty, Genl Grant would be willing to ask an appropriation to enable non-comd, officers to be sent there." AES, *ibid.* After Satterlee reported that Alexander Dunbar was not associated with the college, Townsend endorsed this report on Nov. 7. "Respectfully submitted to Gen Grant and not approved by him" AES, *ibid.*

To Lt. Gen. William T. Sherman

Jan. 13th *1867.*

Dear General,

Whilst you were absent on your Mexican Mission I did not write to you because I did not know how to address you except through the Sec. of State and I have nothing to do with that functionary where it can be avoided. Since your return, although I have been in the office almost daily, I have been so unwell that I do nothing but what I am compelled to do. For the last day or two I have felt much better and am in hopes that I will have no relapse.

The termination of your Mission to Mexico caused, I think, no disappointment as the whole scheme failed when I refused to go. It may be that when Juariz can be reached you will be called on again to accompany our Minister to his Capital merely to save appearances. But I doubt even this being asked of you.

My dispatch to you to come to Washington was written by direction of the President.[1] If you do not desire to come to Washington this Winter you need not do so unless you receive further orders which I will not give without being directed again to give them. You can however interpret the orders you have as authorizing a pilgrimage to this Capital at any time you feel disposed to make it. There was unquestionably a great desire to commit you to a support of the present Administration, against Congress, wright or wrong, as there has been me. In this particular there is but little difference between parties. No matter how close I keep my tongue each try to interpret from the little let drop that I am with them. I wish our political troubles were settled on any basis. I want to turn over the command of the Army to you for a year or so and go abroad myself. But to leave now would look like throwing up a command in the face of the enemy.

My family are all very well and join me in wishing to be kindly remembered to Mrs. Sherman and the children. I did not repeat my visit to see Mrs. S. when I was in St. Louis because I understood that I would not likely see her.

If you come to Washington, eith[er] alone or with some members of your family, we would be glad to entertain you during your stay.

Yours Truly
U. S. GRANT

To LT. GN. W. T. SHERMAN,
ST. LOUIS, MO.

ALS, DLC-William T. Sherman. On Jan. 10, 1867, Lt. Gen. William T. Sherman had written to USG. "The event I have been awaiting came off last night, and I now have a boy added to my already full family to provide for. Mrs Sherman is also as well as possible, so that I feel willing to say that by the time you receive this and can write back, say in one week, I can come to Washington if needed. Of course I have not the remotest idea of how or in what manner I can do any good, yet this is not left for me to determine and though proposing to stay quietly here, yet will try to conform to Yours and the Presidents will in all public matters. I was glad to read in the Republican of yesterday that at last you had succeeded in getting a Judgmt against White. Whether complete & satisfactory I know not—Lest you have not heard I will merely say it was reported as a Judgmt for 400 & odd dollars for past rent, and 16.66 per month as long as he retains possession. I suppose however you want him ousted. General Price is expected here tomorrow. I will simply see that his parole is formal, and leave him to scramble with these Missouri Radicals who will try and make some fuss at his coming back. I learn that he is broken down in Spirit health and pocket, an object of pity rather than fear. After you have notified the President & received his answer please let Comstock write me in general terms of the probabilities. If I am allowed to stay at home quietly this Spring I will interest myself in some project here—looking to the future. Spite of all economy I find expenses awful, and I should dislike to have Schencks pay bill pass—According to Mr Wells Report the value of money in proportion to what it would fetch in 1860, is 95 per cent discount, or in other words our salaries are only half what they were then. I dont believe Congress wants to pinch us, if the subject were properly presented them. Had you or I served a European Govt we would not have to be bothered by petty family expenses. The income tax should be remitted to the whole army, and pay proper should be equivalt to Gold, and the other allowances made approximate to actual cost. Sorry you have been unwell, but hope you are now strong as usual." ALS, USG 3. On Jan. 17, Sherman wrote to USG. "I have your very welcome letter of January 13, and thank you for it. I do not want to come to Washington this winter for many reasons, but chiefly because every act and word would be reported as you say and construed by Politicians for their selfish purposes. We ought to be allowed to confine ourselves to our pure Military business, which will be as much as can be done, looking to the mixed questions and interests that are forced on us. General Augur is now here, looking over all the despatches & letters that have passed between this office and General Cooke during the past few months. He will tomorrow go to Omaha, via Chicago, the quickest way at this season.—I feel certain that he can soon master that Department and bring those Sioux into order. Hancock is taking the most lively interest in his command, but Ord seems to be too much concerned by the everlasting squabbles between the Whites & Blacks of his Departmt. There is some danger in Arkansas of a War of Races. The Whites & Blacks are nearly balanced in numbers, and a general War between them would be an ugly case for us, though it would partake of the character of the Bear fight, when the woman said she did not much care whether the Bear or husband whipped. Grierson is here also to inspect horses for his Regiment. He is making slow progress, because he has no officers to send out to make recruits. If you can hurry up the appointments for the 10th Cavalry it will help us some. I next look for trouble in Terrys vast Departmt. They will also clamor for troops as soon as a Road is opened from Minnesota to Montana, but for the present all is frozen up there. I have failed utterly to get full accounts of the Phil Kearny massacre, but Augur will be instructed to make a thorough investigation & Report, as also to send me approximate account at once on arrival. My family is prospering, and we are slipping along as quietly as a Country village. If I get impatient for travel, I will turn towards the Plains rather than Washington. I agree with you *emphatically* that you should not leave when so many exciting political questions are unsettled. Present me kindly to Mrs Grant, the children, Mr Dent, and all of your household. Again thanking you for your invitation to yr house, . . ." ALS, *ibid.*

1. On Jan. 4, noon, USG had telegraphed to Sherman. "The President would like to have you visit Washington as soon as you can make it convenient." ALS (telegram sent), DNA, RG 107, Telegrams Collected (Bound); telegram sent, *ibid.*; copies, *ibid.*, RG 108, Telegrams Sent; DLC-USG, V, 56. On the same day, Sherman telegraphed to USG. "Dispatch recd. Please say to the President if he wants me I can start on a days notice but there are strong family reasons why I should stay at home all this month   If he reiterates his request I will come at once" Telegram received (at 4:30 P.M.), DNA, RG 107, Telegrams Collected (Bound); *ibid.*, RG 108, Telegrams Received; copy, DLC-USG, V, 55. On Jan. 5, 10:45 A.M., USG telegraphed to Sherman. "It is not important that you should come to Washington immediately." ALS (telegram sent), DNA, RG 107, Telegrams Collected (Bound); telegram sent, *ibid.*; copies, *ibid.*, RG 108, Telegrams Sent; DLC-USG, V, 56.

On Feb. 1, Sherman telegraphed to USG. "Can I go to New York to attend wedding to start sunday" Telegram received (at 11:15 A.M.), DNA, RG 107,

Telegrams Collected (Bound); *ibid.*, RG 108, Telegrams Received; copy, DLC-USG, V, 55. At noon, USG telegraphed to Sherman. "Certainly you can go to New York." ALS (telegram sent), DNA, RG 107, Telegrams Collected (Bound); telegram sent, *ibid.*; copies, *ibid.*, RG 108, Telegrams Sent; DLC-USG, V, 56.

To Lt. Gen. William T. Sherman

Washington, D, C, Jan. 14th *1867* [*9:50* A.M.]

LT. GN. W. T. SHERMAN,
ST. LOUIS, MO,

Gen. Augur[1] left last evening for Omaha via St. Louis. Are you having an investigation into the Fort Phil. Kearny Massacre? A report will probably be called for and it is import that we should know all that can be learned about it as soon as possible.

U. S. GRANT
General.

ALS (telegram sent), DNA, RG 107, Telegrams Collected (Bound); telegram sent, *ibid.*; copies, *ibid.*, RG 108, Telegrams Sent; DLC-USG, V, 56. On Jan. 14, 1867, Lt. Gen. William T. Sherman telegraphed to USG. "Despatch of to-day rec'd—I ordered Gen'l Cooke to make a full report of the Phil Kearney massacre & also to report to me all the facts about it that reached him—The following despatch is this minute recd, which is not full enough & I will renew my orders to Gen Cooke on the subject—'Omaha Jany 14th 1867 BVT MAJ GEN W A NICHOLS Asst Adjt Genl—Thirtieth Infy just arrived four hundred & ninety (490) men about thirty (30) women, no field offices. Gen Palmer reports today reinforcements near Reno expected to arrive there one the 11th. No Indians have made their appearance either at Ft Phil Kearney or Reno since the massacre—Palmers mail party attacked by thirty (30) Indians & lost wagon & mules, forty five miles west of Laramie—He concludes, "quite a heavy snow yesterday & much drift"—The roads must be impassable for a day or two (signed) P ST GEO COOKE Bt Maj Gen'" Telegram received (at 3:20 P.M.), DNA, RG 107, Telegrams Collected (Bound); *ibid.*, RG 108, Telegrams Received; copy, DLC-USG, V, 55.

On Jan. 3, Bvt. Maj. Gen. Philip St. George Cooke, Omaha, had written to Bvt. Maj. Gen. William A. Nichols concerning Indian hostilities and requesting reinforcements. LS, DNA, RG 94, Letters Received, 4P 1867. On Jan. 9, Sherman endorsed this letter. "Respectfully forwarded to the Adjt. Genl USA The best evidence the case admits of goes to show a serious combination on the part of the Indian tribes East of the Rocky Mountains & North of the Platte. I submit this paper of Genl Cooke Comdg Dept of Platte which I construe asks for two Rgts of Cavalry and two of Infantry. The Country occupied by the indians is so vast that it is hard to limit the number of men required to defeat & destroy them, and I submit this paper to the Genl Comdg to enable him to do as much for that quarter of our Country this Spring as the strength of the Army will admit of." AES, *ibid.* On Jan. 16, Bvt. Brig. Gen. Orville E. Babcock wrote to Sherman. "The report of Gen'l P. S. Geo. Cooke asking for two regiments of Cavalry and two regiments of Infantry with your endorsements reached Gen'l Grant this morning. He directs me to inform you that all the cavalry of the army is now assigned to duty in departments having Indians to watch. So it will be impossible to send any more cavalry to the Department of the Platte. He has ordered the Adjt. Gen'l to send sufficient number of recruits to fill the regiments in the Dept. of the Platte to the maximum under existing orders. If it is possible more infantry will be sent" Copies, DLC-USG, V, 47, 60; DNA, RG 108, Letters Sent.

On Jan. 19, Sherman wrote to Bvt. Maj. Gen. John A. Rawlins. "I now have the honor to send you General Cookes letter of the 14, with its enclosures, which is the nearest approach to accounting for the unhappy affair at Fort Phil Kearney. I have already transmitted a copy of a telegraphic despatch from Gen Cooke notifying me that a full Report is on its way by the Regular Mail from Fort Laramie. Until the Reports of Col Carrington and Gen Wessels are on hand, I cannot advise either a formal Court Martial, or Court of Inquiry." ALS, *ibid.*, Letters Received. The enclosures are *ibid.* On Jan. 23, Secretary of War Edwin M. Stanton referred to USG an extract from a letter of Dec. 15, 1866, from C. W. Hines, Fort Phil Kearny, Dakota Territory, to John B. Hines describing a skirmish near the fort in early Dec. during which U.S. forces responded in much the same manner as on Dec. 21. AES and copy, *ibid.* On Jan. 28, 1867, Sherman wrote to "Dear General," presumably USG. "Knowing your anxiety to hear some thing definite and comprehensible of the Fort Phil Kearney matter, I have had a copy made of a letter from a serjeant there to a Clerk in this office, which seems to explain the Case fully. As soon as the other official Report comes I will send it also" ALS, *ibid.* The enclosure is *ibid.*

On Feb. 2, USG wrote to Stanton. "I have the honor to return Senate resolution calling for information 'which may tend to explain the origin, causes and extent of the late massacre of the United States troops by Indians at, or near, Fort Phil Kearney in Dakota Territory'—and referred by you to me for report, I send herewith 'all official reports, papers and other facts' in possession of these Headquarters, bearing upon the subject." LS, *ibid.*, RG 46, Senate 39A–G3, Reports, Secretary of War. The enclosures are *ibid.* See *SED*, 39-2-16; *ibid.*, 40-1-13. On Feb. 7, Maj. George K. Leet wrote to Sherman. "The General-in-Chief directs that Brevet Major General C. C. Augur, Commanding Department of the Platte, be ordered to cause a thorough investigation of and report upon the origin, probable cause and results of the late massacre near Fort Philip Kearney of U. S. officers and men by Indians" Copies, DLC-USG, V, 47, 60; DNA, RG 108, Letters Sent. On Feb. 25, Sherman wrote to Leet. "In order to ascertain authoritatively all the facts, and if necessary to apply a remedy, I recommend that a Court of Inquiry be ordered by the President to meet at Fort Phil Kearny say about ~~May~~ April 1, 1867, to enquire into ~~all~~ the facts attending and preceding the destruction of the party of Officers & Soldiers commanded by Lt Col Fetterman Dec 21, 1866, and to report their opinion of what measures if any are necessary by way of punishmt. The following officers are near at hand and available for detail. Bvt Maj Genl John Gibbon, Lt Col L. P. Bradley 27. Inf. and Maj James Van Voast, 18th Inf. Bvt Col Alex Chambers is a very suitable person for Recorder. I have already sent you the official Reports of Colonel Carington and Genl Wessels and cannot expect more complete details without the agency of a Court of Inquiry, which by Law can only be ordered by the President, in the absence of a demand for enquiry by parties whom the Inquiry may compromise." ALS, *ibid.*, RG 94, Letters Received, 239M 1867.

1. On Jan. 7, USG wrote to Bvt. Maj. Gen. Edward D. Townsend. "Please make orders assigning Gen. Augur to the Command of the Dept. of the Platte, placing him on duty with his Bvt. rank. Assign Gn. Cooke to duty as President of the Chicago Board, relieving the present President." ALS, *ibid.*, 14A 1867. On Jan. 8, 10:40 A.M., USG telegraphed to Sherman. "I have assigned Gn. Augur to Command of Dept. of the Platte ~~relieve~~ relieving Cooke for other duty. I think you will be much pleased with Augur. He has had long experience among Indians both hostile and peaceable." ALS (telegram sent), *ibid.*, RG 107, Telegrams Collected (Bound); telegram sent, *ibid.*; copies, *ibid.*, RG 108, Telegrams Sent; DLC-USG, V, 56. On the same day, Sherman telegraphed to USG. "Dispatch announcing Genl Augur to Command Department of Platte most acceptable" Telegram received (at 3:30 P.M.), DNA, RG 108, Telegrams Received; copy, DLC-USG, V, 55. On the same day, Cooke telegraphed to USG. "I have been hard at work organizing a campaign for next month—Applied by letter for Col Gibbon to be assigned to Brigadier, Brevet—Shall I work on planning what may be all changed or complained of after the disgrace you put upon me? I have at least great Indian experience and if success is a criterion I certainly do not deserve this inconsiderate action in my case" Telegram received (at 5:00 P.M.), DNA, RG 107, Telegrams Collected (Bound); *ibid.*, RG 108, Telegrams Received; copy, DLC-USG, V, 55. On the same day, Sherman again telegraphed to USG. "The enclosed just recd from Gen Cooke, 'From Omaha dated 8th, received January eighth, eighteen sixty seven, twelve thirty P M. LIEUT GEN W. T. SHERMAN Letter of Gen'l Palmer Jany 2nd, has reason to believe five thousand warriors were on the road to make desperate attempts before grass, The Snakes, promised to join in Spring when ten thousand warriors, they say, will stake all upon a big fight to keep one hunting ground—Thermometer has been twenty three degrees below zero, moderated somewhat and six companies only about four hundred men march January third—Cavalry recruits without arms went by to Fort MacPherson last night (signed) P ST GEO COOKE Brevet Maj Genl' 'From Omaha dated 8th, received Jany 8th 1867, 2 45 P M LIEUT GEN'L W. T. SHERMAN I am in full prepartion for a vigorous Campaign next month with the troops that have been sent me Applied for Gibbon to be assigned as Brig and second in command. You can avert this cruel blow calculated to disgrace me only I fear it may have come from you—I fought & whipped the Sioux and am very nearly equal physically to my best day (signed) P ST GEO COOKE' Gen Cooke of course refers to his being relieved" Telegram received (at 10:00 P.M.), DNA, RG 107, Telegrams Collected (Bound); *ibid.*, RG 108, Telegrams Received; copy, DLC-USG, V, 55. On Jan. 9, 9:45 A.M., USG telegraphed to Cooke. "You will be governed by orders from Gn. Sherman as to whether you will go on with your present preparations for an Indian Campaign." ALS (telegram sent), DNA, RG 107, Telegrams Collected (Bound); telegram sent, *ibid.*; copies, *ibid.*, RG 108, Telegrams Sent; *ibid.*, RG 393, Dept. of the Platte, Telegrams Received; DLC-USG, V, 56. On Jan. 17, Sherman telegraphed to USG. "The Subjoined telegram has this moment been recd

'Omaha Jany Seventh (7) eighteen hundred & sixty seven (1867)   LT GEN W T. SHERMAN. Following despatch just recd   Fort Phil Kearney Jany fourth (4) to Adjt Gen Dept Platte   The mail takes full report of fight Dec twenty first (21st)   All bodies rec'd. Severe cold and drifting snows with mercury once at twenty two (22) below Zero has so far prevented further Indian depredations their losses may also explain this   the facts disclosed show that the Detachment was several miles from the wood train they were sent to relieve & pushed over lodge trail ridge in order of pursuit after orders three times given not to cross that ridge   I found Lieut Grummonds body also   Fetterman & Brown evidently shot each other   signed H. B CARRINGTON Col eighteenth Infy.   Respectfully P ST G COOKE B M G"   Telegram received (at 4:30 P.M.), DNA, RG 107, Telegrams Collected (Bound); *ibid.*, RG 108, Telegrams Received; copies, *ibid.*, RG 107, Letters Received from Bureaus; DLC-USG, V, 55.

On Jan. 19, Cooke wrote to the AG protesting his relief from command and requesting a court of inquiry. ALS, DNA, RG 94, Letters Received, 42P 1867. On Feb. 8, USG endorsed this letter. "Respectfully forwarded to the Secretary of War. The application for a Court of Inquiry is disapproved. Gen. Cooke was relieved from command of the Dept. of the Platte solely because it was deemed for the good of the service to do so, and he has no right to question the motives which led to his removal." ES, *ibid.* On July 3, Cooke, Louisville, wrote to USG. "In my view,—as you know—I have been made the subject of injustice and illegal treatment;—it may be well for me, and not lost time to you, that I should present the matter with candour and some fullness. I was assigned by the *President* to the command of the Department of the Platte in March 1866; and again in August when it's boundaries were modified more fully to embrace the scenes of all indian warfare existing for several years.   in January 1867, in the midst of my preparations for a campaign, you displaced me, by the Colonel of a regiment not present   You have stated that I was not removed from my command in consequence of any fault, but to give place to a much younger man &c   On what evidence,—on what probability, did you assume that I was too old to command efficiently an indian campaign in person? It was my intention to take the field although *not*, in the precipitate winter campaign ordered by Lt General Sherman, which I could not approve   My original plan as I wrote was to attack the indians at the first springing up of grass, when their horses are at the very weakest;—I confidently believe that I could and would have crushed the body and soul of the hostile combination, on the Montana road in May, if I had been let alone, and at small expense; for I belong to the old school in that; & have marched with a cavalry regiment, rapidly, above 2000 miles on grass alone. But so soon as I was relieved, peace commissioners were sent out, and the campaign indefinitely suspended! I was ordered here on a Board to examine infantry officers; which the law requires shall 'be composed of officers of that arm of service.' I am *not* of that arm of service: and as the very highest officer of any arm of service is a Colonel, it is plain that I have been degraded, and illegally. The law of July 17th 1862 prescribes when an officer *may* be superannuated—at 62, or after 45 years of service; and as an additional, thorough precaution, the act of Aug. 3d 1861, prescribes the method of retiring officers at any less age or service; 'if any commissioned officer of the army . . . shall hereafter become incapable of performing the duties of his office, he shall be placed upon the retired list, and be withdrawn from active service and command,'—(but by the decision of a Board.)— Is not the conclusion irresistable that these complete provisions of law remove all

excuse for such personal decisions? History is not wanting in cases of commanders eminently successful at ages much greater than mine. I was 58 last
month, and have served forty consecutive years; so that I am four or five years
within the legal limits: My indian service and experience amount to the sum total
of those of perhaps *any* three of the general officers of the army; and it is only
a fact, and on record, that I have been invariably successful against them, in
conducting a campaign and otherwise. I am considered young in constitution for
my age, quite healthy, light of weight and active. Why then, am I, the only
general officer cast aside, and by what right? Can it be argued that the 200 brevet
Major generals,—and innumerable Brigadier generals,—are on the same legal
footing with the general officers of the legal military peace establishment? the
law says 'there shall be . . . five Major generals and ten brigadier generals';—Is
there a right, at will, to instal five captains of the army (with brevet commissions of Major general) in the commands of the five Major Generals,—setting
them adrift on boards &c? Just as much as in my case. If you considered me too
old to command an important department, there are departments not so important; and there is the position of Superintendent of the general recruiting Service,
which an existing order from the War Department—No. 245 of July 28th 1863—
prescribes shall be filled by 'a brigadier general of the regular army', and now
not so filled:—if not respect to my very office—conferred too by Mr Lincoln of
his own motion—common courtesy would, at not a far day back—have suggested
a change to one of these positions. When lately an ex-member of congress was
appointed a brigadier general (to *commence his* career in the military peace establishment a grandfather like myself,) why was displaced for him, the distinguished
colonel & Bt Maj general Steele? Was it not simply a just respect to the law of
rank and command? Having some—to me very important—property interests at
stake in the city of New York,—and having had, in the last nine years but ten
days leave to go where I pleased, I applied lately for 30 days' leave of absence.—
It is refused me. If I should claim to be retired, under the law entitling me to it,
since July 1st instant, I apprehend that in the extreme letter of that law—made in
time of war—my stay here on a board, may be treated as an exigency of the public Service. General, I would be too glad, to be convinced that any of these slowly
and sorrowfully formed conclusions were ill founded; and I have striven to write
with all professional courtesy, and respect for your high office" ALS (ellipses in
original), *ibid.*, 571C 1867. On July 12, USG endorsed this letter. "Respectfully
refered to the Sec. of War with the recommendation that Gen. Cooke be relieved
from the 'Board' on which he is now serving & ordered to New York to await
orders." AES, *ibid.* See letter to Maj. Gen. George H. Thomas, April 30, 1867;
PUSG, 16, 418–23.

To Edwin M. Stanton

Washington D. C. Jan. 15th *1867*

HON E. M. STANTON
SEC. OF WAR,
SIR:

In a report by General Sherman forwarded with my annual report dated Nov. 21st 1866, the following passage occurs:

"I propose the coming year (with your consent, and with that of the Secretary of the Interior, in whose control these Indians are supposed to be), to restrict the Sioux north of the Platte, west of the Missouri river, and east of the new road to Montana which starts from Laramie for Virginia City by way of Forts Reno, Philip Kearny, C. F. Smith, etc. All Sioux found outside of these limits without a written pass from some military commander defining clearly their object, should be dealt with summarily. In like manner I would restrict the Araphoes, Cheyennes, Camanches, Kiowas, Apaches, and Navajoes south of the Arkansas and east of Fort Union. This would leave for our people exclusively the use of the wide belt, east and west, between the Platte and the Arkansas, in which lie the two great railroads, and over which passes the bulk of travel to the mountain Territories. As long as these Indians can hunt the buffalo and antelope within the described limits we will have the depredations of last Summer and worse yet, the exaggerations of danger raised by our own people, often for a very base purpose. It is our duty, and it shall be my study, to make the progress of construction of the great Pacific Railways that lay in this belt of country as safe as possible, as also to protect the stage and telegraph lines against any hostile bands, but they are so long that to guard them perfectly is an impossibility, unless we can restrict the Indians as herein stated. I beg you will submit this proposition to the honorable Secretary of the Interior, that we may know that we do not violate some one of the solemn treaties made with these Indians, who are very captious, and claim to the very letter the execution on our part of those treaties, the obligation of which they seem to comprehend perfectly."

I approve this proposition of General Sherman provided, it does not conflict with our treaty obligations with the Indians now between the Platte and Arkansas Rivers. The protection of the Pacific Railroad so that not only the portion already completed shall be entirely safe, but that the portion yet to be constructed shall in no way be delayed, either by actual or apprehended danger, is indispensable.

Aside from the great value of this road to the country benefited by it, it has the strongest claims upon the military service as it will be one of its most efficient aids in the control of the Indians in the vast regions through which it passes.

I respectfully request that I may be informed at an early day whether this proposition is approved by you and the Secretary of the Interior, that measures may be taken to carry it into effect.

Very respectfully,
Your obe'dt Ser'vt
U. S. GRANT
General

LS, DNA, RG 108, Letters Received. See following letter; letter to Edwin M. Stanton, Feb. 1, 1867; *PUSG*, 16, 387–89; *HED*, 39-2-71. On Jan. 15, 1867, Secretary of the Interior Orville H. Browning wrote to Secretary of War Edwin M. Stanton concerning sending a commission to treat with Indians near Fort Phil Kearny, Dakota Territory, and enclosing additional correspondence. LS and copies, DNA, RG 94, Letters Received, 10I 1867. On Jan. 21, USG endorsed these papers. "Respectfully returned to the Secretary of War. I dissent entirely from the views of the Commissioner of Indian Affairs. The policy being carried out by Gen. Sherman I believe to be the only one by which a permanent peace can be secured with these Indians, and recommend that he be allowed to execute his plans without restriction. If a joint commission should be appointed I would object to both officers mentioned." ES, *ibid*. On Jan. 29, Bvt. Maj. Gen. Edward D. Townsend wrote to USG. "The Secretary of the Interior having requested that Generals A. Sully, and H. E. Maynadier, be ordered to report to him for duty connected with the Indian Department, the Secretary of War desires to know whether you see any objection to such order being given. General Sully is now on the Board to examine Candidates for Commissions in the Infantry, in session in New York—and General Maynadier is with his regiment, the Twelfth Infantry, in this City, the regiment being commanded by its Lieut. Colonel, Wallace." ALS, *ibid*., 88A 1867. On Jan. 30, Col. Ely S. Parker endorsed this letter. "Respectfully returned. No objection is known to both of the within named officers being ordered to report to the Secretary of the Interior for special duty. The continued practice however, of ordering officers of the army to service in the Indian Bureau under the Interior Department is unqualifiedly disapproved." AES, *ibid.*

On Jan. 24, Parker wrote to USG. "In compliance with your request I have the honor to submit the following proposed plan for the establishment of a permanent and perpetual peace and for settling all matters of differences between the United States and the various Indian tribes." ALS, *ibid.*, RG 46, Senate 39A–E7, Committee on Military Affairs. Parker appended detailed recommendations later printed in *HMD*, 39-2-37, pp. 1–8. On the same day, USG endorsed these papers. "Respectfully forwarded to the Secretary of War, with request that copies of the within be sent to each of the Military Committees of the U S Senate and House of Representatives.—I concur generally in the views submitted by Col. Parker." ES, DNA, RG 46, Senate 39A–E7, Committee on Military Affairs.

On Jan. 25, Bvt. Maj. Gen. John Pope, Washington, D. C., wrote to USG at length submitting recommendations on Indian policy. ALS, *ibid.*, RG 108, Letters Received. *HMD*, 39-2-37, pp. 8–11. On Jan. 27, USG endorsed a copy of this letter. "Respectfully forwarded to the Hon. Secy. of War, with request that these copies be sent to the military committees of the U S. Senate and House of Representatives, and the Hon. Secretary of the Interior." ES, DNA, RG 46, Senate 39A–E7, Committee on Military Affairs.

To Lt. Gen. William T. Sherman

Washington. D. C. Jany. 15th 1867

LT. GEN. W. T. SHERMAN
COMDG. MIL. DIV. OF THE MO.
GENERAL:

Your letter enclosing one from Gen. Dodge to Gen. Cooke is received.[1] I am just having a letter written to the Sec. of War, to be submitted to the Sec. of the Interior, endorsing your recommendation as to colonizing hostile & friendly Indians. In the mean time you may go on with your preparations to carry out your views in the matter and if you receive no further instructions you may regard your plans sustained.

In conversation with the Sec. of War on the subject of treatment of Indian affairs, more than six months since he said that in general the whole matter would be left to you being satisfied that with your facilities for information you would know better what should be done than he could by any possibility. I have never had any experience among hostile Indians myself and have never been in their country. I am satisfied however that the Indian Bureau should be transferred to the War Dept. and Indian Agencies, from among civilians, abolished. Then no license should be given to traders among them. Trade with the Indians might be thrown open to all citizens leaving the Military authority to specify what articles should be sold to them, or rather what articles should not. Keeping arms and munitions from them,[2] trade in all other articles would weaken them more rapidly than campaigns.—I have strong hope that the transfer of the Indian Bureau will be made this session of Congress. Every member of Congress I have spoken to on the subject seems to favor the proposition

> Very respectfully
> Your obt. servt.
> U. S. GRANT
> General

Copies, DLC-USG, V, 47, 60; DNA, RG 108, Letters Sent.

1. On Jan. 11, 1867, Lt. Gen. William T. Sherman had written to Bvt. Maj. Gen. John A. Rawlins. "Gen Hancock reports to me by telegraph that a courier crossing over from Fort Morgan on the South Platte, to Fort Wallace on the Smoky Hill encountered many Indian lodges on the tributaries of the Republican Fork. Although their actions were friendly, still Gen Hancock was of opinion that some of them were Sioux who had been engaged in War above Laramie, and had come down for the Winter, and on that theory I instructed him to Capture all, and bring them upon one of his Military Reserves there to be taken in hand by the Indian Bureau. But I have since heard from Gen Cooke, that the bands in question, Spotted Tail, and Big Ribs are and always have been friendly and are Treaty Indians. Whereupon I instruct Genl Hancock to continue his preperations but await further orders before proceeding to seize these tribes. I have not yet received from your HeadQuarters any response to my application to clear out the space between the Platte and Arkansas of all Indians, whether hostile or friendly. The rapid progress of the Great Railroads, and our obligation to protect the mail routes in this belt makes action on our part imperative. I beg you will urge this matter upon the attention of the War & Interior Departments because it will be far more satisfactory if the authority proceeds from them than from us. It would have a bad effect if I were to have my action reversed, after the preperations were made. It would probably form a just cause for a delay in the work on the Railroads so essential to our military plans against Hostile bands beyond. It will be cheaper to have all friendly Indians brought in even to Leavenworth and there fed, than to run the risk of having them forced to join hostile bands by the acts of unthinking citizens. No matter what these Indians do, they will be charged

with all sorts of wrongs, and complicity with the Hostile Sioux. if nothing else can be said now, I would like General Grant to commit himself so far as to say, that I am at liberty to do what I deem necessary to ensure a General state of Peace on the Plains the Coming year. Orders must now be made as we must not give the indians time to recuperate their ponies after this Winter. I am conscious that all is being done that can be, to effect the transfer of the Whole Indian question to the War Dept, which is the first and great step to the end in view." ALS, *ibid.*, Letters Received. On Jan. 4, Grenville M. Dodge, Union Pacific Railroad Co., Omaha, had written to Bvt. Maj. Gen. Philip St. George Cooke requesting military protection during the next construction campaign. Copy, *ibid.* On Jan. 11, Sherman endorsed this letter. "This paper is just received, and I send it forthwith with my letter of this date as illustrative of the feeling of the parties interested. Last fall I passed without escort over every foot of this route, but workmen are not so confident, and so many stories are put afloat that Gen Dodge wisely asks the maximum possible protection." AES, *ibid.*

2. On Nov. 9, 1866, Secretary of the Interior Orville H. Browning had written to Secretary of War Edwin M. Stanton concerning modification of General Orders No. 10, Dept. of the Platte, July 31, forbidding the sale of arms and ammunition to all Indians. LS, *ibid.*, RG 107, Letters Received from Bureaus. On Nov. 26, USG endorsed this letter. "Respectfully returned with the recommendation that Department Commanders be invested with discretionary authority respecting the sale of arms and ammunition to friendly Indians." ES, *ibid.* USG enclosed a letter of Nov. 12 from Bvt. Maj. Gen. Alfred H. Terry, Fort Snelling, Minn., to Rawlins. "I have the honor to call the attention of the General Commanding the Army to a recent order from the Department of the Interior prohibiting the sale by traders of powder and lead to Indians. However necessary such an order may be in certain parts of the country where outbreaks have already occurred or are imminent, in other localities where the the Indians are friendly, it is, in my judgement much better adapted to promote than to prevent outrages. Without powder & lead many of the Indians in this department must be subsisted by the Government, must commit depredations or must starve. Their principal food during the winter is buffalo meat, and this cannot be obtained in sufficient quantities unless fire arms be used. It is true that *mounted* Indians can successfully pursue the buffalo with the bow and arrow alone, but there are not in the possession of the different bands a sufficient number of horses to enable them to obtain a supply in this manner; and besides many of Indians having abandoned the bow for fire-arms, have lost their skill in its use. It is hardly to be supposed that if the alternative of starvation or theft be presented to the Indians they will choose the former & I do not understand that it is the intention of the Government to provide them with subsistence. The Indians upon the Missouri River look upon this order as a breach of the treaty made by General Curtis with them during the past summer: they say that the Commissioner promised them supplies of powder and lead among the presents that were to be sent to them, and now when in addition to the failure to send the expected goods, this order deprives them even of the privilege of purchasing these articles so indispensable to their existence they not unnaturally doubt the good faith & good intentions of the Government toward them. One other considerations is of some importance. It is impossible to prevent the Indians & half breeds of the Red River settlements in the British Possessions from smuggling powder across the frontier and with the powder they bring whiskey: the effect of the order in question will be to

stimulate this illicit traffic and to increase the evil influence which these British Indians already have over the tribes on this side of the border. I therefore earnestly recommend that Indian Traders at or near military posts in this department be permitted to sell ammunition in small quantities under the supervision and control of the post commanders, subject to such rules and regulations regarding the quantity kept on hand and sold as may be prescribed by the Dept. Commander. At Fort Rice until the late order was issued the ammunition belonging to the traders located there was kept in the magazine of the fort: a specific quantity was issued to the traders weekly: a register was kept by them of the names of the Indians to whom it was sold and of the amount sold to each. This register was regularly inspected by the officer of the day of the post. I am persuaded that under similar regulations ammunition may be safely sold to friendly Indians & that unless it is sold to them in sufficient quantities to enable them to procure game & furs the present friendly feeling of nearly all the tribes in this department will be changed and that disturbances and outbreaks may be expected as the result of the prohibition" Copy, *ibid.* Additional papers are *ibid.* On Dec. 2, Col. Isaac V. D. Reeve, 13th Inf., Fort Rice, Dakota Territory, wrote to Bvt. Lt. Col. Edward W. Smith, adjt. for Terry, requesting permission to sell arms to friendly Indians to keep them friendly. LS, *ibid.*, RG 94, Letters Received, 32M 1867. On Jan. 16, 1867, USG endorsed this letter. "Respectfully forwarded to the Secretary of War with request that this communication be submitted to the Secretary of the Interior. I respectfully renew my recommendation of Nov. 27 1866, (on a communication from the Secretary of the Interior bearing upon this subject) 'that Department Commanders be invested with discretionary authority respecting the sale of arms and ammunition to friendly Indians.' " ES, *ibid.* On Jan. 19, Bvt. Maj. Gen. Edward D. Townsend telegraphed to Sherman and Terry. "The Secretary of War directs that General Orders No. 10, Headquarters, Department of the Platte, of July 31st, 1866, relating to the sale of arms and ammunition to Indians, be so modified that Department Commanders are invested with discretionary authority to permit sale of ammunition for hunting purposes to friendly Indians within their respective commands where it can be done with safety; the respective commanders being responsible for the exercise of proper caution in permitting such sales." Copy, *ibid.*, 58M 1867. On Jan. 21, Sherman telegraphed to Townsend requesting permission to supply arms and powder to friendly Indians from military supplies and to prohibit citizens from selling the same to Indians. Telegram received (at 11:00 A.M.), *ibid.* At 1:50 P.M., USG telegraphed to Sherman. "There is no authority except it be obtained by Act. of Congress to issue powder, lead &c. ~~from~~ to Indians, from public supplies. You can however prohibit sale of such articles except by traders doing business within specified posts, and you can limit the quantity to be sold to any one Indian, and the mithod of granting permits for such purchases, as you think proper." ALS (telegram sent), *ibid.*, RG 107, Telegrams Collected (Bound); telegram sent, *ibid.*; copies, *ibid.*, RG 108, Letters Sent; DLC-USG, V, 56. See letter to Edwin M. Stanton, Feb. 1, 1867.

To William Elrod

———

Jan. 15th *1867*.

DEAR ELROD.

I have been waiting to see the result of the law suit for possession of my land in St. Louis Co. before writing to you to go out there. Besides a number of cabins on my place, which by the way I have directed shall all be pulled down, there are three good houses. One at the end of the place furthest from St. Louis is a fine house well furnished. It is not properly situated for any one to live in to attend the farm the body of the cleared land being from one to two miles distant from it. Besides I want to keep that to occupy a few weeks each year myself. The house I intend you to occupy permanently is in the middle of the place. It is the house occupied by my father-in-law for the last forty years. This place was leased out before I purchased it however and although I offered the tenant $500 00 to give up his lease, which has but one year to run, he refuses to take it. This leaves me therefore the two ends of the farm on one of which there is no cleared land except what is in orchard, the other is occupied by Mr. White who has kept me out of the place for eight years without paying a cent for it or even the taxes. I have got judgement against him now however and unless he appeals I will get possession before you can get out there. This is the place I want you to occupy until I get possession of all my land when I want you to move to the house Mr. Dent has lived in so long.

You may start out as soon as you like. When you get to St. Louis enquire for the Gravoist Rock Road. You will want to go first to Mr. Sebastian Sappington's who is my agent. Mr. S. lives

AL (incomplete), Illinois Historical Survey, University of Illinois, Urbana, Ill. See *PUSG*, 16, 375–76, 408–9.

To William Elrod

———

Jan. 18th *1867*.

DEAR ELROD.

Since writing to you a few day I have come to the conclution that it will be better that you should not go to Mo. before March, or until I write to you again on the subject. I shall endeavor to go out in March to stay a few weeks until every thing is farely started. I will have my family with me and will want to live in the house I wrote to you that you would go into in case White was not removed from my place. Should he take an appeal and hold the place for another year I have still possession of land enough to keep you employed until I get the main part of the land. There is also a double log cabin, with hall between the rooms, where you will have to live until I get possession of the better buildings. There are also about one dozen log cabins on the place which I have directed to be torn down as soon as you go out. One or two of them can be moved and put up so as to give you additional room. They have windows, doors, floors &c. so that it would take but a short time, with help, to make you quite comfortable.

Yours Truly
U. S. GRANT

Please answer this.

ALS, ICarbS.

To Mary Jane Safford

———

Washington, Jan. 21st *1867*.

MY DEAR MISS SAFFORD.

I owe you an apology for not earlyer acknow[l]edeing the beautiful token of remembrance which you were so kind as to send me about one month ago. The box containing it came duly to hand and supposing it to be a box of cigars, a present which I often get, it was sent to the house where I have several dozen boxes just like it, though with different contents. I supposed that a letter would come along through the Mail announcing who had favored me, as is usually the case. But no letter came and the matter was forgotten until last evening I had occasion to open a fresh box of cigars, and accidentally opened the one you sent me, and there found your letter and beautiful present. It was the first I knew of your return from Europe. I was indeed glad to hear from you and shall also prize most highly both your letter and the cigar holder which I shall preserve in remembrance of the donor.

I had hoped ere this to have visited Europe. The unsettled condition of our country, politically, has however prevented me doing so up to this time.

Remember me kindly to your brother and Mrs. Safford. Mrs. Grant and the children also join me in this and in desiring to be remembered to you.

Yours Truly,
U. S. GRANT

ALS, Cairo Public Library, Cairo, Ill. See *PUSG*, 4, 419.

To Edwin M. Stanton

Washington, D. C. Jan. 25th *1867*.

HON. E. M. STANTON,
SEC. OF WAR;
SIR:

I have the honor to recommend Bvt. Lt. Col. E. C. Beman,[1] of the Volunteer service, for appointment of Com.y of Subsistence, Regular Army, Vice Capt. E. D. Brigham resigned.

Col. Beman has served faithfully and efficiently for about six years in the Subsistence Dept. The Com.y Gn. is anxious to have this appointment made because he regards Col. Beman one of the very best Com.y he has had from the Volunteer service. He is young and a single man and therefore more available for service in our Mountain territories, where his services are now wanted, than if he had a family.

> Very respectfully
> your obt. svt.
> U. S. GRANT
> General,

ALS, DNA, RG 94, ACP, B117 CB 1867; copies (dated Jan. 23, 1867), *ibid.*, RG 108, Letters Sent; DLC-USG, V, 47, 60.

1. Edgar C. Beman was appointed capt. and commissary as of Nov. 14, 1861. On Sept. 28, 1867, Maj. Gen. Oliver O. Howard, Bureau of Refugees, Freedmen, and Abandoned Lands, wrote to USG, secretary of war *ad interim*. "Capt Edgar C. Beman C. S., I understand is still in the service. I am very anxious to have him retained in the service and assigned to duty temporarily in this Bureau for Disbursing Officer in Tennessee. He might do all the Commissary duty besides the duty required of him in the Bureau, I send this through the Commissary General for his endorsement and recommendation." LS, DNA, RG 94, ACP, H990 CB 1867. Beman was mustered out as of Sept. 1, 1868.

To Lt. Gen. William T. Sherman

———

Washington, D. C., January 26th. 1867.

DEAR GENERAL,

I have carefully read the enclosed letter from General Dodge, an in accordance with your request return it. Now that Government has assumed the obligation to guarantee the bonds of the Pacific Railroad, it becomes a matter of great pecuniary interest to see it completed as soon as possible   Every protection practicable should be given by the military, both to secure the rapid completion of the road and to avoid pretexts on the part of the builders to get further assistance from the Government.

I do not see my way clear now to furnish you further reinforcements beyond one regiment of Infantry. As soon as one regiment of the Invalid Corps is organized, I can have the Canada frontier garrisoned by it, with a few companies of Artillery, and send you the 4th Infantry, now on duty there. It might be further practicable to send you a regiment of Invalids to occupy such depots as are necessary to be kept up, and thereby relieve more active men from duty in the front. I will not send them however without an intimation from you that they can be made available. You might be reinforced to some extent by increasing the standard of companies to the maximum number allowed by law.

Yours truly.
U. S. Grant,
General.

To Lieut. Genl. W. T. Sherman,
Comdg. Mil. Div. of the Missouri.

Copies, DLC-USG, V, 47, 60; IaHA; DNA, RG 108, Letters Sent; *ibid.*, RG 393, Dept. of the Platte, Letters Received. On Jan. 14, 1867, Grenville M. Dodge, Council Bluffs, Iowa, had written to Lt. Gen. William T. Sherman concerning the progress of the Union Pacific Railroad and offering suggestions about campaigning against Indians. Copy, *ibid.* On Jan. 19, Sherman, St. Louis, endorsed this letter. "Please read this carefully—It is very important indeed—We ought to back Dodge as much as possible—for if he can finish the road to Fort Sanders this year it will be all important to the Military interests of the Country. When you have read, please send it back to me. *Augur* will study his case and then notify me the least possible force he will need—and then if you can give it well— if not, we will do our best with what we have" Copy, *ibid.* On Jan. 18, Sherman had written to Dodge. "I have just read with intense interest your letter of the 14, and though you wanted it Kept to myself, I believe you will sanction my sending it to Gnl Grant for his individual perusal, to be returned to me. It is almost a miracle to grasp your proposition to finish to Fort Sanders this year, but you have done so much that I mistrust my own judgmt and accept yours. I regard this Road of yours as the solution of our Indian affairs, and of the Mormon question, and therefore give you all I possibly can but the demand for soldiers *every* where, and the slowness of enlistmt especially among the Blacks, limits our ability to respond—. . . Augur will be with you before this, and you will find him prepared to second you to the utmost of his power. I want him to study his problem and call on Grant through me for the *least* force that is adequate for we must respect the demands from other quarters. Of course I am disposed to find fault that our soldiers are now tied up in the Southern States, but in the light they are now regarded, it would be inpolitic and imprudent for me to say so publicly. All I can do is to keep General Grant well informed so that he may distribute his army to the best advantage for the Whole Country. . . ." ALS, Dodge Papers, IaHA. On Jan. 22, Sherman wrote to Dodge. "Yours of Jan 9. for some reason did not reach me till today. I had nothing to do with Cooke's removal—the order originated at Washington and came to me complete without my being consulted, and I do not know what influenced Genl Grant, but never supposed Genl Cooke was in the least to blame for the Phil Kearney Massacre. That Post had been completed, and the Garrison increased to the largest estimate made by anyone up to that time and I would have volunteered to General Cooke this explanation, only the instant I sent him a copy of the telegram he replied that he presumed I was the Cause of his removal, which debarred me from making any explanation. . . ." ALS, *ibid.*

On Sept. 1, 1866, U.S. Delegate Walter A. Burleigh of Dakota Territory, Yankton, had written to USG. "I learn that no order has yet been received to continue the Military Posts, Fort James and Fort Dakota, the former on the Dakota River and the latter on the Big Sioux River, between this City and the country inhabited by the hostile Sioux's Northwest of us. You will recollect that I called on you in relation to these Posts, and that you at once called to the attention of Gen. Sherman, the great importance of maintaining them. I hope this will be done. The abandoning of these Posts at the present time would be one of the greatest evils that could possibly befall our Territory, as the Valley of the Dakota or James River is, and has been, the established route of war parties from the hostile tribes in their murderous raids upon our defenceless settlers. I sincerely hope that you will at once order the continuance of these very important frontier Posts." LS, DNA, RG 108, Letters Received. Governor Andrew J. Faulk and Surveyor Gen. William Tripp, Yankton, endorsed this letter. "We fully concur in the forgoing and respectfully urge that the forgoing request of Mr. Burleigh be complied with—" AES (undated), *ibid.* Burleigh enclosed a petition of Sept. 1 to USG on the same matter. DS, *ibid.* On Nov. 12, Bvt. Maj. Gen. Alfred H. Terry endorsed these papers. "Respectfully returned to the Head Quarters Mil Div of the Mo. Previous to my assumption of the command of this Dept. Bvt Major General Cooke issued an order discontinuing Fort James and removing its garrison to Fort Randall. When I was at the latter place on the 10th ult. the troops were on the march in obedience thereto. No order has been given for the abandonment of Fort Dakota on the Big Sioux river, nor is such abandonment contemplated" AES, *ibid.* On Dec. 15, Terry, Fort Snelling, Minn., wrote to Bvt. Maj. Gen. John A. Rawlins. "Lieut. General Sherman has strongly impressed upon me the necessity of adequately protecting the navigation of the Upper Missouri and the new stage mail and emigration route which will be opened the coming summer from this state to the mining regions of Montana. I have examined the subject and I am prepared to make recommendations in regard to the disposition of the troops, and the construction of the posts which will be required, and as the absence of General Sherman renders it impossible to present my views to him, I respectfully ask the attention of the General Commanding the Army to them. . . . To recapitulate I recommend that Fort Rice be rebuilt; that Fort Ridgely be removed to, or beyond the western boundary of Minnesota; that a post be built near Berthold; that two posts be built between Abercrombie & Berthold; that Buford be enlarged; that a post be built on the Sun River, and that the post at Crow Creek be abandoned." LS, *ibid.*, RG 92, Consolidated Correspondence, Terry. On Jan. 10, 1867, USG endorsed this letter. "Approved and respectfully forwarded to the Secretary of War, with the recommendation that the funds necessary to carry out the within programme be furnished upon the requisitions of the Chief Qr. Mr., Dept. of Dakota." ES, *ibid.* On March 15, USG endorsed papers concerning Terry's letter. "Respectfully forwarded to the Secretary of War—with recommendation that Lt. Gen. Sherman be authorized to use so much as may be necessary for the erection of these posts, of the unexpended portion of the $1.000.000 placed at his disposal for the purpose of sheltering troops in his Military Division." Copy, *ibid.*, RG 108, Register of Letters Received.

On Jan. 18, Solomon L. Spink, secretary, Dakota Territory, wrote a letter received at USG's hd. qrs. enclosing a memorial concerning defense against Indians. *Ibid.* On Jan. 26, USG endorsed these papers. "Respy. referred to Lt. Gen. W. T. Sherman, and attention called to the recommendation to have Fort James re-occupied. It may be possible to give you one more regiment of Infantry to your entire Military Division, but, I think not more." Copy, *ibid.* On Feb. 20, Sherman wrote to Maj. George K. Leet. "I have before me the Memorial of the Territory of Dahcotah asking for more troops in that Territory and more especially the Post of Fort James be reestablished. Dahcotah has already, a large proportion of the troops at our disposal, and it will be impossible to spare more this year in that Quarter. The subject of the Post at Fort James has been fully considered by the Departmt Commander General Terry, who thinks he can better afford protection to Minnesota by the new Posts contemplated west of Fort Wadsworth. I concur with him in this opinion, yet will give the matter my personal attention this spring. I have also the Memorial of the Legislature of the State of Kansas, asking that a Post be established halfway between Forts Harker and Kearney. This will be referred to the Departmt Commander General Hancock who is on the point of moving a considerable body of troops to the west of that point and can then better judge of its necessity. These new Posts are very costly and must be avoided unless indispensably necessary" ALS, *ibid.*, Letters Received.

On March 9, Bvt. Brig. Gen. Cyrus B. Comstock wrote to Terry. "Some time since a memorial from the ~~legislation~~ Legislature of Dakota was recived at these Hdqrs, urging the reestablishment of Fort James (about 75 miles north of Yankton). On reference of the question to Gen. Sherman he as well as yourself opposed the request. A delegation is now here urging the reestablishment of that post, stating that it is essential to prevent the incursions of Indians; that timber, hay, and water are convenient; that quarters for one company are already erected, &c. The General in Chief desires that you will in reply, state in detail your views in the case" Copies, DLC-USG, V, 47, 60; DNA, RG 108, Letters Sent. On April 3, Terry, St. Paul, wrote to Comstock. "I have the honor to acknowledge the receipt of your letter of the 9th ult., in relation to the re-occupation of Fort James in Dakota Territory. My delay in replying to it has arisen from the facts that when it arrived here I was absent in St Louis, and that since my return I have been confined to my house by illness. The opinion upon which I based my report to Lieut General Sherman that the post aught not to be reoccupied, are substantially as follows; viz:—1st I think that one company posts in the Indian country are almost useless, they have hardly sufficient strength for self protection, they, in common with stronger posts, can easily be avoided by hostile bands and no detachment can be made from them without perilling the safety of the posts themselves 2d I can assign to South Eastern Dakota only one regiment, the 22d Infantry; the distribution of it as approved by Lieut General Sherman will be one company to Fort Dakota on the Big Sioux; one to Fort Randall; four to Fort Sully and four to Fort Rice. I could not place a company in Fort James without diminishing the garrison of Sully or Rice, or discontinuing Randall or Dakota. I think that Dakota might well be given up, I have refrained from recommending that it be abandoned out of deference to the views and wishes of the same people who are now applying for the reoccupation of James, I think that it would in no degree meet their wishes were the company now there transferred to Fort James. Fort Randall should have two companies. I have reluctantly been compelled to order a reduction of its garrison to one company in order to give sufficient strength to Sully and Rice. I esteem it of great importance to the quiet of the inhabited portions of the territory that the posts on the Missouri should be sufficiently strong to keep the hostile Indians west of the river, or to furnish detachments to operate against them if they should cross it. Sully and Rice are the two important posts for this purpose. I believe that four companies at Sully will protect lower Dakota far better than three at Sully and one at James. The same may be said in regard to Rice. 3rd I have recommended the construction of a line of posts from Abercrombie to Fort Berthold; this recommendation has been approved of by Lieut General Sherman, General Grant, and the Secretary of War. When the new posts are completed South Eastern Dakota will be completely encircled by military stations; as follows: Forts Randall, Sully, Rice, and Berthold on the Missouri. A new post on the Headwaters of the James, a new post on the Shyenne, Fort Abercrombie on the Red River of the North, Fort Wadsworth and Fort Dakota, and I do not think that the Indians thus surrounded will dare to attempt hostilities. It might be well to place a garrison at Fort James were there troops dispozable for the purpose, but with the number of troops at my command I believe that the defense of the territory would be weakened rather than strengthened by so doing." LS, *ibid.*, Letters Received. On April 20, Sherman endorsed this letter. "Respectfully forwarded to the Headquarters of the Army. I entirely approve of General Terrys reasoning & conclusion in this matter. It is the worst possible policy to scatter our men to satisfy local interests & people—" AES, *ibid.* On April 27, Terry wrote to Comstock. "I have the honor to acknowledge the receipt of your letter of the 17th inst. enclosing telegraphic despatch from Messrs Rice and Thompson of this place to the Hon. Alexander Ramsey of the United States Senate, in reference to the practicability of conveying the mail hence to Montana on ponies, and directing me to make such remarks upon it as I might deem pertinent to the subject. My attention was first called to the matter by citizens of St. Paul after the despatch had been sent. I therefore have not had time to investigate the matter fully, but as far as I can form a judgement upon it, I am strongly of the opinion that no valuable mail service can be rendered between Abercrombie and Montana, unless frequent stations with ample relays of horses, stock keepers, and all the appurtenances and appliances of a stage route upon the frontier be maintained along the line. My opinion is based upon our experience in this department during the past winter. In the autumn I instructed the Commanding Officers at Forts Rice and Abercrombie to keep up a weekly mail between their posts. Strenuous efforts were made for this purpose, and in the early part of the season one or two mails were gotten through, although with great hardship to the carriers. Afterwards all attempts failed, and finally no one, white man, half-breed, or Indian could be induced to encounter the perils and suffering of the undertaking. During the larger part of the winter the only communication with Fort Rice has been by mounted mail parties to Fort Sully, thence to Randall &c. I am informed that between Rice and Sully these parties have encountered great difficulties, and that as a rule, some of the men in each party have arrived at their destination more or less frost-bitten. Both of the routes above named are in much lower latitudes than the major portion of the Montana route. Should stations be build along the line in as great numbers as they must be on a stage route; should these stations be placed in charge of experienced stock-keepers; should they be well supplied with provisions, fuel and forage; should an ample number of animals to provide for all contingencies be kept there, I think that the mail may be carried on ponies, but under no other conditions could it be carried with celerity, safety, and certainty." LS, *ibid.*

On May 25, 1:00 P.M., USG telegraphed to Terry. "At what time should Gen Comstock be at St. Paul to go with you on your inspection—" LS (telegram sent), *ibid.*, RG 107, Telegrams Collected (Bound); telegram sent, *ibid.*; copies, *ibid.*, RG 108, Telegrams Sent; DLC-USG, V, 56. On the same day, Terry telegraphed to Comstock. "I have expected to leave here June 3rd but can wait a day or two for you   We will look out for your outfit" Telegrams received (2—at 9:40 P.M.), DNA, RG 107, Telegrams Collected (Bound). On May 26, USG wrote to Comstock. "You will proceed to St. Paul Minnesota and thence make an inspection of the Dept of Dakota. Commanding officers and quartermasters are hereby directed to furnish you such escort and transportation as you shall deem necessary. Having accomplished this duty you will report at these Head Quarters." LS, DLC-Cyrus B. Comstock. At 9:00 A.M., Comstock telegraphed to Terry. "I start for St Paul direct tomorrow morning." ALS (telegram sent), DNA, RG 107, Telegrams Collected (Bound); telegram sent, *ibid.*; copies, *ibid.*, RG 108, Telegrams Sent; DLC-USG, V, 56. On May 27, Monday, Terry telegraphed to USG. "Your telegram of the 25th just received. Gen. Comstock should be here by Saturday night." Telegram received (at 6:45 P.M.), DNA, RG 107, Telegrams Collected (Bound); *ibid.*, RG 108, Telegrams Received; copies (one sent by mail), *ibid.*, Letters Received; DLC-USG, V, 55.

To Edwin M. Stanton

Washington, D. C. Jan. 28th *1867.*

HON. E. M. STANTON,
SEC. OF WAR:
SIR:

I have the honor to recommend Lt. Ed. F. Norvell, of Detroit Michigan, for a Lieutenancy of Cavalry. Lt. Norvell enlisted as a private at the begining of the War, in the Cavalry, and served faithfully until mustered out of service less than one year ago. Out of seven brothers six of them went into the Volunteer service and the seventh was only kept out by his youth. I know the family well and have known them for many years most favorably.

Lt. Novell was twice breveted for gallantry during the war.

> Very respectfully
> your obt. svt.
> U. S. GRANT
> General.

ALS, DNA, RG 94, ACP, N123 CB 1867. On Dec. 24, 1866, Isabella H. Norvell, Detroit, had written to USG. "I hope you will forgive the liberty I take in addressing a private communication to you on the subject of my son Edwin Forrest Norvell. At the commencement of the War, when not eighteen years of age, he enlisted in the 1st Michigan Cavalry, under Col. Brodhead. During the first year he was made 'Commissary Sergeant' and 2nd Lieut. and in three months more a 1st Lieut. After the death of Col. Brodhead he was detailed to the Staff of Genl Custer, where he remained untill ordered to his regt. to be mustered out, nearly one year after the close of the War   For his conduct while on Genl Custers Staff, he was brevetted a Capt. and Maj. and before he left the Genl in Texas an application was made to the 'War Department' for a Commission in the Cavalry branch of the Service signed by Genls Sheridan, Custer and others. Not having a *father* or any *influencial* friends to push the matter, nothing has been heard of the application since it was made. This induces me to apply to you for your influence, feeling confident that you will give it, unless, you know of some cause why it would be impossible for you to do so. Having served nearly five years with the Army and not having been educated for any business or profession, he naturally prefers it to any other, independent of being thrown on the world, at twenty three years of age, without the means of support, for I am, myself, dependent upon my children. If you cannot comply with my wishes for the Army, do you think it would be possible for him to get employment in any of the Military Departments in Washington. I enclose you a Copy of the communication sent by Genl Custer to the 'War Department' recommending him for brevets, also the Genls last order before they parted. I hope you will excuse my intruding upon you in this manner and attribute it, to its true cause, the great anxiety I feel about my son" ALS, *ibid*. The enclosure is *ibid*. On Jan. 5, 1867, USG endorsed these papers. "Respectfully forwarded to the Secretary of War, recommended f[o]r 2d Lt. of Infantry." ES, *ibid*.

On Oct. 1, Norvell, Grosse Ile, Mich., wrote to USG. "I wish very much to secure the appointment of my son Alfred C. Norvell as a second Lieutenant in the Infantry. He enlisted early in the war in the 23rd Infantry from this State, and rose from the ranks to be a first Lieutenant, and served faithfully untill disabled by long continued illness, when he was mustered out. His illness was brought on by over exertion in pursuit of the rebel General Morgan, his regiment having been mounted for the purposes of pursuit. He has suffered, more or less, until the last few months, but is now I hope permanently recovered. He would like to return to the Service and it would gratify me if he could receive an appointment. I have never thanked you for your kindness in securing the appoint-

ment of my son E. F. Norvell as Lieut. in the Cavalry, although much to my disappointment, he failed to pass his examination before the Board at Washington.
I was not aware of the strictness of the examination or I might not have asked
for his appointment, for he enlisted at seventeen, when he should have been at
school, and served during the whole war most gallantly. Hoping it may be in
your power to grant me the favor now asked (the appointment of Alfred C.
Norvell as Lieut. of Infantry,) . . ." ALS, *ibid.*, P603 CB 1867. On Oct. 7, Maj.
and Bvt. Brig. Gen. Orlando M. Poe wrote to USG recommending Alfred C.
Norvell. ALS, *ibid.* No appointment followed.

To Edwin M. Stanton

Washington, D. C. Jan. 28th *1867*.

HON. E. M. STANTON,
SEC. OF WAR:
SIR:

Col. J. G. Dudley, of New York, has applied to me for a recommendation for a Cadetship at West Point for his son. The young
man has the higest testimonials from his teachers of qualifications
for such an appointment. I prefer however limiting my recommendations to the sons of officers of the Army & Navy, classes who have
no representation in Congress, consequently no way of getting
these appointments except "At large," and to young men who have
won such consideration by services in the Volunteer Army.

Col. Dudley has shown me letters which indicate that these
appointments have been offered for sale from some Districts, a
practice demoralizing to the Military Academy and which I hope
can be stopped and those engaged in selling these appointments
exposed.

Very respectfully
your obt. svt.
U. S. GRANT
General,

ALS, DNA, RG 94, Correspondence, USMA. William H. Dudley of Sing Sing,
N. Y., son of Jonas G. Dudley, entered USMA in 1867 and died on June 10, 1870.

To Edwin M. Stanton

Respectfully forwarded to the Secretary of War.—Attention is invited to that part of the within communi[c]ation which refers to the condition of Union men and freed men in Texas, and to the powerlessness of the military in the present state of affairs to afford them protection. Even the moral effect of the presence of troops is passing away and a few days ago a squad of soldiers on duty was fired on by citizens in Brownsville, Texas, a report of which is this day forwarded.[1]

In my opinion the great number of murders of union men and freed men in Texas not only as a rule unpunished but uninvestigated, constitutes what is practically a state of insurrection; and believing it to be the province and duty of every good government to afford protection to the lives, liberty and property of her citizens, I would recommend the declaration of martial law in Texas to secure these ends.

The necessity for governing any portion of our territory by martial law is to be deplored. If resorted to it should be limited in its authority and should leave all local authorities and civil tribunals free and unobstructed until they prove their inefficiency or unwillingness to perform their duties. Martial law would give security or comparative security to all classes of citizens without regard to race, color or political opinions, and could be continued until society was capable of protecting itself or until the State is returned to its full relations with the Union. The application of martial law to one of these States would be a warning to all and if necessary could be extended to others.

U. S. GRANT
General.

HDQRS. A U S
JAN. 29. 67

ES, DLC-Andrew Johnson. Written on a copy of a letter of Jan. 25, 1867, from Maj. Gen. Philip H. Sheridan, New Orleans, to USG. "From the enclosed dispatch you will see that there is some little trouble in Texas about honors to be paid to the remains of Sidney Johnson and that General Griffin has taken action in the premises. I very much fear continued disturbance in that State. The condition of Freedmen and Union men in remote parts of the State is truly horrible. The Government is denounced; the Freedmen are shot and Union men are persecuted if they have the temerity to express their opinion. This condition exists in the northeastern counties of the State to an alarming extent. I have been unable to spare troops for these counties, but will try and send a detachment or company to some point north of Jefferson. Applications come to me from the most respectable authorities for troops, but troops have so little power that they are efficient only in the moral effect which their presence has. It is currently reported in these counties that the object of the Governor in calling for troops for the frontier is to get the soldiers removed from the interior, so that there could be no interference in the perpetration of these fiendish actions. There was no trouble here upon the removal of the remains of Sidney Johnson from this city. The newspapers invited the friends of the deceased to attend the funeral and there was simply a funeral without any Confederate display. The 20th Infantry is at the mouth of the river. This will give me as many troops as I want for my command, and the last two remaining regiments of Colored Volunteers will be ordered mustered-out before long." LS, DNA, RG 108, Letters Received. The enclosures are *ibid*. On Jan. 29, Sheridan forwarded to USG information concerning a proposed escort for the remains of C.S.A. Gen. Albert Sidney Johnston through Galveston, Tex., for reburial in Austin. ES and copies, *ibid*., RG 94, Letters Received, 115G 1867. On Feb. 14, USG endorsed these papers. "Respectfully forwarded to the Secretary of War, for his information." ES, *ibid*.

In Jan., Sheridan forwarded papers received at USG's hd. qrs. concerning an order by the district court of Galveston to arrest Bvt. Maj. Gen. Samuel P. Heintzelman for protecting from arrest an agent of the Bureau of Refugees, Freedmen, and Abandoned Lands. DLC-USG, V, 43. On Jan. 28, USG endorsed these papers. "Respectfully forwarded to the Secretary of War. The course pursued in this matter thus far meets my approval, and I would respectfully request information as to whether Gen'l Heintzelman, will be sustained by the Government." Copies, *ibid*.; (incomplete and incorporated in a letter of Jan. 29 from Secretary of War Edwin M. Stanton to President Andrew Johnson requesting instructions) DNA, RG 107, Letters Received from Bureaus.

1. On Jan. 19, Col. Joseph J. Reynolds, 26th Inf., Brownsville, Tex., had written to Bvt. Maj. Gen. John A. Rawlins. "On the night of the 16th Inst, a ~~difficulty~~ patrol of Colored Troops, in charge of a non-comd Officer, while in the discharge of their legitimate duty, was fired upon by some drunken policemen in Brownsville—The patrol returned the fire, promptly & properly, resulting in mortally wounding two white men; one a policeman, the other, the proprietor of a drinking saloon where the affair occurred—The patrol acted right and is in no way to blame. The occurrence has been fully investigated by the Mayor, at which I had an officer present,—We have all the testimony which clearly justifies the action of the guard—I forward this concise statement of the facts in the case for the information of the General in Chief lest the papers through defective information should give a false impression with regard to this affair—" ALS, *ibid*.,

RG 108, Letters Received. On Jan. 29, USG endorsed a copy of this letter. "Respectfully forwarded to the Secretary of War for his information." ES, DLC-Andrew Johnson.

To Edwin M. Stanton

Washington, D. C. Feb. 1st *1867*.

HON. E. M. STANTON,
SEC. OF WAR;
SIR:

The enclosed papers just received from Gen. Sherman are respectfully forwarded and your special attention invited. They show the urgent necessity for an immediate transfer of the Indian Bureau to the War Dept. and the abolition of Civil Indian Agts. and licensed traders. If the present practice is dto be continued I do not see that any course is left open to us but to withdraw our troops to the settlements call upon Congress to provide means, and troops, to carry on formidable hostilities against the Indians until all the Indians or all the Whites upon the great plains, and between the settlements on the Mo. and the Pacific slope, are exterminated.

The course Gen. Sherman has pursued in this matter, in disregarding the permit of Mr. Bogy and others, is just right. I will instruct him to enforce his order until it is countermanded by the President or yourself. I would also respectfully ask that this matter be placed before the President and his disapproval of licensing the sale of Arms to Indians asked.

We have treaties with all tribes of Indians from time to time. If the rule is to be followed that all tribes with which we have treaties, and pay annuities, can procure such articles without stint or limit it will not be long before the matter becomes perfectly understood by the Indians and they avail themselves of it to equip perfectly for war. They will get the Arms either by making treaties themselves or through tribes who have such treaties.

I would respectfully recommend that copies of the enclosed communications be furnished to the Military Committees of each house of Congress.

Very respectfully

your obt. svt.

U. S. GRANT

General

ALS, DNA, RG 108, Letters Received. On Jan. 26, 1867, Lt. Gen. William T. Sherman, St. Louis, had written to USG. "The enclosed papers are so important that I ask for them your special attention. The sale of arms and amunition to Indians is the most delicate operation conceivable. The recent despatches passed between us have been sent to my Dept Commanders for their Govt, but of course I expect the sale to be controlled by Post Commanders & limited in quantity to the powder & lead absolutely needed by Indians known to the local commanders and for the purpose of killing meat for food. Now it seems the aggregated Indian Agents and Commissioners for the Comanches, Kioways, Cheyennes & Arapahos, (all bold daring and active indians inclined all the time to break out into open War) have given an unlimited authority to Mr D. A. Butterfield and to 'any other regularly licensed Indian Trader' to sell arms and amunition 'to any Indians that are at peace with, and receiving annuities from the United States Governmt.' The thing seems to me so monstrous that I would not credit it, unless I had the paper well authenticated before me, and I have ordered Gen Hancock to disregard it, and to restrict the sales to ~~the~~ small quantities, which alone are compatible with the present attitude of things on the Vast Plains and which it is the most difficult problem I have ever had to handle, to make comparatively secure. If the Indian agents are to be entrusted with this matter I may have to withdraw our troops, for it is even now almost impossible to protect the trains going to and fro. These Indians are only nominally friendly, and for buffalo Robes can buy the best carbines, revolvers, and guns of all kinds with the amunition to match. It is absurd to suppose a Trader who makes money by each sale, and generally makes profits by Indian Wars will be prudent in these sales, and I call your attention to the fact that the Commissioned Agents, who might be construed as to have some interest in the Peace of the Frontier—have surrendered all control of the matter to the licensed Traders. I beg you will show this and its enclosures to the President, with this conclusion of mine that the Trader for a profit of ten dollars the pistol, will involve us in a war that will cost the Treasury millions of dollars. I was aware that the Indians were getting arms in dangerous quantities but presumed that they purchased of passing teamsters, but now I see, that one Departmt of our National Governmt is arming them, at the Expense of life, and a vast Cost to another Departmt of the same ~~same~~ Govt. The very Traders, and agents who signed this paper, are now appealing for our scanty ~~buildings~~ Quarters at Fort Larned, deeming it prudent to move from the agency at Zarah, from the very indians named in their 'permit to sell arms.' I am now convinced more than ever that in addition to the Sioux we will have the Cheyennes & Arapahos to fight this year." ALS, *ibid.*, RG 94, Letters Received, 115M 1867. The statement of Charles Bogy and four other Indian agents, Nov. 15, 1866, authorizing the sale of arms and ammunition to peaceful Indians is in *HMD*, 39-2-40.

On Jan. 13, 1867, Maj. Henry Douglass, 3rd Inf., Fort Dodge, Kan., wrote to Sherman's adjt. concerning the sale of arms and ammunition by Indian agents and traders of the Dept. of the Interior to Indians and reporting that Kicking Bird, a Kiowa chief, had informed him that Indians were accumulating surplus weapons and ammunition in preparation for a general war in the spring. ALS, DNA, RG 94, Letters Received, 89M 1867. On Jan. 25, Sherman endorsed this letter. "Respectfully forwarded to Headquarters Armies of the U. S., with request that it be laid before the Committee [on] Indian Affairs. I know 'Kicking Bird,' very well: he is intelligent, and I consider full faith can be given to his statements." ES, *ibid.* On Jan. 31, Col. Ely S. Parker endorsed this letter. "Respectfully returned with request that this communication be laid before the Military Committees of Congress." AES, *ibid.* See *HMD*, 39-2-41.

On Feb. 5, Henry B. Whipple, Episcopal bishop of Minn., Faribault, wrote to USG. "Permit me to thank you for your firm and decided course in behalf of the poor Indians who have so long suffered from our wretched Indian system—and which has made them our relentless enemies and caused the death of thousands of innocent people on the border. In doing this you have been true to the traditions of the army which has always protested against this shameless system. Eight years ago I was brought face to face with its workings and since then I have watched it closely. From first to last it is evil and only evil. It thwarts the merciful designs of the Government, it robs the Indians and sends the pioneer citizen to sleep in nameless graves. For three years I plead with the Department and with the people to redress the evils which I knew was slowly working out a harvest of blood in Minnesota. I saw the dark cloud so clearly that in every parish of my diocese, in letters to the press and in appeals to our rulers I warned them that the massacre would surely come. I was laughed at as a fanatic—It came. The record of its causes are in Washington. For your own satisfaction I wish you would examine them. You will find that in 1858 the Sioux sold us 800.000 acres of their reservation, the plea was the need of money for civilization. After four years they had received nothing save a quantity of goods well nigh worthless was sent to Yellow Medicine—all but about $880—of the amount going to the Lower Sioux was absorbed in claims—This was not enough, they laid hands on the annuities and altho' the treaty provided that the payment should take place in June, 7000 wild men were called together and kept from June till the 18th of August—The traders told them that one half of their annuities were gone and gave this as a reason for refusing credits. The whole of the money did come but the warrant on the treasury shows that a large part of that for the Lower Sioux was taken from other funds and thus hoped to save the massacre—It was too late. I have no heart to write the history of affairs in the Chippewa country. I could tell of dead mens names on pay rolls, of civilization funds squandered, of schools which were a sham and I have been told where the moneys appropriated by Congress for the houses of chiefs had been retained and goods turned out in its place. I have no heart to write this record which is a shame to our boasted civilization. The evil cannot be cured under our present system. The Indian agent is appointed as a reward for political service and he is expected to carry on his agency to pay political campaign expenses. It is a proverb here that an agent can amass a fortune on 1,500 a year—Recently I made a protest against the appointment of an Indian trader and the Secretary of the Interior sustained me. I procured the appointment of a man of the most unimpeachable character and yet it is a question if he can be confirmed—I see no redress for these things except in an entire change of the system. We have allowed matters to drift until we have managed to stir up the whole of the tribes beyond us to mutiny—Three years ago I wrote: 'These questions cannot be buried. The two advancing waves of civilization from the Atlantic and Pacific are soon to meet. The Indians wrongs will now be righted or else, which God forbid, this nation will hear such a wail of agony from the horrors of Indian war as we have never heard. Savage men whose feet are by an open grave will requite an awful vengeance and it will fall where it has fallen on the innocent people of the border—' Pardon me for writing as I do. Your name is more powerful today than any man in America and you have in good Col. Parker of your staff a witness that with God 'there is no respector of persons.' Civilization is as good for one race as another There is a manly heart in the American people which although slow to act will redress wrongs. Much as I have suffered in reproaches and hatred for my pleadings for the poor, it is a happier path to fear God than to fear man." Copy, DNA, RG 108, Letters Received. On Feb. 11, USG wrote to U.S. Senator Henry Wilson of Mass., chairman, Committee on Military Affairs. "I take the liberty of enclosing to you a letter just rec'd from Bishop Whipple, of Minn. a gentleman that I know, and who has, for a number of years, taken a humane and christian interest in 'Indian Affairs.' It has some bearing on the question of transfer of the Indian Bureau now before the Senate" Copy, *ibid*.

To William Elrod

Feb.y. 2d *1867*.

DEAR ELROD:

I received your letter acknowledging receipt of checks for $500 00 this morning. I had previously written to Uncle Samuel to let you know that I had written such letter fearing, as I got no answer, that you had not received it. I hope you received one from me written two days after saying that I would not want you to go to Mo. before March and that I would write to you before you go? Your Post Office address will be Sappington Post Office, St. Louis County, Mo.

You need not go out until I write to you to start. That will not be earlyer than March some time. I expect to go out then and stay for a few weeks and start you all fair.

It will be a year before I get possession of all my place. Then, if it can be done, I will hire as many men with their own teams to come and break up land and get the whole place in meadow at once. After that there will be no land to cultivate but the orchards and my idea is that three men will be sufficient to keep the year round. Many more will have to be hired in [ha]rvest and probably in fruit picking.

Yours Truly,
U. S. GRANT

ALS, Dorothy Elrod, Marissa, Ill.

To Edwin M. Stanton

———

Washington, February 4 1867.

HON. E. M. STANTON
SECRETARY OF WAR.
SIR:

I have the honor to transmit herewith the report of the Board of Officers convened by Special Orders No. 264, War Department, A G O of date June 5th 1866, "for the purpose of recommending such changes in the authorized Infantry tactics as shall make them simple and complete, or the adoption of any new system that may be presented to it, if such change be deemed advisable."[1]

Having examined this report, I concur fully with the Board and recommend the immediate adoption of "Upton's Infantry Tactics, Double and Single Rank", as the text-book for the Military Academy and the standard tactics for the Armies of the United States.

I have seen the system applied to company and battalion drills and am fully satisfied of its superior merits and adaptability to our service—besides it is no translation but a purely American work. The board by which it was examined and recommended was composed of officers of ability and experience, and I do not think any further examination by boards necessary.

> Very respectfully
> Your obedt servt
> U. S. GRANT
> General.

LS, DNA, RG 94, Letters Received, 312A 1869.

On Jan. 4 and 8, 1867, William H. Morris and Col. and Bvt. Maj. Gen. Silas Casey, 4th Inf., had written letters to Secretary of War Edwin M. Stanton protesting the board's decision. ALS, *ibid.* On Oct. 9, 1865, Morris, "Home Journal Office," New York City, had written to USG. "I have the honor to enclose a communication for the Secretary of War, presenting recommendations by our most eminent generals and of some twenty state Adjutant Generals of my simplified system of Infantry Tactics. I respectfully request that you will forward it with your endorsement; for I feel certain that an expression of your willingness to have the wishes of your generals gratified by the adoption of this system, would ensure the favorable action of the Secretary of War." ALS, *ibid.*, 2596M 1865. The enclosures are *ibid.* On Oct. 16 and 18, USG endorsed this letter. "Respectfully forwarded to the Secretary of war, as requested." "Respectfully returned to the Secretary of War, with the opinion that the exigencies of the service do not at present warrant the expense necessarily incurred by the change of tactics requested by Gen. Morris. Our present tactics, tho' perhaps defective, have been sufficient during the maintenance of a large army, and are sufficient for our present organization" ES, *ibid.* See *PUSG*, 13, 495–97.

On Jan. 11, 1866, Lewis Wallace, Crawfordsville, Ind., had written to USG. "I have nearly completed a volume of tactics, upon a new system, simpler than the old one, and intended specially for the flank companies of a regiment, and for mounted infantry, which I would like to submit before leaving the army. The system is that of a one rank formation, resolvable in a moment, and while the company or regiment is on the march, into thre two or three ranks. Its unit is a six, doubling in flank movements into files of threes, instead of fours. Its company sub-divisions are three sections, reducable as above stated, into two platoons. Its advantages are simplicity and greater celerity of movement; at the sametime that it offers the option of fighting in any formation, from one to threes ranks, as the object in hand and the nature of the ground may suggest. It presents, moreover, a complete and perfect system of *skirmishing*—the great desideratum in our present tactics, as at present authorized. As relates to *mounted infantry*, its chief feature is that, by it, four regiments in march can be put in a column of the depth of one regiment on an ordinary country road: thus, reducing the depth of a column of twelve regiments in route to that of three regiments—an advantage which I know you will percieve at a glance. The volume, applicable only to companies, will make be in print a little larger than the present first volume of our authorized infantry tactics. The present *organization* is in no way disturbed by it. I am at loss to know how to proceed in submitting the work. Please advise me on the subject, and withhold the acceptance of my resignation until I can have an opportunity to present it as you may direct. I feel sure it is at least worthy consideration. For about three weeks ~~past~~, I have been confined to my house with ague. Please accept my thanks for ~~you~~ kind and flattering mention you make in your report of my conduct at the Monoccacy." ADfS, InHi. On March 2, Wallace, Washington, D. C., wrote to USG. "I have the honor to submit to you a work entitled Rifle Tactics, which I have prepared for the use of the flank companies of regiments as at present organized in the U. S. Army. You will greatly oblige me by laying it before the Hon. Sec. of War, that a commission may be appointed to examine and report upon it, with a view to its authorization by the President and Sec. of War. As the work is yet in *MS.* it would probably facilitate the duty of the Commission appointed, if I were permitted to be present at the first reading. Waiting your directions in the matter, . . ." ALS, DNA, RG 94, Letters Received, 160W 1866. On the same day, USG endorsed this letter. "Respectfully forwarded to the Hon. Secr.y of war, with the recommendation that the subject be referred to a Board of three infantry officers." ES, *ibid.* A board, convened at Washington, ". . . carefully examined the system of 'Rifle Tactics' proposed by Maj General Lew Wallace, and find little to recommend, either, in the deviations from the authorized System, or in the additions thereto. . . ." DS, *ibid.* The board recommended reviewing recent changes in tactics. On April 5, USG endorsed this report. "The report of the Board is approved except as to examination of changes in the present system of tactics which is not approved." ES, *ibid.* See *Lew Wallace: An Autobiography* (New York, 1906), II, 571–72.

On Feb. 6, 1867, Lt. Col. and Bvt. Maj. Gen. Emory Upton, Washington, D. C., wrote to Bvt. Maj. Gen. John A. Rawlins. "For the information of the General in Chief, I desire to make the following statement in regard to my Infantry Tactics—The book is published by D. Appleton & Co of New York, who give me a percentage on the retail price of every book sold by or for them—The retail price of the book is fixed, by contract, at two dollars $2.00—Should its Tactics be adopted by the Government I expect no compensation therefrom, neither would I expect compensation should the Tactics at any time be superceded—The retail price of the book is fifty cents lower than that of either Scotts or Caseys—I understand that the publishers are to furnish the Government at wholesale prices—" ALS, DNA, RG 94, Letters Received, 312A 1866. On the same day, USG endorsed this letter. "Respectfully forwarded to the Secretary of War" ES, *ibid.* On March 28, USG endorsed papers concerning the need to revise art. and cav. tactics. "Respectfully forwarded to the Secretary of War, with recommendation that Upton's Infantry Tactics be first adopted, and afterwards the Artillery and Cavalry Tactics be made to conform as nearly as practicable, in the general movements, to the Infantry Tactics" ES, *ibid.*, 125G 1867.

On July 2, Bvt. Maj. Gen. James A. Hardie, inspector gen., Washington, D. C., wrote to USG. "I beg to be permitted to invite your attention to a Paragraph on Page 351 of 'Upton's Infantry Tactics' which has just come to my notice, and which I think objectionable. It interpolates, in what purports to be an application of the new system of Infantry manoeuvre to the ceremonial of review and Inspection &c., a regulation concerning the place and duties of the Inspector or Inspector General when junior to the Commanding Officer of the troops under inspection, which is at variance with the existing regulation, and with what, I think, is the proper view of the position of an Inspector General. . . ." LS, *ibid.*, RG 108, Letters Received. On July 8, Bvt. Maj. Gen. Edward D.

Townsend wrote to USG. "I have the honor to enclose herewith papers relative to General Upton's system of Infantry Tactics, for the consideration of which the Board of Officers convened by Special Orders 300, June 11th 1867 from this Office was detailed to assemble at West Point on the 9th instant." LS, *ibid.*, RG 94, Letters Received, 312A 1869. See *ibid.*, 512H 1867.

On July 15, USG, West Point, wrote to the AG. "Inclosed herewith, please find the 'Proceedings of the Board of Officers,' which convened at this Post on the 9th inst. per S. O. 300. C. S. from War Department." LS, *ibid.*, 312A 1869. USG enclosed the proceedings of the board. ". . . The Board therefore recommend that the system of Infantry Tactics prepared by Bvt Major General E. Upton, U. S. Army be adopted as the system for the Armies of the United States in the place of all others, . . ." DS (six signatures), *ibid.* On Aug. 1, Stanton adopted the Upton tactics through War Dept. General Orders No. 73. (Printed) *ibid.*, 975S 1870. See Stephen E. Ambrose, *Upton and the Army* (Baton Rouge, 1964), pp. 59–66.

On Sept. 23, Bvt. Maj. Gen. Philip St. George Cooke, Brooklyn, N. Y., wrote to USG. "I wrote a work on the tactics and instruction of cavalry, new in some principles, which especially simplified the old French system. After a very severe scrutiny, it was in fact approved by the War Department of 1860: in November 1861 it was officially adopted & published by the New Administrati[on.] I received many assurances of its approval in the armies of the West & Southwest— I will enclose as a specimen a letter from Gen. T. C. H. Smith—& its claim, of peculiar adaptation—to our national policy, of volunteer armies,—by greatly reducing the time of instruction, was verified. A change to this new system in the Army of the Potomac was suspended by it's commander, as being imprudent in face of the enemy. This exception led to others; and to the confusion of its issue with the old system to the same commands, until,—a last edition being exhausted, I am told its adoption was *verbally countermanded* I have now received and examined the new 'Upton's infantry tactics'; I find it an application of my system to infantry;—adopting my general use of 'fours';—rendered *possible* in cavalry by the single rank formation; the innovation of ignoring inversions &c Amid differences of opinions, I have never heard one against the superiority of my new system over the French one,—now in actual use—for *indian Warfare* Nothing is ever *perfected*: my cavalry tactics could well be revised, and made somewhat simpler; and I was convinced of at least one practical defect in it,—the omission of the command *March*, in certain important cases of a changed condition of the march. If so ordered, I feel confident that I could in a few months make it acceptable to any intelligent practical Board. I will add, below, a few remarks of comparisons of the two works, which may be worth your attention." ALS, DNA, RG 94, Letters Received, 312A 1869. On Oct. 7, Bvt. Brig. Gen. Horace Porter endorsed this letter. "Respectfully returned to the Adjutant General. It is deemed inexpedient to convene a Board for the examination of Gen. Cooke's tactics at present. The whole system of tactics must soon be revised. When a Board for this purpose is ordered, Gen. Cooke's tactics can be brought before it." ES, *ibid.*

1. On May 10, 1866, Maj. Gen. John Pope, Fort Leavenworth, had written to USG. "I have the honor to invite your attention to a System of Infantry Tactics prepared by Bvt Brig: Genl E. Upton. U. S. A. They greatly simplify all tactical movements from the drill of a company to the evolutions of a Corps d'Armeé and

render the instructions of the Soldier infinitely less difficult and more simple. They seem to me to possess remarkable advantage over any tactiscs now in use and are well worthy of carefull examination with the view to introduce them generally into our Army I. feel so confident of their great merit and simplicity that I respectfully solicit a careful examination of them by a Board of Officers of Rank who have commanded in the Field. I need not speak of Genl Upton himself as he is well Known to you both as to his personal character & his efficiency & ability as an Officer I feel satisfied that if you will give his Tactics even a cursory examination you will be impressed with the desirability of ordering a proper Board to report upon them" Copy, *ibid.*, RG 393, Dept. of the Mo., Letters Sent. On May 31, Rawlins directed Bvt. Maj. Gen. Edward D. Townsend to issue special orders. "A board of officers will assemble at West Point, N. Y., on June 25th 1866, or as soon thereafter as practicable, for the purpose of recommending such changes in authorized infantry tactics as shall make them simple and complete, or the adoption of any new system that may be presented to it; if such change be deemed advisable. The board will examine & report on any system of infantry tactics that may be presented to it and the Superintendent of the Military Academy will give it facilities for testing with the battalion of cadets the value of any system. Bvt. Brig. Gen. Upton is authorized to visit West Point to present his system to the board. Detail for the board: Bvt. Brig. Gen. Chas. Griffin, Bvt. Colonel H. B. Clitz, Bvt. Colonel T. G. Pitcher, Captain J. J. Van Horn, Recorder" ES and ADf, *ibid.*, RG 94, Letters Received, 442A 1866.

To Robert C. Winthrop

Washington, D. C.
Feb.y 5th 1867.

Hon. R. C. Winthrop,
Dear Sir:

Your note of this evening asking an interview with me for tomorrow morning is just received. I had intended to do myself the pleasure to call on Mr. Peabody[1] and yourself in the morning. I will do so soon after breakfast. Should I not find you in I will be at my office, corner of 17th & F. Streets, the balance of the day where I will be glad to see you at any hour, before 2 p. m. that may best suit your convenience.

With great respect,
your obt. svt.
U. S. Grant

ALS, MHi. Robert C. Winthrop, born in 1809 in Boston, served as a Whig U.S. representative (1841–50) and U.S. senator (July 30, 1850–Feb. 1, 1851) before his defeat by Charles Sumner. See letter to Robert C. Winthrop, May 22, 1867.

1. George Peabody, born in 1795 in Mass., prospered as a merchant in the U.S. and London. Among many philanthropies, he established the Peabody Education Fund in Feb., 1867, to encourage education in the South for both blacks and whites, and selected USG to serve on the board of trustees. On Feb. 7, Peabody, Washington, D. C., wrote to Winthrop, USG, and other trustees. "I beg to address you on a subject which occupied my mind long before I left England, and in regard to which one at least of you (the Hon. Mr. WINTHROP, the distinguished and valued friend to whom I am so much indebted for cordial sympathy, careful consideration, and wise counsel in this matter) will remember that I consulted him immediately upon my arrival in May last. I refer to the educational needs of those portions of our beloved and common country which have suffered from the destructive ravages, and the not less disastrous consequences, of civil war. . . . The details and organization of the Trust I leave with you, only requesting that Mr. WINTHROP may be chairman, and Governor FISH and Bishop McILVAINE Vice-Chairmen, . . ." *Proceedings of the Trustees of the Peabody Education Fund . . .* (Boston, 1875), I, 1–7. USG attended the first board meeting held at the Willard Hotel on Feb. 8. *National Intelligencer*, Feb. 9, 1867; Lawrence A. Frost, *U. S. Grant Album* (Seattle, 1966), p. [150].

On Feb. 17, USG wrote to Alexander T. Stewart concerning his desire to get away from official business for a few days. American Art Association, Anderson Galleries, Inc., Sale No. 4098, April 4–5, 1934, p. 181. On March 14, Peabody, New York City, telegraphed to USG. "Please telegraph early today what day next week you will dine at hotel and if on either of these days you and Mrs. Grant have friends you would like invited—Please send them invitations or give me their names by telegraph and I will write them today" Telegram received (at 10:00 A.M.), DNA, RG 107, Telegrams Collected (Bound). At 11:00 A.M., USG telegraphed to Peabody. "For Wednesday & Thursday I have accepted invitations. Either the 19th or 22d will be at your service. As I dine with A. T. Stewart & Judge Pierpont would suggest their names to you." ALS (telegram sent), *ibid.*; telegram sent, *ibid.* On March 20, Peabody wrote to the board. "Understanding that a doubt has been expressed in regard to my intentions and instructions on the subject of the distribution of the fund entrusted to your care for the purpose of education in the Southern and South-western States, I desire distinctly to say to you, that my design was to leave an absolute discretion to the Board of Trustees, as to the localities in which the funds should from time to time be expended. . . ." *Proceedings*, I, 21–22. USG attended the second board meeting held on March 19–22 at the Fifth Avenue Hotel in New York City and Peabody's dinner on March 22. *New York Times*, March 23, 1867.

To Edwin M. Stanton

Washington, February 8th 1867.

HON. E. M. STANTON,
SECRETARY OF WAR,
SIR:

I have the honor to return herewith the copy of a call by the Senate for information as to the violations of the Civil Rights Bill and of a report of the Attorney General, both referred to me by you on the 23d ultimo.

In the reports of officers of outrages committed on the freedmen, reference is rarely or never made to the Civil Rights Bill, and I am accordingly unable to report its violations. I enclose, however, a statement of murders committed in the Southern States as in part pertinent to the inquiry.

Very respectfully
Your obedt Servant
U. S. GRANT
General.

Copies, DLC-USG, V, 47, 60; DLC-Edwin M. Stanton; DNA, RG 108, Letters Sent. See *SED*, 41-3-16. USG enclosed a table listing nineteen "outrages committed in Southern States, and reported to Head Quarters Armies, U. S., during the year, 1866." Copy, DLC-Edwin M. Stanton. On Jan. 18, 1867, USG had written to Maj. Gen. Oliver O. Howard. "Confidential . . . Will you be kind enough to send me a list of authenticated cases of Murder, and other violence, upon Freedmen, Northern or other Union men, refugees &c. in the southern states for the last six month or a year. My object in this is to make a report showing that the Courts in the states excluded from Congress afford no security to life or property of the classes here refered to, and to recommend that Martial Law be declared over such districts as do not afford the proper protection." ALS, DNA, RG 105, Letters Received. Possibly on the same day, Howard wrote to USG. "I will have such cases as I have drawn off, and send them to you." Copy (undated), Howard Papers, MeB.

On Dec. 6, 1866, Howard had written a memorandum concerning the unwillingness of local authorities to investigate the murder near Vicksburg of Abraham H. Zook and the disappearance of his brother Noah, both former constituents of U.S. Representative Thaddeus Stevens of Pa. Copies, DNA, RG 105, Letters Received. On Jan. 2, 1867, Bvt. Maj. Gen. Thomas J. Wood forwarded papers in the case which USG endorsed on Feb. 7. "Respectfully forwarded to the Secretary of War for his information. Copies of the enclosed report of Bvt Major Gen'l T. J. Wood have not been furnished either Maj. Gen. Howard or Hon. Thaddeus Stevens." ES, *ibid.* On Jan. 4, Wood wrote a report concerning the unsolved murders of Purvis Spears, a British subject, and James A. King, former capt., 49th Colored, near Vicksburg. LS, *ibid.*, RG 94, Letters Received, 14T 1867. On Feb. 7, USG forwarded this report. ES, *ibid.* These cases were included in USG's list of Feb. 8.

On Feb. 15, Secretary of War Edwin M. Stanton wrote to President Andrew Johnson concerning violations of the Civil Rights Act of 1866. Copy, DLC-Edwin M. Stanton. See *SED*, 39-2-29. Also on Feb. 15, Stanton wrote to Johnson. "I have the honor to refer to you for your consideration and instructions a report made by General Grant on the 12th instant to this Department in respect to sandry alleged murders and violations of the Act of Congress known as the 'Civil Rights Act', . . ." LS, DNA, RG 60, Letters from the President. See John A. Carpenter, *Sword and Olive Branch: Oliver Otis Howard* (Pittsburgh, 1964), pp. 129–30.

Interview

[*Feb. 16, 1867*]

Q.—The rebellion was put down by the strong arm of military power under your direction, and surely the work was well done. Now the question is, what policy shall be pursued for the reorganization of the late rebel States?

A.—No, the work is not all done. The fighting is finished, but the very important matter of reconstruction is yet to be completed. I think if the Southern States had accepted the Amendment instead of rejecting it so hastily, they would have been admitted by Congress in December, but now I think they will have to take the Amendment, and manhood suffrage besides. Congress will insist upon this.

Q.—How are affairs at the South, General? Is it true that in Texas and many other sections no adequate protection is given to Union men?

A.—It is true that in a large proportion of Texas a Union man is not safe if beyond the limits of military protection. In and about Galveston a better state of things exist, and a majority of the people, I have no doubt, would be glad to have the laws enforced. In many other sections of the South loyal men have no proper security for life and property unless they are so located as to be taken care of by the military. The Civil Courts fail to punish offences against

Union citizens, white and black. And as for that matter they were always remiss. I am told that no murderer who had held what is called a respectable position before he committed the crime was ever hung or otherwise punished in the State of Virginia, and I believe the same is true of most, if not all, the late slave States.

Q.—You say, General, the Civil Courts have failed to protect Unionists at the South. Well, are not the so-called State Governments there the greatest of all failures?

A.—That is a political question for Congress to decide. I only give facts, and others may construe them as they please. I believe that large numbers at the South would be glad to have the laws enforced impartially; in some parts this is the sentiment of the majority. But the trouble is they are overborne by the lawless element, and cannot enforce justice.

Q.—Well, in any event there can be no more fighting?

A.—Oh, no, unless BROOKS[1] and WOOD[2] and that Copperhead set get up their threatened war, and there is some doubt I think whether they will undertake to carry out their threats.

One of our party, Mr. C. O. GREENE, of Troy, who is on his way to Augusta, Ga., here made the inquiry whether a Union man is perfectly safe in traveling South?

A.—Oh, yes, perfectly safe. There is no danger at all on the regular lines of travel. But then if you should stop and get into angry political discussions, there would be danger in some places no doubt. In that case shooting would probably be passed off as justifiable homicide, if the murderer was arrested at all.

New York Times, Feb. 20, 1867. The article is printed as "Special Correspondence of the Troy Daily Times."

1. U.S. Representative James Brooks of N. Y., a Democrat.
2. On Feb. 20, U.S. Representative Fernando Wood of N. Y., a Democrat, wrote to USG. "I enclose the copy of a purported conversation between yourself & a friend, in which you are reported to have said that I had threatened war with reference to the unsettled questions at the South—Assuming that this conversation is correctly stated the object of this is to assure you that I have never spoken nor written one word ~~capable~~ susceptible of such a construction—~~Upon~~ On the contrary I have upon all occasions deprecated such language—. . . P. S. If I am not the 'Wood' referred to it is due to me that the other Wood should be hereafter designated—" ALS, DLC-Adam Badeau.

To Lt. Gen. William T. Sherman

Washington, D, C. Feb. 19th *1867*. [*10:00* A.M.]

Lt. Gn. W. T. Sherman,

St. Louis, Mo.

Let Gn. Hancock carry out his views in Indian matters as fore-shadowed in your dispatch of yesterday unless orders should be sent hereafter prohibiting the proposed issue of rations ~~proposed~~. I will try to get authority for that at once and will inform you of the result.

U. S. Grant
Gen.l

ALS (telegram sent), DNA, RG 107, Telegrams Collected (Bound); telegram sent, *ibid.*; copies, *ibid.*, RG 46, Senate 40A–G3, War Dept. Reports; *ibid.*, RG 107, Letters Received from Bureaus; *ibid.*, RG 108, Telegrams Sent; DLC-USG, V, 56. Also on Feb. 19, 1867, 10:40 A.M., USG telegraphed to Lt. Gen. William T. Sherman. "Authority granted to issue rations when, in Gen. Hancocks judgement, it is deemed expedient" Telegrams sent (2), DNA, RG 107, Telegrams Collected (Bound); copies, *ibid.*, RG 46, Senate 40A–G3, War Dept. Reports; *ibid.*, RG 107, Letters Received from Bureaus; *ibid.*, RG 108, Telegrams Sent; DLC-USG, V, 56. On Feb. 18, Sherman had telegraphed to USG. "As time approaches when we must act in Indian matters I use the telegraph to send you Gen'l Hancocks despatch herewith & ask your answer as soon as possible 'Ft Leavenworth Feby sixteenth (16) Eighteen Sixty Seven (1867)   Gen Nichols Asst Adjt Gen'l   Please inform me when Gen'l Sherman returns   I wish to write him what I propose doing, As soon as the weather changes & the troops are supplied with proper arms Camp equipage &c. Generally, I Propose marching all the disposable troops before the grass springs up probably to Fort Hays and there to demand of the Indian Chiefs on the Smoky Hill an interview, if not satisfactory I will advance my troops towards them & if they do not respond proba~~b~~perly will attack them. If I can be assured that they are peaceful & that I can be safe in issuing them provision at Ft Riley or Elsewhere until the matter is disposed of I will bring them in. As to the matter of rations I wish to be informed as the Action of Congress as developed seems to be in opposition to feeding Indians not already in our Custody   I Can immediately afterwards settle any outstanding difficulties with the Cheyennes or other tribes by going in their direction & having an interview with their chiefs, or by taking such other Subsequent action as may be necessary   Signed W S. Hancock Maj Gen Comdg'   We want to let the Indians feel that if they want fight they can now have all they want.   ~~I~~Like other people as we want to fight they want peace, but if we want peaceful & submissive they are boastful, offencive,   I want Gen'l Hancock to act just as he suggests & he is a Just and fair man & would not abuse the trust. Still he Must be armed with authority to Kill the hostile & draw away the peaceful part of each tribe & that may compel us to feed the latter merely. Now is the time for action For if we wait for grass their ponies will get fat & an indian with a fat pony is very different from him with a starved one. I Know that you have done all that is possible to get an exclusive Control over these Indians & would not trouble you now only the time compels me" Telegram received (at 3:45 P.M.), DNA, RG 107, Telegrams Received; copies, *ibid.*, RG 46, Senate 40A–G3, War Dept. Reports; *ibid.*, RG 107, Letters Received from Bureaus; *ibid.*, RG 108, Letters Received; *ibid.*, RG 192, Special Orders; DLC-USG, V, 55. On Feb. 19, USG endorsed a copy of this telegram. "Respectfully forwarded to the Secretary of War with request that authority be granted to issue rations to the Indians, when in the judgment of Gen. Hancock it is deemed expedient." ES, DNA, RG 108, Letters Received. On the same day, Sherman telegraphed to USG. "Your two despatches of today are received and Gen. Hancock is instructed accordingly This will force the Indians to come to terms very soon" Telegram received (at 5:00 P.M.), *ibid.*, RG 107, Telegrams Collected (Bound); *ibid.*, RG 108, Telegrams Received; copies, *ibid.*, RG 107, Letters Received from Bureaus; DLC-USG, V, 55.

On Feb. 20, noon, USG telegraphed to Sherman. "What do you think of giving to the Governor of Montana 2500 stand arms to enable him to organize Citizens for defence against Indians." ALS (telegram sent), DNA, RG 107, Telegrams Collected (Bound); telegram sent, *ibid.*; copies, *ibid.*, RG 108, Telegrams Sent; DLC-USG, V, 56. On the same day, Sherman telegraphed to USG. "I think very well of your proposition to let the governor of Montana have twenty five hundred 2500 stand of arms to arm the Militia of the Territory There is a good class of people in Montana & if they can protect themselves it relieves us to that extent" Telegram received (at 6:30 P.M.), DNA, RG 107, Telegrams Collected (Bound); *ibid.*, RG 108, Telegrams Received; copies, *ibid.*, RG 156, Letters Received; DLC-USG, V, 55. USG noted on a telegram received. "Please return this by bearer." ANS (undated), DNA, RG 108, Telegrams Received. On March 26 and 29, USG endorsed a copy of this telegram. "Respectfully forwarded to the Secretary of War with the recommendation that 2500 Infantry arms and a Battery of Mountain howitzers be issued to the Territory of Montana, to be distributed under the directions of Gen. Sherman." "I would suggest that Three hundred rounds per gun, both small arms & howitzers, be furnished on the within orders." ES and AES, *ibid.*, RG 156, Letters Received. See *SRC*, 49-1-154.

On March 23, Sherman telegraphed to USG. "Please procure authority for me to issue to boats navigating the Missouri two (2) twelve (12) pounder Guns, and say twenty (20) muskets each to be returned to the Arsenal on return of the boats" Telegram received (at 5:00 P.M.), DNA, RG 107, Telegrams Collected (Bound); *ibid.*, RG 108, Telegrams Received; copies (one sent by mail), *ibid.*, Letters Received; *ibid.*, RG 156, Letters Received; DLC-USG, V, 55. On March 25, USG endorsed a copy of this telegram. "Respectfully forwarded to the Secretary of War, recommended." ES, DNA, RG 156, Letters Received. On the same day, Bvt. Maj. Gen. Edmund Schriver, inspector gen., wrote to USG approving this request. ADfS, *ibid.*, RG 107, Letters Received from Bureaus. On March 26, 11:15 A.M., USG telegraphed to Sherman. "Your recommendation to issue ordnance & stores to steamers assending the Mo. is approved." ALS (telegram sent), *ibid.*, Telegrams Collected (Bound); telegram sent, *ibid.*; copies, *ibid.*, RG 108, Telegrams Sent; DLC-USG, V, 56.

To Henry Wilson

Washington, D. C.
Feb.y 20th 1867.

HON. H. WILSON,
CH. MIL. COM. U. S. SENATE,
DEAR SIR;

Hearing that representations have been made calculated to influance the Committee over which you preside to report against the confirmation of Maj. Justis Steinberger,[1] Paymaster U. S. A. I venture to address you, informally, on the subject. I have known Major S. intimately for more than fourteen years. His present appointment was given him probably as much on my recommendation as on any other recommendations he may have had. I know him to be abundantly qualified for the position and believe him to be in every way worthy of the trust bestowed upon him.

Maj. Steinberger volunteered early in the War and served until honorably discharged. I think it would be hard to reject him now, and thinking so would esteem it a favor if his case should be favorably reported upon.

With great respect,
your obt. svt.
U. S. GRANT
General,

ALS, OrHi.

1. On July 30, 1866, Justus Steinberger, Washington, D. C., had written to Secretary of War Edwin M. Stanton requesting an appointment in the U.S. Army. ALS, DNA, RG 94, ACP, S1263 CB 1866. On July 31, USG endorsed this letter. "I have known Col. Steinberger personally for many years and heartily endorse the statements of Senator Nesmith in his behalf. I would be pleased to have favorable concideration given to this application and heartily recommend it." AES, *ibid.* Probably in late July, USG and ten others wrote to President Andrew Johnson recommending Steinberger for appointment as lt. col. of inf. DS (undated), *ibid.* On Oct. 18, Steinberger wrote to the AG requesting appointment as maj. and paymaster. ALS, *ibid.* On Oct. 23 and 26, USG endorsed this letter. "I have known Justus Steinburger for many years. He is a good business man and a man of probity. In matters of Staff appointments I prefer having the endorsement of the Chief of the Corps for which the application is made

before making a positive recommendation. With his approval to this application I would concur. Col. Steinburger has served as a volunteer during the greater part of the rebellion with credit." "I heartily concur in the recommendation of the Paymaster General." AES, *ibid.* Steinberger, appointed as of Nov. 8, was confirmed on Feb. 23, 1867. See *PUSG*, 10, 367–68.

On Aug. 23, Bvt. Maj. Gen. Rufus Ingalls wrote to Bvt. Maj. Gen. Benjamin W. Brice, paymaster gen. "I have the honor to call your attention to the merits of Major Justus Steinberger of your Dep't—He was appointed an Asst. Adjt. Genl early in the war,—in 1861, and the same year, was made *Colonel* of the 1st Wash. Ter. Volunteers—He went to that country, organized his Regiment, and served several years with great credit to himself and service to the country— He was very highly complimented by his commanding officer—the late Genl George Wright. Under existing laws, the *Brevets* of *Lieut-Col.* and *Colonel* can be conferred on him 'for faithful, distinguished, and meretorious services during the war'—I recommend it—May I ask you to endorse and forward this paper to the Genl-in-Chief and Sec-of War?" ALS, DNA, RG 94, ACP, I79 CB 1867. On Oct. 12, USG endorsed this letter. "Approved for Brevet Lieutenant Colonelcy" ES, *ibid.*

To Lt. Gen. William T. Sherman

Washington, Feb. 21st *1867* [*noon*]

Lt. Gen. W. T. Sherman
St Louis, Mo.

You will afford all the aid and assistance in your power to facilitate and make successful the mission of the special Commissioners appointed by the President to visit and confer with Indian tribes in the neighborhood of Fort Phil. Kearney, and furnish them with such necessary escorts & protection as they may require. The Commission is to meet at Omaha Feby 25th.

U. S. Grant
General

Telegrams sent (2), DNA, RG 107, Telegrams Collected (Bound); copies, *ibid.*, RG 108, Telegrams Sent; DLC-USG, V, 56. On Feb. 21, 1867, Lt. Gen. William T. Sherman telegraphed to USG. "Despatch of twenty first 21 received General Augur will be instructed to telegraph to Provide fully for the wants and safety of the commissioners appointed to treat with the Sioux" Telegram received (at 5:00 P.M.), DNA, RG 107, Telegrams Collected (Bound); *ibid.*, RG 108, Telegrams Received; copy, DLC-USG, V, 55. On Feb. 20, Bvt. Maj. Gen.

John A. Rawlins had written to Secretary of the Interior Orville H. Browning. "I have the honor to inform you that Gen. Sherman will be directed by telegraph to furnish the necessary escorts for the special commission going to Fort Phil Kearney &c. under your instructions." Copies, *ibid.*, V, 47, 60; DNA, RG 108, Letters Sent. On Feb. 16, Browning had written to USG. "I herewith transmit for your examination a copy of the instructions which I propose to issue to Gen'l. Sully and others Special Commissioners, appointed by the President to visit and confer with the Indian tribes, on our North Western frontier. If in your opinion any modification of, or addition to these instructions is desirable, I will be obliged to you for such suggestions upon the subject as you may think proper to make, assuring you that your views will receive the most careful and respectful consideration. I wish the Commissioners to assemble at Omaha, Nebraska, on the 25th inst., and proceed without delay to the theatre of their duties. They have all reported and are now ready to receive orders, except Genl. Sully. Will you have the kindness to inform me when I may expect him to report to this Department." LS, *ibid.*, Letters Received. The undated instructions to the six-member special commission (including Col. Ely S. Parker) to investigate Indian affairs around Fort Phil Kearny are *ibid.* Printed with a date of Feb. 18 in *SED*, 40-1-13, pp. 55–56, which also includes reports of the commissioners. See telegram to Lt. Gen. William T. Sherman, Jan. 14, 1867; letter to Edwin M. Stanton, Jan. 15, 1867.

On March 7, Sherman telegraphed to USG. "General Augur reports from Omaha that he has a message from General Wessells at Philip Kearney of date February twenty first that all was well there and that he had opened communication with C. F. Smith where all was well But terribly Cold and much snow. The couriers on their return from C F Smith were attacked by Indians, losing their mail & animals" Telegram received (at 6:20 P.M.), DNA, RG 108, Telegrams Received; copy, DLC-USG, V, 55. On Jan. 21, Lt. Col. and Bvt. Brig. Gen. Henry W. Wessells, 18th Inf., Fort Phil Kearny, wrote to the adjt., Dept. of the Platte, reporting on the Dec. 21, 1866, massacre. Copy, DNA, RG 94, Letters Received, 256M 1867. On March 9, 1867, USG endorsed this letter. "Respectfully forwarded to the Secretary of War, for his information." ES, *ibid.* On Feb. 27, Bvt. Maj. Gen. Christopher C. Augur wrote to Sherman's adjt. concerning the need for suitable reservations for Indians driven from the Platte River. LS, *ibid.*, 267M 1867. Additional papers are *ibid.* On March 8 and 30, Sherman and USG endorsed these papers. "Respectfully forwarded to the HdQrs of the Army for reference. If we the military are to provide for these Indians we should Know it, for if they wander about at pleasure no matter how peacefully disposed they will be charged with the acts of others and be Embroiled with the whites. They should be located, and an agent should be with them all the time." "Respectfully forwarded to the Secretary of War, with request that these papers be submitted to the Secretary of the Interior. I concur fully in the views expressed by Bvt Major General Augur and Lieut General Sherman" AES and ES, *ibid.* On March 30 and April 1, USG forwarded to Secretary of War Edwin M. Stanton additional papers concerning Indian affairs and requested that the first set be transmitted to Browning. ES, *ibid.*, 301M 1867; *ibid.*, 383M 1867.

On March 14, Parker, Omaha, wrote to Rawlins. "*Unofficial* . . . Here we are snow bound. We can go neither east nor west,—The rail road west will be open by sunday or monday next, and then we will make a break for Ft McPherson. From there we go to Ft Sedgwick and thence to Laramie. We have taken a large amount of testimony in relation to the Phil Kearny massacre, and thus far, I am perfectly satisfied, that Carrington had no sort of discipline in his garrison, and although the Indians had been hostile ever since his arrival there, he took no unusual precautions against them—but herded his stock without the protection of the fort & with very slight guards, and he consequently lost every thing—he also sent out his wood trains some 6 or 7 miles from the Fort, guarded by from 40 to 80 soldiers under charge of a non-commissioned officer—he continued this although his trains were now and then attacked, and were constantly liable to be attacked—The massacre occurred about 3½ miles from the Fort, and almost in sight of it,—Fetterman had disobeyed positive orders in going where he did, yet no one was sent out to ascertain why he disobeyed his orders, nor was any rein-forcements sent out until about 3 hours after Fettermans guns were heard—The whole conduct of Indian Affairs shows a great lack of judgment and efficiency on some one's part. So far as Indian affairs are developed, I must say that I regret Hancock's proposed expedition up the Republican—The concurrent testimony of every body in the west, agree that all the Indians on the Republican, in fact all the Indians between the North Platte and the Smoky Hill route, are friendly, and to send troops among them, or even the simple passage of troops through their territory will alarm them and drive nearly all of the young men to join the hostile bands north of the Platte and south of the Arkansas. Hancock's proposed route has no hostile Indians, and none are to be found until you reach the Powder river country, and that is beyond Hancock's bailiwick. His expedition is therefore un-necessary and will be fruitless, unless he turns his attention towards the Arkansas, and let Augur take care of this route. The true way of campaigning against these northern hostile bands, is to approach them from the Missouri on the north, drive them south against a cordon of troops stretched out on this line, and in that manner hem them in until they sue for peace. If you operate only from the south, they will retire before your advance, they will go north of the Missouri, and you may follow them into the British possessions & never catch one of them. For the purpose of operating from the north and south, Terry's Hdqrs. should be moved from St Paul to Sioux City (and war or no war Sioux City is the point where the Hdqrs Dept. of Dakota should be, it has eastern and northern tele-graphic communication & will very soon have a rail road to it, and then Hdqrs would be in close contact with the Indian country, the management of which is the only active duty this Dept. has to do—)—Hancock should there fore be diverted toward the south, instead of being permitted to march against Indians who are all friendly—I write this unofficially, because I have not yet seen the Indians on the Republican. Next week I shall see them & will know for certain their feelings. To initiate the Northern campaign, I suggest, may require too much time, but I can assure you until that is done, there never will be peace in the northwest. The country between the Platte & Arkansas is practically a peace country, and hostilities only occur as hostile bands are passing either north or south between these points, their actual or assumed residence being either north or south of the Platte or south of the Arkansas. The real points for military operations is north of the Platte & south of the Arkansas & not between those two streams. Regards to all." ALS, *ibid.*, RG 108, Letters Received. On April 2, Sherman wrote to Maj. George K. Leet. "I have received the Copy of Colonel Parker letter of March 14, from Omaha, and laest General Grant may be disturbed by it I will repeat what has heretofore been reported that General Hancock is not operating against the band of Indians who are now between the Platte and the Republican, but against the Cheyennes and Arapahoes, Kiowas and Comanches *South* of the Arkansas. As to General Terry, as soon as the Missouri River opens he will go in person to the Missouri River and assend it to any point where his pressure may be necessary. He has not and we cannot give him, nor can he support a force of Cavalry to carry on war against the Sioux from the Missouri River. The distance are so great that we cannot drive these Sioux against a closed line. The interval are and will necessarily be so great that the Indians can and will pass between the Posts. In any event any campaign will be in conclusion, and we can only destroy the hostile Indians in detail as opportunity offered. As soon as the Commissioners Report we will be ready to take these Indians in hand, but I have no hope that we can do much if anything as long as our action must be kept subordinate to the opinions and interests of Indian Agents." Copy, *ibid.*, RG 393, Dept. of the Mo., Indian War. On April 1, Parker, Fort McPherson, Neb., wrote to Rawlins. *"Unofficial . . .* We reached this post two weeks ago to day, & until saturday were daily occupied in taking Col Carrington's testimony. Not one tenth of the testimony he has given relates to the subject matter of our mission. In my opinion he is not fit to be in this Indian country. He is no fighter and does not understand the Indian character or their mode of warfare. I do not know to what extent he was to blame in the Phil Kearney affair.—But it is certain, that active hostilities on the part of the Sioux commenced immediately upon his arrival at Kearney in July, last. Nearly all of his stock was stampeded, and never recovered, within a few days of his arrival. Indians were daily in sight of the camp or post, and frequent depradations made at Reno and along the route to Kearney, & yet no organized attempt was ever made to pursue the Indians & bring them to a fight or drive them out of the country. Many soldiers were killed within sight of the Fort, some within a few hundred feet of it, and yet all attempt at drill & perfect military discipline was neglected. The force was too much occupied in building magnificent quarters for the Col & his family, the other officers, then for themselves & finally constructed an immense stockade surrounding every thing—A large portion of the garrison, infantry and cavalry were recruits, which the Indians appear to have divined, & were consequently very bold in all their operations, until finally they ambuscaded and massacred Fettermans Entire party. Since then not an Indian has been seen about the Fort. Carrington claims that to do all the work which he was required of him, he had repeatedly applied, though unsuccessfully, for reinforcements. Cooke, on the contrary thinks he had men enough, but was not using them properly. Arms and ammunition were plenty at the Fort. On the day of the massacre somebody was to blame in not promptly reinforcing Fetterman, because every shot fired in his fight was distinctly heard at the Fort. The Court of Inquiry, which has been ordered in this case, will I suppose however, develope much more than we have obtained. Gen Augur reached here saturday evening, having been eleven days coming from Omaha. The run from Omaha is usually made in 12 hours, but the roads have been badly blocked by snow. He it was who told us about the Court of Inquiry & that it was ordered upon his application—I do not therefore feel much interest in any further investigation into this matter on our part, since it can result in no good, and our work would be 'love's labor lost'—We have not yet met any Indians. We sent a messenger to them nearly 3 weeks ago & have not heard either from him or them—Traders coming in from the Indian camps on the Republican report the snow as very deep & the weather extremely cold. There has been great suffering among the Indians on account of the severe cold, and large numbers of their ponies have either been frozen or starved. I am very glad that Hancock is not coming this way, ~~because~~ and now I ~~am satisfied~~ have hopes that we can save the Indians on the Republican & keep them out of the war, yet it is problematical—They can raise some 600 or 700 warriors, not more. We as a Commission have communicated to Browning, that we did not want military operations for the coming season delayed on our account, or for our not reporting promptly our opinion of the condition of affairs. We have therefore notified him that a state of war exists on the part of the Tongue river & Powder river Sioux, & that since the 1st of Jany./67 they have been making the most desperate efforts to have all the northern tribes combine with them in a general war against the whites. It is certain that they have not yet succeeded with the Crows, who are a powerful tribe, though inferior to the Sioux. The Crows have always been friendly & want to remain so. To their friendship ~~and~~ may be attributed the safety of C. F. Smith. If the Indian Confederation succeeds, C. F. Smith will have to succumb, because reinforcements cannot reach there before it will be assailed. Such being our convictions, we have urged the Secretary to open immediate communications with the Indians of the Upper Missouri to prevent this confederation, leaving the Sioux to fight his battles alone—We may be able to reach the Crows, but in doing so we must fight our way through the hostile Sioux, who occupy with their war parties the Tongue river and Powder river regions. There are other Indians on the Missouri that we cannot reach as readily as by going up the Mo. river—These hostile Sioux will not come to terms and they should be promptly & severely punished—I think General when you come out here next summer you will be delighted with the country. The air is very dry & will just suit your case. Mc-Elroy, of the 2nd Cav. has just gone to Washington & he can tell you a great deal about the country. By the time I get through, I can also tell you considerable, but then my information would be too late for you. You had better arrange & go out with Augur. He will hardly make an impression upon the Indians this summer, because he is not in good condition. His troops are raw and his cavalry principally recruits. To fight Indians successfully you want the best of experienced soldiers under command of officers of large experience in Indian warfare. Give my regards to all at HeadQuarters. Jno. E. has not yet got along & it is just as well, for the snow is yet so deep that nothing can move—" ALS, *ibid.*, RG 108, Letters Received. See letter to Edwin M. Stanton, April 10, 1867.

On Feb. 25, H. W. Johnson, Salem, Iowa, wrote to USG. "Allow me to make some remarks in regard to Goverment &. Indian affairs on the plains. for the last 16 years I have bin crossing the plains to & from the pacific & over the rocky mounts, generaly, as I alwas feel at home when in the mountains or in & un expored region. I have bin familiar with all the now hostile Indians I have crossed the planes several times in the last 3 years 2 years a go last October I took my family to the mountains I was 3 months getting from Missouri River to the mountains on account of the Indians the war murdering men women & children evry day before and behind us I was in a train of 80 wagons & about 100 men I was appointed captain of the train I took it through safe, I was anoyed & and agrevated with the soldiers & goverment officers beyond discription the war placed along the road from 15 to 25 miles a part   I suposed the should be thare, to pertect the emigration,   I look uppon those military posts on platt river wors than the Indians,   going out I dident thank them for any protection   I had plenty of men in my train   I saw small squads of men coming in from the mountains stop at those posts just at knight & want to camp within gun shot of the fort for protection   the war driven a way by the officers & soldiers one mile from the fort   thare the war massecreed murdered & culped be for morning   the hollowed murder as long as the could   the soldiers herd the guns & cries wanted to go to ther aid   the officer said he would shoot the first man that started *this I saw with my one Eyes*,   this was at plum creek station   this is the regulation at all the forts between here and the mountains   the let no emigrant camp within 1 mile of the fort   I have just crost the back here with my family   I stoped to camp ¾ of a mile from fort kerny   the sent the soldiers out and we war driven a way like dogs   thare is not a single man that has crost the plains for the last 3 years but what will say the would rather thare was not a soldier on the plains,   as we come home we war stoped at Ft Wordwirth & kept till we numbered 30 wagons & 40 well armed men   the comander then appointed a capptain out of the company and gave us papers to go down plat throu the Indian cuntry   that was all *rite*,   what next   well the next fort we come to we ware stoped & marched off 2 miles from the fort & kept thare to make us feed there corn & hay at 10 cents a pound   some times kept us days & some times weks then turn us loose   this is the rotene that evry man has to go throu that croses the planes   that is all the duty soldiers do on the planes to devel the emigrants & make money out of them,   last winter goverment fed 4000 Indians up to the 27 day of may, when goverment sent their anueties to them such as Blankets guns & amunitions   the next knight the stold the goverment herd proceded down platt & a crost on to the arkansaw murdering & plundering the trains with the guns & amunitions that goverment gave them,   for we owe them nothing for the have Broke their treaty   General I see by the papers you ar taking an Intrest in indian affairs   I dont no ho con troles the matter   I want them that do to no how the matter is conducted   2 years ago this winter the colorado first at *Ft* Lyon ishued rashens to 500 Indians nearly all winter & charged Goverment with it   the got twice the worth of the rashins in robes & Buckskins   col Shivington went down to Sand creek & killed 400 of the red devels the only good act that has bin don in that cuntry for 4 years   I was thare at the time,   I dont no as I will cross the planes a gain the soldiers of the planes or make some different arangement   I hope you will not think I am after office I dont want any   I have enough to do me,   if you want to no whether I am reliable or not I refer you to R. L. B Clark   I think he is in the quarter masters Generals department or E killpatrick both of them ar in the city   on the first day of this month 60 freight waggons & cargo was destroyd & 46 men murdered by the Indians on the Smokey hill rout . . . P S I want it under sud I am no kind to Andy"   ALS, DNA, RG 108, Letters Received.

To Lt. Gen. William T. Sherman

Washington, D, C Feb. 25th *1867*. [*10:45* A.M.]

LT. GN. W. T. SHERMAN,

ST. LOUIS, MO.

Do you know by what authority Carleton is kept in Command of New Mexico? If not by higher authority than mine order him to his regiment at once.

U. S. GRANT
General,

ALS (telegram sent), DNA, RG 107, Telegrams Collected (Bound); telegram sent, *ibid.*; copies, *ibid.*, RG 108, Telegrams Sent; DLC-USG, V, 56. See *PUSG*, 16, 164–65; USG endorsement, Dec. 23, 1867. On Feb. 25, 1867, Lt. Gen. William T. Sherman telegraphed to USG. "Oct. 19th last General Hancock being new in command asked to be permitted to retain Gen Carleton in New Mexico You answered by telegraph Oct 20th to retain him as requested and subsequently your special order no. five twenty three 523 of same date confirmed it. General Hancock wants Genl Getty to command out there as his regiment is to go there but General Getty has not joined If General Carleton is relieved Colonel Gerhart of the hundred and twenty fifth 125 will be senior unless you name Gen Sykes according to his Brevet rank. Genl Carleton shall be ordered to his regiment forthwith but I know that Genl. Hancock will want Genl. Getty to join forthwith or an order putting Genl. Sykes on duty with his Brevet of Brigadier General" Telegram received (at 5:00 P.M.), DNA, RG 107, Telegrams Collected (Bound); *ibid.*, RG 108, Telegrams Received; copy, DLC-USG, V, 55. On Feb. 26, 10:00 A.M., USG telegraphed to Sherman. "You may order Gen. Sykes to releive Gen. Carleton from command in New Mexico until Getty arrives." ALS (telegram sent), DNA, RG 107, Telegrams Collected (Bound); telegram sent, *ibid.*; copies, *ibid.*, RG 108, Telegrams Sent; DLC-USG, V, 56. On Jan. 24, Maj. Gen. Winfield S. Hancock, Fort Leavenworth, had written to Sherman's adjt. requesting that Col. and Bvt. Maj. Gen. George W. Getty, 37th Inf., command the District of New Mexico at bvt. rank. LS, DNA, RG 94, ACP, 3456 1886. On Jan. 24 and Feb. 14, USG endorsed this letter. "Respectfully forwarded to the Secretary of War, approved." "It is recommended that Gen. Getty be assigned to duty according to his brevet rank of Brigr General." ES, *ibid.*

On Sept. 24, 1866, Governor Robert B. Mitchell of New Mexico Territory, Santa Fé, had written to USG. "It is rumored here that an application has been made at Army Head Quarters to supercede Genl Carlton in command of the District of New-Mexico by Genl Sykes on the ground of lineal rank in the Army. There is no person holds Genl Sykes in higher esteem than myself, knowing him to be both a soldier & a gentleman, but I really think it would be a great injustice to Genl Carlton as well as this country to relieve him now from command in the very midst of his usefulness. He has been in command here for four years and has accomplished more than any other Commander ever did in the suppression of Indian difficulties; his policy of reservations with the Navajoes is accomplishing a very great and lasting benefit to this country; and a change of commanders at this time would in all probability work an entire change in the reservation policy, and would leave the country in as bad condition as when his policy was originally adopted. In addition to all this he is familliar with the Indian character here, and the customs of these people, and is better qualified to manage the Military Dept here than almost any other officer you could assign. As to the matter of rank there are other military gentlemen serving in this District that have more grounds of complaint on the ground of rank than Genl. Sykes. If I am not wrongly informed there are three full Colonels serving here in the Volunteer service, either of whom would rank Genl Sykes unless he was assigned with his brevet rank; all of whom are good and deserving soldiers, but neither of which would for a moment seek to supercede Genl Carlton in command, knowing as they all well do his ability to manage the affairs of this territory successfully. General I sincerely hope you will not find it necessary to make a change of commanding officers here at present, and untill the hostile Indians are subjugated, and peace and prosperity once more established in this territory. All good citizens here who are not engaged in manufacturing political capital for a selfish purpose would endorse the retention of Genl Carlton in command here. I hope to be in Washington in December next, and if this change is delayed untill then, I will be able to give you many more reasons, why in my judgement this change should not take place." LS, *ibid.*, RG 108, Letters Received.

On March 6, 1867, 2:30 P.M., USG telegraphed to Sherman. "You are authorized to assign Gn. Sykes to his Bvt. rank of Brig. Gn. and the command of district of New Mexico until relieved by Gen. Getty." ALS (telegram sent), *ibid.*, RG 107, Telegrams Collected (Bound); telegram sent, *ibid.*; copies, *ibid.*, RG 108, Telegrams Sent; DLC-USG, V, 56. On March 30, 10:30 A.M., USG telegraphed to Sherman. "If Gn. Sykes is to come in on the arrival of Gn. Getty, either by promotion or by the movement of his present regiment, you may order him in, as soon as relieved, without delay." ALS (telegram sent), DNA, RG 107, Telegrams Collected (Bound); telegram sent, *ibid.*; copies, *ibid.*, RG 108, Telegrams Sent; *ibid.*, RG 393, Dept. of the Mo., Letters Received; DLC-USG, V, 56. On the same day, Sherman telegraphed to USG. "Dispatch received. Has Genl Getty yet started for New Mexico to relieve Genl Sykes? He has not been here yet" Telegrams received (2—at 6:00 P.M.), DNA, RG 107, Telegrams Collected (Bound); *ibid.*, RG 108, Telegrams Received; copy, DLC-USG, V, 55. On the same day, Sherman wrote to USG. "Your despatch of today about Genl Sykes is received. I will send it forward to General Hancock to day, that he may order accordingly. I construe your despatch to mean that General Sykes be allowed to come in as soon as he is received by General Getty. General Getty has not yet come, and I have no means of telling when he can be promised to reach NewMexico, but until he does it will not be prudent to allow General Sykes to come away as he is the only reliable General out there. General Hancock's orders which he sent me in the rough, before making public, provides for bringing in the 5th Infantry, of which Sykes is the Commanding officer, as soon as the Posts now occupied by that Regimt can be replaced by General Getty's Regimt the 37th, now ordered to march out. This march can not well begin till late in April, as the mules & oxen that have the baggage can depend on the grass. General Hancock in the same orders assigns Gen Sykes to the Command of a district of the Upper Arkansas, HeadQuarters at Fort Harker. Gen Hancock telegraphs me today from the Solomons Fork, which he had to pontoon across, but the weather has modified wonderfully in the past two days, and I hope he will have no more trouble this side of the Arkansas. Your despatch about General Sykes should reach him in three days at Fort Harker, from which point he can send on to NewMexico the necessary orders." ALS, DNA, RG 108, Letters Received. On April 2, 2:20 P.M., USG telegraphed to Sherman. "Gen. Getty will leave this week for New Mexico." ALS (telegram sent), *ibid.*, RG 107, Telegrams Collected (Bound); telegram sent, *ibid.*; copies, *ibid.*, RG 108, Telegrams Sent; DLC-USG, V, 56.

On April 1, Sherman had telegraphed to USG. "General Carleton March fifteenth (15) acknowledges receipt of his orders of relief & to join his Regiment in the Department of the Gulf, He asks a years leave of absence and to be permitted to remain in New Mexico off duty, Without your sanction I must reiterate the orders from you for him to join his Regiment His application is mailed to you today" Telegram received (at noon), DNA, RG 107, Telegrams Collected (Bound); *ibid.*, RG 108, Telegrams Received; copies (one sent by mail), *ibid.*, Letters Received; DLC-USG, V, 55. On March 15, Lt. Col. and Bvt. Brig. Gen. James H. Carleton, Santa Fé, had written to Hancock requesting permission to stay in New Mexico Territory for three months and enclosing earlier requests for a one-year leave. LS, DNA, RG 94, Letters Received, 258C 1867. On April 9, Maj. George K. Leet endorsed these papers. "Respectfully returned to the Adjutant General, approved for three months permission to delay compliance with the orders to join his regiment, and for leave of absence for one year at expiration of that time." ES, *ibid.*

On March 11, J. L. Johnson of New Mexico Territory, Washington, D. C., wrote to USG. "The enclosed petition, was entrusted to me by the people of New Mexico, to hand to Govenor Mitchell, who was at that time in this City. Finding the General has left for Santa Fe, I have the honor, as a citizen of New Mexico to submit the petition to you, and request your careful and favorable consideration of it." LS, *ibid.*, RG 393, Military Div. of the Mo., Letters Received. The enclosed undated petition to Secretary of War Edwin M. Stanton protested plans to move army hd. qrs. from Santa Fé to Fort Union. On Feb. 19, Bvt. Col. Nelson H. Davis, inspector gen., Fort Bayard, New Mexico Territory, wrote to the AG defending himself and Carleton against charges raised in Congress. ALS, *ibid.*, RG 94, Letters Received, 94D 1867. On March 28, USG endorsed this letter. "Respectfully forwarded to the Secretary of War with the recommendation that a copy of this communication be sent to Hon. Henry Wilson, U. S Senate, in accordance with the request of Col. Davis." ES, *ibid.*

On May 16, Bvt. Maj. Gen. William A. Nichols, adjt. for Sherman, St. Louis, twice telegraphed to USG. "The fifth 5 Infantry was ordered in from New Mexico in Hancocks general orders number fifty five 55 of march Twenty eighth 28. General Sykes will be ordered to come in in advance of the troops General Sherman not yet returned" "General Hancock telegraphs that he will order Genl Sykes in from NewMexico but asks where shall he be ordered to, To Fort Harker the Hd Qrs of his Regt when it arrives there or where?" Telegrams received (at 1:15 P.M. and 4:40 P.M.), *ibid.*, RG 107, Telegrams Collected (Bound); *ibid.*, RG 108, Telegrams Received; copies (sent by mail), *ibid.*, Letters Received; DLC-USG, V, 55. On May 17, 9:30 A.M. and 10:10 A.M., USG telegraphed to Nichols and to Sherman. "Order Gen. Sykes in to report at Fort Harker. August 10th with permission to be absent from the Dept. during the interval." "What orders have been given for the return of Gen. Sykes from New Mexico? If his regiment is coming in order him to come in advance of the troops." ALS (telegrams sent), DNA, RG 107, Telegrams Collected (Bound); telegrams sent, *ibid.*; copies, *ibid.*, RG 108, Telegrams Sent; DLC-USG, V, 56. On the same day, Nichols telegraphed to USG. "Gen'l Hancock has sent your order by telegraph to NewMexico for the in come of General Sykes" Telegram received (at 3:45 P.M.), DNA, RG 107, Telegrams Collected (Bound); *ibid.*, RG 108, Telegrams Received; copies (one sent by mail), *ibid.*, Letters Received; DLC-USG, V, 55.

To Lucius S. Felt

———

Washington, D. C.
Feb.y 25th 1867.

L. S. FELT, Esq,
DEAR SIR:

Not knowing the initials of Mrs. Richardson's name I take the liberty of enclosing to you a letter for her, and also a draft for $30 00 payable to your order, to be given to her. Will you do me the favor to send the money and letter to Mrs. R.

I have rec'd one letter from Washburne[1] from Paris. His health is not improved and altogether he seems a little discouraged. My family are quite well and join me in sending regards to yourself and family.

Yours Truly
U. S. GRANT

ALS, PPRF. On March 28, 1867, USG wrote to Lucius S. Felt concerning the health of a mutual friend. *ABPC*, 1975, 1090.

1. See letter to Elihu B. Washburne, March 4, 1867.

To Bvt. Maj. Gen. Edward O. C. Ord

Washington, D. C. March 1st *1867*.

GENERAL:

Rumors very unfavorable to the management, even to the loy-alty, of some of the Clerks under the Quartermasters Dept. in Arkansas are received at these Hd Qrs. This particularly applies to two of them at Fort Smith. The order to relieve Col. Montgomery[1] was intended to obviate this condition of affairs without investigation. Constant efforts have been made, since the date of the Col's order for removal, to retain him, most of them by ex-rebels. I wish you would see that the order for his removal to Buffalo is executed as soon as he can be relieved, and cause an investigation into the management of the affairs of the Dept. at Ft. Smith. If investigation justifies such a course see that all objectionable employees are discharged and worthy men put in their places.

If the bill which has passed Congress becomes a law your Command will probably be taken out of the Mil. Div. of the Mo. and made an independent Dept. with Hd Qrs. at Vicksburg.[2] This is my notion. If however you think any other point more elegible write to me and the question will receive consideration.

Yours Truly
U. S. GRANT
General,

TO BVT. MAJ. GEN. E. O. C. ORD,
COMD.G DEPT. OF THE ARK.

ALS, Ord Papers, CU-B.

1. On Feb. 8, 1867, Ark. Senator Andrew Hunter, Little Rock, had telegraphed to President Andrew Johnson. "Important to all our interest that Col A Montgomery Chief Quarter Master ordered relieved be detained here as Chief Quarter master" Telegram received (at 10:30 P.M.), DNA, RG 94, Letters Received, 186H 1867. On Feb. 15, USG endorsed this telegram. "Respectfully returned to the Secretary of War, disapproved, and recommending that the order relieving Lt Col. Montgomery from duty in Dept Arkansas, be carried into effect." ES, *ibid*. On March 12, Bvt. Maj. Gen. Edward O. C. Ord, Little Rock, wrote to USG. "Your note relating to Col Montgomery is recd I have called his attention more than once to rumors relating to the rebel sympathies & of his

employees—he has denied having such—and I think the matter will be finally disposed of when he leaves—the employees at Fort Smith are reported as all right by the late post commander but Col Peirce is ordered up there to discharge all suspected of rebel proclivities and administer the test oath to the remainder The Editor Dell who ~~Genl Howard~~ has been reporting offices was a rebel during the war when Fort Smith was in the hands of the rebels and now his best claims to being a loyal man is based on his abuse of former friends—he is not reliable— Should I be retained in Command of a military district—I shall ask for as few troops as possible—I am having much less trouble with my freedmens Bureau— The threat to move the whole freed population from Counties where they could not be protected has had a wonderful effect   that county has sent me three petitions to come and see how kindly and affectionally they treat freed people— but the law will probably require a pretty large no—of officers of some sort to carry it out especially in Counties where there are *not* union men enough to hold the County offices—I telegraphed you in cypher to call attention to an apparent inconsistency in the law—Districting the south—I presume the particular matter has ere this been disposed of—We have a mail here but twice a week—& this fails often—. the tops of the telegraph poles between this and Memphis & the wire, are several feet under water—So we can not telegraph—our latest dates to day are the 2d from Washington . . . Montgomery leaves next boat after to morrow" ALS, *ibid.*, RG 108, Letters Received. On April 9, Maj. Alexander Montgomery, Buffalo, N. Y., wrote to USG. "I received the first intelligence of the rejection of my nomination as Lt Colonel, and of the promotion of Majr Myers to fill the vacancy, on my arrival at Cincinnati, on the 1st inst, on my way to this station. I hope this proceeding did not have your sanction, though I have been told by a friend that you were unfavourably impressed towards me because General Ord applied for an officer of the Qr Mr's Department to assist me in conducting the operations of the Department in that Department Military—The application was made at my instance because General Ord informed me that he could not spare an officer of the line to attend to the establishment of national cemeteries and the reinterment therein of the union Soldiers who fell in battle or who died in hospital in that Department. Moreover I was the only officer of the Qr Mrs Dept on duty with the Troops in the Dept of Arkansas, and in addition to the duties of Chief Qr Mr of the Department I had been charged with the care of the Depot at Little Rock, which was then about to be removed to Fort Smith, where it was essential that a bonded officer should be stationed, especially as General Ord had expressed his intention to relieve me of the Depot duties in order that I might the better supervise the operations of the Department generally, visiting the different Posts and giving special instructions to the Arty Arm Quarter Masters, all of whom were inexperienced in their duties as such—Genl Ord also informed me that he contemplated building three or more new Posts within the Department limits—I cannot think that the General intended that his application should be construed to my prejudice. The terms in which he speaks of me in his Order re- lieving me, a copy of which is herewith enclosed, forbids such construction of it. It is humiliating that there should even seem to be any necessity for these re- marks, but I am aware that I have some bitter and active personal enemies who would not scruple to seize any occasion to prejudice your mind against me; and that these others who have been seeking promotion, without much regard to means, & who have been promoted through the wrong done me. I feel that I have been greatly outraged, and I should forfeit all claim to respect if I should submit to it without protest, and the employment of all honorable means to have justice done me—I hope you will so regard it, and will feel prompted to assist me in my efforts for redress—I appeal to you, as the head of the Army, to protect my rights in this matter, with full conviction of the justice of my appeal and of your desire to *defend the right* in every and all cases. When I received a notification of my appointment as Lt Colonel although I felt that I had not been treated fairly in having junior officers thrust over my head, I was in hopes that the relentless persecution which had so long pursued me was exhausted, at last; but the treacherous subsidence of the storm was intended only, it appears, to throw me off my guard, and leave me unprepared to resist the next effort of its violence, to go down before it while indulging a false security. Not dreaming that the Senate would refuse to confirm my appointment I made no effort to secure their favourable action, giving my whole attention to the discharge of my public duties, remote from the scene of struggle among *lobby officers*, and with no stomach for such work, but trusting solely in the justice of my claim, and in the plain letter of the law—I trust you will find, in its importance to me, an excuse for the length of this communication—" ALS, *ibid.* On April 1, Ord wrote to Bvt. Maj. Gen. John A. Rawlins. "I have the honor to enclose for the information of the General Commanding, a report in regard to the loyalty and antecedents of the principal employees of the Quartermaster's Department at Fort Smith, Arkansas. All were present, except Wagenmaster's en-route to or from Fort Arbuckle, who were not aware of the examination. They will be examined and special report in their cases forwarded, as soon as they return to the Post. It will be seen that no disloyal men were employed by direction of the late Chief Quartermaster, Colonel Montgomery, who, though at times an invalid and likely thereby to leave matters to his subordinates, was, I am sure, always loyal, honest and economical in the administration of his duties. The employees herein reported as unable to take the test oath, have been discharged." LS, *ibid.* On Aug. 24, Edgar Cowan, Greensburgh, Pa., wrote to USG, secretary of war *ad interim.* "Maj. Alexr Montgomery was dismissed the Service at one time by Mr Stanton, and afterwards restored—but Mr S. refused his pay for the period of his dismissal, This I think was wrong and unjust and what I desire now is, that you rescind the order forbidding payment, so as to allow the order of restoration to be carried out. 'as if he had not been dismissed' I have known Maj. M. from boyhood, and have never heard his integrity or honor impeached—He had the misfortune however to have been a Democrat and to have incurred the enmity of Hon Thos Williams—During the early part of the War, the Maj. was Qr. Master at Pittsburgh—got into a brawl with Williams on politics—&. was reported to Mr Stanton—and dismissed—Every body was shocked, because nobody wants to see the power of the Govt turned to purposes of private revenge, and with the aid of Gen Morehead & some of the more moderate friends the President was prevailed upon to put him back as before, Then his pay was refused. I trust you will see this matter as I do—I am Satisfied there is no cool unprejudiced man here, who knows any thing of the facts, but will heartily approve your action if you can relieve Maj. Montgomery in ther behalf He is poor—really so—and if he was entitled to be restored to the Army—and to wear its uniform and to associate with its officers—no reason can be given why that restoration should not be perfect—and not upon terms and conditions tending to degrade him as a criminal—If he is expected to do his duty, his honor ought to have no imputation upon it" ALS, *ibid.*, RG 94, ACP, M520 CB 1868. On

May 30, 1872, E. P. Dorn, Buffalo, wrote to USG. "Will you allow me to write to you informally in relation to Major Alexander Montgomery's case. I wrote General Dent awhile ago and asked his kind offices in the premises. Every one here who knows Montgomery sympathises with him and desires that he be placed in his proper rank and position. In the letter that I wrote General Dent were set forth most of the causes that had placed Montgomery where he is at present in inferior rank. In the bill that passed the House yesterday there seems to be some hope if it passes the Senate of accomplishing what we want in his case. Friends of Montgomery and of the Administration, men who have stood by the right in all its phases for our Country have written and telegraphed to Senators Wilson and Conklin and asked them to aid Montgomery to get his desired and proper rights. May we ask the Executive and General Grant as a soldier to aid us and thereby to do an act of justice to a brother soldier—and gratify the ardent desires and wishes of Montgomerys hosts of friends and to bind us all with gratitude to you forever." LS, _ibid_. Montgomery was promoted to lt. col. as of June 6.

2. On Feb. 15, 1867, Ord wrote to USG. "private . . . I think I could be of some service now at Washington in giving information on the subject of affairs in this Dept—to the President, and Congress—if necessary—which information might aid in the reconstruction—my observations relate to the social status— prospects of the Freedmen—feelings of the People South—and the General want of confidence in the future because of the bad present and worse past—I think (and no doubt so do you) that a good many more troops are needed—the planters and property owners in this section would be glad to see them and if eight or ten Regiments of Volunteers ts could be provided, with 25 Laundresses (White) to a Company—sent to each southern State for a year and these all discharged there with 9 months rations _all around_, the reconstruction would be Complete—lives and property would have safety where every company settled—and civilisation— population—and Common Schools would be started among the 'Poor white men' of the south—I think by talking with some of the leading Radicals I could prove this—and could satisfy the President that something of the sort must be done; so—I want to try—The poor class of white men in the south will run off, and kill off, the negroes before long—if troops do not prevent it—hence the welcome troops will receive from the planters—The poor whites want Soldiers—(volun- teers)—to come among them and show them how to work and live—. the rich men want them to buy their lands—and the farmers who are industrious want them to buy their corn and meat—and the U S Govt wants them to breed loyal useful citizens, who have not been whipt—What do you think—Cant you Order Ord to Washington—he is too poor to pay his own expenses—. . . My best re- spects to the Madam—& Miss Jennie" ALS, _ibid_., RG 108, Letters Received. On Feb. 18, Ord wrote to Secretary of State William H. Seward making similar proposals. ALS (with enclosures), _ibid_.

On Feb. 25, Ord telegraphed to USG. "If the act creating new Departments is through or any change in statutes occurs it is important I should see you. Shall I report in person." Telegram received (at 3:15 P.M.), _ibid_., Telegrams Received; copy, DLC-USG, V, 55. On Feb. 27, 12:15 P.M., USG telegraphed to Ord. "Telegram of twenty fifth received. It would be inadvisable to leave your Department at this time. Please communicate your views by letter or telegraph. Act has not yet become a law." Telegrams sent (2—in cipher), DNA, RG 107, Telegrams Collected (Bound); telegram received (in cipher), _ibid_., RG 393,

4th Military District, Miscellaneous Records; copies, *ibid.*, RG 108, Letters Sent; DLC-USG, V, 56. On March 1, Ord twice wrote to USG. "privt,—. . . Enclosed I send you what I think (in part) on the subject of your telegram, and the pending law—Only the Property holders south are Conservative—and they are not in the majority—a bad public opinion is growing up here—The weight of the freedmen in *favor* of the Government is overestimated, force alone is respected by them and by a majority of the Whites in the South Give me 5000 men, half of them mounted to scatter over this state and loyal men will want no *law*, for their protection, or for reconstruction—let these 5000 men let these 5000 men be discharged in the state in 6 months, with rations for them selves and their wives till a crop is raised, and they want no law for reconstruction—they will reconstruct the country themselves—Without such a force all the laws which congress can pass are not worth the ink it takes to write them—we have too many such laws now; unknown to the ignorant majority and freedmen, and unheeded except where our troops are—or the interest of the planter makes obedience a necessity—Agents of the government sent to execute odious laws, (without soldiers), among a well armed and fighting community—become laughing stocks—I wanted if it is not too late to represent to leading M-Cs that such laws in this state, without strong force to back them only render this country every day more uninhabitable to union men—and clinch the hold which the rebel leaders have on their adherents—and which *we* loosened only with cold iron—I want to tell them that the experiment of negro suffrage will not do—that in a few cities loyal or northern men may control the negro vote—but in the country on the plantations—where nearly all the freedmen are,—they will vote with the men who they fear and Obey—and who give them their daily bread—the planters—, that if Congress wants a preponderating union sentiment here they must send it in the shape of loyal colonists—and make it their interest to stay—not tax them one third their crop—or rouse the hostility which exhists between the white and black labourer whenever they are brought into Competition—General if the law *has* passed my note is useless—but I hope you will put me on duty on my Brevet rank and let me select my head qurs, or select them in some healthy place for the sake of my family—as for myself all places are alike—I think I can get along with almost any people—my persistency in the matter of a volunteer colonising force in the south—is simply with a view to a permanent settlement on a tried basis of this great question, instead of an untried experiment—please excuse my pushing my sentiments forward so often—but I thought you were pretty much of my opinion when I last saw you, and I have learned some facts since then which I thougt you would like to hear. I do not know that I shall be retained in command of a Southern Department if not—Halleck would I think be glad to give me a share of California—the Southern part with Arizona I would be at *home* there—Any where, however—. . ." "I am of opinion that sooner or later the administration of the laws for the government and good of Freedmen will have to be left to the legitimate authority in the States and that in this State the interests of the soil and its possessors require that laws for the protection of Freedmen, having been enacted, shall be inforced. If, therefore, this interest of the possessors of the soil, can be called into action and the execution of the laws be left to them, there will be no necessity for any interference by the Military with the civil laws in this State. At the present time, however, there are in this State, many poor and laboring white men, who feel themselves aggrieved and degraded at having to compete with negroes as tenants and laborers, especially where the negroes underbid them and from the fact of being accustomed to plantation labor and used to obey are preferred to the white laborers. These latter willnot tolerate the presence of such negro labor, if they can help it. They will disregard the laws, or having a controlling voice in elections, will elect only such justices and judges as will defer to their feelings and who will not punish outrages upon freedmen by a strict administration of the laws. This feeling, which is growing in the South, especially in sections, where a short crop bears heavily on all poor men, may be compared to the feeling which caused the riot in New-York in 1864 and which in 1862, when large numbers of freedpersons with their families were sent north from the armies, to Illinois and scattered through the State, induced the civil authorities of the State and the city of Chicago to apply to the War Department for an order prohibiting the wholesale importation within their limits, of people liable to pauperism and with whom the white laborers did not harmonize. This prejudice or cast feeling breaks out in the more passionate and ignorant of the white population here, when a freedman resents, what he deems an injury or attempts to redress his own wrongs; then the pistol, worn by almost every white man in Arkansas, settles the dispute As the whites make the law and elect its Officers, and as the negro is servile, ignorant and unused to firearms, one white man can dictate to a hundred negroes. It would therefore be impossible to correct this state of things, by—or expect the negro to use for his own advantage—the right of suffrage, if it were granted them. They are so much accustomed to submit, and the feeling against their taking a place alongside the white man, is so strong, that they would not dare present themselves at the polls, even were they supported by an armed force, except perhaps in a few cities, where they might be taken to the polls by white employers. As this hostility of race is not confined to persons engaged against the Government in the late war, but is natural and common to all white men who are brought into competition with the negro, the remedies which alone are applicable to this growing hostility, between the laboring whites and blacks, as I before observed, to call into action the interests of the owners of the soil, who require the negro labor to cultivate their lands, and encourage them to protect their only labor, when this interest is not strong enough to make the white laboring men defer to the laws, in spite of their hostility to the negro, then defer to them and remove the negroes or freedmen to where they will be protected or can protect themselves. No Steamboat-Captain or Overseer in this country will think of mixing white and black hands; they will not work together. To protect both races socially and under equal laws, they must be separated. To do this gradually and with due regard to the interest of all parties and protect the freedmen from damage in the meanwhile, a large military force is necessary in many parts of the State. Their presence would show badly disposed men, that in case the civil law should be interrupted, military aid to enforce it, was provided by the Government. I also consider that such Military force should be composed of short term Volunteers with a sufficient number of white laundresses to encourage one half of the whole force to bring their wives. Men with their families are more interested in the preservation of civil and social laws and would, if properly encouraged, when their short term of service should expire, remain as settlers in the country, thereby helping to build it up. The presence of such a force would do no violence to the feelings of intelligent citizens of this State, from whom in several instances, I have had applications for a Military force to protect from violence the freedmen employed by them. On the contrary it would have a good effect on all parties, replacing with industrious, white men the freedmen, who are fast passing away" ALS and LS, DNA, RG 108, Letters Received.

On March 25, Bvt. Brig. Gen. Orville E. Babcock wrote to Ord. "The General-in-Chief directs me to reply to your several communications of Feb. 15th, March 1st and March 12th; and to say that the duty now required of you is the execution of the 'Acts of Congress for the more efficient government of the rebel States'—in the States of Arkansas and Mississippi, and that you must use all means provided in said Acts to the best of your ability. It is probable that one more regiment of Infantry can be sent to your District. If you employ faithfully all the means provided you, and the object of the Acts of Congress is not accomplished, the responsibility will not rest upon you. It is the wish and intention of the General to furnish you all the assistance possible. He also thinks it best to try thoroughly the laws now enacted before asking for others, or for changes in those existing. It is believed that the spirit of the above mentioned Acts require the District Commander should be located at the point where he can best communicate with all parts of his District. In accordance with this view Vicksburg was designated as the Headquarters of the District to which you are assigned. The General trusts this letter will be received in the kind spirit intended." LS, Ord Papers, CU-B.

The First Reconstruction Act passed over Johnson's veto on March 2. On March 8, Ord twice telegraphed to USG. "Can I not make Natchez Hd Quarters" "The law creating military districts authorizes commanders to allow local civil tribunals to try offender. Does this mean existing tribunals regardless of eligibility under sixth section." Telegram received (first only—on March 11, 5:30 P.M.), DNA, RG 107, Telegrams Collected (Bound); (the first received on March 11, 5:30 P.M., the second at 5:35 P.M.) *ibid.*, RG 108, Telegrams Received; copies (second only), *ibid.*, RG 46, Senate 40A–F5, War Dept. Messages; DLC-USG, V, 55. On March 13, 12:30 P.M., USG telegraphed to Ord. "You have been assigned to Command of District of Ark. & Miss. Hd Qrs. Vicksburg. Orders by Mail." ALS (telegram sent), DNA, RG 107, Telegrams Collected (Bound); telegram sent, *ibid.*; telegram received, *ibid.*, RG 393, 4th Military District, Miscellaneous Records.

On March 10, Governor Isaac Murphy of Ark. wrote to USG. "On yesterday I called on Gen Ord Comd this department—in relation to difficulties represented to exist between the Union and Late Rebel elements, in Foulton County—I wished him to send an intelegent officer with a small guard into the county to investigate, the mutual charges—and give the influence of the U S Government to the peacable citizens—He expressed entire willingness to do so—but assured me that neither the officer or men could at present be furnishd: that his force was not sufficient to meet the varied demands of the service required of him I am not informed as to the number of troops now in this state—but from appearances suppose it not to exceed five or six hundred rank and file—not sufficient to produce much moral effect—In the present condition of the public mind, I deem that at Lest five thousand soldiers should be distributed throughout the state with full compliment of officers—Elections will soon be held under the requirements—of the military reconstruction act—I fear that without a show of military power in the several counties—that the newly enfranchised voters will not be able to freely express their sentiments at the polls—It is gravely important, to the Govt and to the peace and security of the state, that the first elections under the reconstruction policy now adopted should be held under such protection—as to make evy voter feel safe in voting his real sentiments The state Government being declared, merely provisional—and subordinate to the militry—I have thought it my duty to call the attention of the General in Chief to the condition of the state The Labouring and business portion of the people are Law abiding—and disposed, to accept in good faith the decrees of Congress, and be governed thereby—The great want of this class is somthing fixed and settled—a permanant security—and full protection in all their personal and political rights—To them it is not so important who votes or who holds office—as it is to feel assured that they have a Government that will protect them in their various pursuits—from agression and, pilage The war has Left a heavy debris of Lawless reckless men who glory in rebelion—and war—They are continually singing the praises of the dead *cause* and cursing—congress, the Union and its defenders This class is a terror to the quiet peacable Citizen, and exercise a very great influence over those who have been fully identified with the rebelion and realy give tone to the Rebel Journals—generally—a show of militry power in different sections of the state would soon destroy the influence of this class—and peace order and harmony— would be the result—At present the Political parties are divided as they were during the war—all the Feds—are Union—all the Confeds are conservative—The one sustains Congress the other—bitterly denounces the action of Congress The presence of a sufficient show of the boys in blue in the several counties of the state would Lead to great and rapid changes in sentiment—I Know that a Large number of those who were most deeply involved in the rebelion as soon as they can be relieved from the sarcasm and sne[e]rs, of reckless politician will be hereafter devotedly true to the Government—and act earnestly with the Union element—Four or five thousand troops kept in the state and properly distributed— would in twelve months—be able to Leave the state—in a thoroughly organized condition—at peace among themselves—and regardles of the divisions of the war I trust, that you will find it in your power to Largly increase Gen Ord's forces— so that he may have it in his power to exercise the influence for good that he desires—Gen Ord has the confidence of all who Know him—here—and we trust that He will be continued in command of this district—As provisional Governor I will not take any steps, to introduce the provisions of the military reconstruction act—untill I receive instructions—. . . P. S. I respectfully urge an idea recieved from Gen Ord, 'that the troops sent here be Volunters inclined to emigrate to the state, with their families—to be enlisted for one year and to be discharged within the state—a policy of this Kind would soon secure the controle of the state to the Loyal Element—and introduce the thrifty habits of the north" ALS, *ibid.*, RG 108, Letters Received.

On March 17, Ord telegraphed to USG. "Genl Gillem telegraphs quarters scarce and high at Vicksburg owing to recent great fire If part of Tennessee West of that river were assigned me staff officers could get quarters & I think Gen Thomas would feel glad Memphis is more central & more important than Vicksburg. No eastern mail here last ten days" Telegram received (on March 18, 8:40 A.M.), *ibid.*, RG 107, Telegrams Collected (Bound); *ibid.*, RG 108, Telegrams Received; copy, DLC-USG, V, 55. On March 27, Ord wrote to Rawlins concerning this matter. LS, DNA, RG 108, Letters Received; ADfS (addressed to USG), Ord Papers, CU-B. On March 23, Ord telegraphed to USG. "Can Brevet Major Genl Henry J Hunt report to me by Brevet as Military Commande[r] and Commissioner Freedmens Bureau for this State? I learn that he desires to come and would suit" Telegram received (at 5:00 P.M.), DNA,

RG 107, Telegrams Collected (Bound); *ibid.*, RG 108, Telegrams Received; copy, DLC-USG, V, 55.

On March 27, Ord twice wrote to Rawlins. "I respectfully enclose the within requisition for the action of the General Commanding, the horses being indispensable to mount parties of Infantry as guards to Officers who have to make the registration of Voters in the State of Arkansas, as the only mode of traveling in the state from County to County being by horse, or in wagons, when the County seat is not on a navigable river—I hope the horses will be sent as soon as possible" LS, DNA, RG 108, Letters Received. "In accordance with instructions I have the honor to enclose copy of Order No. 1—General Gillem, District Commander informs me that the 24th Inft. is the only Regiment, or troops, in this State—that he has but fifteen Company Officers for duty—I have not, (owing to failure of eastern mails up to the 23d inst,) received Genrl. Grant's Order No. 10, or official copy of either law of Congress, defining duties of District Commanders, please send me special Copies—From what I can learn there are but few Counties in this state where loyal men can be found to perform the duties of registering voters—In a majority of Counties in this state and in Arkansas, a military force will be the first thing applied for by persons appointed to register voters, upon the grounds that they would be unsafe without military protection. I shall have to forward these applications because the force at present in this state, or available, will not suffice for one third the Counties, *nor is any of it mounted*—I propose organizing for the registering duty as many parties of mounted men as possible, and to require them to take the Counties in succession—Genl. Gillem, is of opinion that the parties should not be less than twenty each. I therefore have directed the Chief Quarter master to apply for five hundred horses, to mount fifteen or twenty parties, half the horses will probably break down on the first march—I shall require *all* the Company and regimental officers as the Non-Commissioned, are recruits and unfit to be trusted with independent Commands—I propose in appointing the registers of voters, and Judges of elections, to select two out of every three from the late Volunteer Officers of our Army, when it is practicable, and the third as loyal a Citizen as can be found, when there is one—In order to reach the freedmen on plantations *at all* with the law of Congress, the Freedmens Bureau, should have an agent in every County, now there are but eleven in the 60 Counties of this State, and but fifteen who can be of use in the 55 Counties of Arkansas—I intended to visit every County in the latter state, and make appointments but nearly half the state is under water, all travel is suspended in that half, and a large part of Missippi presents the same gloomy waste of waters—I hope General, I shall receive for this District a fair share of funds appropriated by the law of Congress, to defray the expenses of organizing it—My impression is that Genl. Sickles, for a District but little more than half as large as this, has nearly twice the number of troops—Genl. Sherman, has authorized me to keep the 28th Infantry but four of its Companies will have to remain at Forts Arbuckle, and Gibson, until relieved, which will probably not be until July, or August—too late for use. I can however get along in Arkansas with 16 Companies, here in Mississippi I should have two regiments at least, and during the registering I think Genl. Thomas or the Department of the Cumberland having no such work, could spare at least one regiment—that at Memphis—" LS, *ibid.*, RG 94, Letters Received, 866M 1867; ADfS, Ord Papers, CU-B. On March 28, Ord wrote to USG. "To promply register legal voters, I propose, with the aid of the 25th Infantry—now at Memphis—to divide this state into ten Dists of 6 counties each, a garrison of two Companies in center of every district—four of the garrisons along each of the two Rail Roads running from end to end of the State   this will give me perhaps 40 men at each garrison who after a little practice can stick a horse—or two parties of 20 each, with which I can take three of the 6 counties in succession, a week to each—so that if you can telegraph the Western Quarter Masters to send me the 500 head of horses—for each state as fast as possible—I may get my garrisons in position— and organised in time to complete the registration—Both in Arkansas and Mississippi mail communications are almost unknown off the rivers or R Roads—in the latter state I must depend entirely upon the military—two companies at each of the stations will give me enough men who can ride and a reserve to care for supplies and do garrison duties with probably an officer to each party of 20 men—(the Non Commissioned recruits can not be trusted)—without the horses I can only reach the countyseats on R Roads or navigable rivers—it would therefore be impossible to make a complete registration—with but 10 companies of Infy to each state I could mount only ten parties, each of which would have to travel over 6 counties—about four times the distance, each of the 20 parties would have to travel—I report my plan in advance for your action—and to get an early start especially in ~~Oregon~~ Arkansas—the Quarter Masters will for each state telegraph when the detachments of horses should be sent if Genl Meigs is authorised to furnish them—I will return the 25th Regt to Genl Thomas as soon as the election is over—please telegraph me if my plan is approved—I return to Little Rock via Memphis & Jackson Miss—to morrow—(the shortest route) to meet a union convention which assembles on the 2d proximo—shall be back here and at work in twelve days—cant you send me a quarter master for Little Rock—have none in Arkansas at all—. . . P S.—General I ask early action because it will take two and three months to get my garrisons in position in Arkansas—and the troops should start while the rivers are up—there—we have no telegraphs—no common or R Roads—except 45 miles—and a very wild country worse than the plains—" ALS, DNA, RG 94, Letters Received, 874M 1867; ADf (dated March 27), Ord Papers, CU-B. On April 3, Babcock wrote to Ord. "The General in Chief directs me to reply to your communication of march 27th—asking for 500 horses and to say that the supposition is that the people will not oppose the execution of the Act of Congress creating the Mil. Districts, &c. and that unless the people do resist the mounted force you ask for can be dispensed with. The sending of a military force before the people have had an opportunity to act might invite a resistance or at least prevent a willing cooperation. If upon trial it is found necessary to send a military force throughout the states of Ark. and Miss.—all assistance possible will be given you" Copies, DLC-USG, V, 47, 60; DNA, RG 108, Letters Sent.

On March 30, Ord, Memphis, telegraphed to USG. "Had an interview with Gov'r Humphrey's yesterday. I am on my return to Little Rock. Have no cipher with me. It is very important that I should see you. Shall I come on?" Telegram received (at 4:00 P.M.), ibid., RG 107, Telegrams Collected (Bound). On April 11, Ord, Vicksburg, telegraphed to Johnson. "Peculiar situation of affairs in Mississippi and Arkansas require that I should confer with you before final action. Can I do so in person?" Telegram received (at 3:00 P.M.), ibid., RG 108, Telegrams Received; copy, DLC-USG, V, 55. Johnson endorsed this telegram. "Genl Ord will be permitted to visit W. for the purpose of confering with the Pres' as requested in his despacth—" AES (undated), DNA, RG 108, Telegrams Received. On April 12, 10:00 A.M., USG telegraphed to Ord. "Your repeated applications for authority to visit Washington, instead of attending to the pressing business of your District, have been uniformly disapproved by me.— By direction of the President you will report in person to him for the interview sought for by yourself." ALS (telegram sent), *ibid.*, RG 107, Telegrams Collected (Bound); telegram sent, *ibid.*; copies, *ibid.*, RG 108, Telegrams Sent; (incomplete) Ord Papers, CU-B; DLC-USG, V, 56.

To Elihu B. Washburne

Washington, D. C. March 4th *1867*.

DEAR WASHBURNE;

I owe you an apology for not writing sooner but have no good excuse to offer. General indolence I suppose has kept me from writing.

Your telegraphic dispatch in favor of the confirmation of Gn. Dix, also your letter, partly on the same subject, were duly received. I lost no time in communicating the substence of your dispatch to as many Senators as I could. I am glad to be able to announce to you this morning, a fact which you will no doubt learn by telegraph long before this reaches you, that the Senate has confirmed him.

Reconstruction measures have passed both houses of Congress over one of the most ridiculous Veto messages that ever emianated from any President. Jerry Black is supposed to be the Author of it.[1] He has been about Washington for some time and I am told has been a great deal about the White House. It is a fitting end to all our controversy, (I believe this last measure is to be a solution unless the President proves an obstruction,) that the man who tried to prove at the begining of our domestic difficulties that the nation had no constitutional power to save itself, is now trying to prove that the nation has not now the power, after a victory, to demand security for the future. I hope you will see this Message, Reverdy Johnson's[2] remarks and Gov. Brown's[3] (of Ga.) letter and contrast the two latter with the former.

I am sorry to learn from your letter that your health has not improved. I thoght that freedom from care, with the witticisms of Jones, would cure you. Hope it will yet have the affect.

I see no chance of getting abroad this year. Do not show what I have said on political matters to any one. It is not proper that a subordinate should critisise the acts of his superiors in a public manner. I rely upon our personal relations however to speak to you freely as I feel upon all matters.

Give my kindest regards to Jones. Tell him not to fail to keep his journal up ready for publication on his return. I rely on the proceeds of ~~that jo~~ the sale of that journal to save the earnings of our Horse Rail Road to go into the hands of the stockholders. You know Jones must be supported and the Horse concern is a "bird in hand."

Hoping to hear soon from you again, and that your health is much improved, I remain, as ever,

Your Friend
U. S. GRANT

ALS, IHi. On Feb. 8, 1867, U.S. Representative Elihu B. Washburne, Paris, had written to USG. "Mr. Jones and myself are safely here. Our passage was a rough one but on the whole quite up to the average of a winter passage—a little over ten days to Liverpool. We liked the 'Persia' very much and were much obliged to Mr. Smythe for his good offices in that regard. Our stay in England was three days, but quite long enough. I am not yet fully determined as to how long I will remain here. I am now looking around for medical treatment. I find myself very much as I was before leaving home, and did I not flatter myself that I may be benefitted, I should feel quite wretched. I have sent two or three letters to Mrs. W. to your care. If she shall have left W. please forward. Anything for me will reach me here care of the American Legation. Jones joins me in kind regards to yourself and family and to the members of the staff Genl Dix, our Minister here is getting along admirably and I have no doubt that he should be confirmed, and if you fall in with Mr. Sumner I hope you will tell him so." ALS, USG 3. On Feb. 17, Washburne cabled to USG. "General Dix should be immediately Confirmed See Senators. Have written" Cable received (at 7:30 P.M.), DNA, RG 107, Telegrams Collected (Bound).

1. Jeremiah S. Black of Pa., attorney gen. and secretary of state for President James Buchanan, was the principal author of President Andrew Johnson's message vetoing the First Reconstruction Bill. William A. Dunning, "More Light on Andrew Johnson," *American Historical Review*, XI, 3 (April, 1906), 584–94; HRC, 40-1-7, 271–73.

2. U.S. Senator Reverdy Johnson of Md. voted for the First Reconstruction

Bill and to override Johnson's veto as the best means to achieve "the restoration of the Union as it was prior to the insurrection." *CG*, 39–2, 1973.

3. On Feb. 26, Joseph E. Brown, former Ga. governor, published a letter advising Southerners to accept the terms of congressional Reconstruction. *New York Times*, Feb. 26, March 1, 1867. See Joseph H. Parks, *Joseph E. Brown of Georgia* (Baton Rouge, 1977), pp. 367–70.

To Edwin M. Stanton

Washington, D. C. Mch. 9th 1867

Hon. E M. Stanton
Sec. of War,
Sir:

In response to your directions of the 8th inst. for me to report to the War Dept. what military expeditions are in progress, or in contemplation to be carried on, in the Indian Territory, or against the Indians in the West, I have the honor to enclose you the within dispatches and orders which embrace all the information I have on the subject. The papers enclosed give information of all hostilities contemplated until the Indians make, by their own acts, further operations against them necessary. Present preparations look more to preventing further massacres than to hostile action towards the Indians on the plains

Very respectfully
Your obt. servt.
U. S. Grant
General

Copies, DLC-USG, V, 47, 60; (dated March 8, 1867) DNA, RG 46, Senate 40A–G3, War Dept. Reports; (dated March 8) *ibid.*, RG 107, Letters Received from Bureaus; *ibid.*, RG 108, Letters Sent. See telegrams to Lt. Gen. William T. Sherman, Jan. 14, Feb. 19, 1867. On March 8, 1867, Secretary of War Edwin M. Stanton had written to USG. "Please report to this Department at your earliest convenience what military operations are in progress, or in contemplation to be carried on, in the Indian Territory, or against the Indians in the West." Copies, DNA, RG 46, Senate 40A–G3, War Dept. Reports; *ibid.*, RG 107, Letters Sent to the President; *ibid.*, Letters Received from Bureaus; *ibid.*, RG 393, Dept. of the Mo., Letters Received.

On March 13, Lt. Gen. William T. Sherman, St. Louis, wrote to Maj.

George K. Leet. "I have the honor to acknowledge the receipt of the communication of the Hon. the Secretary of War addressed to General Grant dated March 8th inst. and endorsed to me from your office on the 9th instant requesting 'early information of military operations in progress or in contemplation in the Indian Territory or against Indians in the West' and in answer thereto beg to state, that. All the troops in the Departments of Dakotah, Platte, and Missouri, embracing the Indian country have been and are now being placed in position to afford the best protection to the Telegraph and Mail routes across the Plains, as well as to protect the four principal roads by which the emigrants travel, or merchants send their goods destined to the mountain Territories. These troops will occupy posts, rudely built but designed for defense by a portion of the Garrison, whilst the balance can operate as escorts, or expeditions between the posts. Commanding officers of these Posts or Stations will act against all people who violate the Laws of Congress, or who endanger the lives or property of our people, be they white, black or copper-colored. Where there are no courts or civil authorities to hold and punish such malefactors, we must of necessity use the musket pretty freely, the only weapon with which the soldier ought to deal. Peaceful people, whites, blacks, or Indians will be left to be dealt with by the civil authorities and agents. General Hancock in the Dept. of the Mo. has organized a special force of about (1500) Fifteen Hundred men mostly of the 7th Cavalry (a new regiment) and some Infantry drawn from the Inner Posts with which he will proceed in person to the country of the Cheyennes, Kiowas, and below the Arkansas, and will then confer with them to ascertain if they want to fight, in which case he will indulge them. If however they will assure him that they will remain at peace subject to their treaties and Agents, he will not disturb them, but impress on them the imprudence of assuming an insolent manner and tone when they visit our posts, and he will impress on them that it is to their interest to keep their hunting parties and their young warriors off our main lines of travel, where their presence gives the occasion for the many rumors which so disturb our people. After he has done this he will distribute this force so as to be again easily assembled if the occasion calls for it. His final orders are not yet made out, but will be in a few days, and I will endeavor to make them so as to leave him free to act but not to create any trouble which should be avoided. In like manner General Augur in the Department of the Platte has prepared a force of about (2000) two thousand men, composed of the 2d U. S. Cavalry and of Infantry grouped about Fort Laramie to be sent under a competent commander, General Gibbon, to the region of country on the head of Powder and Yellow Stone Rivers, to punish the bands of hostile Sioux who have infested that Road for the past year have killed many people, and are at open war. No mercy should be shown these Indians, for they grant no quarter nor ask for it. General Augur was instructed if possible by means of runners to notify all Sioux who wished to avoid the fate of their hostile fellows, to come in to some one of our military Posts on the Platte where we would feed them temporarily and turn them over to the care of their proper agents. But inasmuch as Congress has lately provided for a commission to visit these Indians, and as these Commissioners have reached Omaha, the Headqrs. of General Augur, I have instructed him to delay actual hostilities until these commissions have exhausted their efforts and reported to him their inability to influence the conduct of the hostile Sioux by pacific measures. I have not yet made final orders for this movement, and will delay them till we learn by telegraph at Fort Laramie that the country about Forts Phil. Kearney and C. F. Smith is practicable for military operations. In reference to these two expeditions, which are all we can undertake with our present force, I will remark that defensive measures will not answer against Indians. We are tied down to long routes, and our detachments are necessarily small, hardly enough to build shelters and gather firewood the materials for which have to be hauled two and three hundred miles, whilst the Indians move hundreds and thousands of miles, taking along with them, their ponies, lodges, wives and children. They are thus enabled at one time to attack or molest our roads at one point and a month or so make their appearance at another hundreds of miles distant. Our troops must get amongst them, and must kill enough of them to inspire fear, and then must conduct the remainder to places where Indian Agents can and will reside amongst them, and be held responsible for their conduct. There may be Indian Agents duly commissioned for these Indians that we know to be hostile, but they do not reside with the Indians, and they are not as competent to judge of their hostile character, as our military officers who come into constant contact with them." Copies, *ibid.*, RG 46, Senate 40A–G3, War Dept. Reports; *ibid.*, RG 108, Letters Received; *ibid.*, RG 393, Dept. of the Mo., Letters Received; (2—one incomplete) *ibid.*, Special File, Indian War. On March 18, USG endorsed this letter to Stanton. Copy, *ibid.*, RG 46, Senate 40A–G3, War Dept. Reports. On March 13, Governor Samuel J. Crawford of Kan. wrote to Maj. Gen. Winfield S. Hancock concerning Indian policy. Copy, *ibid.*, RG 107, Letters Received from Bureaus. On March 23, Sherman endorsed this letter. "Respectfully forwarded for the information of the General in chief to show the feeling of uneasiness on the part of people. They dont look to the Indian agents but to us for protection and these Indians all have agents and annuities, and are the very ones that have been so well supplied with arms and amunition by the Indian agents and traders with the full sanction of the Interior Departmt. Gen Hancock will do his best, but he cannot break up his command into little detachmts to be used up in detail. I hope his present move will accomplish the desired result, but there is no telling." AES, *ibid.* On March 28, USG endorsed this letter. "Respectfully forwarded to the Secretary of War, for his information, and attention especially invited to the endorsement of Lieut Gen. Sherman. I respectfully request that a copy be furnished to the Secretary of the Interior" ES, *ibid.*

General Orders No. 10

HEADQUARTERS OF THE ARMY,
ADJUTANT GENERAL'S OFFICE,
Washington, March 11, 1867.

GENERAL ORDERS No. 10.

I.. The following Act of Congress is published for the information and government of all concerned: . . .

II.. In pursuance of the act of Congress entitled "An act to provide for the more efficient government of the rebel States," the President directs the following assignments to be made:

First District, State of Virginia, to be commanded by Brevet Major General J. M. SCHOFIELD.[1] Headquarters, Richmond, Va.

Second District, consisting of North Carolina and South Carolina, to be commanded by Major General D. E. SICKLES.[2] Headquarters, Columbia, S. C.

Third District, consisting of the States of Georgia, Florida, and Alabama, to be commanded by Major General G. H. THOMAS.[3] Headquarters, Montgomery, Ala.

Fourth District, consisting of the States of Mississippi and Arkansas, to be commanded by Brevet Major General E. O. C. ORD.[4] Headquarters, Vicksburg, Miss.

Fifth District, consisting of the States of Louisiana and Texas, to be commanded by Major General P. H. SHERIDAN.[5] Headquarters, New Orleans, La.

The powers of Departmental Commanders are hereby delegated to the above-named District Commanders.

BY COMMAND OF GENERAL GRANT:

E. D. TOWNSEND,
Assistant Adjutant General.

Copies (printed), DNA, RG 94, Letters Received, 532L 1869; *ibid.*, M834 1869; (incomplete) *ibid.*, 239S 1867. An undated df of paragraph II is *ibid.* USG filled in the names of commanders for the First through Fourth Districts; he entered the name of Bvt. Maj. Gen. Edward O. C. Ord for the Fifth District, cancelled the name, and entered the word "Blank." AN, *ibid.* On March 9, 1867, USG met with President Andrew Johnson for three hours to discuss commanders for the military districts. See Theodore Calvin Pease and James G. Randall, eds., *The Diary of Orville Hickman Browning* (Springfield, 1925–33), II, 135; Howard K. Beale, ed., *Diary of Gideon Welles* (New York, 1960), III, 62–65. On March 8, Lt. Gen. William T. Sherman, St. Louis, telegraphed to USG. "General Hancock is here in consultation about early movement on the plains this mornings papers announced positively that he and I are both to be detailed away under the military reconstruction bill Please give me earliest possible notice affecting either of us as a change now would influence our plans & actions" Telegram received (at 10:45 A.M.), DNA, RG 107, Telegrams Collected (Bound); *ibid.*, RG 108, Telegrams Received; copy, DLC-USG, V, 55. On March 11, 1:00 P.M., USG telegraphed to Sherman. "Your assignment to the District of La. & Texas will depend on the reply you may send to this dispatch expressive of your feeling in the matter." ALS (telegram sent), DNA, RG 107, Telegrams Collected (Bound); telegram sent, *ibid.*; copies, *ibid.*, RG 108, Telegrams Sent; DLC-USG, V, 56. On March 12, Sherman telegraphed to USG. "If it depends on my choice I would not go to Louisiana & Texas I dont want to adminster such a govt. but if necessary then I prefer the District you name." Telegram received (at 9:20 P.M.), DNA, RG 107, Telegrams Collected (Bound); *ibid.*, RG 108, Telegrams Received; copies, *ibid.*, RG 94, Letters Received, 161P 1867; DLC-USG, V, 55. On March 12, USG endorsed a copy of this telegram. "Respectfully submitted to His Excellency the President." ES, DNA, RG 94, Letters Received, 161P 1867. On the same day, Johnson endorsed this telegram. "General Grant will fill the blanks with the names originally suggested by him, including that of Major Genl Sheridan.—The Cabinet will meet at twelve o'clock today, and would be pleased to hear any suggestions that he may think proper to submit." ES, *ibid.* On March 13, Sherman wrote to USG. "I received your very clever letter of March 7, last evning and think best to answer at once that you may know exactly how I feel and what I think in the ever changing aspect of things. I was completely taken aback when I saw my name and Hancocks mixed up with the execution of the Law, for Reconstructing the South. I dont think I ought to be sent for the Republicans who have the power are suspicious of me, thinking I am imbued with old prejudice against the Negros, and they would hold me responsible for the defects of the Law itself. If each District embraced but a single state and that made a 'seperate Department, the Military Commander could let the Governor, Legislature and Courts do the bulk of the business, and would only have to interfere in case of the failure to enforce criminal Law in particular parts, but for one officer, to manage two such discordant States as Louisiana & Texas, or Arkansas & Mississipi will be about as hard to manage as two round floating logs drifting down the Mississipi. I think I observe that the Cabinet made one selection, and you the other, and up to this moment I have no positive notice of the result. I am awaiting it, and though I think the detail should be left to you, if it is officially made and my name is included I will leave my family here and go forthwith to the place assigned and do my best. I would hate to displace Sheridan for I believe he is fully as qualified as I am, and having no particular friends there he is less likely to be swerved from a just course I would be embarrassed & importuned beyond measure, by an old class of personal friends, all of whom were active enemies, but now profess to wish Peace, Good order and Good Governmt. Also I understand now the local geography and wants of the Great West, and think I can save you much trouble in this quarter, but repeat that you may act without the least hesitation & take it for granted that I will undertake cheerfully anything you may put me at. As to the Mediterranean voyage, which you so kindly approve, I drop it absolutely till matters in our whole country assume a more quiet and stable character. Congress has put on the army so heavy a load, that I have no business to shirk my share. I think Hancock will not have to fight this year. The Cheyennes profess all sorts of good things, but I think Hancock had better go right in among them and spend a week or so there that they may see that we are ready. He can assure them of Peace or War, as they choose. Of course also Gen Augur must defer positive war against the Sioux till the Peace Commission exhaust the subject but sooner or later the Sioux must be taught a severe lesson. I expect Gen Terry down in a few days for consultation. As soon as the Missouri River is open, say in all april I will have him reinforce the Upper Posts, so that they will not only be safe against the whole

Sioux nation, but be able to sally out and attack hostile parties should they threaten the River. Of course I reckon Arkansas now out and that Hancock will take in the Indian Country. In it ultimately we must collect the Tame Indians, and I am in hopes Parker will go there to make out of the fragments a sort of Indian State. Our weather is still severe, and the whole Plains & Mountains are impracticable by reason of floods and snows." ALS, *ibid.*, RG 108, Letters Received.

On March 15, USG wrote to the five district commanders. "In executing the requirements of the Act of Congress entitled 'An Act to provide for the more efficient government of the rebel States', you will forward to these HeadQuarters as soon as issued, copies of all your orders or instructions under or relating to said Act, sending them usually by mail, but in cases of emergency, or of great importance, by telegraph. When the telegraph is used a copy should also be sent by mail." LS (addressed to Bvt. Maj. Gen. John M. Schofield), *ibid.*, RG 393, Dept. of Va. and N. C., Letters Received; (addressed to Maj. Gen. Philip H. Sheridan) *ibid.*, 5th Military District, Letters Received; copies (dated March 16—the first addressed to Bvt. Maj. Gen. John Pope), *ibid.*, RG 46, Senate 40A–F2, Messages; *ibid.*, RG 108, Letters Sent; DLC-USG, V, 47, 60; (dated March 9—addressed to Sheridan) DLC-Andrew Johnson.

1. On March 9, Secretary of War Edwin M. Stanton had written to USG. "Please direct Gen. Schofield to report immediately to the President, in person." Copy, DNA, RG 94, Letters Received, 162P 1867. At 8:00 P.M., USG telegraphed to Schofield. "Report in person to the President without delay." ALS (telegram sent), *ibid.*, RG 107, Telegrams Collected (Bound); telegram sent, *ibid.*; copies, *ibid.*, RG 108, Telegrams Sent; DLC-USG, V, 56.

2. On March 14, Bvt. Brig. Gen. Louis H. Pelouze, AGO, referred to USG a letter of March 9 to Johnson from Maj. Gen. Daniel E. Sickles setting forth his eligibility to command the Second Military District. AES and ALS, DNA, RG 108, Letters Received. On March 21, Sickles, Charleston, telegraphed to USG. "I have the honor to report my arrival at this place yesterday and have assumed command today" Telegram received, *ibid.*, Telegrams Received; copies, *ibid.*, RG 46, Senate 40A–F5, War Dept. Messages; *ibid.*, RG 393, 2nd Military District, Telegrams Sent; DLC-USG, V, 55. On March 26, Sickles wrote to Secretary of the Treasury Hugh McCulloch through USG's hd. qrs. concerning operating funds. LS, DNA, RG 107, Letters Received from Bureaus. On March 28, USG endorsed this letter. "Respectfully forwarded to the Secretary of War. It is believed that $50000 will be sufficient to cover the expenses incurred in the Second Military District during the ensuing quarter, and I recommend that the Chief Quarter master of that, and the other Military Districts be designated as the officer who shall receive and disburse these funds." ES, *ibid.*

3. On March 13, 12:30 P.M., USG telegraphed to Pope and to Maj. Gen. George H. Thomas. "You have been assigned to command of Dept. of Cumberland, Hd Qrs. Louisville. Orders by mail." "You have been assigned to command District of Ga. Ala. & Florida, Hd Qrs. Montgomery. Orders by Mail." ALS (telegrams sent), *ibid.*, Telegrams Collected (Bound); telegrams sent, *ibid.*; copies, *ibid.*, RG 108, Telegrams Sent; (2nd) *ibid.*, RG 393, Dept. of the Cumberland, Telegrams Received; DLC-USG, V, 56. On the same day, Thomas, Louisville, telegraphed to USG. "Your dispatch of this date recd. What objection would there be to my Commanding a Department of which the District named

should form a part, with my Hd Qrs at this place?" Telegram received (at 8:30 P.M.), DNA, RG 107, Telegrams Collected (Bound); *ibid.*, RG 108, Telegrams Received; copies (one sent by mail), *ibid.*, Letters Received; *ibid.*, RG 393, Dept. of the Cumberland, Telegrams Sent; DLC-USG, V, 55. On March 14, 11:00 A.M., USG telegraphed to Thomas. "It is doubtful whether it would be a strict conformance with law to give District commanders territory beyond their Districts. Their authority in Civil matters is such too that it ~~would be improper to~~ seems that parties exercising it should be within the territory over which it is exercised." ALS (telegram sent), DNA, RG 107, Telegrams Collected (Bound); telegram sent, *ibid.*; copies, *ibid.*, RG 108, Telegrams Sent; *ibid.*, RG 393, Dept. of the Cumberland, Telegrams Received; DLC-USG, V, 56. On the same day, Thomas twice telegraphed to USG. "As Gen'l Pope is as competent as myself to command the District of Alabama why can he not be assigned to that District and I to the Dep't of the Cumberland? He will be much more acceptable to the inhabitants than myself." "Have seen the order ~~organizing~~ assigning District commanders as published in the papers this morning. If allowed a choice I should choose the Department of the Cumberland and I hope the order may be changed to permit of such arrangement" Telegrams received (at 12:50 P.M. and 3:05 P.M.), DNA, RG 107, Telegrams Collected (Bound); *ibid.*, RG 108, Telegrams Received; copies (one of the 2nd sent by mail), *ibid.*, Letters Received; (one of the 1st addressed to Stanton) *ibid.*, RG 94, Letters Received, 146A 1867; (the 1st addressed to Stanton) *ibid.*, RG 393, Dept. of the Cumberland, Telegrams Sent; DLC-USG, V, 55. On the same day, USG endorsed a copy of the 1st telegram. "Respectfully refered to the Sec. of War for his information. If it is the desire of the President to gratify Gn. Thomas in his desire to remain in command of the Dept. of the Cumberland either Gen. Pope can be substituted for the command of the Dist. or he can replace any other General who may be prefered. I think however no better selecti[on] can be made for Dist. Commander than Gn. Thomas" AES, DNA, RG 94, Letters Received, 146A 1867. On March 15, Bvt. Maj. Gen. Edward D. Townsend issued General Orders No. 18 making the change. Copy (printed), *ibid.*, 267S 1867. On March 16, Sherman telegraphed to USG. "Gen Pope has this minute received the dispatch of yesterday He starts for Cincinnati today" Telegram received (at 4:30 P.M.), *ibid.*, RG 107, Telegrams Collected (Bound); *ibid.*, RG 108, Telegrams Received; copy, DLC-USG, V, 55. On March 17, Pope, Cincinnati, wrote to USG. "I received in S Louis in the 13th where I had gone to attend my mother's funeral your telegram of that date assigning me to the command of the Dept of the Cumberland but yesterday afternoon as I was on the point of leaving for this place en route to Louisville Sherman handed me a telegram of later date assigning me to the command of the 3rd District—At least so I understand it although it is not clearly expressed—The first assignment was very agreable and satisfactory—Of the last I had best perhaps say nothing—I am quite sick & shall probably be laid up here for several days by the Doctor but it will not delay my getting to Montgomery as it is now unpracticable to get there owing to the late Freshets which have rendered the rail roads unpassible for the next week or ten days—My object in writing to you is to ask that you will send me some good & reliable officers of the General Staff—Thomas retains all his staff & you know I have none—There is probably no command in the Army where good discreet & prudent Staff officers are needed so much as at the Hd Qrs of these districts—& I beg that you will send me—a good a. a. G.   a q. m.   a. c. s. Medical officer & Inspector—Aside from their proper military duties, they will necessarily be obliged to attend to much civil business & ought to be men of intelligence & discretion   I particularly desire that one of the Judge Advocates retained in the Army who is a good civil lawyer be sent me—for reasons you will understand—All these officers or such of them as you can send should report to me here by 25th at latest—My present purpose is to leave here for Montgomery this day week—and I trust you will send me such officers as you may think necessary to report here by that time—I do not venture to suggest any names except to say that I would be glad to have Fred Myers—I write with difficulty as I am unable to be out of bed long at a time but I think I have said what is necessary—I send the letter by Col Dayton who will deliver it sooner than it would reach you by mail—. . . My address here is 'care of L. E. Mills Esq." ALS, DNA, RG 108, Letters Received. On March 19, Pope wrote to USG. "If there be a vacancy among the 1st or 2nd Lieutenants, I respectfully ask the appointment of Capt & Bvt Major James Sawyer of Milwaukee Wisconsin—Maj Sawyer received a military education, served two & a half years in the War with distinction & is in every respect qualified for the position—I beg this appointment for him as a personal favor coupled with the request that he be ordered to report to me as A. D. C—I will be extremely obliged to you if this appt and order can be made soon as I would like very much to have Maj Sawyer with me as soon as possible—" ALS, *ibid.*, RG 94, ACP, S324 CB 1866. On March 25, USG endorsed this letter. "Respectfully forwarded to the Secretary of War. Capt. Sawyer is recommended for a 2d Ltcy of Infantry." ES, *ibid.* On March 22, Pope telegraphed to USG. "Still confined to house, Hope and expect to leave monday All roads south impassible on account floods Shall probably have to go by River to Vicksburg thence across, have any of Officers I asked for been ordered to report to me here?" Telegram received (at 9:15 P.M.), *ibid.*, RG 107, Telegrams Collected (Bound); *ibid.*, RG 108, Telegrams Received; copy, DLC-USG, V, 55. On March 25, Pope wrote to USG. "I leave for Montgomery via Nashville, Chattanooga &c this afternoon though I am still far from well—I wrote you a few days ago about the appointment of Capt James Sawyer of Milwaukee as 1st or 2nd Lieutenant— & I venture to repeat my request as I am very earnestly interested in having him as my A. D. C—He is an uncommonly fine young fellow, & will do credit to the service—In the Spring of last year he was appointed a Lieutenant but declined on account of some opposition of his father's—He has since written to me that he would gladly accept such an appointment & I beg that you will give it to him—I would be glad (if you can do so) if you will have him ordered by telegraph to report to me in Montgomery without delay—Whilst the assignment to the 3rd or in fact any other Military District under the Reconstruction Act—is not pleasant I trust you will believe that I shall go very cheerfully & do the best I can—I know you intended & arranged to give me a much more satisfactory command & I am greatly obliged to you for it." ALS, DNA, RG 108, Letters Received. At 11:10 A.M., USG telegraphed to Pope. "Staff officers will be ordered to report to you at Montgomery without delay." ALS (telegram sent), *ibid.*, RG 107, Telegrams Collected (Bound); telegram sent, *ibid.*; copies, *ibid.*, RG 108, Telegrams Sent; DLC-USG, V, 56.

On March 27, Stanton endorsed to USG a telegram concerning city elections in Augusta, Ga. AES, DNA, RG 108, Letters Received. At 3:00 P.M., USG telegraphed to Thomas and to the commanding officer, Augusta. "Direct commanders of the states of Ala. & Ga. to disallow all elections, State or local, until Gen. Pope arrives and assumes command." "Prohibit all elections within your command until Gen. Pope arrives and gives his orders in the matter. Answer" ALS (telegrams sent), *ibid.*, RG 107, Telegrams Collected (Bound); telegrams sent, *ibid.*; copies, *ibid.*, RG 108, Telegrams Sent; DLC-USG, V, 56. On the same day, Maj. and Bvt. Col. Thomas W. Sweeny, 16th Inf., Augusta, telegraphed to USG. "Telegram recd   Your instructions will be fully Complied with at this post" Telegram received (at 5:45 P.M.), DNA, RG 107, Telegrams Collected (Bound); *ibid.*, RG 108, Telegrams Received; copies, DLC-USG, V, 55; DLC-Edwin M. Stanton. On March 28, USG endorsed a copy of this telegram. "Respectfully forwarded to the Secretary of War for his information." ES, *ibid.* On April 1, Pope, Montgomery, Ala., telegraphed to USG. "Arrived and assumed command this morning. Orders sent by mail." Telegram received (at 3:40 P.M.), DNA, RG 107, Telegrams Collected (Bound); *ibid.*, RG 108, Telegrams Received; copies, *ibid.*, RG 46, Senate 40A–F5, War Dept. Messages; *ibid.*, RG 393, Dept. of the South and District of Ala., Telegrams Sent; DLC-USG, V, 55.

4. See letter to Bvt. Maj. Gen. Edward O. C. Ord, March 1, 1867.

5. On March 8, Sheridan, New Orleans, telegraphed to USG. "It is important that the District Commander under the late act of Congress be made as soon as possible for this District as the Mayor of this city & the Governor of the State are exciting the public mind over question of authority pending his appointment & presence here" Telegram received (at 10:00 P.M.), DNA, RG 107, Telegrams Collected (Bound); *ibid.*, RG 108, Telegrams Received; copies, *ibid.*, RG 46, Senate 40A–F5, War Dept. Messages; *ibid.*, RG 94, Letters Received, 943W 1867; DLC-USG, V, 55; (2) DLC-Philip H. Sheridan; DLC-Andrew Johnson. On March 9, USG endorsed a copy of this telegram. "Respectfully forwarded for information of the Sec. of War. I would recommend that orders be sent to Gn. Sheridan, by telegraph, assigning him to the Command of the Dist. of La. & Texas temporarily under the provisions of the law refered to by him." AES, *ibid.* At 3:05 P.M., USG telegraphed to Sheridan. "An official copy of the Act of Congress entitled An Act to provide for the more efficient government of the rebel states will be transmitted to you immediately by telegraph. It is now law. Answer." ALS (telegram sent), DNA, RG 107, Telegrams Collected (Bound); telegram sent, *ibid.*; telegram received, *ibid.*, RG 393, Dept. of the Gulf, Telegrams Received. On the same day, USG drafted a telegram. "Use the Military to prevent conflict and riot (under the authority granted by Civil Rights Bill and recent Act of Congress). The law can decide after district commanders are named in relation to legality of means resorted to by opposing parties in New Orleans. The President is now taking steps to put the recent Act of Congress into effect. The President directs that order be preserved and the law enforced." Dodd, Mead & Company, Catalogue No. 66, Jan., 1903, no. 81. Also at 3:05 P.M., USG telegraphed to Sheridan. "The President direct that order be preserved in New Orleans and the laws enforced." ALS (telegram sent), DNA, RG 107, Telegrams Collected (Bound); telegram sent, *ibid.*; telegram received, *ibid.*, RG 393, Dept. of the Gulf, Telegrams Received. On the same day, Sheridan telegraphed to USG. "Your telegrams received   There will be no trouble here—I had taken the necessary steps to prevent it after the Legislature to-day had refused to postpone the Election" LS (telegram sent), *ibid.*, RG

107, Telegrams Collected (Bound); telegram received (on March 10, 10:55 A.M.), *ibid.*; *ibid.*, RG 108, Telegrams Received. On March 11, Sheridan telegraphed to USG. "I have transmitted to you by todays mail a copy of the order which I deemed necessary in order to preserve quiet in the city. It has had the desired effect" Telegram received (at 5:08 P.M.), *ibid.*, RG 107, Telegrams Collected (Bound); *ibid.*, RG 108, Telegrams Received; copies, DLC-USG, V, 55; (2) DLC-Philip H. Sheridan; DLC-Edwin M. Stanton. On March 13, 12:30 P.M., USG telegraphed to Sheridan. "You have been assigned command of district of La. & Texas. Orders gone by mail." ALS (telegram sent), DNA, RG 107, Telegrams Collected (Bound); telegram sent, *ibid.*; telegram received (at 9:30 P.M.), *ibid.*, RG 393, Dept. of the Gulf, Telegrams Received. On March 14, Sheridan telegraphed to USG. "Your despatch of March 13th recd I hope this assignment will not break up my contemplated trip to Texas to establish frontier post I am now all ready to start I have already commenced the movement of troops for this purpose" Telegram received (at 10:00 P.M.), *ibid.*, RG 107, Telegrams Collected (Bound); *ibid.*, RG 108, Telegrams Received; copies, DLC-USG, V, 55; (2) DLC-Philip H. Sheridan; DLC-Edwin M. Stanton; DLC-Andrew Johnson. On March 15, 10:00 A.M., USG telegraphed to Sheridan. "Before starting to Texas it will be well to get all the machinery of your new command adjusted and at work." ALS (telegram sent), DNA, RG 107, Telegrams Collected (Bound); telegram sent, *ibid.*; telegram received (at noon), *ibid.*, RG 393, Dept. of the Gulf, Telegrams Received.

To Edwin M. Stanton

Washington, March 11th 1867

Hon. E. M. Stanton.
Sec. of War
Sir:

Medical Purveyors Lt. Col. E. H. Abadie & Lt Col. Chas. Sutherland not having been confirmed by the Senate I would respectfully recommend their reappointment. They were not rejected by the Senate but their cases were not acted upon.

Both these officers have served for many years in the army and were full Surgeons in the regular army before the creation of the grade of Medical Purveyor. They were appointed to these places by selection and the vacancies created by their promotion filled up. If they are not re-appointed now it necessarily throws out of service two officers who were selected for their merit for promotion.

I would respectfully ask that these appointments be made without delay for the reason stated

> Very respectfully
> Your obt. servant
> U. S. Grant
> General

Copies, DLC-USG, V, 47, 60; DNA, RG 108, Letters Sent. Both Eugene H. Abadie and Charles Sutherland were renominated on March 12; Abadie was rejected, Sutherland confirmed. See *SRC*, 54-1-172.

To Edwin M. Stanton

Respectfully forwarded to the Secretary of War. The sutlership of Judge Carter should necessarily be discontinued from the 1st of July 1867. But as Gen Babcock, after making an inspection of the post at Fort Bridger, recommended a reduction of the reservation at that place, I would recommend that Judge Carter be allowed to continue his farming and milling operations, and that all the reservation be given up except one square mile around the post and two miles square of timberland—all to be selected by, or under, the supervision of the post commander. It is desirable to encourage settlement and cultivation on the line of travel in the Indian Country.

> U. S. Grant
> General.

Hdqrs. A U S
Mch. 18. '67

ES, DNA, RG 108, Letters Received. Written on a letter of March 12, 1867, from William A. Carter, Washington, D. C., to Secretary of War Edwin M. Stanton. "I beg leave most respectfully to state that the accompanying Order, issued in persuance of the 25th Sect. of the Act of Congress of July 26th, 1866. to increase and fix the Military Peace establishment of the Army of the United States, was recently made and sent to me at this place by Brvt. Lieut Col. Anson Mills, Com'dg Fort Bridger U. T. Should this Order be strictly enforced, the greater portion of my means, accumulated during almost a lifetime of toil and exposure with the Army on our distant fronteirs, will be swept away, all that I have being invested in my buildings, machinery, agricultural implements, freight wagons, merchandise &c, at Fort Bridger. . . . My situation is worse than that of any other Sutler on the fronteir as the Reservation is so much larger than those elsewhere, embracing within its limits all the good land and desirable locations in the vicinity, thus preventing instead of encouraging settlement in its vicinity. Trusting that you will appreciate my unfortunate Condition and grant my requests so far as the same may be in your power, . . ." ALS, *ibid.* On March 22, Stanton unfavorably endorsed this letter. AES, *ibid.* On March 30, Carter wrote to USG. "I most respectfully beg leave to apply for the position of 'Trader' at Fort Bridger Utah, Territory, under the law of Congress of March 30th, 1867. . . ." ALS, *ibid.* See letter to Charles W. Ford, April 28, 1867. Carter, born in Va., enlisted in the U.S. Army while young and fought against the Seminole Indians. He was appointed post sutler at Fort Bridger in 1857, and in 1858 was also appointed justice of the peace and probate judge. See Fred R. Gowans and Eugene E. Campbell, *Fort Bridger: Island in the Wilderness* (Provo, 1975), pp. 145–55; W. N. Davis, Jr., "The Sutler at Fort Bridger," *Western Historical Quarterly,* 2, 1 (Jan., 1971), 37–54.

On April 3, 1867, Robert Campbell & Co., St. Louis, wrote to USG. "We have been requested to adress you in favour of three old friends, who for years past, have been Sutlers at posts, on the plains & territories. It seems that by a recent act, or joint resolution of Congress, the right is confered on you, to appoint former Sutlers, or others, to be *traders*, at, or near, the Military posts. Not having seen the law, we know nothing of its purport, and shall therefore confine ourselves, to an expression of opinion with regard to those, whom we know; and whose appointment might be most desireable for the service. From an acquaintance of many years;—and from a knowlege of the efficiency, experience, and ample capital of the parties alluded to, we beg leave to recommend for appointment as traders;—*Wm H. Moore & Co* (W H. Moore & W. C. Mitchell) who have for many years been Sutlers at Fort Union, N. Mexo; *Seth E. Ward*, of Fort Laramie, Dak: Terry; for years the Sutler there; *William A. Carter*, who has a long time been Sutler at Fort Bridger, U. T. All of those gentlemen have stocks of goods on hand, adapted to the wants of the Military residents, and to the emigrants. Unless *for cause*, we feel assured, that on 1st July next, you would not drive them out of a region, where they have spent years with credit to themselves, and usefullness to the service. The loss by removal would be ruinous. We can vouch for the honour, fairness in dealing, and responsibility of each of them." DS, DNA, RG 108, Letters Received. On March 30, Seth E. Ward, Washington, D. C., had written to USG. "I beg leave respectfully to apply for the position of 'Trader' at Fort Laramie, Dakotah Territory, under the law of Congress of March 30th, 1867, authorizing the Commanding General of the Army to permit a trading establishment to be maintained at certain Military Posts, and also for permission to retain possession of my buildings at said Post. Fort Laramie is situated on the travelled route, through the South Pass of the Rocky Mountains, and far distant from any source of supply. I respectfully refer to Robt Campbell & Co of St. Louis—and to the army officers with whom I have been associated for so many years." LS, *ibid.*

On March 5, 1869, Carter, Washington, D. C., wrote to USG. "I have the honor, most respectfully to solicit, for myself the appointment of Governor of the new Territory of Wyoming. For the information of your Excellency, I have the honor to state that I now am, and have been, for the past twelve (12) years, a resident of this Territory, have made its internal resources the subject of my constant study and believe my efforts have contributed materially to their development. From my long residence there, and my intimate acquaintance with the inhabitants, I have every reason to believe that my appointment would be acceptable to the great majority of them. Having but a slight acquaintance with your Excellency, I beg leave to refer you to Genl. W. T. Sherman, U. S. A. Genl. J. A. Rawlins, U. S. A Genl. C. C. Auger, U. S A. and Genl. G. M. Dodge of Ioway, all of whom, I believe, will endorse me favorably. In soliciting this appointment I am not actuated by pecuniary considerations, but by a desire to promote the interests and development of this Territory, which I have so long made my home. If appointed by you you I will deem it a great honor and endeavor, to the utmost of my ability, faithfully and honestly to discharge the duties of my official position." ALS, *ibid.*, RG 59, Letters of Application and Recommendation. On March 11, Carter wrote to Secretary of War John A. Rawlins withdrawing his application. ALS, *ibid.*

To Charles W. Ford

March 24th *1867*.

DEAR FORD,

I do not remember whether or not I ever gave you directions what to do with the Irvin trust deed on my Gravois place? I do not want satisfaction entered until the whole matter is settled up. It may yet be necessary for me to sell the place under that deed.

I have given up the idea of going to Mo. this Spring. I shall however be out there before the end of the year. Hereafter I hope to spend several months in the year in the place. If I am not disappointed I shall in the course of a few years be breeding there some fine horses. I have now four mares worth from eight to ten thousand dollars, all of them very fast, two to have colts this Spring and Sumer, and all four of them next Spring, from the finest trotters in the East.

We are all well here and looking forward with a good-deal of confidence to a final settlement under the Sherman Bill.[1]

Yours Truly
U. S. GRANT

ALS, DLC-USG.

1. U.S. Senator John Sherman of Ohio had introduced the bill enacted as the First Reconstruction Act.

To Isaac N. Morris

———

Washington, March 27th *1867.*

HON. I. N. MORRIS,
DEAR SIR;

Your kind letter proposing to send a fine brood mare to my farm, and asking directions how to send her, is received. Please send her to Arnot[1] & Bro. Chesnut St. St. Louis, to be kept until called for by Mr. Wm Elrod, with order from me. I will send out directions at once.

Your letter speaks of annoyance from remarks by Wendil Phillips[2] in a recent speech! I never feel annoyed at anything he has to say. Phillips is one of the class of men whose enmity is better than his friendship.

I think reconstruction is now in a fare way of being finally and favorably consumated, unless obsticles are thrown in the way from the North. I hope for the best however.

My family are all well and join me in the desire to be rembered to Mrs. Morris.

Your Truly
U. S. GRANT

ALS, ICarbS.

1. See *PUSG*, 2, 168.
2. Late in 1866, Wendell Phillips began to criticize USG as ineffective in protecting the freedmen and as a poor prospect for president. Irving H. Bartlett, *Wendell Phillips: Brahmin Radical* (Boston, 1961), p. 304; James M. McPherson, *The Struggle for Equality: Abolitionists and the Negro in the Civil War and Reconstruction* (Princeton, 1964), p. 417.

To Maj. Gen. Philip H. Sheridan

———

Washington, D. C. March 29th *1867.*

DEAR GENERAL:

I have just seen your order No. 5.[1] It is just the thing, and meets the universal aprobation of the loyal people at least. I have no doubt but that it will also meet with like approval from the *re-*

constructed. It will at least prove advantageous to them and to the quiet and prosperity of New Orleans, and of the State of La.

I only write this to let you know that I at least approve what you have done.

Yours Truly
U. S. GRANT

To GN. P. H. SHERIDAN.

ALS, DLC-Philip H. Sheridan. See letters to Maj. Gen. Philip H. Sheridan, April 5, 21, 1867. On March 28, 1867, Bvt. Maj. Gen. Edward D. Townsend issued General Orders No. 33 transmitting to district commanders the Second Reconstruction Act. *HED*, 40-1-20, pp. 5–7. See General Orders No. 10, March 11, 1867. On April 1, Maj. Gen. Philip H. Sheridan, New Orleans, wrote to USG. "*Personal* . . . The Supplemental Bill has not yet reached me, but I have been pushing things along in advance of its receipt and will soon be in readiness to commence the registration of this State. I will have no trouble, I think, in carrying out the provisions of the Military bill in Louisiana: and, perhaps, in Texas. The extent of Texas is so great and the counties so large, that the work there will be much more tedious. I will put a small force in all the remote parishes in Louisiana, so that there may be a fair canvass of each parish; but I very much fear that the State will be carried by the same sentiment which now holds power over it: the civil offices being held by those of rebel antecedents in most cases. The city here may be carried by the union people; but, if so, they will have to settle the many differences which now exist. They are now like the Kilkenny cats— destroying each other." LS, DNA, RG 108, Letters Received.

Also on April 1, Sheridan telegraphed to USG. "In consequence of diversity of opinion I have the honor to request an authoritive decision showing who are prohibited from voting under the Military bills Covering all cases" Telegram received (at 1:15 P.M.), *ibid.*, RG 107, Telegrams Collected (Bound); *ibid.*, RG 108, Telegrams Received; copies, *ibid.*, RG 46, Senate 40A–F5, War Dept. Messages; *ibid.*, RG 94, Letters Received, 150G 1867; *ibid.*, 1112M 1867; (sent by mail) *ibid.*, RG 108, Letters Received; DLC-USG, V, 55; (2) DLC-Philip H. Sheridan; DLC-Edwin M. Stanton; DLC-Andrew Johnson. On the same day, USG endorsed a copy of this telegram. "Respectfully forwarded to the Secretary of War" ES, DNA, RG 94, Letters Received, 150G 1867. On April 2, Townsend wrote to USG. "The Secretary of War acknowledges the receipt of copy of a telegram from Major General Sheridan, dated April 1st in relation to prohibition from voting, and directs me to inform you that it was submitted to the President in Cabinet, and instructions deferred until the Attorney General completes his opinion upon the same point heretofore presented by General Schofield and on reference by the President, now under consideration of the Attorney General." ALS, *ibid.*, RG 108, Letters Received. At 1:00 P.M., Sheridan telegraphed to USG. "I transmit by mail today a communication from General Griffin in which he asks for the removal of Governor Throckmorton of Texas I feel like Griffin on this subject that he ought to be removed and I fear I will be obliged to remove the Governor of Louisiana—He is impeding me as much as he can—I will commence the registration of Louisiana as soon as the supplemental bill reaches me officially—I feel myself fully equal to the new task and hope to get through with it creditably to the Military I send Griffins application and this telegram asking the benefit of your judgment It is my intention to make but few removals" Telegram received (at 7:30 P.M.), *ibid.*, RG 107, Telegrams Collected (Bound); *ibid.*, RG 108, Telegrams Received; copies, *ibid.*, RG 46, Senate 40A–F5, War Dept. Messages; (sent by mail with enclosure) *ibid.*, RG 94, Letters Received, 876M 1867; *ibid.*, 873M 1867; *ibid.*, 961M 1867; *ibid.*, 1102M 1867; DLC-USG, V, 55; (2) DLC-Philip H. Sheridan; DLC-Edwin M. Stanton; (3) DLC-Andrew Johnson. On April 3, USG endorsed a copy of this telegram. "Respectfully forwarded to the Secretary of War." ES, DNA, RG 94, Letters Received, 961M 1867. At 11:30 A.M., USG telegraphed to Sheridan. "I would advise that no removal of Governors of states be made at present. It is a question now under concideration whether the power exists, under the law, to remove except by special Act of Congress, or by trial under the 6th section of the Act ~~already~~ promulgated in Orders 33." ALS (telegram sent), *ibid.*, RG 107, Telegrams Collected (Bound); telegram sent, *ibid.*; copies, *ibid.*, RG 46, Senate 40A–F5, War Dept. Messages; *ibid.*, RG 108, Telegrams Sent; DLC-USG, V, 56; DLC-Edwin M. Stanton; (2) DLC-Andrew Johnson. On April 5, Sheridan telegraphed to USG. "There is not one word of truth in the rumored Indian Massacres in Texas near Camp Verdi—These reports are now manufactured wholesale to affect the removal of troops from the interior to the frontier its being known that it is contemplated Sending a small detachment of troops to nearly every parish in Louisiana and in as many counties in Texas as I can so there may be a just registration and a fair vote" Telegram received (at 5:45 P.M.), DNA, RG 107, Telegrams Collected (Bound); *ibid.*, RG 108, Telegrams Received; copies, *ibid.*, RG 46, Senate 40A–F5, War Dept. Messages; *ibid.*, RG 94, Letters Received, 877M 1867; *ibid.*, 1113M 1867; *ibid.*, 458W 1867; *ibid.*, 580W 1867; (sent by mail) *ibid.*, RG 108, Letters Received; DLC-USG, V, 55; (2) DLC-Philip H. Sheridan; (misdated April 6) DLC-Edwin M. Stanton; DLC-Andrew Johnson. On April 6, USG endorsed a copy of this telegram. "Respectfully forwarded to the Secretary of War, with request that a copy be furnished His Excellency the President." ES, *ibid.* At 10:30 A.M., Sheridan telegraphed to USG. "I am in readiness to commence the registration in this city—Will in a few days commence throughout the whole state of Louisiana. A reply to my telegram asking an authoritative decision on what classes are disfranchised is very important" Telegram received (at 3:00 P.M.), DNA, RG 107, Telegrams Collected (Bound); *ibid.*, RG 108, Telegrams Received; copies, *ibid.*, RG 46, Senate 40A–F5, War Dept. Messages; DLC-USG, V, 55; (2) DLC-Philip H. Sheridan; DLC-Edwin M. Stanton; DLC-Andrew Johnson. On April 7, noon, USG telegraphed to Sheridan. "Your question as to who are ineligible for registration was submitted to the Atty. Gen. No answer has been received. Go on giving your own interpretation to the law until answer is given." ALS (telegram sent), DNA, RG 107, Telegrams Collected (Bound); telegram sent, *ibid.*; telegram received (marked as sent on April 8, received at 5:00 P.M.), *ibid.*, RG 393, 5th Military District, Telegrams Received.

1. On March 27, Sheridan had issued General Orders No. 5, Fifth Military District, removing from office La. Attorney Gen. Andrew S. Herron, Mayor John T. Monroe of New Orleans, and Judge Edmund Abell, first district court, New Orleans. *SED*, 40-1-14, p. 240.

To William Elrod

————

Washington, D. C. March 31st *1867*.

DEAR ELROD:

I have no special direction to give you, with regard to farming, further than you have already received with the exception that I want you to bear in mind that I want to get all the ground in grass as soon as it can be got rich enough, except what will be in fruit. I will put from 25 to 40 acres in fruit as soon as we get possession of the whole place. I also want to get, as soon as I can, all the land fenced, the outside fence with board. There is now, or ought to be, a pile of cedar logs about the house which I intend to occupy when there. You might take them, at your convenience, to a saw mill and have them sawed into posts. You can then make plank fence, as far as they will go, on the outer line of the farm where you think ... In the course of next year I hope to be able to put up good stabling on the place you will occupy and to commence the raising of good stock. I do not want to put more than $5000 00. more money in the place, if I can help it, except what comes off of it. All the income from the place for the next ten years however I expect to spend on it. This year I know you will be much short of making expenses, and, as I say next I will probably spend $5000 on it.

I still have a little money, tho' but very little, with Benoist & Co. St. Louis. I wish you would find how much and I will send you a check for it.

Get a Blank Book and keep an account of all the money you receive and expend.

Yours Truly
U. S. GRANT

ALS (possibly incomplete), Dr. John T. Bickmore, Dayton, Ohio.

On March 1, 1867, 1:30 P.M., and March 27, 2:30 P.M., USG telegraphed to Lackland and Martin, St. Louis. "Let Sappington occupy White place until I send a man." "Elrod will go soon to take charge of my farm. Let Sappington remain in possession until he arrives." ALS (telegrams sent), DNA, RG 107, Telegrams Collected (Bound).

To Maj. Gen. Philip H. Sheridan

_____

Confidential   Washington, D. C. Apl. 5th *1867*.

MY DEAR GENERAL,

When I telegraphed you a few days ago advising nonaction, for a while, in the matter of further removals from office, under the authority of the reconstruction act, it was because I knew that the Atty. Gen. had taken the ground that the bill gives no such authority to Dist. Commanders. ~~and~~ He is probably preparing an opinion to this effect.

The fact is there is a decided hostility to the whole Congressional plan of reconstruction, at the "White House," and a disposition to remove you from the command you now have. Both the Sec. of War and myself will oppose any such move, as will the mass of the people. In the course you have pursued you are supported by more than party. I thought it well however to advise you against further removals, if you can get along without making them, until we see the *opinion* which is, probably, forthcoming.

There is nothing clearer to my mind than that Congress intended to give district Commanders entire controll over the Civil government of these districts, for a specific purpose, and only recognized present Civil Authorities, within these districts, atall, for the convenience of their Commanders, to make use of, or so much of, as suited the~~ir~~m ~~convenience~~, and as would aid them in carrying out the Congressional plan of restoring loyal, permanent, government.—I think the 1st & 6th Sections of the bill "For the better government" &c. taken together, clearly authorize removals from Civil offices, by district commanders. I am glad to hear that the Hon. Reverdy Johnson, certainly an able lawyer, sustains this view.

One thing is very certain; the law contemplates that district commanders shall be their own judges of the meaning of its provisions. They are responsible to the country for its faithful execution. Any opinion from the Atty. Gen. should be duly weighed however. The power of removing district commanders undoubtedly exists with the President, but no officer is going to be hurt by a faithful performance of his duty.

My advice to you is that you make no more removals than you find absolutely necessary. That you make none whatever, except it be for the gravest disregard of the law, and your authority, until you see what decissions are to be made. ~~by the law officers of the government.~~ That then you make up your mind fully as to the proper course to pursue, and pursue it, without fear, and take the consequences.—I would not advise you to any course that I would not pursue myself, under like circumstances, nor do I believe that I advise against your own inclinations. I will keep you advised, officially or otherwise, of all that affects you.

I think it will be well for you to send me a statement of your reasons for removing Herron, Able[1] & Monroe. It may not be called for, but twice the question has been asked, why you removed them.

Yours Truly
U. S. GRANT

TO MAJ. GN. P. H. SHERIDAN
NEW ORLEANS, LA.

ALS, DLC-Philip H. Sheridan. See letter to Maj. Gen. Philip H. Sheridan, April 21, 1867. On April 19, 1867, Maj. Gen. Philip H. Sheridan wrote to USG. "On the 27th day of March last I removed from office Judge E. Abell of the Criminal Court of New Orleans, Andrew S. Herron, Attorney General of the State of Louisiana, and John T. Monroe, Mayor of the City of New Orleans. These removals were made under the powers granted me in what is usually termed the 'Military Bill', passed March 2nd 1867, by the Congress of the United States. I did not deem it necessary to give any reason for the removal of these men, especially after the investigations made by the Military Board on the massacre of July 30th 1866, and the report of the Congressional Committee on the same massacre; but, as some inquiry has been made for the cause of removal, I would respectfully state as follows: The Court over which Judge Abell presided, is the only criminal court in the City of New Orleans, and for a period of at least nine months previous to the riot of July 30th he had been educating a large portion of the community to the perpetration of this outrage, by almost promising no prosecution in his court against the offenders, in case such an event occurred. The records of his court will show that he fulfilled his promise, as not one of the guilty has been prosecuted. In reference to Andrew S. Herron, Attorney General of the State of Louisiana, I considered it his duty to indict these men before this criminal court. This he failed to do, but went so far as to attempt to impose on the good sense of the whole nation, by indicting the victims of the riot instead of the rioters: in other words, making the innocent guilty and the guilty innocent. He was therefore, in my belief, an able coadjutor with Judge Abel, in bringing on the massacre of July 30th. Mayor Monroe controlled the element engaged in this riot, and when backed by an Attorney General who would not prosecute the guilty, and a Judge who advised the Grand Jury to find the innocent guilty and let the murderers go free, felt secure in engaging his police force in the riot and massacre. With these three men exercising a large influence over the worst elements of the population of this city, giving to those elements an immunity for riot and bloodshed; the General-in-Chief will see how insecurely I felt in letting them occupy their respective positions, in the troubles which might occur in registration and voting in the reorganization of this State." LS, DNA, RG 108, Letters Received. On May 8, USG endorsed a copy of this letter. "Respectfully forwarded to the Secretary of War for his information." ES, DLC-Andrew Johnson.

On April 12, 2:00 P.M., Sheridan telegraphed to USG. "I have already issued the order for the registration of New Orleans and by next Monday or Tuesday will issue the order for registration of the State of Louisiana and will then go over to help General Griffin—I am very much embarrassed for want of funds. Can some be sent me for Louisiana and Texas—" Telegram received (at 5:40 P.M.), DNA, RG 107, Telegrams Collected (Bound); ibid., RG 108, Telegrams Received; copies, ibid., RG 46, Senate 40A–F5, War Dept. Messages; (sent by mail with enclosures) ibid., RG 108, Letters Received; DLC-USG, V, 55; (2) DLC-Philip H. Sheridan; DLC-Edwin M. Stanton; DLC-Andrew Johnson. On April 13, 11:35 A.M., USG telegraphed to Sheridan. "Direct paymaster to make requisition for one months supply of funds in pursuance of accompanying order." ALS (telegram sent), DNA, RG 107, Telegrams Collected (Bound); telegram sent, ibid.; copies, ibid., RG 46, Senate 40A–F5, War Dept. Messages; ibid., RG 108, Telegrams Sent; DLC-USG, V, 56; DLC-Andrew Johnson. On April 16, 11:00 A.M., Sheridan telegraphed to USG. "The registration was commenced in this city yesterday and is progressing without trouble or ill feeling, colored and whites registering at the same offices—I will send by todays mail a memorandum showing what classes are disqualified, under the Military Bill, in this State" Telegram received (at 1:40 P.M.), DNA, RG 107, Telegrams Collected (Bound); ibid., RG 108, Telegrams Received; copies, ibid., RG 46, Senate 40A–F5, War Dept. Messages; ibid., RG 107, Letters Received from Bureaus; DLC-USG, V, 55; (2) DLC-Philip H. Sheridan; DLC-Edwin M. Stanton. On the same day, USG endorsed a copy of this telegram. "Respectfully forwarded to the Secretary of War for his information." ES, DNA, RG 107, Letters Received from Bureaus. Also on April 16, Sheridan wrote to USG, sending a copy of this telegram and other enclosures. LS and copies, ibid., RG 94, Letters Received, 878M 1867. On April 19, 2:00 P.M., Sheridan telegraphed to USG. "The registration in the City is progressing well—There is some dissatisfaction among a few Sore heads because we cannot interpret the law to suit them—No one will be refused registration of his name in my Command who is legally entitled to it Opportunity is given for the correction of any errors that may occur" Telegram received, ibid., RG 107, Telegrams Collected (Bound); ibid., RG 108, Telegrams Received; copies, ibid., RG 46, Senate 40A–F5, War Dept. Messages; (sent by mail) ibid., RG 108, Letters Received; DLC-USG, V, 55; (2) DLC-Philip H. Sheridan; DLC-Edwin M. Stanton.

1. On June 13, Edmund Abell, New Orleans, wrote to President Andrew Johnson, USG, and Sheridan. "Nothing could astonish me more than to find the

extraordinary statements contained in a telegram from General Sheridan to Major General Grant dated the 6th Inst, So far as it relates to me nothing could be more at variance with the record and facts of the case. It seems to me that they are not only made in error, but are most incredible. . . ." ALS, DNA, RG 108, Letters Received.

To Elihu B. Washburne

Washington, D. C.,
April 5, 1867.

Everything is getting on well here under the Congressional Reconstruction Bill, and all will be well if administration and copperhead influence do not defeat the objects of that measure. So far there has been no absolute interference with the acts of district commanders, all of whom are carrying out the measures of Congress according to the spirit of their acts, but much dissatisfaction has been expressed at Sheridan's removal of the New Orleans civil officers. Sheridan has given public satisfaction, however. In his private[1] capacity he shows himself the same fearless, true man that he did in the field. He makes no mistakes.

I see no possible chance of getting abroad this year. I am not egotistical enough to suppose that my duties cannot be performed by others just as well as myself, but Congress has made it my duty to perform certain offices, and whilst there is an antagonism between the executive and legislative branches of the Government, I feel the same obligation to stand at my post that I did whilst there were rebel armies in the field to contend with. . . .

James Grant Wilson, ed., *General Grant's Letters to a Friend 1861–1880* (New York and Boston, 1897), pp. 55–56. Wilson may have extrapolated the date from a slightly variant version printed by Adam Badeau, who stated that USG had written to U.S. Representative Elihu B. Washburne at the same time that he wrote to Maj. Gen. Philip H. Sheridan on April 5, 1867. Badeau, *Grant in Peace* (Hartford, Conn., 1887), pp. 60–62. See preceding letter. Badeau also quoted a fragment of a USG letter to Washburne, implausibly dated May, 1866 (Badeau placed Washburne in Europe in 1866 when he was not there until 1867), but more likely written a year later. "But little is heard now about impeachment. It is sincerely to be hoped that we will not, unless something occurs hereafter to fully justify it." Badeau, p. 134. This fragment may come from the text above, or USG may have written to Washburne in both April and May. On May 21, Washburne, Hamburg, wrote to USG. "I was very much gratified to receive your letter of the 3d inst. forwarded to me from Paris. I have been very much interested in the re-construction matter. Though I see most of our leading Journals, including the 'Galena Gazette,' nothing has been so satifactory as your account of the way in which things are progressing. It is my earnest hope that Sheridan will be fully sustained. The President should not only abstain from any interference with you, but he ought to give the weight of his influence for the adoption of the scheme by the rebel States. It is evident that it is the best and onl[y] thing they can do. They too[k co]urage from the copperhead triumph in Connecticut, but that will do them no good. The Supreme Court having kicked the nonsense of Old Sharkey and Bob Walker out of Court, every influence should now be used to have the rebels 'accept the situation'. and come in with a will. I trust the good work will now go on, and that nothing will impede it. The telegraph brings us the news that Bill Kelley has been mobbed in Mobile and that many persons were killed. I do not know how serious the affair is, but all such occurrences are very unfortunate, and tend to retard the great work. If the row has been a serious one, it will inflame the Country and may bring a quorum of Congress together in July, which I think would be very unfortunate. The wise thing would be not to have Congress convene till December and to let the impeachment die a natural death. The movement, as I clearly fo[re]saw from the beginning, is an unfortunate one ~~from the beginning~~ for the Union party, and it contributed more than anything else, in my judgment, to the loss of Connecticut. The times require wise and enlightened statesmanship, and I hope the present Congress will prove itself equal to the emergencies. We want moderation, but firmness and a more incorruptible personal integrity. A stop must be put to profligate, extravagant and corrupt expenditures and a more rigid economy introduced into all departments of the government. There is more to be feared from a decay of public virtue than there ever was from the rebels. I was satisfied when I left home that you would not be able to get abroad this year. If re-[co]nstruction be accomplished and the Indian war is over, you may get away next year—Jones sailed for home last Wednesday, having 'done' Europe from Naples to St. Petersburgh. I am glad to hear of the general good health of the staff and more than rejoiced at what you say of Rawlins. In the long and dreary weeks and months that I have been Crossing as an invalid, I have thought much of him and I pray that his summer trip may fully restore him. I have been at this celebrated watering place now more than three weeks, and have been pursuing a rigid course of treatment in taking the waters, in diet and in exercise. I am encouraged to hope that in the course of two or three months I may be fully restored. All the doctors agree that my trouble arises from a torpid liver, resulting in those congestive chills and a congestion of the envelopes of the lower part of the spine. The waters here are considered almost a specific for all liver troubles, and I propose giving them a fair trial, or as Capt. Cuttle would say, 'lay my head to the wind and fight it through.' I have improved very much since I have been here, but there is room for further improvement. I shall probably remain here till the last of June and start for home towards the middle of July. I shall go direct to Maine to spend sometime with my family at our place at Elm Hill, and I want to insist upon your taking Mrs. Grant and the children and making us a visit after my return. You will also have to go to Galena to spend a few weeks in the fall. *It is important that you should retain your resi-*

dence there. Genl Washburn writes me that he hopes to be able to come abroad, with his two daughters, in July, but he will not be likely to get over before I leave for home. Nature and art have made this place one of the most attractive I have ever been in. The town and country around are surpassingly beautiful. The great feature here, and one which shocks the moral senses is the gambling, which is carried on on the most extensive scale, by a chartered Company, protected by law. And here they gamble every day and every night, Sundays and all, during the whole year, and here gather all the great gamblers of Europe, and all the fast men and women, fond of play. The gambling house, called the 'Kursaal' is an immense building, equal to many of the palaces of Europe. It has its magnificent *salons*, its theatre, its concert room, its billiard room, its reading rooms and its splendid dining halls, and outside are gardens and walks and flowers and fountains. But Capt. Morehouse of Galena, who is now stopping at this place, and who has been there, says Weisbaden, beats this place for gambling. But enough for once. Kindest regards to Mrs. G. and to the members of the Staff and Mr. Dent. . . . Address me as before." ALS, USG 3.

    1. Badeau printed this word as "present."

To Edwin M. Stanton

Washington, April 9 *1867*

Hon. E M. Stanton
Secretary of War,
Sir:

    I would recommend the transfer of the Headquarters, of the Third Military District from Montgomery, Ala., to Atlanta, Ga. The States of Georgia, Florida and Alabama each form a sub-district, with their Headquarters at the Capital of the State. Atlanta will be more central than Montgomery, and a position from which the District Commander can better communicate with his entire command.

    Maj. Gen. Pope is very anxious for this change.

Very respectfully, Yr. obedt. svt.
U. S. Grant
General.

LS, DNA, RG 94, Letters Received, 212A 1867; copies (misdated April 4, 1867), *ibid.*, RG 108, Letters Sent; DLC-USG, V, 47, 60. On April 8, Bvt. Maj. Gen. John Pope, Montgomery, Ala., had telegraphed to USG. "I go to Georgia in a few days, as most of my time will be spent there for reasons given you by mail I ask authority to move Hd Quarters to Atlanta,   Please answer by tele-graph,   No staff officers reported except Colonel Dunn"   Telegram received (at 11:40 p.m.), DNA, RG 107, Telegrams Collected (Bound); *ibid.*, RG 108, Telegrams Received; copies, *ibid.*, RG 393, Dept. of the South, 4th Army Corps, Letters Sent; DLC-USG, V, 55. At 3:30 p.m., USG telegraphed to Pope. "I will recommend the change of Head Quarters you request"   Telegrams sent (2), DNA, RG 107, Telegrams Collected (Bound); copies, *ibid.*, RG 108, Telegrams Sent; DLC-USG, V, 56. On April 13, 1:45 p.m., USG telegraphed to Pope. "You are authorized to move Hd Qrs. of the District to Atlanta, Ga. Staff of-ficers have been ordered to report to you." ALS (telegram sent), DNA, RG 107, Telegrams Collected (Bound); telegram sent, *ibid.*; copies, *ibid.*, RG 108, Tele-grams Sent; DLC-USG, V, 56.

On March 28, Pope, Louisville, had written to USG. "I leave here tonight & expect to be in Montgomery on Sunday morning—At the suggestion of Genl Thomas, I ask authority in case I find it judicious to move my HdQrs to Atlanta— It is equally convenient of communication with all parts of the District, more easy & direct of Communication with Washington & far more healthy during the Summer—Will you please telegraph the necessary authority to me at Mont-gomery—I am not sure I shall change but if I conclude to do so I would like to have your authority in advance—Of course the District Commanders in Alabama, Georgia & Florida will be posted at the Seats of Government of those States—At the suggestion also of Genl. Thomas I ask that Capt and Bvt Maj S. C. Green 24th U. S. Infy now here be ordered to report to me—He has served on Genl. Charles R Wood's Staff for several years and is entirely acquainted with the con-dition of affairs in Georgia & Alabama as well as with the people—" ALS, DNA, RG 108, Letters Received. On April 2, Pope, Montgomery, wrote to USG. "I have the honor to transmit enclosed my order assuming command of the 3rd Military District   The paragraph suspending elections until the registration of voters is completed and they can be conducted in compliance with the act of Congress you will readily see the necessity of—I thought it necessary in retain-ing the present civil officers to provide against the exercise of their official in-fluence whilst holding such offices, to prevent the people from taking action in the reconstruction of these State Governments—This was the more necessary as most of the Civil officers are understood to be active secessionists and disposed to consel the people to inaction or open opposition—The effect of the Reconstruction Bill upon the people of this section of country has been excellent and it seems certain that in Alabama reconstruction will be accomplished as speedily as the act of Congress will permit—In Georgia there will be more opposition to any action in that direction though the Advocates of Reconstruction are bold & active & feel assured that by the time the Registration is completed the public mind will have been made up to support the necessary measures—As I have said no difficulty is apprehended in Alabama where the Governor & most of the State Officers are actively committed to reconstruction and for that & other reasons I deem it judicious to transfer my HeadQuarters to Georgia—Genl Swayne the Comdg Officer in this State is an intelligent and earnest officer, fully alive to his duties and interested in the success of the Reconstruction policy   He is in en-tire harmony with Governor Patton and matters will work smoothly & well—In Georgia the Governor has not yet pronounced himself & matters are more doubt-ful—Neither is there in that State an officer in command who is likely to so ef-ficient or so much interested in the success of the Reconstruction measures, and

my immediate presence is urged by many of the most prominent men at the head
of the movement for the restoration of the State Government—With you assent
therefore I will move my Head Quarters to Atlanta on or before the 10th (Inst.)—
I have no Staff officers and need them extremely—I ought to have an efficient
AdjtGenl. The official correspondence is already very g[r]eat and I cannot possibly attend to it—There are very few officers with the troops, not more indeed
than are absolutely necessary with their Companies   They are besides young
men entirely unacquainted with such duties—I trust you will send me Staff officers as soon as possible. Will you please telegraph me authority for the removal
of HdQrs—to Atlanta" ALS, *ibid.*, RG 94, Letters Received, 860M 1867. The
enclosure is *ibid.* On March 9, William J. Hardee had telegraphed to USG. "The
People of Alabama unanimously desire the appointment of Maj Gen Wager
Swayne to command the state under the late act of Congress—" Telegram received (on March 10, 11:00 A.M.), *ibid.*, RG 107, Telegrams Collected (Bound);
ibid., RG 108, Telegrams Received; copy, DLC-USG, V, 55.

On April 7, Pope wrote to USG. "I have the honor to ask what is your understanding of the Status of officers of the Rebel Army paroled at the Conclusion of
the War. Do these paroles Still hold good or are they set aside by any proclamations of the President? I ask because I desire to know what action I shall be
authorised to take against the Rebel officers thus paroled who may actively and
openly counsel the people in this District to resist the execution of the late Act
of Congress providing for Reconstruction in the Southern States—Does not that
provision of their parole which requires them to go to their homes & obey the
laws require them also to refrain from inciting others to neglect or resist the
laws of the U. S.—Is not an attempt on their part to keep up difficulty & prevent
the settlement of the Southern question in accordance with the Act of Congress
a violation of parole?—In Alabama I think there will be no trouble whatever in
completing the Registration & carrying out the objects of the Act of Congress—
The Governor of the State and all or nearly all the State officers as well as a very
large Majority of the prominent men in the State are in favor of reconstruction
under the Act and are actively canvassing the State with what may be safely
considered certainty of success—In Georgia there will be far more difficulty—I
am going to that State at the urgent request of many citizens, in a few days and
as a large part of my time will be necessary spent there I have telegraphed for
authority to move my HeadQuarters to Atlanta which being the centre of rail
road communication affords very great facilities for easy communication with
all parts of the District—I have just made an order for the Registration which
I enclose herewith—To determine the compensation of the Registers I would be
glad to have from the Census Bureau a table of pay for their employées—The
object of graduating the pay of Registers by the number of recorded names is to
make sure that the entire freedmen's vote will be brought out. It is for the interest of the Registers that no name of a qualified voter is omitted—I do not apprehend any difficulty in executing the Law as far as it refers to the protection of
persons in their rights of person & property and no disturbance whatever is anticipated—There are however in the Northern parts of Alabama & Georgia bands
of mounted robbers who depredate upon the people & especially upon the Negroes.—These bands are beyond the control of the Civil authorities and Infantry
forces are useless against them—For the same reason that Genl Thomas finds it
necessary to keep four companies of Cavalry in Tennessee, I find some companies of Cavalry necessary in Northern Georgia & Alabama & I trust a few

companies will be sent me as soon as practicable—In Florida every thing is quiet—She will follow the lead of Georgia & Alabama.—No staff officers have yet reported to me except Genl Dunn—Even if I could take officers enough from their companies for Staff duty (which I cannot do without leaving the companies without officers) they are wholly unacquainted with staff duties and are unfit besides for any such position—I presume that an Adjt Genl & Quartermaster at least have been sent me—For these duties I need the best & most discreet officers—" ALS, DNA, RG 94, Letters Received, 861M 1867. The enclosure is *ibid.* On April 10, Pope wrote to Secretary of War Edwin M. Stanton through USG's hd. qrs. requesting operating funds. ALS, *ibid.*, RG 108, Letters Received. On April 13, Bvt. Brig. Gen. Orville E. Babcock wrote to Pope. "In reply to your communication of April 7th the General-in-chief directs me to say that your views upon the obligation of a parole, are in strict accordance with his own. Application will be made to the Secty. of the Interior for the information you desire from the Census Bureau. Staff Officers have been ordered to report to you." Copies, DLC-USG, V, 47, 60; DNA, RG 108, Letters Sent. On April 15, USG wrote to Stanton. "I have the honor to recommend that the Secretary of the Interior be requested to furnish for the information and guidance of the Commanding Generals of the five military districts, copies of the census report of the Southern states for 1860; also the rates and manner of payment of persons employed to take the census throughout the United States." Copies, *ibid.*, RG 46, Senate 40A–F5, War Dept. Messages; *ibid.*, RG 107, Letters Received from Bureaus; *ibid.*, RG 108, Letters Sent; DLC-USG, V, 47, 60. On April 18, Bvt. Brig. Gen. Louis H. Pelouze, AGO, referred to USG a letter of April 17 from John C. Cox, chief clerk, Dept. of the Interior, to Pelouze stating that information had been sent directly to the five district commanders. AES and ALS, DNA, RG 108, Letters Received.

On April 16, 1:40 P.M., USG telegraphed to Pope. "Instruct Gen. Swayne, Comd.g Sub. District of Ala. to comply implicitly with telegraphic instructions this day sent to him by the Sec. of the Treasury, with regard to the First National Bank of Selma, and the officers of said Bank. . . . Send Copy of this direct to Gn. Swayne." ALS (telegram sent), *ibid.*, RG 107, Telegrams Collected (Bound); telegram sent, *ibid.*; copies, *ibid.*, RG 46, Senate 40A–F2, Messages; *ibid.*, RG 107, Letters Received from Bureaus; *ibid.*, RG 108, Telegrams Sent; DLC-USG, V, 56. At 1:50 P.M., Bvt. Maj. Gen. John A. Rawlins telegraphed to Pope. "Two Companies 5th Cavalry will be ordered from here by rail, via Lynchburg, to report to you   Notice will be given when they start that you may direct their movements before reaching Atlanta if desired"   Telegrams sent (2), DNA, RG 107, Telegrams Collected (Bound); copies, *ibid.*, RG 108, Telegrams Sent; DLC-USG, V, 56. On April 25, Pope telegraphed to USG. "Please order Wall Tens to be sent with the Cavalry Companies   No other shelter here for them until Huts can be built" Telegram received (at 5:10 P.M.), DNA, RG 107, Telegrams Collected (Bound); *ibid.*, RG 108, Telegrams Received; copies, *ibid.*, RG 94, Letters Received, 263P 1867; DLC-USG, V, 55. On April 26, Maj. George K. Leet endorsed a copy of this telegram. "Respectfully referred to Brevet Major General E. R. S. Canby, Command'g Department of Wash'gton. If the Companies of the 5th Cavalry ordered to report to Gen. Pope have not gone and are unprovided with tents, the Q. M. Department will be ordered to furnish them at once." ES, DNA, RG 94, Letters Received, 263P 1867.

On April 19, Pope, Atlanta, wrote to Rawlins. "I have sent today an official communication to Maj Leet in regard to the detail of Dr Getty as Medical Director of this District—He is a kind hearted & entirely harmless man for whom I have real sympathy & regard & I do not wish to injure him in any manner—He is however from personal habits as well as business habits unfit to be Medical Director of any command—I had him in Milwaukee & during his service I received letters constantly complaining that his business was not attended to—When he was relieved by Surgeon Swift that officer reported to me that he found Getty's office strewed with papers, (sick certificates certificates of Disability &c &c) which had been accumulating for months & had been entirely neglected—I do not doubt the fact at all because at the time Getty was Medical Director I recd many complaints of the same kind myself—The truth is that he drinks too much & is really not competent to do much business as is required from a Medical Director—I will not make any official or other charges against him—He is a good clean kindhearted man, but utterly unfit for duty—You have doubtless seen many such—I feel sure the Surgeon General must know of Dr Gettys habits & it is not right that because they do not want such men in Washington & prefer other & more efficient officers for comfortable positions in New York Detroit or elsewhere, they should such men as Getty to such a command as this where we ought to have the best officers—I wish you would show this note to the Genl that he may understand why I object to Getty—I trust any application that he be relieved will be complied with, without doing Getty any injury" ALS, OClWHi. On the same day, Pope wrote to Leet officially requesting the change. LS, DNA, RG 108, Letters Received. On April 22, Leet endorsed this letter. "Respectfully referred to the Surgeon General. It is believed that the interests of the service would be promoted by relieving Surgeon Getty and assigning some other officer as Medical Director of the 3d Military District. During the war Gen. Pope had Surgeon Getty as his Medic'l Director and did not find him an efficient officer for that position. The General-in-Chief suggests a change, and that Surg'n Getty be sent to some other command." ES, *ibid.*

To Edwin M. Stanton

Washington, D. C. Apl. 10th *1867.*

HON. E. M. STANTON,
SEC. OF WAR;
SIR:

I have the honor, very respectfully, to reniew my recommendation that all Military organization of the regular army, now serving West of the Mississippi river, or that may hereafter be sent West of that river, unless otherwise directed, be authorized to be filled to the Maximum number of men allowed by law.

At present no troops from the East of the Miss. can be spared for the defence of the settlements, and lines of travel, in the Indian country. From many quarters the cry is: more protection. On the part of numerous tribes war already exists against the whites. In support of this declaration I enclose, herewith, extracts from a report by Gen. Sully, to the Interior Dept., from Col. E. S. Parker, to these Hd Qrs. ~~from~~, letter from J. D. V. Reeve, Col. 13th Inf.y, and ex. from letter of Gen. Sherman.[1]

In further support of this recommendation I would also refer to the dispatch from the Gov. of Montana, sent to the War Dept. to-day, and also the repeated applications from the Governor, and other citizens, of Texas for more protection.

Very respectfully
your obt. svt.
U. S. GRANT
General.

ALS, DLC-Andrew Johnson. On April 3, 1867, Lt. Gen. William T. Sherman, St. Louis, had written to Maj. George K. Leet. "I have the honor to acknowledge the receipt of the communication from the Hon. O. H. Browning, Secretary of the Interior under date of March 19th 1867, and forwarded to me through the Secretary of War, and your Office under date of March 23rd 1867.—Although the subject matter has been treated of in many of my official letters heretofore; it is proper I should repeat. There is no military expedition on foot or in contemplation against the Indians who are now in the belt of Country between the Platte and Arkansas. I did recommend their removal to some other quarter of an unoccupied country, because I thought and believed their presence there along our travelled road would sooner or later result in collisions, which would be to the detriment of the Indians. My recommendation was not approved, and I have long since dropped the subject to await the action of time. General Hancock's present movement is to the south of the Arkansas, to show a force to the Cheyennes, Arapahoes, Kiowas and Commanches, who have repeatedly threatened our Posts along the Arkansas, and to stop all travel along that and the Smoky Hill routes, by which our people reach the settlements in Colorado and New Mexico.—In my annual report I used the word 'supposed' because in person I had travelled through those Indians, and saw for myself that they did not even pretend to confine themselves to their Reservations or to pay much heed to the requirements of their Agents, whose control over them is no control at all. As to the Sioux north of the Platte it is idle for us to close our eyes to the fact that they are at war. They declare it openly and without reserve. It is hardly fair to attribute the utter annihilation of Colonel Fetterman's party to the misconduct or incapacity of Colonel Carrington. The Sioux had for months hung around Fort Phil: Kearney and were only deterred from an open attack on the Post by the natural fear of heavy loss to themselves; but by their well known powers of deciet they drew out Lt. Col. Fetterman's party beyond reach of the Fort, and by overwhelming numbers, massacred every man. Even to hold Council with such Indians, is a weakness that will cost us dear. I wish I could feel as confident as the Hon. Secretary of the Interior of the peaceful disposition of the Indians, but he must pardon me if I cannot, and accept the reports of our Military Commanders who live in contact with these Indians. In this connection I enclose a report just received from Colonel I. V. D. Reeve, Comd'g the District of the Upper Missouri; and merely state the fact that the public is at this moment agitated by a report that has reached us through Indian sources that Colonel Rankin and the entire garrison of Fort Buford at the mouth of Yellow Stone have been massacred. Our communication with that Post since about the midde of January has been cut off by the severe weather and by the Indians, so that we are unable to contradict the report. With these facts staring us in the face and the entire unanimity of opinion of the Military and Civilian population directly interested in the condition of Indian affairs, it is hard for us to hold our hands and remain passively on the defensive because a different opinion prevails elsewhere. I recognize the fact that Congress has sent out Peace Commissioners and that the lawful control of the Indian vests in the Department of the Interior, so that legally and rightfully the Military can not be held to an accountability for the consequences, and I should be glad if our Government would go further, and assume that war against any Indians should not be begun and undertaken, except on a formal 'Declaration of War' when of course Congress would provide by law for the force needed to carry the War to a successful conclusion. This state of quasi-war where we are held to protect our vast frontiers and lines of travel measured by thousands of miles with our troops forced to remain on the defensive to be dealt with in detail, by Indians who say they are at War and mean a war of utter innihilation and no quarter shown, is not a state of facts pleasing to a military mind. Still I suppose we must submit to it like law abiding men, till the problem produces its necessary solution." LS, DNA, RG 108, Letters Received. The enclosure is *ibid.* On April 8, USG endorsed these papers. "Respectfully forwarded to the Secretary of War, inviting special attention to these communications, and with request that copies be furnished to the Secretary of the Interior." ES, *ibid.*

On April 9, Act. Governor Thomas F. Meagher of Montana Territory, Virginia City, telegraphed to USG. "The most populous & prosperous portion of our Territory immediately adjoining the wild region where are located Forts Phil Kearney and Fort C F Smith is threatened by the Sioux. The greatest alarm reasonably prevails   Projected movement from East against these Indians are forcing them upon outer settlements in that direction   Danger ins imminent & will overpower unless measures for defence are instantly taken. Until therefore regular troops are reinforced on Yellow Stone we earneastly entreat permission from War Department to raise a force of one thousand 1000 Volunteers for menaced quarters to be paid by general government while serving in field & to be releived by reenforcements early in Summer. Major Clintons command at Judith no use whatever to settlements spoken of   Fort Smith too far from latter & too weakly manned to be of service   people of territory will generously and bravely do their duty successfully defending themselves if privelege asked be granted." Telegram received (at 5:20 P.M.), DNA, RG 107, Telegrams Collected (Bound); *ibid.*, RG 108, Telegrams Received; copies, *ibid.*, Letters Received; *ibid.*, RG 393, Military Div. of the Mo., Indian War; DLC-USG, V, 55; DLC-Andrew Johnson. On April 10, USG endorsed a copy of this telegram. "Respectfully re-

fered to the Sec. of War. If there is the danger which Governor Maher appre-
hends, and there wood seem to be, judging from all the information reaching us,
the Citizens of Montana ought to have some organization to defend themselves
until the troops of the United States can give them the required protection. I
think however the Governor should know what self defense requires these Citizens to do, and if the services rendered by them warrant it, they should, afterward, look to Congress for compensation." AES, *ibid*. On April 27, Meagher and
Chief Justice Hezekiah L. Hosmer telegraphed to Secretary of War Edwin M.
Stanton requesting authority to raise vols. Copy (marked as received on April
28), DNA, RG 108, Letters Received. On May 3, USG telegraphed to Hosmer.
"There is no law authorizin the calling out of Militia. The law of self defence
will justify the Governor of the Territory in calling out troops for the protection
of her citizens and Congress must be looked to afterwards for reimbursment. . . .
P. S. Note to Sec. of War. In substance this same reply was made to Gn. Meaghr's
first dispatch about three weeks since." ALS (telegram sent), *ibid*., RG 94, Letters Received, 286W 1867; copy, *ibid*., RG 393, Military Div. of the Mo., Indian
War. See letter to Lt. Gen. William T. Sherman, May 17, 1867.

    1. In addition to enclosing extracts from Sherman's letter of April 3 con-
cerning the Sioux, USG enclosed a letter of Feb. 24 from Col. Isaac V. D. Reeve,
13th Inf., Fort Rice, Dakota Territory, to Bvt. Lt. Col. Edward W. Smith.
"From the information which reaches these HeadQrs from time to time relating
to Indian affairs in the Dept. of Dakota, there is every probability that hostilities
will commence on the part of the Indians as soon as the weather shall prove
favorable. So far as relates to those in this Dist. I have no doubt but such will
be the case. The interruption of our mails between this post and Fort Buford,—
the attack on that post in Dec'r last, the threats made to 'destroy all the whites
in the country', messages to the friendly Indians to 'keep out of the way', and in
fact all that we hear from or of them goes to prove that their designs are *war*.
The combination amongst them for that purpose is very powerful. . . . The whole
number of warriors which can be brought into the field—probably somewhere
from eight to ten thousand—will make dreadful havoc,—notwithstanding all the
restraining influences which the Govt can, or *will* bring against them. . . ." Copy
(ellipses in document), DLC-Andrew Johnson. USG also enclosed a letter of
March 25 from Bvt. Brig. Gen. Alfred Sully, Fort McPherson, Nebraska Territory, to Secretary of the Interior Orville H. Browning. ". . . Beyond doubt a large
number, located in the region of Tongue river, are, and have been for some time
back, in a state of war. There appears no alternative but that these Inds must
be *severely* punished, or driven out of the country, or that section of the country,
and line of communication, to Montana must be entirely abandoned. . . . Hostility
exists on the part of certain Indians. It is impossible to tell how far it may extend, and how many, now friendly or disposed to be so, may be driven into it. . . ."
Copy (ellipses in document), *ibid*. USG also enclosed an extract from a letter of
April 1 from Col. Ely S. Parker, Fort McPherson, to Bvt. Maj. Gen. John A.
Rawlins. See telegram to Lt. Gen. William T. Sherman, Feb. 21, 1867.

To Edwin M. Stanton

Respectfully forwarded to the Secretary of War.

Gen. Thomas was entirely unwarranted in publicly charging Gen. Hunt with the authorship of "A memorial of the officers of the Army" unless he had positive proofs of the fact, in which case the charge should have been made through the proper official channel. If Gen. Hunt did write the above mentioned pamphlet, and attribute it to the "officers of the Army" without their authority and consent, he has been guilty of an offense which deserves the severest censure. Nothing is more subversive of discipline in an army than the circulation of documents tending to array one class of officers against another, and destroy that harmony between officers of the Staff and line upon which the efficiency of an army in so great a measure depends.

It is therefore recommended that no further action be taken in reference to the charge.

U. S. GRANT
General.

HDQRS. AUS
Ap. 10. '67.

ES, DNA, RG 94, Letters Received, 485H 1867. Written on a letter of April 8, 1867, from Lt. Col. and Bvt. Maj. Gen. Henry J. Hunt, 3rd Art., Washington, D. C., to Maj. George K. Leet. "I have the honor to submit to the General Commanding, a charge and Specifications against Bt Major Genl. L. Thomas Adjt Genl. of the Army" ALS, *ibid.* The enclosure is *ibid.* On Aug. 25, Hunt, Fort Sullivan, Eastport, Maine, wrote to Bvt. Maj. Gen. Edward D. Townsend. "I have the honor to acknowledge the receipt of your letter of June 26, containing the endorsement of the general-in-chief—on the charges submitted by me on the 8th of April last, against Adjutant General Thomas. . . . My principal object in preferring these charges was to vindicate my own character, openly and publicly, against false charges made in my absence by an officer of high rank and position, and kept so far as possible concealed from my knowledge, but for the circulation of which unusual means had been adopted. As to the additional charge now brought against me by the general-in-chief, in his endorsement, accusing me of writing a pamphlet and attributing it to the officers of the Army, 'without their authority and consent,' it is a duty which I owe to myself to declare that this new charge is wholly gratuitous and unfounded, nor am I justly obnoxious to the comments by which it is followed. I will add that I am astonished that General Grant should make such a charge against me even under its conditional form

No action having been taken by the War Department it would seem that I am refused the redress I have sought through the proper official channel against the false charges of General Thomas. To guard myself (so far as it is possible, under existing circumstances) against the effects of the further injurious charge on which this denial of justice is based, I have to request that this letter be brought to the notice of General Grant, and filed with his endorsement on my charges against General Thomas,—which charges however I do not withdraw—" ALS, *ibid*. On Aug. 10, 1868, Hunt wrote to Townsend requesting that his letter of Aug. 25, 1867, be filed with USG's endorsement of April 10. ALS, *ibid*. On Nov. 10, 1868, Townsend endorsed these letters. "At suggestion of Dr Craig, brother in law of Genl. Hunt not submitted to Genl Grant until after receipt of his letter of Aug. 10, 1868." AES, *ibid*. Probably on Nov. 10, USG wrote a note, presumably to Townsend. "State Gn. Hunts letter of Aug./67 has just been submitted to Gn. in Chief. Ask does he deny authorship of 'Memorial to Congress'? If the author, had he the authority of the 'Officers of the Army' to speak in their behalf? If he is not the author then no reflection is contained in the indorsement of the Gn. in Chief, or if he had authority to speak for any considerable number of the 'Officers of the Army' Gn. Hunt is only reprehensible to the extent that he may have misrepresented the views of his brother officers in his 'Memorial.' " AN (undated), *ibid*. On Dec. 10, Hunt wrote to Townsend. ". . . In reply I have to say that I am the author of the *body* of that 'Memorial,' I mean all except the 'Heading' which gives it the form of a Memorial; and I will state the circumstances under which it was written, and appeared, this explanation being essential to a full understanding of the matter—In the summer or fall of 1866, my attention was called to a *Table*, in the hands of a staff officer in Washington, setting forth what purported to be the pay and allowances of the officers of 'Heavy,' Artillery, and Infantry. This Table was in manuscript and was in form and substance exceedingly likely to mislead any one not thoroughly, acquainted with the practical working of the actual pay-system of the Army. I represented to its supposed author, in whose hands I saw it, the unfairness of the statement, and in what respect it was calculated to do injustice to the officers, especially those employed on active service, who were charged with receiving certain allowances. He did not see the matter in the same light that I did, and as I was, in common with other officers habitually 'serving with troops,' deeply interested in the result, and had every reason to believe that the 'Table' had been prepared for the express purpose, and would be used to defeat, in the Senate a bill (known as Genl Schenck's) which had already passed the House of Representatives; and would be likely to affect injuriously any other effort to obtain an increase of compensation to those officers, I prepared a paper which I hoped would aid in setting the question in its true light, serve to correct the false inferences which might be drawn from the '*table*,' and meet the principal arguments which were being urged against the bill—This paper was not in the form nor was it intended as a Memorial to Congress: It was addressed to and intended for Genl Wilson, Chairman, of the Senate Military Committee and was designed to call his attention, and that of the Members of his Committee, should he see fit to submit it to them, to a thorough examination of the whole subject—. . . This paper although intended for the use of Genl Wilson I read to several officers, both of the line and staff; who had served with troops in the field, and I gave copies of it to two or three persons. They all, without an exception so far as my memory serves, approved of the paper, and indorsed the correctness of its statements so far as known to them, as many others have since done. Yet I spoke in that paper only in my own name, I am its sole author, hold myself responsible for its contents, and have not attributed it, or any part of it, to any other person or persons whatsoever, officers or citizens whether with or without their authority or consent. A copy of this paper, somewhat modified for publication, but substantially the same as the original, and almost identical with it, was with my consent, printed by another officer, who however probably desiring that it should be adopted, as well as read by the officers of the army who approved it, put it under the form of a Memorial to Congress. . . . I have never signed the 'Memorial,' as such, nor do I know of its having been signed by any other officer, or presented to Congress, and thus perfected, so that it could be attributed to any one; but as it is substantially the same paper which I addressed to Genl Wilson, so soon as I ascertained that Adjutant General Thomas had, over his official signature, publicly given my name as the author, charged that the arguments were 'most disingenuous,' and some of the statements 'untrue,' I took prompt measures by preferring charges against him 'through the proper military channels' to bring his assertions to the test of trial. . . ." ALS, *ibid.* See *CG*, 39–2, 1030, 1894–95; Edward G. Longacre, *The Man Behind the Guns: A Biography of General Henry Jackson Hunt . . .* (South Brunswick and New York, 1977), pp. 228–29.

To Lt. Gen. William T. Sherman

Washington, D, C,
Apl. 10th 1867. [*11:00* A.M.]

Lt. Gn. W. T. Sherman,
Omaha, Nebraska.

Make no change in your plans against Indians the coming Summer, without more positive orders than any that have yet been given, except as your judgement should dictate a change. Do not delay on account of the Commission sent out by the Interior Dept.

U. S. Grant
General.

ALS (telegram sent), DNA, RG 107, Telegrams Collected (Bound); telegram sent, *ibid.*; copies, *ibid.*, RG 107, Letters Received from Bureaus; *ibid.*, RG 108, Telegrams Sent; *ibid.*, RG 393, Military Div. of the Mo., Indian War; DLC-USG, V, 56. On April 11, 1867, 10:30 A.M., Lt. Gen. William T. Sherman telegraphed to USG. "Cipher despatch received; am glad you take the responsibility as it will enable me to give General Augur clear and distinct instructions" Telegram received (at 1:00 P.M.), DNA, RG 107, Telegrams Collected (Bound); *ibid.*, RG 108, Telegrams Received; copies, *ibid.*, RG 107, Letters Received from Bureaus; DLC-USG, V, 55. On the same day, USG endorsed a copy of this telegram. "Respectfully forwarded to the Secretary of War for his information" ES, DNA, RG 107, Letters Received from Bureaus.

On April 20, Sherman, St. Louis, telegraphed to USG. "Am back from Omaha General Augur is delayed by highwaters but is doing all that is necessary by way of preparation." Telegram received (at 3:30 P.M.), *ibid.*, RG 108, Telegrams Received; copies (one sent by mail), *ibid.*, RG 94, Letters Received, 428M 1867; DLC-USG, V, 55. On the same day, Sherman wrote to Maj. George K. Leet. "I am just back from Omaha. I went by Chicago and the North Western Railroad that crosses the State of Iowa. The upper part of that State had heavy falls of snow during the winter. They are now melting and have raised the Missouri and its lateral streams, so that the railroad itself is now much damaged and is impassable. But I have no doubt it will soon be repaired and put in order. On arriving at Omaha, I found also that the lateral streams of Nebraska had risen to an unusual height and had seriously damaged the Pacific Railroad, so that trains could not pass at all. The waters were so high about the Elk-horn, Loup Fork and the Platte itself that many miles of the track were under water and could not be reached. I expect however that by the experience, energy, and well-organized labor of the parties in charge of that road, it also will be all right in a few days. The ice in the Missouri passed down when I was at Omaha, and the waters rose to an unprecedented height for April. This rise evidently came from the side streams and not from the mountains, which can be ~~safely~~ expected in all June, so that I think we may safely count on three good months for the navigation of the Missouri River. Since my return, I find that all our boats destined for the Upper Missouri, are off, and very soon we will know all about the condition of affairs about Fort Buford, the terrible reports about which have occasioned so much distress, and which even yet we are unable to contradict positively. As to General Augur. He has now the posts of Laramie, Reno and Phil. Kearney strongly garrisoned, but was uneasy about C. F. Smith, though the garrison had not been disturbed, up to latest dates, by the Indians. General Wessells at Phil. Kearney has orders to reinforce the place as soon as the intervening country becomes passable. All those posts are troubled by attacks on their trains, and on their mails and couriers. A mail party of four men was reported killed by Indians near Fort Reno while I was at Omaha, and a herd of mules belonging to a contractor was driven off by Indians at Fort Mitchell, this side of Laramie. General Augur was of opinion that these acts were perpetrated by small parties of Sioux. The Peace Commissioners were at Fort McPherson, but had sent out runners to the Sioux and Cheyennes south of the Platte to meet them at Fort Sedgwick last Saturday. These Indians are and have been peaceable, and I don't see what is the use of treating with them. The hostile Sioux are evidently above, in the neighborhood of the Yellowstone, and it is with them we have to deal. After a full and free conversation with General Augur, I prepared for him a letter of instructions, a copy of which is herein enclosed; and to it I refer for all points connected with the summer and fall campaign I doubt much that we can accomplish anything positive by following these Sioux, but now they are boastful and insolent and it is possible they will accept battle, which will be the best thing to hope for, but a movement of troops in a circuit from Phil. Kearney down to the mouth of the Yellowstone, and back round by the North, will have a good effect. In that district of country there are no peaceful Indians, and General Augur can hardly go amiss. He will have about ten companies of the 2nd US. Cavy., the whole of the 30th U. S. Infantry, Col.

Stevenson and out of the 18th and 37th he can make up garrisons and an additional force of Infantry to complete a column of, say, 2500 efficient men. The 4th Infantry Brevt Maj Genl Colonel Casey was camped at Omaha, but will be moved out along the Pacific Railroad for the summer. If we can keep the Indians off the Platte this year, it will enable the Pacific Railroad Company to complete their road to the Black Hills, which will be a great achievement, and will be of infinite use to us in the future. I feel somewhat apprehensive that these Indians may learn the weakness and vulnerability of the steamboats navigating the Missouri River, but captains and owners have been cautioned, and are now well supplied with guns and muskets for self defence. I think we have now done in that direction all that prudence and the occasion call for, and must await the developmenents of time." LS, DNA, RG 108, Letters Received. The enclosure is *ibid.*

On March 27, noon, Bvt. Brig. Gen. Cyrus B. Comstock had telegraphed to Bvt. Maj. Gen. Alfred H. Terry. "The General desires me to ask for the latest news from Fort Buford. Do you give any credit to the rumor of a massacre there on January 15th." ALS (telegram sent), *ibid.*, RG 107, Telegrams Collected (Bound); telegram sent, *ibid.*; copies, *ibid.*, RG 108, Telegrams Sent; DLC-USG, V, 56. On the same day, Terry, St. Paul, Minn., telegraphed to Comstock. "Latest dates from Buford are to January first   I do not credit the rumor. The Indians were troublesome there during December but no harm was done to the garrison as soon as troops can be moved I shall Send four 4 more companies to the post" Telegram received (on March 28, 9:35 A.M.), DNA, RG 107, Telegrams Collected (Bound); *ibid.*, RG 108, Telegrams Received; copy, DLC-USG, V, 55. On May 8, Sherman telegraphed to USG. "Gen. Augur reports the arrival at Omaha of a citizen who left Fort Buford Apl. sixteenth 16   Col Rankin & garrison are all well   The report of massacre originated in Chicago" Telegram received (at 10:20 P.M.), DNA, RG 108, Letters Received; copy (sent by mail), *ibid.*, RG 94, Letters Received, 526M 1867. See *ibid.*, 542M, 543M, 554M, 567M 1867.

On April 22, Sherman wrote to Leet. "I have now before me several papers, referred to me from your Headquarters, upon which I have to remark as follows. W. F. Walton asks protection for miners in the neighborhood of Hardyville. I have no knowledge of where Hardyville is, and infer from his reference to the name of General R. C. Drum, who was in the Military Division of the Pacific, that Hardyville is in that Division, and not in that of the Missouri. I therefore return the paper. Hon. O. H. Browning applying for an escort to Commissioners to examine and determine the point of the Pacific Railroad to be considered the base of the Rocky Mountains   That point is beyond all controversy near the head of Lodge Pole or Crow Creek, a country as safe as Missouri, where the Commissioners can go in a stage traveled daily by women and children, and where I have been myself without wishing an escort. Still, if the Commissioners need one, General Augur at Omaha will be instructed to furnish one from Fort Sanders, just over the first ridge known as the Black Hills. The Commissioners will doubtless go via Omaha, where they can apply to General Augur in person. James S. Goodall, of Kansas, calling attention to the danger of attack on the frontiers by Indians. General Hancock is at this moment among those Indians, and will give the frontier of Kansas all the protection the case admits of. I rather think the frontiers of Kansas are more likely to disturb the Indians, for the settlements are pushing out faster than they should with a due regard to ordinary selfprotection. Copies of letters from General Sully and Colonel Parker,

Commissioners for the Interior Department in relation to Indian Affairs. These will be sent to General Augur, who is at this moment preparing to act against the hostile Indians, and who will take every possible precaution not to involve those who are peaceably inclined." LS, *ibid.*, RG 108, Letters Received. On April 29, USG forwarded to Secretary of War Edwin M. Stanton an extract of Sherman's remarks concerning the military escort. ES and extract, *ibid.*, RG 94, Letters Received, 544M 1867.

To Lyman Trumbull

Washington, April 10th 1867

Hon. L. Trumbull
U. S. Senate
Dear Sir:

In the matter of the non confirmation of Gen. Simpson,[1] to the rank of Bvt. Maj. Gen'l I have been informed that it was partially on the ground of my non concurrence in his recommendation that this course was pursued, by the Senate, I would state that generally the subject of brevets, for the Staff Corps, except such of them as did line duty during the rebellion did not come before me. In the case of Gen. Simpson, however, it did, & I endorsed my nonconcurrence in the recommendation for the brevet. Gen. Simpson has always been an acknowledged faitful and efficient officer, & no fault has ever been found, that I ever heard of with his performance of his duties. Two of his juniors who did no duty outside the subsistence Dept. during the rebellion have been confirmed as Maj. Gen. and for this reason I withdraw my disapproval to his promotion, and add that I think he should have the same rank with Gens. Clarke & Beckwith,[2] the juniors referred to.

I have the honor to be
Very respy Your obt. servt.
U. S. Grant
Gen'l

Copies, DLC-USG, V, 47, 60; DNA, RG 108, Letters Sent.

1. On Sept. 17, 1866, USG unfavorably endorsed an undated petition to U.S. Senator Henry Wilson of Mass. recommending Lt. Col. Marcus D. L. Simp-

son, asst. commissary gen., for appointment as bvt. maj. gen. ES and DS, DNA, RG 94, ACP, S128 CB 1863. Simpson, rejected on April 5, 1867, was reconsidered and confirmed on April 10.

2. In late Feb., USG had favorably endorsed a letter of Feb. 16 from U.S. Senator Luke P. Poland of Vt. to Secretary of War Edwin M. Stanton recommending Maj. and Bvt. Brig. Gen. Amos Beckwith for appointment as bvt. maj. gen. AES and ALS, *ibid.* On Feb. 25, USG wrote to Stanton. "I would respectfully ask to withdraw my recommendation for the appointment of Amos Beckwith, C. S. as Bvt. Maj. Gen. or else to recommend Bvt. Brig. Gen. H. F. Clarke, C. S. Gen. Beckwiths senior, and who saw as much of field service, for the same commission." ALS, *ibid.* Beckwith and Lt. Col. Henry F. Clarke, asst. commissary gens., were both confirmed as bvt. maj. gens. on March 2. On April 28, 1875, U.S. Senator George F. Edmunds of Vt. wrote to USG. "I beg leave, respectfully, to express the earnest wish that General Beckwith may receive the appointment of Commissary General. He is a native Vermonter and went to West Point from our state, to which I believe he has done honor in his military career ever since. I believe his rank, his age, his character, and his qualifications, make it preeminently fit that he should have this honorable promotion. Hoping that you will find it consistent with your sense of duty to make this selection . . ." ALS, *ibid.* On April 16, Bvt. Maj. Gen. Edward D. Townsend had issued orders assigning Beckwith to duty as act. commissary gen. (*ibid.*), but no appointment as commissary gen. followed.

To Edwin M. Stanton

———

Washington, April 13th *1867*

HON. E. M. STANTON
SECRETARY OF WAR
SIR:

I have the honor to forward herewith a list of Captains in the regular army, recently appointed from volunteers, who are recommended for the brevet promotion indicated in the list.

It is recommended that these brevets be dated March 2d 1867., the date of the law authorizing them.

There are many other Captains of this class who deserve brevet promotion and who will be recommended hereafter. At present their records in the Adjutant General's Office are not sufficiently full to enable a proper selection to be made of special battles or services for which they should receive their brevets.

Very respectfully
Your obedt. Servant
U. S. GRANT
General.

LS, DNA, RG 94, ACP, G177 CB 1867. The enclosure is *ibid.*

On March 25, 1867, USG had written to Secretary of War Edwin M. Stanton. "I have the honor to forward herewith a list of recommendations for promotion by brevet, of field officers in the regular army, recently appointed from volunteers. I recommend that all such brevets date from the approval of the Act of Congress authorizing them: March 2d 1867." LS, *ibid.*, G129 CB 1867. The enclosure is *ibid.* On March 27, USG wrote to Stanton. "I would respectfully ask to change my recommendation for the brevets to be given to Gen. Sickles so that his Brevet of Major Gen. shall read 'for Gettysburg' instead of 'Chancellorsville.'" ALS, *ibid.* On March 29, USG wrote to Stanton. "I have the honor to make the following recommendations for brevets to date March 2d 1867, in addition to my list of March 25th 1867: . . ." LS, *ibid.*, G363 CB 1867.

To James Longstreet

Washington, April 16, 1867.

DEAR GENERAL:

I have received yours, dated April 10. With regard to the railroad from New Orleans to Mazatlan (Mexico), there is no doubt that it is feasible and that a similar railroad would have value both commercially and politically. I have, nevertheless, to refuse my consent or the use of my name in connection with the enterprise, because my name has been requested in so many enterprises that require a great amount of capital that I believe myself forced to establish a rule of rejecting every case. I would applaud very much were this road made to which you refer, with the consent of the liberal Government of Mexico. There can be no doubt that one can obtain this consent unless one has the idea that we try to promote the future acquisition of Mexican territory. In this matter, my firm conviction is that one ought to apply the same rule to the acquisition of a neighboring territory that we would apply to the acquisition as private individuals, of a piece of land adjacent to ours. So much has been said by some newspapers of our country about the United States acquiring the states of Northern Mexico, that the Mexican Government may see with jealousy the enterprise of which you are speaking, unless the idea that one can take its territory without its free consent be effectively combatted.

I have seen with great interest your two letters on the duties of the South in the present circumstances.[1] These ideas freely expressed by one who occupies a position like yours, have to exercise a beneficial influence. I hope that reconstruction is realized without great difficulty.

> Yours very truly,
> U. S. GRANT.

To GENERAL JAMES LONGSTREET, NEW ORLEANS.

Translated from translation in Matías Romero, comp., *Correspondencia de la Legacion Mexicana en Washington durante la Intervencion Extranjera 1860–1868* (Mexico, 1870–92), IX, 479. On April 10, 1867, James Longstreet had written to USG. "I have the honor to acknowledge the receipt of your esteemed favor of the 23d Ult. The subject of *great interest* between Col Casey and myself is a proposed Rail Road route from this city via Houston & Ringold Barrack Texas, and Monterey, Durango and Mazatlan Mexico. A few moments examination of a map will show you the great advantages of this route over any other to the Pacific Coast. The distance from the City of New York to Mazatlan by this route will not exceed twenty six hundred hundred miles—by other routes it cannot be less than thirty two hundred miles—Our route is tolerably well settled already, a very well watered route and affords greater facilities, of construction in the way of timber than any other—It can be reached by water transportation at intervals of one and two hundred miles until it leaves the Rio Grande, and we shall only have a distance of five hundred miles to run through the interior from the Rio Grande to Mazatlan: two hundred and fifty from each point. There are no indians on the route and it is entirely practicable at all seasons. It will pass through some of the richest mining portions of Mexico, and has a very strong recommendation, in its political bearing in that country. I write to ask if you may permit us to use your name as one of the patrons of this route. Hon L. D. Campbell has undertaken to secure the aid of Gen Sheridans name. Then we want besides the two, other prominent names, say two more from the north (Citizens) and from this part we propose to associate Beauregard and myself with the names of two other of our citizens, making in all eight names for the purpose of under writing the scheme This will not involve a necessity upon your part of taking stock. Or of being in any other way connected with it unless it should be your pleasure—Hoping to hear from you at your convenience." ALS, ICHi.

1. On March 18 and April 6, Longstreet wrote public letters, eventually printed in many newspapers, urging cooperation with military governments established under the Reconstruction Acts. *New Orleans Times*, March 19, April 7, 1867; William Garrett Piston, *Lee's Tarnished Lieutenant: James Longstreet and His Place in Southern History* (Athens, Ga., 1987), pp. 104–6.

To Bvt. Maj. Gen. John Pope

Washington D. C. ~~Dec. 8th 18678~~ April 21st 1867
MY DEAR GENERAL

Having read Gov. Jenkins' address to the Citizens of Ga., I was on the eve of writing you a letter, advising his suspension, and trial before a Military Commission, when your dispatch announcing that the Governor had given such assurances as to render your order, in his case, unecessary, was received. I am now in receipt of the order itself, and your accompanying letter, and have just prepared the enclosed endorsement to go with it.[1]

My views are that District Commanders are responsible for the faithful execution of the reconstruction Act of Congress, and that, in Civil matters, I cannot give them an order. I can give them my views however, for what they are worth, ~~and above all I can advise them of views and opinions here which may serve to put them on their guard. When Gen. Sheridan removed three Civil officers in the State of Louisiana, an act which delighted the loyal North, and none more than the supporters of the Congressional reconstruction bill, in Congress, it created quite a stir and gave expression to the opinion, in other quarters, that he had exceeded his authority.~~ I presume the Atty. Genl. will give a written opinion on the subject of the powers of District Commanders to remove Civil officers and appoint their successors. When he does I will forward it to all the District Commanders.

It is very plain that the power of District Commanders to try offenders by Military Commissions exists. I would advise that Commissions be resorted to, rather than arbitrary removals, until an opinion is had from the Atty. Gen'l or it is found that he does not intend to give one.

~~I will say here General that I have watched your course closely, as I have that of all the District Commanders, and find nothing you have done that does not show prudence and judgement. Rest assured that all you have done meets with the approval of all who wish to see the Act of Congress executed in good faith.~~

Yours truly

U. S. GRANT

General

To MAJ. GEN. J. POPE
COMDG. 3D DIST

Copies (incomplete), DLC-USG, V, 47, (complete) 60; DNA, RG 46, Senate 40A–F2, Messages; *ibid.*, RG 108, Letters Sent. The cancelled material, apparently excised at the time USG's letter was copied for transmission to Congress, was presumably received by Bvt. Maj. Gen. John Pope. On April 24, 1867, Pope, Atlanta, twice wrote to USG. "I have just received your kind letter of the 21st and I am much gratified to know that my course thus far has met your approval—I find the situation here very perplexing and it is not always easy to decide what is best to be done—I shall endeavor however to do the best I can to carry these acts of Congress to a successful [—] & I have the confident hope that by judicious mangement I shall meet with a satisfactory success—I enclose you an extract from a paper of this place which contains my correspondence with Governor Jenkins.—I send by this mail also proper official manuscripts of the correspondence—When I telegraphed you I had just concluded a long conversation with Gov Jenkins in which he gave me satisfactory assurances, & explanations and in substance informed me that he would not repeat the offence—His letter however is a little ambiguous & perhaps was so worded as to let himself down as easily as possible from a rather humiliating position—His influence in the State will be greatly impaired if not altogether destroyed by this correspondence—Nearly all the State officers are rebels & opposed to the execution of these Acts of Congress but I had rather keep them where they *are* (*silenced*) than by displacing them, make martyrs of them as well as active and influential participants in the Struggle to defeat a Convention—Of course if they fail to comply strictly with my order I will remove them without hesitation & bring them to trial if necessary—While I can keep them 'tightly corked' they are harmless— I shall not hesitate to remove any civil officers whatever in this District for cause, and this in spite of any opinion of my powers pronounced by the Atty-Genl—I do not believe and for good reason, that he will give any opinion on this subject adverse to the exercise of such power & if he does, I have still higher ~~power~~ authority than his to sustain me—In his message to Congress vetoing the Reconstruction Act, the President himself lays down his interpretation of the powers conferred upon the District Commanders by this act and the Atty Genl if he did not write the message himself, is well known to have concurred in its Statements—this is the highest Executive interpretation of the Law, & they cannot now go back upon it without acknowledging that it was an attempt knowingly to mislead & deceive the public—I say then that I do not believe that the Atty Genl will give any opinion adverse to the exercise of the power of removal by District Commanders and if he does I have the authority of the President & Cabinet against him—I am grea[tly obl]iged to you for ~~the~~ your expressions of confidence & encouragement in the performance of my duty & I shall hope to profit much by your advice on the Subject from time to time—I am arraying the Boards of Registration as fast as I can, though with the movement of the public mind in the direction of reconstruction under these acts I shall be in no hurry to complete the registration—Time is needed to bring the people to any thing like satisfactory reconstruction and I shall give the out & out Union party all the time I can under the law—I mean to appoint Boards of Registration to consist of two white white men & one negro, a fair arrangement as the Negro vote is less than the white—I think besides that this arrangement will keep many of the 'dignity party' who would otherwise register & vote against a convention, entirely aloof— They will not be willing to be questioned & cross examined ~~by~~ & compelled to take an oath administered by a darkey—In Alabama there is no doubt & there will be no trouble—It is rather mixed here yet but every thing seems to be working in the right direction—" ALS, *ibid.*, Letters Received. "I have the honor to transmit enclosed copies of a correspondence with Provisional Governor Charles I Jenkins of Georgia—I have concluded in view of a lengthened conversation with Governor Jenkins to take no further action in his case for the present. I think it judicious to retain in office the present civil officers in Georgia most of whom are still rebels provided they can be restrained from using any influences to prevent the people from complying with the acts of Congress & so long as they administer the laws with impartiality & justice—By this arrangement they will be prevented from doing the injury to the cause of Reconstruction that they might do if allowed in an unofficial capacity to take an active part in the political discussions which will arise in the progress of registration & election As soon as I find that they are not thus restrained I will remove them [fr]om office & if necessary bring them to trial—I shall in a few days publish an order prohibiting the newspapers or speakers in their discussions about the policy of Reconstruction under the late acts of Congress, from abusing or denouncing the Govt or any of its Departments or using personal epithets or misrepresentation personally of any officer of the U. S. Government for any acts done in performance of his duty In fact from any abuse whatever that may tend to weaken the authority or bring into contempt or excite any feeling of ill-will toward any such officer" ALS, *ibid.*, RG 94, Letters Received, 865M 1867. The enclosures are *ibid.*

On May 8, Pope wrote to Bvt. Maj. Gen. John A. Rawlins. "I need two or three good detective officers in this District to keep me posted about matters in the interior which I am not otherwise able to ascertain—Such officers are not to be had in this Country & I have the honor to request that they be sent me as soon as practicable—I presume the War Dept knows of & could send me the men and I would be greatly benefitted in the performance of my duties if they could be sent at once" ALS, *ibid.*, RG 108, Letters Received.

On May 13, USG wrote to Pope. Carnegie Book Shop, Catalogue 310 [1969], no. 170. On May 16, Pope twice wrote to USG. "I am just in receipt of your note of the 13th enclosing papers &c in relation to Taxes, in Florida, & the letter of Mr Richards—I have long since forbidden the State Government of Florida to pay any money out of the State Treasury for ~~payment of~~ pensions or other purposes for the benefit of soldiers of the Rebel Army or their families—The State Treasurer is held responsible that no such payments are made on any body's order & he is notified that no vouchers for such payments will be passed to his credit—He has been farther notified that a failure to comply strictly with these instructions will ensure his being tried by Military Commission—I do not think it advisable to arrest or interfere with the collection of Taxes in any of the States, but will take care that no money thus collected is appropriated to such purposes as are mentioned in Mr Richard's letter—" "I have the honor to acknowledge the receipt of a petition of certain Citizens of Florida addressed to you and asking a general removal of the Civil Officers of that State for reasons therein Set forth.— In many opinions your petitioners are mistaken.—1st The Reconstruction Acts retain in office the present State Officers except in cases where they obstruct the law or fail to administer it faithfully. It is only provided that in all elections held under the Provisional State Govts. certain persons Shall and Shall not be eligible to office. This provision applies to future elections and not to the present Status. 2nd The Military power has been established for the express purpose of Seeing that the laws are fairly and equally administered and any failure to do So on the part of any Civil Official need only to be reported to be corrected and the Offender punished. 3rd. So far from Sharing the belief of your petitioners that the removal of the civil officers in Florida would strengthen the Union Sentiment and increase the prospect of Success of reconstructio[n] in that State, I am decidedly of opinion that the very reverse would be the fact. The dismissal from Office of So large a number of Civil Officers without charges of Offence actually committed would Simply make Martyrs to what will be called Military Despotism of a large number of influential persons and introduce them into the political campaign of this Autumn with greater activity and influence than they ever had before. Retained in Office and Silenced on these questions they are harmless. Any neglect of duty or wrong done to any person by these Officers will be at once corrected and punished by the Military Authorities.—I think the measures being perfected and carried out for the States in this District will result in putting the State Governments in all their Departments into the hands of loyal men and in a manner to give them assured possession.—Over zeal or the indulgence of feelings natural well warrented and to be respected as they deserve to be, will lead to difficulty if not indeed to disaster in the attempt to Secure a great and final result. I hope the earnest Union men of Florida have by this time begun to See that they are not more determined than I am on this Subject, and I trust that they will recognize that the measures being put in operation are well calculated to Secure the most Satisfactory results." ALS and LS, DNA, RG 108, Letters Received. See *PUSG*, 15, 403, 408–12.

1. Possibly on April 17, Pope had written to USG. "I have the honor to transmit enclosed a copy of an order which it is my purpose to publish as soon as I have ascertained from Provisional Governor Jenkins whether at the time he issued his address to the people of this State he had seen or had knowledge of my Order No 1 The course of Governor Jenkins is disapproved and deprecated by every man in the State who favors reconstruction. It is doing great injury by

keeping the people disturbed and uncertain what to do and in arresting the general movement which was going on for active participation in re-establishing the State Government. In addition to this I am mainly concerned in the total neglect of his duties and the embarrassment in the execution of the laws and the maintenance of good order arising from the fact that there is no L't Governor and no one in the State who can act for him   Already it has been necessary to interfere with the military authorities to arrest the execution of a man who was recommended to Executive Clemency by both Judge and Jury but who would inevitably have been hanged because the Provisional Governor had absented himself and was not present to perform his duties. Provisional Governor Jenkins course in attempting to make Georgia a party to a suit without authority of law and without the consent of either Legislature or people is creating great disatisfaction, and is embarrassing me very much in the performance of my duty   His address to the people of this State advising them to take no action under the late acts of Congress and denouncing these acts in a manner to excite ill feeling if not actual disturbance in their execution is a positive violation of my Order No 1 and if not promptly noticed will render that order null and of no effect and at once array the whole army of State Officials against the execution of these Acts. The ill effects of permitting the whole power of the Provisional State Government through all its civil departments and in all its ramifications to be used to frustrate the acts of Congress and to keep up the disturbed condition of the public mind cannot be overstated. No reconstruction is possible and it will be next to impossible to secure faithful administration of the laws while such influences are allowed to go on unchecked unless the entire Civil government is overthrown and the military substituted. I deem it of the last importance to arrest it now in the person of Provisional Governor Jenkins. If he is permitted to set authority at defiance it will be useless to notice such offences committed by the minor officers. I shall wait until the receipt of this letter and order is acknowledged which I request may be done by telegraph when if I am not restrained I will then publish and execute the order" LS (undated), DNA, RG 94, Letters Received, 862M 1867. The enclosures, a printed letter of April 10 from Governor Charles J. Jenkins of Ga., Washington, D. C., to the people of Ga. and unnumbered Special Orders, Third Military District, April 17, removing Jenkins from office, are *ibid.* On April 20, Pope telegraphed to USG. "The explanation made by Govr. Jenkins & his assurances for the future are satisfactory & render unnecessary any further consideration of the order I sent you by mail—" Telegram received (at 10:45 A.M.), *ibid.,* RG 108, Telegrams Received; copies, *ibid.,* RG 94, Letters Received, 863M 1867; *ibid.,* 1109M 1867; DLC-USG, V, 55. On April 22, USG endorsed these papers. "Respectfully forwarded to the Secretary of War for his information. The telegraphic dispatch herein enclosed shows that Gov. Jenkins of Georgia has given such pledges to the commander of the 3d District as to induce him to withhold, for the present, his order suspending the Governor. The conduct of Gov. Jenkins demonstrates, however, how possible it is for discontented civil officers of the reconstructed States to defeat the laws of Congress if the power does not exist with District Commanders to suspend their functions for cause, in some way. It seems clear to me that the power is given in the Bill 'for the more efficient government of the rebel States', to use or not, at the pleasure of District Commanders, the *provisional* machinery set up, without the authority of Congress, in the States to which the reconstruction Act applies. There being doubt, however, on this point, I would respectfully ask an early opinion on the subject. If the power of removal does not exist with District Command'rs, then it will become necessary for them to take refuge under that section of the Bill which authorizes Military Commissions." ES, DNA, RG 94, Letters Received, 862M 1867.

To Maj. Gen. Philip H. Sheridan

Private   Washington, D. C.
                                                              Apl. 21st 1867.

My Dear General,

As yet no decission has been given ~~yet~~ by the Atty. Gn. on the subject of the right of District Commanders to remove civil officers and appoint their successors. It is likely however that he will give attention to that subject, and all other questions submitted to him arrising under the reconstruction act, as soon as he is through with the Mississippi motion to file a bill of injunction against certain parties to restrain them from executing the laws of Congress.[1] In the mean time I would advise that in case any of the Civil officers obstruct the laws they be suspended, and tried by Military Commission. This right certainly does exist on the part of District Commanders, and I have no doubt myself on the subject of their powers to remove arbitrarily. The lawmakers clearly contemplated providing Military governments for the rebel states until they were fully restored in all their relations to the general government. They evidently only recognized present state governments as provisional, for convenience, to be made use of by District Commanders just so far as they could be used in carrying out the will of Congress, and no further.

Many questions have arisen out of different interpretations given to the meaning of different sections of the re-construction Act, all of which have been submitted to the Atty. Gen. and will receive his attention soon.—On the subject of who can register, under the law, I think it was the intention to exclude only those who are excluded from holding office, under the Constitutional Amendment, and those who have been previously disfranchised for infamous crime, such as were recognized before the rebellion as sufficient cause for disfranchisement. Of course there is no greater crime than that of attempting to overthrow the government. But that is the particular crime which is forgiven by the re-construction Act, except to certain offenders who are supposed, from their previous relations ~~with~~ to the general government, to be more guilty than the rest. The supplementary bill, particularly the oath ~~provided~~ prescribed to be taken, before registration, would seem to provide for the disfranchisement of a class of Citizens that ought always to be disfranchised, in every community, for their gross violation of law, and could not have been intended as a further punishment, or the punishment of other classes, for the crime of treason against the government.—By the same rule of judging I do not think that a class of Citizens who heretofore have not had the elective franchise can be excluded for acts which would have disfranchised them had they ~~heretofore~~ possessed the privilege of voting.

I give this only as my views on the subject. If I were commanding a District however I would require registering officers to keep two lists. On one I would register the names of all about whose right to register there could be no doubt, and on the other all those about whom there might be doubt.

There has ~~been~~ nothing new transpired affecting you. I think your head is safe above your shoulders, at least so that it can not be taken off to produce pain.

Yours Truly
U. S. GRANT

To MAJ. GN. P. H. SHERIDAN
COMD.G 5TH DIST.

P. S. Did you receive a private letter written by me a few weeks since?

U. S. G.

ALS, DLC-Philip H. Sheridan. On April 26, 1867, Maj. Gen. Philip H. Sheridan, New Orleans, wrote to USG. "*Private* . . . Your note of the 21st instant. came this morning: the previous one of April 5th was duly received; but, I have been so busy that I did not answer it. In reference to the right to remove from office, I did not doubt it for a moment: and do not yet doubt it: in fact the Military Bill is a cipher unless this right is given. When I made the removals I first looked at the law and then at the Presidents veto and did not for a moment doubt the right. The moment that the office holders here find out I have not the power to remove them; that moment they become defiant and I lose nearly all my strength: They will use their official positions to influence elections, and will, to some extent, carry them. The North will make a mistake if they allow themselves to be deceived by the late apparent change in sentiment in these States. It is as deceptive as ever and if the elections are carried the cloven foot will again be shown in all probability. In this city they supposed at first that the colored vote could be managed; but it cannot, and there are now indications that they will give up the contest for the city: in fact they now want to compromise. In reference to the classes disfranchised, I have applied the provisions of their own State Constitution to the Military Bill: if my judgement is in error, the corrections can at once be made on the receipt of the authoritative decision. I have rejected all doubtful cases; but give them a chance to register, in case the decision of the Attorney General will permit. So far as oaths are concerned, there is not much conscience here. Men who have held high judicial positions before the Rebellion; and during the Rebellion have taken the oath to support the Confederacy; think nothing of taking the prescribed oath of the Military Bill, when it comes to the question of holding office: in fact they will not hesitate taking the 'Iron Clad' oath of 1862. There is much demoralization in reference to oaths, and they are taken, to a great extent, as they were during the Rebellion. So in registration, it is necessary to question closely, and adopt every precaution to prevent fraud   The simple test of submitting the oath, will not do; it would be taken as a thirsty man would take a drink of lemonade   I am getting along well, and with but little annoyance, considering the complicated state of affairs here. Throckmorton has taken in his horns, and Wells still annoys me by creating new issues having only his own personal interest involved   I sincerely thank you general for your support, & beg of you to believe that your interests are mine, as they always have been, & that all I desire is to be your faithful friend & assistant" LS, USG 3.

On April 21, Sheridan had written to USG. "I issued my order for the registration of the State of Louisiana yesterday, giving until the 30th June to accomplish the work. Should I not be able to accomplish it in that period an extension of the time will be given   I anticipate no trouble in the work: the people generally will register. I have in no way sought by consultations with governors, legislatures or public assemblies, to mould the public mind by such political machinery, to an acceptance or non-acceptance of the law; but, I have given them clearly to understand that the law would be enforced and the reorganization accomplished and I believe my course is not unacceptable to the majority of the people in the State. By pursuing this course I am freed, as I ought to be, from any just charge of giving partizan support. My only desire is to faithfully carry out the law as a Military order. Some of the public prints in the city are loud in denouncing the Boards of Registrars here: but it is unjust. There has been, from the developements already made, the most unparalleled frauds in the voting here in this city, and I am now not surprised at the conduct of some of the best citizens here in never voting, or that bad men should have ruled in the city Government   In the appointment of Registrars for the State, I have in nearly every case selected two citizens, residents of the Parish, and one

Ex-Army Officer from the city of New Orleans. This gives me a check on each board by having a good and tried man as Chairman of each. Then in addition I have the boards supervised by intelligent army officers. I deem this caution necessary for many good reasons. The Attorney General should not hamper me too much: no one can conceive or estimate, at so great a distance, the precautions necessary to be taken in the present condition of society here." LS, DNA, RG 108, Letters Received. On May 8, USG endorsed a copy of this letter. "Respectfully forw'd to the Secretary of War for his information" ES, DLC-Andrew Johnson. USG also forwarded to Secretary of War Edwin M. Stanton other official messages from Sheridan. On April 24, 1:30 P.M., Sheridan telegraphed to USG. "The registration is going on quietly & with fairness. The General condition of affairs in this state is good" Telegram received (at 8:30 P.M.), DNA, RG 107, Telegrams Collected (Bound); *ibid.*, RG 108, Telegrams Received; copies, *ibid.*, RG 46, Senate 40A–F5, War Dept. Messages; DLC-USG, V, 55; (2) DLC-Philip H. Sheridan; DLC-Edwin M. Stanton. Maj. George K. Leet noted on a telegram received. "Mr. Tinker will please send this telegram to Phil. Care Gen. Meade & oblige" AN (marked 10:00 A.M.), DNA, RG 108, Telegrams Received. On May 4, Sheridan telegraphed to USG. "The registration in the city & in the state is progressing very well The proportion of colored voters registered in the city is much in excess of the white for the reason that the colored people are excited & crowd the registration offices. The white people preferring to wait until the colored people finish their registration when they will register politicaians are trying to make it appear that the few white voters registered is on account of the stringency in registration but this is not the case The white people are waiting until the colored get through It must not be disguised however that quite a large number of whites will not register because they do not like the military bill." Telegrams received (2—at 4:40 P.M.), *ibid.*, RG 107, Telegrams Collected (Bound); *ibid.*, RG 108, Telegrams Received; copies, *ibid.*, RG 46, Senate 40A–F5, War Dept. Messages; (2—one sent by mail) *ibid.*, RG 107, Letters Received from Bureaus; DLC-USG, V, 55; (2) DLC-Philip H. Sheridan; DLC-Edwin M. Stanton.

On May 7, Stanton wrote to USG. "In General Sheridans order relating to the registering of voters in the Parish of New Orleans, he directs that the registry must be completed by the 15th of this month. The President is of opinion that the time allowed by General Sheridans order, as above mentioned, is too short for a full and fair registry and that so much of said order as limits the registry to the 15th of May should be rescinded You will please communicate this to Major General Sheridan." ALS, DNA, RG 393, 5th Military District, Letters Received; ADfS, DLC-Edwin M. Stanton. On May 9, 10:30 A.M., USG telegraphed to Sheridan. "The President, thinks the 15th of May too short a time for the registration of voters in the Parish of Orleans and thinks so much of the order as limits registration to that date should be rescinded." ALS (telegram sent), DNA, RG 107, Telegrams Collected (Bound); telegram sent, *ibid.*; telegram received, *ibid.*, RG 393, 5th Military District, Telegrams Received. On May 10, 10:30 A.M., Sheridan telegraphed to USG. "I have the honor to acknowledge the receipt of your cipher telegram of the ninth (9th) I had already extended the time in the City until the thirty first (31st) of May" Telegram received (at 1:30 P.M.), *ibid.*, RG 107, Telegrams Collected (Bound); *ibid.*, RG 108, Telegrams Received; copies (misdated May 18), *ibid.*, RG 46, Senate 40A–F5, War Dept. Messages; (dated May 10) *ibid.*, RG 107, Letters Received from Bureaus;

DLC-USG, V, 55; (3—one misdated May 18) DLC-Philip H. Sheridan; DLC-Edwin M. Stanton; DLC-Andrew Johnson. Misdated May 18 in *SED*, 40-1-14, p. 207; *HED*, 40-1-20, p. 75.

On May 9, President Andrew Johnson wrote to Stanton. "The Secretary of War will please furnish the President with copies of all orders issued or instructions given to General Sheridan, relating to the discharge of his duties since his assignment to the command of the Fifth District, created by an act entitled 'An act to provide for the more efficient government of the Rebel States" Copies, DLC-Andrew Johnson; DNA, RG 108, Letters Received. On the same day, USG wrote to Stanton. "In pursuance of directions received this day I have to honor to forward the enclosed orders, and dispatches, sent from these Hd Qrs. to the Commander of the 5th District, and such dispatches from Gen. Sheridan as called forth replies." ALS, DLC-Andrew Johnson. The enclosures are *ibid.*

At 1:10 P.M., USG telegraphed to Sheridan. "What has been done in Walkers case? Please send report of ~~ease~~ proceedings before executing sentence." ALS (telegram sent), DNA, RG 107, Telegrams Collected (Bound); telegram sent, *ibid.*; telegram received, *ibid.*, RG 393, 5th Military District, Telegrams Received. On May 10, 11:00 A.M., Sheridan telegraphed to USG. "The proceedings in the case of Walker will be forwarded today & the execution of the Sentence deferred until further orders. He was sentenced to hard labor at Ship Island for six months for shooting a freedman with shot—This had been the third case in the neighborhood of shooting with shot guns, the object being not to kill—that was too much risk—but to punish severely" Telegram received (at 2:00 P.M.), DLC-Andrew Johnson; DNA, RG 107, Telegrams Collected (Bound); *ibid.*, RG 108, Telegrams Received; copies, *ibid.*, RG 94, Letters Received, 1103M 1867; (sent by mail) *ibid.*, RG 108, Letters Received; DLC-USG, V, 55; (2) DLC-Philip H. Sheridan; DLC-Edwin M. Stanton.

Also on May 10, Sheridan telegraphed to USG. "The bitterness which has existed in this city for the last two weeks about the street car question has subsided I advised the Companies to make no distinction as there was no law state or municipal to support them and that ultimately the colored people would be permitted to ride in any car. This view they cheerfully adopted and the excitement died out at once—There is no trouble now—" Telegram received (at 6:00 P.M.), DNA, RG 107, Telegrams Collected (Bound); (2) *ibid.*, RG 108, Telegrams Received; copies, *ibid.*, RG 46, Senate 40A–F5, War Dept. Messages; (sent by mail) *ibid.*, RG 108, Letters Received; DLC-USG, V, 55; (2) DLC-Philip H. Sheridan; DLC-Edwin M. Stanton. On May 11, Sheridan wrote to Bvt. Maj. Gen. John A. Rawlins. "I have the honor to enclose herewith copies of orders given for the distribution of troops in the State of Louisiana, pending registration and voting under the 'Military bill'" LS, DNA, RG 108, Letters Received. The enclosures are *ibid.* On the same day, Sheridan telegraphed to USG. "The reports of the progress of registration from the different parishes in this State are now coming in & indicate that the machinery is in good working order—I have to contend with all kinds of attempted fraud in this City today I have to dismiss the clerk of the 5th District Court for issuing false certificates of naturalization & the same thing has been done in one other & in perhaps all of the courts, but I have been too sharp for them—I will go to Texas with Porter & Babcock tomorrow Will be back in about six days" Telegrams received (2—at 3:00 P.M.), *ibid.*, RG 107, Telegrams Collected (Bound); *ibid.*, RG 108, Telegrams Received; copies, *ibid.*, RG 46, Senate 40A–F5, War Dept. Messages; *ibid.*, RG 94,

Letters Received, 748M 1867; *ibid.*, 1108M 1867; DLC-USG, V, 55; (2) DLC-Philip H. Sheridan; DLC-Edwin M. Stanton.

On April 13, Leet had written to Bvt. Brig. Gen. Orville E. Babcock, sending an identical letter to Bvt. Brig. Gen. Horace Porter. "You will proceed in company with Bvt. Brig. Gen'l Horace Porter, Aide de Camp, without delay to the principal posts in each of the Military Districts of the South, inspect the present quarters of the troops, and direct each District Commander to cause careful estimates to be made for the erection of suitable barracks for all the permanent garrisons in his command. Upon the completion of this duty you will make the inspections designated in your verbal instructions, after which you will rejoin these Headquarters" Copies, DLC-USG, V, 47, 60; DNA, RG 108, Letters Sent. On May 10, Babcock, New Orleans, wrote to Col. Adam Badeau. "The Genl wished us to inform him from time to time about the reconstruction of the south &c We have been on such constant motion that we could find no good time to report, and besides we needed to see a considerable of the South before we could draw any comparisons We found Schofield progressing with his work in a very satisfactory manner. The negroes in Va. seem to be all employed on the plantations and a good prospect for a crop. The negro is learning very fast. they will soon be the best educated *class* in the South, if they continue at their present rate of progress. In North Carolina we saw more evidence of prosperity than in Va. and perhaps more than in any other Southern state we have been in. Gen Sickles seems to be master of the position and is hard at work. South Carolina will be one of the first to come into ranks. The good union people in N. C. and S. C. though a small number, seem to wish to aid Genl S. In Ga. Fla &. Ala. things do not look as well, especially Ga & Fla. This Mil Dist is far behind either of the others we have visited. In Ga. the police in most of the cities are in a grey uniform, the real *confederate* uniform. You will see the uniform very often. The 'Lost Cause,' ~~you~~ one would think would soon be saved. In Fla we found the people generally very quiet and indifferent—In fact the state seems a great way behind each of the other states in all general matters. It took us four days to go from Savannah to Tallahassee and find the Head Qrs of the Dist of Fla. We had to ride 40 miles in a buggy or wait 4 2 days to get to St Augustine. No Telegraph. On our arrival we found the Hd Qrs. but the Comdg officer had gone to Atlanta—Tallahassee is the place for the Hd Qrs of the Dist—It might as well be at Key West as where it now is. Except St Augustine is a pleasant place to live,—We found Genl Pope at Atlanta. He is satisfied with his progress. We went after two oclock and he had gone to his house. we called there but he asked to be excused without seeing our card so we did not see him but once. I asked him why Col Sprague's Hd Qrs and Col Sibley were not at the Capitol of the State as he had said in his letter they were to be. He said he had changed his mind—He complains of the quality of the officers under him, especially the younger line officers.—We went to Macon, and found a nice camp, and all progressing well there. At Montgomery Ala. we met Genl Swayne. He makes a more favorable report than either of the other Dist Commanders in the 3rd Mil Dist He is at the Capital of the State where he can take advantage of the machinery of the civil government and can accomplish more than in any other place in the State. I think Each Dist. that is Sub Dist. Commander should be placed at the Capitals of the states. The sooner the better. Alabama shows less damage from the war than any other portion of the South we have visited. I am fully satisfied of two things. First, The Negro will vote the right ticket notwithstanding the attempt of his old master to convince him that he is his best friend—Second. The amt of suffering by starvation is very much exagerated. In some of the states there is a great scarcity of food. I have been unable to hear of a single authenticated case of starvation. In this state I would judge the registration and work of reconstruction is going on finely. Two citizens of each parish and an ex officer form Each parish board. Genl Pope thinks he is going to do the thing up by putting a Negro on each board. I question the propriety for he cannot find Negroes of sufficient education to do the work, and they must become ornamental members of the board. Time will decide all of this. Genl Pope very much desires Genl Kelton be sent to him as his Asst. Adjt Genl. We promised to do all we could for him. Genl Sheridan is quite well, that is he looks quite well, but I think there is no doubt but the climate is undermining his health. He will not admit it but I think he will be obliged to do so before the year ends. We start (with Genl Sheridan), tomorrow for Texas.—Genl Sheridan and all the people here made enquiries about the Genl and family. We meet a great many people who enquire after Badeau, and 'when will his book be out'? McAlister of the Engineers, says Palfrey writes to him that Comstock is anxious to get away from Head Qrs. Weitzel told Palfrey. Remember us to Genl and Mrs Grant, Rawlins, Leet, Dent &c &c. You may leave out the people at 397, 20th St. Many thanks for your kindness to Mrs B. 'Your kindness I never shall forget'." ALS, USG 3. Late in May, Porter wrote to Badeau. "We returned to this city last night, after having visited Galveston, Brazos, and Brownsville, Texas. This is, by far, the worst State in the Union, and it is only by the adoption of strict and decided measures that it is kept from giving a great deal of trouble. Griffin is doing as well as any man could in his position. It is hard for persons at a distance to understand the difficulties that surround him. His order requiring jurymen to take an oath of loyalty was promulgated after mature deliberation, and should be sustained. It was not intended to force negroes upon juries, but only loyal men. Gen. Sheridan accompanied us to Galveston, but returned the same day to N. Orleans, upon hearing of a probable riot. He wants to be on hand now upon all such interesting occasions. Everything, however, is quiet here. The registration is progressing rapidly, and fairly. It will be completed in this State early in June. Texas will require a longer time   Sheridan is greatly respected by all classes, though the editors will occasionally enter upon a not very flattering biography of him. One paper says it is no use trying to make him the hero of a battle, in the Valley which had already been won by Wright, and endeavoring to make a 'fast ride' out of a 'damned slow walk.' He thinks he can survive all this, however. Kelley was not half as much to blame at Mobile as we at first supposed. The Chivalry carried out a preconcerted plan to break up his meeting, and by interruptions and insulting remarks spurred him on to using the violent language he uttered. Then a general attack was made upon the stand. Sheridan gets this report, which he deems authentic." Copy, DNA, RG 94, Letters Received, 345P 1867. On May 30, USG endorsed this letter to Stanton. AES, *ibid.*

On May 18, Sheridan telegraphed to USG. "I have the honor to report my return from Galveston. Genl Griffin issued his orders for registration while I was there and the machinery is now in full operation in Texas   There has been some excitement in NewOrleans during my absence but without much political significance—it was a strike on part of Colored laborers which produced a stampede and consequent exaggeration—all is now quiet & will continue so—The night before I arrived at Galveston there was some little trouble at a political meeting but of little significance or importance   Genl's Porter & Babcock have gone to the Rio Grande"   Telegram received (at 5:00 P.M.), *ibid.*, RG 107, Telegrams Collected (Bound); *ibid.*, RG 108, Telegrams Received; copies, *ibid.*, RG 46, Senate 40A–F5, War Dept. Messages; DLC-USG, V, 55; (2) DLC-Philip H. Sheridan; DLC-Andrew Johnson. Stanton noted on a copy of this telegram. "Read to President in Cabinet May 23 1867 (extra session)" ANS, DNA, RG 94, Letters Received, 978M 1867.

1. See Charles Fairman, *Reconstruction and Reunion 1864–88* (New York and London, 1971), I, 374–91.

To Charles W. Ford

Apl. 28th *1867*.

Dear Ford;

Enclosed I send you a deed for some land which I purchased from Mrs. Casey which I wish you would have recorded and the deed returned to me.

I have written to you several times lately but do not recollect whether I answered your request to get some of the trading posts authorized by resolution of Congress? The previous Congress abolished the office of Sutler, to take effect July 1st 1867. Some of these Sutlers having a good thing of it which they did not want to give up, and believing me more pliable than the Sec. of War, got the resolution passed through Congress leaving it discretionary with me to continue *traders* at Military posts West of 100° W. Longitude. I do not intend to continue one of them unless on the report of Post Commanders of the necessity ~~of~~ for continuing them.[1]

I have not yet been called on for the $2000 00 which you had drawn on me for.[2] Will probably be to-morrow however.

Yours Truly
U. S. Grant

ALS, DLC-USG.

1. See *PUSG*, 16, 75–76; endorsement to Edwin M. Stanton, March 18, 1867; *U.S. Statutes at Large*, XIV, 336; *ibid.*, XV, 29. On March 28, 1867, George F. Hooper, San Francisco, wrote to USG. "I have the honor to state that in the year 1846, 1847, & 1848 that I was in the Military Service of the U. S. both

as a Volunteer & a 2d Lieut in the 15th Infty then on duty in Mexico, that from January "52 continuously until the present time I have held & now hold the appointment of Sutler at Fort Yuma, that in & about that business I have erected permanent improvements, consisting of buildings & store houses, at an expense of from $5000. to $6000.—That Francis Hinton of the firm of Geo F Hooper & Co, of which the undersigned is the senior member, now occupies & for the past year has held the position of Sutler at Camp McDowell Arizona Territory. That said Hinton was for upwards of a period of 5 years a member of the 1st Reg't of U. S. Dragoons. That by recent action had in Congress I am advised that from & after the 1st day of July next ensuing the office of Sutler is to be abolished   I am also advised that a joint resolution has passed Congress authorizing Military Commanders to permit Traders upon the line of Emigration to remain on Government Reservations. As emigrants are constantly passing & repassing the Military Reserve at Fort Yuma as well also at Camp McDowell. That such emigrants require to be supplied with provisions & other necessaries, I would therefore respectfully ask that I may be permitted to remain at Fort Yuma as a Trader, & that my partner Francis Hinton may be allowed to remain at Camp McDowell as a Trader subject to Military rules & regulations at said posts respectively." ALS, DNA, RG 108, Letters Received.

On April 8, Capt. and Bvt. Lt. Col. Thomas C. Williams, 19th Inf., *et al.*, Fort Gibson, Indian Territory, wrote to USG. "We the undersingned Officers of the 19th U. S. Infantry stationed at the military Post of Fort Gibson, in the Indian Territory, would most respectfully solicit the appointment of Mr J. S. Evans as 'Trader' at this Post. We are induced to make this request from the fact, that, under an act of congress abolishing Sutlers in the Army after 1st of July, 1867, the prices of articles required for Officer's use and wear, will be greatly enhanced, if not, in many instances, entirely beyond our reach. Stationed as we are in the Indian Country, there are no Express Companies represented here, and past experience has Taught us, that the means of obtaining articles from the States, constantly needed, are altogether unsafe and unreliable. Mr Evans has been trading at this Post for the past six months in the capacity of Sutler, and has given us entire satisfaction, and we beleive him to be a thorough gentleman, and fully deserving of the appointment we now solicit at your hands." DS (thirteen signatures), *ibid.*

On April 10, U.S. Delegates Allen A. Bradford (39th Congress) and George M. Chilcott (40th Congress), Colorado Territory, wrote to USG. "We respectfully ask that F W Portoff Esq be permitted to maitain a *trading* establishment after the first day of July eighteen hundred and sixty seven at the Military Post of Fort Garland Colorado Territory,   Said Post is not in the vicinity of a City or Town and we believe that a trading posts establishment at said Fort is needed for the accomadation of emigrants freighter and other cities   We take pleasue in recommending Mr Portoff as a gentleman of the strictest integrity and well qualified to conduct such an establishment" LS, *ibid.*

On April 15, Robert Wilson, Denver, Colorado Territory, wrote to USG. "Understanding that a Military Post is about being established at or near Pueblo, on Arkansas River Col. Ter. I respectfully apply to you for the position of Sutler. I have been Sutler at Fort Karney Neb Ter. Fort Hall Utah, Forts Dalls & Vancouver in Oregon, and for ten (10) years previous to 1864 at Fort Riley Kansas— I have addressed letters to Genl I N Palmer Genl P St Geo Cook. Genl James Totten Genl Sturgess. Genl Sackett and Genl Denver—asking their reccomendations to you. All these Officers were acquainted with me during my Sutlership and I feel confident will endorse me favourably. As soon as these documents are returned, with endorsements, I will forward them to you. Soliciting your favourable consideration of this application . . ." ALS, *ibid*. On the same day, Wilson wrote to James W. Denver concerning the appointment. ALS, *ibid*. On April 30, Denver, Washington, D. C., endorsed this letter. "Respectfully submitted to Gen. U. S. Grant with the remark that if Mr. Wilson is correct as to the law, the undersigned would regard it as a personal favor if he will grant Mr. Wilson his request. PayMaster Gen. Brice is well acquainted with Mr. Wilson." AES, *ibid*.

On April 20, Lt. Gen. William T. Sherman, St. Louis, wrote to Maj. George K. Leet. "I have the honor to acknowledge receipt of a letter from General Grant, concerning the appointment of Traders at Posts west of the 100th Parallel.—I have made a Circalar, which will be sent out at once, and which I think will accomplish what the General wants.—I would entertain no application unless made by parties on the spot, for the General will otherwise be flooded by applications of every adventurer, hanging about, for something to turn up.—The Post Commanders on the spot can regulate trading at their own posts, easily, to satisfy all reasonable demands of trade." LS, *ibid*. On May 2, Leet wrote to Sherman. "General Grant directs me to acknowledge the receipt of your letter of April 20th, with accompanying Circular relative to the appointment of Traders at Military Posts, under the Resolution of Congress approved March 30th, 1867, and to say that what he desires to ascertain more particularly, from the Commanding Officers of the Posts where such Traders are authorized, is, whether it will be necessary to have Traders at all after the 1st of July next, If they are needed he thinks those who have been sutlers, should have the preference." Copies, DLC-USG, V, 47, 60; DNA, RG 108, Letters Sent.

2. On April 19, USG had telegraphed to Charles W. Ford, St. Louis. "Pay Mr. Dent Two Thousand (2000) dollars & draw on me. I will settle the balance soon." ALS (telegram sent), *ibid*., RG 107, Telegrams Collected (Bound).

To Lt. Gen. William T. Sherman

Apl. 29th *1867*.

DEAR GENERAL;

On my return from Philadelphia I found your letter of the 20th inst.[1] I understand well the embarassment Seward's letter places you under, and how little you have to thank him for it. I would advise you however to make no difference on account of that letter, but on the first occasion let it be understood that you are making your first trip to Europe, dont know when another opportunity will present itself, have but a short time to stay, and want to see as much of the country as possible in the time at your disposal. I would feel myself under no obligation to return civilities further than to return ~~calls~~ cards to such as call.

With a leave of absence you would lose all your rations for commanding a Division, and one half the balance. This I intended to obviate however by ordering you here, when the time came, and then getting permission for you to delay returning to your command for the time you wish to be absent, with authority to go beyond the United States. There will be no difficulty about this I imagine and it will give you full pay and allowances.

I have been spending a very pleasant week in Phila. I would prefer a trip on the plains however to these excursions which give a person neither day nor night for rest.

My kindest regards to Mrs. Sherman and the children.

Yours Truly

U. S. GRANT

To LT. GN. SHERMAN

ALS, DLC-William T. Sherman. See letter to Lt. Gen. William T. Sherman, May 23, 1867. On May 3, 1867, Lt. Gen. William T. Sherman, St. Louis, wrote to USG. "I have yours of April 29 and if you can without making a troublesome precedent fulfill your plan as to me to save half pay, it will be a most timely help. I had figured on losing commutation and half pay, reckoning that Mrs Sherman could keep the family on the remainder, and to use some $2500 of other money that I had laid by for the children for the European trip, on the theory that the whole would be chargeable to Minnie for education. But if you can with propriety leave me in ~~full~~ possession of full pay I will be easy & snug in finances. I will go up next week to Fort Leavenworth, Riley & Harker, to meet Gen Hancock & talk over his matters   I have no doubt he can cover the progress of the Union Pacific Railroad this summer, so that the Company may finish the 200 miles contracted for, but the terrible extent of the Country and apparent ease with which the Indians hide, we must always expect such dashes as occurred at Lookout Station. I will be back here May 20, and will then seriously begin to think of the 'Excursion'. If all is as well as can be expected, I ought to leave here Sunday June 2, reach Washington Tuesday, & NewYork Thursday, to embark Saturday June 8 the day appointed. A Miss Linton daughter of Doctor Linton of this City will go with Minnie. Of course I can come to Washington with advantage, and only lose one or two days in time to NewYork, but at this City (NewYork) I have nothing to do which I may not accomplish in one business day. I was in hopes ere this to have something positive from Fort Buford. Boats by the dozen have passed Omaha for the Upper Missouri, but the season has been very backward. Hancock had snow on the Arkansas as late as Apl 23, and on the Upper Missouri the weather in March & April was as bad as in Mid Winter.   An official letter sent you yesterday from Genl Terry explains why he utterly discredits the rumor of disaster, and how he accounts for the non receipt of a mail from Col Rankin. I will be sure to advise you by telegraph of the first definite news that reach me. Mrs Sherman begs me to thank you specially for your kind message to her and she sends in return her warmest acknowledgmts. Present me kindly to Mrs Grant, and the members of your family." ALS, USG 3.

On March 21, Sherman had written to USG. "The parties in NewYork who are getting up that European trip, continue to urge me for a definite answer as doubtless some gentlemen will make their engagemts dependant on mine. All the wealth of creation wont tempt Mrs Sherman to cross salt water, but Minnie now sixteen, wants to go: but you observe it makes a difference on board a ship between a man & wife who occupy a single room, and a man & daughter who would be seperate. I have written to Capt Duncan that if his invitation may be construed as embracing me and my daughter Minnie I will go, provided the President will consent. You have given yours. Now I have conferred with Hancock who is all ready for his years work, and is only embarrassed by the necessity of garrisoning the Indian Country west of Arkansas, but in time we can fill up Hazens and Griersons new black Regimts and can spare enough to hold Gibson, & Arbuckle & patrol the country roundabout—Terry is here, and we have perfectly agreed upon what he has to do. I will go up to Omaha, by or before April 12, to see Genl Augur before he begins to act. So that I dont really think the public service will be damaged in the least by my absence. Still I have no right to think of going outside of the United States without the consent of the President and I would like to know before I make the formal request. Will you be kind enough to ascertain if he will consent to my going—say for 4½ months from June 1. next—on the express condition that I will be prepared to come back, on the shortest notice by the Atlantic Cable. I dont want to make the formal official application till in May, when I will know that all things are or are not working well. If the President or Secretary of war will simply say that there will be no objection if you are satisfied I could then give a positive answer to Capt Duncan, who has doubtless an interest to know for certain." ALS, *ibid.* On March 27, 11:25 A.M., USG telegraphed to Sherman. "The President authorizes me to grant the leave you propose asking for." ALS (telegram sent), DNA, RG 107, Telegrams Collected (Bound); telegram sent, *ibid.*; copies, *ibid.*, RG 108, Telegrams Sent; DLC-USG, V, 56. On March 28, Sherman wrote to USG. "I received your despatch last evning saying that the President had authorized you to grant me the leave I proposed to ask for. I will therefore notify Capt Duncan to count me in. I suppose you have seen a paragraph copied from a Chicago paper saying that a letter had been received there that the Indians are reported as having massacred all the Garrison at Fort Buford Jan 15. It so happens that our latest dates from that Post are to Jan 13—two days before the massacre is reported to have occurred. I can hardly credit the Report though I confess I am uneasy. Rankin had 88 men for duty, and had been threatened by the Sioux Decr 23, 4 & 5—but drove them off without loss to himself. He expressed himself confident of being able to defend himself, but wanted more men & some horses to enable him to go out & pursue. Terry designs to strengthen the Post to Five companies, but we cant get there till the ice moves out of the Missouri. All I propose for Terry is to make the line of the Missouri a kind of barrier, so that the Indians will not cross to its East, and to supply his posts, so as to afford supplies to any column that may reach the Missouri River from Augurs Command. I want Augurs troops

to act offensively from the direction of Laramie, Reno, and Phil Kearney. Apl 12, is the date fixed by himself (Augur,) to be all ready at Omaha, and I will be there by or before that date for conference.—I will then come back to St Louis, and afterwards go out on the Union Pacific RR to its terminus & on to Fort Harker to meet Gen Hancock, who is now off to look after the Cheyennes & Kioways. He expects to get back to Harker in May. By that time I can pretty well judge of the probabilities for the Summer, and can then make official application for a leave of absence, to embrace the time of the proposed absence of 4½ months, to date from June, the time fixed by Capt Duncan—As to myself I feel little enthusiasm for the trip, but I know it will be of immense advantage to Minnie, who has set her heart on it, and as it is about her only chance to travel I feel disposed to indulge her. But if in the meantime any thing occurs I can drop it."
ALS, DNA, RG 108, Letters Received.

1. On April 20, Sherman wrote to USG. "I got back yesterday and will write you fully & officially of General Augurs preperations & purposes.—I have noticed the prominence Capt Duncan has given to my proposed joining his excursion & especially that he has applied to Mr Seward, and procured a letter that puts the Quaker City on the footing of a national vessel, and me as willing and expecting public notice abroad. This so differs from my wishes that I feel strongly inclined to back square down and go with Augur up to the Sioux Country for the Summer, or to change destination to the Holy Land of Utah, our own 'Dead Sea'. I hardly know what to do or to say. Mr Sewards letter which I see in the newspapers *only*, is so kindly meant, so flattering, and so public that it embarrasses me beyond measure. He cannot know that when I apply for leave, which I have not yet done formally & officially, my pay falls down *one half*, or say to $7000. a year, which reduced to Gold & foreign money is less than 1000£ sterling. Now how can Mr Seward expect me to maintain a large family at home and abroad to accept public honors, that will bring me in contact with public men whose servants can eclipse me in dress, style & travel. The fact is I wanted to go in this excursion purposely for economy, and absence of display, hardly expected to put on my uniform, & hoped to glide along like any other modest citizen. I wish Mr Seward had first heard from me, before accrediting me abroad, for now I can hardly back out without occasioning surprise and disappointmt to others, and if I go, it is with a foreknowledge that foreign ministers, consuls, and officers ~~may~~ are expected to show me attentions that will absorb my time & subject me to associations that will humiliate me, unless I can equal them in external appliances. Poor Minnie has set her heart on it, and if I back out now she will be dreadfully disappointed, and yet if I go with Mr Sewards public manifesto I will hardly be able to attend to a child in foreign lands. You have often come to my relief in hard times. Can you now suggest any escape from this dilemma. I can borrow money enough, but when I get back there comes the hard scratch of saving to pay back. If forced to receive public attention I would far rather go *alone* with Commodore Alden in the splendid Minnesota that makes substantially the same voyage this Summer, but in her I could not take Minnie the real and chief object of going at all" ALS, *ibid*. On April 10, Secretary of State William H. Seward had written a circular letter to U.S. ministers, consuls, and consular agents authorizing special status for Sherman during his proposed trip. *National Intelligencer*, April 15, 1867.

To Maj. Gen. George H. Thomas

Washington, Apl. 30th *1867*.

DEAR GENERAL:

Your letter in relation to Gen. Cooke was duly received here during my absence in Phila. I do not think Gn. Cooke has any secret enemy here, working against him. I know nothing of the cause of his removal from duty during the rebellion. His last removal was not in consequence of any fault committed by him but because it was thought that Gn. Augur, being a much younger man, would be much better able to conduct an active campaign, in person, than Gn. Cooke. Hostilities were, and are, threatened in the Dept. from which he was relieved. The right to select commanders for important service was acted upon.

Yours Truly,

U. S. GRANT

To GN. G. H. THOMAS,
LOUISVILLE, KY.

ALS, ViHi. See telegram to Lt. Gen. William T. Sherman, Jan. 14, 1867.

To Benjamin S. Ewell

Washington, D. C.
Apl. 30th 1867.

DEAR SIR:

Your letter of the 27th of Apl. asking a recommendation from me in favor of aid for the re-establishment of Wm & Mary College, Va. is just received. The advantages secured to a government by educational privileges being extended to all the youths of the country is are appreciated by every one. That the South, as a result of the rebellion, is unable to rebuild at once, from her own resources, college buildings destroyed, and to provide the necessary means for securing instruction for the massess, is also well understood. I hope therefore you may be successful in procuring the means to re-establish Wm & Mary College, over which you preside, on as good a basis as it has ever had, and that it will continue to teach loyalty to the general government as I understand it has done under [your] able supervision.

The North, and more prosperous sections of our country, has been very liberal in providing for the pressing wants of the South. Education is a material want to a nation if it is not to each individual, and I hope, in making contributions, this want will receive a due proportion of the bounty bestowed.

With great respect,
your obt. svt.
U. S. GRANT
Gen.l U. S. A.

To BENJ. S. EWELL, ESQ,
PRES. WM & MARY COLLEGE, VA.

ALS, College of William and Mary, Williamsburg, Va. Benjamin S. Ewell, born in Georgetown, D. C., USMA 1832, resigned from the U.S. Army in 1836. Appointed professor of mathematics at the College of William and Mary in 1848, he became its president in 1854. Although opposed to secession, he was appointed col., 32nd Va., and later served as adjt. and chief of staff for Gen. Joseph E. Johnston. On April 27, 1867, Ewell, Washington, D. C., had written to USG. "Having understood you were not unwilling to give me a personal interview, I called to day at your Head Quarters, & found to my regret you were not in the District—Aware of your engagements in New York last March I did not press myself on you there; though desiring to pay my respects, and to obtain your approval of an attempt I am making I have taken the liberty of writing to you before on the subject of William & Mary College, & its destruction during the late Civil War—I informed you that the teachings of the Institution are loyal, & would, I trusted, continue so. It ought to be restored because of the national men it has educated, if for no other reason. To begin to rebuild now would avert destitution in the vicinity, & encourage industry. To restore would furnish education, so sadly needed I am on my way to New York to solicit contributions A word from you approving—or, better, recommending the scheme would prove of great service. For this I ask—If you think proper to write anything on this matter it may be forwarded to my address by Dr Smith—U. S. Army Be kind enough to pardon this request, & believe me to remain whether you think fit to grant it—or not—. . ." ALS, OClWHi. On Jan. 27, 1866, Ewell, Williamsburg, had written to USG. "With great hesitation I presume so far, as to enclose for your consideration a short article published in one of the Richmond papers—relating to the College of William, & Mary. For a private matter my unwillingness to intrude on you would be much greater—The sketch is correct in the main. It was written by me, & its statements, especially those referring to the destruction of the College property during the war, can be fully substantiated—In 1859 the College suffered heavy losses by fire—To repair these liberal contributions were made by the North. Without like contributions now the College must remain a ruin for an indefinite time Any favorable expression from you, however general, in relation to the matter might, & would conduce much to a successful issue—Hence my application to you—Trusting that my communication may not be deemed impertinent—or improper—I have the honor to remain—. . ." ALS, USG 3. On Feb. 8, Bvt. Col. Adam Badeau wrote to Ewell. "Lieut. Gen. Grant directs me to acknowledge the receipt of your communication of Jany. 27th relative to the College of William and Mary, at Williamsburg, Va., and to say that he takes a decided interest in the Success of any educational enterprise or institution ~~of learning~~ at the South, in which the principles of loyalty to the government, and devotion to the unity and prosperity of the entire country, are inculcated." Copies, DLC-USG, V, 47, 109; DNA, RG 108, Letters Sent.

On Dec. 22, 1868, USG wrote a testimonial. "I take pleasure in recommending to the Public who have the means & disposition to give to the cause of education Wm & Mary College as deserving the patronage of Union loving citizens. The course of Prof Ewell the head of Wm & Mary College since the close of the rebellion is evidence of what I have say of the Institution over which he presides." Copy, DLC-William T. Sherman. See *HRC*, 41-3-53; *ibid.*, 42-2-9; *ibid.*, 44-1-203; *SRC*, 52-1-393; *HRC*, 52-1-562.

To Charles W. Ford

Apl. 30th *1867*.

DEAR FORD:

Your dispatch asking for special protection for the Ex. Co. on the plains was rec'd. Sherman, in his instructions to Dept. Commanders, directs them to give the best protection they can especially to the Mails & lines of rail-road now being built. I presume your Express runs on one of these lines. By calling on Sherman you can find exactly what is being done, as well as what he can do, and make your calculations accordingly. I want to get out to St. Louis this Summer if I can. Now that I have commenced farming there I feel an interest in being on my farm as much as possible. I think you had better go out to my house and keep Bachelor's Hall for a while. I feel but little hope of your ever keeping house in any other way. You are not as old yet however as Dr de Camp was when he commenced the second time. But then previous experience taught him how good a thing it is. You and Andrew Elliot had better start out soon.

Yours Truly

U. S. GRANT

ALS, DLC-USG. On April 30, 1867, 10:00 A.M., USG telegraphed to Charles W. Ford. "Sherman gave orders for the protection of Mail & rail-roads on the plains." ALS (telegram sent), DNA, RG 107, Telegrams Collected (Bound); telegram sent, *ibid.*; copies, *ibid.*, RG 108, Telegrams Sent; DLC-USG, V, 56. On April 26, Ford, St. Louis, had telegraphed to USG. "The express Company have recently lost about thirty (30) horses two (2) Stations burnt and three men Killed on the Smoky Hill route by the Indians. We are apprehensive of a stampede of our men & the consequent abandonment of the route unless we receive some aid from the Government. If a few soldiers put at the Stations together with our own men I think the route Could be Kept open. Can that be done? I send Out today four thousand rounds of ammunition for our men" Telegram received (at 8:40 P.M.), DNA, RG 107, Telegrams Collected (Bound); *ibid.*, RG 108, Telegrams Received; copies, *ibid.*, RG 393, Military Div. of the Mo., Indian War; DLC-USG, V, 55.

To Bvt. Maj. Gen. John M. Schofield

———

Washington, May 6th *1867*.

BVT. MAJ. GN. J. M. SCHOFIELD,
COMD.G 1ST DISTRICT,
GENERAL,

Your letter of the 22d of Apl. enclosing copy of regulations for the registration of voters in your command was received during my absence from the city and either from my neglect or that of some one else I have only just read them. The order is without number and without date from which I infer you are waiting to hear whether there are any suggestions to offer before publishing it. I hasten therefore at this apparently late date to reply.

The order seems to me to meet every point and to be good. I asked the Sec. of War to know whether he had any suggestion to offer. He said that he had read the order and found nothing to suggest in relation to it.

Very respectfully,
Your obt. svt.
U. S. GRANT
General,

ALS, DNA, RG 393, 1st Military District, Letters Received. On April 22, 1867, Bvt. Maj. Gen. John M. Schofield, Richmond, had written to USG. "I send you herewith a copy of my proposed regulations for the registration of voters and will be glad of any suggestions that may occur to you or to the Secretary of War. I intend to add instructions concerning disfranchisement, based upon the opinion of the Attorney General when that opinion is received." ALS, *ibid.*, RG 94, Letters Received, 856M 1867. The enclosure is *ibid.* On April 23, Bvt. Maj. Gen. John A. Rawlins endorsed this letter. "Respectfully forwarded to the Secretary of War." ES, *ibid.* Bvt. Maj. Gen. Edward D. Townsend noted on the docket. "Submitted to the President and returned to the War Department." AN, *ibid.* See letter to Bvt. Maj. Gen. John M. Schofield, June 3, 1867.

On May 14, Schofield telegraphed to USG. "Jefferson Davis was yesterday brought before the U. S. Circuit Court discharged from Military custody and released upon bail. He left the city and started north this morning. The most perfect order and the utmost good feeling have prevailed throughout the city during the proceedings of the Court and since the release of the prisoner The troubles which occurred a few days ago were only a temporary ebulition easily suppressed. The excitement is rapidly passing away." Telegram received (at 12:30 P.M.), DNA, RG 107, Telegrams Collected (Bound); *ibid.*, RG 108, Telegrams Received; copies, *ibid.*, RG 46, Senate 40A–F5, War Dept. Messages; *ibid.*, RG 393, 1st Military District, Telegrams Sent; DLC-USG, V, 55.

On May 16, Schofield, Fort Monroe, telegraphed to USG. "I think it necessary to establish a quarantine at this port without delay, and respectfully request that the Quartermaster Department be ~~requested~~ directed to furnish a suitable steamer for that purpose." ALS (telegram sent), DNA, RG 107, Telegrams Collected (Unbound); telegram received (at 1:00 P.M.), *ibid.*, Telegrams Collected (Bound); *ibid.*, RG 108, Telegrams Received. On the same day, USG endorsed a copy of this telegram. "Respectfully forwarded to the Secretary of War, with recommendation that the Surgeon General be directed to establish Quarantine regulations for all the unreconstructed states on the seaboard" ES, *ibid.*, RG 107, Letters Received from Bureaus.

To Edwin M. Stanton

Respectfully returned to the Secretary of War. It is evident that
this application is made by Gen. Granger with a view to securing
his detail as a member of the Commission should it be appointed.
He has already received unusual and extraordinary indulgences,
and as there seems to be no necessity for a Commission of this character the application is disapproved.

Attention is invited to the fact that Gen. Granger sends his application direct to the President instead of communicating through
the regular military channel: a violation of the Army regulations
which is inexcusable in an officer of his experience and length of
service.

U. S. GRANT
General.

HDQRS. AUS
MAY 7. 67.

ES, DNA, RG 94, Letters Received, 369G 1867. Written on a letter of April 30,
1867, from Col. and Bvt. Maj. Gen. Gordon Granger, 25th Inf., New York City,
to President Andrew Johnson concerning the need for a commission of experienced officers to examine changes in the militia systems of Europe. ALS, *ibid.*
On May 15, Johnson endorsed this letter. "Returned to the Honorable the Secretary of War. The President does not understand the communication of Genl.
Granger to be an 'application' The suggestions which it makes were, at the
President's request, submitted to him in writing, and were referred to the Secretary of War for his consideration as to the propriety of appointing a commission
for the purpose indicated by Genl. Granger The remarks contained in the endorsement of Genl. Grant would seem to pertain more particularly to General
Granger than to the suggestions which the latter officer submits, and would be
more relevant had it been determined to appoint a commission, and the question
had arisen as to whether or not Genl. Granger should be detailed as one of its
members." ES, *ibid.* On May 13, Thomas Ewing, Jr., New York City, had written to Johnson. "Maj: Gen Gordon Granger wants to be ordered to inspect and
report on the militia systems of the chief Powers of Europe for the information
of the Executive and Congress in establishing an uniform system for the United
States. . . ." ALS, *ibid.* Perhaps later in May, USG wrote an undated note to
Maj. George K. Leet. "Send me Granger's letter to the President, with my endorsement, also papers relatin to cruelty to prisoners at Dry Tortugas." Stan. V.
Henkels, Catalogue No. 1194, June 8, 1917, p. 92. On May 6, USG had endorsed
papers concerning mistreatment of prisoners at Fort Jefferson, Dry Tortugas, Fla.
"Respectfully forwarded to the Secretary of War. Although the action of Captain
McConnell was harsh and unjustifiable, yet, in view of the reported bad conduct

of the soldiers at Fort Jefferson, I respectfully recommend that the order for his trial be recalled. If soldiers are refractory and disobedient, they should be placed in confinement and tried by CourtMartial at the earliest practicable moment." ES, DNA, RG 94, Letters Received, 830A 1866.

On May 22, Bvt. Maj. Gen. Edward D. Townsend wrote to Granger ordering him to report immediately to his regt. ALS, *ibid.*, 369G 1867. On May 23, Granger wrote to Townsend. ". . . I have been instructed by the President of the United States to ask a Suspension of your orders of the 22d inst. Until my letter of the 30th ult addressed to him at his own request Shall have been finally considered by himself & the War Department . . . Upon this application the Secretary of War has given me verbal permission to await until further orders." ALS, *ibid.*, 258G 1867. Granger noted on this letter: "Seen by Genl Grant & the Secretary of War, May 24/67." ANS, *ibid.* Granger remained on leave until he assumed command of the District of Memphis on Sept. 1.

On Oct. 14, 1866, Granger had written to the AG requesting a six-month extension of leave with permission to leave the U.S. ALS, *ibid.*, 571G 1866. On Oct. 20, USG endorsed this letter. "General Granger has already had greater indulgence than is consistent with the interests of the service. His application for further extension of leave, no sufficient reason for its being granted, being assigned, is therefore not recommended." ES, *ibid.* On Jan. 17, 1867, Granger wrote to Townsend requesting a six-month leave for business reasons. ALS, *ibid.*, 27G 1867. On Jan. 22, Townsend endorsed this letter to USG by listing Granger's leaves, quoting USG's endorsement of Oct. 20, 1866, and noting that Granger had been given an additional three-month leave at USG's direction on Oct. 22. On Feb. 2, 1867, Leet unfavorably endorsed Granger's request. ES, *ibid.* On Jan. 27, Granger had written to Townsend enclosing a surgeon's certificate stating that Granger could not leave New York City for at least two months on account of illness. ALS and DS, *ibid.*, 40G 1867.

On Jan. 25, 1868, noon, Maj. Gen. George H. Thomas, Louisville, telegraphed to USG. "Brevet Maj Gen Gordon Granger absented himself from his Command early in this month without my Knowledge or consent His address was not left with his AAAG and he has no idea where he now is, Further particulars will be forwarded by mail" Telegram received (at 1:30 P.M.), *ibid.*, RG 107, Telegrams Collected (Bound); *ibid.*, RG 108, Telegrams Received; copies, DLC-USG, V, 55; (misdated Jan. 24) DNA, RG 94, Letters Received, 69C 1868. Papers in the matter, later forwarded by Thomas, included an explanation and apology from Granger, and USG accepted Thomas's recommendation that the matter be dropped. *Ibid.*

On Feb. 22, 9:45 A.M., USG telegraphed to Thomas. "Is Gen. Granger absent from his command and in this city by authority?" ALS (telegram sent), *ibid.*, RG 107, Telegrams Collected (Bound); telegram sent, *ibid.*; copies, *ibid.*, RG 108, Telegrams Sent; DLC-USG, V, 56. On Feb. 23, Thomas telegraphed to USG. "General Granger has leave of absence for twenty (20) days, with permission to apply for an extension on his application, for the leave, to attend to pressing private business" Telegram received (at 9:15 A.M.), DNA, RG 107, Telegrams Collected (Bound); *ibid.*, RG 108, Telegrams Received; copy, DLC-USG, V, 55.

On April 10, Johnson wrote to USG. "Will you please furnish me a list of all officers, above the rank of Captain, who are now awaiting orders or are on leave of absence; stating the length of time they have been so awaiting orders or for which they have been granted leave of absence, and the authority under which they have been instructed to await orders or have been granted leave. The list should also embrace the names of officers, above the grade of Captain, who have permission to delay reporting to their commands." LS, DNA, RG 108, Letters Received. On April 13, USG wrote to Johnson. "In compliance with your request of 10th inst to be furnished with a list of all officers above the rank of Captain now on leave of absence awaiting orders, or having permission to delay reporting to their commands, showing the authority under which they are on leave or awaiting orders, I have the honor to forward herewith a list giving, in detail, the information desired." LS, DLC-Andrew Johnson. The enclosure listed 34 officers; only Granger received orders directly from Johnson. Copy, DNA, RG 108, Letters Received.

On April 27, Granger, Washington, D. C., wrote to the AG requesting a thirty day extension of permission to delay joining his command, and Leet favorably endorsed this letter on April 30. ALS and AES, *ibid.*, RG 94, Letters Received, 120G 1868.

On Aug. 8, 1867, Townsend had written to Bvt. Maj. Gen. Benjamin W. Brice, paymaster gen. "General Grant, commanding the Army, directs me to report to you Brevet Major General Gordon Granger, Col 25th Infantry as absent from duty without any authority known to him, in order that General Granger's pay may be stopped until his unauthorized absence shall be satisfactorily explained." Copy, *ibid.*, 225P 1868. On May 1, 1868, Townsend endorsed a letter inquiring about Granger's pay. "Respectfully returned to the Paymaster General. The stoppage made against Genl. Granger's pay in letter of Aug. 8., 1867, will be considered as applicable to amount due during the time of his unauthorized absence prior to that date. He is now absent with proper authority and entitled to draw his pay." AES, *ibid.*

To Bvt. Maj. Gen. Edward O. C. Ord

Washington, D, C, May 11th *1867.* [*1:30* P.M.]

BVT. MAJ. GEN. E. O. C. ORD,
VICKSBURG, MISS.

There is no legal authority for employing a Civilian as Judge Advocate. A Judge Advocate of the Army will be sent from here to report to you at once. Delay trial until he arrives.

U. S. GRANT
General.

ALS (telegram sent), DNA, RG 107, Telegrams Collected (Bound); telegram sent, *ibid.*; copies, *ibid.*, RG 46, Senate 40A–F5, War Dept. Messages; *ibid.*, RG

108, Telegrams Sent; DLC-USG, V, 56. On May 10, 1867, Bvt. Maj. Gen. Edward O. C. Ord had telegraphed to USG. "I am about to order the first Military Commission under the reconstruction act—Have no competent officer for Judge Advocate except my principal staff officers who Cannot be spared from more necessary duty—Can I employ a citizen as special Judge Advocate? The cases to be tried are important." Telegram received (at 5:50 P.M.), DNA, RG 107, Telegrams Collected (Bound); *ibid.*, RG 108, Telegrams Received; copies, *ibid.*, Letters Received; *ibid.*, RG 393, 4th Military District, Telegrams Sent; DLC-USG, V, 55. On May 11, USG endorsed a copy of this telegram. "Respectfully forwarded to the Secretary of War, for his opinion and instructions." ES, DNA, RG 108, Letters Received. On the same day, Secretary of War Edwin M. Stanton endorsed this telegram. "The Judge Advocate General has been directed to detail a competent officer to proceed immediately to Vicksburg & report to Genl Ord. There is no legal authority for General Ord to employ a civilian & his request for a suitable officer will be met without delay" AES, *ibid.*

On April 15, Ord had forwarded to Bvt. Maj. Gen. John A. Rawlins three letters concerning Reconstruction affairs in Ark. Copies (3), *ibid.* See *HED*, 40-1-20, pp. 55–56. On April 26, Ord forwarded to Rawlins additional papers concerning Ark. Copy, DNA, RG 108, Letters Received.

On April 19, Ord, Washington, D. C., wrote to Rawlins. "I beg leave to state, that the Union men of the State of Arkansas, lately in Convention at Little Rock, have, through this Committee of Conference, represented to me, that there are fifteen or twenty counties of this State in which registers under the recent act of Congress, for the better government of the rebel states, cannot go with safety to perform their duties without a military guard, which in every instance must be mounted—That I have at Little Rock, available for such service, only seventeen (17) horses, and that I have made requisitions for five hundred horses for mounting guards, but have heard nothing of their being approved—Throughout the State of Arkansas, (and from what I can learn) of Mississippi, it is the custom for the white population to go armed, and at elections, the lower classes take it for granted they can indulge freely in whiskey, and fighting; the freedmen who I am expected to protect in voting, for the first time, are timid, and unarmed, accustomed to submit—The whites, of whom I speak as accustomed to go armed, are in my District, exasperated, and generally bitterly opposed to Negro suffrage, and unless the freedmen are protected at many of the Precincts by the vicinity, or presence, of an armed force, provided with horses to pursue and punish rioters, I do not believe the freedmen will even present themselves at the polls, except at a few towns where they are brought forward, and protected, by armed white men who desire to control their votes—Under this state of things, I deem it of great importance, and necessity, that I should be provided with at least five hundred horses, to mount parties for the purposes above mentioned—To give an idea of the Country, I will mention that in the town of Little Rock, where recently a convention of union men assembled, and a few freedmen, were allowed to unite with them, this attracted a number of other freedmen from the plantations, some of whom doubtless had arms, but the common white people are so excitable on this question, that many of the Citizens kept guards on their premises, and kept their families ready to fly at night, in case the expected mob, and riot, should begin; and I have been especially petitioned by the principal inhabitants, wealthy men, to keep guards in the town, and use every precaution against assembling large crowds of the exciteable hostile elements—A similar condition of things exists in Mississippi, so that, where I have but a single Regiment of about six hundred infantry, just ten men to every thousand square miles, and not a single mounted man, except two orderlies, I regard it absolutely necessary to have at least two regiments in that state, have them full, and horses enough to mount twenty parties of twenty each to guard Registers, and more particularly, protect freedmen from attack on election day, so that no such bloody affairs as recently occurred in New Orleans, and Memphis, may happen in my District." LS, *ibid.* At 11:05 A.M., USG telegraphed to Maj. Gen. George H. Thomas. "Send the 34th Inf.y to Corinth Miss. to report to Gn. Ord for orders. ~~If the 20th Inf.y is with you send that regiment also.~~ Send also two Companies of Cavalry to Vicksburg." ALS (telegram sent), *ibid.*, RG 107, Telegrams Collected (Bound); telegram sent, *ibid.*; copies, *ibid.*, RG 108, Telegrams Sent; *ibid.*, RG 393, Dept. of the Cumberland, Telegrams Received; DLC-USG, V, 56.

On May 7, Robert W. Flournoy, Pontotoc, Miss., wrote to USG. "Permit me to call your attention to order No 5 issued by Gen Ord and particularly to the third paragraph of said order. There is no mistaking the intention of order or its effects. There is an intention to organize a Republican Party in this state, the foundation of which must rest upon the freedmen, the question has been put directly to Gen Ord, to know if he would protect such a movement. It was not expected that either you or Gen Ord would aid in the advancement of that end. But we had the right to expect, and did hope that no official position would be used against the right of the citizen to freely discuss, and form any party not inimical to a loyal adherence to the government of the United States. We consider the order above alluded to as a rebuke intended to prevent an expression of opinion. He does not inculcate any desire, that the white people should not engage in political discussions, but that the freedmen who are altogether uninformed upon political subjects should abstain from any means to inform themselves. And leaves those of the dominant race who are disposed to aid them at the mercy of those who above all things desire the overthrow of this government. It is not only dangerous but impossible to form a Republican here unless we are assured of the protection of the government to prevent our being mobbed and murdered Are the freedmen to be used to swell a party, who at heart are traitors, to the country. That is the important question and to that point I beg leave to direct your attention   All we ask is that we shall be protected in this movemet equally with all other men in the course we intend favoring and which we think of vital importance, to the future peace and prosperity of the whole country. We think Gen Ord should issue an order informing the people that there shall be no restriction in the formation of what they believe to be a loyal party, but that every citizen shall be protected in the free expression of, and action upon this subject. And to the security of this important object, I write you emboding as it does the wishes of the loyal people here both white and black. We had indulged the hope, that this right was secured and would be enforced under the bills passed by congress. I lay this matter before you, hoping you will feel it to be your duty to direct Gen Ord in the premises. I have written to him. And shall if it becomes necessary make the whole matter public,   we shall not tamely submit to official interference in the exercise of our rights." ALS (marked as copy), DNA, RG 108, Letters Received. On the same day, Flournoy wrote a similar letter to Ord. ALS (marked as copy), *ibid*. On May 15, Maj. Oliver D. Greene, adjt. for Ord, endorsed this letter. "Respectfully returned to Mr R W Flournoy Pontotoc Miss. with the information that the Gen commanding holds the opinion that the most important duty devolving upon freedmen is that of providing by their own labour for their support, and cannot see that this opinion can be construed to the benefit of 'Rebels, or Union men' as classes. To prevent poverty and starvation among the masses the soil must be tilled. Par III of general orders No 5 means this and this only, and has no political bearing whatever. As the General Commanding has no connection with political parties, he will neither prevent or assist party organizations" Copy, *ibid*. On April 15, Ord had issued General Orders No. 5, Fourth Military District. ". . . III. The most important duty devolving upon freedmen in their new condition, is that of providing by their own labor for the support of themselves and families. They now have a common interest in the general prosperity. This prosperity does not depend so much on how men vote, as upon how well each member of society labours and keeps his contracts. Freedmen are therefore urged not to neglect their business to engage in political discussions, but continue to comply with their contracts and provide for themselves and families, for unless they do so, a famine may come and they will have no food. When the time comes for them, to have their names entered in the books of voters, which will be before next September, the General Commanding will send them word through proper United States or county officers and send the books to places near by their homes, so that every voter can have his name registered and can afterwards vote without going far from his home. Only those residing in towns will be registered or vote there." Copy (printed), *ibid*. On May 23, Flournoy wrote to Stanton enclosing papers, concluding: ". . . What we desire is the removal of Gen Ord, or that he should be required to give assurance to the loyal people of protection in the free exercise of their political ~~their political~~ rights, to free discussion, and the organization of any party loyal to the government. And in this behalf we appeal to you. And shall unless in a short time you are pleased to take action in the matter appeal to the president. And if after exhausting all the means afforded us by the bills, we fail to secure that protection, which is our right, submit the whole subject to Congress." ALS, *ibid*.

To David Wills

May 14th *1867*.

DEAR SIR;

   Your letter of the 13th enviting me to visit Gettysburg some time in June to meet the "Board of Commissioners" is received. It has been my desire to visit the "Battlefield of Gettysburg" ever since the close of the rebellion; but it has so happened that when others were going who I wanted to accompany other engagements prevented. I will be but too glad to meet the Commissioners there any time after the 16th of June.

Yours Truly
U. S. GRANT

To DAVID WILLS,
PRES. SOLDIERS NATIONAL CEMETERY
GETTYSBURG, PA

ALS, Mrs. Thomas Dukehart, Towson, Md. David Wills graduated from Gettysburg College in 1851, studied law in the office of Thaddeus Stevens, and began a practice at Gettysburg in 1854. As president, Gettysburg Soldiers' National Cemetery Commission, he had made arrangements for the dedication in 1863. On June 8, 1867, USG wrote to Maj. Gen. George G. Meade. "Your letter of the 7th extending the invitation of Mr. Childs for me to be present in Phila on the 20th inst. is received. As you mention in your letter I have accepted an invitation to be at Gettysburg on that date but will be most happy to accept the invitation of Mr. Childs if the meeting at Gettysburg can be put off until the next day. I would like particularly to have you with me on on the Gettysburg occasion." ALS, Union League of Philadelphia, Philadelphia, Pa. On June 19, Wills telegraphed to USG. "Please inform me of how many your party will consist & whether you will leave Washington tomorrow morning according to previous arrangements" Telegrams received (2—at 5:00 P.M.), DNA, RG 107, Telegrams Collected (Bound). At 7:00 P.M., USG drafted his answer to Wills at the foot of a telegram received. "Myself & one staff officer leave to-morrow morning in early train for Gettysburg." ADfS, *ibid.*; telegram sent, *ibid.* USG arrived at Gettysburg during the afternoon of June 20 and toured the battlefield the following morning. *New York Times*, June 20–22, 1867.

On Feb. 20, and April 5, 1869, Wills wrote to USG requesting appointment as minister to Italy. ALS, DNA, RG 59, Letters of Application and Recommendation.

To Lt. Gen. William T. Sherman

Washington, May 17 1867

LT. GEN. W. T. SHERMAN
COMDG. MIL. DIV. MO.
GENERAL:

Herewith I return your proposed circular letter to Governors of Western States and Territories, with a letter from the Secretary of War giving his approval to it.

Inasmuch as most of the Governors would likely be glad to get their unemployed citizens into nominal government service, I would suggest that your letter only be sent to such of them as have represented the necessity for having militia organized to protect them from hostile Indians and such others as you think yourself should take this precaution.

Very respectfully
Your obt svt
U S Grant
General.

Copies, DLC-USG, V, 47, 60; DNA, RG 108, Letters Sent; *ibid.*, RG 393, Military Div. of the Mo., Indian War. See letter to Secretary of War Edwin M. Stanton, April 10, 1867. On May 5, 1867, Lt. Gen. William T. Sherman, St. Louis, had written to USG. "The Secretary has telegraphed me twice about organizing and accepting the service of Volunteers in the remote Territories, should the danger of Indian Hostilities make it necessary. I cannot be on the spot, and must necessarily devolve the matter upon Dept or District Commanders. I know that in New Mexico, and it may be in Colorado it would not be safe to trust the Governors, for they would gain popularity by getting their people employed in nominal service by the United States. I have made a rough draft of a letter which before sending out I would like you & Mr Stanton to revise, and if you sanction it send it back to me, and I will issue at once. All of these Governors must be familiar with the forms and if they will organise and hold a regimnt, we can call for it *only* if needed. I also write a letter to the Secretary about the Fort Buford matter which also read, and send to him. I am writing out home on Sunday, and do not keep copies as the matter is private or preliminary. I will meet Genl Hancock next week up about Fort Harker. I feel certain he can protect the Smoky Hill, and the Settlements of his Departmt, but Terry and Augur have a shorter season & longer distances. If I am up in Kansas when this draft comes back I will instruct Nichols to issue it, and send copies to the Dept Commanders. If the Governors of Minnesota Montana, Colorado & New Mexico will respond by the organization of a Regimt each, I do not think any will be called out, though the fact when known will give confidence to the People. The newspapers so mingle the little truth with so much falsehood, that every body is scared, though the plains are as safe now as ever. The Sioux are openly hostile up about Powder River & Yellowstone, but the others are as they always were, mixed. T[he] stages to Colorado & Utah go daily and there is as much travel as ever." ALS, DNA, RG 108, Letters Received. The enclosure is *ibid.* On May 10, USG endorsed these papers to Secretary of War Edwin M. Stanton. AES, *ibid.*

On the same day, Stanton wrote to USG. "The letter of Lieutenant General Sherman and his proposed Circular to the Governors of Western States & territories in relation to the organization of a local militia or volunteer force for defence against the Indians by referred by you to this Department have received consideration. There is no Act of Congress authorize now in force providing for calling volunteers or organizing the organization of militia in the territories and

I do not know that any laws have been passed in the States or territories referred to by Lieutenant General Sherman ~~been made~~ in relation to the subject. But ~~Tt~~he urgent necessity for defence of the Western Settlements from imminent danger now threatning them and the obvious advantages of the plan proposed by the Lieutenant General seem to justify & even require immediate provisional measures of defence subject to the future sanction ~~by~~ of Congress. The plan indicated by the proposed circular appears to this Department to be well adapted to the purpose and is therefore approved with ~~the following~~ such suggestions ~~that should be~~ as may appear to you proper to be made. It should ~~be~~ distinctly ~~declared~~ appear in the circular ~~that~~ 1st That the organization being ~~for~~ local ~~defence~~ the right to supplies and pay for officers and men will not commence until they are actually called and mustered into the service of the United States by the proper Division or Department or District Commander and will end with their muster out of the service of the United States   2d That in States or territories where there is no militia law prescribing the mode of appointing & commissioning of officers ~~the appointments~~ in order to secure proper and competent officers the appointment ~~must~~ should be subject to the approval of the Division ~~Distric~~ Department or District Commander & without ~~which~~ such approval no officer will be recognized by the War Department or be entitled to receive any pay. Any further regulations that may occur to you or to Lieutenant General Sherman as proper ~~either~~ to ~~control~~ limit the expense of the contemplated organizations or secure their efficiency will receive the sanction of this Department. The letter of General Sherman & proposed Circular are herewith returned. . . . P S Although General Sherman Circular appears to be addressed to several States & territories I ~~am~~ do not ~~aware~~ know that any application for authority to raise local forces has been made except in Montana. He probably contemplates only to issue the circular to those territories &c where danger is imminent or just grounds of apprehension exists ~~of imminent danger.~~ I ~~think it~~ would suggest whether it would not be better to be limited only to those cases rather than extend it in advance and thus afford occasion to the territorial authorities to claim that they acted at the request and instance of the Government and not from any impulse of their own   Past experience shows how such pretences may be used to fasten a claim upon the public treasury." ADfS (undated), *ibid.*, RG 94, Letters Received, 286W 1867; (postscript only—possibly added on May 16) DLC-Edwin M. Stanton; copies (dated May 10), DNA, RG 108, Letters Received; *ibid.*, RG 393, Military Div. of the Mo., Indian War. The enclosures are *ibid.*, RG 94, Letters Received, 286W 1867. On May 16, Stanton wrote to Sherman. "Your letter to me of the 4th inst ~~reached here at a time when I was by tempo~~ and your letter of the 5th to General Grant with the Circular proposed to be issued to the Governors of certain States & territories have received my careful attention. With your general views on the important subject discussed I fully accord, ~~and~~ The absence of any legislation by Congress to meet the case and ~~also~~ the probable want of any laws in the respective States & territories providing for the organization & officering of Militia or Volunteer forces occasioned some embarrassment. But after full reflection the urgent existing necessity seems to require action by the Department and your proposed plan meets my cordial approbation. The great point to be guarded is that indicated in your letter ~~the~~ the opportunity for needless expense by territorial authorities and whatever check or limitation you can ~~be placed~~ place upon that is advisable. ~~I have~~ In a note to General Grant which he will communicate to you with his own suggestions the views of the Department are expressed with ~~the~~ authority to you for carrying your plan of organization into effect. . . . P. S. In conversation with General Grant this morning it occurred to us to suggest the expediency of issuing the Circular only to those States and Territories that had applied for local force or where danger was imminent. This suggestion is mentioned in a postscript to my letter to him and he will express his views. You will act in the matter according to your own judgment." ADfS, DLC-Edwin M. Stanton. On May 22, Sherman wrote to USG. "I have the honor to acknowledge the receipt of your letter of May 17th: enclosing one of the 16th from the Honorable Secretary of War and the rough draft of a letter I had prepared and submitted in the nature of a circular to the Governors of States and Territories bordering on the Indian country. At the time of my submitting that draft, I had in view a long absence from my command, but now I have resolved not to ask leave to go away, but to remain. I will therefore be able to fulfill yours and the Secretary's orders and instructions in detail instead of as proposed in the aggregate, and will therefore address only such as make application for the privilege of organizing Volunteers and Militia in their own defence, and clearly prescribe that the United States will not be liable for expenses of any sort, until I call for the troops and until after they are mustered and accepted into the service of the United States   On this point I will exercise great caution, as I think I comprehend the motives of some of the Governors whom I would not entrust with a picket post of fifty men, much less with the discretionary power to call out troops at the national cost   The season is now favorable, and I hope the movements in progress and the reinforcements reaching their respective destinations will give reasonable security to the frontiers; but no amount of men and foresight can guard against such mischief-makers as are employed to invent and circulate stories like that of Fort Buford in the interest of rival roads." LS, DNA, RG 94, Letters Received, 633M 1867. On May 29, USG forwarded this letter to Stanton. ES, *ibid.* On June 3, USG forwarded papers to Stanton concerning calling out vols. in Colorado Territory. ES, *ibid.*, 632M 1867. On the same day, Governor Alexander C. Hunt of Colorado Territory *et al.* telegraphed to President Andrew Johnson. "We are menaced by hostile Indians   Our line of Communication Cut off, the U S mails Captured, Coaches and stations destroyed The occupants murdered Private trains are plundered burned & the men murdered & scalped   The arts of peace suspended & the people suffering from a feeling of insecurity which paralyses every branch of industry & all from the foe the lives of the whole of which are & should be considered by the authorities ~~ares~~ worthless Compared with that of one American Citizen   This we have suffered more or less for some time & yet no adequate protection or relief has been afforded us. In the name of God & Humanity we make this appeal to you & ask that the too long continued temporising policy towards these merciless Devils shall cease and that you will at once direct that prompt & decisive measures be taken for protection of the Country"   Telegram received (on June 6, 5:05 P.M.), *ibid.*, 286W 1867; copy, *ibid.*, RG 393, Military Div. of the Mo., Indian War. On June 7, USG endorsed the telegram received. "Respectfully returned to the Secretary of War, with recommendation that this telegram be referred to Lt Gen. Sherman. I would respectfully suggest that Govr Hunt be informed that all the force that can possibly be given to protect our frontiers has been put under the charge of Gen. Sherman, and that all communications on the Subject of further protection be directed to him." ES, *ibid.*, RG 94, Letters Received, 286W 1867.

On July 2, Sherman wrote to Stanton through USG. "I think you had better ask of Congress the right to call out, say, the equivalent of four regiments of Volunteer Cavalry, and to place an appropriation of money at your disposal, enough to pay them for six months' service. I do not propose to call out anything like that number, but if the Indians continue to oppose the progress of the Railroads, we will be forced to drive them out between the Arkansas and Platte, and then to invade their country north and south to attack them in their own camps." LS, *ibid.*, RG 107, Letters Received from Bureaus.

On Oct. 15, Henry N. Blake, Virginia City, Montana Territory, wrote to U.S. Senator Henry Wilson of Mass. "An attempt will be made by certain parties to procure the passage of a bill by Congress appropriating money to defray the expenses of an irregular organization termed the Montana militia, which was created by General Meagher and destroyed by Genl. Terry. A small force was required near the confluence of Twenty-five Yard Creek and the Yellowstone River to prevent bands of thieving Indians from molesting the residents of Gallatin County. About 400 soldiers were recruited for this purpose and nearly 100 officers, embracing many Colonels, were commissioned to take charge of them. Upon the question of paying these men and those who furnished them with supplies, a just and reasonable compensation I have nothing to say. But I respectfully protest against the passage of any bill relating to the subject until a thorough investigation has been made by an upright commission duly authorized by Congress to scrutinize every item of alleged expenditure. I am ready to substantiate the following facts whenever the investigation takes place. First:—The prices charged for supplies are exorbitant and unjust. Horses worth about $30 or $40 were sold to the Territory and payment was made in vouchers at rates varying from $217.50 @ $225. Flour not worth more than $600 or $700 was sold for $23 @ $26. Beef furnished to regular troops at 12¾ per lb. cost the militia $30 @ $40. Clothing of the most worthless description was furnished by swindling Jews and the same extortionate prices were claimed and allowed. I could enlarge the list if it was required. Second:—Certain officers signed receipts and certificates for grain, forage and other articles that were never furnished; or, if furnished, the *quantity* was much less than the amount specified in the papers. The contractors paid bribes to these dishonest men varying from $50 to $250. One freight train, that was never employed, plays a conspicuous part in this thievery operation. Third:—A captain Hughes, who departed with over 100 men with their arms, saddles and equipments, when the organization was disbanded, is charged in all the departments with carrying away more articles than he actually had and vouchers have been furnished to the so-called losers. Hughes had 3 or 4 mules; he is charged with about 25 or 26. He had two gold pans; he is charged with 12. This list could be extended considerably. Fourth.—A large number of so-called Colonels have drawn the rations allowed to those of corresponding rank in the regular army and also claim the same pay, while the size of the command never justified the appointment of one officer of this rank. Fifth.— In several cases, parties who were willing to furnish supplies for moderate sums were prevented under various pretexts in order that accomplices in cheating the Government could be favored. Sixth.—A comparison of the prices charged for furnishing supplies to Fort Ellis near Bozeman with those specified in the vouchers will reveal remarkable differences between what should be and what has been the rule. If a Commission is appointed by Congress I earnestly trust that Gov. G. Clay Smith and most of our Territorial officials will not be named. I have the best of reasons for saying that Smith and others are implicated in the rascality connected with the movement, and will profit enormously, if the vouchers are paid by the National Government. Our delegate J. M. Cavanaugh, will leave no means untried to win. He will labor for the cooperation of the Democratic members of both houses. Several Republican lobbyists will be employed to work upon their party friends. $100000 will be cheerfully paid by those interested to gain the desired end—an appropriation by Congress. By resisting this measure you will protect the Treasury and defeat a vile crowd of cormorants. I have written to General Butler and requested him to resist the proposed bill. Please make a free use of this communication. It will make me many enemies but I cannot sit by and see the country, in behalf of which I have fought, imposed upon and swindled by speculators. The newspapers support the project and only one voice comes from them. The citizens, who think that the money will benefit the Territory if put into circulation, even if it is acquired by robbery, also endorse the measure." Copy, *ibid.*, Letters Received, W412 1867. Wilson endorsed this letter. "Respectfully referred to General Grant, requesting him to read and return to me. I know the writer *well* and have no doubt of the truth of his statements." Copy, *ibid.* See Vivian A. Paladin, ed., "Henry N. Blake: Proper Bostonian, Purposeful Pioneer," *Montana, The Magazine of Western History*, 14, 4 (Autumn, 1964), 31–56. On March 1, 1870, William J. Snavely, Helena, wrote to USG. "I have Beene Reading in the Last Papers that theare has Beene Some Ressolution Offerd in Regard to The Montana Indian war that has happent in sixty seven And what I Know About it I think It was Got up for A speculation theare was A Large Immagration in sixty six And the Got the Imigrants to Beleive that if the would stop till Next spring that the could fill the Pockets and Go home   when spring Opend the found out theay was sold and dead Broake and no work that thee Could Get   theare was something to be Done the That Meatings and Came to the Conglution that the Best way to Get up an Indian Excitement and Let the Goverment pay the Bill   the Got Govener Meagher to Issue A Procclamation to Raise Vollenteerse But it was an uphill Buisness till the Got up an Excitement that the order Come from General Sherman to Governor Meagher to Raise five Hundred Vollenterse to Protect the Cittiens in Gallintin Valley   the Citticen of Galtinvalley did Not Apprahent Eney danger till the Excitement Commence in Helena And virginna   I talk with some of the Citticents of Gallitin   thea told Me that the did Not Apprahent Eney Daneger from the Indians that it was Got up for A speculation By the Left Wing of Pap Prices Armey to swindel the Goverment and the have succeded In the first And if the Can Blind the Govverment By such A Man as James. M. Cavanaugh wich has Belong to Everry Party that has Ever Excisted he happent to Meete with the the Rite stripe heare in Montana   Mr Jeames bot the Left wing tide heare to hoald the Ballence of Power with his Irish Friends. He told the Left Wing if the did Not Nominate him he would Play them the same trick that he playd in Colorado   the Bill that he Interduce in the House May Be well enuff But for eney such Amount of Money as is ask by him an Mr Howard in the senate Mr Jeames ask for Commisioner to Be Appoint and send to Montana to Ixamine the Claimes   that is all Right Enuff Providing the Are the wright Men there in Case that is hard to Get at   the out fit of the soulders was verry Poore and was Put in at verrey high Prices and it takes Men that is Acquainted how thease sharpers Manageit to Get the old truck of there parts at High Prices After the Got on the yellow stone the Laid done till theare time Nearley Exspired and some got tired the Exeact Number I Dont no But theare was over one hundred that toock theare Horsses Guns and what the Neaded and put for Parts Onknown and the wrest Returned to Helena & Virginiai and Got theare this Charge and sold theere Vouchers from fifteen to twenty five cents on a Dollar In trate and Left the County in ingush   Mr Grand you Must Excuse Me for writing this Letter to you as i have but won Acquaintans in Washington City that is the vice President Colfax   I have written him A Letter to Send to Mr Howard And I hope he will do so"   ALS, DNA, RG 75, Letters Received, Montana Superintendency. Although the Montana legislature requested $1.1 million, on March 3, 1873, Congress appropriated $513,343.10 to pay the expenses of the Montana vols. See *HED*, 43-2-9; Robert G. Athearn, *Thomas Francis Meagher: An Irish Revolutionary in America* (Boulder, 1949; reprinted, New York, 1976), pp. 157–66.

To Edwin M. Stanton

Washington D. C., May 21 *1867*

Hon E. M. Stanton
Secretary of War
Sir:

I have the honor to recommend that Department Commanders, West of the Mississippi river, be authorized to throw open to settlement so much of the military reservations within their respective commands, as they deem expedient, the reservation, however, not to be reduced below one hundred & sixty acres in any case. In throwing open these reservations it would be with the view of having those who might settle upon them become the owners of the soil either under existing laws for acquiring public lands, or under such rules as may hereafter be established by Congress. When these reservations were established it was desirable to have the military authorities control sufficient extent of territory to preclude a class of traders who are always ready to follow in the wake of troops, and who by their trade demoralize them without rendering any good. Now that settlements are springing up throughout the mountain regions between the Mississippi and the States on the Pacific; and lines of travel are clearly defined and traversed yearly by great numbers of people, it seems there would be inducements for good and permanent settlements on these lines, if settlements could have protection. With large reservations they must locate too far from the troops for this.

Settlements become strong and self-sustaining, as against hostile Indians. By cultivation, supplies, to a limited extent at least, will be produced near the troops, and thus much heavy transportation may be avoided.

Very respectfully
Your Obedt Servant.
U. S. GRANT
General.

LS, DNA, RG 107, Letters Received from Bureaus.

To Bvt. Maj. Gen. Daniel H. Rucker

Washington, May 21st, 1867.

GENERAL D. H. RUCKER
A. Q. M. GENL.
GENERAL:

Enclosed I send you bids, by Sylvester Mowry[1] for delivering Government supplies in the Territory of Arizona, which have been left at these Headquarters for transmittal. The route over which he proposes to transport supplies is shorter than that now in use which will make a saving to Government even if the same price per hundred miles is paid. In addition to this I believe his bid is below what it has been customary to pay. If these conditions are so I would recommend a trial of the route from Guaymas Libertad.

Very Respectfully
Your obt Servt
U S GRANT
General.

Copies, DLC-USG, V, 47, 60; DNA, RG 108, Letters Sent. On May 25, 1867, Bvt. Maj. Gen. Daniel H. Rucker, act. q. m. gen., wrote to USG. "I have the honor to acknowledge the receipt of your communication of May 21st transmitting proposition of Sylvester Mowry for transportation of Military Supplies into Arizona via Guaymas or Libertad and recommending conditionally a trial of these routes. It would be injudicious for me to take any positive action upon this proposition without consultation with the Chief Quartermaster of the Military Division of the Pacific, who may have already made arrangements for the supplying of the posts in Arizona for the coming year. I have therefore referred the communication of the General of the Army with its enclosures to Bvt Maj. Genl. R. Allen, Chief Qr. Mr. Mil. Div. of the Pacific, with instructions to give the subject full consideration and after conference with the Commanding General of the Military Division of the Pacific report to me thereupon. If these routes lay within the Territory of the United States, they would seem to be, from the representations which have been made of them, decidedly the most advantageous for the supply of Arizona. But as they pass through foreign territory I should not feel at liberty to forward over these routes the public stores turned over to this Department for transportation, even though they be shown to be for private freighters the most advantageous, unless I were expressly authorized to do so. If this authority were to be given, it would seem to be proper, that the official sanction of the Government of the country, through which the routes pass, should be obtained through the State Department. It might also be thought necessary that a military escort should in so unsettled a country accompany the trains. The economical advantages of the routes irrespective of these considerations I will meanwhile ascertain and report to you." LS, *ibid.*, Letters Received.

On Sept. 7, Rucker wrote to USG, secretary of war *ad interim.* "I have the honor to submit for your consideration the following statement of facts compiled from reports of officers of the Quartermaster's Department and other data on file in this office relative to the transportation of supplies for military posts in the Territory of Arizona south of the Rio Gila, and to invite your approval of the measures to be taken for the establishment of a more direct, economical and reliable route for this transportation than that hitherto traveled. Slowness, delay and uncertainty as to supplies have heretofore been the chief obstructions to military operations in Arizona; these have been unavoidably caused by the unsettled state of affairs in the Republic of Mexico, but the time has now arrived for removing these obstructions, and to a considerable extent relieving the Government of the heavy cost of forwarding supplies to posts in that Territory. . . ." LS, *ibid.*, RG 92, Reports to the Secretary of War (Press). On Sept. 13, USG wrote to Secretary of State William H. Seward. "At the instance of the Qr. Mr. Genl. of the Army, I have the honor to send herewith his communication of Sept. 7th relative to the *transportation* of *military supplies* for posts in *Arizona*, through the *Mexican Ty.*, with the hope that the privilege desired may be obtained from the Mexican Government." Copy, *ibid.*, RG 107, Letters Sent to the President. On Sept. 14, Seward wrote to USG. "I have the honor to acknowledge the receipt of your letter of yesterday accompanied by one addressed to you by the Quarter Master General upon the subject of shortening the transportation of army supplies to the territory of Arizona, by carrying them thither in part across Mexican territory from the ports of Guaymas or Libertad. In reply. I have the honor to inform you that pursuant to the 4th article of the treaty between the united States and the Mexican Republic of the 30th of December 1853, commonly called the Gadsden treaty, the privilege referred to requires the express consent of the government of that Republic, which will be asked for through Mr

Plumb, the Chargé d'Affaires of the united States at Mexico. The Mexican government has already been requested, at the instance of private parties, to make Libertad a port of entry, but sufficient time has not yet elapsed for an answer to be received to the application." LS, *ibid.*, Letters Received from Bureaus. On Nov. 19, Seward wrote to USG. "I have the honor to furnish you a copy of a despatch received from Edward L. Plumb Esqr Secretary of Legation and acting Chargé d'Affaires of the United States near the Government of Mexico, likewise of his correspondence with Mr Lerdo de Tejada Minister for Foreign Affairs of that Government in relation to the transportation of United States Army supplies from the Port of Guaymas, or that of Libertad in the state of Sonora to Arizona" LS, *ibid.*, RG 92, Letters Received. The enclosure is *ibid.*

On Oct. 25, Seward had written to USG. "I submit herewith for your information a copy of a letter which by direction of the President, I have written to the Secretary of the Navy, and also a copy of instructions which I have sent to Mr Plumb, Chargé d'Affaires ad interim of the United States in Mexico, concerning the detention of military stores of this Government at the port of Guaymas as mentioned in the telegram of Major General Halleck of the 21st of October, which was submitted by you to the President at a meeting of the Cabinet on the 25th of October." LS, *ibid.*, RG 94, Letters Received, 1069S 1867. The enclosures are *ibid.* On Dec. 26 and 27, Seward wrote to USG about problems in sending supplies through Guaymas. LS, *ibid.*, RG 92, Letters Received. On Jan. 11, 1868, Rucker wrote to USG concerning this matter. LS, *ibid.*, Reports to the Secretary of War (Press).

1. Sylvester Mowry, USMA 1852, born in R. I., resigned from the U.S. Army in 1858 to develop a silver mine in Arizona Territory. He was imprisoned briefly for disloyalty during the Civil War and his mine seized. He fought the seizure, eventually regained control, and used the mine as the basis for unscrupulous financial schemes. See Constance Wynn Altshuler, "The Case of Sylvester Mowry: The Charge of Treason," *Arizona and the West*, 15, 1 (Spring, 1973), 63–82; Altshuler, "The Case of Sylvester Mowry: The Mowry Mine," *ibid.*, 2 (Summer, 1973), 149–74. On April 9, 1867, USG favorably endorsed a request from Mowry seeking information about U.S. Army posts in Arizona Territory that needed supplies. Copy, DNA, RG 108, Register of Letters Received. On April 17, Mowry, Washington, D. C., submitted a bid to supply the posts via Mexico. *Ibid.* See *ibid.*, RG 107, Letters Received, M546 1866, M314 1867. On April 16, Mowry wrote a letter received at USG's hd. qrs. requesting troops to protect his mine. *Ibid.*, RG 108, Register of Letters Received. On April 18, Maj. George K. Leet endorsed this letter. "Respy. referred to M G. H. W. Halleck Comdg. Mil. Div of the Pacific. If troops can be stationed as within requested and give protection to greater interests—and as much protection to settlements and travel as where they now are, it would seem advisable to so station them. [T]he Commander of the Mil. Div. will please give this matter his attention, and act upon his own judgment." Copy, *ibid.* On Oct. 31, Mowry, Union Club, New York City, wrote to Lt. Gen. William T. Sherman asking his recommendation for minister to Mexico and claiming USG's support. ALS, DLC-William T. Sherman.

To Jesse Root Grant

May 21st *1867.*

DEAR FATHER;

Your letter in relation to relief for Capt. Lawson & Miss Landrum was received just before I started to Richmond. When you first wrote to me on the same subject I looked up Capt. Lawson's whereabouts which I thought was all that was wanted. A subsequent letter however showed that more was wanted. I do not see that anything further can be done. Original appointments, except to the rank of Lieutenant, and about all of them, are filled. No more officers can be detached from their commands for duty and I am trying all I can to get some of them now absent back again. In relation to Miss Landrum's papers I sent a staff officer to hurry them up on the receipt of your first letter. The reply was that when accounts of deceased soldiers are presented for settlement they are numbered in the order in which received and are taken up and settled in turn. There can be no departure from the rule.

In relation to your Ky. politics the military have no controll whatever. What Congress will do I have no means of knowing. It looks as though you were sending from there a fair representative for the Congress which was sitting in Richmond two & a half years ago, if the papers are reliable.

The family are all well. Fred. & Buck will probably pay you a short visit during vacation, and some time during the Summer or Fall Julia and my self will go West and stop two or three days in Covington.

Yours Truly
U. S. GRANT

J. R. GRANT, ESQ.
COVINGTON, KY.

ALS, DLC-USG, I, B. See letter to Jesse Root Grant, May 28, 1867.

To Robert C. Winthrop

———

Washington, D, C, May 22d *1867*.

DEAR SIR;

Your favor of the 13th inst. notifying me of a special meeting of the "Trustees of the Peabody Educational Fund," and also forwarding two volumes, by yourself, to be added to my "Boston Library," was duly received.

It will not be convenient for me to be present at the meeting on the 28th inst, nor do I suppose my presence would do any good. The working Committees are all that can be desired and I feel that their judgement can be relied on for carrying out the wishes of the donor of the fund.

Please accept my acknow[l]edgment of the kindness you have shown in sending me the volumes which will be added, as you request, to my library. I hope you a very pleasant trip to Europe and am only envious that I cannot go too.

With great respect
your obt. svt.
U. S. GRANT

To Hon. ROBT. WINTHROP
BOSTON, MASS.

ALS, MeB.

To Lt. Gen. William T. Sherman

———

May 23d *1867*.

DEAR GENERAL:

I am just in receipt of your letter of the 19th inst. I am very glad to learn that you have *almost* concluded not to go to Europe at this time and hope you will quite conclude before this reaches you. I have felt for some time that it was almost as important for you to be at your post this Summer as it was during the War. When the Summer Campaign is over, or it is demonstrated that the Indians intend peace, you can go without the necessity of confining yourself to a particular route, or any definite time at each stop.

I sent orders to you yesterday to report here which you will understand was merely intended to give you a start. You will not be arrested or tried for disobedience of orders if you do not comply.

Yours Truly
U. S. Grant
General,

To Lt. Gen. W. T. Sherman,
St. Louis. Mo.
P. S. Since writing the above I find the order which I directed yesterday has not been mailed. It will not be sent now unless requested.

U. S. G.

ALS, DLC-William T. Sherman. On May 19, 1867, Lt. Gen. William T. Sherman had written to "Dear General," presumably USG. "I got back yesterday, at Leavenworth I had a full conversation with Genl Hancock and am satisfied his Early movement ~~may have~~ Checked any disposition the Comanches, Kioways and Cheyennes may have had to a general Coalition for hostile purposes. The Camp that was stampeded on Pawnee Fork was composed of Cheyennes and Sioux. He thinks the Cheyennes have gone mostly south of the Arkansas and the Sioux north to the Republican   As these have been driven over to Gen Augurs line I thought it but fair that Gen Hancock should send 8 companies of the 7th Cavalry up to the Platte about McPherson, to operate there awhile, and then swing back to the Smoky Hill by the West. I dont like at all the R[e]servation made by Genl Sully & Rankin—viz between the Platte & Smoky Hill. I dont care what the Indians do, they will be charged with every theft on both these Roads, and such a clamor kept up by Express & transportation Companies, by the working & exploring parties of the Railroads, and the People generally that we will have to move them again, and this gives the Indians the opportunity to accuse us of bad faith.—I went to Riley and Harker, the Railroad being done within 15 miles of the latter, 205 miles out from Kansas City. At Fort Harker I met Genl A. J. Smith who has charge of the Smoky Hill route[.] He assured me of his belief that there were no hostile Indians within 200 miles. Gen Augur reports thefts & depredations on the Utah Road, beyond Saunders near old Fort Halleck, & thinks that to protect this overland Road he may have to modify his former plan of operations towards the Yellowstone, but I have ordered him to go on to attack the Sioux on Powder & Big Horn. The thefts & depredations are done by small bands who disappear and cannot be traced[,] whereas the Sioux alone are bold & defiant and must be fought. We must insist on the frontier people, and the teams to defend themselves until we can strike the Indians who will stand to fight. In view of the fact that both Genls Terry and Augur must go to the remote parts of their commands, and the very unsettled state of the Indian Wars, I am convinced I ought not to go away. There exist other reasons also why I ought not to go with the Duncan Expedition, and I am almost concluded not to go at all. Unless I write or telegraph specifically asking for leave let the matter stand. In a day or so, I will give you a positive request one way or the other. For myself I had little inclination, but the Girls were crazy to see Foreign lands—I think they must moderate their desires and postpone their sight seeing to a later day. I could better be spared in mid winter than now, the only season when offensive steps can be taken. I have no doubt you are now bothered by all sorts of Reports from Montana to New Mexico, but if I am to go away you would have them in increased numbers. Every little neighborhood wants the whole Army for its prot[ec]tion, and it requires great care, not to get our troops too much scattered. One of my children is quite ill, but I hope not dangerous. Tomorrow from the office I will see all matter accumulated in my absence"   ALS, DLC-Edwin M. Stanton.

On May 27, Sherman wrote to USG. "I have your letter of May 23d. I have announced in former letters that I have determined to give up the Duncan trip for this summer; but if next winter I could in a quiet way go out in some naval vessell destined for the Mediterranean Squadron, I would like it, and could cast off at some port, and come home by England. Even this I will not ask till the time approaches, nor if it in any way interferes with your plans. The Indians are restless and mischievous everywhere. Every road and every settlement appeals for military protection, and you understand how this divides up our troops, rendering them powerless for any combined movement whatever. I have now by me a long letter from General Dodge which is a fair sample of what I get from every quarter, each party, as a matter of course, exaggerating their difficulties and necessities, and underrating that of others. I rather think, however, we ought to have a battalion, [Despatch is received, and I will do the best with the Cavalry in hand.] say, half a regiment of cavalry, that should remain as it were at the head of the working parties of the Railroad, where their presence will give the workmen the necessary confidence. You know enough of railroad construction to see that though there may be two or three thousand workmen strung along the road, they can not carry arms and protect themselves. After the road is done, towns and stations are built, and the people will naturally arm in self-defence. I am anxious that this Railroad should reach the base of the Black Hills this year, which General Dodge has assured me will be the case, if they have sufficient guards. Augur has only the 2nd Cavalry and will need it all up about Phil. Kearney all summer and fall. Hancock has the 3d Cavalry in New Mexico, and if I wanted I could not get it in till fall: and then a clamor would be raised in that quarter. The 7th Cavalry has its hands full on the Smoky Hill; and the 10th Cavalry, Grierson's, is progressing very slowly. I hate to avail myself of the right to call for Volunteers, as it would stampede the whole country. In Montana we have no troops save at Camp Cooke and Sun River. The stampede there is further to the south and west, and to that point I have ordered from Utah a single officer, Major Lewis, and have authorized him to call for and use the battalion raised by Acting Governor Meagher, for two months only. If Major Lewis had enough men to feel out to Gallatin Valley I doubt if he would use the Volunteers at all, and I regard this as experimental only. I expect we shall be all summer fighting with little bands of horse-stealing Indians, and doubt if we can prevent them; but increased emigration to Montana and increased population along the Platte and Smoky Hill will divide the northern and southern Indians permanently, when we can take them in detail. I will write to General Dodge and have him keep his people at work, at all events this side of Fort Sanders." LS (bracketed insertion in Sherman's hand), DNA, RG 108, Letters Received. Sherman enclosed a letter of May 19 from U.S. Representative Grenville M. Dodge of Iowa, Council Bluffs, to Sherman expressing doubts that there were enough troops to mount a campaign against Indians in Dakota Territory and also to protect railroad construction crews. LS, *ibid.* On May 22, Bvt. Maj. Gen. Christopher C. Augur, Omaha, wrote to Sherman concerning the shortage of troops to defend railroad, telegraph, and stage lines while also engaging in offensive operations. Copy, *ibid.*, RG 94, Letters Received, 614M 1867. On May 24, Sherman endorsed this letter. "Respectfully forwarded to Headquarters U. S. Army, for the information of the General Commanding.—If we assume the pure defensive as suggested here, the Sioux will be free to roam at will, and attack any point of our defensive line.—We have now five or six months of good weather, during which, the camps that have been so insultingly placed almost in sight of Kearny and C. F. Smith can be attacked, and war carried into their country.—It will be bad war to allow the 300 dog soldiers bounced by General Hancock on the Pawnee Forks, to hold in check over 2000 spare troops that have been prepared for this very purpose.—I have no doubt the horses of General Augur are jaded by escort and patrol duty; but surely they must be in as good condition as those of the Sioux after a winter the severest known for years.—I have ordered Gen'l Augur to go ahead, and take the chances.—" ES, *ibid.* On April 27, Sherman had telegraphed to USG. "My opinion is that if the commissioners locate Indians as proposed between the Platte & Smoky Hill we will be subject to endless trouble for the rail road & stage companies are afraid of them and their constant demands for protection at their several stations will absorb all our troops." Telegram received (at 3:45 P.M.), *ibid.*, RG 107, Telegrams Collected (Bound); *ibid.*, RG 108, Telegrams Received; copies, *ibid.*, RG 94, Letters Received, 545M 1867; (sent by mail) *ibid.*, RG 108, Letters Received; DLC-USG, V, 55. On April 29, USG endorsed this telegram to Secretary of War Edwin M. Stanton. ES, DNA, RG 94, Letters Received, 545M 1867. On May 13, Stanton transmitted this telegram to Secretary of the Interior Orville H. Browning. Df, *ibid.*

On May 26, 2:30 P.M., USG telegraphed to Sherman. "There is no Cavalry that can possibly be sent to Gen. Augur this side of Texas. Can you not give a Battalion from Hancocks command or let Gn. Augur make his expedition with less Cavalry than he first proposed? Answer." ALS (telegram sent), *ibid.*, RG 107, Telegrams Collected (Bound); telegram sent, *ibid.*; copies, *ibid.*, RG 108, Telegrams Sent; DLC-USG, V, 56. On May 27, Sherman twice telegraphed to USG. "Maj Lewis has reached Virginia City from Salt Lake & reports a great scarcity, I have authorized him to deEmploy for two (2) months a Battalion of Eight hundred (800) men to drive out of Montana the Sioux and open communication with Ft Benton This will give time for the arrival of the arms for Governor Smith to reach his post & for Genl Augurs expedition to the Yellow Stone to produce its effect" "Both Gen Augur & Simpson report that the Indians have attacked the Rail Roard parties along the LodgePole & that the work on the Rail Road may cease unless we give more protection Infantry is powerless to prevent or pursue, Cavalry is alone useful, Gen Augur must take his single Regiment up to the Yellowstone for which he starts next tuesday If you could possibly spare us a Battalion of Cavalry for the Summer it would be invaluable, It would be a National Calamity if the work on the Pacific Rail Road should cease" Telegrams received (at 12:40 P.M.), DNA, RG 107, Telegrams Collected (Bound); *ibid.*, RG 108, Telegrams Received; copies (sent by mail), *ibid.*, RG 94, Letters Received, 600M 1867; *ibid.*, 601M 1867; (of the second) *ibid.*, RG 393, Military Div. of the Mo., Indian War; DLC-USG, V, 55. On May 28, Sherman twice telegraphed to USG. "Dispatch of twenty seventh (27) received. Will do our best with the Cavalry now in hand The enlistment of the tenth (10) [(]Griersons) proceeds too slowly. Can Butterfield help with general service recruits. Black will go up to the Platte in a day or so" "If you will order the head quarters & the four 4 companies of the Sixth 6 Infantry named in Special Orders Two hundred & sixty five 265 paragraph five 5 of May Twenty third 23 Adjt. Genls. Office to Hancock instead of Augur to go to the Indian country he can spare me the battalion of the seventh 7 Cavalry for the Platte The sixth 6 Infantry could embark at Pittsburg for Fort Gibson Augur has enough Infantry but is short of Cavalry I am sure the reports of Damage to rail road and mail parties are exaggerated party from natural fear & a good deal by interested parties Hancock will go in person up the Smoky Hill & I will go up the Platte & find out how Indians can be so *universal*" Telegrams received (the first at 1:30 P.M., the second at 5:00 P.M.), DNA, RG 107, Telegrams Collected (Bound); *ibid.*, RG 108, Telegrams Received; copies (one of the second sent by mail), *ibid.*, RG 94, Letters Received, 608M 1867; DLC-USG, V, 55. On May 29, Maj. George K. Leet endorsed Sherman's first telegram. "Respy. referred to the AG, who will telegraph instructions to Gen Butterfield and the supt. Mounted Recruiting service to enlist all the colored men they can get for the 10th Cav." Copy, DNA, RG 108, Register of Letters Received. At 9:40 A.M., USG telegraphed to Sherman. "Hd. Qrs. & four companies Sixth Infantry will be sent to Hancock as you request" Telegrams sent (2), *ibid.*, RG 107, Telegrams Collected (Bound); copies, *ibid.*, RG 108, Telegrams Sent; DLC-USG, V, 56. On the same day, Sherman telegraphed to USG. "Dispatch about the sixth Infantry recd I will start for Omaha and the plains tomorrow" Telegram received (at 1:40 P.M.), DNA, RG 107, Telegrams Collected (Bound); *ibid.*, RG 108, Telegrams Received; copies (one sent by mail), *ibid.*, RG 94, Letters Received, 631M 1867; DLC-USG, V, 55. See letter to Lt. Gen. William T. Sherman, May 29, 1867.

On May 23, Thomas C. Durant, vice president, Union Pacific Railroad Co., wrote to USG. "I have the honor to transmit herewith for your information, the enclosed copies of despatches from the line of this road, dated the 17th 21st, & 23d inst respectively, from which you will observe that the Indians are interfering very seriously with our operations, both in the location of the line west of the Black Hill range of the Rocky Mountains, and in the construction of the road in the upper end of the Platte-Valley, and across the Black Hill Range— Unless some relief can be afforded by your Department immediately, I beg leave to assure you that the entire work will be suspended—as it will be impossible to keep a force of men & teams employed upon the work, without adequate Military protection—Being aware to some extent of the scarcity of troops now in the field in that Military department, I will take the liberty of suggesting that if those that are now there could be massed along, or in the vicinity of the line of the Pacific Railroad, they would be able to afford ample protection to the work: and at the same time be the means of keeping the hostile Indians considerably to the Northward of the Territory contiguous to the Road." ALS (press), Union Pacific Historical Museum, Omaha, Neb. On May 28, Sherman wrote to Durant. "Yours of May 23d is received. I had received from General Augur the same information and more, and considering that similar calls come from a hundred other quarters, I have half a notion to accept your proposition to draw off your scattered forces, which would leave me the better able to defend the balance. But you have no such idea, nor have I. We are not going to let a few thieving, ragged Indians check and stop the progress of a work of national and world-wide importance; but it is right we should modify and conform our acts to the actual state of facts. . . ." Copy, DNA, RG 94, Letters Received, 597M 1867. Sherman forwarded this letter to USG. ES (undated), *ibid.*

On May 3, Governor William R. Marshall of Minn., St. Paul, had written to Stanton concerning possible removal of troops from the Minn. frontier. ALS, *ibid.*, 634M 1867. On May 22, Sherman endorsed this letter. "Respectfully returned to the Headquarters of the Army. Governor Marshall states this case well. I will write him direct, and explain to him that it was only to show General Terry how to act in case the whole Sioux nation, if pursued from the direction of Laramie, should turn towards their old homes in Minnesota. It is hardly possible that this contingency will happen, but if it do, the 10th Infantry moved on to the Missouri would meet the Sioux beyond the State limits instead of in the State. I will explain to him how and in what event he may raise for temporary use a few companies, say, four or five: to protect the public property in the State while the National troops are engaged elsewhere" ES, *ibid.* On May 29, USG endorsed this letter to Stanton. ES, *ibid.*

To Maj. Gen. Winfield S. Hancock

Washington, D, C, May 23d *1867.* [*3:30* P.M.]

MAJ. GN. W. S. HANCOCK
LEAVENWORTH, KANSAS.

Reports from Indian Agt. Wynkoop[1] to effect that Schyennes have committed no hostilities against the whites to justify the destruction of their village the Interior Dept. desire to know if in good faith their losses should not be made good. Report by telegraph briefly reasons for destroying their property, whether they should be fed and equipped again, and report at length by mail in reply to letters of Wynkoop & Leavenworth[2] sent you by Mail.

U. S. GRANT
General.

ALS (telegram sent), DNA, RG 107, Telegrams Collected (Bound); telegram sent, *ibid.*; telegram received, *ibid.*, RG 393, Dept. of the Mo., Telegrams Received. See letter to Lt. Gen. William T. Sherman, May 29, 1867. On May 23, 1867, Maj. Gen. Winfield S. Hancock telegraphed to USG. "Your despatch of this date received I burned the Sioux & Cheyennes villages deliberately in Col. Wynkoops presence I understood he then objected to my course but that I had expected, for I have seen no agents who do not attempt to shield their indians Col. Wynkoop presented as an argument for my not burning the villages that the Government would be the only losers as the property destroyed would be returned by the Indian Department as had been done before If I had not felt satisfied of the wisdom & propriety of my course it is scarcely probable that I would have acted as I did I have made a full report of my operations which will be transmitted to Lieutenant Genl. Sherman. within twenty four hours I also daily I may say from my camp sent him full reports of all that occurred of moment on my tour so that he had the means of laying these matters before you as they transpired We have a war now on hand with the Sioux & Cheyennes between the arkansas & the Platte They have attacked a mail station & an engineering party on the Smoky Hill within the last few days & were in Each case driven off once with certain loss. one or two depredations have recently been committed on the Arkansas so reported I would suggest that as we have a war with these Indians the matter of restoration of lodges &c had better be deferred until the war is over My report states that my reasons for burning the villages were as follows: The Indians broke faith with me in leaving their camp after they had promised to remain & have a conference with me They left a little captive girl about eight 8 or nine years of age said to be part white In their camp whom they had brutally outraged & abused notwithstanding that I had informed two days previously that if they abused captives again as they had done before I would punish them for it notwithstanding the above matters I remained by the villages guarding them as Sacredly as I could from the fourteenth 14 until the nineteenth April to ascertain whether or not they intended to commence a war as we had been previously informed they would do this spring when I learned from Genl. Custar who investigated these matters on the spot that directly after they had abandoned the villages they attacked & burned a mail station of the Smoky Hill Killed the white men at it disemboweled and burned them fired into another station endeavored to gain admittance into a third fired on my expressmen both on the smoky Hill & on their way to Larned I concluded that this must be war and therefore deemed it my duty to take the first opportunity which presented to resent their hostilities & outrages and did so by destroying their villages. As to Col. Leavenworths letter to which you refer I may say that serious charges have been made against him both by Indians & whites which have been transmitted If they are true it would seem that he is not a very reliable witness in this case. The Influence of trade with the Indians in this country which is almost entirely under the control of the Indian Agents in giving licenses to traders is so great as to render it questionable as to whether they are biased in these matters. War & the destruction of Indian villages prevents trading transactions for the time being That the sioux & Cheyennes who were living together in the villages which were destroyed were endeavoring to engage the southern Indians in the war which is now pending in the north I have not the least doubt we have been repeatedly so informed by the Chiefs of the southern tribes and by our officers. many depredations have been committed on the Smoky Hill since I have been in this Department & many before. They have all to my knowledge been traced to the Sioux & Cheyennes & although most undoubted evidence was furnished to the agent of the Cheyennes in reference to the depredations of the last nine months not a single demand has been forcibly made by the Indian Dept. for the depredators although in some cases the evidence was undisputed I have informed the Agents that If they requested me to enforce such demands I would do so   I furnished evidence in some cases which they did not even dispute" Telegram received (on May 24, 3:30 P.M.), DNA, RG 107, Telegrams Collected (Bound); *ibid.*, RG 108, Telegrams Received; copies (one sent by mail), *ibid.*, Letters Received; *ibid.*, RG 393, Military Div. of the Mo., Indian War; DLC-USG, V, 55; DLC-Andrew Johnson. On May 24, USG forwarded a copy of this telegram to Secretary of War Edwin M. Stanton. ES, *ibid.* On July 31, Hancock wrote to Maj. George K. Leet at length concerning his decision to burn Indian villages on April 19. LS, DNA, RG 94, Letters Received, 1093M 1867. Printed in *HED*, 41-2-240, pp. 111–18.

On May 8, USG had forwarded to Stanton a lengthy synopsis of Hancock's correspondence concerning Indians. ES, DNA, RG 94, Letters Received, 523M 1867. The reports are *ibid.* On April 16 and 30, May 11, and June 3, USG forwarded to Stanton papers concerning Hancock. ES, *ibid.*, 395M, 523M, 553M 1867; *ibid.*, RG 108, Register of Letters Received. See *ibid.*, RG 94, Letters Received, 521M, 590M, M102 1867.

1. Edward W. Wynkoop, born in Philadelphia in 1836, moved to Kansas Territory in 1858 and was appointed sheriff of Arapahoe County. During the Civil War, he served in the 1st Colo. Cav., fought at Apache Canyon and Glorieta Pass, and was promoted to maj. Following the 1864 attack on a Cheyenne village at Sand Creek, Wynkoop conducted investigations that condemned the brutal actions of the troops. He was appointed Indian agent at the Upper Arkansas Agency in 1866. See Thomas D. Isern, "The Controversial Career of Edward W. Wynkoop," *Colorado Magazine*, 56, 1–2 (Winter–Spring, 1979), 1–18.

2. Jesse H. Leavenworth, born in Vt. in 1807, USMA 1830, left the army in 1836 to pursue a career as civil engineer. He organized and commanded the 2nd Colo. Inf., but was discharged in 1863 after raising another regt. without authority. In 1864, Leavenworth was appointed agent for the Kiowas and Comanches. See *PUSG*, 16, 118–20.

To Maj. Gen. Daniel E. Sickles

Washington, May 23rd 1867

MAJ. GEN. D. E. SICKLES
COMDG 2D DISTRICT
GENERAL:

Orders are just issued sending Hd. Qrs. and four companies 6th Inft'y to Omaha to report to the Commander Dept of the Platte.

In selecting companies to go, take those having the greatest number of men enlisted in the Southern States.

Please answer on receipt of this and state whether you deem it necessary to have the troops thus taken from you replaced by others. It is possible to give you two companies of artillery, and, if absolutely necessary, two companies of Infantry from the 1st District. I hope you will call for no more than you deem indispensibly necessary.

All that you have said on the subject of Quarantine has been duly submitted and, I am informed, answer sent to you from the War or Surgeon General's Office

> Very Respectfully
> Your obt Servant
> U S Grant
> General

Copies, DLC-USG, V, 47, 60; DNA, RG 108, Letters Sent. On May 27, 1867, Maj. Gen. Daniel E. Sickles, Charleston, wrote to USG. "I have the honor to acknowledge the receipt of your letter of 23d instant and also Special Orders 265., Head Quarters of the Army, Adjutant Generals Office, same date; and in reply to your inquiry whether I deem it necessary to have the troops ordered to Omaha replaced by others, I am constrained to state that I do deem it necessary. It is proper to add that so far nothing has yet seriously disturbed the tranquility and order of my District. Nevertheless, I am satisfied this should be attributed in a large measure to the excellent discipline of the troops, the system of Post Administration—with one or two Company garrisons,—in troublesome places; the cooperation of zealous and efficient officers in such localities; and *the possession of a small reserve force* available for special service in places where meetings are called or where any other occasion justifies the apprehension of probable disturbance. It is precisely this small reserve of which I am deprived by the order now received and to replace it other troops are indispensable, in my judgement. Although a few men have been enlisted for the 6th Infantry here, most of them have deserted and very few—not more than six, belonged South. Nearly all were Northern and Western men who had been in our service and had come South in search of employment and failing to find employment, enlisted. The number so enlisted is so small as not to be an appreciable element and I wish you would relieve me from the restriction expressed in your letter, so that I may designate those companies best suited in general for service on the frontier. If, instead of Artillery, you could send me two companies of Cavalry they would be of the greatest possible utility in the approaching work of Registration in the Bushwhacking counties, where I apprehend negroes will be intimidated from Registering by the unsafe condition of the country in some bad localities. If possible also I beg that the Head Quarters of the 6th Infantry may remain, as I feel most sensibly the loss of *so many officers of experience in this sort of half civil administration, so difficult to learn.*—I will send General Green in any case, in command. I thank you, General, for your prompt action in reference to my unofficial letter to yourself on the important subject of quarantine.—Last year I did not have *one case* of *cholera or Yellow fever* in my Department, and if possible I wish to keep pestilence away from these unfortunate people this year also. . . . P. S. Enclosed please find a list showing the nativity of men now serving in the 6th Infantry who were enlisted in the South." LS, *ibid.*, Letters Received. On May 29, 9:40 A.M. and 10:10 A.M., USG telegraphed to Sickles. "Order the Hd. Qrs. & four Companies Sixth Infantry to Ft Gibson, to report to Maj. Gen. Hancock, instead of sending them to Omaha as heretofore ordered" "Other troops will be sent at once to replace the four Companies Sixth Infty ordered to Hancock" Telegrams sent, *ibid.*, RG 107, Telegrams Collected (Bound); telegrams received (the 2nd), *ibid.*, Telegrams Collected (Unbound); *ibid.*, RG 393, Dept. of the South, Telegrams Received. At 2:15 P.M., Sickles telegraphed to USG. "I respectfully acknowledge receipt of your two telegrams of this date. I have ordered Gen'l. Greene, Headquarters, companies "C" D. "E" & F. 6th Inf to ~~prepare~~ proceed at once to ~~leave for~~ Fort Gibson" LS (telegram sent), *ibid.*, RG 107, Telegrams Collected (Unbound); telegram received (at 3:30 P.M.), *ibid.*, Telegrams Collected (Bound); *ibid.*, RG 108, Telegrams Received.

On June 19, USG unfavorably endorsed a letter of the same day from Col. and Bvt. Brig. Gen. James D. Greene, 6th Inf., Washington, D. C., to the AG requesting permission to delay reporting to Fort Gibson, Indian Territory. AES and ALS, *ibid.*, RG 94, ACP, 388G CB 1867. On June 24, Bvt. Brig. Gen. Robert Williams, AGO, wrote to Greene. "The General-in-Chief directs that you proceed at once to join the Head quarters of your regiment and that you leave Washington City in compliance with this order within twenty-four (24) hours." Copy, *ibid.*, 391G CB 1867. On June 25, Greene wrote to the AG tendering his resignation. ALS, *ibid.*, 388G CB 1867. On the same day, USG endorsed this letter. "Respectfully forwarded to the Sec. of War with the following information and recommendation. May 31. 1867 Col. Greene with Hd. qrs and four Co's. of 6th Inf'y. was ordered to Ft. Gibson, C. N. to report to Maj. Gen. Hancock. Without permission from these Hd. Qrs. and instead of complying with above order, Co'l. Greene left the troops en route and came to this City. June 19th he applied in person 'for permission to delay until further orders joining the Hd. qr's. of his Reg't. at Ft. Gibson, C. N. in order to attend to some business important to myself and of value to the public Service.' This being refused, Col. Greene on the 24th applies directly to the President of the United States for permission to delay thirty days for the same purpose. Disapproving this I ordered Col. Greene to proceed within twenty four hours to join the Hd. Qr's. of his Reg't. On receipt of this Col. Greene tenders his resignation as Col. 6th Infty, U. S. A. This practice of tendering resignation on disapproval of application for leave or other indulgence—for the purpose of obtaining the same is very prejudicial to military discipline. The reasons given for delay are not believed to be sufficient to warrant the granting of the indulgence. I would therefore recommend the resignation be accepted at once, and that no application for reinstatement be entertained." Copy, DLC-USG, V, 43. On July 1, Greene wrote to President Andrew Johnson seeking withdrawal of his resignation. ALS, DNA, RG 94, ACP, 391G CB 1867. On July 6, USG endorsed this letter. "Respectfully returned to the Secretary of War, disapproved. Under instructions from these Headquarters,

Major General Sickles, Comdg. 2d Mil. Dist., on the 29th of May '67, or-
dered Bvt. Brig. Gen. J. D. Greene, Col. 6th Infantry, with his regimental Staff,
Records, non-commissioned Staff, and Cos. "C," "D," "E" and "F", 6th Infantry,
to proceed without delay to Fort Gibson, C. N., to report to Maj. Gen. W. S.
Hancock, Comdg. Dept of the Missouri.—By S. O. No. 66 Hdqrs. 2d Mil. District,
June 9 '67 the Comdg. Officer Post of Charleston was directed to send the Reg'l
Staff, N. C. Staff, Records, and Cos. "D" and "F" 6th Infantry, to Branchville,
S. C., to report to Bvt. Brig Gen. J. D. Greene, Col. 6th Infantry, *who will then
conduct the entire command to Ft. Gibson, C. N.*' (copies of orders enclosed.)
Gen. Greene instead of complying with these orders and without permission from
his superior officer—see enclosed copy of telegram from Maj. Gen. Sickles—left
his command and came to Washington where he applied in person to these Hdqrs
for permission to delay until further orders joining the Hdqrs of his regiment at
Ft. Gibson. This application having been disapproved, Gen. Greene addressed
himself direct to the President, asking permission to delay joining the Hdqrs. of
his regt. for thirty days. On reference to me of this application I ordered Gen.
Greene to proceed at once to join the Hdqrs. of his regt., and to leave Washington
City in compliance with the order within twentyfour hours—copy of letter to
Gen. Greene enclosed herewith—Gen. Greene then tendered his resignation,
which was accepted. Having by this means secured a delay he now asks to withdraw his resignation which he claims was hastily tendered. In the course pursued
by Gen. Greene he not only grossly and repeatedly violated the Army Regulations, but he committed the grave offence of absenting himself from his command without a shadow of authority. In my opinion the application to withdraw
his resignation should not be granted." ES, *ibid.*

On April 18, Sickles had written to USG. "Enclosed please find Copy of an
Extract from a letter received yesterday from Gov. Orr, and also Copy Extract
from a Communication from Gov. Worth. All the indications point so far to the
successful administration & Execution of the recent Acts of Congress for the
reorganization of these States. Govs Orr & Worth have recently passed a few
days here with me, by my invitation; we talked over a good many of the
matters appertaining to the work in hand and upon most questions they acceded
without much pressure to my views, and in all things assured me of their acquiescence & Cooperation. Such is I believe the general disposition throughout
the Carolinas." LS, *ibid.*, Letters Received, 859M 1867.

On June 17, Sickles telegraphed to USG. "Sixth section of first Military
Government Act authorizes the removal of nearly every Civil officer in the South
from Governors down. Not one in twenty could take the oath if required to do so
by a Military order of three lines. This may become necessary to the successful
execution of the Reconstruction measures passed by Congress. Not more than
twelve removals have yet been made in the Carolinas and these for positive
misconduct in office" LS (undated telegram sent), *ibid.*, RG 107, Telegrams
Collected (Unbound); telegram received (dated June 17, received at 12:20
P.M.), *ibid.*, Telegrams Collected (Bound); *ibid.*, RG 108, Telegrams Received. On June 18, Sickles telegraphed to USG. "The Charleston Daily News of
this date organ of the Reconstruction party of South Carolina in a powerful
leader on the published semi-official Synopsis of the Attorney Generals opinion
dissents from its conclusions; and in the interests of the South and of Reconstruction as well as of order Earnestly appeals to the President to adhere to the
views expressed in his veto message and to his patriotic purpose to execute the

Reconstruction Acts as Military measures. The Daily News represents the opinions of four fifths of the people of South Carolina" LS (telegram sent), *ibid.*, RG 107, Telegrams Collected (Unbound); telegram received (at noon), *ibid.*, Telegrams Collected (Bound); *ibid.*, RG 108, Telegrams Received. On June 19, USG endorsed a copy of this telegram. "Respectfully forwarded to the Secretary of War for his information." ES, *ibid.*, RG 94, Letters Received, 937M 1867.

To Maj. Gen. Philip H. Sheridan

Private   Washington, D, C, May 26th *1867.*
MY DEAR GENERAL,

Your letter of the 22d is received. I have no doubt but that the reports of your contemplated removal have eminated from a high source. It has unquestionably been in contemplation. But it can not hurt, though it may embarrass you. Every loyal man in the country admires your course in civil affairs, as they they did your Military career. You have to the fullest extent the confidence of the Sec. of War, the loyal people generally and of myself. Removal can not hurt you if it does take place, ~~which~~ and I do not believe it will. You have carried out the Acts of Congress and it will be difficult to get a General Officer who will not.

Let me say dismiss all embarassment on account of rumors of removal. Such an act will not reflect on you.

Yours Truly
U. S. GRANT
General.

ALS, DLC-Philip H. Sheridan. On May 22, 1867, Maj. Gen. Philip H. Sheridan, New Orleans, had written to USG. "*Private* . . . There has been a great deal of discussion here for the last month about my contemplated removal by the President, and which has been an additional embarrassment for me to overcome. I wish to say on this subject that there is as little reason for my removal from my present command, as there would have been to have removed me from the troops which I commanded at the battles of Stone River Missionary Ridge, Cedar Creek or Five Forks, after those battles had been fought. I have managed affairs here with fair ability, honesty and truth and the constant embarrassment of threatened removal is annoying." LS, USG 3.

On May 20, Sheridan had telegraphed to USG. "On the fourth I telegraphed you stating the reason why there was such a preponderance of Colored voters registered in this City was because the whites stayed away from the registration offices until the Colored got through—this proves to be true and the tables are now turned & the ratio is about one hundred whites to thirty Colored daily The white is increasing on the ~~black~~ colored very fast" Telegram received (at 7:20 P.M.), DNA, RG 107, Telegrams Collected (Bound); *ibid.*, RG 108, Telegrams Received; copies, *ibid.*, RG 46, Senate 40A–F5, War Dept. Messages; *ibid.*, RG 94, Letters Received, 979M 1867; DLC-USG, V, 55; (2) DLC-Philip H. Sheridan; DLC-Edwin M. Stanton. On May 21, USG forwarded a copy of this telegram to Secretary of War Edwin M. Stanton. ES, DNA, RG 94, Letters Received, 979M 1867. Also on May 20, Sheridan wrote to Bvt. Maj. Gen. John A. Rawlins. "I have the honor to enclose for the information of the General-in-Chief specimens of spurious certificates of naturalization papers issued by the 5th District Court of New Orleans, for which the clerk was dismissed from his office. A great many of thes papers were and are issued." LS, *ibid.*, RG 108, Letters Received. The enclosures are *ibid.*

On May 22, Sheridan telegraphed to USG. "There is a persistent effort made to construe the order of Genl Griffin in Circular number thirteen (13) as forcing Colored Jurors on the Courts in Texas. General Griffin tells me he had no such intention but it was to force the Courts to put on loyal citizens of which there is in each County sufficient number to give security to Union people and to relieve himself from the pressure of applications of this class of the Country for redress in the most grievous wrongs" Telegram received (at 5:00 P.M.), *ibid.*, RG 107, Telegrams Collected (Bound); *ibid.*, RG 108, Telegrams Received; copies, *ibid.*, RG 46, Senate 40A–F5, War Dept. Messages; *ibid.*, RG 94, Letters Received, 746M 1867; *ibid.*, 1106M 1867; DLC-USG, V, 55; (2) DLC-Philip H. Sheridan; DLC-Edwin M. Stanton. On May 23, USG forwarded a copy of this telegram to Stanton. ES, DNA, RG 94, Letters Received, 746M 1867. On May 29, Bvt. Maj. Gen. Charles Griffin, Galveston, wrote to Sheridan at length concerning the matter, and Sheridan forwarded this letter to USG. Copy and ES (undated), *ibid.*, 880M 1867. For Griffin's Circular No. 13, April 27, see *HED*, 40-1-20, pp. 73–74.

On May 23, Sheridan telegraphed to USG. "The most encouraging reports are coming in from every section of the State of the progress & sucess of Registration If the Attorney Genl is to give an interpretation it should be sent as Soon as possible otherwise the registration may be unnecessarily delayed beyond the time allotted viz the 30th of June" Telegram received (at 7:00 P.M.), DNA, RG 107, Telegrams Collected (Bound); *ibid.*, RG 108, Telegrams Received; copies, *ibid.*, RG 46, Senate 40A–F5, War Dept. Messages; *ibid.*, RG 94, Letters Received, 747M 1867; *ibid.*, 1115M 1867; DLC-USG, V, 55; (2) DLC-Philip H. Sheridan; DLC-Edwin M. Stanton. On the same day, USG endorsed a copy of this telegram to Stanton. ES, DNA, RG 94, Letters Received, 747M 1867. On May 30, Sheridan telegraphed to USG. "On the Twenty seventh 27 inst. I extended the time for registration in this city to June twentieth 20. The most cheering reports are sent in by the boards Throughout the state of the success of registration and the good will with which they are received by all classes. There is a very good condition of affairs throughout my command Last night the largest political assembly which ever collected together in this city mostly of colored people paraded the streets without the slightest disturbance I had made every prepration should any disturbance occur but did not show public a single soldier I desired to make this case a test one and the result was most satisfactory" Telegram received (at 5:45 P.M.), *ibid.*, RG 107, Telegrams Collected (Bound); *ibid.*, RG 108, Telegrams Received; copies, *ibid.*, RG 46, Senate 40A–F5, War Dept. Messages; DLC-USG, V, 55; (2) DLC-Philip H. Sheridan; (torn) DLC-Edwin M. Stanton. On May 31, USG forwarded a copy of this telegram to Stanton; on the same day Stanton endorsed this copy. "Respectfully transmitted to the President for his information" ES and AES, *ibid.* On June 4, Sheridan telegraphed to USG. "Have returns of registration from most of the parishes of this state Also the reports of the Officers Supervising and can report to you the greatest success & the best of feeling existing among the people" Telegram received (at 2:00 P.M.), DNA, RG 107, Telegrams Collected (Bound); *ibid.*, RG 108, Telegrams Received; copies, *ibid.*, RG 46, Senate 40A–F5, War Dept. Messages; DLC-USG, V, 55; DLC-Philip H. Sheridan; DLC-Edwin M. Stanton; 5th Military District Papers, Duke University, Durham, N. C. On the same day, Maj. George K. Leet noted on a telegram received. "The General has gone to West Point. Please forward these telegrams to him & oblige . . ." ANS, DNA, RG 108, Telegrams Received. On June 5, Rawlins forwarded a copy of this telegram to Stanton. ES, *ibid.*, RG 94, Letters Received, 816M 1867.

On May 22 or 23, Sheridan had written to USG. "In my recent trip to Galveston I met a man from the extreme Northern portion of Texas and accumulated a good deal of information in reference to the strength and position of the Cammanche Indians, who inhabit the Canadian River country. He represents that there are about (12,000) twelve thousand warriors and that the Cheyennes and Sioux Indians will eventually join them and be friends, and that probably some of them have already taken up their abode in the Canadian River country, as they fraternise with the Cammanches readily The Canadian River country is a fine country: has plenty of grazing, and the Indians are in possession of large herds of horses, cattle and sheep &c. My informant has driven (19,000) nineteen thousand head of cattle from Texas to New Mexico within the last two years and was at no time molested. He has frequently seen small bands of Cammanches but was not molested: there being at the same time no intercourse. The route he pursued with his cattle was from the head waters of the Concha across to the Pecos striking it at the Horse Shoe crossing; thence up the Pecos to New Mexico. I think his estimate of the Cammanche warriors is perhaps exaggerated There is now no destruction on the Indian frontier of Texas: it has disappeared since I thought of removing Governor Throckmorton; but I have deemed it best to accumulate a small supply of munitions of war at the Arsenal at San Antonio." LS (dated May 22), *ibid.*, RG 108, Letters Received; (dated May 23) *ibid.*; copies (dated May 23), *ibid.*, RG 393, Dept. of the Mo., Letters Received; (misdated June 8) *ibid.*, 5th Military District, Letters Sent; (dated May 23) DLC-Philip H. Sheridan.

To Jesse Root Grant

———

May 28th *1867*

DEAR FATHER:

If you will write me the full particulars of the claim of Miss Landrum, giving name of party whos services are unpaid, &c. I will have the matter looked into again. I can not recollect these matters and I do not preserve private letters.

It will be out of the question for young Landrum to get an appointment this year. There were hundreds of applications for the Ten, at Large, many of whom are recommended by the Presidents personal & political friends who would have much more weight than I would.

Yours Truly,
U. S. GRANT

ALS, Boston Public Library, Boston, Mass. See letter to Jesse Root Grant, May 21, 1867.

To Lt. Gen. William T. Sherman

———

Washington, May 29th 1867.

LT. GEN. W. T. SHERMAN,
COMDG. MIL. DIV. OF THE MO.
GENERAL:

For several days back there has been a conflict going on between the Interior and the War Depts. which I have been compelled to enter into, growing out of Indian Affairs. On the statements of Agents Leavenworth & Wynkoop Mr. Browning was very ready to condemn Hancock's policy.[1] At first the only question seemed to be whether the Army would destroy camp equipments, provisions &c. if they were sent to the Cheyennes to replace those destroyed by Hancock. I suggested that Hancock had better be heard from before action, maintaining that there always is two sides to a question and that a man who had won his own way to a Major Generalcy might be regarded as reliable as an Indian Agt. The Sec. of the Interior thinking there was no time to lose in this matter I telegraphed directly to Hancock for a report, by telegraph and mail. His reply by telegraph has been received, and, I presume you have been furnished a copy.[2]

I can not describe to you, on paper, the two interviews I have had, in Cabinet, (being sent for) on the subject of Indian matters. There will be a war with the Indians let the Army do what it may. If inactive we will be justly blamed; if active, the Interior Department will endeavor to show that the army are responsible for the war and that interference with their legitimate duties has produced it.

The last turn we had on Indian affairs was to know whether Indian Agts. would be allowed to issue annuities,[3] including arms, powder, lead, &c. (which are not stipulated as part of these annuities, but are regarded as necessary to the support of the Indian) on their own judgment ~~as to the~~ as to the propriety of giving them without interference from the Military. I replied no: war existed and we could not fight them with one branch of the Government and equip and feed them with ~~the~~ another with any kind of justice to those who are called on to expose their lives. Then the question arose as to whether these issues could be made, in the way specified above, to peaceable Indians. My reply was that the Military must be the judge of who are peaceable Indians, and which of them it would be prudent to make issues to. I suggested that the goods purchased be sent to Military posts on the frontier and that the Indian Agts. be directed to communicate with Military Commanders, and issue their goods to such tribes of Indians, and at such time and places as they, the Military, might authorize.

If you can spare time from St. Louis, I do not know but it will be well for you to come on here for a few days. If you do not come on write me an official letter suggesting such plan as you would propose, whilst hostilities exist, for delivering Indian goods.

The Sec. was indignant at the idea of Indian Agts. being subordinate to the Military. I do not believe he will issue goods unless he can do it entirely independent of us unless we can get the order from the President compelling it. I think he is inclined to hold us responsible for treaty stipulations not being carried out.

Very respectfully
Your obt. Servt.
U S GRANT
General.

Copies, DLC-USG, V, 47, 60; DNA, RG 108, Letters Sent. On June 1, 1867, Bvt. Maj. Gen. William A. Nichols telegraphed to USG. "Your letter of May twenty ninth (29) received this morning.—General Sherman is at Omaha—I have telegraphed him in the case." Copy (sent by mail), *ibid.*, RG 94, Letters Received, 656M 1867. On June 6, Sherman, Fort Sedgwick, Colorado Territory, telegraphed to USG. "Am here, plenty of Indian attacks in every direction in small bands Will attend to them" Telegram received (at 7:40 P.M.), *ibid.*, RG 107, Telegrams Collected (Bound); *ibid.*, RG 108, Telegrams Received; copies, *ibid.*, RG 94, Letters Received, 753M 1867; DLC-USG, V, 55. On June 7, USG endorsed a copy of this telegram to Secretary of War Edwin M. Stanton. ES, DNA, RG 94, Letters Received, 753M 1867. On June 8, Sherman twice telegraphed to USG. "On the application of Govr. Hunt of Colorado I authorized him to raise four 4 companies of mounted Militia to move rapidly to the head of the Republican to catch in motion the Indians who will thus attempt to escape General Custar application comes to buy horses Equipments &c which is refused but an offer of forty 40 cents a day made for the use of private horses If they dont succeed tomorrow I will not use them at all but trust to the regular troops in hand. The Indians are very widely scattered and are engaged mostly in stealing horses They may combine and do mischief and the country is awfully long. Genl. Augur goes up the south Platte Gen. Gibbon up Pole Creek. I remain here a central location I have not yet heard from Gen Custer and await his coming" "Major Lewis who was sent to Montana reports 'That all the excitement here was founded on the murder of Boseman' I will not therefore accept any volunteers and major Lewis will return to Salt Lake" Telegrams received (on June 10, the first at 10:30 A.M., the second at 11:00 A.M.), *ibid.*, RG 107, Telegrams Collected (Bound); *ibid.*, RG 108, Telegrams Received; copies, *ibid.*, RG 94, Letters Received, 753M 1867; DLC-USG, V, 55. On June 10, USG endorsed copies of these telegrams to Stanton. ES, DNA, RG 94, Letters Received, 753M 1867. See letter to Lt. Gen. William T. Sherman, May 17, 1867.

On June 10, Sherman telegraphed to USG. "No recent attacks in the road by Indians Telegraph poles and wire badly damaged by Indians and lightning but are being rapidly repaired. Major Lewis reports from Montana that all the trouble reports sent by the governor and others had no other foundation than the murder of Boseman. He will not therefore accept any more Volunteers there. Govr. Hunt of Colorado also reports he cannot raise the three hundred 300 horses and therefore his volunteers cannot do what I wanted and will not be accepted The Indians are doubtless confining their attacks to small parties and unexpected points. Genls Augur and Gibbon have gone forward by separate routes and I will remain here until the railroad is finished. This far till Genl. Custer arrives and things settled down or take a positive direction We are relied upon to protect mail and stage lines." Telegram received (on June 12, 8:55 A.M.), DNA, RG 107, Telegrams Collected (Bound); *ibid.*, RG 108, Telegrams Received; copies, *ibid.*, RG 94, Letters Received, 753M 1867; DLC-USG, V, 55. On the same day, Sherman wrote to USG. "Yours of May 27 [29], did not reach me till today, and I hasten to reply. All doubts as to the intentions of the Indians whose Camp Gen Hancock burned last April on Pawnee Fork, are set at rest, for these same Indians besides killing and burning the three men on the Smoky Hill have made at least a dozen open and bloody attacks on people living along the Platte, or on Stages and emigrants travelling this road. To restore to them their lodges or the value thereof would be a premium for Murder and highway Robbery. As to giving to Traders who have an interest, or to Indian Agents who do not actually live with the Indians a right to sell arms and munitions either as barter for Buffalo Robes, or as part of their Governmet Annuities, I wish to be even more Emphatic than heretofore. The very Indians that the Agents and Butterfield Equipped last winter at Zara, and the Arkansas have this year used Spencer Carbines and Colts pistols skilfully in riding down the Overland Stages. So skilful have they become, and so well supplied are they that citizens and soldiers manifest more fear of them than I have ever noticed before. If the faith of the nation is pledged to this traffic we may have to draw off our troops, abandon our Territories, and forego our Overland Stages, Telegraph and Railroads. This cannot be tolerated for a moment, and therefore I wish to be construed as agreeing with you perfectly that no arms or munitions should go to any of the Plain Indians except by and through the Military officers. If the Commissioner of Indian affairs will deposit with the commanding officer of the nearest Military Post what arms and munitions a tribe claims or is entitled to, I will order their issue in such manner as to approach ordinary prudence and safety. As to issues under former Treaties, To the tribes who have fixed Reservations and who really and in fact sojourn there with an agent right among them I agree that the annuities should be paid with the greatest regularity, and that no trader should have a lien on this annuity. What is due by Governmt to Indians should go to them absolutely, & traders should be confined to a barter for their furs, skins, or whatever they may manufacture or raise. This should apply to the Cherokees, Creeks, Choctaws, Pawnees Winnebagos and indeed all the Tribes whose reservations are clearly defined. There is now no objection to the annuities being paid to the Cheyennes & Arapahoes, the Kioways and Comanches to the south of the Arkansas, but as many of their warriors are out on the War path, their payments should be at their Camps, or on the south Bank of the Arkansas opposite Forts Larned & Dodge, and witnessed by some officer to be designated by the Departmt Commander. No goods or payments should go to any of the Sioux Nation, except to Spotted Tails Band, that we propose to put on an Island in the Platte, near Fort McPherson, where we can hold the families as hostages, and can see for ourselves whether they bring in from their hunts, stolen horses. There are also some bands of Sioux along the Missouri River who have remained peaceable & Dependant. This conflict of authority will exist as long as the Indians exist, for their ways are different from our ways, and either they or we must be masters on the Plains. I have no doubt our people have committed grievous wrong to the Indians and I wish we could punish them but it is impracticable but both races cannot use this country in common, and one or the other must withdraw.

We cannot withdraw without checking the natural progress of Civilization. The only course is for us to destroy the hostile, and to segregate the peaceful and maintain them. The Interior Dept has not the means to accomplish this, and should at once consent to relinquish all control of tribes that are not localized. With the wandering or nomadic Indians we are forced to deal, and should have absolute control. With such as are localized we do not wish to deal, and these could be left as now. The line may be difficult to draw, but not impossible. The recent events along this Line of Road demonstrate what I state, and will I think have convinced Mr Browning that he is in error. I think the Interior Departmt should place at our disposal, all funds due under treaties to the Sioux, Cheyennes, Arapahoes, Kioways, Comanches, Utes and Apaches, and leave us to disburse them so as to segregate & maintain the peaceful and well inclined parts of these tribes, and to pursue & destroy the hostile All other Indian funds could continue to be disbursed as heretofore." ALS, DNA, RG 108, Letters Received. On June 11, Sherman wrote to USG. "I have been here long enough to have a pretty good idea of things and suppose you are in a mist by reason of the thousand and one stories that are afloat. An excursion party with Wm B. Ogden at its head turned back yesterday 100 miles out of Omaha—from which I infer they have a scare down there.—I am just 400 miles from Omaha, and the Railroad is finished to within 22½ miles. The grading parties are a little behind hand but I hope these 22½ miles will be finished in ten days.—You know the map. Settlements in Nebraska strong enough to feel safe against a dozen Indians, do not exist 50 miles out of Omaha, thence to the Pacific will be this single track, with a board station house every 10 or 20 miles, and a Country incapable of maintaining inhabitants. This is now our task to guard, beside a telegraph line South of the Platte along the Old Stage Road, and a string of wagons hauling goods & stores to all the the Territories. To defend my old line of 300 miles to Atlanta against Forest & the Guerillas was easy as compared with this. The clamor for guards at every stage station, every telegraphic hut, for every passing train, for every party engaged in getting ties, grading, or laying track consume our troops and will leave us little or nothing to carry war into the Enemys Country. Then this Enemys Country is a land as big as the whole settled United States and one may travel, weeks, months years without seeing an indian, a pony bush, tree, or any thing. of course we have no interest or desire to produce Universal War on the Plains, nor if we had armies could we maintain them. Even our small forces scattered as they are can hardly procure the food for themselves and corn for their horses, and all are worn out with pursuing the faint tracks of some little thieving band that comes from no one knows where, and have gone in like manner. General Augur can hardly get to Laramie Reno & c food & forage for his garrisons much less a supply with which to carry an adequate force into that unknown land about the Yellowstone where we think the great Sioux tribes rendezvous, if they ever do rendezvous, so that the Indian Expedition I had designed may be thwarted this season, or at least deferred too late to prevent these constant raids on the Roads. Both General Augur & I agree that the first great essential is to hurry up the Construction of the Railroad at least to the Black hills, so that corn & stores can be accumulated early in the year with which to proceed on these distant expeditions, so for the present his troops will be arranged pretty much as follows. . . . This absorbs all his command, and a part of each garrison is taken up as little detachmts at stage & telegraph stations and guarding trains in route. If these Indian raids diminish

Gen Augur can assemble about Laramie a part of each garrison and go for the Indians if he can find out where they are. Since I have been here two severe thunder storms destroyed many telegraph poles, and coming at the time of the Indian raids, the repairs have progressed slowly, and has added to the Confusion. One or two of the repair parties which are small were caught by the Indians and were killed, adding to the difficulty. We can now telegraph by Denver to San Francisco, but the Line round by Laramie is not yet repaired.—We also reach the telegraph wire at the end of the road by sending Couriers—but the line on the South of the Platte is not yet repaired. I have just learned of the arrival at McPherson of Gen Custar with six Cos of the 7th Cavalry. Col Carrington who is still there notifies me of this fact by a Courier who rode to Bishops opposite North Platte, 22 miles this side of McPherson. I have sent back to Gen Custar by the Same messenger his orders to this effect. After a Couple days rest to start in this direction one day, then despatch his train here by the Valley Road, and himself by a rapid night march to cross over the wide prairie to the South West, on the Republican, and scour it thoroughly to its head and come in here for supplies and further orders. I think the Cheyennes are on the Republican from which they have depredated on this Road by small parties. If Custar can act rapidly I hope he may catch & destroy this party of Indians, at all events it is worth the effort. After this I will have his Cavalry to act all summer to cover the working parties of the Railroad, leaving Gen Augur to use Stevensons Regimt 30th for other purposes. To understand the difficulties out here you should see this River Platte—it is now runing about 7 miles an hour, half a mile wide, so shallow in parts that a skiff drawing 4 inches has to be hauled over its quick moving sandy bottom—at other points deep enough to swim a horse. To cross a boat with load they have to put in the water from 30 to 50 men. Some wade ahead pulling at a rope and have of course to swim at the deep places. Others cling to the boat, pushing and swiming as they go. Already two men have been drowned, and two men escaped within an inch of their lives yesterday. It is about the meanest river I ever saw. A pontoon bridge cannot be built because no anchor will hold, as all the bottom is travelling down stream as well as the water, and a pile bridge would cost as much as a pin bridge over the Mississipi. It may run down in a month so that horses and wagons may ford. The valley is flat, wide, and absolutely devoid of bush or plant higher than ordinary grass, so that an object may be seen as far as on water. The hills that bound the valley are rounding and not high, so that you can gallop a horse up them anywhere, but instead of being a plain, it is a high plateau with innumerable ravines in which the bands of Indians conceal themselves absolutely, and from some high point they see every train, horse & man pass. That the valley is watched at all points, is believed, yet all attempts to run down and catch these fellows have proved failures. The Indians see a small band of horses or Cattle grazing, they slip down—surround and drive them off, and hide them before pursuit can be made. In like manner when a single Stage or wagon, or small party are seen on the road, they move parallel out of sight until the Road approaches the foot hills, when they stream down and their victims rarely have a minutes notice for preperation. They take no prisoners and always scalp the dead. It is this that enrages the People in Denver, Montana & else where, that depend on these Roads for all they buy. They are clamorous for extermination which is easier said than done, and they have an idea that we are moved by more humane sentiments. They cry for the Chivington process—but what I recall of that affair was that Chivington did not fall upon a band that was hostile but one that was in the Custody of the Commanding officer at Fort Lyon. I would not hesitate to approve the extermination of a camp such as I believe may exist on the Republican, from which they send out these thieving murdering parties to kill and steal on this Road, but I would not sanction the extermination of such a Band as Spotted Tail's, which is camped near Fort McPherson, with the approval of General Augur. You know that Governor Hunt of Colorado wanted to make a Campaign, and I inquired when and against what Indians he would move, he answered down the Smoky Hill and down the Platte, and the movemt would develope the whereabouts of the Warriors—This was absurd, for on both the lines he named he could move a hundred men, and would not see a Warrior. Thinking that probably a force moving from Denver down the Republican in cooperation with Custar moving up, might catch some Indians and hearing from him that he only had 300 Carbines, I authorized him to raise 300 Mounted Volunteers and start them on that line. Then through Ihrie he asked for authority to buy horses, wanted Quarter Masters Commissaries &c. I answered offering to pay 40 cents a day for the use of horses for the two months, ample time to do all that was needed. At first he said he would start the party, but finally said he could not raise the horses and would have to abandon the whole matter. On Sunday last I got a Denver paper in which I saw he had published one of my despatches on which the papers made furious comments, whereat I notified the Governor that I considered the publication of one of my despatches without my consent a breach of honor. He is very much hurt thereat but it is true. These Civilians cannot appreciate what we do unless they appeal to the people of their neighborhood. Like Meagher in Montana, and Hunt in Colorado they must use events of this kind as means to secure local popularity. They cannot forget themselves in an occasion that demands personal sacrifice. I have notified all the People that they must lend their aid unbought if they would save their lives & stock. Notwithstanding the danger, there is a carelessness on the part of trains that is almost criminal and tempting to Indians. Col Potter and other officers tell me what I have seen myself of Cases, where two or three bold highwaymen Indian or white would be tempted to Capture whole trains. Not a single train organised under our orders more than a year old, has been successfully attacked, and all the attacks have been made on the weakest Ranches. The only stage Coach captured was the one up at Moores, where was but one unarmed passenger inside who escaped, and the driver and another man behind leading 4 horses, so both these men had four horses, and fell an easy prey to a small band that was of course tempted by the Eight good horses, which they got with two scalps. Still I am looking for the Indians after they have got enough horses to make a descent on the Road on a larger scale and it is against that that I am now guarding. I hope Custars movemt will anticipate them on the south side of the Road, but the danger on the North side cannot be met so punctually or so effectually because the Country is so much larger and more difficult. If this condition of affairs indicates peaceable Indians I would like Mr Browning to define to us, what war & peace means. This whole state of things cannot be traced to any single cause, and we should not charge it solely to Indian Agents or Traders, nor should they charge it on us. It is an inevitable conflict of races, one that must occur when a stronger is gradually displacing a weaker. The Indians are poor, & proud. They are tempted beyond their power of resistance to steal of the herds & flocks, they see grazing so peacefully in this valley. To steal they sometimes must kill. We in our turn cannot discriminate—all look alike, talk alike and under the same pressure act alike, and to get the rascals, we are forced to include all. I dont ask you for more men, because if we had them we could hardly maintain them now. Nor do I propose War in its strict sense, but hostilities between the races will continue till the Indians are all killed or taken to a Country where they can be watched. I wish our Cavalry could keep their horses on grass alone like the Indians, but they cannot, and the Ghosts of horses I see here are good proof. Excuse so long a letter, but I suppose you want to hear. . . . P. S. Augur has gone up the South Platte, and Gibbon up the Lodge Pole, but they can do but little, as the Indians can watch them every foot of the way, and will be as likely to strike the road three miles behind them as a hundred miles away,—but the troops will all be kept in motion somehow—" ALS (tabular material omitted), *ibid.* On June 19, USG endorsed to Stanton copies of these letters. ES, *ibid.*, RG 107, Letters Received from Bureaus.

On June 18, 2:35 P.M., USG telegraphed to Sherman. "It is represented that the abandonment of Fort Thompson D. T. as now ordered, will expose settlers to ~~great~~ certain danger. Would it not be well to countermand orders for abandonment of that post?" ALS (telegram sent), *ibid.*, Telegrams Collected (Bound); telegram sent, *ibid.*; copies, *ibid.*, RG 108, Telegrams Sent; DLC-USG, V, 56. On June 20, Sherman, North Platte, Neb., telegraphed to USG. "Dispatch about Fort Thompson is received. It was not considered a Military Post. I will send your dispatches to Gen Stanberry [*Stanley*] & ascertain from him the facts & instruct him if necessary to keep an Outpost there in the nature of a Detachment from Fort Sully. These detachments so diminish our garrisons that they are prevented from doing more than to defend themselves leaving the Indians free to go where they please" Telegrams received (2—one on June 22, 4:00 P.M., the second at 6:15 P.M.), DNA, RG 107, Telegrams Collected (Bound); *ibid.*, RG 108, Telegrams Received; copy, DLC-USG, V, 55. On June 18, Sherman, North Platte, had telegraphed to USG. "All the Indians between the Arkansas and Platte have had ample time to come in to Military Posts for protection. May I now permit civil authorities and citizens generally to clear out that region to have all captured stock not claimed as stolen. The Indians are so scattered that without absolutely filling the span with Cavalry they will elude us. There is no doubt of their hostility" Telegram received (on June 21, 10:05 A.M.), DNA, RG 107, Telegrams Collected (Bound); *ibid.*, RG 108, Telegrams Received; copies (2), *ibid.*, RG 94, Letters Received, 809M 1867; *ibid.*, RG 393, Dept. of the Platte, Telegrams Received; DLC-USG, V, 55. On June 22, USG endorsed a copy of this telegram to Stanton. ES, DNA, RG 94, Letters Received, 809M 1867. On June 19, Sherman telegraphed to USG. "Gen. Sanborn is just down from Laramie & says 'that some friendly Sioux are coming down to join Spotted Tails band near here. Runners have gone out & allow thirty 30 days for the rest to come all others to confer with you. I suppose you cannot do much but propose during these thirty 30 days'. The Cheyennes south are also cutting up and I have calls for eCustars Cavalry. Had we not better Keep it in motion between Fort Morgan & the Smoky Hill   Nothing here or along the line.   will go down to Omaha tomorrow & stay till I hear from you at Laramie. Railroad will reach Julesburg saturday" Telegram received (on June 21, 10:30 A.M.), *ibid.*, RG 107, Telegrams Collected (Bound); *ibid.*, RG 108, Telegrams Received; copies (2—misdated June 21), *ibid.*, RG 94, Letters Received, 808M 1867; *ibid.*, RG 393, Dept. of the Platte, Telegrams Received; DLC-USG, V, 55. Misdated June 21 in *HED*, 41-2-240, p. 110. On June 22, USG endorsed a copy of this telegram to Stanton. ES, DNA, RG 94, Letters Received, 808M 1867. At 10:10 A.M., USG telegraphed to Sherman, Omaha. "I do not like the idea of ~~authorizing~~ giving Civil Authorities all the plunder they can capture as a reward for protecting themselves against hostile indians. We want to capture however all the stock of hostile indians and you may use as you deem most advantageous such as you do capture. Carry out your own views as to movement of Custer's Cavalry." ALS (telegram sent), *ibid.*, RG 107, Telegrams Sent; telegram sent, *ibid.*; telegram received (on June 23, 9:00 A.M.), *ibid.*, RG 393, Dept. of the South, Telegrams Received. On June 24, Sherman, Fort Leavenworth, telegraphed to USG. "Dispatch of June twenty second (22) is received, Genl, Auger is now at Laramie and Genl Hancock is near Denver Each is capable of managing his own Department and I will return to St Louis tomorrow" Telegram received (at 8:20 P.M.), *ibid.*, RG 107, Telegrams Collected (Bound); *ibid.*, RG 108, Telegrams Received; copy, DLC-USG, V, 55.

On June 26, Sherman, St. Louis, telegraphed to USG. "I am now back. The troubles on the Plains will not cease till we Can invade the country north of the Platte and South of the Arkansas where reside the families of the hostile. We have not regular troops enough for this and would have to call into service at least five thousand 5000 mounted Volunteers Will the Secretary of War Sanction this or had we better lay the whole matter before Congress and ask Special legislation At present the troubles are quieted down along the Platte but are renewed on the Arkansas and Smoky Hill. Shall I address you a formal report on the whole case to be laid before Congress" Telegram received (at 3:00 P.M.), DNA, RG 107, Telegrams Collected (Bound); *ibid.*, RG 108, Telegrams Received; copies (one sent by mail), *ibid.*, RG 94, Letters Received, 798M 1867; *ibid.*, RG 393, Military Div. of the Mo., Indian War; DLC-USG, V, 55. On June 27, noon, USG telegraphed to Sherman. "I do not think it advisable to call any Volunteers into service except such assistance becomes necessary for preservation of existing settlements and lines of travel. I should like a formal report on Indian matters to presnt to Congress." ALS (telegram sent), DNA, RG 107, Telegrams Collected (Bound); telegram sent, *ibid.*; copies, *ibid.*, RG 108, Telegrams Sent; (incomplete) *ibid.*, RG 393, Dept. of the Mo., Letters Received; DLC-USG, V, 56. On the same day, Sherman telegraphed to USG. "Despatch of today is rec'd Your conclusion is exactly right and I have called for no Volunteers at all and am only Committed to accepting a small number of mounted Volunteers at Fort Harker if Gen A J Smith calls for them, of Governor of Kansas" Telegram received (at 5:20 P.M.), DNA, RG 107, Telegrams Collected (Bound); *ibid.*, RG 108, Telegrams Received; copies (one sent by mail), *ibid.*, RG 94, Letters Received, 799M 1867; DLC-USG, V, 55.

On July 1, Sherman wrote to USG. "*Private* . . . Whilst Dayton is copying my official letter, I will write you a few words to keep you as fully posted as you care to be. I wrote you a long letter from Sedgwick—As soon as the People got on their guard and fought the Indians, and as soon as I had got Custars & other cavalry behind them the Indians quit the Platte and the Excitemt subsided. It is now turned up on the Smoky Hill, and I have the same claimor from them and threats to abandon the Stage Line and the Railroad. Every Contractor and Stage driver thinks we have nothing to do but guard him, and every one wants to take Command of the Army. If they make much more fuss I will tell them the truth and let them abandon the Stage Line. to secure the price of half a dozen passengers per day, they would have us spend a Couple thousand dollars, by way of protection. I will go up again to Fort Harker to see for myself on Thursday of this week and will judge for myself.—I fear A. J. Smith takes too many toddies, & sees more than double. He did not like my sending Custar and six of his companies over to the Platte and as quiet is now prevalnt on the Platte I have sent orders to Custar by way of Sedgwick to work back to the Smoky Hill about Fort Wallace. I will meet Hancock on his way in, and will arrange for a permanent distribution of Cavalry. I gave the 4 Cos of the 6th Infantry for the Indian Territory to Hancock with a clear bargain to have a like quantity of cavalry for Augur, who has only the 2nd Regular Cavalry which is worn down by constant Escort duty, and distant Scouts. I am sure that we must treaty as no treaty forbid all Indians going betwn the Platte and Arkansas. There are only War parties there, and by clearing them out and keeping them out, we permanently divide the Sioux of the north from the Cheyennes and prevent these combinations.—If we can do that then we can take each of these warlike tribes in hand one at a time, instead as now, having them together. I notice the fixed purpose of the Interior Dept to give this middle ground to the Indians for Hunting.—Look at the Report made last winter by Mr Doolittle, and on Page 6. you will see clearly stated what I have also urged that of necessity Game & Indians must disappear betwn the two great Railroads. Our season has been so backward & the contractors for hauling have been so embarrassed that I fear Gen Augur will not be able to make his Expedition to the Powder River & Yelowstone this year. I have therefore consented that he confine his attention to the better protection of the overland Routes, and existing settlements, at all costs until the commission of which Gen Sanborn is a member has exhausted its efforts to seperate the friendly from the hostile Sioux—I know the almost utter impossibility of bringing the hostile Sioux to battle, except when they have every advantage, but sooner or later they must be whipped, so that they fear us which is not the case now. Mrs Sherman & children will go up to Madison Wis. next week—I will go to Fort Harker & remain till Gen Hancock gets there, and then up to Omaha & out to Sedgwick till I can observe how things are progressing, when I will return here or go on up to Terry's Dept—all the Dept Commanders are in the Field: and all the Soldiers are either at Posts in the Indian Country or marching." ALS, USG 3. On the same day, Sherman wrote at length to Maj. George K. Leet concerning Indian affairs. ALS, DNA, RG 94, Letters Received, M102 1867. Printed in *HED*, 40-2-1, II, part 1, pp. 65–68.

1. On June 3, Monday, Secretary of the Interior Orville H. Browning, Quincy, Ill., telegraphed to Act. Secretary of the Interior William T. Otto. "Had a brief interview with Genl. Sherman on Friday and with Agent Leavenworth this morning. I am clearly of opinion that the Military between the Platte and Arkansas should be confided [confined] to the protection of the roads and not be allowed to scout the country till commissioners can be sent to confer with the Indians, between these rivers and south of the Arkansas, if this can be done, further hostilities in that region will be prevented if Commissioners are sent & suggest for consideration the names of Dole Irwin of the Indian Bureau & Wm W. Bent, now near Fort Lyon. If appointed others should be added—Leavenworth and Wynkoop should be directed to get the Indians together." Copy (brackets in original), DNA, RG 107, Letters Received from Bureaus. On June 21, USG endorsed this telegram. "Respectfully returned to the Secretary of War. I have no information to warrant the belief that the result predicted by the

Secretary of the Interior can be reached by sending Commissioners, and the delay would leave the Indians free to commit their depredations with out hindrance by the military authorities. There is no objection to the Secretary of the Interior sending Commissioners, provided they do not interfere with the operations of Lt. Gen. Sherman." ES, *ibid.*

2. See telegram to Maj. Gen. Winfield S. Hancock, May 23, 1867.

3. On July 19, Sherman wrote to Leet. "The communication of the Honorable the Secretary of the Interior enclosing copies of his letters of instruction for the distribution of the annuity goods, dated May 30, 1867, was received at this office June 14, and forwarded to me at Fort Sedgwick, C. T., but before they reached me I had returned to Saint Louis and gone up to Fort Harker, where I received them about the 10th instant. I made enquiries at once as to where the good in question were, and communicated to Mr Murphy, Superintendent of Indian Affairs, that I did not want any annuity goods to go to the Cheyennes, Arapahoes, Kiowas, or Camanches, as they were in open hostility. In the mean time the goods had been hauled to Emporia, Kansas, where I understand they are held subject to General Hancock's notice. I enclose herewith General Hancock's instructions to Captain E. Byrne, 10th Cavalry, who has his company at the mouth of the Little Arkansas about forty miles west of Emporia. In case the agents, Wynkoop or Leavenworth move these goods further towards the Indian country, General Hancock has ordered they be escorted to Fort Larned, and there held. The Indians will soon learn that these goods were en route to them, but are held because of their recent acts of hostility on the Smoky Hill and Arkansas; and I doubt the wisdom of their ever again having annuity goods till they are punished for their late acts. At all events, General Hancock and I are unwilling that these goods should be distributed till this whole question is settled on a basis satisfactory to the Government." LS, DNA, RG 94, Letters Received, 955M 1867.

To Maj. Gen. Henry W. Halleck

Washington, May 29th, 1867,

MAJ GEN. H W. HALLECK,
COMDG. MIL. DIV. OF THE PACIFIC
GENERAL:

Enclosed I send you copy of letter from the Sec. of State to the Sec. of War, and reply of the latter thereto. These letters give all the information that can now be given as to the time when we can send troops to occupy the possessions acquired from Russia.—You will see the letter of the Sec. of War contemplates your going in person to receive the formal delivery of the Territory known as North American Russian Provinces.

Four companies of troops, all Infantry, or part Infantry, and part Artillery as you can best spare them, will be sufficient Military force to occupy that Country. You may designate this force, with a suitable Field Officer for the command, to hold themselves in readiness to start on the shortest notice when the proper time comes.

I suppose a years provisions, from the 1st of July, should be taken for whatever force goes. This however you may judge of and act at your own discretion.—As you will be with the troops first landing upon our new possessions you will designate the points to be garrisoned.—At first, and until otherwise directed, the newly acquired territory, under whatever name may be given to it, will comprise a "District" and will be attached to the Department of California.

If you have any suggestions to make in addition to the instructions here given, or recommending changes in them, please communicate them.

> Very respectfully,
> Your obt. Servant,
> U S GRANT.
> General.

Copies, DLC-USG, V, 47, 60; (typescript) DNA, RG 94, Letters Received, 456P 1867; *ibid.*, RG 108, Letters Sent.

To Bvt. Maj. Gen. John M. Schofield

Washington, D, C, June 3d *1867.*

BVT. MAJ. GN. J. M. SCHOFIELD,
COMD.G 1ST DISTRICT;
GENERAL:

Your letter of the 2d inst. enclosing copy of General Orders on the subject of registration, which you propose to publish as supplemental to Gen. Orders No 28 of May 13th 1867, and asking for suggestions in relation to said orders, is received.

The order seems to me very full and complete and I think of nothing to add to it. In the 4th par. you innumerate the classes who are to be excluded from Registration if they have engaged in giving aid or comfort to rebellion as described in the three following paragraphs. I am not prepared to express an opinion as to the correctness of this innumeration without looking, as I have not doubt you have done, at the laws of Va. to see what the special duties are of the State Officers. Par. 8 gives, in my opinion, proper direction to Boards of registration for their action where they feel a doubt as to the right of an applicant to register, if any direction is to be given on the subject. But a doubt arises in my mind whether it would not be better to let the Boards settle the question of the right to register, under the other instructions contained in your orders, without any guide but their own judgement in doubtful cases.

> Very respectfully
> your obt. svt.
> U. S. Grant
> Gn.l

ALS, DNA, RG 393, 1st Military District, Letters Received. On June 2, 1867, Bvt. Maj. Gen. John M. Schofield, Richmond, had written to USG. "I send you herewith a copy of Instructions for the Government of Boards of Registration which I propose to issue as an Appendix to the regulations prescribed in my General Order No. 28 of May 13th. These instructions are based upon my understanding of the Acts of Congress of March 2d and 23d, And, it will be seen, differ in some respects from the opinion of the Attorney General—But the registers when completed, including the lists of those 'rejected upon challenge,' will include the names of all persons who apply for registration and take the prescribed oath, that is of all persons who are entitled to vote according to the Opinion of the Attorney General. Hence if I prove to be wrong in any interpretation of the law no harm will be done—the registration will still be correct. I shall be thankful for any suggestions on this subject which the President, Secretary of War, or yourself may be pleased to make. I have nearly completed my preparations for making the registration and intend to commence the work in a few days." ALS, ibid., RG 108, Letters Received.

On June 27, Schofield wrote to USG. "I have the honor to enclose, herewith, a list of the Civil appointments, which have been made by me in this Military District, Each appointment has been reported to the Governor of Virginia, who has thereupon issued his Commission according to the laws of the State" LS, ibid., RG 94, Letters Received, 857M 1867. The enclosure is ibid.

To J. Russell Jones

June 3d *1867*.

DEAR JONES,

Rawlins leaves here for the West in a day or two.[1] He will stop in Chicago on his way out and if you want him, now that his hand is in in a literary way,[2] will revise and correct up your journal ready for publication.

I attended to your request with the Atty. Gen. and made it all right. I suppose you want to report to him your return. I also attend[ed] to your other request in seeing that that elegant work of art, received from Rome, should go into the possession of Mrs. Jones. Corwith delivered it in person so I know it went strait

All are well here. Babcock has just returned from a long Southern tour.

Yours Truly
U. S. GRANT

ALS, George R. Jones, Chicago, Ill.

1. On June 5, 1867, Maj. George K. Leet wrote to Bvt. Maj. Gen. John A. Rawlins. "You will make a tour of inspection through such parts of the Military Division of the Missouri as the General Commanding has verbally directed, . . . Capt. Wm. McK. Dunn, Jr., 21st U. S. Infantry will accompany you on the tour of inspection above named." Copies, DLC-USG, V, 47, 60; DNA, RG 108, Letters Sent. On June 12, noon, Bvt. Brig. Gen. Orville E. Babcock telegraphed to USG, Washington, Pa. "Genl Rawlins babe died this morning. Mrs Rawlins does not think it necessary for him to return—Every thing will be attended to." ALS (telegram sent), *ibid.*, RG 107, Telegrams Collected (Bound); telegram sent, *ibid.* USG sent Rawlins on a lengthy western inspection tour to allow him to recover his health. James Harrison Wilson, *The Life of John A. Rawlins* (New York, 1916), pp. 338–47.
2. Rawlins delivered a speech on national affairs at Galena on June 21. *Galena Gazette*, June 22, 1867. See *ibid.*, June 18, 24–28, 1867. Wilson states that USG read and approved the text of Rawlins's address. Wilson, p. 338. The text is printed (misdated June 14) *ibid.*, pp. 470–502. Newspapers reporting the speech noted that USG's and Rawlins's views were probably identical. See *Chicago Tribune*, June 24, 1867; *Chicago Times*, June 24, 1867; *New York Times*, June 26, 1867.

To Maj. Gen. Philip H. Sheridan

Private   Washington, D, C, June 7th *1867*.

DEAR GENERAL:

I was absent from here, on my way to West Point, when the correspondence commenced between you and the Sec. of War which culminated in the removal of Gov. Wells. I knew nothing of it, except what was publishe[d] in the papers, until my return here yesterday. The Secretarys dispatch was in obedience to an order from the President written on Saturday[1] before starting South but not delivered to the Sec. until Monday after I had left my office.—I know Mr. Stanton is disposed to support you not only in this last measure but in every official act of yours thus far. He cannot say so because it is in Cabinet he has to do this and there is no telling when he may not be overruled and it would not be in keeping with his position to anounce beforehand that he intended do differ with his associate advisers. I have no doubt myself but that the removal of Governor Wells will do great good in your command if you are sustained, but great harm if you are not sustained. I shall do all I can to sustain you in it. You have acted boldly and with good judgement and will be sustained by public opinion as well as your own conscience no matter what the result.

It has been my intention to order you to Washington as soon as your command is in a condition that you can leave it for a few weeks to give you an opportunity of taking a run up North. A little relaxation for a few weeks will do you good, bodily, and give you an an opportunity of coming in contact with people who supported the government *during the rebellion.*

Yours Truly,

U. S. GRANT

To MAJ. GN. P. H. SHERIDAN,
NEW ORLEANS, LA.

ALS, DLC-Philip H. Sheridan. On June 7, 1867, 1:30 P.M., USG telegraphed to Maj. Gen. Philip H. Sheridan. "I see a dispatch from Washington announcing that the Sec. of War and myself favored a reprimand for your action in removing the Governor of La. I was not even in the City at the time. There is not one word of truth in the story." ALS (telegram sent), DNA, RG 107, Telegrams Collected (Bound); telegram sent, *ibid.*; copies, *ibid.*, RG 46, Senate 40A–F5, War Dept. Messages; *ibid.*, RG 108, Telegrams Sent; DLC-USG, V, 56; DLC-Edwin M. Stanton. On June 13, Sheridan wrote to USG. "Confidential . . . I am just in receipt of your letter of the 6th instant. I have not doubted for a moment that Mr Stanton would support me. I see that the newspapers are doing me injustice in supposing that I acted wholly on the Secretarys telegram. I had contemplated the removal of Governor Wells for some time: in fact, General, it was a necessity. He embarrassed me by making tests and by violations of the law, which I had to annul, and was in every way inimical to my administration   In addition he was the most zealous advocate for the removal of all officers but above all this he has no principle; is totally unreliable and nobody could trust him. I want to say, General, upon the subject of removals: that if they are not permitted, the 'Military Bill' is no use in these lower States so far as changing their status. The very moment that the civil authorities know that they are beyond the power of the Military commander; that moment they will defy him and impede the law. To attempt to reach cases by Military Commissions is impracticable: In the first place I have no officers and it would require many Military Commissions to be constantly in session. Then the extent of the territory over which I have jurisdiction would make it impossible to carry on this system of justice. The only way that I can give protection is by removal whenever the incumbent impedes the law. Under this fear but few will impede the law; because they have a greater love for office in this section than anywhere else. I have not removed any one without a just cause: and will not. I have not given away one iota to any political party in this respect and that is why Governor Wells and his few adherents attacked me. I have not issued any orders excercising a surveillance over the civil officers as has been done in some of the States: as I did not wish to have too many irons in the fire or too many complications; besides, those orders are buncombe so far as any good practical results can be obtained in my command. We have not the military strength in this State or Texas to work out any good in that way. It should be recollected that Texas is a State a thousand miles across in almost any direction, and there is no way to control it but to have the power to remove. Nevertheless, I believe it should be used with discretion and as little as possible. I will do no injury to those who passed the bill by any indiscretion on my part. The President has embarrassed me very much by raising the question of the right to remove   No one in this country doubted it until it was thus raised, and until it is definitively settled there will be the strongest opposition to the Military Commanders. I have again to renew my thanks to you, General, for your unwavering support and for your kindness in proffering to order me North. I have worked hard ever since I came down here and will take advantage of your kindness; but not until I get things so far a head here as will suit me   This Ste will come in as a Union State if the President will let me alone" LS, USG 3. Sheridan prepared a lengthy memorandum discussing the involvement of Governor J. Madison Wells of La. in a fraudulent scheme to sell La. bonds to repair damaged levees along the Mississippi River. AD (undated), *ibid.*

On June 4, 12:30 P.M., Sheridan had telegraphed to USG. "I found it necessary yesterday to remove Governor Wells. He has embarrassed me very much since I came in command by his subterfuges and political chicanery   This necessary act will be approved here by every class and shade of political opinion He has not a friend who is an honest man. I enclose by mail copy of the order removing him" LS (telegram sent), DNA, RG 107, Telegrams Collected (Bound); telegram received (at 1:45 P.M.), *ibid.*; (at West Point) *ibid.*, RG 108, Telegrams Received. On June 6, Sheridan telegraphed to USG. "Mr F. J. Durant having declined the appointment of Governor of this state Mr B T Flanders has been appointed in his stead The backbone of the trouble has been broken by the removal of Gov Wells I think you need not hereafter have any anxiety about the Condition of affairs here" Telegram received (at 11:10 P.M.), *ibid.*, RG 107, Telegrams Collected (Bound); *ibid.*, RG 108, Telegrams Received; copies, *ibid.*, RG 46, Senate 40A–F5, War Dept. Messages; *ibid.*, RG 94, Letters Received, 957M 1867; DLC-USG, V, 55; (2) DLC-Philip H. Sheridan; DLC-Edwin M. Stanton. On June 7, USG forwarded a copy of this telegram to Secretary of War Edwin M. Stanton. ES, DNA, RG 94, Letters Received, 957M 1867. On June 8, 12:30 P.M., Sheridan telegraphed to USG. "Governor Flanders assumed the duties of his office this morning. He is a man of integrity & ability and I now feel as though I was relieved of half my labors. As it has been heretofore there was no security and I feel, as the people of the whole state feel, that we have gotten rid of an unprincipled Governor and the set of disreputable tricksters which he had about him. Nothing will answer here but a bold and strong course and in taking it I am supported unanimously by every class & party" Telegram received (at 2:45 P.M.), *ibid.*, RG 107, Telegrams Collected (Bound); *ibid.*, RG 108, Telegrams Received; copies, *ibid.*, RG 46, Senate 40A–F5, War Dept. Messages; DLC-USG, V, 55; (2) DLC-Philip H. Sheridan; DLC-Edwin M. Stanton.

On June 4, Sheridan had written to USG. "I have the honor to enclose herewith a communication from the Hon W. B. Thompson of Hidalgo County Texas, and respectfully invite your attention to the endorsements thereon by Genls Griffin and J. J. Reynolds. Letters Similar to this in tone and statements reach my Hd Qrs frequently. I simply forward these as specimen cases; and request that you return these papers to me. I have made no removals of Judges and do not know that I will" LS, DNA, RG 108, Letters Received. On June 20, Sheridan telegraphed to USG. "I forward by todays mail the reasons for the reinstating of the two Union Judges in Texas The reported conduct of the officer at ElPaso is a humbug However the post is yet and has been under General Shermans Command doubtless the people of El Paso County sought justice in the courts of New Mexico as that county used to be do formerly because when Judge Bacon who lives there was Legislated out of office & that county joined to another district no courts could be held on account of the great distance and the necessity of having a large escort between San Antonio and ElPaso" Telegram received (at 3:30 P.M.), *ibid.*, RG 107, Telegrams Collected (Bound); *ibid.*, RG 108, Telegrams Received; copies, *ibid.*, RG 46, Senate 40A–F5, War Dept. Messages; *ibid.*, RG 94, Letters Received, 884M 1867; *ibid.*, 1107M 1867; DLC-USG, V, 55; (2) DLC-Philip H. Sheridan. Probably on June 20, Sheridan forwarded to Bvt. Maj. Gen. John A. Rawlins papers concerning the removal from office of a deputy sheriff and constable in Jefferson, Tex., for refusing to arrest the accused white murderer of a Negro. *SED*, 40-1-14, p. 234; dated June 25 in *HED*, 40-1-20, p. 102. On June 21, Sheridan forwarded to Rawlins papers concerning the murder of a Negro in Natchitoches, La. *SED*, 40-1-14, p. 226. On June 22, Sheridan wrote to Rawlins. "I respectfully call the attention of the General in

Chief to the enclosed report of one of my Staff Officers Showing the manner of administrating justice in the parish of Lafourche, Louisiana." LS, DNA, RG 94, Letters Received, 887M 1867. The enclosures are in *HED*, 40-1-20, pp. 95–99; *SED*, 40-1-14, pp. 227–30.

On June 10, Sheridan had written to USG. "I desire to call your attention to the inadequacy of the appropriation made by Congress to carry out the act passed March 2nd 1867 and the act supplemental thereto. Most of those employed in this reorganization are very poor and cannot work without their pay and when the amount already furnished is exhausted, much embarrassment will occur." LS, DNA, RG 107, Letters Received from Bureaus. On May 11, Maj. George K. Leet had written to the five military district commanders. "The estimates for funds to carry out the Act of Congress 'for the more efficient government of the rebel States,' being in excess of the amount appropriated by Congress, District Commanders are informed that the Paymaster General will inform them of the amount each can receive from the present appropriation. Any expense incurred beyond the present appropriation cannot be paid until Congress supplies the means." LS, *ibid.*, RG 393, 5th Military District, Civil Affairs, Letters Received; *ibid.*, 2nd Military District, Letters Received; *ibid.*, 1st Military District, Letters Received; copies, *ibid.*, RG 108, Letters Sent; DLC-USG, V, 47, 60. On the same day, Bvt. Maj. Gen. Benjamin W. Brice, paymaster gen., issued a circular apportioning the funds. DS, DNA, RG 393, 5th Military District, Civil Affairs, Letters Received. On July 8, 2:30 P.M., Sheridan telegraphed to USG. "It will be necessary for Congress to make an additional approp[riation] to carry out the prov[i]sio[ns] of the military bill" Telegram received, *ibid.*, RG 107, Telegrams Collected (Bound); copies (2), DLC-Philip H. Sheridan.

1. June 1.

To Edwin M. Stanton

Washington, D, C, June 8th *1867.*

HON. E. M. STANTON,
SEC. OF WAR:
SIR:

I have the honor to recommend Jas. S. Rawlins for the appointment of 2d Lt. of Infantry, regular Army. This applicant is a brother of Gen. Rawlins, Chief of Staff. He was a most excellent soldier and served faithfully from the early part of the rebellion until appointed a Cadet to West Point in 1863. He was eighteen months at West Point and was a member of the class now graduating.

If appointed now Mr. Rawlins can not present himself for examination and get through before the class to which he belonged is commissioned   His address is Mobile, Ala.

> Very respectfully
> your obt. svt.
> U. S. GRANT
> General.

ALS, DNA, RG 94, ACP, 384R CB 1867. Bvt. Maj. Gen. Edmund Schriver, inspector gen., noted on the docket. "This person entered the Mil. Academy (appointed from NoCa) in July 1863—He passed the Jan'y examination of 1864, (being 71 in class of 84) and the June examination in same year (being the foot of class of 74) but at the Jan'y examination in 1865, he was found deficient in Mathematics, reported as being of little aptitude, variable in habits of study and very inattentive to Regulations, having 98 demerit in 6 months, two short of being declared deficient in conduct—He was discharged upon the recommendation of the Academic Board—" AN (undated), *ibid*. No appointment followed.

To George Bancroft

—————

Washington, D, C, June 8th *1867*.

HON. GEO. BANCROFT,
MINISTER &c.
MY DEAR SIR:

How can I apologize for not earlyer answering your kind letter of the 31st of May, expressing regret that your Mission abroad will prevent the visit Mrs. Grant and myself contemplated making you at New Port, this Summer? I can only confess inexcusable neglect and ask suspension of judgement.

Mrs. Grant & myself had promised ourselves a pleasant visit to your very pleasant retreat in July or August. We will probably still pay New Port a visit, but will not remain as long as we would, had you and Mrs. Bancroft been there. I shall hope now to pay you a visit in Berlin, long before you return from there.

Allow me to congratulate you on the very important mission, probably at this time the most important mission abroad, for which you have been selected, and to express the belief that it will be filled in a way most acceptable to this country.

Please give my best regards to Mrs. Bancroft. Mrs Grant also desires to be remembered to her & yourself.

Yours Truly
U. S. GRANT

ALS, MHi.

To Edwin M. Stanton

———

Washington, June 11 *1867*

HON. E M. STANTON
SECRETARY OF WAR
SIR:

I have the honor to transmit herewith a list of recommendations of applicants for appointment in the Army.

The number of existing vacancies are:

		Captains	1st Lieut's	2d Lieut's
Cavalry	White	2	7	31
	Colored	3	8	10
Infantry	White	1	7	35
	Colored	1	8	3
	Total	7	30	79

I have selected the seven Captains from the Regular Army: it being entitled to that number. I have recommended a sufficient number of Lieut'nants from each State to fill up its quota except Illinois, from which there has not been a proper number of well-recommended applicants. In addition thereto I have selected the names of seventeen applicants at large.

There remain fifteen vacancies in the Cavalry, for which I have made no recommendations for the reason that there is not at present a sufficient number of applicants properly qualified for that arm of the service.

> Very respectfully
> Your obedt serv't.
> U. S. GRANT
> General.

LS, DNA, RG 94, ACP, G338 CB 1867. The list is *ibid.*

On June 24, 1867, USG endorsed a list of officers (including John R. Howard, Hastings, Minn.) who had accepted appointments in the U.S. Army but had not reported for examination. "Respectfully returned to the Secretary of War, with recommendation that the appointments of the within named officers be cancelled." ES, *ibid.*, A285 CB 1867. On Aug. 20, U.S. Representative Ignatius Donnelly of Minn., Hastings, wrote to USG. "The writer of this rec'd: an appt as Lieut. in the Regular Army from my Dist: but for the reasons set forth was unable to report at the time designated. I would respectfully ask that a new notice of appt be sent him, and as the distance is great that a liberal allowance of time be given in which to report." ALS, *ibid.*, D479 CB 1867. The enclosure is *ibid.*

To Brig. Gen. Andrew A. Humphreys

June 11th *1867.*

GEN. A. A. HUMPHREY
CHIEF ENG.
GENERAL:

This will introduce to you Mr. J. T. Ryan, of California, who has invented a plan by which he thinks large guns can be handled, in action, with small cost of labor. He wishes to submit to you his plans and if possib[le] have it tested.—I have looke[d] at the drawings representing his theory but not closely enough to express an opinion as to its practicability. I think it well worth examination however.

> Yours Truly
> U. S. GRANT
> General,

ALS, DNA, RG 94, Letters Received, 223W 1869. Additional papers are *ibid.*
See *HED*, 41-2-18. On March 14, 1867, USG had written to U.S. Representa-
tives John A. Logan of Ill., Grenville M. Dodge of Iowa, and Cadwallader C.
Washburn of Wis. "Permit me to introduce to your acquaintance Mr. Jas. T.
Ryan, of California, the builder of the Iron Clad which was sunk in the Bay of
San francisco whilst in the course of construction. I knew Mr Ryan well, and
favorably, whilst I was stationed on the Pacific Coast and can recommend him
to your favorable concideration." ALS, IaHA.

To Bvt. Maj. Gen. Edward O. C. Ord

Washington, June 23d 1867

Bvt Maj. Gen. E. O. C. Ord
Comdg. 4th Mil. Dist.
General:

Copy of your final instructions to Boards of registration of
June 10th 1867 is just received.[1]

I entirely dissent from the views contained in Par IV. Your
views as to the duty of registrars to register every man who will
take the required oath, though they may know the applicant per-
jures himself, is sustained by the views of the Attorney General.[2]
My opinion is that it is the duty of the Board of Registration to see,
so far as it lays in their power, that no unauthorized person is allowed to register. To secure this end the registers should be allowed
to Administer oaths and examine witnesses. The law however
makes District Commanders their own interpretors of their power
and duty under it, and in my opinion the Atty. Gen. or myself
can no more than give our opinion as to the meaning of the law,
Niether can enforce their views against the judgment of those made
responsible for the faithful execution of the law, the District Commanders

Very respectfully
Your obt. servt.
U. S. Grant
General

Copies, DLC-USG, V, 47, 60; DNA, RG 46, Senate 40A–F5, War Dept. Messages; *ibid.*, RG 108, Letters Sent. On June 28, 1867, Bvt. Maj. Gen. Edward O. C. Ord, Vicksburg, wrote to USG. "your letter of the 23d I recieved yesterday—before answering I would like to say that I have more respect and regard for (you and) your opinion than for that of any other person I know I am sure *you* are honest and give me credit for the same—now for the answer—I enclose a letter from Genl Kautz—many like it are received and all show that few disqualified persons offer to register—under my instructions—which were conceived and written before I had an idea what the Attorney Generals opinion would be except that it was telegraphed as coming out and reversing the action of Genl Sheridan—I had waited for the opinion until there was no more time left to wait, and *I had to* write my own; which I did after careful study of the law and the circumstances around me—The practical difficulties in the way of giving Boards the right to decide in all doubtful cases were such that I think you would be satisfied were you aware of them that I had to act as I have done, to complete my registration in time—and successfully—To get my Boards I had to take *all* the union officers I could hear of and get—I had to send officers through the country to hunt up the few union men (ellegible) in it, who when found, have generally no business capacity, the result was that Boards *will not take the responsibility* of deciding doubtful cases—a flood of letters poured in on me on each of the few cases in a county—to send answers to such letters from remote parts of Arkansas takes from 30 to 60 days—the work is just commenced their—and to keep Boards waiting replies on queries on doubtful cases would have taken till next December and cost about a hundred thousand dollars—(the boards in the District cost about 4000$ a day)—and all to settle the status of a few hundred voters—when in the end the black vote (registering double the white—) will decide questions—If I had have been in an eastern state with mail facilities and plenty of sensible registrars I could have acted differently—my intention now is to scatter military commissions thro both states and try every man registered, and reported 'doubtful'—Mr Mygatt a registrar for this county has just answered my querry—of 'how many will register who are disqualified, under my order'— With 'not any in this county' the union men south,—who are hard to please— are satisfied with my order—Col Goodfellow just from Washington as judge advocate—says it covers the law and excludes disqualified about as perfectly as could be—and General it *is* working well—But General unless we get funds soon the whole thing will fall through registrars are at heavy expenses and can not get about without cash, they are *all* poor; can not borrow, one registrar walked here 60 miles to get funds to pay expenses—some counties are so destitute of mules & horses that boards have to travel in ox carts—I enclose copy of my letter to the Secty on this subject—I have heard of but one case of obstruction to freedmens registering, if on enquiry it proves as stated—obstructor will be arrested and tried—" ALS, *ibid.*, Letters Received; ADfS, Ord Papers, CU-B. The enclosures are *ibid.*

On May 15, Ord, Helena, Ark., had telegraphed to USG. "Many conscioenscious union men ask if they can register as voters when they have furnished a child clothing while in rebel army. Can I get opinion of Attorney General *hereon*" Telegram received (at 12:15 P.M.), DNA, RG 107, Telegrams Collected (Bound); *ibid.*, RG 108, Telegrams Received; copy, *ibid.*, RG 46, Senate 40A–F5, War Dept. Messages. On June 7, Ord, Vicksburg, wrote to USG. "Govr Morton was attended to by Genl Smith & sent to the Springs—I am just

back from inspection of southern Ark—had a rough ride all our waggons broke
& Ambulances capsized—country inundated—people glad I broke up the legislature—I have over 300000$ in that State Treasury have just directed part of
it invested in U S Bonds and left in U S Treasy Dept—the state will reconstruct
I think and if they do not I think every year of military Govt, will add to
strength of northern men there—This state will register with little trouble—but
will I think vote no convention—there is much poverty and apprehension for the
future all along the valleys of the western rivers—at least half Louisiana & much
of Mississippi, and Arkansas are still under water & have been so over two
months—it is a question of bread—with a great many of the freed & white men—
I have just approved sentence of 5 years confinement for two horse thives & have
some 30 men for trial—much joy among planters & hands at the prospect of safe
mules in Miss—I am about to issue a Stay law to protect hands from having lands
taken by sale while they are cultivating—I am getting along very well and shall
get through my work only the appropriation of 500000$ for the 5 Dists is about
⅛th enough—I write to morrow calling attention to fact that I will have to stop
as soon as the money sent me 99000$ gives out, unless Congress meets and ap-
propriates more—in July—My best respects to Mrs Grant and to the members of
your staff—I think I understand why you didnt want me to go to Washington
but the kind offers and offices of the powers were all declined I shall go straight
ahead, and not do any thing that I think you would not do in my place" ALS,
USG 3. On June 15, Ord wrote to USG. "Confidential but important—. . . I am
afraid the Chief Qur Mr of my Dept—Col Pierce is becoming too much interested
in the Little Rock ~~Ban~~ National Bank—which is the public Depostary of his
funds—I applied for Col Chandler to relieve him—the order is out but Pierce is
pretty confident he can (with the aid of the Bank) get it rescinded—as both he
& his chief clerk are stock holders in it and the Bank controls much influence in
fact all it wants in the State—and as Montgomery would have been kept in his
place by it had you not have interfered and as They ~~did~~ managed pretty much
all the telegraphing to you and the President about not removing my head Qurs
to Fort Smith.—I hope therefore General you will not allow the order sending me
Chandler to be rescinded I have ordered ark State funds to be ~~sent~~ deposited
in the US Treasy—the Bank is trying to stop that—, now these Banks are *not*
to be trusted in this country—I took charge of the funds of the State just in
time—the Bank which had recieved & used the State funds formerly and which
expected them—not receiving them *broke*, and the state lost two thousand dollars
by them—all it had there, ~~And~~ the public interest and my directions have both
been opposed by this national banks interfering, or requesting the Quarter Master
to act as *they* wished—in forwarding funds to remote posts, and in the disbursements—I dont object to Quarter masters and Pay Masters owning Bank stock—
but it had better be of Banks ~~Els~~where they are not stationed, and have funds— . . .
Col Chandler is up the Missouri but will return in time—" ALS, DNA, RG 108,
Letters Received. Probably in early July, Ord forwarded to USG a letter and
papers concerning voter registration and finances in Ark. AES (2), *ibid.* On
July 1, Ord telegraphed to USG. "The Cholera has broken out badly here and
among troops at Head Quarters, Shall have to move them probably, Is there
any objection to taking Hd Qrs to Mississippi City for a month? Registration
progressing in all the Counties of this State & Registers appointed & books furnished throughout Arkansas" Telegram received (at 7:50 P.M.), *ibid.*, RG 107,
Telegrams Collected (Bound); *ibid.*, RG 108, Telegrams Received; copies, *ibid.*,

RG 46, Senate 40A–F5, War Dept. Messages; (sent by mail) *ibid.*, RG 108, Letters Received; DLC-USG, V, 55.

1. On June 15, Ord had written to USG. "I enclose a copy of my final order in the matter of registering doubtful cases. You will perceive that the number of State officials excluded by me is greater than the number excluded by General Schofield. I have I think as near as may be, covered the intention of Congress. I also separate all who the Boards may deem disqualified from those they may consider qualified, and place before the former the penalties of the only law under which cases of persons disqualified by the law can be decided. I think with the certainty of trial before them, but few who should not, will register. This I believe accords with the intention of Congress. The system of colored or white chalengers is utterly impracticable in this District. I can hardly find loyal men enough for registrars." LS, DNA, RG 94, Letters Received, 869M 1867. Paragraph four of the enclosed circular, 4th Military District, June 10, states: "Boards are informed that the Acts of Congress, providing for this registration, are the sole guide and rule for their action. The Board of Registration is not empowered to decide in doubtful cases, upon the question of qualification or disqualification, but is required to register and grant certificates of registration to all persons who take and subscribe the prescribed oath. In the first instance, the applicant himself must determine on his own responsibility and at his peril, his ability or disability: and, afterwards, the tribunal authorized to try those who falsely take the oath, and not the registrars, is the arbiter appointed to decide this question. But the registrars are expected promptly to report to these Headquarters for investigation by a Military Commission, all cases in which it shall appear that any disqualified person has taken and subscribed the oath. . . ." (Printed) *ibid.* Also on June 15, Ord telegraphed to USG. "Registration progressing satisfactorily in thirty five (35) Counties of Mississippi & in a few of Arkansas where it has been detained by succession overflows" Telegram received (at 7:20 P.M.), *ibid.*, RG 107, Telegrams Collected (Bound); *ibid.*, RG 108, Telegrams Received; copies, *ibid.*, RG 46, Senate 40A–F5, War Dept. Messages; *ibid.*, RG 94, Letters Received, 935M 1867; *ibid.*, RG 393, 4th Military District, Telegrams Sent; DLC-USG, V, 55.

2. See following letter.

To Maj. Gen. Philip H. Sheridan

Washington, D, C, June 24th *1867.*

DEAR GENERAL,

The dispatch of Gen. Townsend, sent by direction of the President, directing you to extend the time of registration in your district to the 1st of August had probably better be complied with.[1] It will silence all charges of attempting to defeat the Atty. Gen.s construction of the reconstruction act.² Before publishing the order extending the time I would answer the dispatch of the Adj. Gen. however. In fact I would not publish the order extending the time of registration until a few days before the expiration of the time already given. In the mean time Congress may give an interpretation of their own acts differring possibly from the one given by the Atty. Gen.

The shape in which the views of the Atty. Gen. have been communicated to district commanders is such as not to entitle them to the force of ~~an~~ orders. As district commander I would not be controlled by them further than I might be convinced by the argument.

Yours Truly,
U. S. Grant
General,

To Maj. Gn. P. H. Sheridan,
Comd.g 45th Dist.

ALS, DLC-Philip H. Sheridan. On June 24, 1867, 10:00 a.m., USG telegraphed to Maj. Gen. Philip H. Sheridan. "I will write you by mail to-day on subject of extending time of registration. Make no order until my letter is received." ALS (telegram sent), DNA, RG 107, Telegrams Collected (Bound); telegram sent, *ibid.*; copies, *ibid.*, RG 108, Telegrams Sent; DLC-USG, V, 56. On June 28, 5:00 p.m., and June 29, Sheridan, New Orleans, telegraphed to USG. "Your letter which was to have been mailed on the twenty fourth (24) has not yet reached me, Was it mailed at that date?" "I have rec'd your letter and will continue the registration and have notified the Adjt General" Telegrams received (on June 28, 6:44 p.m., and June 29, 6:40 p.m.), DNA, RG 107, Telegrams Collected (Bound); *ibid.*, RG 108, Telegrams Received; copies, DLC-USG, V, 55; (2 of each) DLC-Philip H. Sheridan.

On June 10, Sheridan had telegraphed to USG. "I have returns up to the present date from twenty five parishes of this state & find that over fifty seven thousand 57000 voters have been registered and everything going on well" Telegram received (at 1:50 p.m.), DNA, RG 107, Telegrams Collected (Bound); *ibid.*, RG 108, Telegrams Received; copies, *ibid.*, RG 46, Senate 40A–F5, War Dept. Messages; (sent by mail) *ibid.*, RG 94, Letters Received, 1117M 1867; DLC-USG, V, 55; (2) DLC-Philip H. Sheridan; DLC-Edwin M. Stanton. On June 18, Sheridan telegraphed to USG. "I have the honor to report that I have extended the registration in the parish of Orleans until the Thirtieth 30 June at which time registration will be closed in this city In the state there are now Eighty thousand voters registered which indicates that the registeration in the state is nearly completed in eighteen hundred & sixty 1860 the vote of the state was fifty thousand 50000 I will extend the time until tenth July in some of the parishes where the population is large so as to give no just grounds for complaint I have to say again that the registration throughout the state has been harmonious The boards having been kindly received every where." Telegram received (at 12:45 P.M.), DNA, RG 107, Telegrams Collected (Bound); (at 12:40 P.M.) *ibid.*, RG 108, Telegrams Received; copies, *ibid.*, RG 46, Senate 40A–F5, War Dept. Messages; *ibid.*, RG 94, Letters Received, 936M 1867; DLC-USG, V, *55*; (2) DLC-Philip H. Sheridan; DLC-Andrew Johnson. On June 19, Sheridan telegraphed to USG. "Since my telegram of yesterday I have additional information of the Registration in La. The latest returns made the number of registered voters eighty seven thousand four hundred & eighty eight (87488) There will be a large number of whites in the state who are entitled to register but who decline on account of objection to the Military bill" Telegram received (at 5:50 P.M.), DNA, RG 107, Telegrams Collected (Bound); *ibid.*, RG 108, Telegrams Received; copies, *ibid.*, RG 46, Senate 40A–F5, War Dept. Messages; (misdated June 16) *ibid.*, RG 94, Letters Received, 817M 1867; DLC-USG, V, *55*; (2) DLC-Philip H. Sheridan. On June 21, Sheridan telegraphed to USG. "I have extended the registration in the state of Louisiana until the fifteenth 15 of July I consider the registration now nearly closed but deemed it best to give fifteen days grace. I wrote you some time ago about the necessity for additional funds some will be necessary but not as much as I expected. My expenses so far are only thirty six thousand 36000 dollars Our system has been very Complete, thorough & economical—" Telegram received (at 1:45 P.M.), DNA, RG 107, Telegrams Collected (Bound); *ibid.*, RG 108, Telegrams Received; copies, *ibid.*, RG 46, Senate 40A–F5, War Dept. Messages; *ibid.*, RG 94, Letters Received, 886M 1867; *ibid.*, 1116M 1867; DLC-USG, V, *55*; (2) DLC-Philip H. Sheridan; DLC-Andrew Johnson.

On June 28, Sheridan telegraphed to USG. "Returns from forty three 43 parishes out of forty eight 48 in this state show eighty seven thousand nine hundred and forty one 87,941 registered voters as far as reported up to present date." Telegram received (at 12:50 P.M.), DNA, RG 108, Telegrams Received; copies, *ibid.*, RG 46, Senate 40A–F5, War Dept. Messages; DLC-USG, V, *55*; (2) DLC-Philip H. Sheridan. On July 2, Sheridan telegraphed to USG. "The latest returns from forty seven (47) parishes of this State show one hundred and two thousand one hundred and twenty six, (102,126) voters registered. As some of the returns are fifteen days old there will be considerable increase up to the present date." Telegram received (at 7:45 P.M.), DNA, RG 107, Telegrams Collected (Bound); *ibid.*, RG 108, Telegrams Received; copies, *ibid.*, RG 46, Senate 40A–F5, War Dept. Messages; *ibid.*, RG 94, Letters Received, 892M 1867; DLC-USG, V, *55*; (2) DLC-Philip H. Sheridan. On July 10, Sheridan wrote to USG. "I have the honor to enclose herewith a statement, showing the number of registered voters in this State, so far as heard from." LS, DNA, RG 107, Letters Received from Bureaus. On July 17 and 19, Sheridan wrote similar letters to USG. LS, *ibid.*, RG 108, Letters Received.

On July 3, Sheridan wrote to USG. "I enclose herewith a copy of a telegram sent to the President by Genl Steedman on June 19th. When he first arrived here he called on me & was loud in advocating your claims for Pesidential honors and apparently, to me, seeking to get an expression of opinion on that subject from me, but, he did not succeed. I did not. believe he was sincere, and evry action of his since confirms me that I was not mistaken—He is not your friend & has not been mine I am getting along very well—of course since the publication of Mr Stansbery opinion there has been a, great change and excitemt among the professional office holders & seekers in this state who are disfranchised by the

rulings of our boards of Registratn but among the masses & the thinking men
there is the greatest regret that the Pesidnt should again stir up strife. The
issue at stake was great & was wheather the state would cast its vote for the
union party or the Ddemocracy. & I suppose that is what the fight is for. *The
state will be union if congress comes to the scratch*" ALS, USG 3. The enclosure
stated. "Want of respect for Gov. Wells personally alone represses the expression
of indignation felt by all honest and sensible men at the unwarranted usurpation
of General Sheridan in removing the civil officers of Louisiana. It is believed here
that you will reinstate Wells. He is a bad man and has no influence I believe
Sheridan made the removals to embarrass you believing the feeling at the north
would sustain him. My conviction is that on account of the bad character of Wells
and Monroe you ought not to reinstate any who have been removed, because you
cannot reinstate any without reinstating all; but, you ought to prohibit the
exercise of this power in the future" Copy, *ibid*. A telegram received is in DLC-
Andrew Johnson.

1. On June 22, Sheridan had telegraphed to USG. "I am in receipt of a
telegram from the President through Brevet Major General E D Townsend Asst.
Adjt. Genl. USA. directing me to extend the registration in this city and state
until August first unless I have some reasons to the Contrary and ordering me to
report such reasons for his information. Also stating that in his judgment this
Extension is necessary to a full & fair registration and that the time should be
thus extended because the other district Commanders will not get through before
that time My reasons for closing the registration in this city were because I
had given the city two and a half months and there were no more to register I
have given the state two and a half months and the registration will be exhausted
by that time. I did not feel warranted in keeping up boards of registration at
large expense to suit New issues coming in at the eleventh hour. The registration
will be completed in Louisiana at the time specified unless I am ordered to carry
out the law under Mr. Stanberys interpretation which practically in registration
is opening a broad macademized road for perjury & fraud to travel on. I do not
see why my registration should be dependent on the time when other district
commanders get through I have given more time for the registration of Louisiana
than they propose to give in their commands for I commenced six 6 weeks before
they did. I regret that I should have to differ with the President but it must be
recollected that I have been ordered to execute a law to which the President has
been in bitter antagonism If after this report the time is to be extended please
notify me and it will be done I would do it at once but the Presidents telegram
was conditional and there is sufficient time left to issue the necessary order"
Telegram received (at 3:25 P.M.), DNA, RG 107, Telegrams Collected (Bound);
ibid., RG 108, Telegrams Received; copies, DLC-USG, V, 55; (2) DLC-Philip
H. Sheridan; DLC-Andrew Johnson. On the same day, Secretary of War Edwin
M. Stanton wrote to USG. "I have received the copy of General Sheridan's telegram. I do not remember when he proposed to close the registration, but think
it was the 10th or 15th of June [*July*?]. There appears to be no necessity for
any action until we can confer together, and in the meantime General Sheridan
can let his orders, if he has made any, stand until he gets instructions from you."
Adam Badeau, *Grant in Peace* (Hartford, Conn., 1887), p. 83. On June 25,
Bvt. Brig. Gen. Horace Porter wrote to Sheridan. "Gen Grant was highly disgusted to see, in yesterday's 'N. Y. Tribune', the publication of your dispatch of

the 22d inst, and has directed me to inform you of the circumstances. The dispatch was Sent to his house, direct from the telegraph office, on Saturday evening. No one connected with our Head Quarters knew of its arrival until Monday morning, (yesterday) It had then already been published. Though the General is not sorry to have the people know the contents of your dispatch, and believes that its publication will be of personal benifit to you, yet he is exceedingly annoyed to find publicity given to a communicated which he regarded as Semi-Confidintial. The act was certainly that of a spy, and the General will spare no pains to trace the matter to its source. Congress will meet *without doubt*, and we hope that a brief and active session will undo the mischief that has lately been done. It is now pretty well decided that the Administration will not *order* an enforcement of the doctrines embodied in the Attorney-General's opinion. The opinion will therefore have no more weight than that of any other good lawyer. Your course is more and more applauded by every loyal man, and you cannot fully realize, till you come North, how universally you are supported. With kind regards to all the staff, and renewed thanks for the hospitalities enjoyed under your roof, . . ." ALS, DLC-Philip H. Sheridan. On July 13, USG wrote to Stanton. "I have the honor to request the withdrawal of the dispatch of the 22d of June, from Maj. Gn. P. H. Sheridan to me, which was transmitted through mistake. The dispatch I regarded as private and its transmission was purely a mistake." ALS, DLC-Andrew Johnson. On the same day, President Andrew Johnson endorsed a copy of this letter. "The within despatch of the 22d ultimo, from major General P. H. Sheridan to Genl U. S. Grant, was received at this office on the 11th instant, with other despatches and papers transmitted by the Secretary of War in answer to a resolution of the Senate of the 3d instant, calling upon the President for certain information in respect to the operation, construction, and execution of the military reconstruction acts. This despatch is now returned to the Secretary of War in compliance with the request contained in his endorsement upon a letter this day addressed to him by Genl Grant, in which application is made for the withdrawal of this despatch, for the reason that it is regarded by him as private, and that its transmission to the War Department, with other despatches and papers, requested by the resolution of the Senate, was purely a mistake" ES, DNA, RG 94, Letters Received, 1070M 1867.

On June 29, USG telegraphed to Sheridan. "I think it advisable for you to extend the time for restration in La. to the 10th of July throughout the state. The President will have returned before that and deside as to the further extension." ALS (telegram sent), *ibid.*, RG 107, Telegrams Collected (Bound); telegram sent, *ibid.*; copies, *ibid.*, RG 46, Senate 40A–F5, War Dept. Messages; *ibid.*, RG 108, Telegrams Sent; DLC-USG, V, 56; DLC-Andrew Johnson. On July 2, 6:30 P.M., Sheridan telegraphed to USG. "I did not get your dispatch of June 29th until today, It was mislaid in the Washington Office—I had already ordered the extension in the state except parish of Orleans until the 15th of July & after receipt of your letter of the 24th the extension was made indefinite, The boards now have nothing to do in this City & in most of the parishes" Telegram received (at 8:40 P.M.), USG 3; DNA, RG 107, Telegrams Collected (Bound); *ibid.*, RG 108, Telegrams Received; copies, *ibid.*, RG 46, Senate 40A–F5, War Dept. Messages; *ibid.*, RG 94, Letters Received, 891M 1867; DLC-USG, V, 55; DLC-Andrew Johnson.

2. On May 24, Attorney Gen. Henry Stanbery had issued an opinion concerning the right to vote and hold office under the Reconstruction Acts, and, on

June 12, a second opinion discussing the duties and obligations of military district commanders. *SED*, 40-1-14, pp. 262–87. On June 18–20, Johnson discussed these opinions in cabinet. Johnson recorded cabinet votes on points in Stanbery's opinion, including Stanton's frequent dissents. See George C. Gorham, *Life and Public Services of Edwin M. Stanton* (Boston and New York, 1899), II, 360–71; Howard K. Beale, ed., *Diary of Gideon Welles* (New York, 1960), III, 109–14. Under Johnson's orders, Bvt. Maj. Gen. Edward D. Townsend, on June 20, transmitted a summary of Stanbery's opinions to military district commanders. *HED*, 40-1-20, pp. 8–11; *SED*, 40-1-14, pp. 9–12. See *ibid.*, pp. 284–87. On June 27, Sheridan telegraphed to USG. "The result of Mr Stanberys opinion is now beginning to show itself by a defiant opposition to all acts of the Military Commander by impeding and rendering helpless the Civil officers acting under his appointment, for instance The Mayor of this City notifies the Common Council that one and a quarter (1¼) million of illegal money has been issued by the Comptroller & Treasurer, The Common Council refuses to investigate to ascertain the facts, The City Attorney refuses to sue it on injunction to stop the issue, I fear the Chaos which the opinion will make if carried out is but little understood, Every Civil Officer in the State will administer justice according to his own views, many of them denouncing the military bill as uncostitutional, will throw every impediment in the way of its execution and bad will go to worse unless this embarrasing Condition of affairs is settled by permitting me to go on in my just course which was endorsed by all the people except those disfranchise[d] most of whom are Office holders or desired to be so" Telegram received (at 4:35 P.M.), DNA, RG 107, Telegrams Collected (Bound); *ibid.*, RG 108, Telegrams Received; copies, *ibid.*, RG 46, Senate 40A–F5, War Dept. Messages; DLC-USG, V, 55; (2) DLC-Philip H. Sheridan. On June 28, 10:45 A.M., USG telegraphed to Sheridan. "Cypher . . . Your dispatch of yesterday received. Enforce your own construction of the Military Bill until ordered to do otherwise. The opinion of the Atty Genl has not been distributed to district commanders in language or manner entitling it to the force of an order nor can I suppose that the President intended it to have such force." LS (telegram sent), DNA, RG 107, Telegrams Collected (Bound); telegram sent, *ibid.*; copies, *ibid.*, RG 46, Senate 40A–F5, War Dept. Messages; DLC-USG, V, 10, 56. At 11:00 A.M., Sheridan telegraphed to USG. "I am in receipt of a Communication from the Adjutant Generals department dated 20th June in reference to registration. I am at a loss to know whether it is an order or not. The form and phrasealagy is not that of an order but I may be mistaken and ask for information whether I am to regard it as an order." Telegram received (at 1:00 P.M.), DNA, RG 107, Telegrams Collected (Bound); *ibid.*, RG 108, Telegrams Received; copies, *ibid.*, RG 46, Senate 40A–F5, War Dept. Messages; *ibid.*, RG 94, Letters Received, 1130M 1867; DLC-USG, V, 55; (2) DLC-Philip H. Sheridan.

Testimony

———

[*June 26, 1867*]

ULYSSES S. GRANT, General United States army, sworn and examined:

By Mr. PIERREPONT:

Q. At what time were you in command at Vicksburg?

A. In the early part of 1863—the first half of the year 1863; there and opposite Vicksburg, on the Mississippi, near Vicksburg.

Q. Will you tell the jury at what time, if any, you met Jacob Thompson, and under what circumstances?

(Mr. BRADLEY desired to have objection to this testimony noted.)

A. I met Jacob Thompson some time during the first or second month I was at Milliken's Bend, in the beginning of 1863. I cannot state the exact time.

Q. State the circumstances and what claim he there made.

A. One of our picket-boats discovered a little sail or row boat with a few persons in it, up the river, near the shore on the Mississippi side, about abreast of where we were lying at the time, or where the flag-ship of Admiral Porter was lying. I sent out to bring them in. When we were near to them we discovered that they had a little white flag, like a flag of truce. We brought them in, and I met Thompson at that time at the flag-ship of Admiral Porter.

Mr. BRADLEY objected to any conversation between General Grant and Thompson, or anybody else not connected with the conspiracy.

Mr. PIERREPONT stated that the prosecution had connected Jacob Thompson with money. They had a man who went there the same day, and expected to have a man who took the money. They wanted to show who Jake Thompson was and what relation he held.

Mr. MERRICK asked whether the prosecution expected to connect Jacob Thompson with the conspiracy to kill the President.

Mr. PIERREPONT said he expected to show that he was in it and aided in it by the use of money.

The COURT understood counsel for the prosecution to say he expected, in the examination of witnesses hereafter, to show the connection of the prisoner at the bar with Jacob Thompson in regard to the disbursement of money in the prosecution of this conspiracy. If he could make that connection, the evidence would be relevant. If not, it would be irrelevant. For the present, the testimony was admitted.

Mr. BRADLEY desired an exception to the ruling to be noted.

WITNESS, continuing: I met Thompson on Admiral Porter's flag-ship and had some conversation with him. He represented himself as a staff officer, stating some ostensible business. I think he represented himself as acting inspector general of the rebel army. I do not think he stated that he held a commission at all in the confederate army, but represented himself as an acting staff officer. It was in the early part of 1863, when I was at Milliken's Bend.

Mr. BRADLEY. That is to say March, 1863?

A. I think in February, 1863.

Trial of John H. Surratt . . . (Washington, 1867), I, 336–37. See *PUSG*, 15, 33–34.

On Oct. 11, 1867, Henry B. Sainte-Marie, Montreal, wrote to USG. "At the time of the assassination of President Lincoln, your predecessor Mr. Stanton offered a reward of $25.000 for any information that might lead to the capture of J. H. Surratt. Subsequently the order offering such reward was revoked. A year ago on my information and through the agency of Genl. Rufus King then Minister at Rome, J. H. Surratt was captured and brought to the United States for trial much to my astonishment one of the first things I learnt on landing in the United States was there was no reward for the capture of Surratt. I think Genl. King too much of a gentleman not to have informed me of the revocation of that order, if he himself had been aware of its revocation. Surely the Government of the United States cannot think that mileage and expenses from Italy here a sufficient remuneration for the dangers I have been and still am exposed to. I have been here now about six months and it is impossible for me to get anything to do. I am surrounded by numerous enemies and liable to suffer at any moment from the vengeance of Surratt's sympathizers. My name has been thrown to all the world and there is no place on earth where I can go on my own name. It is not my province to enlarge on the many surmises which the capture of Surratt gave rise to, and the disclosures expected to inculpate even the first magistrate. Now these things are set at rest and the public mind is satisfied. I will thank you from my heart to inform me if you would be disposed to pay that reward or even part of it as I am at present depending on my brothers for support and my position is far from being agreeable. . . . P. S. Any letters addressed C. H. Walters Cuvellier & Co. Montreal, Canada East, will reach me safely." Copy, DNA, RG 94, Letters Received, 1521M 1867. See *HED*, 40-2-36. On Oct. 25, Judge Advocate Gen. Joseph Holt wrote to USG recommending that Sainte-Marie be paid for his role in the capture of John H. Surratt as stated in War Dept. General Orders No. 164, Nov. 24, 1865, which revoked a $25,000 reward and offered instead a "liberal reward" for information leading to the arrest of conspirators still at large. Copy, DNA, RG 153, Letters Sent. On Nov. 6, 1867, Bvt. Maj. Gen. Edward D. Townsend wrote to Sainte-Marie informing him that a board of officers would determine the amount of this reward. ADf (initialed), *ibid.*, RG 94, Letters Received, 1521M 1867; copy, *ibid.*, Letters Sent. A response of Nov. 26 from Sainte-Marie to USG is *ibid.*, Letters Received, 1521M 1867. On Dec. 9, USG wrote to Speaker of the House Schuyler Colfax. "I have the honor to send, herewith, for the consideration of Congress the application of *H. B. St. Marie*, claiming compensation for the information furnished by him which lead to the capture of *J. H. Surratt*; together with a report of a Board of officers to whom the subject was referred and the recommendation of the Judge Advocate General in the case" Df, *ibid.*, RG 107, Letters Received, S375 1867; copy, *ibid.*, Reports to Congress. The board recommended payment of $15,000 to Sainte-Marie. Copy, *ibid.*, RG 94, Letters Received, 1521M 1867.

On Feb. 4, 1868, Sainte-Marie wrote to USG. "I have to thank you in my name and that of all my family, for your kind action in my case, gratefull for what you have done for me, in the miserable position I am placed, it is with diffidence I venture to ask a new favor. my case is now before Congress. how long can it remain there I do not know. at the same time I am here without any means and dependent on my family for support. I do not know if it is becoming for me to ask you to press the issue of the commissions report before Congress. Still I hope you will excuse me for intruding on your precious time, persuaded as I am that if the thing is practicable, you will do what is consistent with your position to help me." ALS, *ibid.*, RG 107, Letters Received from Bureaus. On Feb. 6, USG endorsed this letter. "Respectfully forwarded to the Sec. of War." AES, *ibid.* Paid $10,000 by Congress in 1868, Sainte-Marie spent the remainder of his life unsuccessfully pursuing additional payment. On Dec. 7, 1872, Sainte-Marie wrote to USG concerning this case. ALS, *ibid.*, RG 94, Letters Received, 1521M 1867. The U.S. Supreme Court rejected his claim after his death. *U.S. Statutes at Large*, XV, 234; *New York Times*, Sept. 12, 1874; Joseph George, Jr., "H. B. Ste. Marie and His Role in the Arrest of John H. Surratt," *Lincoln Herald*, 85, 4 (Winter, 1983), 269–79.

To Bvt. Maj. Gen. John Pope

Washington June 28th 67 [*10:45* A.M.]

MAJ GENL J POPE
ATLANTA GA.

Your despatch of yesterday received. Enforce your own construction of the Military Bill until ordered to do otherwise. The opinion of the Atty General has not been distributed to district commanders in language or manner entitling it to the force of an order, nor can I suppose that the President intended it to have such force—

U. S. GRANT
General,

LS (telegram sent), DNA, RG 107, Telegrams Collected (Bound); telegram sent, *ibid.*; copies, *ibid.*, RG 46, Senate 40A–F2, Messages; *ibid.*, Senate 40A–F5, War Dept. Messages; *ibid.*, RG 108, Telegrams Sent; DLC-USG, V, 56. On June 27, 1867, Bvt. Maj. Gen. John Pope had telegraphed to USG. "Day before yesterday I received a copy of the opinion of the Attorney General on registration sent me for my information through the Assistant Adjutant General by order of the President. Ten days ago I had made and published instructions to Registers which will have to be dropped if the Attorney General's opinion is enforced. The opinion sent me by the President's order does not seem to be an order to me on the subject, but as there may be room for doubt I ask that I be informed by Telegraph whether or not I am ordered by the President to conform my action to the Attorney Generals opinion. I stand ready to obey the Presidents orders on the subject, but I wrote you fully on the subject yesterday, the probable result of enforcing Attorney Generals opinion in this District—enclosing also copies of my orders and instructions about registration. Please answer by telegram as soon as possible as it is manifest that there should be no delay in my being informed of the President's purpose" Telegram received (at 2:00 P.M.), DNA, RG 107, Telegrams Collected (Bound); *ibid.*, RG 108, Telegrams Received; copies, *ibid.*, RG 46, Senate 40A–F2, Messages; *ibid.*, Senate 40A–F5, War Dept. Messages; DLC-USG, V, 55. On June 25 and 26, Pope had written to USG. "I received today, from the Adjutant General's Office, a paper issued, it appears, by order of the President, and by his direction transmitted to the respective Commanders of the Military Districts created by the Acts of Congress known as the Reconstruction Acts, communicating to these Commanders for their information what the President accepts as a practical interpretation of the Acts on the points therein presented. The occasion for issuing this paper is therein stated to be, that several Commanders of Military Districts have expressed doubts as to the proper construction of the above-mentioned Acts, and have applied to the Executive for information in relation thereto. I deem it proper to state that I am not one of the Commanders who so applied. Before the receipt of this paper I had made out and published orders regulating the Registration provided for by the Acts of Congress referred to, and which orders are in my judgement in accordance therewith. I have carefully examined the opinion of the Attorney General, and whilst in most respects my orders concerning Registration are believed to be in general harmony with his interpretation of the law, in one essential particular they are widely different. This difference is found in the duties of Boards of Registration and the mode of determining the qualifications of applicants to register. According to the interpretation of the Attorney General any and every applicant who takes the oath prescribed in the Supplemental Act is entitled thereby to have his name registered as a voter. This oath is held to be conclusive as to the facts therein stated, so far as relates to the right of suffrage. It may be perfectly apparent to the Board of Registers that the applicant to register is a lad or a woman, or it may be known to them personally that such applicant is a foreigner who has not been twelve hours in the country, or unquestionable proof may be in the hands of the Board that he is excluded from registry by some other plain disqualifying provision of the law, yet the Board can raise no inquiry and make no objection, but must register and report as a lawful voter, one, thus well known not to be so. It is said that the Act, (to guard against falsity in the oath,) provides that if false, the person taking it shall be tried and punished for perjury. I need not discuss the probability of either the prosecution or conviction of such offenders in this District and under present circumstances especially such as are disqualified for participation in the Rebellion—The tendency to falsity in the oath is obvious. Persons who regard restrictions upon registry as unjust impediments to the exercise of a right; who have been instructed by prominent political characters and leaders, not to regard as binding on their consciences oaths imposed upon them by laws they do not consider constitutional; and who readily believe all laws to be unconstitutional which are not in accordance with their ideas of the proper relations of the National to the State Governments, cannot reasonably be expected under the excitement on the subject now existing to be very scrupulous about taking the prescribed oath. By the Supplemental Act above referred to, it is made *my* duty as the Commander of this Military District 'to cause a Registration to be made of the male citizens of the U. S. twenty one years of age and upwards, resident in each County or parish included in this District *which Registration shall include only those persons* who are qualified to vote for delegates by the Act of March 2nd 1867 *and* who shall have taken and subscribed the following oath or affirmation &c' As I interpret this law it does not mean that all who take the prescribed oath are entitled to registry. It makes two things necessary to registry—First—the applicant must in the judgement of the Board of Registration be a qualified voter under the law. Secondly—he must make oath that he is so qualified. In determining whether the applicant is entitled to be registered the Board of Registrars is not bound by the oath of the applicant. He is required to take the oath, so that he cannot deceive the Board as to his qualifications without also committing the crime of perjury. The oath is not the *only*, but is an *additional* security against illegal registry. The law imposes upon me the duty of causing a registration to be made which shall *include only* those persons who are qualified to vote. It authorizes me 'to appoint as many Boards of Registration as may be necessary, consisting of three loyal officers or persons to make and complete the registration.' In my opinion these Boards have something more to do than merely to administer oaths and enter names on the registry of voters. I supposed Congress provided for Boards of Registration, that through their supervision, qualified voters might be registered, and disqualified persons might be prevented from registering. In this view of the duties and powers of the Boards of Registration, I am confirmed by the interpretation of the Supplemental Act made by the President of the United States in his veto message of March 23d 1867, speaking of these Boards he therein states 'Yet these persons (the registers) are to exercise most important duties, and are vested with unlimited discretion—They are to decide what names shall be placed upon the Register, and from their decision there is no appeal.' Whilst I do not consider the Boards of Registration to be vested with such supreme powers, yet substantially my views on the subject are in accord with the opinion of the President above quoted. If however the duties of these Boards are, as the Attorney General states, simply ministerial, illegal registry is made easy and comparatively safe, and a Registration so made, would not in my judgement, be such a registration, as I am commanded by the Act of Congress 'to cause to be made.' As the responsibility for a correct and legal Registration is imposed on me, alone, by the Acts of Congress, and as I farther believe my published instructions are well calculated to secure a registration in accordance with the intentions and provisions of these Acts, I shall proceed with the Registration in this District in accordance with these orders and instructions, unless I receive specific orders to the contrary from higher authority. Should I receive orders to conduct the Registration in accordance with the 'opinion' of the Attorney General I will of course execute them, but I shall consider myself relieved thereby from any responsibility for the character of the Registration, and shall probably feel it to be my duty to report of any election based on such Registration that it was not an election in which those voted and those only, who were qualified to do so under the Acts of Congress. I have the honor to enclose herewith the paper, above referred to, and copies of my orders concerning Registration in Georgia and Alabama   It is proper to say that the Codes of Georgia and Alabama have been carefully examined to determine who are Judicial and Executive Officers under their respective State Constitutions, and that in every case it has been the purpose, as far as the law would allow, to enlarge and not restrict the number of qualified voters under the Acts of Congress. Although the paper above referred to, as transmitted to me by the order of the President is drawn up in the usual form of orders, it does not seem to convey any order to me on the subject of Registration nor to have passed through the General of the Army; yet as it is construed by the people of this Military District as a positive order to me in regard to Registration, and is considered to be only in advance of other orders of the President ratifying and promulgating the farther opinion of the Attorney General on the powers and duties of the Military Commanders; and as much excitement and hitherto repressed hostility are being occasioned thereby I deem it proper and just both to the Commander and citizens of this District, that I should be plainly informed whether I am to consider the paper sent me, as above stated, a specific order to me to conform my action to the opinions of the Attorney General, therein expressed. I therefore respectfully and plainly ask to be informed in direct terms whether or not I am to regard this paper above referred to as the specific order of my Military superior which I am expected to obey." "I have mailed to you today an official letter in regard to a paper sent to me by the order of the President, conveying certain opinions of the Atty Genl on the subject of registration— Whilst this paper has all the form of an order & in ordinary times would be considered an order, yet a careful examination of it shows that the only *order* given

by the President is to *transmit* certain opinions for *the information* of certain officers—The paper however is so worded & invested with such outward formality
of appearance & diction that it is understood every where in this District as a
positive order to me to conduct Registrations in accordance with Mr Stanberry's
views—It is also considered the precursor of another order from the President
ratifying & promulgating the opinion of the Atty Genl. in the powers & duties of
the District Commanders—These ideas among the people based upon the peculiar
form of the paper above referred to, & justified by it, are creating great com-
motion in this District and all the ill-feeling & bitter hostility to the Govt, repressed before, is again finding utterance & will probably lead to acts of violence—
It is most unfortunate for the country & for reconstruction in the South that this
ill advised 'opinion' of the Atty Genl. has been given to the public—I will not
comment upon the matter further than to say that unless the President's dis-
avows or authorizes District Commanders to disavow, any purpose to enforce
these opinions by positive orders to the District Commanders, the condition of
this District will be worse than it has ever been & reconstruction in any sense
contemplated by the Acts of Congress entirely defeated—I have given my views
about registration in my official letter to you & have asked specifically to be informed whether the President considers the paper he sent me an *order* to be
executed—I think that you will insist, that as justice to me & to the people of
this District as well as of the whole country, that a specific answer be made to
this question—I shall not act in any manner until I get an answer, upon the subject of the paper—Every thing in this Command was going on so well & promised
so fairly that it is to the last degree provoking that it should be obstructed in this
way—Will you please communicate to me by telegraph the substance of the
President's answer to my question concerning the paper above referred to—"
LS and ALS, USG 3.

On July 6, Pope wrote to USG. "I have the honor to transmit herewith copies
of correspondence and circulars in relation to Civil Affairs in this District. In
Georgia you will perceive that but two Civil officers have been removed viz the
Sheriff and Deputy Sheriff of Cass (Bartow) County.—They were removed for
gross neglect of duty after investigation by a careful officer at the request of many
citizens of that county. In Alabama the Mayor, Board of Alderman Chief of
Police and other City Officers of Mobile were removed for causes already reported
to you.—I will not trust the City Government of Mobile to Such persons whilst I
am held responsible by the law for 'peace' and good order in that City.—These
persons were elected at about the Same time and from the Same motives which
prompted the election of Raphael Semmes, Probate Judge in Mobile—The riot
which occasioned their removal was the natural result of the administration of
City affairs by men thus elected.—A few other minor Civil Officers in Alabama
were displaced for cause after abundant evidence of their unfitness and and wrong
doing, mainly on the representation of the Citizens of their own Section of country. The last Legislature of Alabama made Several new Counties, all the offices
in which were vacant when I took command. It was necessary to fill Some of
these offices for the discharge of County business.—The Governor of the State
had no power under the State Constitution to fill Such vacancies.—No elections
could be held under the Reconstruction Acts until registration was completed—
I accordingly filled Such offices as were actually necessary by my own appointment Subject to an election when Registration is completed.—In Florida a few
changes have been made for Substantially the Same reasons. I enclose a full list

of all Civil Officers thus appointed to fill vacancies as well as a list of those deposed from office. You will See from all these papers just how far and why I have interfered with Civil Officials in this District.—I enclose also my General Order No 25 the 2nd & 3d paragraphs of which contain Substantially my views of the relations between the Military Authorities of the United States and the Provisional State Governments in this District under the Reconstruction Acts.— My orders on the Subject of Registration are also transmitted" LS, DNA, RG 108, Letters Received. The enclosures are *ibid*.

To Maj. Gen. Philip H. Sheridan

[( )Cypher)   Washington, D, C, July 13th *1867.* [*11:00* A.M.]

MAJ. GEN. P. H. SHERIDAN,

NEW ORLEANS, LA,

There is every indication that a conspiracy is now on foot, having for its object the invasion of Mexico, in violation of our neutrality laws. One Hd Qrs. is said to be in New Orleans. If you find preparations being made within your command for such invasion prevent it. Arrest and imprison leaders if necessary to vindicate the law.

U. S. GRANT

General.

Show to Sec. of War before transmittel.

U. S. G.

ALS (telegram sent), DNA, RG 107, Telegrams Collected (Bound); telegram sent, *ibid*.; copies, *ibid*., RG 108, Telegrams Sent; DLC-USG, V, 56; Seward Papers, NRU. On July 13, 1867, 5:30 P.M., Maj. Gen. Philip H. Sheridan telegraphed to USG. "I am in receipt of your telegram of this date, I will act very promptly on it should I discover any organization for purpose named, I heard this morning that a small party had left this city for Mexico but I think if true I would have known it—There are many Imperial soldiers on the streets here, The old rebel feeling was stirred up here by the total loss of the Imperial cause— Some newspapers have been assiduous in stimulating the bad elements in the population of New Orleans to a difficulty with Mexico but the excitement on the subject is subsiding" Telegram received (at 8:00 P.M.), DNA, RG 107, Telegrams Collected (Bound); *ibid*., RG 108, Telegrams Received; copies, *ibid*., RG 94, Letters Received, 946M 1867; DLC-USG, V, 55; (2) DLC-Philip H. Sheridan. On July 17, Sheridan telegraphed to USG. "I am pretty well satisfied that the Mexican fillibustering project is entertained but has not come to any head in this City yet, I will watch it closely, On the twenty ninth of June the

Steamer Irene sailed for some point in Cuba via Havana, I think in connection with the fillibustering project. She cleared under British colors" Telegram received (at 6:15 P.M.), DNA, RG 107, Telegrams Collected (Bound); *ibid.*, RG 108, Telegrams Received; copies, DLC-USG, V, 55; (2) DLC-Philip H. Sheridan. On July 20, Secretary of State William H. Seward wrote to Secretary of War Edwin M. Stanton concerning a congressional request for documents on Mexican affairs. LS, DNA, RG 107, Letters Received from Bureaus. On Aug. 1, USG endorsed this letter. "Respectfully returned to the Secretary of War, with copies of two telegrams, which are the only communications relative to this subject on record at these Headquarters." ES, *ibid.* See *HED*, 40-2-25. On Aug. 9, USG endorsed papers reporting no evidence of an expedition under preparation. "Respectfully forwarded to the Secretary of War, inviting attention to the report of Bvt. Maj. Gen. J. J. Reynolds" ES, DNA, RG 107, Letters Received from Bureaus.

On Jan. 29, Sheridan had written to USG. "I have the honor to enclose herewith copy of a communication just received from Paso Macho regarding Mexican affairs." Copy, DLC-Philip H. Sheridan. On March 2 and 4, Sheridan wrote to Bvt. Maj. Gen. John A. Rawlins transmitting information on Mexican affairs. LS, DNA, RG 107, Letters Received from Bureaus. On March 9 and 12, USG endorsed these papers to Stanton. ES, *ibid.* On March 21, Sheridan wrote to Rawlins transmitting information on Mexican affairs. LS, *ibid.*, RG 94, Letters Received, 749M 1867. On March 26, USG endorsed these papers to Stanton. ES, *ibid.* On March 25, Sheridan wrote to Rawlins transmitting a report of Feb. 26 from an agent accompanying Mexican forces. LS and copy (signature removed), *ibid.*, RG 108, Letters Received.

On April 18, Sheridan telegraphed to USG. "Late news from Mexico shows increased Liberal successes, There is scarcely a hope of the escape of Maximillian It is barely possible he may get from Queretara as a fugitive but his escape from the Country as a fugitive is very uncertain," Telegram received (at 5:00 P.M.), *ibid.*, RG 107, Telegrams Collected (Bound); *ibid.*, RG 108, Telegrams Received; copies, DLC-USG, V, 55; (2) DLC-Philip H. Sheridan; DLC-Edwin M. Stanton. On May 26 or 27, Sheridan telegraphed to USG. "Queretaro was captured at 8. o'clock a. m May 15th. Maxamilian, Mejia, and Miramon are prisoners." LS (telegram sent dated May 26), DNA, RG 107, Telegrams Collected (Bound); telegram received (dated May 27, marked as sent at 11:30 A.M., received at 12:30 P.M.), *ibid.*; *ibid.*, RG 108, Telegrams Received.

On June 13, Sheridan wrote to USG. "I have the honor to transmit enclosed the latest information concerning Mexican affairs" LS, USG 3. Sheridan enclosed a letter of May 29 from an agent, San Luis Potosí, to Sheridan. ". . . A secret Court-Martial has been sitting in Queretaro for the last three days for the trial of Maximilian, Mejia, and Miramon, who, meanwhile are kept in solitary confinement under double guard and hear none of the evidence; if evidence there is. . . . If they are shot it will be *because* of the U. S recommendation that they should *not* be and a direct defiance of the United States. . . ." Copy (signature removed), *ibid.* On June 13, Sheridan endorsed this letter. "This note has a little informal coloring, but, from other sources there is without doubt, serious fears of the execution of Maximillian but it is not to be attributed to American intervention; although the course of Mr Seward is not popular in Mexico." AES, *ibid.* On June 18, Sheridan telegraphed to USG. "I have information which is reliable that Maximillian is safe His trial is indefinitely postponed" Telegram received (at 11:05 P.M.), DNA, RG 107, Telegrams Collected (Bound); *ibid.*, RG 108, Telegrams Received; copies, DLC-USG, V, 55; (2) DLC-Philip H. Sheridan. On June 29, Sheridan telegraphed to USG. "The following news has just reached me—I do not fully Vouch for its Authenticity—Maximillian was condemned and shot on June 19th, body not delivered—Austrian Maximillian troops at Vera-Cruz are requesting transportation from that point home—badly scared. President Juarez refuses to deliver body of Maximillian—If this is true it is but the end of the Rebellion which had its Commencement in this country and its tragic ~~end~~ termination in Mexico" LS (telegram sent), DNA, RG 107, Telegrams Collected (Bound); telegram received (at 9:10 P.M.), *ibid.*; *ibid.*, RG 108, Telegrams Received. On July 1, Sheridan wrote to USG. "*Private* . . . There are certain parties in this city, aided and abetted by the public press, who are attempting to get up ill will against the Liberal Government in Mexico, by the publication of false reports, and the assertion that the Liberal Government is hostile to our own. Among those most prominent in this work are General Steadman and a Mr. King of the 'New Orleans Times', and it appears very much as though they were carrying out the instructions of higher authority for some purpose. The appointment of the new minister seems to be in accordance with this work of embarrassing our relations with the Liberal Government; for he will scarcely be accepted. He has been an Imperialist and is a very disagreeable man to the Liberals. I very much fear, from what I have seen here within the last ten days, that there is an attempt being made to involve us in trouble." LS, USG 3. On Aug. 9, Sheridan wrote to USG. "I have the honor to herewith enclose for your information a copy of a communication regarding affairs in Mexico. The writer is a reliable man." LS, *ibid.* The enclosure is *ibid.*

Testimony

Washington, D. C.
Thursday, July 18th, 1867.

Gen'l Ulysses S. Grant,
    Sworn and examined
      By Mr. Eldridge.

Q. At what time were you made General of the army by your present title?

A   In July 1866.

Q. Did you after that time have interviews with the President in reference to the condition of affairs in the rebel States?

A   I have seen the President very frequently on the subject and have heard him express his views very frequently; but I cannot call to mind any special interview. I have been called to Cabinet meetings a number of times

Q With reference to those matters?

A Generally when I was asked to be at a Cabinet meeting it was because some question was up in which as General of the army I would be interested.

Q. Did you have any interviews with him on the subject of granting amnesty or pardon to the officers of the confederate army, or to the people of those States?

A Not that I am aware of. I have occasionally recommended a person for amnesty. I do not recollect any special interview that I have had on the subject. I recollect speaking to him once or twice about the time that he issued his proclamation. I thought myself at that time that there was no reason why, because a person had risen to the rank of General, he should be excluded from amnesty any more than one who had failed to reach that rank. I thought his proclamation all right so far as it excluded graduates from West Point, or from the Naval academy, or persons connected with the Gov't. who had gone into the rebellion; but I did not see any reason why a volunteer who happened to rise to the rank of General should be excluded any more than a Colonel. I recollect speaking on that point. Neither did I see much reason for the $20.000 clause. These are the only two points that I remember to have spoken of at the time. I afterwards, however, told him that I thought he was much nearer right on the $20,000 clause than I was.

Q. Do you recollect when you had that interview with him where you expressed those opinions?

A. About the time of the proclamation.

Q. Did the President, previous to issuing that proclamation, ask your opinion on the various points of it?

A I do not recollect. I know that I was present when it was read, before it was issued. I do not think that I was asked my views at all. I had the privilege of course, being there, to express my views.

Q. Was not that the purpose of your attendance—to get your views on the subject?

A   I cannot say that it was. About that time I was frequently asked to be present at Cabinet meetings.

Q   Were there other subjects discussed before you at the meetings referred to?

A   Yes Sir. Whenever I was there, all the subjects that were up that day were discussed.

Q.   I speak of that time?

A   I imagine not. My recollection is that it was solely to hear that proclamation read, but I would not be positive as to that. It is my recollection.

Q   Did you give your opinion to the President that it would be better at that time to issue a proclamation of general amnesty?

A.   No Sir. I never gave any such opinion as that. By general amnesty I mean universal amnesty.

Q   Did you give your opinion to the President that his proclamation interfered with the stipulations between yourself and General Lee?

A   No Sir. I frequently had to intercede for Gen'l Lee[1] and other paroled officers on the ground that their parole, so long as the obeyed the laws of the U. S. protected them from arrest and trial. The President at that time occupied exactly the reverse ground, viz: that they should be tried and punished   He wanted to know when the time would come that they should be punished. I told him, not so long as they obeyed the laws and complied with the stipulation. That was the ground that I took

Q.   Did you not also insist that that applied as well to the common soldiers?

A   Of course it applied to every one who took the parole; but that matter was not canvassed except in case of some of the leaders. I claimed that, in surrendering their armies and arms, they had done what they could not all of them have been compelled to do, as a portion of them could have escaped. But they surrendered in consideration of the fact that they were to be exempt from trial so long as they conformed to the obligation which they had taken; and they were entitled to that.

Q You looked on that in the nature of a parole and held that they could only be tried when they violated that parole?

A Yes: that was the view I took of the question.

Q That is your view still?

A Yes Sir, unquestionably.

Q Did you understand that to apply to Gen. Lee?

A Certainly.

Q. That was your understanding of the arrangement which you made with Genl. Lee?

A. That was my understanding of an arrangement which I gave voluntarily. Genl. Lee's army was the first to surrender, and I believed that with such terms all the rebel armies would surrender, and that we would thus avoid bushwhacking & a continuation of the war in a way that we could make very little progress with—having no organized armies to meet.

Q. You considered that the like terms were given by Gen'l. Sherman to the armies which surrendered to him?

A. Yes Sir, to all the armies that surrendered after that.

Q. And you held that so long as they kept their parole of honor & obeyed the laws they were not subject to be tried by courts?

A. That was my opinion. I will state here that I am not quite certain whether I am being tried, or who is being tried by the questions asked?

Mr. Eldridge. I am not trying any body. I am enquiring in reference to the President's proclamation and as to the views which he entertained.

Did you give those views to the President?

A. I have stated those views to the President frequently, and, as I have said, he disagreed with me in those views. He insisted on it that the leaders must be punished, and wanted to know when the time would come that those persons would be tried.

I told him when they violated their parole.

Q. Did you consider that that applied to Jefferson Davis?

A. No sir, he did not take any parole.

Q. He did not surrender?

A. No sir. It applied to no person who was captured—only to those who were paroled.

Q. Did the President insist that Genl Lee should be tried for treason?

A. He contended for it.

Q. And you claimed to him that the parole which Genl Lee had given would be violated in such trial?

A. I did. I insisted on it that Genl Lee would not have surrendered his army and given up all their arms, if he had supposed that after surrender he was going to be tried for treason and hanged. I thought we got a very good equivalent for the lives of a few leaders in getting all their arms and getting themselves under control—bound by their oaths to obey the laws—That was the consideration which I insisted upon, we had recieved.

Q. Did the President argue that question with you?

A. There was not much argument about it, it was merely assertion.

Q. After you had expressed your opinion upon it, did he coincide with you?

A. No sir, not then. He afterwards got agreeing with me on that subject. I never claimed that the parole gave prisoners any political rights whatever—I thought that that was a matter entirely with Congress, over which I had no control—that simply, as General in Chief, Commanding the Army, I had a right to stipulate for the surrender on terms which protected their lives. That is all I claimed. The parole gave them protection and exemption from punishment for all offences not in violation of the rules of civilized warfare, so long as their parole was kept.

Q. Do you recollect at what time you had those conversations— Can you state any particular time, or up to any particular time when they were finished?

A. The conversations were frequent after the inauguration of Mr Johnson. I cannot give the time. He seemed to be anxious to get at the leaders to punish them. He would say, that the leaders of the rebellion must be punished and that treason must be made odious.

He cared nothing for the men in the ranks, the common man. He would let them go, for they were led into it by the leaders.

Q. Was that said to you in conversation?

A. I heard him say it a number of times. He said it to me, and he said it in my presence at the time that delegations were coming up to him from the south.

Q. What persons do you recollect being present at those conversations—I mean what southern men?

A. I did not know them at all. I recollect that on one occasion he talked to a delegation from Richmond in that way. I do not know any of their names.

Q. Was that prior, or subsequent to his proclamation.

A. It was subsequent. I think.

Q. Do you recollect at any time urging the President to go further in granting amnesty than he had gone in his proclamation?

A. Just as I said before, I could not see any reason why the fact of a volunteer rising to the rank of General should exclude him any more than any other grade. And with reference to the $20.000 clause, I thought that a mans success in this world was no reason for his being excluded from amnesty. But I recollect afterwards saying to the President, that I thought he was right in that particular and I was wrong. In reference to the other I never changed my views. If he was going to give amnesty to a soldier at all, I did not see why the fact of a mans having risen to the rank of General should be a reason for excluding him.

Q. Did you not advise the President that it was proper and right he should grant amnesty?

A. I do not think I said any thing on that subject. I only looked at the Proclamation as one which he was determined to issue, and as a thing susceptable to amendment or improvement

Q. Did you not give your opinion at all that amnesty ought to be granted to those people to any extent?

A. I know that I was in favor of some proclamation of the sort, and perhaps I may have said so. It was necessary to do something to establish government and civil law there. I wanted to see that done, but I do not think I ever pretended to dictate what ought to be done.

Q. Did you not advise?

A. I do not think I ever did. I have given my opinions, perhaps, as to what has been done, but I do not think that I advised any course my self any more, than that I was very anxious to see something done to restore civil government in those states.

Q. Did you not give your opinion at all to the President as to what should be done?

A. I do not think I did. After matters were done, I was willing to express an opinion for or against particular clauses.

Q. I suppose the President called on you for your advice on those questions?

A. I say I was in favor, and so expressed myself, of something being done to restore civil rule there immediately as nearly as it could be under the circumstances.

Q. Did you suggest any thing?

A. No sir.

By Mr Woodbridge.

Q. I understand your position to be this—that you did not assume to originate or inaugurate any policy, but that, when any question came up, and your opinion was asked as to what the President was going to do, or had done, you gave an opinion?

A That was it exactly, and I presumed the whole Committee so understood me. I have always been attentive to my own duties and tried not to interfere with other peoples. I was always ready to originate matters pertaining to the army, but I never was willing to originate matters pertaining to the civil Govt of the U. S. When I was asked my opinion about what had been done, I was willing to give it. I originated no plan and suggested no plan for civil government. I only gave my views on measures after they had been originated. I simply expressed an anxiety that something should be done to give some sort of control down there. There were no governments there when the war was over, and I wanted to see some Governments established and wanted to see it done quickly. I did not pretend to say how it should be done, or in what form.

By Mr. Eldridge.

Q. I confined my questions entirely to war and peace. In expressing the opinion that something ought to be done & done quickly, did you make a suggestion of what ought to be done?

A. No sir. I will state here that before Mr. Lincoln's assassination the question about issuing a proclamation of some sort and establishing some sort of a civil government there was up; and what was done then was continued after Mr. Johnson came into office.

Q. Did you give your opinion on that after it was done?

A. I was present. I think twice during Mr. Lincoln's administration, when a proclamation which had been prepared was read. After his assassination it continued right along, and I was there with Mr. Johnson

Q. Did you give President Johnson your opinion on the subject of the proclamation which you say was up before Mr. Lincoln's death & was continued afterwards?

A I say I have given my opinion on particular passages of it.

Q Tell us what conversation you had with President Johnson on the subject, so far as you can recollect it?

A. I have stated once or twice that, so far as I can recollect, I disagreed with two clauses of the proclamation. As to the plan of establishing Provisional Governors there, that was a question which I knew nothing about & which I do not recollect having expressed an opinion about. The only opinion I recollect having expressed on that subject at all was to the Secretary of War. I thought there would be some difficulty in getting people down there to accept offices, but I found afterwards they were ready enough to take them.

By the Chairman.

Q. If I understand you correctly, the only opinion that you expressed & the only advice that you gave were in reference to the military side of the question, & not in reference to the civil side?

A. Nothing further than that I was anxious that something should be done to restore some sort of Government.

Q. But you gave no advice as to what should be done?

A. I gave no advice as to what should be done.

By Mr. Eldridge

Q. State the conversation that you had on the subject?

A. I have had repeated conversations with the President, but I cannot specify what those conversations were any more than I have already done.

Q. Did you recommend certain Generals of the Confederate Army to the President for pardon who fell within the exemptions?

A. Yes Sir. I recommended General Longstreet,[2] I think a year and a half ago, and although I cannot recollect the name of anybody else, I think I recommended several others.

Q. Do you recollect recommending J. G. French,[3] a Graduate of West Point?

A. Yes sir.

Q What part did he take in the rebellion?

A. He was a Brig. General.

Q. Was he a graduate of West Point?

A. He was & a class mate of mine.

Q.[4] Do you not think he was ever a secessionist?

A No sir. I knew a good deal of the circumstances of his being in the rebel service. He had resigned from the Army quite a number of years before—shortly after the Mexican war—and settled in Mississippi. Everything he owned in the world was there. He was offered a position in the Ordnance Department in the rebel army, but he declined and Kept out of the Confederate service until they were conscripting everybody. Then they sent him a Brig. General's commission; and, as he expressed it to me, he knew he must either take that or go in as a private and he accepted the Brig Generalcy.

By Mr. Williams.

Q. When you say he was not a secessionist, you mean he was not a secessionist at heart or from the beginning?

A. Yes sir.

By Mr Eldridge

Q Do you recollect recommending the pardon of Geo. H. Stuart?[5]

A. Yes sir.

Q. What part did he take in the confederate service?

A. He was a General & commanded a brigade or division. He took no very conspicuous part.

Q. Was he a graduate of West Point?

A I think so

Q. He was not a classmate of yours?

A No sir; he came long after me.

Q. Was there any special circumstance in his case which you considered?

A Yes sir. I did that at the instance of Genl. Hunter & as a special favor to him; and I did it because it affected an inheritance. Stewarts wife was a staunch consistent Union woman throughout the war, notwithstanding her husband was in the rebel army I think she never went South and she was as devoted to the Union cause as any woman, whose husband was on our side. There was considerable property in Maryland which had not been confiscated which he inherits and I thought that his wife and his children were entitled to that property. General Hunter thought so to. My recommendation was not out of any favor to Genl Stuart.

Q. Were those circumstances presented to the President as a reason for the pardon?

A I do not know that they were, and I do not know that they were not. I think I merely signed a recommendation.

Q. Did that contain the statement you have given?

A I do not recollect whether it did or not. I do not know that I stated the circumstances to the President.

Q. Do you recollect signing the recommendation of M. D. Ector,[6] a rebel Brig. General?

A. No Sir. I do not recollect there being such a Brig. General in the rebel service.

Q. The report to the House is that he was pardoned on the recommendation of L't. Gen'l. Grant & John Hancock?

A. I do not recollect any such person as John Hancock or the General named.

Q. Do you recollect _____ Lloyd J. Dean? (Beall.)[7]

A. Yes Sir.

Q. Did you sign a recommendation or make an application to the President for his pardon?

A. I do not think that the record will show that I recommended his pardon, but I am not sure as to that. I know that his sent his application through me, with the request that I should forward it to the President with some endorsement. My recollection is, that I made an endorsement as to his general character which was as high up to the breaking out of the rebellion as any man's could be

Q. Were you acquainted with him previous to the breaking out of the rebellion.

A. Oh yes, sir, for many years I do not think that I recommended him, but still I may have done so. My recollection is that I simply endorsed his character on the application. The application was to the President but sent through me.

Q. Do you recollect P. D. Roddy[8] said to be a rebel Brig. General?

A. Yes sir, I do not recollect what my endorsement was in Roddy's case, but I know that, if I had it to do over again, I would recommend his pardon very quickly, and I presume I did so. I had him in my front a good deal during the rebellion & I know that, if he ever applied to me to recommend his pardon I would do so, and, if he is not pardoned yet, I would be very glad to sign a recommendation for him now.

Q. He is reported as being pardoned on your recommendation?

A. It may be so, but I do not recollect anything about it. If he ever applied to me, I know I did recommend him. He gave more protection to Union people & to refugees than we were capable of doing ourselves.

Q. Do you recollect any other officers of the rebel army who were recommended to the President for pardon by you.

A. No sir, I cannot mention any. You have already gone over a bigger list than I thought I recommended.

Q. Do you recollect the case of Gen'l. Pickett?[9]

A. I know that I was urged in that case over and over again, & I can send you from the office exactly what I did in the matter.

Q. Did you sign a recommendation in his case

A. I do not think I did. I recollect receiving letter after letter from him, and letters were sent to me time & again on his behalf. He was specially uneasy lest he would be tried by a Military Commission on account of some men who were executed in North Carolina

Q. Dou you recollect talking to the President about him?

A. I do not recollect ever mentioning his name to the President. I will furnish whatever is in my office about him. I received one appeal after another, not only from Pickett himself and from his relations, but from officers of the Army, who know him very well and favorably prior to the war.

Q. Do you know whether he has been pardoned yet?

A. I do not know

Q. State what the circumstances of his case were, and whether you are in favor of his pardon?

A. I was not in favor of his pardon. I was not in favor, however, of his being tried by a Military Commission. I think that his great anxiety was to receive some assurance that he would not be taken up and imprisoned for offences alledged against him as Commander in North Carolina. He wanted to be able to go to work and make a living. It is likely I may have recommed that he be given assurance that he would not be arrested and imprisoned   I do not think that I ever under any circumstances, signed a recommendation for his pardon. You have no right to ask what my opinion is now.

Q. Was he an active rebel officer?

A. Yes sir. He was charged with executing a number of North Carolina refugees who were captured with a garrison under Gen'l. Wessels in North Carolina   Those men had gone there to evade the rebel concription, or it may be had deserted from the rebel army and they were tried as deserters and quite a number of them executed. Picketts was commanding officer at that time, and there was a good deal said of his having approved the proceedings

Q. Was this man French an active rebel officer?

A. He served in the field. I never heard much of him during the rebellion. He was not generally in the army against which I was personally engaged. He was at one time on the James river when Gen'l. McClellan was in command, and was afterwards in the West but he never filled a conspicuous place

Q. Did you ever advise the pardon of Gen'l. Lee

A. Yes sir

Q. Were you ever consulted on that question by the President?

A. Gen'l. Lee forwarded his application for amnesty through me, and I forwarded it to the President, approved.

Q. Did you have any conversation about it with the President?

A. I do not recollect having had any conversation with him on the subject. I think it probable that I recommended verbally the pardon of Gen'l. Johnston,[10] immediately after the surrender of his army, on account of the address he delivered to his army, I thought it in such good tone and spirit that we should distinguish between him and others who did not appear so well I recollect speaking of that and saying that I should be glad if Genl. Johnston received his pardon on account of the manly manner in which he addressed his troops.

By the Chairman

Q You supposed his pardon would have a good effect?

A Yes, I thought it would have a good effect. I am not sure whether I spoke on the subject to the Sec'y of War or to the President.

By Mr Eldridge

Q Do you recollect having a conversation with the President at any time when Genl. Hillyer was present?

A I remember going with Genl. Hillyer to see the President, but it was on the subject of an appointment which he wanted. I went to state to the President what I know of Genl. Hillyer, I do not recollect the conversation, going beyond that range, at all, though still it might have done so.

Q You do not recollect any other meeting with the President when Genl. Hillyer was present?[11]

A I do not know. I think I met him twice, perhaps, but it was on a subject in which Genl. Hillyer himself was personally interested. Whether the President conversed on other subjects at that time, I do not recollect.

Q. Do you not recollect any conversation with the President in the presence of Genl. Hillyer on the subject of granting amnesty to the people of the South?

A. No sir. I do not recollect any conversation on the subject of general amnesty and I know that I never was in favor of general amnesty. I do not recollect any conversation at that time on the subject of amnesty at all. I have stated here that I never recommended general amnesty and never was in favor of it until the time shall come when it is safe to give it.

By Mr. Williams.

Q. When you say that you did not recommend general amnesty, you mean universal amnesty.?

A. I do not recollect of ever having any conversation on the subject of universal amnesty. I know I could not have recommended such a thing because I never was in favor of it until the time shall come when it is safe.

Q. I merely put the question to your use of the term "general" because it might be supposed from that, that the amnesty in the proclamation was not a general amnesty?

A. I meant "universal amnesty", of course.

Q. You state that you differed with the President as to two points in his proclamation, but that his views afterwards changed. State when the President's mind underwent a change?

A. It would be very hard, I reckon, to fix any period for it.

Q. Was it in the summer of 1865?

A. Yes sir, along in the summer of 1865.

Q. How long after the North Carolina proclamation of the 29th of May?

A. It is impossible for me to say.

Q. Was it more than two or three months?

A. I should think not.

By Mr. Woodbridge

Q. What did you mean by saying that the President's views afterwards changed?

A. I meant to say that while I was contending for the rights which those rebel paroled leaders had, he was insisting on it that they should be punished. My remark was confined to that particular subject.

By Mr. Eldridge.

Q. Did you have any correspondence with the President in writing.?

A. Any correspondence I ever had with the President is official and can be furnished. I had to make frequent endorsements on the subjects of the rights of those paroled prisoners. The only correspondence that I could have had on the subject of amnesty was where I recommended men for pardon, as in the case of French and others.

Q. Did you keep copies of them.?

A. Yes sir, and will furnish them.

Q Do you recollect the proclamation that is called the North Carolina Proclamation?

A. Yes, sir. That was the first one published, giving a State government.

Q. Did you have any conversation with the President as to the terms or purport of that proclamation?

A. I was, as I say, present when it was read. It was in the direction that I wanted. I was anxious to see something done to give some sort of temporary government there. I did not want to see anarchy.

Q. Did you give any opinion in favor of that proposition?

A. I did not give any opinion against it. I was in favor of that or anything else which looked to civil government until Congress could meet and establish governments there. I did not want all chaos left there and no form of civil government whatever. I was not in favor of anything or opposed to anything particularly. I was simply in favor of having a government there. That was all I wanted. I did not pretend to give my judgment as to what it should be. I was perfectly willing to leave that to the civil department. I asked no person what I should do in my duties. I was willing to take all the responsibilities and I did not want to give my views as to what the civil branch of the government should do.

Q. Some of those governors were military officers and held rank in the army?

A. That was during the rebellion. Mr. Johnson was military governor in Tennessee, and Genl Hamilton in Texas. I do not recollect that there were any other military governors. The others were provisional governors. I did not care whether they were called Provisional or Military governors. I looked upon them as equally provisional.

By Mr. Thomas.

Q. You have stated your opinion as to the rights and priveleges of Genl. Lee and his soldiers—did you mean that to include any political rights?

A. I have explained that I did not.

Q. Was there any difference of opinion on that point between yourself and President Johnson at any time?

A. On that point there was no difference of opinion; but there was as to whether the parole gave them any priveleges or rights.

By Mr. Eldridge.

Q. He claiming that it did not, and you claiming that it did?

A. He claiming that the time must come when they could be tried and punished, and I claiming that that time could not come except by a violation of their parole. I claimed that I gave them them no political priveleges, but that I had a right, as Military Commander, to arrange terms of surrender, which should protect the lives of those prisoners. I believe it is conceded by everybody that I had that right. I know that Mr. Lincoln conceded it at the time.

By Mr. Boutwell.

Q. How recently has the President expressed to you the opinion that Genl. Lee or others who had the benefit of the parole ought to be tried and punished?

A. Not since about two years ago.

Q. Have you at any time heard the President make any remark

in reference to admission of members of Congress from the rebel states into either House?

A I cannot say positively what I have heard him say on that subject. I have heard him say as much perhaps in his published speeches last summer as I ever heard him say at all upon that subject. I have heard him say—and I think I have heard him say it twice in his speeches—that if the North carried the elections by numbers enough to give them with the southern members a majority, why would they not be the Congress of the United States? I have heard him say that several times.

By Mr. Williams

Q. When you say "the North" you mean the democratic party of the North, or in other words the party favoring his policy.

A I mean if the North carried enough members in favor of the admission of the South. I did not hear him say that he would recognize them as the Congress. I merely heard him ask the question, why would they not be the Congress.

By the chairman.

Q When did you hear him say that.

A I heard him say that in one or two of his speeches. I do not recollect where.

By Mr Boutwell.

Q Have you heard him make a remark kindred to that elsewhere?

A Yes. I have heard him say that, aside from his speeches, in conversation. I cannot say just when. It was probably about that same time.

Q Have you heard him at any time make any remark or suggestion concerning the legality of Congress with the Southern members excluded?

A He alluded to that subject frequently in his tour to Chicago and back last summer. His speeches were generally reported with considerable accuracy. I cannot recollect what he said, except in general terms; but I read his speeches at the time and they were reported with considerable accuracy.

Q Did you hear him say anything in private on that subject, either during that trip or any other time?

A I do not recollect specially.

Q Did you at any time hear him make any remark concerning the Executive department of the government?

A No, I never heard him allude to that.

Q Did you ever hear him make any remark looking to any controversy between Congress and the Executive?

A I think not.

By Mr Marshall.

Q I understand you to say that you were very anxious at the close of the war that civil governments should be established in some form as speedily as possible, and that you so advised the President?

A I so stated frequently in his presence

Q But that you advised no particular form or mode of proceeding?

A I did not.

Q Were you present when this North Carolina Proclamation was read in the Cabinet?

A I would not be certain, but my recollection is that the first time I heard it read was in the presence only of the President, the Secretary of War and myself.

Q Did you give your assent to that plan?

A I did not dissent from it, That is just in accordance with what I have stated. It was a civil matter, and although I was anxious to have something done, I did not intend to dictate any plan, I do not think I said anything about it or expressed any opinion about it at that time. I looked upon it simply as a temporary measure, to establish a sort of a government, until Congress should meet and settle the whole question, and that it did not make much difference how it was done, so there was a form of government there.

Q Were you present at that time by invitation of the President or the Secretary of War?

A I must have been.

Q Were you not invited for the purpose of getting your views as to whether it was a judicious plan to be adapted for the time?

A I suppose I was free to express my views. I suppose the object was, perhaps, that I might express my views if I could suggest any change.

Q Were you at that time asked your views in reference to it?

A I do not think I was. I think it was merely read over.

Q You think you neither assented nor dissented?

A I know that if I had been asked the question, I would have assented to that or almost anything else that would have given stable governments there.

Q. In reference to the Amnesty Proclamation I wish to know whether you ever gave your opinion to the President as to whether it was too liberal or not liberal enough in its clauses?

A. I think I have answered that question pretty fully. When the Proclamation was published, I told the President that there were two points on which I disagreed with him—that is as to excluding volunteer generals and as to the $20000 clause. I did not say anything as to whether the rest of it was too liberal or too stringent. I can state what I thought about it, but not what I said about it.

Q. I wish to know whether at or about the time of the war being ended you advised the President that it was, in your judgment, best to extend a liberal policy towards the people of the south and to restore as speedily as possible the fraternal relations which existed prior to the war between the two sections?

A. I know that immediately after the close of the rebellion there was a very fine feeling manifested in the south, and I thought we ought to take advantage of it as soon as possible; but since that there has been an evident change there. I may have expressed my views to the President.

Q. What is your recollection in reference to that?

A. I may have done so, and it is probable that I did. I do not recollect particularly. I know that I conversed with the President very frequently. I do not suppose that there were any person engaged in that consultation who thought of what was being done at that time as being lasting—any longer than until Congress would meet and either ratify that or establish some other form of government. I know it never crossed my mind that what was being done was any thing more than temporary.

By Mr. Churchill

Q. You understood that to be the view of the President?

A. I understood that to be the view of the President and of every body else. I did not know of any difference of opinion on that subject.

Q. Did you not understand that to be his view as other proclamations appeared to be from time to time?

A. I cannot say as to that. It would seem that he was very anxious to have Congress ratify his own views.

By Mr. Woodbridge.

Q. I understand you to say that Mr. Lincoln prior to his assassination had inaugurated a policy intending to restore those governments?

A. Yes, sir.

Q. You were present when the subject was before the Cabinet?

A I was present I think twice before the assassination of Mr. Lincoln when a plan was read.

Q. I want to know whether the plan adopted by Mr. Johnson was substantially the plan which had been inaugurated by Mr. Lincoln as the basis for his future action?

A. Yes sir, substantially. I do not know but that it was verbatim the same.

Q. I suppose the very paper of Mr. Lincoln was the one acted on?

A. I should think so.—I think that the very paper which I heard read twice while Mr. Lincoln was President, was the one which was carried right through

By Mr. Churchill.

Q. What paper was that?

A. The North Carolina Proclamation.

By Mr. Boutwell

Q. You understood that Mr. Lincoln's plan was temporary, to be either confirmed or a new government set up by Congress?

A. Yes, and I understood Mr. Johnson's to be so too.

By Mr. Williams.

Q. Was there anything said on that subject or was that your inference?

A. That was my inference.

Q. You never heard the President say that the plan was to be temporary?

A. No; but I was satisfied that every body looked on it as simply temporary until Congress met.

Q. You have stated that the North Carolina Proclamation was a continuation of the *projet* submitted by Mr. Lincoln. I wish to inquire of you whether you ever compared them to ascertain whether they were the same or not?

A. No sir. I never compared them. I took them to be the very same paper. The papers were substantially the same, if not the very same.

By Mr Thomas

Q. Did the President propose at any time to use the military power for the adjustment of the controversy in Baltimore between the Police Commissioners appointed by Governor Swan & those who claimed authority independent of Gov'r Swan?[12]

A. I understood that he wanted to use it, & called his attention to the law on the subject which changed his views & determination evidently. I called his attention to the only circumstance in which the mily forces of the US can be called out to interfere in State matters. It was his intention to send troops there to enable Gov'r Swan, as he termed it, to enforce his decision in the case of those Police Commissioners.

Q. Did the President on account of your opinion change that purpose?

A. I ~~wrote~~ made a communication to him

By Mr. Williams.

Q. Have you a copy of the letter addressed by you to the President?

A. I have a copy of everything official, except conversation.

(witness was directed to furnish the official Documents on the subject)

By Mr. Thomas.

Q. Did the President signify his wish concerning the army in writing or verbally?

A Verbally and in writing.

Q. Were you sent for formally?

A. Yes sir, I was sent for several times—twice, I think, while Governor Swan was there in consultation with the President. Finding that the President wanted to send the military to Baltimore, I ~~sat down & wrote a communication objecting~~ objected to it.

Q. Are you distinct in your recollection as to when the President acquiesced in your views?

A. It was prior to the election, two or three days. When the matter was left entirely with me, I ordered those troops down to join their regiments & to halt at Fort McHenry until after the election.

Q. Was it before or after the arrest of the Commissioners appointed by Governor Swan that the President withdrew his request to you to use the army in that controversy?

A. I cannot state precisely as to that. It was before I ordered the troops from New York. What took place was in conversation until I found that there was rather a determination to send troops there; and then I ~~sat down & wrote~~ communicated officially to the Secy of War my objection to using troops in that way. That called out the opinion of the Attorney General, & it was then that what I proposed was acquiesced in. I thought this was in writing but do not find the paper.

By Mr. Marshall.

Q. The President seemed to think he had a right to send the army under the circumstances?

A Yes Sir; he seemed to think so.

Q. After you sent your written communication, giving your views in reference to it, the President then left the subject entirely in your hands?

A. Yes Sir. he left it entirely in my hands. I think that is in writing.

(witness was directed to furnish a copy of the communication.)

    By Mr Eldridge

Q That was a formal withdrawal of his first opinion?

A. Yes Sir; I think I was sent a copy of the Attorney General's opinion as a sort of order in the matter, virtually leaving it to me.

Q After that time you did have the management of it?

A Yes Sir. I sent Gen'l Canby to Baltimore & went there twice myself, & had troops stop there on their way to the South.

Q. It was entirely within your control?

A. Yes sir

Q. (By the Chairman) They were solely for the purpose of being used in the case of a riot?

A. Solely for that purpose.

Q. (By Mr. Marshall) Merely as a police force?

A. Yes sir.

Transcript, USG 3. *HRC*, 40-1-7, pp. 825–36, 838–40. USG testified before the Judiciary Committee, U.S. House of Representatives, which was considering the impeachment of President Andrew Johnson. On July 19, 1867, E. G. Bowdoin, clerk, Judiciary Committee, wrote to USG. "Please make such corrections as you desire in your testimony, and then return it to me at your earliest convenience." ALS, DNA, RG 108, Letters Received.

On July 11, 11:27 A.M., Maj. George K. Leet had telegraphed to USG. "You are needed here." ALS (telegram sent), *ibid.*, RG 107, Telegrams Collected (Bound); telegram sent, *ibid.*; copies, *ibid.*, RG 108, Telegrams Sent; DLC-USG, V, 56. On the same day, USG, West Point, telegraphed to Leet. "Why am I wanted in Washington? Explain, Send answer to Garrison Station NewYork immediately" Telegram received (at 5:00 P.M.), DNA, RG 107, Telegrams Collected (Bound); *ibid.*, RG 108, Telegrams Received; copy, DLC-USG, V, 55. At 7:05 P.M., Leet telegraphed to USG. "See cipher telegram to General Porter for explanation" ALS (telegram sent), DNA, RG 107, Telegrams Collected (Bound); telegram sent, *ibid.*; copies, *ibid.*, RG 108, Telegrams Sent; DLC-USG, V, 56. At the same time, Leet telegraphed to Bvt. Brig. Gen. Horace Porter. "Telegram of this morning to the General was sent by direction of the Sec. of War, and he desired that his name should not be mentioned. I thought the General would understand." ALS (telegram sent in cipher), DNA, RG 107, Telegrams Collected (Bound); telegram sent (in cipher), *ibid.*; copies, *ibid.*, RG 108, Telegrams Sent; DLC-USG, V, 56. On the same day, USG wrote to John Bigelow. "A despatch just this moment received calls me back to Washington where I must be by to-morrow morning." Carnegie Book Shop, Catalogue No. 162. On July 12 (Friday), 11:40 A.M., USG, Washington, D. C., telegraphed to Julia Dent Grant, Garrison Station, N. Y. "Found your father & all well. Will return Sunday morning." ALS (telegram sent), DNA, RG 107, Telegrams Collected (Bound). On July 13, USG telegraphed to Bvt. Brig. Gen. Henry D. Wallen, Governors Island, N. Y. "Mr. Dent & myself will leave here in 7 O'Clock tran this evening to visit you. Please have boat meet us at Battery on our arrival." ALS (telegram sent), *ibid.*

1. For Robert E. Lee, see *PUSG*, 15, 149–51, 210–12; *HRC*, 40-1-7, pp. 836–37.

2. For James Longstreet, see *PUSG*, 15, 401–2.

3. For Samuel G. French, see *ibid.*, 15, 246–47.

4. The next two questions and answers are omitted from the printed text.

5. For George H. Steuart, see *PUSG*, 16, 570–71.

6. For Matthew D. Ector, see *ibid.*, 16, 530–31.

7. For Lloyd J. Beall, see *ibid.*, 16, 441. On March 26, 1866, William N. R. Beall, St. Louis, had written to Brig. Gen. Frederick T. Dent. ". . . As yet I've not received a pardon from the President. I made my application on the 2d of last Aug. and the President mentioned to a friend that he would let me hear from my application soon, not one word have I heard, and I'm under the impression that it has been overlooked. Lt. Gen. Grant was kind enough to send me word while I was in N. Y. to write to him in reference to it. This I did but have heard nothing, so presume that my letter was lost— . . ." ALS, DNA, RG 94, Amnesty Papers, Mo. On April 2, USG endorsed this letter. "Respectfully submitted to His Excellency the President, through the Hon. Secretary of War, and recommended." ES, *ibid.*; *HRC*, 40-1-7, p. 838. Possibly supplied to the committee in error because of confusion about the name.

8. For Philip D. Roddey, see *PUSG*, 16, 52.

9. For George E. Pickett, see *ibid.*, 16, 120–22; *HRC*, 40-1-7, pp. 837–38.

10. For Joseph E. Johnston, see *PUSG*, 15, 242–43.

11. For William S. Hillyer's testimony of July 18 and 20, see *HRC*, 40-1-7, pp. 845–57. See also following testimony.

12. On Aug. 1, Bowdoin wrote to USG. "I am directed by the Committee on the Judiciary of the House of Representatives respectfully to request that you will furnish to the Committee copies of the orders of the President of the United States referred to in your letter to Genl Canby dated Washington D. C. Nov. 2, 1866, and in the letter of C. B. Comstock to Genl Canby dated Washington Nov. 3. 1866, which letters are appended to and made a part of your testimony before the Committee. To facilitate reference thereto I inclose a copy of the letters referred to." ALS, USG 3. See *PUSG*, 16, 350–55, 362–65; *HRC*, 40-1-7, pp. 840–45.

Testimony

WASHINGTON, D. C., *July* 20, 1867.

General ULYSSES S. GRANT recalled and examined.

By Mr. BOUTWELL:

Q. Do you recollect having an interview with the President in company with General Hillyer, on the return of General Hillyer from the South?

A. Since my attention was called to it I do. I did not remember it when I gave my testimony the last day here.

Q. What is your recollection of what transpired and was said at that interview?

A. My recollection is that General Hillyer called to explain to the President what he had seen in the South, and what he had heard of the views and opinions of the people there; and that what he had seen was an acquiescence on the part of the southern people, and favorable to peace, harmony, and good will. That was said in general terms, but the language I do not remember.

Q. Do you recollect whether, at that interview, there was any expression by the President as to any political policy?

A. No, sir, I do not; I remember General Hillyer said something of having been invited to make a speech in New York, or some place, I do not remember where, and that he should do so, and send me a copy of his speech. I am very sure that he mentioned that in the presence of the President. What he said in that speech I do not remember now, but I presume the speech could be procured. I remember that General Hillyer gave the substance of what leading men said to him in the South. He particularly mentioned Judge Hale, of Alabama. He said that Judge Hale very candidly said that when they went into the rebellion they took their lives, property, &c., in their hands, and that when they were defeated, they should accept such conditions as the government chose to give; and that they claim now that what they did they did in good faith, and would not take it back again. Judge Hale claimed no right whatever after the failure of the rebellion, except such as was granted to them. That was the point he made. The conversation was made up considerably of instances of that sort. I recollect his mentioning meeting a special party in Mobile, and what occurred there.

HRC, 40-1-7, p. 836. See preceding testimony. On July 19, 1867, U.S. Representative James F. Wilson of Iowa, chairman, Judiciary Committee, had written to USG. "The Committee will be pleased to meet you at their room at two oclock tomorrow." ALS, DNA, RG 108, Letters Received.

To Edwin M. Stanton

Washington, July 20th *1867*.

HON. E. M. STANTON,
SEC. OF WAR,
SIR:

I leave this evening for Governor's Island, N. Y. Harbor. On Monday evening I will go to Long Branch N. J. Where any communication will reach me for the balance of next week. If it is desirable to send any dispatches in Cipher Maj. Leet can send them to Gen. Porter who will be with me.

As soon as I receive a copy of the bill which passed Congress yesterday, over the Presidents veto, I will make such orders as seem to me necessary to carry out the provisions of the bill and direct that they be shewn to you before being issued.[1]

Very respectfully
your obt. svt.
U. S. GRANT
Gen.l

ALS, DLC-Edwin M. Stanton.

On July 19, 1867, Friday, 10:15 A.M., USG telegraphed to Bvt. Brig. Gen. Henry D. Wallen, Governors Island, N. Y. "I will not get through business here to leave before Saturday evening." ALS, DNA, RG 107, Telegrams Collected (Bound). On the same day, Wallen telegraphed to USG. "Your despatch rec'd & your reception deferred till Monday afternoon." Telegram received (at 3:25 P.M.), *ibid.*, RG 108, Telegrams Received. At 4:20 P.M., USG telegraphed to Wallen. "Dont have reception on Monday." ALS (telegram sent), *ibid.*, RG 107, Telegrams Collected (Bound).

1. Congress passed the Third Reconstruction Act on July 19. *U.S. Statutes at Large*, XV, 14–16.

To Edwin M. Stanton

(Cipher)   Long Branch, N. J.
                                                  July 23d 1867.

Hon. E. M. Stanton,
Sec. of Washington

Gen. Dent with dispatches from Gen. Thomas arrived before your telegram. I directed Gen. Thomas to give orders for the most vigerous use of the Military to preserve order on election day and not to wait until people are killed and the mob beyond controll before interfering. I will direct Gen. Thomas to go directly to Memphis in person but do not think there is any need of my going to Nashville.

                                                  U. S. Grant
                                                  General,

ALS (telegram sent), Free Library of Philadelphia, Philadelphia, Pa.; telegram received (at 4:00 p.m.), DNA, RG 107, Telegrams Collected (Bound); DLC-Edwin M. Stanton. On July 18, 1867, Maj. Gen. George H. Thomas, Louisville, had written to the AG. "Enclosed, herewith, I have the honor to transmit copies of Correspondence on the subject of an anticipated riot at Memphis on the day of the election, August [1]st 1867, for the information of the General-in-Chief." LS, DNA, RG 94, Letters Received, 614C 1867. Bvt. Maj. Gen. Edward D. Townsend noted on these papers. ". . . Copies handed Bvt. Brigdr Genl. F. T. Dent A. D. C. 3.30. P. M. July 22, 1867, with orders to convey them to Genl Grant by this evenings train." ANS, *ibid.* On July 22, 2:25 p.m., Maj. George K. Leet telegraphed to Bvt. Brig. Gen. Horace Porter, care of Bvt. Brig. Gen. Henry D. Wallen, Governors Island, N. Y. "Important dispatches received from Gen. Thomas. Secretary of War desires that the General remain at Governors Island until receipt of dispatches which he is now preparing." ALS (telegram sent in cipher), *ibid.*, RG 107, Telegrams Collected (Bound); telegram sent (in cipher), *ibid.*; copies, *ibid.*, RG 108, Telegrams Sent; DLC-USG, V, 56. On the same day, Porter, Stetson House, Long Branch, N. J., telegraphed to Leet. "Send dispatches to Long Branch" Telegram received (at 10:15 p.m.), DNA, RG 107, Telegrams Collected (Bound); *ibid.*, RG 108, Telegrams Received; copy, DLC-USG, V, 56. At 2:30 p.m., Secretary of War Edwin M. Stanton had telegraphed to USG, Governors Island. "Despatches have just been received from General Thomas strongly indicating that there is danger of a formidable and bloody riot at Memphis on the first of August, the day of election arising from an organization to prevent negroes voting and the determination of the colored men to vote. General Thomas has ordered some troops to Memphis under command of Lieut Colonel Townsend with directions to report to and act under the civil authorities. In my judgement the emergency is one demanding the ~~utmost~~ most prompt ~~and~~ efficient and discreet action on the part of the military authorities of the government, and that the national peace may depend upon the manner in which it is treated I think therefore that you ought to go immediately in person to Nashville so as to direct on the spot what may be proper to be done in the condition of affairs now existing [a]nd to be apprehended in Tennessee, and that General Thomas should be directed to proceed immediately in person to Memphis establish his quarters there temporarily and take such measures as may be proper to preserve the peace in that city. I have directed copies of General Thomas' communication to be made & forwarded to you by special messenger but the substance is as above stated and I am unwilling to lose a moment of time in communicating the matter with my judgement as to what seems to me to be the proper action on the part by the General Commanding and the Commander of the Department Please acknowledge this telegram and advise me of your determination" LS (telegram sent), DNA, RG 107, Telegrams Collected (Bound); telegram received (at New York City), *ibid.*, RG 108, Telegrams Received. On July 23, USG telegraphed to Thomas. "Go to Memphis in person and remain there until after election. Let it be felt that where the military is law must prevail and the guilty be punished. Do not wait for a riot to take place but use the military vigorously to prevent one commencing" Copies, DLC-USG, V, 56; DNA, RG 108, Telegrams Sent; *ibid.*, RG 393, Dept. of the Tenn., Telegrams Received. On July 24, Thomas telegraphed to USG. "Have received your telegram of yesterday. Will be in Memphis before election takes place" Copy, *ibid.*, Telegrams Sent.

On July 26, 2:10 P.M., Stanton telegraphed to USG. "The President has appointed on Brownings request Sherman Harney and Terry Indian Commissioners. An important cipher despatch will be sent you by Major Leet as soon as he can prepare it. When will you be here." ALS (telegram sent), *ibid.*, RG 107, Telegrams Collected (Bound). See telegram to Edwin M. Stanton, July 25, 1867. Also on July 26, Stanton telegraphed to USG. "Governor Brownlow has applied for one thousand stand of infantry arms and fifty thousand rounds of ammunition to be forwarded to him at Nashville in addition to the two thousand stand of arms heretofore furnished him. They are at Indianapolis Arsenal ready to be forwarded subject to your approval and order. If you think it right and proper under the present condition of affairs in Tennessee, you will issue an order to the Ordnance officer in charge of the Indianapolis Arsenal to forward the arms and ammunition to Nashville or make any other order on the subject you think the occasion requires." ALS (telegram sent), DLC-Edwin M. Stanton; (2—in cipher, incorporated in a telegram from Leet to Porter, marked as sent at 3:25 P.M.) DNA, RG 107, Telegrams Collected (Bound); copies, *ibid.*, RG 94, Letters Received, 430A 1867; *ibid.*, RG 107, Letters Sent to Bureaus; *ibid.*, RG 108, Telegrams Sent; DLC-USG, V, 56. On the same day, USG telegraphed to Leet. "The issuing of arms and munitions to States is entirely subject to the control of the War Department. If left to me I would say send them to Louisville subject to the discretion of General Thomas whether they would be given to Governor Brownlow or not." Telegram received (at 10:36 P.M. in cipher), DNA, RG 107, Telegrams Collected (Bound); *ibid.*, RG 108, Telegrams Received; copies, *ibid.*, RG 94, Letters Received, 430A 1867; DLC-USG, V, 55.

Also on July 26, Friday, USG telegraphed to Stanton. "Despatches from General Thomas received—I have instructed him to send all troops from Kentucky except enough to guard public property to such parts of Tennessee as in his judgement most require their presence to preserve peace during the Election—

I will go to Washington Monday night if I do not go to Nashville before" Telegram received (at 11:30 P.M.), DLC-Edwin M. Stanton; DNA, RG 107, Telegrams Collected (Bound); (at 7:05 P.M. in cipher, incorporated in a telegram from Porter to Leet) *ibid.*, RG 108, Telegrams Received; copies, DLC-USG, V, 55, 56. On the same day, USG telegraphed to Thomas. "Send all troops in Kentucky, except enough to gaurd public property to such parts of Tennessee as in your judgement most require their presence to preserve peace during the approaching election. After the election they can be returned to their proper stations" Telegram sent, DNA, RG 107, Telegrams Collected (Bound); telegram received (at 7:00 P.M. in cipher, incorporated in a telegram from Porter to Leet), *ibid.*; *ibid.*, RG 108, Telegrams Received. On July 27, Thomas telegraphed to USG. "Yours of yesterday received. I have a few troops in Louisville which can probably be spared for service in Tennessee—The balance in Kentucky not already sent will be required to check the murderous propensity of some of the citizens" Telegram received (at 4:15 P.M.), *ibid.*, RG 107, Telegrams Collected (Bound); (2—in cipher, incorporated in a telegram from Leet to Porter, marked as sent at 10:10 P.M.) *ibid.*; *ibid.*, RG 108, Telegrams Received; copies, *ibid.*, RG 393, Dept. of the Tenn., Telegrams Sent; DLC-USG, V, 55. On July 28, 9:30 A.M., Thomas telegraphed to USG. "All the troops in Kentucky are fully occupied in preserving order in that State. I believe we shall be able to prevent riots in Memphis and Nashville and the other larger towns in Tennessee. I shall go to Memphis tomorrow" Telegram received (on July 29, 9:30 A.M.), DNA, RG 107, Telegrams Collected (Bound); *ibid.*, RG 108, Telegrams Received; copies, *ibid.*, RG 393, Dept. of the Tenn., Telegrams Sent; DLC-USG, V, 55; DLC-Edwin M. Stanton. On Aug. 2, Thomas, Memphis, telegraphed to USG. "The Election passed off very quietly yesterday   I hear of no serious disturbance [a]ny where in this state.   will [re]port more fully from [L]ouisville" Telegram received (at 1:40 P.M.), DNA, RG 107, Telegrams Collected (Bound); *ibid.*, RG 108, Telegrams Received; copies, *ibid.*, RG 393, Dept. of the Tenn., Telegrams Sent; DLC-USG, V, 55.

On July 21, Thomas had telegraphed to USG. "James H. Bridgewater late of our army was murdered by a party of citizens of Lincoln County, Ky at Stanford July 18th   Several of his murderers are paroled rebel soldiers. I have ordered their arrest under your general order 44 series '66 & shall hold them to secure their trial by the civil authorities of Lincoln County for the murder. Will I afterwards be authorized to try them for violation of their parole? Something must be done to deter paroled rebel soldiers from committing violence against union men in sections of this State where they are sure of ~~jurymen~~ sympathy from jurymen when brought to trial for the offences they commit. Many other instances of outrages against Union men have occurred recently but none so heinous as the one now reported." Telegram received (at 9:30 P.M.), DNA, RG 107, Telegrams Collected (Bound); *ibid.*, RG 108, Telegrams Received; copies, *ibid.*, RG 94, Letters Received, 494C 1867; *ibid.*, RG 393, Dept. of the Tenn., Telegrams Sent; DLC-USG, V, 55. On July 30, USG endorsed this telegram. "Respy. referred to the Sec of War. It is clear that cold blooded murderers lose all protection by their Paroles—but I ask what can be done with them. If punishment can be given for violation of Paroles it ought to be inflicted." Copy, DNA, RG 108, Register of Letters Received. On Aug. 6, Thomas telegraphed to USG. "Complaints are constantly made to me of oppression and maltreatment of union men and negroes by returned paroled rebels. Am I authorized to arrest and punish them for violation of their parole?" Telegram received (at 3:45 P.M.), DLC-Andrew Johnson; DNA, RG 108, Telegrams Received; copies, *ibid.*, RG 393, Dept. of the Tenn., Telegrams Sent; DLC-USG, V, 55. On Aug. 8, USG endorsed a telegram received. "Respectfully forwarded to the Sec. of War and information asked as to how far the Civil Rights Bill will authorize the punishment of the class of offenders herein spoken of." AES, DLC-Andrew Johnson. On Aug. 7, 1:45 P.M., USG had telegraphed to Thomas. "If civil authorities will not protect Union men from the violence of paroled rebels arrest the guilty for violation of their paroles." ALS (telegram sent), DNA, RG 107, Telegrams Collected (Bound); telegram sent, *ibid.*; copies, *ibid.*, RG 108, Telegrams Sent; (misdated Aug. 6) *ibid.*, RG 393, Dept. of the Tenn., Telegrams Received; DLC-USG, V, 56. Misdated Aug. 6 in *HED*, 40-2-75, p. 2. On June 4, Thomas had endorsed to the AG a request from James H. Bridgewater for protection against former C.S.A. soldiers. ES, DNA, RG 94, Letters Received, 493C 1867. Additional papers concerning similar problems in Ky. and Tenn. are *ibid.* Probably on Sept. 4, USG, secretary of war *ad interim*, noted on these papers. "In ~~clear~~ cases where it is clear that Citizens of Ky. can not get justice at the hands of the Civil Courts on account of their political opinions or for other reasons give such protection as you can under the 'Civil Rights Bill' & Genl [O]rders No 44 of 1866, Army Hd Qrs." AN (undated), *ibid.*; copy (incorporated in an endorsement of Sept. 4 from Bvt. Maj. Gen. Edmund Schriver, inspector gen., to the AG), *ibid.*, RG 107, Orders and Endorsements.

To Edwin M. Stanton

Long Branch, N. J., July 24th *1867.*

Hon. E. M. Stanton,
Sec. of War;
Dear Sir:

Every day that I am absent from Washington I see something in the papers or hear something, that makes me feel that I should be there. At the same time I am very anxious to remain absent all that public duty will allow, this Summer, and write now to ask if you will not inform me when you think it essential that I should go back and allow me to remain absent until it is. Even with permission to be absent all the time I will go back for a day or two at a time occasionally.

The few orders necessary to give under the recent supplementary reconstruction law I can write here and send to Washington to be issued by the Adj. Gen. I cannot do this however until I receive an official copy of the law. I think it will be well however for the Adj. Gn. to notify all the district commanders except Ord in my name, to continue the orders now in force until otherwise directed. Gn. Ord should change his registration order at once so as to authorize registrars to take testimony and reject all persons not entitled to registar even if they are willing to take the required oath.[1]

If at any time you wish to leave Washington I will go back with great pleasure and will be glad to see you go, on your account, because I feel that your health requires it. For myself my health does not require rest but I have got so tired of being tied down that I am nearly ready to desert. Things might so easily ~~might~~ have been different now and given repose to the country and consequently rest to all interested in administering the laws.

Very respectfully
Your obt. svt.
U. S. GRANT
General,

ALS (on Stetson House stationery), DLC-Edwin M. Stanton.

1. See letter to Bvt. Maj. Gen. Edward O. C. Ord, June 23, 1867.

To Edwin M. Stanton

Long Branch N J
July 25th 1867

HON EDWIN M. STANTON
SECY OF WAR.

I would recommend Sherman Hancock and Terry for Commissioners to arrange terms of peace with Indians. It will not interfere with their military duties to serve. Senator Henderson Chairman of the ~~of~~ Commission concurs in the recommendations above

U S. GRANT
General

Telegram received (at 2:40 P.M.), DNA, RG 107, Telegrams Collected (Bound); DLC-Andrew Johnson; copies, DNA, RG 108, Telegrams Sent; DLC-USG, V, 56. See telegram to Edwin M. Stanton, July 23, 1867. On July 19, 1867, Lt. Gen. William T. Sherman, St. Louis, had written to USG. "I see by the papers that you were called from West Point to Washington by the Judiciary Committee, but I cannot make out if you got through at West Point or whether you are to return. I also observe that Congress instead of making a law Commanding all Indians to retire within certain limits, have again referred the whole subject to another joint Commission. of course I dont believe in such things for Commissions Cannot come into contact with the fighting Indians, & to talk with the old ones, is the Same old senseless twaddle. I am however partially reconciled by delay, for our hauling Contracts *all* failed this year: and our upper posts are all short, so that any expedition would have to haul its own food along the whole way. It may be that we had better dally along this year, and hurry up the Railroad, and try to be better prepared next year. I am Convinced that somehow we must whip these Indians terribly to make them fear & respect us. Mrs Sherman & children are now up at Madison Wisconsin where I will join them tomorrow, & afterwards will go up to Minnesota to see to things there, as General Terry has gone across to the Missouri River and will continue on to Montana. Now that Meagher is no longer there, and Governor Smith has reached his Post, I feel satisfied matters in that remote territory will be less threatening. All our Posts on the Missouri River are now strengthened and well supplied, so that I hope we will not again be alarmed by such reports as disturbed us last Winter about Fort Buford. Augur and Hancock are proceeding systematically strengthening their respective lines, and all I can aim to do this season, will be to go after the Cheyennes & Kioways below the Arkansas in Sept & Oct, but even that may become impracticable if new negotiations are attempted. I have instructed Hancock to be all ready by September for such a move if at the time it be necessary. Augur thinks he cannot attempt an invasion of the Yellowstone Country this year, and I believe he is right. He must therefore be somewhat on the defensive. Nichols is at this moment absent but will be back in this month. Dayton in the mean time will be in this office. I will be within easy reach always." ALS, DNA, RG 108, Letters Received. On Aug. 3, Sherman, Madison, Wis., wrote to USG. "I got here from St Paul at midnight of yesterday, and have studied the Railroad tables and find that I can leave here at 8 P M tomorrow Sunday, reach Chicago at daylight of Monday & St Louis same night, so I will be present at the St L Southern Hotel on Tuesday morning the 6th Inst. the date fixed for the meeting of the Indian Commission. General Terry passed Fort Buford, going up the Missouri July 17, expecting to reach Camp Cooke on the 27, and the Post on Sun River about this time. I telegraphed him from Saint Paul, by Omaha, & Virginia City that he was on the Commission but I wanted him not to slight his present work, but to do all in that quarter that he could, and then to join us where ever we might be, either by descending the Missouri River, or coming round by Salt Lake and Denver. In the Meantime General Harney & I must do our best that the Civil Commissioners who can outvote us two to one do not have it all their own way. I have very little faith that this Indian Commission can do much more than fashion some scheme for Congress to enact into a Law—but the present act requires us to confer with the Hostile Indians & personally inspect the lands selected as reservations. To do this in any thing like a perfect way, would require years instead of the few months that are left us between this and November when I suppose the Commission must be through or adjourn over, as the Congressmen would have to leave. Mr Stanton telegraphed me that I was to be the head of the Commission. I would choose a more subordinate place, as I fear whatever we may do will fail for the same reason that all previous commissions have failed, viz because the Indians are so scattered, and have so little governmt, that they do not feel bound by the acts of their so-called Chiefs. They will always find it easier & more profitable to steal than to work. I see you are having your share of trouble about the District Commanders. If Sheridan is removed & Hancock sent there I suppose they will change places. Of course I dont want any change for Hancock has just been over the ground and knows it best. He is not satisfied with Custar who has not fulfilled our wishes. He has had our best Cavalry force & instead of going after the Indians has simply moved in order from place to place, with the Indians moving about him. On his arrival at Wallace instead of starting at once after the Cheyennes he came into Fort Riley to see his wife. Gen Hancock reports to me that he has arrested him.—Grierson still remains in Fort Leavenworth, his Regimt incomplete—The fact is our Cavalry officers come down to their small commands with evident reluctance, and we must afford opportunities for still younger men to grow up to the occasion. I dont see as I can do better than to have the Dept Commanders to work out the question in their own commands. In Minnesota I saw Governor Marshall and he is well satisfied with matters on his frontier. Terry has established two posts between Abercrombie & the Missouri River, one at Reavis Den Hillock and the other on Devils Lake. I will have copies of his Reports sent you the momt I reach Saint Louis. My family will stay here for the summer—and if I am away in September Mrs S will bring Minnie to put her in Georgetown convent for the winter." ALS, *ibid.* On Aug. 14, USG, secretary of war *ad interim*, wrote to Secretary of the Interior Orville H. Browning. "I have the honor to transmit herewith for your information a copy of a letter from Lieut. Genl. Sherman, dated the 8th inst. acknowledging receipt of his commission and other papers relating to the Indian Commission; and reporting the proposed movements of the commission." Copies, *ibid.*, RG 107, Letters Received from Bureaus; *ibid.*, Letters Sent to the President. See letter to Lt. Gen. William T. Sherman, Sept. 18, 1867; *HED*, 40-2-97.

On July 2, Sherman, St. Louis, had telegraphed to USG. "Mailed my report yesterday. Genl A J Smith reports cholera at Fort Harker nine 9 cases & four 4 deaths on Sunday This added to Indian troubles will I fear be the *Coup de Grace* to work on that road this year. I will go myself there on Thurdsay & do what I can to keep parties at work" Telegram received (at 11:00 A.M.), DNA, RG 108, Telegrams Received; copy, DLC-USG, V, 55. On July 4, Sherman telegraphed to USG. "I am on the point of starting for the Smoky Hill It occurs to me that Sheridan can help us very much if he were to have a Cavalry Command. A Regiment would be ample on the upper Red River a little to the west of Fort Arbucle to strike without regard to boundary lines northwest about the Wichita Mountains where the Kiowas and Camanches are represented to have sent their families & where they hold some captives taken by them from Texas. I will not precipitate matters at all or send an invading force south of the Arkansas River unless it becomes necessary to draw the Cheyennes down to look after their own families & plunder and thus keep them off our roads. That rumor of Custers being defeated is one of a series of inventions designed by malicious persons. I left him in person June seventeenth at the forks of the Platte. Next day he started with his whole command of three hundred and fifty (350) fully equipped Cavalry for the Republican. On the twenty fourth (24) he sent an Officer into Sedgwick with a report that all was well and on the twenty Eighth (28) one of his Companies with some empty wagons came into Fort Wallace for supplies I sent him orders that if he found the Indians had gone south from the Republican to follow & at Fort Wallace he would encounter Hancock or receive fresh orders. He had force enough in his own & my opinion to whip all the Indians between the Platte & Arkansas and all I fear is this they will not find him but avoid him as usual by scattering. Every thing is reported quiet up the Missouri and Platte & no recent damage on the Smoky Hill" Telegram received (at 5:30 P.M.), DNA, RG 107, Telegrams Collected (Bound); *ibid.*, RG 108, Telegrams Received; copies, *ibid.*, RG 94, Letters Received, 916M 1867; DLC-USG, V, 55. On July 10, Maj. George K. Leet endorsed a copy of this telegram. "Respy. referred to Maj Genl. P. H. Sheridan, Comdg. 5th Mil. Dist. for his information and compliance with suggestion of Lt Genl Sherman if he deems it advantageous, or if Genl Sheridan can think of any thing better, he will act according to his own plan, and communicate with Lt. Genl. Sherman." Copy, DNA, RG 108, Register of Letters Received. On July 17, Maj. Gen. Philip H. Sheridan, New Orleans, wrote to USG. "I am in receipt of the copy of Lieutenant General Sherman's letter on Indian troubles. I think it would not be well to carry out his suggestions at the present time,—even if I was in a condition to do so, which I am not. The Indians in the Wachita Mountains have not engaged in hostilities on the Texian Frontier; nor do I believe they have on any frontier; nor am I satisfied that the families of the Indians, now making war on the Plains, have been sent to the Wachita country. I think they have been sent to the Canadian River country. If I were to send a regiment to the Wachita Mountains, it would not be sufficient to accomplish much, I would stir up a Hornet's nest and a large one too. If Sherman invades the Canadian River country and and the Wachita country he will have a difficult campaign. The troops in Texas are very much scattered by this civil business and I very much prefer to let these Indians alone until we get through with it, which I hope will be by next spring. Then, if these Indians are to be cleaned out, I would like to try my hand at it. My opinion is, that the Government might as well lay out reservations for nearly all of the Indian tribes at once, and then make arrangements to so far subdue them by force of arms, as to compel them to occupy them. Treaties may be made, but only to be broken by both sides." Copies, *ibid.*, RG 393, Dept. of the Mo., Letters Received; DLC-Philip H. Sheridan. On July 31, Leet forwarded this letter to Sherman. Copy, DNA, RG 108, Register of Letters Received.

On July 9, Lt. Col. Lewis M. Dayton, military secretary for Sherman, had telegraphed to USG. "The following telegram just recd 'Fort Harker July sixth (6) TO COL L M DAYTON, Arrived here last night No cause of alarm here by reason of Cholera, Have agreed to accept eight (8) Companies of Cavalry from Kansas up to wednesday tenth (10) Doubt if they will be raised, Think we can soon quiet down the people about Indians and keep the Rail Road progressing, High water has done more damage than Indians Weather good now for work signed W T SHERMAN'" Telegram received (at 8:20 P.M.), *ibid.*, RG 107, Telegrams Collected (Bound); (marked as forwarded to USG at West Point on July 10) *ibid.*, RG 108, Telegrams Received; copies, *ibid.*, RG 94, Letters Received, 971M 1867; DLC-USG, V, 55. See DNA, RG 94, Letters Received, 911M, 948M, 963M 1867. On July 16, Sherman telegraphed to USG. "I am just in from Fort Harker. Gen Hancock has made all possible provision for guarding the Smoky Hill line and the Arkansas having just come over the road from Denver, only four (4) Companies of Kansas Volunteers could be got up to Saturday and they are mustered in for four (4) months No more will be received unless Gen Hancock absolutely requires them, Gen Augur will remain on the Platte line to give it his personal attention I may have to go up to Minnesota whilst General Terry is up the Missouri The Cholera still prevails at Fort Harker but does not seem to alarm the parties who are building the Rail Road. It is graded nearly up to Fort Hays, & rails are laid five (5) miles beyond Harker & progressing well ~~Will The~~ Santa Fe stages have ~~to~~ run regularly but for some reason the Smoky Hill Denver Stages stopped running some time ago ~~through~~ though Gen Hancock who has just passed twice along the whole line says all the Stations are safe and ample guards have been offered for the Coaches, I have ordered a thorough investigation & unless the Agents can show better reasons than they offered me shall infer they stopped for the purpose of making claim for damages & loss of property I hope the Post Master General will withhold compensation till the matter can be fully investigated" Telegram received (at 4:40 P.M.), *ibid.*, RG 107, Telegrams Collected (Bound); *ibid.*, RG 108, Telegrams Received; copies, *ibid.*, RG 94, Letters Received, 1096M 1867; DLC-USG, V, 55; DLC-Edwin M. Stanton. On July 17, Sherman wrote to Leet. "I have the honor to report that I have just returned from Fort Harker, whither I went on the 4th of July to see the state of affairs there, and to meet General Hancock on his return from Denver. I reached the Fort on the night of July 5th, by the Pacific Railroad, which is now in full operation to that place. Cholera had made its appearance there, and Dr. Mills, Medical Director of the Department of the Missouri, had repaired there in person with two assistant surgeons, in addition to the three already there. What was the cause of the appearance of Asiatic cholera was, and still continues to be, a mystery. To all appearances the locality is as salubrious as possible, and the cases were not confined to any one camp, or to any one class of men. I was at Fort Harker ten days, during which time the disease continued to manifest its presence, and it still lingers there; but there is every possible care taken by the medical officers, and there was and is no seeming fear of its extension. The Railroad construction party is now at work some five miles above Fort Harker laying rails, whilst grading is progressing up to and beyond Fort Hays, 73 miles. During all June, the Indians were quite active along the whole line, and for a time there was danger of the working parties abandoning the road, but Mr. Shoemaker (contractor) is now satisfied with present arrangements, he can keep his people at work, and he calculates to finish one hundred miles of Railroad beyond Fort Harker, in all 1867. General Hancock arrived at Fort Harker on the 12th of July, from Denver. In going and returning, he examined personally all the posts and stage stations, and I enclose herewith his reports to me of his observations, and of the orders he has given the District Commander, General A. J. Smith, to complete the arrangements deemed necessary to give the best possible protection to the important interests along that line. By the terms of my Circular issued June 21, 1867, I invited the Governor of each state and territory bordering on the Indian country, to organize a battalion of mounted troops, ready to be called into the service, when Department Commanders called for it. On the 26th of June, I received from Governor Crawford so pressing a message that I agreed to accept six or eight companies, if General A. J. Smith, commanding the District on the border of Kansas would call for them. This was done, as General Hancock was beyond Fort Wallace, and difficult to be reached. On a further representation of Governor Crawford, I made the call myself for eight companies, on the 29th of June, the men to be ready for muster, at the end of the Railroad, by July 6th: and I accordingly ordered up a mustering officer, Captain Bates, of the Retired List, and repaired there in person myself. On the 6th: at Fort Harker, I received another message from Governor Crawford, asking an extension of time to Wednesday, July 10th, which was promptly granted. On the night of the 10th, the Governor arrived also, but up to Saturday, the 13th, had not completed four companies; but on Sunday I instructed the mustering officer to accept enough dismounted men to complete the organization of the four companies of the minimum standard. All were reported as ready for muster in, on Monday, the 14th, the day I left; so that I take it for granted Captain Bates on that day mustered in four companies of Kansas Volunteers for four months. These are the only Volunteers that I have thus far received into the service of the United States, and I doubt much if we can under present circumstances rely on raising any more Volunteers, in case they be imperatively needed. Governor Crawford, however, promised to persevere and raise eight more companies to complete a full regiment, so as to be ready if we needed them Our first duty is, of course, to make the roads comparatively safe, and to hunt up and attack all the straggling bands that infest the country between the two Railroads; and that, you will observe is General Hancock's instruction to General A. J. Smith; but before we can hope for perfect security, we must seek the camps and families of the hostile Indians, which are believed to be down towards Red River, back of the 'Indian Territory.' The danger of invading that country is that we may attack the wrong people, and may arouse the tribes of Camanches that have taken but little part in the recent hostile operations. General Hancock has sent a confidential scout down into the Indian camps, who should be back in time to enable him to act by or about the 1st of September. General Hancock reports that the Indians thus far have not taken a single station, but have everywhere been repelled, and that they have sustained a loss equal if not greater than we. None of our well organized trains have been lost, and wherever the Indians had the advantage was where men exposed themselves too much, or were over confident. Now all are on their guard, and such things should not occur again. We are resolved that the Railroads shall progress uninterruptedly, and if the stage lines do not run regularly it will be their own fault. The work on the Platte Road is also progressing well, but fears are entertained for the safety of a party of Lieutenant Kidder, 2nd Cavalry,—ten men and a guide sent from Fort Sedgwick on the 29th ultimo, with my orders for General Custer. My orders were intended to reach Fort Sedgwick in time to meet there a messenger he had sent in from his camp on the Republican, but, reaching there too late, General Potter dispatched it by Lieutenant Kidder and party. General Custer had broken up his camp on the Republican and marched for the Platte at Riverside Station to the west of Fort Sedgwick, and it is probable Lieutenant Kidder fell in with a band of hostile Indians who followed Custer in. General Custer after getting some supplies started back, and should be at or near Fort Wallace to-day. I am very anxious that Congress at its present session should take some decided course in regard to these Indians; for we cannot act with any vigor, or to any distinct end, until we

know what view they take of these matters. From a letter of the Governor of
Colorado (Honorable A. C. Hunt), I do not suppose we can raise any Volunteers
there unless we provide them horses, which I do not think prudent; but in Kansas,
Nebraska and Iowa I think we could soon raise enough if the money were provided for their prompt payment." LS, DNA, RG 108, Letters Received. The
enclosures are *ibid.* On July 22, Dayton telegraphed to USG. "The following
telegrams rec'd. 'Jefferson Barracks. To. COL L. M. DAYTON   General Custer
left Wallace on the [t]hirteenth 13.   he found the bodies of Lieut Kidder Second
2nd Cavalry & ten 10 men killed & scalped on Beaver Creek forty seven 47 miles
north of Ft Wallace   sig. W. S. HANCOCK Major General' ['JFrom Fort Harker.
July twentieth 20th   To COL DAYTON   I have [r]eliable information that Bishop
Lamy & party passed Fort Dodge 55 miles west of Fort Larned on the sixteenth
16 in company with a large train. The report of the capture by Indians must be
incorrect   sig A. J. SMITH Brevet. Major Gen'   I send you the last because a
report is going the rounds of [t]he press that this party had been captured &
murdered" Telegram received (at 11:25 A.M.), *ibid.*, RG 107, Telegrams Collected (Bound); *ibid.*, RG 108, Telegrams Received; copy, *ibid.*, RG 94, Reservation File, Fort Kearny, Neb.

To Bvt. Maj. Gen. Edward O. C. Ord

Cypher)   Washington D, C,
                                                    July 30th/67 [2:00 P.M.]

MAJ. GN. E. O. C. ORD,
VICKSBURG, MISS.

Complaints are made of the very partial manner in which
justice is administered by Gen. Gilham between laborers & ex
rebel employers. Examine this matter and if the charge is just
apply such remedy as the degree of culpability seems to require.

                                                    U. S. GRANT
                                                    General.

ALS (telegram sent), DNA, RG 107, Telegrams Collected (Bound); telegram
sent, *ibid.*; telegram received, Ord Papers, CU-B. On Aug. 2, 1867, Bvt. Maj.
Gen. Edward O. C. Ord telegraphed to USG. "Your telegram relating to Administration of Justice by the Assistant Comissioner of the Freedmens Bureau
here is just received. Can I be furnished with the charges advanced that special
investigation of each can be made   If a Mr Adams who was removed by Gen
Gillem from position make the allegations they should be received with caution"
Telegram received (at 5:40 P.M.), DNA, RG 107, Telegrams Collected (Bound);
ibid., RG 108, Telegrams Received; copies, *ibid.*, RG 105, Letters Received;
(sent by mail) *ibid.*, RG 108, Letters Received; DLC-USG, V, 55. On Aug. 12,

Ord wrote to USG. "I have examined the management of the Bureau by Genl. Gillem: he has tried to do justice to the freedmen; his force of Agents has been entirely inadequate, and some of them, having become accostomed under instructions from former Asst. Commissioners, to refer contracts to civil authorities, do not thoroughly investigate such complaints, or make arrests of offenders as ordered, but confine themselves to reporting cases they hear of the indifference or neglect of civil authorities to do justice to freedmen—Post Commanders have at Genl. Gillems request, been made Agents of the Bureau—Frequent arrests have been made for offences against the rights of freedmen, and offenders have been punished   innumerable frivolous complaints, are of course received, and on account, of the inaccessibility of the agents of the Bureau to freedmen scattered on remote plantations, no doubt abuses are committed upon them which cannot be redressed. Civil authorities in many parts of the state, doubtless ignore their complaints (it is not easy to eradicate the habit of generations, which has been to allow the master to settle with his servant) such civil authorities should be removed, but there are counties in this state containing *no* intelligent man who can take the oath of office now required so that were I to remove the judges and majistrates, who fail to do the freedmen justice, I would as rule have *no one* to replace them—With one Bureau Agent to about every three thousand square miles of forest and swamp, with not loyal northern men enough to fill vacancies occurring in state offices, with scarcely a southern man who can take the oath of office, a portion of the thousand per day of real and imaginary complaints which freedmen in this state may have, must go unheard, and abuses of the simple and ignorant by the powerful and depraved, cannot be prevented   In countries where it is not deemed advisable to keep police agents, or armed men enough to hold all the vicious in check, an enlightened public opinion, the interests of the community, and the selection of good and wise citizens to administer justice, are I think the best preventives to such evils   Officers from the north including Agents of the Bureau in this country, generally associate with persons of their own color, and preferably with the intelligent, all their associates and they themselves are employers of freed people, who are the only servants in the land, they find the freedmen in the country occupying no other positions than those of servants and operatives under whites, and they find the intelligent white men (themselves and their associates) with some exceptions the sole employers; In administering justice between them, they endeavor to maintain the same relations that exist elsewhere between employer and employee, this encourages industry, and the freedmen (who are mostly working for a share of the crop) are benefitted in proportion—Should however the agent of the Bureau, *not* associate with white men, consult the inclinations of his associates rather than their interests, and advise them not to work if they can help it, not to keep their contracts because they thereby add to the white mans wealth, such advice would if generally followed, result in idleness and pauperism of the operatives, and much hostility to them— The position of the two classes in Mississippi, places the ignorant and submissive freedmen, at the mercy of the white class, and the humanity and interests of the latter are almost the only safeguard of the former—The Bureau is for these reasons much more necessary, among an ignorant, and not very humane white population,—who are are hostile to the colored race, because being themselves compelled to work enough to obtain subsistence, they regard the blacks as competitors,—than among educated and intelligent men who have no fear of competition, and who know that anything which adds to the comfort of their employees will in proportion, increase their usefulness—I enclose a letter from Judge Hill, U S District Judge in Miss. to show how difficult it is to fill vacancies now occurring in offices in this state but one of the persons he names can (I think) take the oath of office and I doubt if he will accept the position—" LS, DNA, RG 105, Letters Received; ADf, Ord Papers, CU-B. On Aug. 8, U.S. District Judge Robert A. Hill, Oxford, Miss., had written to Ord concerning judicial appointments and on the same day Ord endorsed this letter to USG. ALS and AES, DNA, RG 108, Letters Received. On Aug. 20, Bvt. Brig. Gen. Frederick T. Dent wrote to Ord. "The Gen Commandg directs me to inform you that the letter of Judge Hill U S Dist Judge in regard to filling vacancies of Judgeship now or to be vacant forwarded by you for his information has been received   The Gen desired me to say to you that his acquaintance with the legal proffession in your District is not sufficient for hi to warrant him in suggesting or giving an opinion of any one who may be deemed proper candidates to fill vacancies but the general does reccomend to you in filling vacancies to select only such men as will not only be able to qualify, but will also administer justice impartially to all irrespective of race and former political status—. that he would not appoint any man who was not in favour of carying out the laws of Congress as they now exist. The gen desires me to say he will approve of any appointments you make." ADfS, *ibid*.

On July 30, Ord had written to USG and then to Col. Adam Badeau. "The House of Representatives having—no doubt intententionally—omitted my name in voting thanks to the District Commanders—And as I am indirectly in the receipt of intimations from such leading republicans as Genls Schenck and Wilson that my course is disapproved by them—And in consideration of the fact that Congress has given you supervisory power over the District Commanders—And that—judging from indications recently given—*that I have not your entire confidence as District Commander*—Should my fear in this last respect prove true— and without remedy—then I consider it a grave duty that I should request to be relieved from Command of this District, which I do—I have to add that the duties of my Command are exceedingly unpleasant—that I have only been deterred from previously asking to be relieved by a sense of duty and the belief that I possessed your confidence and would receive your support if attack'd for maintaining what I believed the right and your views—" ALS, *ibid*. "The enclosed to Genl Grant will explain itself—I hope you will take advantage of some time when the Genl is well and after Sealing it—hand it to him—that is if you by enquiry can learn that my opinion in regard to my fear that I have incurred the Genls disapprobation is well founded—I dont care a fig for the abuse of politicians but the action of the H of R—and the *unpleasant fact that my last* telegram to the *General*, sent when the Cholera was raging—and a man had just died of it at my privt quarters and my Staff were all more or less stampeded so as almost to incapacitate them from duty—two of them were sick—well my telegram asking permission to remove temporarily my Head Quarters—*was unnoticed*—now General—it may be that Genl Grant never received this telegram or that he accidentally forgot it—but the silence coming just at the same time when I was being snubbed by the H of R & and was being abused by the republican whippers in— and when I was covered with boils—made me uneasy—and after Cogitating over the matter I have Concluded to send in my request to be relieved *provided* I have not the Entire Confidence of the Genl Commanding—I send it thro you for fear if I donot it may not reach the General at first hand—I have enough Enemies at

Washington to make the Generals Support necessary to me here" ALS, USG 3. See letter to Bvt. Maj. Gen. Edward O. C. Ord, June 23, 1867. On Aug. 5, noon, USG telegraphed to Ord. "You cannot be relieved from your present duty. Push the work entrusted to you with your usual energy, and according to the clear meaning of the law, and you will be supported." ALS (telegram sent), DNA, RG 107, Telegrams Collected (Bound); telegram sent, *ibid.*; copies, *ibid.*, RG 108, Telegrams Sent; DLC-USG, V, 56.

On July 31, USG wrote to Secretary of War Edwin M. Stanton. "I have the honor to recommend the removal of Surgeon Joseph R. Smith, U. S. A. from the 4th Mil. District to some point out of the Non reconstructed States." ALS, DNA, RG 94, Letters Received, 433A 1867. On Aug. 9, Lucien J. Barnes, Little Rock, wrote to USG. "The loyal men of this state almost unanimously rejoice at the reported removal from this District of Dr. Joseph R Smith recently on the staff of Major General Ord. The encouragement given by Dr. Smith to those who oppose reconstruction under the laws of Congress has been greater than *could* have been given by any state official or private citizen. It is hoped that Dr. Smith will be permanently relieved from duty in this District and sent far enough away to prevent his further influence in the affairs of Arkansas." ALS, *ibid.*, RG 108, Letters Received.

On Aug. 8, Dent wrote a circular. "By direction of the General Commanding I herewith enclose circular no. 13, April 27th 1867, Headquarters District of Texas, with his request that orders of like import be published to the District you command." LS (addressed to Bvt. Maj. Gen. John Pope), Meade Papers, PHi; (addressed to Maj. Gen. Daniel E. Sickles) DNA, RG 393, 2nd Military District, Letters Received; copies (addressed to Ord), *ibid.*, RG 108, Letters Sent; DLC-USG, V, 47, 60. See letter to Maj. Gen. Philip H. Sheridan, May 26, 1867. On Aug. 14, Ord telegraphed to USG. "Your request that I issue circular thirteen District of Texas will subject whites generally in Mississippi to trial by negro juries or none for there are not white men in the State who can qualify to fill vacancies among sheriffs Is not a military decree now reversing laws in force touching them while they are obedient to such laws a violation of the terms on which rebels surrender They were promised protection if obedient to such. I see propriety of circular in Texas and Arkansas where disloyalty shelters under juries" Telegram received (at 6:00 P.M.), DNA, RG 108, Telegrams Received; copy, DLC-USG, V, 55. On Aug. 15, 10:50 A.M., USG telegraphed to Ord. "You need not adopt the Texas Jury order but make such order as suits your particular command and will secure justice to all classes of citizens and not protect the rebel at the expense of the loyal man." ALS (telegram sent), DNA, RG 107, Telegrams Collected (Bound); telegram sent, *ibid.*; copies, *ibid.*, RG 108, Telegrams Sent; DLC-USG, V, 56. On the same day, Ord telegraphed to USG. "Have issued such orders, cases of assaults on the loyal & persecution by authorities are held for trial by Commissions, disputes over wages or sharing crops are taken from Courts & referred to arbitrators, Many Civilians confined for trial, find by experience that I cant base action on Statement of interested extremists, Along Misssissippi very orderly, Freedmen registering fully They will number about sixty five thousand, whites forty five thousand, Genl Smith reports progress in Arkansas satisfactory & will complete except in few counties by twentieth (20th) August" Telegram received (at 8:30 P.M.), DNA, RG 107, Telegrams Collected (Bound); *ibid.*, RG 108, Telegrams Received; copy, DLC-USG, V, 55.

On Aug. 20, Ord telegraphed to USG. "A Quartermaster is much needed here vice Capt Scully who is waiting Sentence & who in any event having had sharpers around him should not be retained here on duty" Telegram received (at 5:10 P.M.), DNA, RG 94, Letters Received, 300Q 1867; *ibid.*, RG 107, Telegrams Collected (Bound); *ibid.*, RG 108, Telegrams Received; copy, DLC-USG, V, 55. On Aug. 23, Maj. George K. Leet endorsed this telegram. "Respectfully referred to the Adjutant General. In view of the fact that Capt. Scully is now available for duty in the 4th Military District, it is thought unnecessary to order Bvt. Major Eckerson to report to Gen. Ord." ES, DNA, RG 94, Letters Received, 300Q 1867. On Aug. 29, Ord telegraphed to USG. "The order returning Capt Schully to duty on the Staff of Gen Gillem and at my head Quarters places that Officer who proferred charges and believes them true and myself who approved the proceedings in an anomalous position. will not the President assign him another Station" Telegram received (at noon), *ibid.*, RG 107, Telegrams Collected (Bound); *ibid.*, RG 108, Telegrams Received; copies, *ibid.*, RG 94, Letters Received, 315Q 1867; DLC-USG, V, 55. On the same day, Leet endorsed a copy of this telegram. "Respectfully referred to the Quarter Master General, who will relieve Capt. Scully from duty in the 4th Military District, and assign another officer to duty in his stead." AES, DNA, RG 94, Letters Received, 315Q 1867.

On Aug. 23, Ord, Corinth, Miss., telegraphed to USG. "Can you send me an Adjutant General vice Green who would like Missouri" Telegram received (at 6:15 P.M.), *ibid.*, RG 107, Telegrams Collected (Bound); *ibid.*, RG 108, Telegrams Received; copy, DLC-USG, V, 55. On Aug. 24, 12:25 P.M., USG telegraphed to Ord. "No other officer of the ~~Asst.~~ ~~G~~ Adjutant Generals Department can be sent to you" Telegrams sent (2), DNA, RG 107, Telegrams Collected (Bound); copies, *ibid.*, RG 108, Telegrams Sent; DLC-USG, V, 56.

To Andrew Johnson

Private   Washington, D, C, Aug. 1st *1867.*

HIS EXCELLENCY, A. JOHNSON,
PRESIDENT OF THE U. STATES
SIR;

I take the liberty of addressing you privately on the subject of the conversation we had this morning feeling as I do the the great danger to the welfare of the country should you carry out the designs then expressed.

First: on the subject of the displacement of the Sec. of War.[1] His removal can not be effected against his will without the consent of the Senate. It is but a short time since the United States senate was in session and why not then have asked for his removal if it was desired? It certainly was the intention of the Legislative branch of the Govt. to place Cabinet Ministers beyond the power of Executive removal and it is pretty well understood that, so far as Cabinet Ministers are affected by the "Tenure of Office Bill," it was intended specially to protect the Sec. of War who the country felt great confidence in. The meaning of the law may be explained away by an astute lawyer but common sense, and the mass of loyal people, will give to it the effect intended by its framers.

On the subject of the removal of the very able commander of the 5th Military District[2] let me ask you to consider the effect it would have upon the public. He is universally, and deservedly, beloved by the people who sustained this government through its trials; and feared by those who would still be enemies of the Government. It fell to the lot of but few men to do as much against an armed enemy as General Sheridan did, during the rebellion, and it is within the scope of the ability of but few in this or other country to do what ~~Gen. Sheridan~~ he has. His civil administration has given equal satisfaction. He has had difficulties to contend with which no other District Commander has encountered. Almost, if not quite, from the day he was appointed District commander to the present time the press has given out that he was to be removed, that the Administration was dissatisfied with him &c. &c. This has emboldened the opponents to the laws of Congress, within his command, to oppose him in every way in their power, and has rendered necessary measures which otherwise may never have become necessary.

In conclusion allow me to say as a friend desiring peace & quiet, the welfare of the whole country, North & South, that it is in my opinion more than the loyal people of this country, (I mean those who supported the Government during the great rebellion) will quietly submit to to see the very man of all others ~~that~~ who they have expressed confidence in, removed.—I would not have taken the liberty of addressing the Executive of the United States thus but for the conversation on the subject alluded to in this letter, and from a sense of duty feeling that I know I am right in this matter.

With great respect,

Your obt. svt.

U. S. GRANT

General,

ALS, DLC-Andrew Johnson.

1. See letter to Edwin M. Stanton, Aug. 12, 1867.

2. See letters to Andrew Johnson, Aug. 17, 26, 1867. On Aug. 2, 1867, Bvt. Brig. Gen. Orville E. Babcock wrote to Maj. Gen. Philip H. Sheridan. "General Grant wishes me to write to you to tell you that President Johnson has made up his mind to remove you and also the Sec of War. He sent for General Grant yesterday and told him this. The General said all proper for him to say against such a course, and when he came back he put his views in writing, and sent them to Mr Johnson. I send you a copy of his. The General wishes me to say to you to go on your course exactly as if this communication had not been sent to you. and without fear of consequences. That as long as you pursue the same line of duty that you have followed thus far in the service, you will receive the entire support of these headquarters. The General and all on Staff are quite well." Copy, DLC-Philip H. Sheridan. On Aug. 5, Sheridan, New Orleans, telegraphed to USG. "I very much fear that if the President removes me Governor Flanders will resign and that the excellent condition of affairs now existing in Louisiana will be thrown into confusion. I say this not on my own account, but in the interest of the State." LS (telegram sent), DNA, RG 107, Telegrams Collected (Bound); telegram received (at 2:00 P.M.), *ibid.*; *ibid.*, RG 108, Telegrams Received.

On July 13, Sheridan had telegraphed to USG. "Gen Griffin telegraphs of yesterdays date that two 2 of the Board of Registars of Washington County Texas were shot & badly wounded—No particulars given—" Telegram received (at 2:55 P.M.), *ibid.*, RG 107, Telegrams Collected (Bound); *ibid.*, RG 108, Telegrams Received; copies, *ibid.*, RG 94, Letters Received, 947M 1867; DLC-USG, V, 55; (2) DLC-Philip H. Sheridan. On July 14 and 20, Sheridan wrote to USG. "I take the liberty to enclose you a letter received from Jo McKibbin a few days ago. I did not answer it, but if I had the following would have been the answer: 'I have no aspirations for Presidential honors, & would decline any nomination, tendered me—There is a little breach of confidence on my part in sending this letter to you & I beg of you to destroy it—It is perhaps of no [co]nsequence & originated simply in the mind of McKibben, but in these tricky times I have the sincerest desire to let you know that the only motive which has governed me out side of my professional duty is to be of benefit to you, because I think now, as when I saw you in Washington, that you will be obliged to again lend yourself to secure the union & development of the country." *"Private . . .* Genl Rousseau has been in the city for the four days past. much of the time in conference with Steedman. I think there is a determination to hatch out an other political dodge. It looks like an advice to the people of this state to vote against the convention or it may be the fillibusting project. However I see a Slight tendency on part of politicians to go against convention, & reconstruction. Mississippi is strongly that way, Texas is beginning to look that way, & Georgia also. They will have no success in Louisianna. Rousseau called on me yesterday and opened the question of city & Genl Politics. I told him that I had nothing to do with politics and that any officer of the Army who had was wrong & doing an injustice to his profession. Everything is very [quiate] here. Affairs in Texas are not so satisfactory. The whole population here has turned against the city governmt. which is about as corrupt as was the First National Bank. I will make an ajustment by some changes in a few days." ALS, USG 3. On July 23 and 24, Sheridan wrote to USG. "Private . . . General Rousseau, after spending some days here in conference with Steedman and others has gone up to Baton Rouge, apparently awaiting the developement of some new phase of politics by the President. When he first arrived here he notified the executive that he had arrived and would soon be ready to go to the Pacific Coast; then subsequently notified him that the above information was only to let him know of his arrival here. Then Mr Johnson asks him the condition of affairs and Rousseau is now awaiting telegrams from the President. Should he come about me again and have no authority as an Inspector General; he will probably get rapped over the knuckles. He is engaged in dirty business for one of his rank in the Army." "*Private* . . . I enclose herewith a communication sent by General Rousseau to day This will explain the object and purposes of his visit to this city." LS, *ibid.* In the second letter, Sheridan enclosed a copy of a telegram of the same day from Bvt. Maj. Gen. Lovell H. Rousseau to President Andrew Johnson. "Matters here gloomy, people generally greatly depressed. Any change that may be made will be received with universal satisfaction" Copy, *ibid.* On Aug. 3, Sheridan wrote to USG. "I have the honor to submit for your information the following. That the State of Louisiana is registered in accordance with the Act of Congress dated March 2nd 1867 and the Bills supplementary thereto: the Poll books are nearly made out and the Commissioners of election for each polling precinct appointed: the number of registered votes will be slightly over One-hundred and twenty thousand: the State will in all probability come in as a Union State. In accomplishing this registration I have had no opposition from the masses of the people, on the contrary much assistance and encouragement, but, from the public press— especially that of the City of New Orleans—and from office-holders and office-seekers disfranchised, I have met with bitterness and opposition. The greatest embarrassment with which I have had to contend, was the constant rumors of my removal published nearly every day in the papers of this City. It was a serious embarrassment as it was breaking down the confidence of the people in my acts, but notwithstanding this we worked patiently and industriously, having in view only right and justice, and the law in its spirit. I have as I have heretofore stated to you permitted no political influence nor political machinery to help or influence me in this work. Receiving the law as an order, it was so executed. I regret that I have to make the charge against Brigadier General L. H. Rousseau U. S. A. of visiting my command recently, and without exhibiting any authority, interfering with my duties, and suggesting my removal." LS, DLC-Andrew Johnson. On Aug. 8, USG endorsed this letter. "Respectfully forwarded to the Secretary of War for his information, and with the request that it be laid before the President, and his attention called to the unofficerlike conduct attributed to Gen. L. H. Rousseau." ES, *ibid.*

On Aug. 12, Rousseau, Washington, D. C., wrote to Johnson. "On to day during an interview with General Grant, I told him I understood that Major

General Sheridan had written him a letter in which he had charged me with assailing him and his administration of affairs in his District during my late visit to New Orleans, and asked him for a copy of that letter if it was official. He said in reply he had recieved a letter from General Sheridan in which allusion was made to me, but that it referred to other matters, and had been immediately forwarded to the President, and was now in his possession. I have the honor, therefore, to respectfully request a copy of so much of that letter as refers to myself." ALS, DNA, RG 107, Letters Received from Bureaus. On Aug. 22, Rousseau, New York City, wrote to USG. "The New York papers to day publish what purports to be, and what I take for granted is, an official letter from Major General Sheridan to yourself, in the course of which he Says: 'I regret that I have to make the charge against Brig. Genl. L. H. Rousseau, U. S. A. of visiting my command recently and, without exhibiting any authority, intefering with my duties and suggesting my removal'. So much of the above charge as alleges that I visited General Sheridan's command and intefered with his duties, is false. As to suggesting his removal:—I did Say, in answer to a telegram from Washington inquiring of me how things looked in Louisiana,—that the state of affairs was gloomy—that the people were much depressed—that any change would be almost universally acceptable. This telegram referred to matters and things in general, and was intended as such, including General Sheridan in its Scope.—If this was suggesting the removal of that officer, all right. But his name was not mentioned   Whilst I claim the right, in common with all other citizens, to criticize So much of General Sheridan's administration as is not purely military and which solely concerns the civil policy of the country, yet, on my late visit to New-Orleans, I Scrupulously refrained from doing So; and So far as I now remember, I expressed no opinion for or against his policy to anybody in his district. I had no purpose or motive to do so. And my recollection I think is as distinct about this as it usually is, or as it can be about anything. As I know there is no sufficient Evidence on which to base this charge I cannot concieve how it was possible for General Sheridan to make it. I am therefore reluctantly forced to the present conclusion that it has no better foundation in his mind than conjecture or suspicion.—I concur with General Sheridan in his 'regrets.' I am really Sorry that So inconsiderable a man as myself was not permitted to visit New Orleans without being made the medium for any Sort of sensation wherewith to thrill the public pulse; and it seems as unnecessary as it is unfortunate that it fell to my lot to be made Such a medium in the hands of General Sheridan, who now, on what is universally declared to be his conspicuous merits, fills So large a space in the nation's admiration. General Sheridan might have let me pass I think and no harm would have followed my Escape from the collision which has forced this letter. In order wholly to relieve General Sheridan's mind, let me Explain in a word my late mission to New Orleans. Ordered to a command in a very distant Department, and having also to go into our Russian Possessions, I thought that before So long a journey I would go south and say good bye to a part of my family and to many of my kindred who were in New Orleans, Baton Rouge, and Pass Christian.—I took my last chance to pay that visit, and was so much interested and occupied in it, that I Even declined all outside Social calls at the request of my many hospitable friends. And when I got through with that domestic mission I left.—. . . P. S. As these charges have reached the Ears of the President I have taken the liberty to Send him a copy of this reply." LS, *ibid.*, RG 108, Letters Received.

On July 24, Sheridan had written to USG. "I have the honor to enclose for your information a copy of a letter received from General Griffin this morning. I feel the importance of removing some of the civil officers in Texas as fully as General Griffin. There is but little security in Texas for those who love the Government, and the military commander has a heavy load to pull up the hill in the concientious execution of his duties, when the laws are executed by those who hate the government and the military commander who is ordered to protect persons and property of its loyal citizens. I will therefore make some changes progressively, but if this does not make a change for the better, I will be forced to make many." LS, *ibid.* The enclosure is *ibid.* On July 25, Sheridan telegraphed to USG. "I have the honor to ~~to~~ report a very good condition of affairs throughout this state—Since the passage of the last supplementary Bill nearly all political excitement has subsided—The registration has been ordered closed on the 31st July and I will be able soon thereafter to give you the sum total registered. Genl Griffin reports crime and defiance of the laws of the Government on the increase in Texas; he attributes this condition of affairs to a disloyal governor and his subordinate Civil officeholders—I forwarded to you by mail yesterday his last communication to me on the subject" Telegram received (at 3:00 P.M.), *ibid.*, RG 107, Telegrams Collected (Bound); *ibid.*, RG 108, Telegrams Received; copies, *ibid.*, RG 94, Letters Received, 427A 1867; DLC-USG, V, 55; (2) DLC-Philip H. Sheridan. On July 30, 2:00 P.M., USG telegraphed to Sheridan. "You are authorized to make such removals from civil offices, and appointments to fill vacancies, as you may deem necessary ~~for~~ to secure a thorough practical execution of the laws of Congress in Texas." ALS (telegram sent), DNA, RG 107, Telegrams Collected (Bound); telegram sent, *ibid.*; copies, *ibid.*, RG 108, Telegrams Sent; DLC-USG, V, 56. On July 31, Sheridan endorsed papers concerning the murder of three former Union soldiers in Tex. "Respectfully forwarded. For the information of the *General Commanding* the *Armies U. S.* As a specimen of the manner in which Civil Officers in the *State* of *Texas* ignore the perpitration, of crimes upon the persons and property of Union Citizens." ES, DNA, RG 108, Letters Received. Misdated July 21 in *HED*, 40-2-57, p. 128. The papers are *ibid.*, pp. 126–28.

On July 26, Sheridan had written to USG. "I have the honor to herewith enclose a tabular statement of the number of voters registered in this State, so far as heard from, up to this date." LS, DNA, RG 108, Letters Received. The enclosure is *ibid.* On Aug. 5, Sheridan telegraphed to USG. "The returns of registration in the State of Louisiana are now nearly all in, they will amount to a little over one hundred and twenty thousand (120.000) The Poll books are nearly made out and the commissioners of election at each Poll Precinct appointed. I see no objection to going on with election for or against convention as soon as the appointment of the state is made out." Telegram received (at 12:30 P.M.), *ibid.*, RG 107, Telegrams Collected (Bound); *ibid.*, RG 108, Telegrams Received; copies, DLC-USG, V, 55; (2—one marked as sent at 10:30 A.M.) DLC-Philip H. Sheridan; DLC-Andrew Johnson. At 3:00 P.M., USG telegraphed to Sheridan. "Close registration & order election when in your judgement all legal voters who wish to register have registered, and when the the Acts of Congress will not be violated by calling the election." ALS (telegram sent), DNA, RG 107, Telegrams Collected (Bound); telegram sent, *ibid.*; copies, *ibid.*, RG 108, Telegrams Sent; DLC-USG, V, 56.

To Bvt. Maj. Gen. John Pope

Washington. D. C. Aug. 3d 1867,

DEAR GENERAL

Your official letter on the subject of reconstruction in the 3d District, and your private letter accompanying it, are received and I have read both with care. I think your views are sound both in the construction which you give to the laws of Congress, and the duties of the supporters of good government to see that when re-construction is effected that no loophole is left open to give trouble and embarrassment hereafter. It is certainly the duty of District Commanders to study what the framers of the reconstruction laws wanted to express, as much as what they do express, and to execute the law according to that interpretation. This I believe they have generally done and so far have the approval of all who approve the Congressional plan of restoration.

I think it hardly advisable to publish your letter now as it might give advantage possibly to the Alabama delegation who, the papers say, are now here trying to effect your removal

On the subject of the arrest of Toombs, and trial for his letter[1] I certainly think he deserves it. He was a voluntary exile from the country and shows himself now insubordinate to its laws whilst he is being tolerated. I think all voluntary exiles who have returned to the country ought to be required to subscribe to the same parole required of those who surrendered in the field.[2]

Very truly yours
U. S. GRANT
General

TO BVT MAJ. GEN'L JNO POPE
COMDG. 3D MIL DISTRICT
ATLANTA, GA.

Copies, DLC-USG, V, 47, 60; DNA, RG 108, Letters Sent; (incomplete) *ibid.*, RG 46, Senate 40A–F2, Messages. On July 24, 1867, Bvt. Maj. Gen. John Pope had written to USG. "I have the honor to send enclosed a Newspaper containing a speech made in this City by B. H. Hill, of this State late a Senator in the Rebel Congress.—This person only a few weeks since was pardoned by the President, and in common with almost every other pardoned rebel, this is the use he makes of the clemency of the Government.—You can readily see from the speech itself the character of the man, who is the representative of a large class, and the hoplessness of any satisfactory reconstruction of the Southern States whilst such men retain influence.—It has been and will continue to be my course to permit and encourage the widest latitude of Speech and of the Press in this District consistent with law and the public peace.—I do not include among those who are permitted to exercise this latitude of Speech the Civil officers of the Provisional State Governments already prohibited by my orders from, 'using any influence whatever to deter or dissuade the people from taking an active part in reconstructing their State Governments under the Reconstruction Acts.—' No such advantage as the use of the machinery of the existing State Governments ought to be or will be given to the Anti-reconstruction party.—I consider it desirable that the Government and people of the United States should thoroughly understand the feelings and purposes of the leading politicians in the South in order that, the country may know by the result of the coming elections precisely the amount of influence possessed by these men and the kind and extent of Legislation required to counteract its baleful effects.—In my opinion no reconstruction can be satisfactory or at all reliable as to future results unless these men are permitted to discuss openly and according to their nature the issues presented.—If they still retain influence enough with the masses of the Whites at the South to enable them by active efforts to defeat reconstruction under the late Acts of Congress it is better that the country should know it before than after the re-admission of the Southern States into the Union.—It would not be difficult to find in the violent speeches of such men abundant cause for silencing them but Reconstruction accomplished in this manner would be no index of the public sentiment and might and probably would result after a year or two in a relapse of the people into the same condition of bondage to these leaders that would lead necessarily to a reproduction of the same condition of things which demanded the passage of the Reconstruction Acts.—It is better that the battle be fought out now and openly—If the people of these States have the common sense and the manhood to withstand the influences of the Secession party and of the, political leaders who have long controlled them, who have led them into their present desperate condition and who seek to plunge them still deeper into misfortune, and if they prove able and willing to reconstruct their State Governments upon the only true principles of Government in defiance of these leaders and against their active opposition there will be good ground for hope that reconstruction will be satisfactory and permanent.—If they cannot do this it may well become a question whether reconstruction on any reasonable terms is possible so long as these unrepentant and reactionary political leaders are suffered to remain in this Country.—It is better that the Country should know the truth on this subject now than run the risk of learning hereafter that an irreparable mistake has been made in the plan and execution of the Reconstruction Acts.—I need scarcely repeat that reconstruction to be in the Spirit of the Acts of Congress and to be permament must be the Act of the people themselves after the fullest and freest discussion.—Congress has done wisely in aiding them to make this fight, by disfranchising the leading rebels and at least making it impossible for them to vote or hold office.—It would have been still better to enforce their permament absence from the country.—The personal influence they might bring to bear if they were candidates themselves is thus greatly weakened and they are forced to discuss issues and not appeal to personal feeling in their own favor.—The people are thus left freer than they ever were before to choose their own Candidates, and are forced to think for themselves as they have not hitherto done.—So far from being willing to see the disfranchised classes relieved from political disabilities, I consider these disfranchising clauses of the Acts to be among their wisest and best considered provisions.—If they do no other good than to relieve the people from the incubus of the old political leaders, they have accomplished incalculable service.—It is not doubted that many worthy and now loyal men who could be safely trusted, are disfranchised by these clauses of the Military Bills, but such a result was unavoidable and can in their cases be easily remedied.—It will no, doubt be wise, at an early day, to relieve by name such of the disfranchised persons as have hitherto proved or shall prove by their conduct in the course of the next six months that they are worthy of it.—Whilst it was unavoidable that some good men would be disfranchised by provisions of law against classes of persons the remedy is easy—To undertake the converse of this, that is to give general amnesty and except individuals by name, would certainly result in leaving large numbers enfranchised who ought not to be.—Such improper persons might decide the coming elections before their unfitness could be ascertained, and even then it would be more than difficult to remedy the evil.—I consider the method set forth in the Reconstruction Acts by far the wiser course of the two and I can hardly understand how any man familiar with the facts can think otherwise.— These disfranchised persons include generally the whole Army of those who now hold or have hitherto held office.—With few exceptions all these persons were active rebels and are bitterly opposed to Reconstruction under the Acts of Congress; opposed in fact to any reconstruction whatever except such as would leave them in precisely the same political condition as if there had been no Rebellion and no War.—Even such a reconstruction as this they would only accept as a necessity of the situation with the purpose to renew in Congress and perpetuate among themselves as nearly as possible the same conditions which existed before the War.—With these re-actionists dominant in the South freedom of Speech and of the Press would not even exist in name.—The Union men and even those who were Secessionists but have advocated reconstruction under the late Acts of Congress would find no peace and no protection in these States.—The last condition of the Freedmen would be worse than the first—I need only point to this speech of Mr Hill, his numerous letters, the letters of Governor Perry of S. C. of Herschel V. Johnson of Georgia, and many other such men for sufficient evidence that I have not overstated the case.—These men are the representatives of a large and powerful element bent on reaction and they have been in the habit of controlling the Southern Whites.—By taking opposite sides of a political question they have in times past divided the Southern Whites on purely personal grounds and have thus created the impression elswhere that among the masses there was a political question decided instead of a purely personal one—United as they now are against reconstruction it is wise to ascertain how far their influence can prevail with the people.—The disfranchising clauses of the Acts of Congress put it out of the power of these men to be Candidates for office—One great element of their strength is thus destroyed, and the people left to choose other leaders and vote for other candidates have really a freedom of action which they never had before, and find themselves under a necessity for thinking which they have not heretofore felt.—Congress has given them this privilege and imposed upon them this salutary necessity.—It remains to be seen how they will use them.—If they can win the battle against their former leaders after an open fight all may be well in the future—If not, then not.—I do not at all agree in the opinion that there are not enough competent men in this District to hold the Civil offices, who are not disfranchised.—I have I think reason to know otherwise—but even admitting that it is so, it is surely better to have an incompetent but loyal man in office, than to have a rebel of whatever ability.—In fact the greater the ability the greater the danger of maladministration—The questions at issue under these Acts of Congress are the most momentous ever presented to a people—The result for good or evil will affect all parts of the Country with more or less force and will leave an impress upon our Institutions which will long remain.—It is easy under existing circumstances to win the first victory and reconstruct these States under the Acts of Congress.—But this victory is only the beginning of the contest and unless it be a victory openly and fairly won and very decisive in its results it may prove not only fruitless but absolutely destructive.—The problem is to perpetuate Reconstruction in the Spirit and on the principles which can alone assure free Government—Should we effect reconstruction even after silencing the open opposition of the old political leaders, we stand committed to admit the reconstructed States into the Union.—Once admitted into the Union the power of Congress over them is reduced practically to the general power which that body has over all States in the Union.—By admitting these Southern States after silencing the old politcal leaders and neutralizing for the moment old political influences Congress and the people disarm themselves.—The moment admission into the Union is accomplished the Military power is suspended and with it all restrictions are removed.—At once these old political leaders, and the old political and personal influences will resume their activity and we may find too late that such reconstruction as we have made is not only not what was needed and expected but what will simply result in a reproduction of the same condition of affairs which made reconstruction measures necessary at all.—Freedom of Speech and of the Press, Education, Equality before the law, and in political rights and privileges are the essentials of any satisfactory reconstruction in the South.—Without securing these we have secured nothing.—How can we know that reconstruction will accomplish these results unless we know in advance the strength and the power of those who oppose it.— Reaction is certain unless the reconstruction party can win the battle by decisive majorities over all the elements which oppose it, left to develope themselves and apply their full force to the contest.—If the reactionists thus left free can defeat such reconstruction as this, we then know what to do, what in fact we must do if we desire to perpetuate free institutions.—It is best to know all these things before readmission into the Union is granted.—It will be too late to learn them afterward.—Now is the time and this is the opportunity to complete this work so that it will stand.—Every dictate of wisdom and patriotism demands this work at our hands.—If hastily or partially done reconstruction will drag with it a train of evils to this Country which can never be remedied.—It is not necessary to say that however we restrain the opposition party now, the moment reconstruction is accomplished this party will regain its activity and we ought to know in advance whether it possesses the power to undo what we thought we had done.—I do not mean to intimate that it would be possible to re-establish Slavery; perhaps it would not even be practicable to take from the Freedmen the right of suffrage, though this latter is doubtful.—These politicians are wiley and sagacious.—They will make no laws which are not equal in their face to all men.—It is in the execution of these laws which seem to bear equally on all, that wrong will be done, and a condition of things produced which bears no resemblance to free Government except in name.—Social exclusion, withdrawal of business relations, open exhibitions of hostility if not indeed actual hostile Acts, interruption of or interference with the Freedmen's and other Schools maintained by charitable contributions from the North; these will be the weapons used against Union men and the colored race.—Acts of wrong and violence will meet in sufficient redress if indeed any redress at all in the Courts.—These are acts which cannot be reached by the General Government, and yet which quietly and silently render justice impossible and establish discrimination against classes or color odious and unbearable—I say then again that unless reconstruction is accomplished after the fullest developement of all the influences against it by decisive majorities we will simply have reproduced and perpetuated in the South what we sought to destroy.—We ought to know in advance if possible whether the presence of the leaders of these incurable reactionists and their active influence in this country are compatible with the peace of the Country and the security of our Institutions.—Another question ought to be and probably will be decided in the course of the coming canvas for and against Convention.—That question is this;—Has the sluggishness of mind and body and the tendency to assail by violence the right of opinion and discussion, engendered by habits acquired during the existence of Slavery and the system of politics in the South unfitted the people for such self Government as is implied by free speech, free press, and the fullest peaceable discussion of all public questions? This is a most important question and one which if answered in the light of existing facts must be answered unfavorably.—Not only do the re-actionary anti-reconstructionists use all the instrumentalities I have named, except such as they are restrained from using by the Military Authorities, but there is little doubt that they would resort at once to the intimidation and violence which long practice has made a habit, if they dared to do so in the presence of the Military forces of the United States.—Candor compels me to say that this tendency to repress freedom of Speech is not confined to either party, but prevails, though to a much less degree, among the Reconstructionists, whether they have been always Union men or have lately joined the ranks of the Reconstruction party.—It becomes the Government of the United States, to frown upon such measures by whatever party proposed, and no rebuke so salutary, or so pregnant of good results can be administered as for the Government to protect all parties in the exercise of free speech.—Results will show what we must expect in the future in establishing in the South, what are cardinal principles of our Government.—The foregoing remarks refer exclusively to the White race in this District.—The condition and future of the Colored race are far more hopeful and encouraging.—The earnest and touching anxiety of the Freed people to learn cannot but awake a profound impression upon the mind of any one who has had the opportunity to observe it.—It may safely be said that the marvelous progress made in education and knowledge by these people, aided by the noble charitable contributions of Northern Societies and individuals, finds no parallel in the history of mankind.—If continued (and if continued at all, it must be by the same agencies) and the masses of the White people exhibit the same indisposition to be educated that they do now, five years will have transferred intelligence and education, so far as the masses are concerned, to the Colored people of this District.—The social and political results of such a change cannot fail to be important and to a great extent decisive of the questions which we are seeking to solve.—It becomes us therefore to guard jealously against any reaction which may and will check this most desirable progress of the colored race.—In this view also we should assure ourselves that the reconstruction we are attempting to set up in the South is of a character and possesses the vitality to encourage and maintain this progress and perpetuate its results.—These, General, are briefly my views upon the condition of affairs in this District and they furnish the reasons why I am pursueing the course in the Administration of my office which I have indicated to you.—It is not improbable that I may be mistaken and that reconstruction forced and hurried may finally result in equal good.—It seems to me however that we will incur a great risk by departing from the course I have marked out for myself; and if by carrying out other measures we fail to accomplish the results we all have at heart, we will have entailed endless evil upon these people and upon the country, and will have disarmed ourselves of the power to remedy it.—I am confident that Reconstruction will be satisfactorily accomplished in this District in spite of the open and active opposition of the disloyal re-actionists.—I can safely say that Alabama will give not less than 'ten thousand' majority of White votes for Reconstruction—and I think it may be said with almost equal certainty that Georgia will give a White majority in the same direction.—Not less than three fourths of the Colored vote in each of these States will be cast for Reconstruction.—The same remarks are substantially true of Florida, and if I have so earnestly invited your attention to the danger of opposite results it has only been to furnish the data necessary to meet the case, and to justify the course I have thought it judicious to pursue.—All the facts that can bear upon these questions I shall continue to report as they come to my knowledge.—It is however my duty to state that in my judgement the condition of affairs in the Southern States, even should reconstruction be satisfactorily accomplished, will of necessity be a reproduction in a more or less modified degree, of what now exists in Tennessee, unless some measures are adopted to free the Country of the turbulent and disloyal leaders of the reactionary party.—Whilst these persons remain in the Country to exercise the baneful influence which they undoubtedly possess there can be no peace.—I believe that in Florida and Alabama the danger from this cause is less than in Georgia, but in all these States there is so much danger of the disorders and violence which mark the daily history of Tennessee that it would seem wise to adopt whatever measures are practicable to remove from the States in process of reconstruction the causes which now endanger loyal Government in Tennessee.—I do not venture to suggest a remedy for the evils that may be developed—Such matters merit and will no doubt command patient examination and careful action, and having laid before you the facts and my own general views upon them I consider my duty performed.—" LS, *ibid.*, RG 108, Letters Received.

On July 17, Pope had written to USG. "As the Act supplemental to the Military Bills of March just passed by Congress, impose farther duties upon the Boards of Registration and make it necessary to keep these Boards in actual service much longer than was anticipated, I feel bound to ask that the proper proportion of the additional appropriation just made be assigned to this District. My arrangements for Registration were based on the plan for taking the census, paying per capita for registering voters. I expected as soon as Registration was completed to discharge these Boards until the day of Election, and made as careful an estimate as possible in that view.—For revising and correcting the Registration lists, and exposing them in public places before an Election, the Boards must be kept in employment and paid by the day from the time Registration is completed to the day of Election. Other expenses incident to this change will of necessity be incurred, and my request therefore, for such proportion of the additional appropriation as the extent and population of this District require, has become necessary." LS, *ibid*. On Aug. 13, Pope wrote to USG. "I have the honor to state that Registration in this District is progressing rapidly and without disturbance.—The results to this date are as follows. Georgia White votes registered 64.719 Colored votes registered 73.344 Excess of colored votes over white. 8.625 The registration in Georgia will probably reach One hundred and eighty thousand with a white excess of five or eight thousand.—Alabama White votes registered 59045 Colored votes registered 76640 [*total*] 135.685 Excess of Colored over White 17595 The complete registration will probably reach 145.000 but the relative white and black will not be materially changed From Florida, owing to difficulty of communication the returns are not sufficient to forward you anything satisfactory.—The entire registration in this District will be completed before September 1st" LS (tabular material expanded), *ibid*.

On Aug. 14, Pope telegraphed to USG. "Shall I publish the order requiring Jurors in this District to take the test oath as by your instructions or on my own authority? I had just made an order but fortunately not distributed it, to require jurors to be drawn from the lists of registered voters" Telegrams received (2— at 4:00 P.M.), *ibid*., RG 107, Telegrams Collected (Bound); *ibid*., RG 108, Telegrams Received; copies, *ibid*., RG 46, Senate 40A–F2, Messages; DLC-USG, V, 55. At 4:30 P.M., USG telegraphed to Pope. "Publish the jury order which you had prepared. The only object of distributing Gn. Griffins order was [to] secure a jury system which [w]ill give protection to all classes." ALS (telegram sent), DNA, RG 107, Telegrams Collected (Bound); telegram sent, *ibid*.; copies, *ibid*., RG 46, Senate 40A–F2, Messages; *ibid*., RG 108, Telegrams Sent; DLC-USG, V, 56. See telegram to Bvt. Maj. Gen. Edward O. C. Ord, July 30, 1867; *HED*, 40-2-1, II, part 1, pp. 331–32.

On Aug. 17, Pope wrote to USG. "I intended to have transmitted to you with my Order 49 a letter of explanation but did not do so as I thought it was sufficiently clear to explain itself.—As an attempt is being made by the Rebel Journals in this District aided by their Copperhead allies in the North to make it appear that this order is an attack upon the freedom of the Press, it will perhaps not be out of place for me to give my reasons for issuing it, somewhat more in detail than they are given in the order.—When I first took Command here I found that nearly every civil officer in this District had been elected almost wholly on the ground of service in the rebel army or other aid given to the Rebellion.— Neither their disloyalty nor their malignity had been in the least mitigated by the result of the war and they were as active and untiring in resisting the settlement of the Southern difficulties as they were during the War.—But two courses were open to me under the circumstances unless indeed it is the purpose of the Government to permit the entire machinery of the Provisional State Governments to be actively used against the execution of the Reconstruction Acts.—The first was to remove all the civil officers and replace them by others who were at least semi-loyal to the Government of the United States.—The second was to require that such civil officers whilst holding their offices should not use any influence against Reconstruction.—I adopted the second course indicated mainly because I feared that any considerable removal of office holders would seriously interfere with the ordinary course of civil business and therefore would to some extent inconvenience the people.—Whilst the feelings and purposes of the civil officers in relation to Reconstruction were well known and of course had their influence upon the people, my order was generally complied with in its literal sense, but I soon found that these civil officers were using their official patronage to support small newspapers all over this District which constantly and bitterly opposed Reconstruction, denounced everybody in favor of it and assailed the civil officers appointed by the Military authorities with abuse and threats for official acts; beside denouncing them for accepting office under a Military despotism. In every way the civil officers appointed by the Military authorities were embarassed and obstructed in the performance of their duty.—Every sort of influence was used to prevent people from going on their bonds by threats of social and business exclusion and by prosecution, and by revenge as soon as Military protection was withdrawn.—In this manner much difficulty has been occasioned in carrying on Civil Government in this District;—Union men being absolutely overawed and overborne by this incessant abuse and vilification by the Rebel papers.—Almost without exception these papers owe their existence entirely to the patronage of the civil officers.—They could not be kept up without the official advertisements and publications which are given to them.—If the support and encouragement of such newspapers by the Provisional civil officers be not obstructing the Execution of the Reconstruction Acts, I know not what could be so considered—Again I had the alternative of removing the civil officers and thus doing away with this evil and by the Supplemental Act I am required to remove such persons from office, but I have been restrained from doing so by the same reasons which prevailed with me at the outset.—In no respect has the 'Freedom of the Press' been interfered with as will be sufficiently manifest from the violent and abusive articles against myself personally which have appeared in them ever since my order 49 was issued The order is not addressed to them at all but to civil officers alone.— These Rebel papers are permitted and will be permitted to publish what they please but I do not propose that they shall be supported in doing so by money paid them from the Treasury of the Provisional State Governments.—My order does not even require these civil officials to advertise in papers which advocate Reconstruction.—Simply that they shall not advertise in papers which are opposing it and denouncing it in gross and outrageous terms every man in the South who is in favor of Reconstructing the State Governments under the Acts of Congress.—The order interferes not at all with freedom of Speech or the Press; it is an order necessary to prevent so powerful an organization as the Provisional State Governments from defeating the execution of the Reconstruction Acts; it is necessary to maintain any civil Government at all in these States during the progress of Reconstruction, and it is in no sense an unfair order.—It seems hardly necessary for me to have said so much on so plain a matter.—It is clear that unless some such order had been issued I should simply have been myself encouraging and permitting the machinery of the Provisional State Governments to be used to defeat the execution of a law of the United States which I am sent here to execute and this law, the very law by whose sufferance alone these Provisional State Governments have any existence at all.—I need not tell you General of the difficulties which necessarily confront an officer in my position who is required to preserve 'peace and good order' in these States in which for some years past violence and disorder have been the rule; to protect all persons in their 'rights of person and property' in communities where for a long time at least there has been scarcely a conception of such things; and to do this through civil officers who oppose every act of the Military authorities, who resist in every manner practicable the execution of the Law which I am placed here to see executed and who so far from assisting me to maintain 'peace and good order' are using all their official patronage to support newspapers whose sole purpose is to inflame the public mind; to incite resistance to the execution of the laws and to create such prejudice and animosity toward any person who accepts a civil appointment under the Military authorities that even if he is bold enough to accept, so embarrass and obstruct him in the performance of his duty that he is rendered next to useless.—The difficulties from these causes have not been so great in Florida and Alabama as in Georgia but they are sufficiently troublesome in all.— I have sent you my correspondence with Governor Jenkins.—You will see what assistance he gives even in the ordinary affairs directly concerning the business and welfare of the people of the State. He declines to appoint officers to fill some such vacancy as that of Judge of Probate, an office absolutely necessary to the people, on the ground that he has no authority to fill such vacancies.—I have written him that no elections can be held under the reconstruction Acts until registration is completed and it is known who are entitled to vote under the Laws of the United States.—that I will myself appoint officers to fill such vacancies if he will recommend suitable persons to me who are not disqualified to hold office— To this he replies that I have the same means of knowing the character and qualifications of people in Georgia that he has and therefore declines.—It may be true that I, a stranger who have only been in the State five four months, know as much about the people as Governor Jenkins who has lived here all his life and whom the people only recently elected Governor of the State, but if so, I am sure he can have no high opinion of the intelligence of a people who have elected as their Governor a man who knows so little about them and who exhibits so little interest in their affairs.—I refer you to this correspondance, some time since transmitted to you.—I present this case merely as an illustration of the difficulty of getting along with people who are possessed by so much prejudice and malignity and so little common sense.—It is not an exceptional case but merely an example of the general rule.—It is necessary to do much here which I hoped to avoid and which I am loth to do, but I cannot escape it without neglecting my duty." LS, DNA, RG 108, Letters Received.

On Oct. 7, Pope wrote to USG. "I have the honor to acknowledge the receipt of a private letter of George. S. Houston of Athens, Alabama, addressed to the President of the United States, and referred to me for remark. I regret that Mr Houston's memory is so treacherous, as not only to occasion him to forget the number of my order of which he complains, but to misrepresent entirely the contents of the order.—He says, 'The order of General Pope, the number of which I have forgotten, *forbids the publication* in the County papers, and requires them to be made in some County, remote in very many cases from the point or County at, and in which, the act is to take place or be performed, and in a paper, almost universaly, that is not taken by a dozen men in the County &c. &c.' I enclose the order in question, which is the only order or instruction I have given in this matter, that you may understand the utter recklessness of statement of even prominent men in this region.—My order as you will see indicates no paper whatever, and does not require the *advocacy* of any thing whatever.—I simply exact from papers, publishing official advertisements, that they shall not seek to overthrow all civil Government whatever in these States.—The order speaks for itself, and has in no manner been changed, or modified, nor have any other instructions, either General or Special, been given on the subject by me or by my knowledge. I transmit enclosed an extract from my official report, covering this subject, which explains very fully the necessity of this order—The report itself will be sent in a few days. I also send you a number of the 'Florence Journal,' the newspaper in which Mr Houston manifests such paternal interest—You need only read it to see what claims it has to the consideration of any loyal man. As to Mr Houston's absurd remarks about 'tyranny and oppression' I have only to say that they are worthy of the character of a man, who ventures to make such an appeal to the President of the United States in favor of such a news-paper.—My official Acts are open and public, and I defy any man in this District to point out a case, in which any person whatever has been wronged or oppressed by me or by my authority, unless indeed it be oppression to punish crime and discountenance violent and unscrupulous rebels.—" LS, DLC-Andrew Johnson. The enclosure is *ibid.* On Oct. 8, Pope wrote to USG. "In connection with my letter forwarded to you yesterday, in reply to a private letter of Mr Geo S Houston, of Alabama, complaining of, and misrepresenting, General Orders, No 49, from these Head Quarters; I respectfully ask your attention to my letter of August 17th, last, on that subject. This letter explains much more in detail, than the extract from my official report sent yesterday, the precise necessities and motives which occasioned me to issue the order in question. I request that it be made part of the official record on the subject." LS, DNA, RG 108, Letters Received.

On Aug. 21, Pope had telegraphed to USG. "Will Lieut. H. J. Farnsworth who has just passed his Examination as 1st Lieut 34th Infantry be permitted to remain here as Depot Quartermaster according to my request sometime since made." Telegram received (at 11:00 A.M.), *ibid.*, RG 94, Letters Received, 277Q 1867; *ibid.*, RG 107, Telegrams Collected (Bound). USG noted on a telegram received. "Gn. Pope can retain Lt. Farnesworth. So inform him." ANS, *ibid.*, RG 94, Letters Received, 277Q 1867. Also on Aug. 21, Pope telegraphed to USG. "will you please let me know what decision you have reached in relation to my recommendation about concentrating troops & building barracks. The season is passing & some winter arrangements for troops must soon be made." Telegram received (at 3:15 P.M.), *ibid.*, RG 107, Telegrams Collected (Bound); *ibid.*, RG 108, Telegrams Received; copies, *ibid.*, RG 46, Senate 40A–F2, Messages; DLC-USG, V, 55. Pope also submitted an undated report to USG concerning military administration. ". . . Whatever be the result of reconstruction in this district, United States troops, under a prudent officer, will be needed here for some years to come. Should reconstruction under the acts of Congress be unfortunately defeated, (though I think there is no possibility of such a result,) the need of troops is obvious. Should it be successful, the aid of United States troops will be necessary to the civil authorities of the reconstructed State governments until passion has subsided and affairs have so settled down that the people, without distinction of party, can be relied on to enforce the laws of the State. . . ." *HED*, 40-2-1, II, part 1, pp. 354–56. On Aug. 24, 12:30 P.M. and 2:00 P.M., USG telegraphed to Pope. "Adj. Gn. Wood is ordered to report to you. He will report about 1st of Sept." "Make your disposition of troops for the winter in the manner suggested in your dispatches. Use the troops as far as possible for building quarters." ALS (telegrams sent), DNA, RG 107, Telegrams Collected (Bound); telegrams sent, *ibid.*; copies (one of the second), *ibid.*, RG 46, Senate 40A–F2, Messages; *ibid.*, RG 108, Telegrams Sent; DLC-USG, V, 56. On Sept. 26, Pope telegraphed to USG. "will you please determine upon the plans for barracks here as soon as convenient—The plans are in the hands of the Quarter-master General—The winter season is fast approaching and we have no time to lose" Telegram received (at 12:10 P.M.), DNA, RG 107, Telegrams Collected (Bound). On the same day, Bvt. Maj. Gen. Daniel H. Rucker, act. q. m. gen., endorsed papers concerning the matter. "Respectfully submitted to the Secretary of War, ad-int. Authority was granted by the War Department Aug 24th '67 for the erection of Barracks &c. at Atlanta Ga for 4 Companies, in accordance with plans herewith enclosed—I respectfully request authority to erect the additional six (6) Barracks &c required, as recommended by Maj Genl Pope upon the same plans as those approved by the War Dept Aug 24th 1867—" ES, *ibid.*, RG 92, Reports to the Secretary of War (Press). On Oct. 11, Rucker wrote to USG suggesting alterations in plans for the barracks at Atlanta. LS, *ibid.*

On Aug. 26 and 29, Pope telegraphed to USG. "Please assign Genl Swayne according to his Brevet rank and leave him for duty in this Department. I can-not possibly spare his services until after the elections are over" "I telegraphed you the other day asking that Swayne be assigned to his Brevet rank of Brigadier General and left in this Department as his services are indispensible until Elec-tions in Alabama are over. Please inform me whether this will be done. Registra-tion complete in Alabama & election order will be issued monday the 2nd Sep-tember. Registration in Georgia will be finished in a few days" Telegrams received (on Aug. 26, 1:00 P.M., and Aug. 29, 3:00 P.M.), *ibid.*, RG 107, Tele-grams Collected (Bound); *ibid.*, RG 108, Telegrams Received; copies, DLC-USG, V, 55. On Aug. 30, 10:30 A.M., USG telegraphed to Pope. "Gen. Swayne was ordered to remain in his present command. He will be assigned to his Bvt. of Brig. Gn." ALS (telegram sent), DNA, RG 107, Telegrams Collected (Bound); telegram sent, *ibid.*; copies, *ibid.*, RG 108, Telegrams Sent; DLC-USG, V, 56.

On Aug. 26 and 29, Pope wrote to USG. "I have the honor to report results of Registration up to this date in this Military District, as follows: STATE of FLORIDA—August 16: Registration progressing. Up to date have been registered *Whites* 2651 *Colored* 6236 Bradford County reports total of 290 without des-ignating color *Total Registered* 9.177 STATE of ALABAMA. August 22d—Registration progressing. Up to date have been registered *Whites* 67,686 *Colored* 84,524 *Total Registered* 152,210 STATE of GEORGIA August 24: Registra-tion progressing. Up to date have been registered *Whites* 75,502 *Colored* 83,109 *Total Registered* 158,611 This report leaves to be heard from nineteen (19) counties, whose population in 1860 was 99,327." "I have the honor to transmit herewith a copy of my letter, dated August 26th 1867, in reply to a letter from A. T. Akerman, of Elberton, Elbert County, Georgia, making inquiries as to what action is to be taken by the Military Authorities in reference to the Stay Laws of the State of Georgia." LS, DNA, RG 108, Letters Received. The en-closure in the second letter is *ibid.* On Sept. 2 and 3, Pope wrote to USG. "I have the honor to transmit herewith, copy of General Order No 59. C. S. from these Head Quarters, relating to elections in Alabama.—" "I have the honor to trans-mit herewith copy of a letter received from Governor C. J. Jenkins dated Milledge-ville August 20 1867, and also copy of my letter in reply to the same.—" LS, *ibid.* The enclosures are *ibid.* On Sept. 4, Pope twice wrote to USG. "I enclosed you yesterday my order for an election in Alabama—I shall send you in a day or two the exact registration for each County in that State so that you can see pre-cisely how the apportionment of Delegates was made—The number of voters registered in Alabama surprised every body.—Hertofore the white vote has never exceeded 75.000—The registration shows 74000 In Georgia the registration has been equally complete—The largest white vote ever cast in the State was 107.000—The usual white vote has been about 90.000—The registration will show very nearly 100.000 white voters.—I attribute this complete registration to the system I adopted for making it.—Instead of paying Registers by the day I adopted the rule of paying them 'per capita' under the same general rules in use by the Census Bureau—The average per voter in the whole District I fixed at 26 cents.—It was therefore the interest of the Registers to register every man that was qualified to vote and to do this in as short a time as possible—The result has been eminently satisfactory both as securing very full registration and doing it at small expense.—The whole number of registered voters will be about as follows. Alabama *163.000* Whites 74.000 Colored. 89.000 Georgia *195.000* Whites 100.000. Colored 95.000. Florida *21.000*. I cannot yet tell the relative strength of white and colored votes in Florida.—The election in Georgia will be ordered by the 12th of this month and will take place about October 25th—In Florida a few days later." "I have the honor to invite your attention to the extracts herewith transmitted from a letter of the 31st Ult, from Colonel J. T. Sprague, Comd'g Dis of Florida, and to state that in my opinion it would be judicious to send, if possible, a company of Cavalry to the District of Florida.—" LS, *ibid*. The enclosure in the second letter is *ibid*.

1. Robert A. Toombs, born in Ga. in 1810, U.S. representative (1845–53) and U.S. senator (1853–61), the first C.S.A. secretary of state, had served as C.S.A. brig. gen. To avoid arrest, he fled to Europe in May, 1865, and returned to Ga. in 1867, where he wrote a fiery letter supporting the Democratic party. *New York Times*, July 10, 1867.

2. Probably on Sept. 3, USG drafted an order. "Commanders of the Five Military Districts will require within thirty days from the receipt of this order, that all persons within their respective commands who (since the 9th of Apl. 1865) voluntarily exiled themselves from any of the ~~seceded states~~, states lately in rebellion, and have since returned to the United States, shall take the same parole oath taken by those who remained ~~in the Country~~ at home and manfully met ~~their~~ all requirements made ~~of~~ upon them." ADf (dated on docket), DNA, RG 94, Letters Received, 631W 1867.

To Julia Dent Grant

———

Washington, Aug. 5th *1867*.

DEAR JULIA:

I had made all my preparation to start to Doubling Gap this evening when a startling piece of news, which will probably be published in the morning papers, which will keep me here indefinately. I do not think it probable that I can get away from here this

week, not even for a day to go after you   You may either come home
or stay until such time as I can go after you. Dr. Sharp ~~would~~ will
come with you to Carlisle if you wish to come and I will meet, or
send Fred. to meet you, at Baltimore. I am getting along here very
nicely and if you are enjoying yourself stay where you are. It would
be more pleasant for me to have you here but it will be better

AL (incomplete), USG 3. See following letter.

To Edwin M. Stanton

Washington, D. C, Aug. 12th *1867*.

HON. E. M. STANTON,
SEC. OF WAR;
SIR;

Enclosed herewith I have the honor to transmit to you a copy
of a letter just received from the President of the United States
notifying me of my assignment as Act Sec. of War, and directing
me to assume those duties at once.

In notifying you of my acceptanc[e] ~~of the duties thus imposed
on me~~ I cannot let the opportunity pass without expressing to you
my appreciation of the zeal, patriotism, firmness and ability with
which your have ever discharged the duty of Sec. of War. ~~and also
the regret I now feel at seeing you withdraw from them.~~

With great respect,
your obt. svt.
U. S. GRANT
General.

ADfS (facsimile), Adam Badeau, *Grant in Peace* (Hartford, Conn., 1887), pp.
[92–93]; ALS, DLC-Edwin M. Stanton. On Aug. 12, 1867, Secretary of War
Edwin M. Stanton wrote to USG. "Your note of this date accompanied by a copy
of a letter addressed to you Aug: 12th by the President appointing you Secretary
of War ad interim, and informing me of your acceptance of the appointment, has
been received. Under a sense of public duty, I am compelled to deny the Presidents right under the Constitution and Laws of the United States to suspend me
from office as Secretary of War, or to authorize any other person to enter upon

the discharge of the duties of that office, or to require me to transfer to you, or any other person, the records, books, papers and other property in my official custody and charge, as Secretary of War. But inasmuch as the President has assumed to suspend me from office as Secretary of War, and you have notified me of your acceptance of the appointment of Secretary of War ad interim, I have no alternative but to submit, under protest, to the superior force of the President. You will please accept my acknowledgment of the kind terms in which you have notified me of your acceptance of the Presidents appointment, and my cordial reciprocation of the sentiments expressed." LS (2), DNA, RG 108, Letters Received; ADf, DLC-Edwin M. Stanton. On the same day, President Andrew Johnson had written to USG. "The Honorable Edwin M. Stanton having been this day suspended as Secretary of War, you are hereby authorized and empowered to act as Secretary of War ad interim, and will at once enter upon the discharge of the duties of that office. The Secretary of War has been instructed to transfer to you all records, books, papers, and other public property now in his custody, and charge." LS, DNA, RG 108, Letters Received; DLC-Andrew Johnson; ADf, *ibid.*

On Aug. 5, Johnson had written to Stanton. "Public considerations of a high character constrain me to say, that your resignation as Secretary of War will be accepted." LS (marked as copy), *ibid.*; copy, DNA, RG 107, Letters Sent to the President. On the same day, Stanton wrote to Johnson. "Your note of this date has been received stating that public considerations of a high character constrain you to say that my resignation as Secretary of War will be accepted. In reply I have the honor to say that public considerations of a high character, which alone have induced me to continue at the head of this Department, constrain me not to resign the office of Secretary of War before the next meeting of Congress." ALS, DLC-Andrew Johnson. On Aug. 12, Johnson wrote to Stanton. "By virtue of the power and authority vested in me, as President, by the Constitution and Laws of the United States, you are hereby suspended from office as Secretary of War, and will cease to exercise any and all functions pertaining to the same. You will at once transfer to General Ulysses S. Grant, who has this day been authorized and empowered to act as Secretary of War ad interim, all records, books, papers, and other public property now in your custody and charge." Copies (3), *ibid.*; DNA, RG 107, Letters Sent to the President. On the same day, Stanton wrote to Johnson. ". . . Under a sense of public duty I am compelled to deny your right under the Constitution and Laws of the United States, without the advice and consent of the Senate, and without legal cause to suspend me from Office as Secretary of War, or the exercise of any or all functions pertaining to the same; or without such advice and consent to compel me to transfer to any person the records, books, papers and other public property in my custody as Secretary of War. But inasmuch as the General commanding the Armies of the United States has been appointed Secretary of War ad interim, and has notified me that he has accepted the appointment, I have no alternative but to submit, under protest, to superior force." LS, DLC-Andrew Johnson. See letter to Andrew Johnson, Aug. 1, 1867; St. George L. Sioussat, ed., "Notes of Colonel W. G. Moore, Private Secretary to President Andrew Johnson, 1866–1868," *American Historical Review*, XIX, 1 (Oct., 1913), 107–10; Howard K. Beale, ed., *Diary of Gideon Welles* (New York, 1960), III, 154–69; Theodore Calvin Pease and James G. Randall, eds., *The Diary of Orville Hickman Browning* (Springfield, 1925–33), II, 154–56.

To Maj. Gen. Henry W. Halleck

Washington Aug. 12th *1867*. [*2:10* P.M.]

MAJ. GN. H. W. HALLECK,

SAN FRANCISCO, CAL,

Russian Commissioner to deliver Russian America to United States, and Gen. Rousseau, Agt. to receive the same leave New York for San Francisco Aug. 21st. Have troops and transports ready so there shall be no delay on their arrival. It probaby will be well to send no more than three companies this year.

U. S. GRANT

General,

ALS (telegram sent), DNA, RG 107, Telegrams Collected (Bound); telegram sent, *ibid.*; copies, *ibid.*, RG 108, Telegrams Sent; DLC-USG, V, 56. See letter to Maj. Gen. Henry W. Halleck, May 29, 1867. On Aug. 12, 1867, President Andrew Johnson had written to USG. "I will be pleased to have you present at one o'clock today, at which time several questions in reference to the newly-acquired Russian territory will be considered" LS, Morristown National Historic Park, Morristown, N. J. On Aug. 14 and 15, USG wrote to Secretary of State William H. Seward. "As the season will have advanced too far to permit the erection of buildings this year at Sitka, it is desirable to be informed as to the extent of the accommodations for troops & their supplies which will be turned over to the United States by the Russian Government, at that point & at any others which it is deemed necessary to be garrisoned by the United States. It is presumed the Russian Commissioner can furnish the information" "I have the honor to acknowledge the receipt of your communication of the 13th inst., transmitting a copy of the treaty between the United States & Russia of the 30th March last for the cession of certain territory to the former; A copy of the instructions of the State Department to Brig. Genl. Rousseau, United States Commissioner and a copy of the instructions of the Russian Government to its agent for transferring the same; and to inform you that copies of the instructions have been sent to Genl. Halleck, Commanding the Military Division of the Pacific, for his information." Copies, DNA, RG 107, Letters Sent to the President.

On Aug. 14, Secretary of the Treasury Hugh McCulloch wrote to USG. "I have the honor to inform you that this Department proposes to appoint a special agent with authority to act as Collector of Customs at Sitka, or New Archangel, until Congress shall make regular provision by law. The business being small, he will have few or no assistants regularly assigned him, but may at times need a force of men, armed or unarmed, to aid or protect him in the performance of his duties. He may also need the countenance, advice and authority of the military force to be stationed there in the adoption of rules and regulations to be observed by the masters and crews of vessels and others while in port. I have the honor therefore respectfully to request that the Commanding Officer of such military force may be ordered to afford all such needed aid, assistance and advice in respect of the matters mentioned, as the said Special Agent shall from time to time require, and, also, to afford him such 'quarters' as may be found necessary for the proper transaction of the public business." LS, *ibid.*, Letters Received from Bureaus. On Aug. 15, USG wrote to McCulloch. "I have the honor to inform you that a copy of your comn of the 14. inst. respecting the acting collector proposed to be sent to Sitka, has been sent to Major Genl Halleck, Com'g on the ~~Western~~ Pacific Coast for proper action in the case." Df, *ibid.*; copy, *ibid.*, Letters Sent to the President.

On Sept. 6, Seward wrote to USG. "In relation to the dispatch of Major General Halleck of the 2nd of September, instant, in which he requests that the President will, by proclamation, declare the newly acquired Russian territory an Indian territory in order to prevent the introduction of ardent spirits among the Indians there, I am instructed to say that the President will retain the same for further consideration. At the same time he desires that Major General Halleck will confer with General Rousseau upon that subject to the end that the matured views of those officers may be submitted to the President as early as practicable. For the information of the War Department, I communicate a copy of an opinion of E. Peshine Smith, Esqre, Examiner of Claims in this Department, which sets forth a view of the laws of the United States bearing upon that question, which view is adopted by this Department." LS, *ibid.*, RG 94, Letters Received, 557P 1867. The enclosure is *ibid.*

On Oct. 28, Seward wrote to USG. "In the absence of specific legislation by Congress for the organization of Land Districts in Alaska, claims of preemption and settlements are not only without the sanction of law but are in direct violation of laws applicable to the public domains. Military force may be used to remove intruders if necessary. Will you have the goodness to instruct Major General Halleck to this effect by telegraph, and request him to communicate the instruction to Major General Rousseau at Sitka." LS, *ibid.*, 1062S 1867. On Oct. 29, USG wrote to Seward. "I have the honor to acknowledge the receipt of your communication of the 28th inst in relation to claims of pre-emption and settlements in *Alaska*, and to enclose herewith for your information copies of the telegram and letter of instructions to Genl Halleck on this subject." Copies, *ibid.*, Letters Sent; *ibid.*, RG 107, Letters Sent to the President. On Dec. 21, USG wrote to Secretary of the Interior Orville H. Browning. "I have the honor to transmit herewith a copy of a com'n from *Maj. Genl. Halleck*, Comd'g Milty. Div. of the Pacific, concerning the Peninsula of *Kenay* in the newly acquired territory of *Alaska*, and to request that his suggestion that these lands be surveyed and brought into market at as early period as possible,—be carried out." Copy, *ibid.*

On Nov. 16, Seward had written to USG. "I have the honor to forward to you for transportation to Brigadier General Lovell H. Rousseau, Commissioner to Russian America, seven boxes of instruments, marked L. H. S. and numbered 1 to 7 inclusively. The inclosed list enumerates the instruments, some of which being of a delicate nature require careful handling." LS, *ibid.*, RG 94, Letters Received, 1144S 1867. The enclosures are *ibid.* On the same day, USG wrote to Seward. "I have the honor to acknowledge receipt of your com'n of this date transmitting, for transportation to *Genl. L H Rosseau* Comr to Russian America, 7 boxes of instruments, and to inform you that instructions have been issued for their immediate transmittal" Copies, *ibid.*; *ibid.*, RG 107, Letters Sent to the President.

On Jan. 8, 1868, Secretary of the Navy Gideon Welles wrote to USG. "I have the honor to inform you that I have transmitted to Rear Admiral H. K. Thatcher, commanding the North Pacific Squadron, a copy of the communication addressed to Major General Halleck by Brevet Major General Jef. C. Davis, on the 5th Nov. last, which you referred to this Department, on the subject of having a vessel of war stationed at Sitka to co-operate with the military force in preserving peace." LS, *ibid.*, Letters Received from Bureaus.

On Jan. 13, McCulloch wrote to USG. "I have the honor to transmit herewith an extract from a report received by this Department from William S. Dodge Esqr. Special Agent of this Department, and Acting Collector of Customs, at Sitka, Alaska, in which, he makes certain suggestions, in regard to the existing trade regulations at that port, so that liquors in limited quantities may be allowed to be brought to that port for sale to the citizens proper thereof; and in regard to the sale of arms and ammunition to the Coast Indians or the Esquimaux tribes along Norton's Sound for hunting purposes. Should you deem it proper to adopt the suggestions of Mr. Dodge, either in whole or in part, this Department will be pleased to coöperate with you, and will, on the receipt of a copy of your instructions to the Military Governor of that Territory, duly issue the necessary regulations for the government of the Officers of the Customs thereat." LS, *ibid.* On Jan. 24, USG endorsed this letter. "Respectfully returned to the Secretary of War. In my opinion the Secretary of the Treasury should establish the necessary rules and regulations concerning the importation of arms, ammunition and liquor into Alaska, subject only to such restrictions, changes and modifications as may from time to time be suggested by the Military Commandant of that Territory, to the officers of the customs placed there." ES, *ibid.*

On Jan. 2, U.S. Senator Henry W. Corbett of Ore. and U.S. Representative Rufus Mallory of Ore. had written to USG. "We respectfully submit for your consideration the enclosed papers relative to the question as to what Military District the newly acquired territory of Alaska ought to be attached—We beg to refer you to the accompanying letter of Brevet Major General Steele lately commanding the Department of the Columbia showing that Alaska ought to be attached to that Department & also to the letter of Brevet Major General Rosseau in which he fully concurs with his predecessor   Their opinions are strengthened by the letter of Mr Brooks Postal Agent for the Northern Pacific Coast—To the above we desire to add that in our judgment public economy & convenience are altogether on the side of the views expressed in the enclosed communications" LS, *ibid.*, RG 94, Letters Received, 123A 1868. The enclosures are *ibid.* On Jan. 27, USG endorsed this letter. "Respectfully returned to the Secretary of War. I do not approve the transfer herein recommended. Alaska being so remote from the Headquarters of both the Pacific Departments, and the communications with them at certain seasons of the year so uncertain, I respectfully recommend that it be made a separate military department, and that Bvt. Maj. Gen. Jeff. C. Davis, Col. 23d Infy., be assigned to the command." ES, *ibid.*

On Feb. 14, Maj. Gen. Henry W. Halleck, San Francisco, wrote to the AG. "Preparations have been made to establish, during the months of April and May next, some four or five new military posts in the Military District of Alaska. This will make the command of Brevet Major General Davis larger, both in territorial extent and in Military force, than some of the Military Departments already existing east of the Rocky Mountains. The peculiarly isolated position of Alaska, especially in the winter, with no mail facilities, and only casually a Steamer or

Sailing vessel from its ports to California or Oregon, renders it exceedingly desirable that the military Commander in that country should have the powers conferred by law and regulations upon the commander of a Military Department. This remark is peculiarly applicable to the subject of General Courts Martial, the discharge and transfer of Soldiers, &c. I therefore respectfully and earnestly recommend that the Military Department of Alaska be constituted, with Head Quarters at Sitka, and that General J. C. Davis be assigned to the command, with his Brevet rank of Major General. I think that General Davis' services, and most excellent character as an officer, render him fully deserving of this compliment. The increase of expenses to the government by this arrangement will be almost nothing, and no new Staff Officers will be required. On the other hand, it will promote Military discipline and greatly facilitate the transaction of public business. I had first intended to ask that General Davis be given simply in orders the powers of a Department Commander, but I find that he cannot exercise *all* of such powers under the law without being made the Commander of a Department." LS, *ibid.*, 119P 1868. On March 17, USG endorsed this letter. "Respectfully submitted to the Presid't. I concur in the recommendation of Major General Halleck." ES, *ibid.* On March 18, 12:20 P.M., USG telegraphed to Halleck. "Orders issued making Alasca Dept. Notify Gn. Davis." ALS (telegram sent), *ibid.*, RG 107, Telegrams Collected (Bound); telegram sent, *ibid.*; copies, *ibid.*, RG 108, Telegrams Sent; DLC-USG, V, 56.

To Bvt. Maj. Gen. Frederick Steele

Aug. 13th *1867*.

DEAR GENERAL,

Your private letter to me was duly received and it was my intention to have answered it promptly. Delaying for a few days however the matter passed out of my mind.—My advice (answering your question) would be to use no political influence to obtain promotion. It is not a satisfactory way of holding rank. Rousseaus[1] appointment was essentially a political appointment and one having no merit in it. My prediction is it will not last long. Believing so I want you when relieved by him, if you are so relieved, to remain on the Pacific Coast for a time to see the action of Congress on Military appointments.

Give my kindest regards to Mrs. Steele and her daughter when you write to them, and express to Ella (that was) my congratulations.

Yours Truly

U. S. GRANT

GEN. F. STEELE,
U. S. ARMY,

ALS, CSt. On Oct. 9, 1866, USG had written to Secretary of War Edwin M. Stanton. "I have the honor to recommend that Gen. Steele be assigned to duty on his brevet of Major General and directed to retain command of the Department of the Columbia until relieved by Gn. Pope or such other officer as may be assigned to that command." ALS, DNA, RG 94, Letters Received, 760A 1866. On Jan. 22, 1867, Bvt. Maj. Gen. Frederick Steele, San Francisco, telegraphed to USG. "Cannot Capt R N Scott fourth (4th) Infantry be appointed Asst Adjt Genl and ordered to duty with me   There is no AAG in my Dept" Telegram received (on Jan. 23, 11:30 A.M.), *ibid.*, RG 107, Telegrams Collected (Bound); *ibid.*, RG 108, Telegrams Received; copy, DLC-USG, V, 55. On Jan. 24, Maj. Gen. Henry W. Halleck, San Francisco, telegraphed to USG. "I respectfully recommend Bvt Lt Col R N Scott for Asst Adjt Genl" Telegram received (on Jan. 25, 9:00 A.M.), DNA, RG 108, Telegrams Received; copy, DLC-USG, V, 55. On March 11, Steele, Portland, Ore., having been mustered out as maj. gen. on Jan. 1, telegraphed to USG. "Please inform me if I am to remain here & on Bvt Rank" Telegram received (at 11:00 P.M.), DNA, RG 108, Telegrams Received; copy, DLC-USG, V, 55. On April 30, former U.S. Senator James W. Nesmith of Ore., Portland, telegraphed to USG. "For Gods sake have Steele retained in Command of this Department   He wishes it and it is the desire of our whole community   Please answer" Telegram received (on May 1, 2:15 P.M.), DNA, RG 108, Telegrams Received; copy, DLC-USG, V, 55. Steele was relieved of command of the Dept. of Columbia on Nov. 23 and died on Jan. 12, 1868.

    1. Lovell H. Rousseau, a friend of President Andrew Johnson, had been confirmed on April 5, 1867, as brig. gen., reconsidered, and confirmed again on April 11 as of March 28. On April 15, USG wrote to Stanton. "I have the honor to recommend Brig. Gn. L. H. Rousseau for the brevet of Major General in the regular army. All the Brigadier Generals, except Gen. Rousseau, and many officers of lower rank, hold the rank of Bvt. Maj. Gen. now. For this reason, and for his services during the rebellion, I recommend this." ALS, Delbert S. Wenzlick, St. Louis County, Mo. On the same day, USG wrote to the AG. "Issue order, obtaining first the consent of the Sec. of War, assigning Gen. Rousseau to the command of the Dept. of the Columbia, giving the authority to relieve Gn. Steele at any time between now and the 1st day of November 1867. Gen. Steele, on being relieved, will be allowed six months delay in reporting at his regimental Hd Qrs." ALS, DNA, RG 94, Letters Received, 258A 1867. Bvt. Maj. Gen. Edward D. Townsend twice endorsed this letter, the second time on April 29. "Submitted to the President by me April 18, 1867—The President directed me to say to Genl Grant that he wished the General would not issue the order 'till he saw him." "General Grant directs that this order be issued to take effect from its date, April

15—1867—" AES, *ibid.* On June 19, Rousseau, Washington, D. C., wrote to USG. "I think under my orders I am entitled to commutation of quarters. But the Quartermaster at Louisville declined to pay me. The circumstances connected with the issuing these orders, and which you will recollect as transpiring in our interview with the President differ my case from what is ordinarily denominated a 'delay order.' On that occasion the President was very Explicit in his inquires as to whether my assignment to the command of the Department of the Columbia, would at all interfere with any other assignment of duty he might choose to make between that time and the first of Nov, and on your replying that it would not, he requested you to make such orders in the premises as you deemed proper. The orders had then been before him for his approval about three weeks, and were not approved for the reason indicated by the President in the conversation before referred to. So I have no doubt that the President understood and desired that I should remain in reach of orders until it was time to start for my command, and that my delay at Louisville was under an order to do so rather than a permission, and that therefore I am justly entitled to commutation of quarters at that point. I respectfully ask for such action in the matter as may be thought proper." ALS, *ibid.*, 282R 1867. On the same day, USG endorsed this letter. "Respectfully refered to the Sec. of War. Gen. Rousseau was assigned to command of the Dept. of the Columbia with the understanding on the part of the President that he should delay at Louisville to be available for other duty should he be wanted. Under these circumstances I recommend that commutation be allowed." AES, *ibid.*

On April 30, Richard H. Rousseau, Jr., Washington, D. C., wrote to Secretary of War Edwin M. Stanton requesting an appointment in the U.S. Army, endorsed by USG on May 3. "Respectfully refered to the Sec. of War. This applicant not having served as a volunteer is not elegible for appointment to an *original* vacancy. I would not recommend his appointment to any other at least until the present 1st Class at West Point graduates & receives appointments." AES, *ibid.*, ACP, R7 CB 1869. On Dec. 25, Rousseau, Jr., 2nd lt., 1st Cav., Portland, Ore., wrote to USG tendering his resignation which was favorably endorsed by Gen. Rousseau on Dec. 26 and by USG on Jan. 23, 1868. ES, *ibid.* On May 29, 1867, Maj. George K. Leet favorably endorsed Gen. Rousseau's request for the assignment of 2nd Lt. David Q. Rousseau, 5th Cav., as an aide. AES, *ibid.*, Letters Received, 226R 1867.

To William H. Seward

Washington City,
August 15 /67.

HON. WM H. SEWARD, SECRETARY.
SIR:

In reply to your communication of the 13th inst., respecting *Gov. Ballard*,[1] I have the honor to state that enquiry having been made of *General Halleck*, he has reported as follows.

"I have no reason to think that Gov. Ballard is neglectful or inefficient, or the pease & safety of *the inhabitants of Idaho* are endangered—I will cause investigation."

Very respectfully
Your obt. servant,
U. S. GRANT.
Secr'y of War Ad interim.

Df, DNA, RG 107, Letters Received from Bureaus; copy, *ibid.*, Letters Sent to the President. On Aug. 13, 1867, Secretary of State William H. Seward had written to USG. "It is represented that the neglect and inefficiency of Governor Ballard in the exercise of his duty as Superintendent of Indian Affairs in the Territory of Idaho renders his continuance in Office hazardous to the peace and safety of the inhabitants. You will oblige this Department by informing me whether the state of our Indian relations in Idaho and vicinity is of such a character as to demand unusual activity and efficiency in the Governor, and justify an immediate suspension for such a degree of neglect or incapacity as might, otherwise and in view of the failure of the Senate at its late session, to ratify the nomination of a successor, be tolerated for a time without danger." LS, *ibid.*, Letters Received from Bureaus. On Aug. 16, U.S. Delegate Edward D. Holbrook of Idaho Territory wrote to USG. "Not being able to see you I submit these papers in addition to the many on file in the Department of State—The present Gov is neglecting every interest in the Territory and I trust he may be suspended—" ALS, *ibid.*, RG 59, Idaho Territorial Papers.

On Aug. 30, USG wrote to Seward. "In addition to the information respecting Governor Ballard, sent to your Department on the 15th instant, I have the honor to enclose herewith a copy of a telegram received this day from Major General Halleck." Copies, *ibid.*, RG 94, Letters Received, 566P 1867; *ibid.*, RG 107, Letters Sent to the President. The enclosure is *ibid.*, RG 94, Letters Received, 566P 1867. On Aug. 31, Seward wrote to USG. "I have the honor to acknowledge the receipt of your letter of the 30th instant, transmitting a copy of a telegram, received from Major General Halleck, of the 30th instant." LS, *ibid.*, RG 107, Letters Received from Bureaus. On Sept. 27, USG wrote to Seward. "Your letter of the 13th August to this Department, respecting the alleged inefficiency of Governor Ballard as Indian Agent in Idaho, was duly received and the telegraphic replies of General Halleck, to whom the subject was referred for investigation, have already been communicated to you. I now send in addition copies of reports on the subject just received from Generals Halleck and Steele." LS, *ibid.*, RG 59, Idaho Territorial Papers. The enclosures are *ibid.* On Oct. 4, USG wrote to Seward. "In addition to the reports from General Halleck and General Steele, heretofore transmitted to you from this Department respecting Governor Ballard's administration of Indian Affairs in Idaho, I have the honor to send herewith for your information a copy of a telegram on the same subject received last evening from General Halleck. 'San Francisco, October 3d 1867. Inspection report of Lieutenant Colonel Roger Jones (Assistant Inspector General) confirms opinion of General Steele heretofore communicated

in regard to Governor Ballard and Indian Affairs in Idaho. Everything is satis-
factory. (Signed) H. W. HALLECK.' " LS, *ibid.* On Oct. 7, Seward wrote to USG.
"I have the honor to acknowledge the receipt of your letter of the 4th instant,
enclosing a copy of a telegram of the 3d of September, ultimo, from General
Halleck, in regard to Governor Ballard and Indian affairs in Idaho." LS, *ibid.*,
RG 107, Letters Received from Bureaus.

1. Republican David W. Ballard, confirmed as governor of Idaho Territory
on April 10, 1866, remained in office through the Tenure of Office Act. See Merrill D. Beal and Merle W. Wells, *History of Idaho* (New York, 1959), I, 381–89.
On Jan. 14, 1870, U.S. Representative Benjamin F. Whittemore of S. C., Washington, D. C., wrote to USG submitting a petition requesting Ballard's retention
in office. LS, DNA, RG 59, Letters of Application and Recommendation. Petitions
addressed to USG for and against the retention of Ballard are *ibid.* On July 12,
Ballard, Boise City, wrote to USG. "As I desire to leave the Territory on the
16th day of this Month, I hereby tender my resignation, as Governor of Idaho to
take effect on that day. With the most Sincere wish for your good health, through
the distant years of the future; and for the Success of your wise and patriotic
administration . . ." LS, Idaho State Historical Society, Boise, Idaho.

To Andrew Johnson

Washington, D, C, Aug. 17th *1867*.

HIS EXCELLENCY, A. JOHNSON,
PRESIDENT OF THE U, STATES
SIR:

I am in receipt of your order of this date directing the assign-
ment of Gen. G. H. Thomas[1] to the command of the 5th Military
District; Gen. G. H. Sheridan[2] to ~~the command of~~ the Dept. of the
Mo. & Gen. Hancock to the Dept. of the Cumberland; also of your
note of this date (inclosing these ~~directions~~ instructions) saying:
"Before you issue instructions to carry into effect the enclosed order
I would be pleased to hear any suggestions you may deem necessary
respecting the assignments to which the order refers."

I am pleased to avail myself of this invitation to urge, earnestly
urge, urge in the name of a patriotic people who have sacrificed
Hundreds of thousands of loyal lives, and Thousands of Millions
of treasure to preserve the integrity and union of this Country that
this order be not insisted on. It is unmistakably the expressed wish

of the Country that Gen. Sheridan should not be removed from his present command. ~~He has executed the laws of Congress faithfully and not in the interest of clique or party~~

This is a republic where the will of the people is the law of the land. I beg that their voice may be heard.

Gn. Sheridan has performed his civil duties faithfully and intelligently. His removal ~~can~~ will only be regarded as an effort to defeat the laws of Congress. It will be interpreted by the un reconstructed element in the South, those who did all they could to break up this government by arms, and now wish to be the only element consulted as to the method of restoring order, as a triumph. It will embolden them to renewed opposition to the will of the loyal masses, believing [that] they have the Executive with them.

The services of Gen. Thomas in ~~batteling~~ [battling] for the union entitles him to some consideration. He has repeatedly entered his protest ~~to~~ [against] being assigned to either of the five Military Districts and especially to being assigned to relieve Gen. Sheridan.

Gen. Hancock ought not to be removed from where he is. His ~~d~~Department is a complicated one which will take~~ing some time for~~ a new Commander some time to become acquainted with. ~~it~~ It ~~will be atten~~ Gen. ~~Hancock is also a Member of on~~ Board ~~of Indian Commission, provided for by Act of Congress, which he ought not to be relieved from now.~~ There are Military reasons, pecuniary reasons, and above all patriotic reasons why this order should not be insisted upon.

I beg to refer to a ~~private~~ letter, ~~whi~~ marked private, which I wrote to the President when first consulted on the subject of the change in the War Dept. It ~~shows~~ bears upon the subject of this removal and I had hoped ~~silenced led to its abandonment.~~ would have prevented it.

> [I have the honor to be
> With great respect
> Your Obt. svt.
> U. S. Grant
> General U. S. A.
> Sec. of War ad interim]

ADf (bracketed material not in USG's hand), PPRF; ADfS (the last two pages of an earlier Df), *ibid.* On Aug. 17, 1867, USG rewrote his letter to President Andrew Johnson. "I am in receipt of your order of this date directing the assignment of Gen. G. H. Thomas to the Command of the 5th Military District; Gen. Sheridan to the Dept. of the Mo. and Gen. Hancock to the Dept. of the Cumberland: Also of your note of this date, (enclosing these instructions) saying; 'Before you issue instructions to carry into effect the enclosed order I would be pleased to hear any suggestions you may deem necessary respecting the assignments to which the order refers.' I am pleased to avail myself of this invitation to urge, earnestly urge, urge in the name of a patriotic people who have sacrificed Hundreds of thousands of loyal lives, and Thousands of Millions of treasure to preserve the integrity and Union of this Country, that this order be not insisted on. It is unmistakably the expressed wish of the Country that Gen. Sheridan should not be removed from his present Command. This is a republic where the will of the people is the law of the land. I beg that their voice may be heard. Gen. Sheridan has performed his civil duties faithfully and intelligently. His removal will only be regarded as an effort to defeat the laws of Congress. It will be interpreted by the un reconstructed ~~in~~ element in the South, those who did all they could to break up this government by arms, and now wish to be the only element consulted as to the method of restoring order as a triumph. It will embo[lde]n them to renewed opposition to the will of the loyal Masses, believing that they have the Executive with them. The services of Gen. Thomas in battling for the Union entitle him to some consideration. He has repeatedly entered his protest ~~to~~ against being assigned to either of the five Military Districts, and especially to being assigned to relieve Gen. Sheridan. Gen. Hancock ought not to be removed from where he is. His Department is a complicated one which will take a new Commander some time to become acquainted with. ~~Gen. Hancock is also a~~ There are Military reasons, pecuniary reasons, and, above all, patriotic reasons why this order should not be insisted on. I beg to refer to a letter, marked private, which I wrote to the ~~p~~President when first consulted on the subject of the change in the War Department It bears upon the subject of this removal and I had hoped would have prevented it" ALS, DLC-Andrew Johnson. See letters to Andrew Johnson, Aug. 1, 26, 1867; letter to Maj. Gen. Philip H. Sheridan, Sept. 8, 1867.

On Aug. 17, Johnson had written to USG. "Before you issue instructions to carry into effect the enclosed order, I would be pleased to hear any suggestions you may deem necessary respecting the assignments to which the order refers." LS, DNA, RG 94, Letters Received, 869P 1867. Johnson enclosed an order of the same day. "Major General *George H. Thomas* is hereby assigned to the command of the Fifth Military District, created by the Act of Congress passed on the second day of March, 1867. Major General *P. H. Sheridan* is hereby assigned to the command of the Department of the Missouri. Major General *Winfield S. Hancock* is hereby assigned to the command of the Department of the Cumberland. The *Secretary of War ad interim* will give the necessary instructions to carry this order into effect." DS, *ibid.* On Aug. 19, Bvt. Maj. Gen. Edward D. Townsend issued General Orders No. 77 incorporating and amplifying Johnson's order. Copy (printed), DLC-Andrew Johnson.

On Aug. 19, Johnson wrote to USG. "I have received your communication of the 17th instant, and thank you for the promptness with which you have submitted your views respecting the assignments directed in my order of that date.

When I stated, in my unofficial note of the 17th, that I would be pleased to hear any suggestions you might deem necessary upon the subject, it was not my intention to ask from you a formal report, but rather to invite a verbal statement of any reasons affecting the public interests which, in your opinion, would render the order inexpedient. Inasmuch, however, as you have embodied your suggestions in a written communication, it is proper that I should make some reply. You earnestly urge that the order be not insisted on, remarking that 'it is unmistakably the expressed wish of the country that General Sheridan should not be removed from his present command.' While I am cognizant of the efforts that have been made to retain Gen'l Sheridan in command of the 5th Military District, I am not aware that the question has ever been submitted to the people themselves for determination. It certainly would be unjust to the army to assume that, in the opinion of the nation, he alone is capable of commanding the States of Louisiana & Texas, and that were he for any cause removed, no other General in the military service of the United States would be competent to fill his place. Genl Thomas, whom I have designated as his successor, is well known to the country. Having won high and honorable distinction in the field, he has since, in the execution of the responsible duties of a department commander, exhibited great ability, sound discretion, and sterling patriotism. He has not failed, under the most trying circumstances, to enforce the laws, to preserve peace and order, to encourage the restoration of civil authority, and to promote as far as possible a spirit of reconciliation. His administration of the Department of the Cumberland will certainly compare most favorably with that of Gen'l Sheridan in the Fifth Military District. There, affairs appear to be in a disturbed condition, and a bitter spirit of antagonism seems to have resulted from Genl. Sheridan's management. He has rendered himself exceedingly obnoxious by the manner in which he has exercised even the powers conferred by Congress, and still more so by a resort to authority not granted by law, or necessary to its faithful and efficient execution. His rule has, in fact, been one of absolute tyranny, without reference to the principles of our government or the nature of our free institutions. The state of affairs which has resulted from the course he has pursued has seriously interfered with a harmonious a harmonious, satisfactory, and speedy execution of the Acts of Congress, and is alone sufficient to justify a change. His removal, therefore, cannot 'be regarded as an effort to defeat the laws of Congress,' for the object is to facilitate their execution, through an officer who has never failed to obey the statutes of the land, and to exact, within his jurisdiction, a like obedience from others. It cannot 'be interpreted by the un-reconstructed element in the South—those who did all they could to break up this Government by arms, and now wish to be the only element consulted as to the method of restoring order—as a triumph;' for, as intelligent men, they must know that the mere change of military commanders cannot alter the law, and that General Thomas will be as much bound by its requirements as General Sheridan. It cannot 'embolden them to renewed opposition to the will of of the loyal masses, believing that they have the Executive with them,' for they are perfectly familiar with the antecedents of the President, and know that he has not obstructed the faithful execution of any act of Congress. No one, as you are aware, has a higher appreciation than myself of the services of Genl. Thomas, and no one would be less inclined to assign him to a command not entirely consonant with his wishes. Knowing him, as I do, I cannot think that he will hesitate for a moment to obey any order having in view a complete and speedy restoration of the Union, in the preservation of which he has rendered such important and valuable services. General Hancock, known to the whole country as a gallant, able, and patriotic soldier, will, I have no doubt, sustain his high reputation in any position to which he may be assigned. If, as you observe, the Department which he will leave is a complicated one, I feel confident that, under the guidance and instruction of General Sherman, General Sheridan will soon become familiar with its necessities, and will avail himself of the opportunity afforded by the Indian troubles for the display of the energy, enterprise, and daring which gave him so enviable a reputation during our recent civil struggle. In assuming that it is the expressed wish of the people that General Sheridan should not be removed from his present command, you remark that 'this is a Republic, where the will of the people is the law of the land,' and 'beg that their voice may be heard.' This, is, indeed, a Republic, based, however, upon a written Constitution. That Constitution is the combined and expressed will of the people, and their voice is law when reflected in the manner which that instrument prescribes. While one of its provisions makes the President Commander-in-Chief of the Army and Navy, another requires 'that 'he shall take care that the laws be faithfully executed.' Believing that a change in the command of the Fifth Military District is absolutely necessary for a faithful execution of the laws, I have issued the order which is the subject of this correspondence, and in thus exercising a power that inheres in the Executive, under the Constitution, as Commander-in-Chief of the military and naval forces, I am discharging a duty required of me by the will of the Nation, as formally declared in the supreme law of the land. By his oath, the Executive is solemnly bound, 'to the best of his ability, to preserve, protect, and defend the Constitution,' and although, in times of great excitement, it may be lost to public view, it is his duty, without regard to the consequences to himself, to hold sacred and to enforce any and all of its provisions. Any other course would lead to the destruction of the Republic; for the Constitution once abolished, there would be no Congress for the exercise of legislative powers: no Executive, to see that the laws are faithfully executed; no judiciary, to afford to the citizen protection for life, limb, and property. Usurpation would inevitably follow, and a despotism be fixed upon the people, in violation of their combined and expressed will—In conclusion, I fail to perceive any 'military,' 'pecuniary,' or 'patriotic reasons' why this order should not be carried into effect. You will remember that in the first instance, I did not consider General Sheridan the most suitable officer for the command of the 5th Military District. Time has strengthened my convictions upon this point, and has led me to the conclusion that patriotic considerations demand that he should be superseded by an officer who, while he will faithfully execute the law, will at the same time give more general satisfaction to the whole people, white and black, North and South." LS, DNA, RG 94, Letters Received, 869P 1867.

1. On Aug. 17, 3:00 P.M., USG telegraphed to Maj. Gen. George H. Thomas. "Please mail copy of your last letter to Sec. of War ~~protesting~~ objecting to assignment to 5th Military District. The letter cannot be found here." ALS (telegram sent), *ibid.*, RG 107, Telegrams Collected (Bound); telegram sent, *ibid.*; copies, *ibid.*, RG 108, Telegrams Sent; *ibid.*, RG 393, Dept. of the Tenn., Telegrams Received; DLC-USG, V, 56. On Aug. 19, Bvt. Maj. Gen. William D. Whipple, adjt. for Thomas, Louisville, forwarded to USG a copy of Thomas's letter of July 4 to Secretary of War Edwin M. Stanton. "A rumor has reached

me in a somewhat authentic form that I may yet be detailed to relieve Genl. Sheridan in command of the 5th Military Dist. I must confess my surprize that such an intention should still be entertained by the President after my last interview with him. By my earnest application to be allowed to remain in command of this Dep't rather than undertake the task of reconstructing the states composing the third Military Dist, stating my reasons for making the application—I also endeavored to impress upon his mind not only how repugnant such politico-military duties were to my mind but also how little influence I could hope to exercise on the citizens of those or any other of the states lately in rebellion, to lead them back to a sense of allegiance to the Government, or to a proper appreciation of their own present and future welfare. With the same sentiments existing in the minds of the citizens of Louisiana and Texas it would be as useless an undertaking on my part to attempt to lead the minds of those people in a loyal direction as in the States of Alabama, Georgia and Florida. The relief of Genl. Sheridan will be sure to revive the hopes and energies of the opponents of reconstruction in those states and in a like proportion embarrass the efforts of his successor and should I be unfortunately selected to take his duties, their hopes of success would be doubled. I could not hope to effect the least good, not even if the people believed I disapproved of his course—I therefore earnestly urge that he may not be relieved but be permitted to complete the service he has commenced with so much vigor and earnestness." Copy, DNA, RG 108, Letters Received.

On Aug. 21, 11:30 A.M., Bvt. Lt. Col. Alexander B. Hasson, surgeon and medical director, Dept. of the Cumberland, Louisville, telegraphed to USG. "General Thomas is absent in West Virginia and has probably not yet seen his orders. He has been under medical treatment this summer for an affection of his liver and it would be a great risk for him to go South at this time" Telegram received (at 3:45 P.M.), *ibid.*, RG 107, Telegrams Collected (Bound); *ibid.*, RG 108, Telegrams Received; *ibid.*, Letters Received; copies, *ibid.*; *ibid.*, RG 393, Dept. of the Tenn., Telegrams Sent; DLC-USG, V, 55. On Aug. 22, USG endorsed a telegram received. "Respectfully forwarded to the President for his information, and recommending a suspension of the order making change in military Commanders." ES, DNA, RG 108, Letters Received. On Aug. 23, Johnson endorsed the telegram received. "In view of the precarious condition of Genl Thomas's health, as represented in the within despatch of Surgeon Hasson, Genl Thomas will, until further orders, remain in command of the Department of the Cumberland." ES, *ibid.*

On Aug. 22, Thomas, Lewisburg, West Va., had written to USG. "I have just seen a copy of the Richmond Despatch of the 20th inst the Editorial of which states that General Sheridan had been relieved by order of the President and sent to the Dept of the Missouri that I had been assigned to the Command of the Fifth Mil. District & Genl Hancock had been assigned to the command of the Department of the Cumberland. Why I should have been assigned to the Command of the Fifth Military District I cannot conceive. I cannot hope to be of any more service in executing the Reconstruction of the states composing that District than Genl Sheridan nor can the citizens of those states be in the least benefited by substituting me for General Sheridan; on the contrary knowing my sentiments I fear that the reconstruction of those states will be very much retarded, if it does not fail altogether, by appointing me to that Command. If it be true that General Sheridan has been removed I earnestly hope in consideratn of my services that General Hancock to whose Department Genl Sheridan is reported to have been assigned, may be designated to relieve him—rather than relieve me in command of my Department—I believe the interests of the service will be eminently more advanced, by permitting me to remain in my present Command, where I believe I have been enabled to secure comparative peace & quiet, than to place me where I could be of no use whatever—I shall be in Louisville by the 27th of this month." ALS, USG 3. On Aug. 24, 10:30 A.M., USG telegraphed to Thomas. "Orders go by mail today relieving you for the present from orders No. 77. (Seventy-seven)" ALS (telegram sent), DNA, RG 107, Telegrams Collected (Bound); telegram sent, *ibid.*; copies, *ibid.*, RG 108, Telegrams Sent; *ibid.*, RG 393, Dept. of the Tenn., Telegrams Received; DLC-USG, V, 55. On Aug. 29, 12:30 P.M., Thomas, Louisville, telegraphed to USG. "I returned yesterday and received your telegram of Aug 24th & the order referred to there in relieving me for the present from orders No 77." Telegram received (at 3:00 P.M.), DNA, RG 107, Telegrams Collected (Bound); *ibid.*, RG 108, Telegrams Received; copies, *ibid.*, RG 393, Dept. of the Tenn., Telegrams Sent.

2. On Aug. 15, USG telegraphed to Maj. Gen. Philip H. Sheridan. "Circular enclosing Copy of Jury order in Texas is intended to secure regulations in all the districts giving such juries as will insure equal justice to all classes of Citizens. ~~you~~ it need not be construed that the Texas order is to be adopted verbatum" Telegram received, *ibid.*, 5th Military District, Telegrams Received; copy, DLC-USG, V, 56. See telegram to Bvt. Maj. Gen. Edward O. C. Ord, July 30, 1867; letter to Maj. Gen. Daniel E. Sickles, Aug. 24, 1867. On Aug. 15, Sheridan, New Orleans, telegraphed to USG. "I have rec'd the copy of the Jury circular & also your telegram of this date I am glad you have given some latitude because while the circular was Just & proper for Texas at the time it was issued it would now when affairs have progressed so far in the state be very embarrasing to issue orders on the subject of empannelling Juries as soon as the returns were all in & officially announced but have had some embarrasment as to the oath to be required. If the oath in circular thirteen 13 is adopted it will cut off from the Jury list a very large portion of the whites who are considered loyal enough to vote to make the laws but not loyal enough to sit on Juries to execute them after presenting these points Please give me your advice for it will give place to much discussion My own opinion is so far as this state is concerned it would be best to let all who are allowed to vote sit on Juries" Telegram received (at 3:00 P.M.), DNA, RG 107, Telegrams Collected (Bound); *ibid.*, RG 108, Telegrams Received; copies, DLC-USG, V, 55; (2) DLC-Philip H. Sheridan. On Aug. 16, 10:30 A.M., USG telegraphed to Sheridan. "Make exactly such Jury order as You think best suited to your command. It would probably be well to make elegeble as Jurors all who can hold office under the law." ALS (telegram sent), DNA, RG 107, Telegrams Collected (Bound); telegram sent, *ibid.*; telegram received (at noon), *ibid.*, RG 393, 5th Military District, Telegrams Received. On Aug. 17, Sheridan telegraphed to USG. "I have the honor to report a very good condition of affairs in my command I have to day issued the order for election of Convention, and will in a day or two issue the necessary order on the Jury question and I think on the basis that all who are entitled to vote are entitled to sit on juries. I think this view is the best for this State under its present stage of reconstruction. Very encouraging reports are now coming in to me from persons who heretofore opposed the law, expressing the greatest desire to, in every way, comply with all its conditions" LS (telegram sent), *ibid.*, RG 107, Telegrams

Collected (Bound); telegram received (at 4:00 P.M.), *ibid.*; *ibid.*, RG 108, Telegrams Received.

On Aug. 23, Sheridan telegraphed to USG. "I am ready to turn over as soon as General Thomas arrives, and will then proceed direct to Washington. Can I publish the copy of letter sent to me by General Porter dated August 1st 1867." LS (telegram sent), *ibid.*, RG 107, Telegrams Collected (Bound); telegram received (at noon), *ibid.*; *ibid.*, RG 108, Telegrams Received. At 5:00 P.M., USG telegraphed to Sheridan. "*Cypher private*) . . . I would not publish Gen. Porter's letter now. You need no vindications and in proper time all will become public." ALS (telegram sent), *ibid.*, RG 107, Telegrams Collected (Bound); telegram sent, *ibid.*; copies, *ibid.*, RG 108, Telegrams Sent; DLC-USG, V, 56. See letter to Andrew Johnson, Aug. 1, 1867. On Aug. 24, USG telegraphed to Sheridan. "Gen. Thomas orders to relieve you are suspended for the present. ~~Continue the policy heretofore~~ Orders will be sent by mail. ~~Your course~~ Relax nothing in consequence of probable change of commands." ALS (telegram sent), DNA, RG 107, Telegrams Collected (Bound); telegram sent, *ibid.*; copies, *ibid.*, RG 108, Telegrams Sent; DLC-USG, V, 56. On Aug. 30, Sheridan telegraphed to USG. "On being relieved by General Griffin I respectfully request a leave of absence for 30 days with permission to apply for an extension I had some private interests with Gen D. A. Russell who was killed in the battle of Opeqon October nineteenth 19 1864 which I desire to settle & then I want some rest I have been on active duty fourteen 14 years continuously having had in that period only one leave of 20 days & that nearly 4 years ago. I have I believe given up during this period every consideration of personal comfort & now beg this indulgence." Telegram received (at 11:20 A.M.), DNA, RG 107, Telegrams Collected (Bound); *ibid.*, RG 108, Telegrams Received; copies, DLC-USG, V, 55; (2) DLC-Philip H. Sheridan. On Aug. 31, 12:48 P.M., USG telegraphed to Sheridan. "As soon as you relieve Gen. Hancock direct the officer next in rank to yourself to take temporary command and come to Washington. You shall have all the leave you want." ALS (telegram sent), DNA, RG 107, Telegrams Collected (Bound); telegram sent, *ibid.*; copies, *ibid.*, RG 108, Letters Sent; DLC-USG, V, 56. On the same day, Sheridan telegraphed to USG. "I respectfully request that Brevet Colonel George A Forsythe Major (9th) ninth Cavalry now on duty with me may be permitted to accompany me. his duties here are of no essential importance to my successor as the work is nearly done I also respectfully request permission to take with me private Henry Brown Company G sixth 6 Cavalry—he has been my Confidential Emanuensis for a long period and is also familiar with all my private records of the War which I have been working on in this City when I had time" Telegram received (at 2:00 P.M.), DNA, RG 107, Telegrams Collected (Bound); *ibid.*, RG 108, Telegrams Received; copies, DLC-USG, V, 55; (2) DLC-Philip H. Sheridan. At 2:30 P.M., USG telegraphed to Sheridan. "You are authorized to take with you Maj. Forsythe & Brown." ALS (telegram sent), DNA, RG 107, Telegrams Collected (Bound); telegram sent, *ibid.*; copies, *ibid.*, RG 108, Telegrams Sent; DLC-USG, V, 56.

To John M. Binckley

August 19 *1867*.

TO THE HONORABLE THE ATTORNEY GENERAL.
SIR.

The communication from your office dated the 17th instant has been received conveying the President's instructions to submit for his personal examination any of the affidavits, also a petition for the pardon of one Dunham, which appeared and are alluded to in the New York Times of the 15th instant, and which the correspondent says are on file in the Attorney General's office, the Bureau of Military Justice and the War Department.

In reply I have to inform you that careful search has been made, and it does not appear that there is no record that any such papers are on file or have ever been received in the War Department, or in the Bureau of Military Justice.

I am, Sir,
Very Respectfully
Your obdt. servt.
U. S. GRANT
Secretary of War [ad int.]

LS (brackets in original), DNA, RG 94, Letters Received, 471A 1867. On Aug. 17, 1867, Act. Attorney Gen. John M. Binckley had written to USG. "I have been directed by the President to address to each of the Heads of Departments the following communication: Your attention is respectfully invited to the enclosed slip from the *New York Times* of the 15th inst., purporting to be a communication from a correspondent of that paper, writing from this city, in which he professes to recite at length a number of affidavits, and also a petition for the pardon of one Dunham, and states that he copied them all from the originals, which, he says, are on file in the Attorney General's Office, the Bureau of Military Justice, & the War Department, & says also that they are on file in the proper Departments, where, he furthermore states, many documents of like character are on file. I have to state, for the information of the Heads of the several Departments, that there has not been found, upon due investigation, any papers corresponding to, or resembling in any degree, those recited in this publication, in the archives of the Attorney General's Office, except those which were recited in full in a Report from this Office addressed to the President, under date of the 5th inst., in relation to an application for the pardon of Charles A. Dunham. The President instructs me to say that if any documents or papers resembling those recited in this publication are in the archives of the government, he desires that they be immediately submitted for his personal examination. In the event of there not appearing to be in the Department committed to your charge, nor in any Bureau or Office thereof, any papers or documents corresponding with the publication referred to, the President further directs me to request that your Report may be as prompt as your convenience will allow." LS, *ibid.* On Aug. 19, Bvt. Maj. Gen. Edward D. Townsend wrote to USG. "In compliance with your instructions I have made careful search on the files of the War Department and of this office, for the affidavits in the New York Times of the 15th instant, alluded to in the letter of assistant Attorney General J. M. Binckley, and have respectfully to report that no such papers appear ever to have been received in either office. The Judge Advocate General reports 'that no such documents as those referred to are or have been on the files of' the Bureau of Military Justice." ALS, *ibid.* For Charles A. Dunham (Sanford Conover) see *PUSG*, 15, 295; *New York Times*, Aug. 10, 15, 1867; Howard K. Beale, ed., *Diary of Gideon Welles* (New York, 1960), III, 143–46, 165, 172–73.

To Bvt. Maj. Gen. Daniel H. Rucker

Washington, D, C, Aug. 21st *1867*.

Bvt. Maj. Gn. D. H. Rucker,
Act. Q. M. Gen. U. S. A.
General:

Sr. Romero, Ministe[r] from Mexico, expresses a desire to purchase Ten Thousand suits, complete, of Uniform as soon as he goes to Mexico and can make arrangements for the payment of it. He wants to get however, before leaving here a statement of the price which he will have to pay. Please inform him if the purchase can be made at private sale, and at what price, or if it would be better to make the purchase, through an agent, at Auction.

Very respectfully
your obt. svt.
U. S. Grant
General

ALS, DNA, RG 92, Consolidated Correspondence, Mexican Minister. On Aug. 22, 1867, Bvt. Maj. Gen. Daniel H. Rucker, act. q. m. gen., wrote to USG. "I have the honor to acknowledge the receipt of your letter of yesterday, in relation to a proposed purchase by the Mexican Minister of ten thousand Suits of uniform clothing, and to enclose a copy of a communication addressed to that gentleman on the Subject, in compliance with your instructions. The clothing now on hand, was purchased during the war, at very high prices, much higher than could now be obtained for it at auction. I have therefore taken the regulation prices of 1861, at which I would recommend the Sale of the clothing to Mr. Romero, at private sale, provided it meets the approval of the Secretary of War." LS, *ibid.*, RG 108, Letters Received. The enclosures are *ibid.* On the same day, Matías Romero, Mexican minister, wrote to Rucker. "I have had the honor to receive your kind letter of this date and the list accompanying it in regard to a purchase of ten thousand suits of uniform [clothing] for the Mexican Army. I am very much obliged to you for the prompt manner in which you have imparted to me the information contained in your letter, which will be communicated to my government." LS, *ibid.*, RG 92, Consolidated Correspondence, Mexican Minister.

To Maj. Gen. Philip H. Sheridan

Washington, Aug. 21st *1867*. [*1:10* P.M.]

MAJ. GN. P. H. SHERIDAN,
NEW ORLEANS, LA.

I have directed the Surgeon Gen. to employ nurses in New Orleans.

U. S. GRANT
General

ALS (telegram sent), DNA, RG 107, Telegrams Collected (Bound); telegram sent, *ibid.*; copies, *ibid.*, RG 108, Telegrams Sent; DLC-USG, V, 56. On Aug. 20, 1867, Maj. Gen. Philip H. Sheridan had telegraphed to USG. "The yellow fever is on the increase & it looks as though it would become Epidemic. We have had it in two 2 Companies of first 1 Infantry & among the Clerks at these Head Quarters severely. Four 4 Officers are down with it—two 2 are out of danger but I have serious fears for Captain DeRussey Lieut Smith son of C. F. Smith is perhaps beyond recovery. I think it of the utmost importance that the Medical Department be authorized to hire nurses—soldiers do not make good nurses for this disease. General Mower is down today, his case appears light but has not yet developed—" Telegram received (at 3:00 P.M.), DNA, RG 107, Telegrams Collected (Bound); *ibid.*, RG 108, Telegrams Received; copies (2), *ibid.*, Letters Received; DLC-USG, V, 55; (2) DLC-Philip H. Sheridan. On Aug. 21, Sheridan telegraphed to USG. "I telegraphed you yesterday about the yellow fever & the dangerous condition of Lieut Smith. he had then been given up as past recovery but during the night changed for the better. I still advise the Employment of nurses by the Medical Dep't. we have five 5 or six 6 new cases in the troops since yesterday." Telegram received (at 12:40 P.M.), DNA, RG 107, Telegrams Collected (Bound); *ibid.*, RG 108, Telegrams Received; copies, *ibid.*, Letters Received; DLC-USG, V, 55; (2) DLC-Philip H. Sheridan.

On July 1, Sheridan had telegraphed to USG. "We have had a few deaths from Yellow fever in this City Lt Dewey of the fourth (4) Cavy died yesterday bringing the disease from Indianola Texas, We have had no case among the troops here as yet" Telegram received (at 5:00 P.M.), DNA, RG 107, Telegrams Collected (Bound); *ibid.*, RG 108, Telegrams Received; copies, DLC-USG, V, 55; (2) DLC-Philip H. Sheridan. On Aug. 6, Sheridan telegraphed to USG. "The yellow fever of a malignant type is now Epidemic at all the Gulf ports of Texas—Doctor Taylor died of it yesterday. Two 2 other officers had previously died. It is prevailing in this City but not yet Epidemic. One 1 officer has died of it—Brevet Col Von Schroder formerly Adjt Gen of Gen Thomas staff died this morning of fever & Congestion of the brain—We have so far here & in Texas prevented its spread among the troops & in fact have had but few cases." Telegram received (at 2:50 P.M.), DNA, RG 107, Telegrams Collected (Bound); *ibid.*, RG 108, Telegrams Received; copies, *ibid.*, Letters Received; DLC-USG, V, 55; (2) DLC-Philip H. Sheridan. On Aug. 10, Sheridan telegraphed to USG. "I very much fear from the indications that the yellow fever of a malignant type may become Epidemic in this City & would respectfully advise that officers absent from their Command should be permitted to remain absent until 15th of Oct. Acting Assistant Surgeon G. W. Shields died of malignant yellow fever in this City this morning" Telegram received (at 12:05 P.M.), DNA, RG 107, Telegrams Collected (Bound); *ibid.*, RG 108, Telegrams Received; copies, *ibid.*, RG 94, Letters Received, 1071M 1867; *ibid.*, RG 108, Letters Received; DLC-USG, V, 55; (2) DLC-Philip H. Sheridan. On the same day, Bvt. Maj. Gen. Edward D. Townsend issued a memorandum giving such permission. Copy, DNA, RG 108, Letters Received.

On Aug. 19, Sheridan wrote to USG. "The yellow fever has abated but very little on the coast of Texas as yet. At Galveston and Indianola it has been very bad and has interfered to some extent with the public service, from the stampede and fright of employees In this city it has as yet only taken hold of two companies, and there are now some signs of improvement. We have now four officers down with it belonging to these companies. One of them,—Lieutenant Smith, son of C. F. Smith.—is very dangerously ill. Lieutenant Alseph of the Engineers took the disease from here to Fort Morgan and there died." LS, *ibid.* On Aug. 23, Sheridan telegraphed to USG. "There is still much distress among the Officers & their families at Galveston from yellow fever. Mrs Colonel Abert is dead also Lieut Kirkmans wife—Col Abert is very low—Mrs Dr Adams very low. Colonel Howell is better. General Mower is better. There are five 5 other Officers down with it here but they are all but one doing well." Telegram received (at 3:35 P.M.), *ibid.*, RG 107, Telegrams Collected (Bound); (at 3:30 P.M.) *ibid.*, RG 108, Telegrams Received; copies, DLC-USG, V, 55; (2) DLC-Philip H. Sheridan. At 3:30 P.M., USG telegraphed to Bvt. Maj. Gen. Charles Griffin. "Telegraph me each day the condition of Col. Abert until he recovers. Stop the dispatches now being sent to his family here." ALS (telegram sent), DNA, RG 107, Telegrams Collected (Bound); telegram sent, *ibid.*; copies, *ibid.*, RG 108, Telegrams Sent; DLC-USG, V, 56. On Aug. 24, Griffin, Galveston, telegraphed to USG. "Col Aberts symptoms not so favorable today as yesterday" Telegram received (at 4:30 P.M.), DNA, RG 107, Telegrams Collected (Bound); copies (one sent by mail), *ibid.*, RG 94, ACP, 406A CB 1863; *ibid.*, RG 393, Dept. of Tex., Letters Sent. On Aug. 25, Griffin telegraphed to USG. "*Colonel Abert* is worse, but little hope of his recovery." Copies (one sent by mail), *ibid.*, RG 94,

ACP, 406A CB 1863; *ibid.*, RG 393, Dept. of Tex., Letters Sent. On Aug. 26, Griffin telegraphed to USG. "Abert died at twelve (12) o'clock last night—" Telegram received (at 2:10 P.M.), *ibid.*, RG 107, Telegrams Collected (Bound); copies (one sent by mail), *ibid.*, RG 94, ACP, 406A CB 1863; *ibid.*, RG 393, Dept. of Tex., Letters Sent. On Aug. 27, 2:50 P.M., USG telegraphed to Griffin. "Send Col. Aberts children to Washington in care of some suitable person." ALS (telegram sent), *ibid.*, RG 107, Telegrams Collected (Bound); telegram sent, *ibid.*; copies, *ibid.*, RG 108, Telegrams Sent; DLC-USG, V, 56. On Aug. 28, Griffin telegraphed to USG. "Col Aberts children shall be sent north in a few days   They are well" Telegram received (at 7:00 P.M.), DNA, RG 107, Telegrams Collected (Bound); copies (one sent by mail), *ibid.*, RG 94, ACP, 406A CB 1863; *ibid.*, RG 393, Dept. of Tex., Letters Sent.

On Aug. 26, 10:52 A.M., USG had telegraphed to Sheridan. "You are authorized to move the troops serving about New Orleans & Galveston to such localities as you select for their health and if the public interest will admit of their removal. Of this latter you can judge." ALS (telegram sent), *ibid.*, RG 107, Telegrams Collected (Bound); telegram sent, *ibid.*; telegram received, *ibid.*, RG 393, 5th Military District, Telegrams Received. On Aug. 27, Sheridan telegraphed to USG. "I am in receipt of your telegram of yesterday. All the troops have been moved out of the City. The two 2 Companies in which the disease was Epidemic were moved out some time since & isolated. Lt Wallace adjutant 1st Inf'y died of yellow fever this morning." Telegram received (at 3:45 P.M.), *ibid.*, RG 107, Telegrams Collected (Bound); (at 3:25 P.M.) *ibid.*, RG 108, Telegrams Received; copies, DLC-USG, V, 55; (2) DLC-Philip H. Sheridan.

On Aug. 25, Sheridan had telegraphed to USG. "My cipher Operator is down with the yellow fever. This need not interfere with cipher despatches   I can get them translated by the old operator who is now here in the Quartermasters Office." Telegram received (at 10:00 A.M.), DNA, RG 107, Telegrams Collected (Bound); copies, DLC-USG, V, 55; (2) DLC-Philip H. Sheridan. On Sept. 3, Sheridan telegraphed to USG. "Mr Keefer Cipher Operator died today from yellow fever. It will be necessary to send an operator to take his place" Telegram received (at 6:00 P.M.), DNA, RG 107, Telegrams Collected (Bound); *ibid.*, RG 108, Telegrams Received; copies, DLC-USG, V, 55; (2) DLC-Philip H. Sheridan; DLC-Andrew Johnson. On Sept. 4, 11:00 A.M., USG telegraphed to Sheridan. "The Sup't of Military Telegraph has been directed to appoint Mr James Newell a former Employee of this Department & now in the telegraph office at New Orleans, to take temporary charge of the cipher held by Mr Keefer. It would be inexpedient to send an operator from here at this time." LS (telegram sent), DNA, RG 107, Telegrams Collected (Bound); telegram received, *ibid.*, RG 393, 5th Military District, Telegrams Received.

On Sept. 3, Sheridan telegraphed to USG. "The following telegram from Gen Griffin has just been rec'd & I respectfully forward it for the instructions of the Gen'l in Chief. The fever is fully Epedemic here. Army Surgeons will be ordered from here to Galveston without delay. Galveston Sept 3d 1867. Doctor Adams just taken with the fever. Dr Payne dying.   not a u. S. Surgeon at the post & private physcians all they can do. Impossible to leave affairs in this condition. Cannot I assume command of the fifth 5 Mil'y Dis't without going to New Orleans.   signed CHS GRIFFIN Bt Maj Gen" Telegram received (at 12:30 P.M.), *ibid.*, RG 107, Telegrams Collected (Bound); *ibid.*, RG 108, Telegrams

Received; copies, DLC-USG, V, 55; (2) DLC-Philip H. Sheridan; DLC-Andrew Johnson. At 1:57 P.M., USG telegraphed to Sheridan. "Gen. Griffin is authorized to retain his Hd Qrs. at Galveston as long as he deems necessary, until relieved by Gen. Hancock if he chooses." ALS (telegram sent), DNA, RG 107, Telegrams Collected (Bound); telegram sent, *ibid.*; copies, *ibid.*, RG 108, Telegrams Sent; DLC-USG, V, 56; DLC-Andrew Johnson; 5th Military District Papers, Duke University, Durham, N. C.

On Sept. 13, Capt. and Bvt. Maj. Henry A. Swartwout, 17th Inf., adjt. to Griffin, telegraphed to USG. "Gen Griffin was taken with the fever last evening Symptoms favorable this morning" Telegram received (at 10:00 P.M.), DNA, RG 107, Telegrams Collected (Bound); *ibid.*, RG 108, Telegrams Received; copies, *ibid.*, RG 393, Dept. of Tex., Letters Sent; DLC-USG, V, 55. On Sept. 15, Swartwout telegraphed to USG. "Gen Griffin will not live through the morning" Telegram received (at 10:45 A.M.), DNA, RG 107, Telegrams Collected (Bound); *ibid.*, RG 108, Telegrams Received; copy, DLC-USG, V, 55. At noon, USG telegraphed to Swartwout. "I am shocked to hear the dangerous condition of Gn. Griffin. Previous dispatches gave me great hope of his speedy recovery." ALS (telegram sent), DNA, RG 107, Telegrams Collected (Bound); copies, *ibid.*, RG 108, Telegrams Sent; DLC-USG, V, 56. At the same time, USG telegraphed to Bvt. Maj. Gen. Joseph J. Reynolds. "Assume command of the Dist. of Texas as Bvt. Maj. Gen." ALS (telegram sent), DNA, RG 107, Telegrams Collected (Bound); telegram sent, *ibid.*; copies, *ibid.*, RG 94, Letters Received, 514A 1867; *ibid.*, RG 108, Telegrams Sent; DLC-USG, V, 56.

On Sept. 16, Swartwout telegraphed to USG. "I request authority to order transportation home for Mrs Gen Griffin & one 1 attendant" Telegram received (misdated Sept. 18, received at 11:30 A.M.), DNA, RG 107, Telegrams Collected (Bound); (dated Sept. 16) *ibid.*, RG 108, Telegrams Received; copies (dated Sept. 15), *ibid.*, RG 393, Dept. of Tex., Letters Sent; (dated Sept. 16) DLC-USG, V, 55. On Sept. 18, 11:45 A.M., USG telegraphed to Swartwout. "Order transportation for Mrs. Griffin & attendent." ALS (telegram sent), DNA, RG 107, Telegrams Collected (Bound); telegram sent, *ibid.*; copies, *ibid.*, RG 108, Telegrams Sent; DLC-USG, V, 56. On Sept. 16, Maj. Gen. Oliver O. Howard had written to USG. "I have this morning received the sad intelligence of the death of Brevet Major General Charles Griffin, Colonel 35th U. S. Infantry. Assistant Commissioner of this Bureau for the State of Texas. In the death of General Griffin the public service has met with a heavy loss—His administration of the duties pertaining to this Bureau has been conducted with marked ability, and has been productive of the most beneficial results. Firmness and justice to all classes have characterized his acts I mingle my heartfelt sympathies with those who are mourning for him." LS, DNA, RG 94, ACP, G216 CB 1863. See letter to Andrew Johnson, Sept. 19, 1867.

To Elihu B. Washburne

[Aug. 21, 1867]

. . . It is not likely that I shall get to Galena or any place else this Fall. I am always hopeful and confident of the final result, but now public affairs look blue indeed.

Goodspeed's Catalogue 593 [1981], no. 55. On Aug. 13, 1867, Bvt. Brig. Gen. Orville E. Babcock had written to U.S. Representative Elihu B. Washburne. ". . . That man Rousseau has been playing the dirty spy on Genl Sheridan. The latter has reported him to the Sect of War. He is a low unprincipled fellow as you can find. He goes to Alaska to receive the Wilderness from the Russian commissioners—Three companies of troops go there from Cal. Genl Halleck was to go, but Rousseau goes in his place. One good thing he will not be where he can be held up as a threat against Sheridan,—I do not think Mr J. will remove Sheridan. He knew the Genl's mind on the subject before he put him in as act Sect of War, If he lets Sheridan alone the call for a convention in La will be made soon—and in a month the convention will meet—They have nearly all the voters registered, They now stand 41000 whites 84000 black, all the other district commanders are far behind Sheridan. Texas to all appearances will not vote to reconstruct, and Miss is doubtful. La. will be the first to be back into the union—If Sheridan is removed Genl will direct his successor to execute all of Sheridans orders and as he has planned them.—. . . Politics run high. Chase. Howard, Stanton. Harlan, &c &c are all in the field—The democrats and Butler stripe of the Republicans keep shy of Grant. The good republicans seem to be a unit on him. They are troting him out too soon. Rawlins speech was most untimely and uncalled for. The democrats look upon it as a bid from Grant. and many of them think—it was all gotten up by you and Jones, and brought about in that way. Rawlins' child died about a week before he made this speech. They say had it he not had an object the respect for his family would have prevented it—The Eastern papers have paid little or no attention to that speech, not a single editorial in a leading New York paper on the speech all but the Tribune I mean the World Times and Herald have come out flat footed for Genl Grant. 'Horace Greely. Jef Davis' &Co are not for him. Butler has had detectives following the Genl. and the story is that they will at the proper time prove 'Grant is a drunkard after fast horses women and whores' It is a fact that Butler has had the detectives on his track—and what mean thing they are up to I cannot tell.—Rawlins is at or near Salt Lake City, all his reports are that he is improving very fast, We cannot credit it but hope it is all true. Parker has not yet returned from the Plains—but he and Sully say the Indians are bad, and must be fought. They are bad all along the lines of both rail roads. the new commissioners may do some good but I guss not—They must be whipped—but first of all the difficulty between the Indian Bureau and War Dept must be reconciled in some permanent way.—Comstock is on the upper Mo river—is on an inspection. Porter Badeau, Leet, Dent and myself are here and quite well. Annie is in Galena. and doing very well indeed, Had a letter this morning, also one from Jones all well. RR earned over 11000. in July. (clear).—Mrs Grant has returned here with her children, and expects to remain the rest of the summer, He will be too busy to get away. ~~now~~ I do not think he can get away to go to Galena.—. . ." ALS, DLC-Elihu B. Washburne. See letter to J. Russell Jones, June 3, 1867.

On Aug. 24, Washburne, New York City, telegraphed to USG. "I shall reach Washn tomorrow morning Early train." Telegram received (at 11:25 A.M.), DNA, RG 107, Telegrams Collected (Bound). On Sept. 5, Col. Adam Badeau wrote to Washburne. "I should have written you several days ago, but I had not your address, and the General could not recollect it. I was very sorry to hear of Mrs Washburne's ill health, but trust she is now sure to recover since you have returned. Please make her my kindest regards. The letter *was* with drawn; Mr. J. sent for the General, and they had a long interview; nothing disagreeable said, and the General came back, saying he had offered to with draw the letter. there was no yeilding of any of the positions; and the same day that order was issued to District commanders, not to reinstate civil officers removed by themselves or their predecessors—I don't believe the Genl. will be disturbed in his position; unless some new developments arise. Mr J. wants him to issue his Proclamation to District Commanders. I suppose there is no doubt it will be followed by an amnesty—Then perhaps an attempt to postpone elections, and registrations, and to compel the registration of every body amnestied. This of course will only delay the return and recognition by Congress of the Southern states—But it may make Complications here. However this is pure surmise. I feel a good deal of anxiety about this Maryland militia business. The review is ~~Oct~~ Sept 10th The General receives crowds of letters daily upholding him. Bab has gone to Hancock; but H. is a weak man; and will try to please *every* body, which nobody can. Schenck was to see the General yesterday; he was strong for impeachment, I shall be very glad when Congress meets, and all responsibility is not thrown on the General I enclose you a letter which Busteed sent me. Please return it. I don't doubt tis correct, as we get numerous confirmations. Please remember me Cordially to Gov. Washburne." ALS, DLC-Elihu B. Washburne. See letter to Andrew Johnson, Aug. 26, 1867.

On Sept. 9, Washburne, Portland, Maine, wrote to USG. "Well, the Amnesty Proclamation appears this morning, and creates a feeling of profound indignation among all loyal men here. It is, in spirit and essence, a proclamation against the re-construction law and intended to hinder and obstruct its execution. The demand for an impeachment is loud and prolonged. I was in Boston last Saturday. A little band of malignants in Massachusetts have worked hard to impair the confidence of the loyal people in you, but the appearance of the letter in regard to Sheridan and your general course since you assumed the War Dept. has in a great measure disarmed them of their venom, and I think you now have the fullest confidence of all the best people in the State. All the leading papers in the State are friendly to you. I am astonished and pained to know that Stanton has done a great deal to prejudice you. He told Mr. Sumner last Friday morning that there was no understanding or communication between you and him in regard to his removal and your assuming the Dept.—that the first he knew of anything in regard to the matter was your letter to him telling him you had been appointed &c.—that he only yielded to you as the head of the army and that he would not have yielded to any one else. He gave the impression that you were in collusion with the President to get him out, and that had it not been for *you* he would have still been in the Dept. This I get from Mr. Sumner, who made the statement at a dinner party. In justice to you and to truth, I stated the precise facts in regard to the matter, greatly to the astonishments of those present. Wilson is your defender and backer every where, and he is as roundly abused by Wendell Phillips and gang as you are. Fessenden is not here and I have not seen him, but I learn that he is very earnest and emphatic in the approval of your course. Indeed, I think there is but one sentiment among the Union men of Maine, on that subject. I take my family to Massachusetts this week, to remain till Congress meets. I shall start west in about two weeks—may go by way of Washington to arrange about a house for the winter. I hear nothing from the agent of the Romero house. If you have time I wish you would give me a confidential word as to the present outlook at W. I feel intensely anxious. Write me at Taunton, Mass." ALS, USG 3. On Sept. 16, USG wrote to Washburne. *ABPC*, 1913, 775.

To William H. Seward

Washington City
August 23. 1867.

Hon W. H. Seward
Secretary of State
Washington. D. C.
Sir;

I have the honor to acknowledge the receipt of your letter of August 8th 1867, stating that *Mr Sasaki Gournk*, the Chief Officer of the *Prince of Echizen* of Japan desires to purchase from the Government of the United States the necessary books, equipment &c, to enable the *Prince of Echizen* to adopt our system in all branches of the military service; and requesting, should there be no objection thereto, the necessary directions be given.

In reply, I have the honor to inform you that the Quartermaster General has been authorized to furnish *Mr Gournk* with one complete outfit for a soldier of each branch of the Service, viz; Engineer, Artillery, Cavalry and Infantry; the Chief of Ordnance to furnish one complete battery of Field Artillery of the smallest calibre now in use, with horse equipments and the latest musket improvement;

and the Adjutant General a complete set of books of instruction, Army Regulations &C.

In regard to so much of your request as relates to an outfit for a marine and a copy of the regulations for the Navy, I would suggest that these matters pertain exclusively to the Naval Department

> I am &c
> U. S. GRANT.
> Sec of War *ad int*

Copy, DNA, RG 94, Letters Sent. See Robert B. Van Valkenburgh, Yokohama, to Secretary of State William H. Seward, May 23, 1867, introducing Sasaki Gouruk, ALS, *ibid.*, RG 59, Diplomatic Despatches, Japan.

To Maj. Gen. Daniel E. Sickles

Washington, D, C, Aug. 24th *1867*.

MAJ. GEN. D. E. SICKLES,
COMD.G 2D MIL. DIST.
GENERAL:

Your course in obstructing the action of Federal Courts, by prohibiting executions and collections, under the second paragraph Nof General Orders No 10 causes a good deal of comment by the Executive, and his advisers, all of whom, leaving the writer of this out, deny unhesitatingly your authority under the Acts of Congress to interfere in any manner with these Courts.[1] My own views always have been that the Military should be subordinate to Civil authorities as far as is consistent with safety and nothing should be regarded as a justification to impede the action of a United States Court unless such Courts were acting clearly in a way to defeat the Acts of Congress for the reconstruction of the "rebel states." In such an event a district command would have to look more to the support of a future session of Congress than to authority given by past acts, to justify his course.—Now I do not know that I clearly understand the nature of the controversy between the Military in North Carolina and Federal officials acting under instructions from the Atty. General of the United States. I know with the latter a hostility exists towards all the laws touching reconstruction. Under such circumstances representations may be unintentionally byiased. I do not like to base a positive order to a district command to revoke an order he has made upon such information alone. I will ask whether in your judgement it will not be better to direct that Par 2, Gen. Orders No 10, Current series, shall not be interpreted to apply in any manner to acts by United States Courts?

If you do not take this view of the case report to me fully, by Mail, as soon as possible, the whole of the controversy between Civil & Military authorities in N. C. the interpretation you give to Par. 2 Gen. Orders No 10 from your Hd Qrs, the Acts of Congress from which you derive the authority; in fact such a report as will give me "the other side" of "the question" so that when I do act it will be understandingly.

> Very respectfully
> your obt. svt.
> U. S. Grant
> General,

ALS, deCoppet Collection, NjP. On Aug. 26, 1867, Tuesday, Maj. Gen. Daniel E. Sickles, Charleston, telegraphed to USG. "Your letter received. Reply mailed to-night. Full report will be forwarded Thursday. It will be satisfactory to you. My report would have been sent sooner but the Marshal for North Carolina refused Col. Franck the information ~~about the Cases~~ I asked for, about the Cases." ALS (telegram sent), DNA, RG 393, 2nd Military District, Telegrams Sent; telegram received (at 10:15 P.M.), ibid., RG 107, Telegrams Collected (Bound). On the same day, Sickles wrote to USG. "Your letter of 24th instant has this moment been received. My views upon the general question of the relation created by the Reconstruction Acts between the Federal Courts in the rebel States and the authority of District Commanders, will be fully stated in my report which I will forward as soon as Col. Frank sends me the information I have called for in regard to the pending cases at Wilmington. ~~My~~ report would have been transmitted sooner but for the refusal of the Marshal of North Carolina to give Col. Frank the information required as to the particular cases now in controversy. It is quite true that the military should in general be subordinate to the civil authority. Congress has however established military Government in the rebel States. We are held responsible for the execution of the Scheme of Reconstruction proposed by Congress. Meanwhile we are required to protect all rights of person and property. To do this, in these States, military authority has been made for the time being paramount to all civil authority except that of Congress.—A great revolution is going on. Order must be maintained. If it be conceded as a proposition that military authority is subordinate in the rebel

States to civil authority, the embarassments and impediments to the execution of the Reconstruction Acts will be multiplied and may become insuperable. Concessions now made to the courts cannot be recalled. In regard to the particular cases at present in controversy it will probably turn out that they do not involve the issue attempted to be made. ~~elsewhere~~. The judiciary act makes the Federal courts dependent for much of their law of procedure upon the laws of the States. It is conceded that I have authority to modify or annul the laws of the two Carolinas. This is precisely what I have done as to certain remedies for the collection of old debts accruing before the surrender. It may ~~turn out~~ be that no more has been required of the Federal court in North Carolina than to exact the same compliance with General Order No 10 that the same Court has always heretofore yielded to the laws of North Carolina.—Registration goes on well.—I have registered more than half of the vote of both States without trouble of any kind. The real contest will begin when the election takes place. The rebel elements will not surrender without a desperate struggle.—Abandoning all other ground they will make their last fight on the issue of Negro rule. They regard all means of resistance as justifiable which may prevent the blacks from obtaining control of these State Governments.—The leaders will not hesitate to bring on a conflict of races, with the hope that such a result will defeat the plan of Reconstruction desired by Congress.—Under these circumstances I cannot hesitate to avow as my sincere and earnest conviction that the successful administration of the military Government established by Congress,—the organization of legal State governments and the preservation of order, all depend upon our retaining & executing full & firm control over the entire administration of affairs in these States, subject only to the limitations expressly made by Congress—." LS, *ibid.*, RG 108, Letters Received. On Aug. 30, USG endorsed a copy of this letter to President Andrew Johnson. ES, DLC-Andrew Johnson. On Aug. 26, Johnson had issued orders for USG. "Brevet Major General Edward R. S. Canby is hereby assigned to the command of the Second Military District, created by the Act of Congress of March 2d, 1867, and of the Military Department of the South, embracing the States of North Carolina and South Carolina. He will as soon as practicable relieve Major Genl Daniel E Sickles, and, on assuming the command to which he is hereby assigned, will, when necessary to a faithful execution of the laws, exercise any and all powers conferred by Acts of Congress upon District Commanders, and any and all authority pertaining to officers in command of Military Departments. MajorGeneral Daniel E. Sickles is hereby relieved from the command of the Second Military District. The Secretary of War ad interim will give the necessary instructions to carry this order into effect." LS (incomplete facsimile), Manuscript Society Sale, May 26, 1990, Superior Galleries, Beverly Hills, Calif., no. 8223; copies, DNA, RG 108, Letters Received; (2) DLC-Andrew Johnson.

On Aug. 31, Sickles sent to USG a forty-seven page explanation of policy. LS, DNA, RG 60, Letters from the President. Printed in *New York Tribune*, Sept. 6, 1867. On Sept. 3, Sickles telegraphed to USG. "all the Charleston journals publish this morning an elaborate opinion from the Attorney General's office reflecting upon my action respecting General Orders Number ten (10) of these Hd Qrs—My report on the subject was made yesterday & transmitted by mail in compliance with your directions of the twenty fourth ultimo.—The point made against me by the Acting Attorney General is that I appealed to you & not to the Courts to decide whether Civil or Military authority prevails in the rebel States—He maintains I should first yield to Marshal Goodloes interpretation of the Reconstruction Acts & then go to law with him to see who is right. Congress having forbidden me to be governed by the opinion of any Civil Officer in the execution of my office it would ~~have been~~ be difficult for me to satisfy the Attorney General & Marshal Goodloe without violating your orders & the law of the land.—Having done my duty as well as I could in accordance with the instructions of my Commanding Officer, I have only to request in order that the ~~publication~~ Justification of my conduct may be made public along with the accusation of the Attorney General ~~I respectfully ask~~ that I may have permission to publish my report." LS (telegram sent), DNA, RG 107, Telegrams Collected (Unbound); telegram received (at 2:30 P.M.), *ibid.*, Telegrams Collected (Bound); *ibid.*, RG 108, Telegrams Received. On Sept. 4, USG telegraphed to Sickles. "You are authorized to publish the report mentioned in your request of yesterday." ALS (telegram sent), *ibid.*, RG 107, Telegrams Collected (Bound); telegram received (at 12:55 P.M.), *ibid.*, RG 393, Dept. of the South, Telegrams Received.

On Sept. 5, Sickles telegraphed to the AG. "I have the honor to report that the returns rec'd yesterday from the boards of Registration shew that one hundred & fifty thousand (150000) voters have been Registered in this District without trouble any where   In compliance with General Orders. number eighty (80) Hd Qrs of the Army, Current series I have today turned over to Brevet Maj Gen Canby Command of Second (2nd) Military District. In reference to the intimation contained in the Proclamation of His Excellency The President dated third (3) September instant that I have disregarded the Commands of the President of the United States I respectfully request permission to put on record my declaration that I have not disobeyed any of the orders or Commands of the President & that in all things I have obeyed all orders & instructions I have received from Superior Authority   I shall have the honor as soon as I reach my station to address you further & less informally on the subject of this & other like accusations made by the President & the Acting Attorney General"   Telegram received (at 6:50 P.M.), *ibid.*, RG 94, Letters Received, 1236M 1867; copy, DLC-Andrew Johnson. On the same day, USG endorsed a copy of this telegram to Johnson. ES, *ibid.* On Sept. 11, Sickles, Brevoort House, New York City, wrote to the AG. "It appearing that in a published report addressed to the President of the United States by John M. Binckley Esq Acting Attorney General, dated the 24th August ultimo, I am charged with 'a high misdemeanor' committed in the exercise of my office as commanding General of the 2d Military District: and it further appearing that in the same official communication I am denounced as 'a contumacious and unfaithful executive agent'; and it further appearing that said report has received executive sanction and has been the basis of executive action; and it further appearing that in a Proclamation by the President of the United States dated the 3d day of September instant, it is declared that in disregard of the command of the President of the United States and while I exercised command of the Second Military District embracing the rebel states of North and South Carolina, serious impediments had been interposed preventing the execution of the laws of the United States within the said territory;—and it further appearing that I am charged by common report with disobeying the commands of the President while in command of said District;—I respectfully deny each and all of the allegations aforesaid, express or implied, and I therefore respectfully demand that a Court of Inquiry be ordered to investigate my conduct as the Commanding General of the Second Military District, in respect to the allegations aforesaid and upon such other accusations as may have been or shall be made." LS, DNA, RG 94, Letters Received, 964S 1867. On Sept. 23, USG endorsed this letter. "Respectfully submitted to the President with a recommendation that the Court of Inquiry asked for by Genl *Sickles* be granted, he having been publicly accused by the Acting Attorney-General of a high misdemeanor, committed in the exercise of his office as Commander of the Second Military District and also denounced as a contumacious and unfaithful executive agent; in consequence of which charges Genl Sickles' professional reputation is suffering, he having been relieved from his command &c." ES, *ibid*. On Oct. 12, Johnson endorsed this letter. "For reasons which were deemed conducive to the public interests, and necessary to the proper administration of justice within the Second Military District, Major Genl *Daniel E. Sickles* was relieved from his command, and all that has since occurred, it seems to me, has confirmed the propriety of the change.—Upon his own request, he has already been permitted to publish his official statement of the facts and circumstances connected with his removal. I do not, therefore, perceive any necessity for a court of inquiry, to investigate the subject, nor do I deem it proper that a court should be ordered merely for his gratification, any more than for the gratification of any other officer who might choose to ask one, under the supposition that he has a right to demand it, and cannot be refused. As the Department has recommended this application of Major Genl *Sickles* for a court of inquiry, on account of differences between him and the law officers of the Government, growing out of a conflict between him, as Commander of the Second Military District, and the Federal Courts, I have thought it proper to make this statement, and to add that the differences between him and the civil officers of the Government are questions which in my opinion more properly pertain to the civil tribunals of the country than to military courts." ES, *ibid*. Johnson had prepared a lengthy endorsement for Sickles's letter (DLC-Andrew Johnson), but made changes after conferring with Secretary of the Navy Gideon Welles. See Howard K. Beale, ed., *Diary of Gideon Welles* (New York, 1960), III, 232–33. On Sept. 13, Friday, USG had written to Bvt. Maj. Gen. Edward D. Townsend. "Order Gen. Sickles between Teusday & Saturday of next week to report in person at Army Hd Qrs." ALS, DNA, RG 94, Letters Received, 509A 1867. On Sept. 25, USG noted. "Make the order directing Gn. Sickles to proceed to New York, &c., include Capt. J. W. Cloues, 38th Inf.y, A. D. C." AN (initialed), *ibid*., 536A 1867.

On Dec. 24, Sickles wrote to USG. "*Private* . . . It was my intention—as you have perhaps heard—to apply for a few months leave of absence with permission to go abroad—Friends of yours as decided as I am in the desire to see you in the Presidential Chair persuade me to defer my purpose for the present, in the belief that my presence may be of some use—although in my opinion nothing is more Certain than your nomination & election I am unwilling to leave any thing I can do in so good a work, undone. I would prefer however if I remain *to be assigned to some duty in this City*—I have heard that Gen'l Butterfield will, in the usual routine of service, be soon relieved as Gen'l. Sup't of Recr.g Service.—If that be done, I would like that assignment—& to be put on duty according to my Brevet rank.—For reasons I need not particularize this post would be advantageous and agreeable." ALS, USG 3.

1. On Aug. 13, 2:20 P.M., USG had telegraphed to Sickles. "Par 2 Gen. Orders No 10, current series, must not be construed to bar action of a United

States Court. Authority confered on Dist. Commanders does not extend in any respect over the acts of Courts of the United States." ALS (telegram sent), DNA, RG 107, Telegrams Collected (Bound); telegram sent, *ibid.*; telegram received, *ibid.*, Telegrams Collected (Unbound); *ibid.*, RG 393, Dept. of the South, Telegrams Received. On Aug. 14, 10:50 A.M., USG telegraphed to Sickles. "My instructions of yesterday in regard to construction of par. 2 of your Gen. Order No 10 you may suspend if deemed proper until a report is received from you giving your views and reasons on the subject." ALS (telegram sent), *ibid.*, RG 107, Telegrams Collected (Bound); telegram sent, *ibid.*; telegram received (at 11:05 A.M.), *ibid.*, RG 393, Dept. of the South, Telegrams Received. On Aug. 15, 11:45 A.M., Sickles telegraphed to USG. "Your telegram of 13th & 14th recd   In the exercise of the discretion given in your telegram of yesterday I deem it expedient to suspend the execution of your previous instructions until your further order. A report on the subject with my views will be forwarded as soon as the necessary papers can be obtained from Raliegh & Wilmington" LS (telegram sent), *ibid.*, RG 107, Telegrams Collected (Unbound); ADfS, *ibid.*; telegram received (at 5:00 P.M.), *ibid.*, Telegrams Collected (Bound); (at 1:20 P.M.), *ibid.*, RG 108, Telegrams Received. On Aug. 17, Sickles telegraphed to the AG. "The Commanding Officer at Wilmington reports to me this morning that the U. S. Marshal for N. C. is. instructed by the Attorney General to Enforce immediately all Executions of the U. S. Courts & to Report the names of persons offering obstructions with a view to proceed against them under the Criminal laws of the United States and asks for instructions. I caused the Commanding Officer to be informed that on the receipt of the report he has been ordered to make in relation to the pending Cases he will receive further instructions & that meanwhile he will not permit the order or decree of any Court to be Enforced in Violation of Existing military orders. These threats of the Attorney General repeated by the marshal are foreshadowed in a false and scanddalous article on this subject published, it seems not without authority in the National Intelligencer on Monday last & to which I respectfully invite attention. I will remark that the Question now raised in this matter is not new. Last July the U. S Court in south Carolina ordered me to surrender four 4 citizens under sentence of death for the murder of (3) three soldiers of the Garrison at Anderson Court House   I refused & the Court ordered the marshal to arrest me. The Case having been reported to the Adjutant General of the Army the Secretary of War instructed me not to give up the prisoners not submit to arrest but to take into custody any and all persons attempting Either. The President afterwards Commuted the sentences of these men to imprisonment for life when they were sent to Fort Delaware & there discharged by a Judge of the U. S. Court. If the U. S. Courts in the rebel states be allowed to control the military authorities the Execution of the Reconstruction acts will for obvious reasons soon become impracticable   Some of these Courts will begin [b]y declaring those acts of [C]ongress void—" Telegram received (at 1:40 P.M.), *ibid.*; copies, DLC-USG, V, 55; DLC-Andrew Johnson. On Aug. 19, USG endorsed a copy of this telegram to Johnson. ES, DLC-Andrew Johnson. On Aug. 17, 3:00 P.M., USG had telegraphed to Sickles. "Your despatch of this date received. Follow the course of action indicated by you as right and regard my dispatch of the 13th as entirely withdrawn." Telegrams sent (2), DNA, RG 107, Telegrams Collected (Bound); telegram received, *ibid.*, Telegrams Collected (Unbound); (2) *ibid.*, RG 393, Dept. of the South, Telegrams Received. On Aug. 20, 10:05 A.M., Sickles telegraphed to USG. "Your gratifying telegram of Saturday was duly received. I hope the question will be allowed to rest where you have left it. Judge Bryan now holding United States Circuit Court at Greenville accepts my orders as establishing the legal relations of partie[s] within this Military District. To hold the people of the Carolinas to one code of laws and allow people from other States to come here and enforce a different code upon them, would be unequal & unjust. To allow United States Courts held here to disregard military regulations made for the government of the District would soon nullify all military authority. By writs of Habeas Corpus they could discharge offenders convicted by military Courts as fast as I could arrest and punish them. Registration and all other matters are going on well in my District and will continue so if new issues be not encouraged by His Excellency the President." LS (telegram sent), *ibid.*, RG 107, Telegrams Collected (Unbound); telegram received (at 10:10 A.M.), *ibid.*, Telegrams Collected (Bound); *ibid.*, RG 108, Telegrams Received.

On Aug. 15, 11:30 A.M., USG had telegraphed to Sickles. "Circular enclosing copy of Jury order in Texas is intended to secure regulations in all the districts giving such Juries as will insure equal justice to all classes of Citizens. It need not be construed that the Texas order is to be adopted verbatum. . . . Operator will send copy to Gn. Sheridan also." ALS (telegram sent), *ibid.*, RG 107, Telegrams Collected (Bound); telegram sent, *ibid.*; telegram received, *ibid.*, Telegrams Collected (Unbound); *ibid.*, RG 393, 2nd Military District, Letters Received. On the same day, Sickles telegraphed to Bvt. Brig. Gen. Frederick T. Dent. "In obedience to instructions contained in Circular letter, dated eighth instant, I have prepared ~~draft of~~ a General Orders which, with a suggestion on the subject, I shall forward by mail for the perusal and further instructions of the General-in-Chief. In South Carolina the test oath will exclude nearly all white persons, so that Jurors here will be mostly blacks, not one in ten of whom can read or write, or comprehend the duty of a Juror." LS (telegram sent), *ibid.*, RG 107, Telegrams Collected (Unbound); telegram received (at 7:30 P.M.), *ibid.*, Telegrams Collected (Bound); *ibid.*, RG 108, Telegrams Received.

On Sept. 13, Bvt. Maj. Gen. Edward R. S. Canby, Charleston, wrote to Bvt. Maj. Gen. John A. Rawlins. "General Grant's telegram in relation to juries together with the draft of an order conforming to the General's suggestions were turned over to me by Major General Sickles—I have given the subject a full & serious consideration and have reached the conclusion that it will be unwise at this time to give so full an extension to the jury lists. In the inland Counties where the population is without material preponderance on either side—it would work well and ensure justice, but in the Sea-board Counties and particularly on the Rice and Sea Island plantations the preponderance of the colored population is so great that the proportion of colored jurors would range from twelve to fifty to one of white. I have therefore considered it proper to defer any further action upon this particular point until after the registration is completed, when it can be done with a better understanding of its necessity—justice and probable results. In the meantime I have abrogated the property qualification and have excluded from the jury-lists all persons who are not qualified to be registered as voters. A copy of this order is transmitted herewith." LS, *ibid.*, Letters Received. See telegram to Bvt. Maj. Gen. Edward O. C. Ord, July 30, 1867; letter to Andrew Johnson, Aug. 17, 1867, note 2.

To Charles A. Stetson

Washington D, C,
Aug. 25th 1867.

DEAR CAPTAIN;

I send my two boys to New York City this evening, the older on his way to West Point and the younger on his way to Long Branch   He is young and has never traveled alone, and has never been to Long Branch. I therefore, take the liberty of consigning him to your care to get breakfast and to ask if you will give directions to put him on his way via Monmouth Landing. I think that is the name of the route. At all events he wants to go by the route which gives fourteen miles of rail-road. He stops with a friend at the villege of Schrewsbury.

Yours Truly
U. S. GRANT

CAPT. CHAS. A STETSON
ASTOR HOUSE, N. Y.

ALS, Goodspeed's Book Shop, Inc., Boston, Mass. Charles A. Stetson, born in 1810, became proprietor of the Astor House in 1838; his son Charles A. Stetson, Jr., worked there as a clerk.

To Andrew Johnson

Aug. 26th *1867*.

[TO HIS EXCELLENCY A JOHNSON
PRESIDENT OF THE UNITED STATES]
SIR,

I have the honor to acknowledge the receipt of the following letter; towit: "   " [1] To it I have the honor to submit the following reply. General Thomas has not yet acknowledged the receipt of the order assigning him to the Command of the 5th Military District. My recommendation to have the

order assigning him to that command suspended was based principally on the fact that the yellow fever had become epidemic, and
some time since orders were issued, at the suggestion of Gen.
Sheridan, authorizing all officers then absent from the 5th Military
District, on application to the Adj. Gn. of the Army, to remain
absent until the 15th of October. A Copy of the dispatch on which
this order, or Circular, was based and the Circular itself was forwarded, with my recommendation for the suspension of Gen.
Thomas' order. Before substituting Gen. Hancock, or any one else,
for Gen. Thomas to command the 5th Military District, his objections, if he makes any, should be heard or else the order for the
change should be based on other grounds. Unless there is very
grave public reasons no officer should be sent to Louisiana now.

Your letter quoted above will leave the 5th [military] district
without a Commander of the rank required by law, during the
period necessary to effect the contemplated change of commanders.
In fact it orders Gen. Sheridan to turn over his command to an officer absolutely incompetant by law to fill it. I assume that you will
change this part of your instructions so as to admit of Gen. Sheridan remaining where he now is until relieved by an officer of the
requisite rank.

The Act of Congress of July 19th 1867 throws much of the
responsibility of executing faithfully the reconstruction laws of
Congress, on the General of the Army. I am bound by the responsibility thus imposed on me. ~~Your~~ I approve all General Sheridans
orders, to this date, and therefore must insist on instructing his
successor to carry out those orders so far as I am authorized to do
so by Acts of Congress.

Having the responsibility placed on me that I have in regard
to the execution of the laws of Congress, in the districts composing
the States not represented in Congress, I claim that I ought to be
consulted as to the Agents who are to aid me in this duty. But The
right existing with the President to name district Commanders, I
can not decline to publish the order so far as it effects change of
Commanders. I do protest however against the details of the order;

I do more, I emphatically decline yielding any of the powers given the General of the Army by the laws of Congress.

In the present changes ~~taking place~~ the Country sees but one object no matter whether they interpret the objects of the Executive rightly or not. The object seen is the defeat of the laws of Congress for restoring peace, Union and representation to the ten States now not represented. ~~It~~ This course affects the peace of the whole country, North & South, and the finances of the Country, ~~to keep up~~ unfavorably. The South is the most affected by it, and through the South the whole country feels the agitation which is kept up. It is patent to every one that opposition to Congress ~~is all that~~ has ~~driven them to~~ induced the measures which now stand in the Statute Books as the laws of the land, ~~or that~~ and has ~~driven~~ induced the loyal people of this Country to sustain ~~such~~ [those] measures. ~~Have they not Congress now gone far enough to secure a lasting peace?~~ will not further opposition necessarily ~~drive Congress~~ [result] ~~into~~ more stringent measures against the South? ~~and the loyal people to the support of Congress.~~ The ~~Country~~ [people] had come to look upon the reconstruction policy of the Country as settled whether it pleased them or not. They acquiesced in it and at heart the great mass of people, irrespective of political creed, desired to see it executed and the country restored to quiet, ready to meet the great financial issue before ~~them.~~ [us]

I would not venture to write as I do if I was not greatly in earnest, if I did not see great danger to the quiet and prosperity of the Country in the course being pursued. ~~I do sincerely~~

> [I have the honor to be
> Very respectfully
> Your obedient servant
> U. S. Grant]

ADf (bracketed material not in USG's hand), OCIWHi; LS, *ibid*. On Aug. 27, 1867, President Andrew Johnson wrote to USG. "Your communication of the 26th instant has just been received. You will, without further delay, issue the necessary instructions to carry into effect the order to which your communication refers." LS, DLC-Andrew Johnson. On Aug. 28, Johnson wrote a note to USG. "I would be pleased to see General Grant this morning, if he can conveniently call." NS, DLC-Adam Badeau. Possibly during the same period, Johnson wrote an undated note to USG. "Will Genl Grant be kind enough to call as he passes on his way home or such other time as my be most convenient—" ANS, *ibid*. On Aug. 28, USG wrote to Johnson. "I have the honor, very respectfully, to request permission to withdraw my letter of the 26th inst." ALS, DLC-Andrew Johnson. On the same day, Johnson wrote to USG. "I have received your communication of this date, and, in compliance with your request, return herewith your letter of the 26th instant." LS, OClWHi. See St. George L. Sioussat, ed., "Notes of Colonel W. G. Moore, Private Secretary to President Johnson, 1866–1868," *American Historical Review*, XIX, 1 (Oct., 1913), 111–13.

On Aug. 29, USG issued Special Orders No. 429. "Commanders of the Military Districts created under the act of March 2, 1867, will make no appointments to civil office of persons who have been removed by themselves, or their predecessors in command—" Df, DNA, RG 94, Letters Received, 485A 1867. On Jan. 6, 1868, Maj. Gen. Winfield S. Hancock endorsed papers relating to the removal of the city council of Jefferson City, La. "Respectfully forwarded to the General-in chief, this being a case which I am prevented from revising by S. O. No 429, Head'qrs of the Army A. G. O., Aug 29 /67. I do not consider after a careful reading of the papers within, that there was any intention by the Council to violate General Sheridan's Special Orders No 7, March 28 /67, (enclosed). I think after the action of the council had been rescinded, and as no intention seemed to have existed to violate the spirit of that order, it would have b[ee]n better had the matter been [pe]rmitted to rest. [N]o military action whatever was [t]aken until fourteen days after the resolution had been rescinded by the council. Mr Fellows is a well known Union man and the Rev. Dr *W. G. Eliot* is a person whose history throughout the late war indicates him to be of the same character. He is well known by all of the principal citizens of New Orleans & Saint Louis." ES, *ibid*., RG 108, Letters Received. The enclosures are *ibid*. On Jan. 10, Hancock endorsed a petition of citizens of St. John the Baptist Parish, La., and other papers. "Respectfully referred to the *general-in-chief* for his consideration, under the provisions of special Orders No 429, C. S. War Department Aug 29 /67, which prevents me from reinstating officers who have been removed from civil offices by my predecessor in command." ES, *ibid*.

1. On Aug. 26, 1867, Johnson wrote to ʼUSG. "In consequence of the unfavorable condition of the health of MajorGeneral George H. Thomas, as reported to you in Surgeon Hasson's dispatch of the 21st instant, my order dated August 17, 1867, is hereby modified so as to assign MajorGeneral Winfield S. Hancock to the command of the Fifth Military District created by the Act of Congress passed March 2d, 1867, and of the Military Department comprising the States of Louisiana and Texas. On being relieved from the command of the Department of the Missouri by Major General P. H. Sheridan, Major General Hancock will proceed directly to New Orleans, Louisiana, and, assuming the command to which he is hereby assigned, will, when necessary to a faithful execution of the laws, exercise any and all powers conferred by Acts of Congress upon District Commanders, and any and all authority pertaining to officers in command of Military Departments. MajorGeneral P. H. Sheridan will at once turn over his present command to the officer next in rank to himself, and, proceeding without delay to Fort Leavenworth, Kansas, will relieve Major General Hancock of the command

of the Department of the Missouri. MajorGeneral George H. Thomas will, until further orders, remain in command of the Department of the Cumberland." Copy in USG's letter, LS, OClWHi; copies (2), DNA, RG 108, Letters Received; (3) DLC-Andrew Johnson. See letter to Andrew Johnson, Aug. 17, 1867, note 1.

On Aug. 27, Hancock, Fort Leavenworth, telegraphed to USG. "without desiring to Embarrass matters I think it proper to state to you that it is not a desire of mine to go to one of the 5 military Dists in the south or Even to the Dept of the Cumberland to which late orders transfer me I state these facts so that my preferences may not be misrepresented hereafter." Telegram received (at 3:40 P.M.), DNA, RG 107, Telegrams Collected (Bound); *ibid.*, RG 108, Telegrams Received; copy, DLC-USG, V, 55. On Sept. 11, 1:30 P.M., USG telegraphed to Hancock. "Come to Washington before proceeding to your new Command." ALS (telegram sent), DNA, RG 107, Telegrams Collected (Bound); telegram sent, *ibid.*; copies, *ibid.*, RG 108, Telegrams Sent; DLC-USG, V, 56. On the same day, Hancock telegraphed to USG. "Tomorrow Gen Sheridan relieves me here, Tomorrow PM I leave for St Louis remaining there a day or two to attend to necessary affairs I then proceed to Washington in accordance with your orders" Telegram received (at 10:30 P.M.), DNA, RG 107, Telegrams Collected (Bound); *ibid.*, RG 108, Telegrams Received; copy, DLC-USG, V, 55.

Also on Sept. 11, Maj. Gen. Philip H. Sheridan, Fort Leavenworth, twice telegraphed to USG. "I have the honor to report my arrival at Ft. Leavenworth & will assume Command tomorrow the twelfth (12) Gen Hancock will leave here same date & desired me to notify" "Being a little apprehensive when I left New Orleans of the Yellow fever I ordered Doctor Asche to accompany me as far as St Louis and on our arrival there Dr Asche was taken down but is doing well I respectfully request that he may be permitted to remain until the first of November should he desire he will not gain his strength again before that time" Telegrams received (at 4:50 P.M.), DNA, RG 107, Telegrams Collected (Bound); *ibid.*, RG 108, Telegrams Received; copies (of the second), *ibid.*, RG 94, Letters Received, 1271M 1867; DLC-USG, V, 55; (2) DLC-Philip H. Sheridan. On Sept. 17, Sheridan, St. Louis, telegraphed to Maj. George K. Leet. "I respectfully request that Asst Surg Morris J. Asch be permitted to delay reporting to his proper station until November first (1). he is just convalscent from yellow fever & will be unfit for duty until then" Telegram received (at 2:10 P.M.), DNA, RG 107, Telegrams Collected (Bound); *ibid.*, RG 108, Telegrams Received; copies, DLC-USG, V, 55; (2) DLC-Philip H. Sheridan. At 3:50 P.M., Leet telegraphed to Sheridan. "Permission to remain at StLouis until November first has been granted Surgeon Asch" ALS (telegram sent), DNA, RG 107, Telegrams Collected (Bound); telegram sent, *ibid.*; copies, *ibid.*, RG 108, Telegrams Sent; DLC-USG, V, 56.

On Sept. 14, Hancock, St. Louis, had telegraphed to USG. "Will I delay too much by starting for Washington monday the sixteenth (16) inst" Telegram received (at 4:00 P.M.), DNA, RG 107, Telegrams Collected (Bound); *ibid.*, RG 108, Telegrams Received; copy, DLC-USG, V, 55. On Sept. 15, 10:45 A.M., USG telegraphed to Hancock. "A detention ~~of a few~~ until to-morrow before starting here will make no matter." ALS (telegram sent), DNA, RG 107, Telegrams Collected (Bound); telegram sent, *ibid.*; copies, *ibid.*, RG 108, Telegrams Sent; DLC-USG, V, 56. See letter to Andrew Johnson, Sept. 19, 1867.

To William H. Seward

Washington City
August 27 /67.

HON. WM H. SEWARD, SECRETARY.
SIR:

I have the honor to acknowledge the receipt of your letter of the 24th inst., enclosing a copy of a communication from *Commissioner Campbell*[1] respecting the relief of *Maj. Genl. Parke* from duty as Astronomer of the North West Boundary Commission—

Genl. Parke has been employed for several years on the work described in Mr. Campbell's letter during a part of which he has exercised the rank of Major Genl. of Vols., without apparently interfering with his work on the Commission—As he does not now seem to be much oppressed with those labors, & as his services are much needed in the Engineer Dept. it is very desirable he should be made assignable to duty therein, while he can continue his operation with Commissioner Campbell until completed.

Very respectfully
Your obt. servant,
U. S. GRANT,
Secr'y of War *ad interim*

Df, DNA, RG 107, Letters Received from Bureaus; copy, *ibid.*, Letters Sent to the President. On Sept. 4, 1867, Secretary of State William H. Seward wrote to USG. "Referring to your letter of the 27th ultimo, relative to the relief of General Parke from duty as Astronomer of the North West Boundary Commission, I have the honor to inclose in reply a copy of a letter of the 2nd instant, upon the subject from Commissioner Campbell, who will, in compliance with your wishes, be instructed to direct General Parke to report for duty to the War Department." LS, *ibid.*, RG 94, Letters Received, 879S 1867. The enclosure is *ibid.*

On Aug. 14, USG had written to Seward. "Special orders No. 478. par. 6 of Sept. 26th 1866 from the Adjutant Genl's office U. S. A. assign *Bt. Major General J. G. Parke* to report for duty to the Hon. W. H. Seward, Secry. of State, to complete his work as Astronomer of the N. W. Boundary commission. I would respectfully ask if Genl. Parke cannot be relieved from that duty & ordered to report to the Chief Engineer, U. S. A." Df, *ibid.*, RG 107, Letters Received from Bureaus; copy, *ibid.*, Letters Sent to the President. On Aug. 24, William Hunter, 2nd asst. secretary of state, wrote to USG. "I have the honor to acknowledge the receipt of your letter of the 14th instant, inquiring whether Major General J. G. Parke can be relieved from duty as Astronomer of the Northwest

Boundary Commission, and in reply to transmit for your information, a copy of a letter upon the subject addressed to this Department on the 20th instant, by Commissioner Campbell." LS, *ibid.*, Letters Received from Bureaus. The enclosure is *ibid.*

1. Archibald Campbell, USMA 1835, resigned from the U.S. Army in 1836, became chief clerk of the War Dept. in 1846, and, in 1857, was appointed U.S. commissioner, Northwest Boundary Commission.

To Hugh McCulloch

August 31st *1867.*

SIR:

It being understood that certain book[s] & papers belonging to G. B. Lamar, Sr.,[1] now in possession of the Treasury Department, are desired by him, but will not be delivered without the consent of the Secretary of War, I beg to say that so far as this Department is concerned, they may be regarded as beyond its control. But if any orders are required for their restoration they would be that all private letters and papers should be returned to Mr. Lamar except such as may be necessary to protect the Government in any action heretofore taken against him or his property or such as could be used as evidence by him in any attempt to recover from the Government property lost by him from his participation in the rebellion—in short I would retain possession of such papers only as would be useful to defend the interests of the Government.

> Very respectfully
> Your obedient Servant
> U. S. GRANT
> Secretary of War ad int.

THE HONORABLE SECRETARY OF THE TREASURY.

LS, DNA, RG 56, Div. of Captured and Abandoned Property, Letters Received. On Sept. 2, 1867, Secretary of the Treasury Hugh McCulloch wrote to USG. "I have the honor to acknowledge the receipt, this morning, at the hands of Mr. Lamar, of your letter of the 31st ulto, relative to the application of that gentleman for the restoration to him of certain books and papers taken from his possession in 1865, and now in the possession of this Department. These documents were taken, it is understood, by the military authorities in Georgia, at the time stated, to be used as evidence against Mr. Lamar on his trial before a military commission on some charges of a grave character, and were subsequently transferred to this Department, as bearing upon matters then before it for consideration, and not yet finally disposed of. An examination showed them to be of very great importance, directly and indirectly, touching claims for a large amount of property or the proceeds thereof, made by Mr. Lamar and other persons against the Government; and I have accordingly heretofore declined to restore them to Mr. Lamar's possession. That gentleman has, however, had access to them, and, on his application I have from time to time furnished him a copy of such of them as he selected, after thoroughly examining them; and if he will make a further application for any specific paper or papers, and state for what purpose it is intended to be used I will, if no objection is perceived thereto, furnish him another copy thereof—duly certified, if such authentication should be necessary for the protection of his interests in any suit or proceeding between himself and other private individuals. Beyond this, I do not think it safe or expedient for the Government to go; and, in view of all the circumstances, it seems to me that this is all Mr. Lamar can reasonably ask. Should your Department, however, choose to take sole jurisdiction and responsibility touching them, and request the return of the books and papers in question, to make other disposition of them, I will, upon being so advised, promptly comply with your requirement." Copies, *ibid.*, Letters Sent Relating to Restricted Commercial Intercourse; *ibid.*, RG 153, MM 3469.

On Aug. 20, Gazaway B. Lamar, Washington, D. C., had written to USG. "When Genl Sherman took the City of Savannah, one A. G. Browne, Treasury Agent, presented to me, as President of the Bank of Commerce, a Military order, for the possession of the Bank, as an Office for his business—On his repeated promises, that all the Books & Papers, both of the Bank & myself, should not be molested, they were suffered to remain—Violating his promises, he sent my Books & Papers to the War Department—notwithstanding I had taken the Amnesty Oath under President Lincolns proclamation, & under orders of Maj Genl Geary Commanding the City—which restored me to all my rights, except property in slaves In July following President Johnson ordered them all to be restored to me, but Mr Stanton retained all my Letter Books & other papers—In December 1865, whilst my Nephew was engaged in preparing to ship my Cotton, from Thomasville under an order from Maj Genl Steedman he & I were both arrested & imprisoned at the instance, of the same man Browne & his son, & all our Books & Papers were again seized & the most important, Bills, Invoices & Receipts for my Cotton, & my Cotton Books, as well as those of a Company of which I was President—are detained from me, & are either in the War Department, or have been, in whole or in part, transferred to the Treasury Department—at my request—During our imprisonment the Brownes took all my Cotton, except some parcels which other persons had previously stolen, or the holders of which, had disposed of it—& for which several suits are now pending—which cannot be safely brought to trial in the absence of my Books & the original papers—more especially as my Agent who bought the Cottons & stored them died in July 1863— These Books & Papers, in both cases, were taken in violation of my rights as a citizen of the U States—without any legal authority, & have been detained not only, without reason, justice or equity, but in violation of them all—It may be proper to state that Mr McCulloch not feeling authorized to restore the Books & Papers, received from the War Department has kindly furnished certified copies of them—but these will not be received in the Courts, because in many cases the hand writing of the parties will require to be proven—But if any of them be of importance to either of Departments, certified copies, will answer all their purposes—And I trust that no Rule in any Department deprive a citizen of the right to his Books & Papers—illegally taken & wrongfully withheld from him—I present these facts, to which many others can be added, for your just consideration with an earnest & respectful request, that all which remain in your Department may be promptly restored; and that you will grant me a written request to Mr McCulloch to restore those transferred from the War Department to the Treasury Department as the Fall Terms of the Court is fast approaching in which the suits for the stolen Cotton are to be tried—All of which is respectfully submitted . . ." ALS, *ibid.* On Aug. 27, USG endorsed this letter. "An application, similar to this, having been made in February, 1867, the subject was examined, and a reference to the records now shows that, the writer having been convicted of high crimes against the United States for which he was sentenced to pay a fine of $25,000, and to be confined until paid, the request was not granted. For the same reasons the present application is denied." ES, *ibid.* On Sept. 9, USG endorsed papers concerning Lamar. "Respectfully forwarded to His Excellency, the President, in relation to the Case of 'Lamar' of Ga." AES, *ibid.* See letter of Sept. 7 from Lamar to President Andrew Johnson, ALS, DLC-Andrew Johnson. On Oct. 14, Judge Advocate Gen. Joseph Holt endorsed papers to USG. "Respectfully returned with copies of the several reports made in the case of *G. B. Lamar,* which will explain its history and present condition. It will be observed that the opinion has been expressed that the sentence pronounced by the Court was fully justified by the law and the testimony, and the enforcement of the sentence has been recommended. The views and convictions are still entertained. It is not known what action, if any, has been taken on the recommendation made." Copy, DNA, RG 153, Letters Sent.

On Oct. 31, USG wrote to McCulloch. "Information rec'd. by this Dept. indicating a purpose on the part of *Mr G. B. Lamar,* of Savannah, to institute legal proceedings against some of its late officers on account of his arrest and imprisonment by military authority in 1865, I have to request that until further advised no books or papers: or copies of the same, in possession or under control of the Treas'y. Dept. pertaining to his case, be furnished Mr Lamar without the assent of this Dept., it being apprehended that he may seek in connection with the proceedings referred to, to obtain from the Gov'mt. the evidences of his criminality now in its possession." Copy, *ibid.,* RG 107, Letters Sent to the President. On Nov. 1, McCulloch wrote to USG. "I have the honor to acknowledge the receipt of your letter of yesterday, asking that, until further advised by you, none of the books or papers claimed by Mr Lamar or copies of the same be delivered to that person. The documents in question are now in the office of the Attorney General for examination; but I have transmitted to that office a copy of your letter requesting that your wishes may be carried out. I will see that the same course is pursued by this Department when the books and papers referred to are returned to it." LS, *ibid.,* Letters Received from Bureaus.

On Oct. 31, USG wrote to Attorney Gen. Henry Stanbery. "Information has been received from Honorable Charles A. Dana, of New York City, late Assistant Secretary of War, that suit has been instituted against him by Mr. G. B. Lamar of Savannah, Georgia, on account of the arrest and imprisonment of the latter, by order of this Department, in 1865.—As any part had by Mr. Dana in these proceedings was in the performance of his duty as a public officer, I have to request that the U. S. District Attorney for the Southern District of New York be instructed at once to take charge of the case, and the requisite authority is hereby given for the employment of counsel, should such be necessary for the proper defense of the suit." LS, *ibid.*, RG 60, Letters Received, War Dept. On Nov. 12, Bvt. Maj. Gen. Edmund Schriver, inspector gen., wrote to Charles A. Dana. "Your letter of the 7th inst., to the Secretary of War respecting the *Lamar* suit against you has been referred to me with directions to inform you that the Department authorizes you to employ *Mr G. P. Lowrey* as Attorney and *Mr. W. M. Everts* as counsel, to defend you when the suit shall be brought. A proper disposition has been made of your letter." Copy, *ibid.*, RG 107, Letters Sent to the President. On Dec. 12, Stanbery wrote to USG. "Your letter of October 31, 1867, addressed to the Secretary of the Treasury, requesting that none of the papers of G. B. Lamar, the legal custody of which was then a question before this office, should be delivered to him, was communicated by the Secretary of the Treasury, in his letter to me of the 1st November, 1867, whereupon, the whole matter was treated as having been withdrawn from my consideration, and all the papers relating to it were, with my letter of the 5th November, 1867, transmitted to the Secretary of the Treasury, conformably to your request. It appears, however, that among the papers so transmitted were some which did not belong to those which were in question, and which, having been duly filed here by Mr. Lamar after the reference, were subject to the exclusive discretion of this office, and ought not to have been transmitted, as happened by inadvertence. These papers comprised certain copies of the originals in question which copies had been regularly made and delivered to Mr. Lamar by the Secretary of the Treasury, in the exercise of his competent authority, and were, therefore, not subject, in any sense, to the discretion of the Government, except for the purposes of this office in the business of Mr. Lamar, then before me, upon the reference aforesaid of the question. When the reference was retracted, it would have been necessary to determine what would be a fit disposition to make of the papers so filed here by Mr. Lamar. I subjoin a schedule of the papers herein referred to, and anticipate, upon this explanation, that you will be pleased to separate them from the other papers, the subject of your letter to the Secretary of the Treasury, of October 31st, 1867, and return them to this office for such disposition as may be found proper, after due consideration." Copies, *ibid.*, RG 56, Letters Sent; *ibid.*, RG 60, Letters Sent. On Dec. 16, USG wrote to Stanbery. "I have the honor to acknowledge receipt of your letter of the 12th instant, requesting that certain described papers pertaining to the case of G. B. Lamar, which were transmitted to the Secretary of the Treasury with your letter of the 1st of November last, be returned to you, and to inform you that as none of the papers named have been received at this Department, a copy of your letter has been referred to the Secretary of the Treasury with the assent of this Department to the return of the papers should such assent be deemed necessary." LS, *ibid.*, Letters Received, War Dept. On the same day, USG wrote to McCulloch. "I have the honor to enclose herewith a copy of a letter from the Hon. Attorney-General, dated the 12th instant, requesting the return to him of certain papers transmitted to you with his letter of November 1st, pertaining to the case of G. B. Lamar. As none of the papers referred to have been received at this Department it is presumed the object of the letter of the Attorney-General is to obtain the assent of the Secretary of War to the return of the papers to his custody, and should this inference prove correct no objection on the part of this Department is offered to their being so returned." LS, *ibid.*, RG 56, Div. of Captured and Abandoned Property, Letters Received.

1. Lamar, born in Ga. in 1798, prospered in shipping and banking. In New York City after 1845 he pursued expanded commercial interests and returned to Savannah in 1861, engaging in banking and blockade running during the Civil War. See Edwin B. Coddington, "The Activities and Attitudes of a Confederate Business Man: Gazaway B. Lamar," *Journal of Southern History*, IX (Feb., 1943), 3–36. On June 25, 1869, Lamar, Savannah, wrote to USG. "Allow me to approach you with all due respect, for your character, and the high Office you hold, as a private citizen, under the same sacred obligations, as yourself, 'to *preserve protect and defend the Constitution'*—in order to set before you, what appears to me to be very clearly the course you should adopt—in regard to all Military Commissions, for the Trial of citizens, who are 'not in the land *or naval forces of the United States—or in the Militia in time of war, or public danger*' . . ." ALS, DNA, RG 60, Letters from the President.

To Henry Stanbery

August 31st *1867*.

SIR:

I have the honor to enclose herewith a communication from Edward R. Hill, sued for damages while acting in the line of his duty as clerk of a United States Quartermaster, with a request that you instruct the District Attorney for the Western District of Tennessee to provide for the proper defence of the suit should it be brought.

Very respectfully
Your obedient Servant
U. S. GRANT
Secretary of War ad int.

THE HONORABLE ATTORNEY GENERAL.

LS, DNA, RG 60, Letters Received, War Dept. On June 13, 1867, Edward R. Hill, Memphis, had written a letter received at USG's hd. qrs. "Protests against suit brought by one Jno. M. Camack (late rebel soldier) against him in Memphis, Tenn. for $2,000 damage for actions done by him (Mr. Hill while in line of duty as clerk to Capt A. R. Eddy in 63 and 64." *Ibid.*, RG 108, Register of Letters Received. On July 3, Judge Advocate Gen. Joseph Holt endorsed papers concerning Hill. "Respectfully returned to the General in chief with the recommendation that this paper be referred to the Attorney General with the request that he will instruct the U. S. District Attorney for the Western District of Tennessee to provide for the defence of this suit, if it shall be ascertained by him that the party is actually prosecuted—as he states—for acts performed in the line of duty and under the orders of his proper superior. It is the experience of this Bureau that by entrusting such cases to the U. S. Attorney a far less expense is ordinarily incurred than where other counsel are employed." Copy, *ibid.*, RG 153, Letters Sent. On July 13, USG endorsed these papers. "Respy. forwd to the Sec of war. I concur in the recommendation of the Judge Adv. Gnl." Copy, *ibid.*, RG 108, Register of Letters Received.

On May 14, William H. Hampton, Altamont, Tenn., had written to USG. "it has become my duty to write you a few lines for myself &, others to inform you that the munciple authoriets, under controll of Late Rebel Enrolling officers Lieut Cols. &C have in violation of your orders & a writen order from maj Genl. Thomas positivly prohibiting the Shiriff or Depty from collecting the cost in the said case between myself & James. Winton which was brought against me for the pitiful sum of *Two sides of Beacon* taken by my Order by my, Lieut for the use of a Det. of, 40 men whil acting as a vidette Between the 21st A, R, C & the Reble Command,   know as soon as the Genl. has Left the State the Rebles have raised the Exicutions & proceeds to sell 3.20 three hundred & twenty acres of Land as my property and who shall I ask for assistence but thoes who have So, gallently led us through the hotest contest of a greate war,   true blue are Scarse in this part and the Rebels have devised all kinds of plans to drive union Soldiers from thire home   the case I have Spoke of is not all.   many union Soldiers have been prossacuted for acts done under orders & while in the service of the U. S. & the Courts have caused them to pay large costs   all this I am led to beleive is in violation of Department Orders & all humanity & Justice   if their is not Some Order Isued directly from the U. S Department to the Civil officers of Grundy County the Soldiers will continu to Suffer—" ALS, *ibid.*, RG 107, Letters Received from Bureaus. On July 5, Holt endorsed this letter. "Respectfully returned to the General-in-chief. Inasmuch as Tennessee is not included in one of the Five Military Districts; and seems to occupy at this time the same political status as that of any other state not lately in insurrection; the only proper ground for exercising the military authority herein suggested, would—it is conceived—be that the state of war, notwithstanding the discontinuance of active hostilities, has not yet legally ceased. But this gives rise to a purely political question, the determination of which belongs to the political power of the Country and not to this Bureau; and to the consideration of that power it is respectfully submitted." AES, *ibid.* On July 13, USG endorsed this letter. "Respectfully forwarded to the Secretary of War." ES, *ibid.* On Sept. 4, USG wrote to Attorney Gen. Henry Stanbery. "The attention of this Department is not unfrequently called to cases of persons against whom suits are brought for alleged trespass while in the performance of public duties under orders from their superior officers of the United States, in States where military force was used for the suppression of the rebellion. The enclosed letter from W. H. Hampton, late Captain 10th Tennessee Cavalry, reports a case of that class and I respectfully ask your attention to it for the purpose of inquiring whether under the provisions of the 'Act to protect all persons in the United States in their civil rights', &c, passed April 9th 1866, protection cannot be given to persons who are persecuted in the manner represented in Hampton's letter." LS, *ibid.*, RG 60, Letters Received, War Dept. On Sept. 7, Act. Attorney Gen. John M. Binckley wrote to USG. "I have the honor to enclose herewith, a copy of the instructions of this date from this office to the United States District Attorney at Nashville, Tennessee, for the information of Captain Hampton, should you think fit to forward them to him, whose letter reached me yesterday with yours of the 4th inst., in which you intimate that similar cases not unfrequently come to the knowledge of your department. I have to state that in every instance where a similar case has come before this Office, the Attorney General has promptly instructed the District Attorney for the proper district to appear for the defendant, as in the present case. The like course will continue to be pursued. I herewith return the letter of Captain Hampton." LS, *ibid.*, RG 107, Letters Received from Bureaus. The enclosure is *ibid.*

On Oct. 1, John M. Ament, Columbia, Tenn., wrote to USG. "As an humble citizen please let me have a few moments of your very valuable time, to ask you a question of the very utmost importance to me, and by answering it, you will confer a lasting favor upon me. To wit:—In 1863, I was furnished with a contract by Gen A Anderson general Supt. U S Military Rail Roads Armey of the cumberland, under Gen McCollum, to furnish The Nashville, Decator & Stevenson Rail Road with wood. The contract was stamped and approved August 1863, and form 30. furnished with said contract in which form it was agreed to furnish the contractor with the timber *free*—from which the wood for the [l]ocomotives was to be furnished; on this contract I proceeded to the work of furnishing wood The timber was cut from various parties lands who were then (most of them) very unloyal to the U. S. and when those who were disloyal applied for their vouchers failed to satisfy the A. A. A Q M of their loyalty, they necessarily failed to get vouchers for their timber, These men then returned home, and as soon as civil authority set the courts in operation, they then instituted suits against me, individually in the circuit court of Maury county Tennessee for all the timber cut by the hands I had employed, under my contract, and the suit was tried before a majestrate of this county, before whome I presented my authority with all the papers thereto pertaining, with such evidence before the majestrate he gave judgment against the plantiffs for the cost. The plantiffs then took appeal on his judgment to the circuit court—in which court it (the suit) is now pending—Now My Dear General as I have laid the facts before you as they now stand, I wish to know what course I aught to persue to defend myself against this unjust prosecution by men who had they been loyal would have been paid for their timber by the government The parties suing me is one James T Moore & _____ McLemore—The damages they claim amounts to some thousand dollars. Gen. please be kind enough to give me some advice how to proceed—or have the matter brough to a terminus by the investigation of my papers, and facts as above stated, by so doing you will do a favor to one who has been a verey consistant loyal man to the U S Govenmt I refer you to Hon S M Arnell member of congress elect Thomas W Keesee assessor for this district James H Gregory Agent of Freedman Beaurue and other loyal men of this county" ALS, *ibid.*, RG 60, Letters Received, War Dept. On Oct. 8, USG wrote to Stanbery. "I have the honor to send herewith a communication of 1st Oct. from John M. Ament who represents himself to be harrassed by civil suit for acts done under the orders of the U. S. authorities; with a request that the U. S. District Attorney in Tenn. may be instructed to defend Mr. Ament when necessary. Mr. Ament has been informed of this reference." Copy, *ibid.*, RG 107, Letters Sent to the President. On Dec. 4, Holt endorsed to USG papers concerning Ament. ". . . It is believed that the defendant is entitled to the aid of the government, inasmuch as the acts complained of were done in pursuance of orders of U. S. Officers, legally issued, and it is advised that the Attorney General be requested to direct the U. S. District Attorney of Tennessee to assume his defence." Copy, *ibid.*, RG 153, Letters Sent. On Dec. 14, USG wrote to Stanbery. "As suggested by the Judge Advocate General of the Army, I have the honor to send herewith papers in the case of John M. Ament against whom suits have been instituted in the Circuit Court of Maury County, Tennessee, for cutting timber for the railroad purposes of the United States with a request that you direct the U. S. District Attorney for Tennessee to assume his defence." LS, *ibid.*, RG 60, Letters Received, War Dept. On Dec. 16, Binckley wrote to USG acknowledging his letter. Copy, *ibid.*, Letters Sent.

To William Elrod

Sept. 4th *1867.*

DEAR ELROD,

I regret to learn that Dr Barrett has been permitted to cultivate this year the orchard opposite to his house. I would have much prefered the old man who lives in my house should have had it. I do not want [— — —] one who does not live on my place to have any thing to do with the land, or to have any pretext entitling them to drive in and through the place. I do not want Mr. Sappington or the Dr to fill my ice house.

It is a good ways from where you live for your children to walk to school but I think you had better not move until you can get the house now occupied by Kesselring. My children used to walk as far or rather Fred did. If there is any possible chance I will go to Mo. and then I should live in my house even if I only remained there a week.

AL (signature clipped), Illinois Historical Survey, University of Illinois, Urbana, Ill.

To Orville H. Browning

September 6th *1867*.

SIR:

In reply to your letter of September 2d, respecting the proposed conversion of the old Penitentiary into an Ordnance Depot, I have the honor to inform you that such conversion has been approved by this Department. There is no objection to allowing the Department of the Interior to have such of the materials of the old Penitentiary as will not be required by the Ordnance Department in its conversion into an Ordnance Depot, and authority is hereby granted to Mr. Faxen, Architect, to inspect the same for the purpose.

Very respectfully
Your obedient Servant
U. S. GRANT
Secretary of War ad int.

THE HONORABLE SECRETARY OF THE INTERIOR.

LS, DNA, RG 48, Miscellaneous Div., Letters Received. On Sept. 2, 1867, Act. Secretary of the Interior William T. Otto had written to USG. "I am informed that authority has been, or would be given by your Department for converting the old Penitentiary into an Ordnance Depot. I am not aware that any such authority has been given, but if it is the intention of the War Department to carry out this project I will thank you to communicate with me on the subject. It is understood that there is a quantity of material in the old Penitentiary that will not be required in its conversion into an Ordnance Depot, and which might be advantageously employed in the erection of the New Jail, and for the purpose of inspecting this material I would respectfully request that a permit be furnished Eben Faxon Esq, the Architect, and that said permit be transmitted to this Department." LS, *ibid.*, RG 156, Letters Received. On Sept. 3, Bvt. Maj. Gen. Alexander B. Dyer, chief of ordnance, had written to USG outlining plans for the alteration of Washington Arsenal. LS, *ibid.*

On Sept. 27, USG wrote a note. "Direct Chief of Ord to remove the bodies of conspiritors buryed in the 'Old Penitentiary,' now being demolished, reburryed within the arsenal grounds and record of graves kept." AN (initialed), *ibid.*, RG 94, Letters Received, 694W 1867. On Sept. 11, Edwin Booth, Baltimore, had written to USG. "Having once received a promise from Mr Stanton that the family of John Wilkes Booth should be permitted to obtain the body when sufficient time had elapsed, I yeilded to the entreaties of my Mother and applied for it to the 'Secretary of War'—I fear too soon, for the letter was unheeded—if, indeed, it ever reached him. I now appeal to you—on behalf of my heart-broken Mother—that she may receive the remains of her son.—You, sir, can understand what a consolation it would be to an aged parent to have the privelege of visiting the grave of her child, and I feel assured that you will, even in the midst of your most pressing duties, feel a touch of sympathy for her—one of the greatest sufferers living. May I not hope too that you will listen to our entreaties and send me some encouragement—some information how and when the remains may be obtained? By so doing you will receive the gratitude of a most unhappy family, and will—I am sure—be justified by all right-thinking minds should the matter ever become known to others than ourselves. I shall remain in Batimore two weeks from the date of this letter—during which time I could send a trustworthy person to bring hither and privately bury the remains in the family grounds, thus relieving my poor Mother of much misery. Apologizing for my intrusion, and anxiously awaiting a reply to this—. . ." ALS, Walter Hampden Memorial Library, New York, N. Y. On Oct. 12, Mary R. Tucker, New York City, wrote to USG. "As to one, whose deeds have been marked with mercy in the prominent situation, you have filled within the last few years; as to the father of children, hence one capable of realizing a parent's feelings, I would appeal, and ask, (if compatible with the position, in which you are now placed) to grant the body of my young friend John Wilkes Booth to his afflicted mother;— she does so yearn to have all, that remains of her cherished child, that my woman's heart has led me to take a liberty, which, under other circumstances, would be unwarrantable, and thus to intrude on your notice by presenting my earnest petition, that the lifeless body may be given to her, who has been sorely tried by the untimely termination of the earthly career of one so loved. Should it not lie with you to comply with this request, will you *influence* those, who can; and thus, be not only the soldier's friend, but that which usually accompanies so honorable a title, the sympathizer in woman's grief." ALS, DNA, RG 107, Letters Received, T163 1867. For the transfer of the body of John Wilkes Booth to his family, under orders from President Andrew Johnson, see George S. Bryan, *The Great American Myth* (New York, 1940), pp. 306–7.

To Maj. Gen. Philip H. Sheridan

Sept. 8th *1867*.

DEAR GENERAL,

By my dispatch to you to turn over your command to the officer next in rank to yourself, as soon as you relieve Gen. Hancock, and to come to Washington I did not mean to hasten your arrival in this city, but meant it as an order for you to come here at your leasure. I want to see you. When you leave Leavenworth however make such visits as suits your own convenience, only do not return to Leavenworth before coming to Washington.

I feel that your relief from command of the 5th District is a heavy blow to reconstruction not that Griffin will not carry out the law faithfully, and Hancock too when he gets there, but that the act of removal will be interpreted as an effort to defeat the law and will encourage opposition to it. So again in the 2d District. I do not know what to make of present movements in this Capitol but they fill me with alarm. In your own personal wellfare you do not suffer from these changes, except as one of the Thirty-five millions of inhabitants of the republic, but may be the gainer so far as personal comfort is concerned. I felt it my duty however to do all I could to keep you where you was until the laws which you were executing so faithfully were carried through and your District restored to the Union. All I can say now is that I have sustained your course publicly, privately & officially, not from personal feeling, or partiality, but because you were right.

You are entitled to a little rest now and I know such a welcome awaits you as will convince you that "Republics" are not always "ungreatful," and that there is still a loyalty in the Country which will save it through any trial.

Yours Truly
U. S. GRANT

TO MAJ. GN. P. H. SHERIDAN,

ALS, DLC-Philip H. Sheridan. See letters to Andrew Johnson, Aug. 17, 26, 1867. On Sept. 15, 1867, Maj. Gen. Philip H. Sheridan, Fort Leavenworth, wrote to USG. "*Personal* . . . I am in receipt of your letter of September 8th 1867. It is an additional bond, if any were necessary, for my friendship for you. My removal from New Orleans, so far as I was concerned personally, was of no consequence to me or any one else; but, it will set back Congressional reconstruction; will promote evil passions and will give much insecurity in Louisiana and Texas, and perhaps throughout the whole country. I was becoming master of all the conflicting elements, and I was getting sufficient influence to have drifted them in the interests of the whole country North and South. It was for this reason, perhaps, more than any other that I was removed. We never can have peace or quiet until the States which were in rebellion surrender their attempts at political power as absolutely as Lee surrendered the Military strength of the rebellion at Appomattox Court House. I think like you, that we have reasons at times to become alarmed, when justice, truth and honor, are so often violated, we must look out that greater evils do not come. Much has been said about me and there is a general approval of my conduct, and I have consequently accumulated strength; but, no other thought has entered my mind, except to be able to use it to assist you, should the trouble which I sometimes fear, may again come to distract the country. This I want you to understand as unequivocally my position. I will be in Washington during the coming week." LS, USG 3.

To Andrew Johnson

WAR DEPARTMENT, *September* 9, 1867.

The prisoner, the record of whose trial is within, had every opportunity he desired to defend himself. His crime is a most fearful, brutal one, and he is without any excuse for its commission. It is the first trial for murder by a military commission under the reconstruction acts, and the sentence should be carried into effect.

Respectfully submitted to the President.

U. S. GRANT,
Secretary of War ad interim.

HED, 40-2-47, p. 22. On Sept. 6, 1867, Judge Advocate Gen. Joseph Holt had written to USG. "The following report is respectfully submitted, upon the proceedings of a Military Commission convened at New Orleans, La. by Maj. Gen. Sheridan, Commd'g 5th Military District, under date of June 17th 1867, for the trial of one A. M. D. C. Lusk & others. The order convening the Court is in the following words: 'Hd Qrs 5th Mily. Dist. New Orleans, La, June 17. 1867 Special Orders, No 70. Extract. 3. *The proper civil authorities having stated that it is impossible* for them to take charge of Albert M. D. C. Lusk of the Parish of Carrol, State of Louisiana, accused of murder, *and that it is impracticable to administer justice in his case through the civil courts*, a Military Commission is hereby ordered to convene in this city at 10 o'clock, a. m. on Thursday the 20th inst, or as soon thereafter as practicable, for his trial, and for that of such other persons as may be properly brought before it. . . .' After completing the formalities required for the legal organization of Military Courts, all of which were strictly performed, the prisoner was arraigned under the following charge: — Murder. In this, that he, Albert M. D. C. Lusk, of the Parish of Carrol, State of Louisiana, did, with malice aforethought, and without cause or provocation feloniously shoot and wound with a pistol ball from a pistol in the hands of him, the said Albert M. D. C. Lusk, Wilson Calcoat, a freedman, from the effects of which shot and wound he, the said Wilson Calcoat, subsequently died. All this at or near the town of Floyd, Parish of Carroll, State of Louisiana, on board steamer 'Lizzie Tate,' on the night of the 1st April, 1867. To this charge and specification the prisoner pleaded *Not Guilty*. He then, through his counsel, C. P. Bemiss, Esq. submitted a protest against the jurisdiction of the Court, on the grounds that the homicide occurred in the Parish of Carroll where there is a regular organized Court of Justice, and that there is no evidence that the proper civil authorities have proved that it is impracticable and impossible for them to administer justice in his case; that his confinement by military authority is without warrant in law, and that no absolute necessity exists for his trial before this Commission. The Commission overruled the objection, and proceeded to hear evidence in the case; and after a trial of twelve days, not including several adjournments at the request of the prisoner, found him as follows:—Of the specification—Guilty   Of the Charge—Guilty.   and sentenced him 'to be hanged by the neck until he be dead, at such time and place as the proper authorities may direct'. Two thirds of the Court concur in the sentence. Gen. Sheridan approves, and forwards the record for the action of the President. . . . It is believed that no record of guilt and crime has ever been examined by this Bureau, calling more loudly for the rigid enforcement of the extreme penalty of the law, than this. Every moment of the three hours during which the steamer was in the possession of this desperado seems to have been employed in acts of cruelty and terror; culminating at last in the pitiless shooting of an unoffending boy, whom he had never seen before, and whose sole offence seems to have been that the color of his skin was a shade darker than that of his assassin. It is respectfully urged that the prisoner be executed." Copy, DNA, RG 153, Letters Sent. Printed in full in *HED*, 40-2-47, pp. 16–22.

To Henry Stanbery

September 9th 1867.

SIR:

I have the honor to enclose herewith a copy of a letter from U. S. Marshal J. R. Jones, (Northern District of Illinois) with a request that you instruct the District Attorney to defend the suit. Under the circumstances of the absence of District Attorney Norton and the urgency of the case, the War Department has this day authorized Marshal Jones to employ the necessary counsel.

Very respectfully
Your obedient Servant
U. S. GRANT
Secretary of War ad int.

THE HONORABLE ATTORNEY GENERAL.

LS, DNA, RG 60, Letters Received, War Dept. See *PUSG*, 6, 220–21; 16, 272–73; George R. Jones, *Joseph Russell Jones* (Chicago, 1964), pp. 24–28. On Sept. 6, 1867, J. Russell Jones, U.S. marshal, Chicago, had written to USG. "During the war, by order of the President, I arrested and conveyed to Fort La Fayette, M Y Johnson and David Shean, subsequent to which, I was sued, and the Scty of War authorised me to employ counsel at the expense of the Govt to defend the suit. I gained the suit in the lower Court, it was taken to the Supreme Court of the State, and the case sent back for a new trial—The Atty General has directed me to have the case tried before a Jury before taking it to the U. S. Courts. Our Dis't Att'y, Judge Norton is absent from home, ill, & will not be able to attend to it, and I will thank you to authorise me to employ Counsel to attend to the matter, and also to attend to another similar case growing out of the arrest of one Dr Carver in Stephenson Co. for disloyal practices. This latter case was tried in the State Circuit Court and I gained it, and the parties have now taken it to the State Supreme Court, and it is set for trial 2d Tuesday in Septr, inst, so that you will see that no time can be lost." ALS, DNA, RG 107, Letters Received, J148 1867. On Sept. 9, 11:00 A.M., USG telegraphed to Jones. "You are authorized to employ council ~~to defend you~~ for defence in the Cases brought by Johnson, Shean and Carver against you." ALS (telegram sent), *ibid.*, Telegrams Collected (Bound).

On July 19, Stanbery had written to USG. "Upon looking into the opinion of the Court in Johnson vs. Jones, et al. and the letter of Mr. Beckwith, I deem it best to adopt the course indicated by Mr. Beckwith and to have the damages assessed by a jury in the State Court before removing the case to the U. S. Court—I therefore respectfully suggest that you so advise Mr. Beckwith—" Copy, *ibid.*, RG 60, Letters Sent. On Aug. 11, Corydon Beckwith, "Cresson Springs," Pa., telegraphed to USG. "Desirable that I should return to Chicago to protect Jones and interest—he represents. he wrote last week for leave of absence for Lieut Chs. S. Smith fourth (4th) Artillery. Can he relieve me." Telegram received (at 4:30 P.M.), *ibid.*, RG 107, Telegrams Collected (Bound); *ibid.*, RG 108, Telegrams Received; copy, DLC-USG, V, 55. On Aug. 12, 10:21 A.M., Bvt. Brig. Gen. Orville E. Babcock telegraphed to Beckwith. "Leave telegraphed to Lieut Smith this morning." ALS (telegram sent), DNA, RG 107, Telegrams Collected (Bound); telegram sent, *ibid.*

On Oct. 15, Judge Advocate Gen. Joseph Holt wrote to USG. "Respectfully returned to the Secretary of War. The within is the claim, amounting to $3080 35/100 of *C. Beckwith, Esq.*, for professional services in the cases of Johnson vs. Jones et al. and Sheehan vs. the same. Jones, who is U. S. Marshal for Illinois, was, with several other defendents, sued by Johnson and Sheehan on account of his action in arresting them, (by order of the President) as members of the Sons of Liberty and abettors of the rebels, and conveying them to Fort Lafayette. The pleas of the defendents having been entertained in the lower court, the case was appealed by the Plaintiffs to the Supreme Court of Illinois; and on May 1st 1866, Mr. Beckwith was authorized by the Secretary of War through the Adjutant General, to aid in the argument on behalf of the defendants in that court. His account now rendered, through Jones, is—$3000 'for argument' in these cases, 'and going to Springfield to argue the same'; and $80 35/100 for cash paid for printing argument and brief, and for copies of official opinions procured from Washington in the case of exparte Milligan—. . . I am clearly of opinion that, notwithstanding the character of the testimony which has been set forth, the charge of $3000 in this case cannot justly be regarded as a reasonable one, but must, on the contrary, be held to be excessive. I have therefore to recommend that the claim, in the form in which it is now presented, be disallowed by the Secretary of War." Copy, *ibid.*, RG 153, Letters Sent. On Oct. 21, Bvt. Brig. Gen. Horace Porter wrote to Jones. "The claim of *Mr Beckwith*, for services in the cases of *Johnson vs. Jones et al.* and *Sheehan vs.* the same, has been referred to the Judge Advocate General, and the sum of $3000 is regarded by him as excessive.—Should you have any additional evidence as to the justice of the present amount of this claim, you will please forward it to this office and it will be duly considered before a final settlement of the claim is made.—A copy of the Judge Advocate General's opinion is forwarded herewith." Copy, *ibid.*, RG 107, Letters Sent. On Jan. 10, 1868, Holt wrote to USG. "Respectfully returned. The former account of *Judge Beckwith*, (Beckwith, Ayer & Kales,) for his services rendered this Department in the within mentioned case, amounting to Three Thousand Dollars, ($3000) with $80.35/100 for disbursements; having been reported upon by this Bureau as 'excessive' and not proper to be allowed; has been withdrawn by the claimant; and a new account of One Thousand Dollars, ($1000,) with the same item for disbursements, has been substituted. This counsel is understood by this Bureau to be a lawyer of high repute and distinguished ability in Illinois; and his charges are—naturally—no doubt so adjusted as to conform in their proportions to his professional eminence. This Bureau, however, having had before it the material upon which to form an intelligent estimate of the value of the services rendered in the case, must regard the modified account as still unusual and by no means moderate or acceptable. But in view of the promptness of the counsel in reducing his bill, upon being advised of the opinion of the Department thereon, and of the material extent of this reduction—viz. two thirds of the whole amount—this Bureau would not be disposed to contend against the allowance of the claim as now presented." Copy, *ibid.*, RG 153, Letters Sent.

To Bvt. Maj. Gen. John Pope

Washington D. C. Sept. 9th 1867

MY DEAR GENERAL;

Your dispatch of the 7th instant asking if you were likely to be relieved from your present command was duly received. I could not answer it because I did not know what the chances of removal were. Except in the case of Sheridan, I was not spoken to about these removals and yet we see they have been made. The newspapers have been filled from time to time with rumors of your removal and the appointment of Swayne to your place. I have not heard a word of this from official sources. All I can say is that I would not involve myself in any contract which would be burdensome if removal takes place were I you.

I am just in receipt of a long and well grounded protest against your removal, from Gov. Jenkins,[1] which I will use, together with

my own support of your official conduct as District Commander
before I will let an order go out for your removal

> With great respect, Your obt servt.
> U. S. GRANT
> Gen'l

To Bvt. Maj. Gen. J. Pope
Comdg. 3d Mil. Dist

Copies, DLC-USG, V, 47, 60; DNA, RG 108, Letters Sent. On Sept. 7, 1867,
Bvt. Maj. Gen. John Pope, Atlanta, had telegraphed to USG. "If consistent with
propriety I would be glad if you would let me know whether there is any probability of my being relieved from this command   I am about to rent a house for
the winter and dont wish to commit myself to the bargain unless I am to retain
command" Telegram received (at 10:30 A.M.), *ibid.*, RG 107, Telegrams Collected (Bound); (at 10:35 A.M.) *ibid.*, RG 108, Telegrams Received; copy,
DLC-USG, V, 55. On Sept. 10, Pope wrote to USG. "*Confidential . . .* I telegraphed you the other day asking to be informed whether it was likely that I
should be removed from the command of this District—As you have not replied
I presume that it either was not proper to inform me or that you found it difficult to answer my question with any certainty—I certainly do not wish to be
removed from this Command just at this time—Two months ago I should have
been rejoiced to be relieved from these duties   As you know I came here with
great reluctance, but now having completed the Registration which has been the
hardest work of all, and being just on the eve of elections which will show the
result of this work, I should be very unwilling to jeopard the certain result of
being replaced by some one else less familiar with the situation than I am—In
this view I shall be very careful to do as little as possible until the elections are
over & to give the President no ground even for any movement against me—
Alabama will give not less than *80.000* majority for Convention probably
100.000—Georgia will surely give *60000* majority & with judicious management will give much more—When once the Conventions in these States are assembled I will put myself in such relations with them that these Ordinances will
be substantially the orders I would myself issue & I will execute these Ordinances, by the aid of such Military force as may be necessary—Shielded behind
these Conventions representing the highest soveregnty of the people of Georgia
& Alabama, & using these Ordinances to secure the action necessary to the welfare & security of the people it will not be easy to find fault with me—I will be
simply *aiding* the Civil authorities to do the thing necessary to be done & if fault
be found, the Conventions and not I are responsible—I shall have no trouble
whatever in getting them to pass as Ordinances any orders I think it judicious to
issue, & I shall be found executing *these* decrees and not my own orders—A
couple of months more will find me thus fortified & meantime I shall be careful
to do nothing I can avoid to give even an excuse for my removal—I received on
Saturday evening your letter advising that Rebel officers who fled the Country
at the Surrender should be required to give their parole within thirty days—
Toombs was the only person in this Category of any prominence in this District
& in fact of whom I knew at all—He is absent in Canada or perhaps now in
Baltimore & has been so for a long time—The President's Amnesty Proclamation

which covers his case reached us on Monday Morning, and as there could be no result to such an order except collision with the President & excitement here I have thought that in view of what I have just written you I would postpone the order until I can hear again from you—If you still think it best to issue the order I will do so at once—I cannot well spare Genl. Swayne from Alabama until the elections are over—I can assign him to command there by letting Shepherd go on leave. Shepherd ranks him as Col but is not judicious & is in complete ignorance of civil affairs in the state—I will give him leave for twenty days with permission to apply for such extension as the Genl in Chief may consider judicious. As I have not recd the order assigning Swayne to his Bvt rank I infer that there is some hitch in the matter—Under all the circumstances I think you will agree with me that great care & circumspection are needed in every action, so as to avoid interference in results which are certain in this District   A couple of months will settle the matter beyond farther controversy—" ALS, USG 3.

On Sept. 24, Pope telegraphed to USG. "Gen'l Swayne has not been assigned to his Brevet and when Shepherd returns from leave he will be Senior Officer in Alabama,   He is wholly unacquainted with the details of Registration or Civil business and as the Election in Alabama comes off in a few days it would be a serious calamity to be deprived of Swayne in charge. If he cannot be assigned I hope you will extend Shepherds leave until December first 1st" Telegram received (at 5:00 P.M.), DNA, RG 107, Telegrams Collected (Bound); *ibid.*, RG 108, Telegrams Received; copy, DLC-USG, V, 55. On Sept. 25, 10:45 A.M., USG telegraphed to Pope. "Gen. Swayne was assigned to his Bvt. rank several days ago." ALS (telegram sent), DNA, RG 107, Telegrams Collected (Bound); telegram sent, *ibid.*; copies, *ibid.*, RG 108, Telegrams Sent; DLC-USG, V, 56. See letter to Bvt. Maj. Gen. John Pope, Aug. 3, 1867.

On Oct. 14, Bvt. Col. H. Clay Wood, Atlanta, wrote to USG. "Since the order of September 24. 1867. assigning General Swayne to duty according to his Brevet of Major General, it has occurred to me that Generals Pope and Swayne occupy rather anomalous positions—General Pope requested the assignment of General Swayne by his Brevet rank, that he might place him in command of the District of Alabama, over Senior Colonels, as being more suited to conduct the administration of the civil affairs in that State—Of this you are already aware—The case now stands as follows: General Pope commands the Third Military District as Brigadier General U. S. Army, while he has, as a Subaltern officer, General Swayne, assigned to duty with his Brevet of Major General, Commanding the Sub-District of Alabama. General Swayne thus ranking his Commanding General, General Pope—Should not General Pope be assigned to duty according to his Brevet of Major General? General Pope, I know, will not ask the assignment, but it seems to me, in the fitness of things, it should be done—I have sent the same letter to General Townsend—" ALS, DNA, RG 94, ACP, 5013 1883. On Oct. 18, Bvt. Brig. Gen. Frederick T. Dent and Bvt. Maj. Gen. Edward D. Townsend endorsed this letter favorably. AES, *ibid.*

On Sept. 30, Pope wrote to USG. "I have the honor to transmit herewith copies of a correspondence with Hon A. Reese a Judge of the Superior Court of Georgia for the Ocmulgee Circuit. As he has positively refused to conform to my orders No 53 & 55 (enclosed) in relation to Juries or to resign his office in order that some other Judge may hold the Courts, I have been compelled to remove him   The new appointee is a gentleman of high personal character & the leading lawyer on the Circuit to which he is appointed   My full details of the reasons for this transaction will be found in the enclosed letters" ALS, *ibid.*, RG 108, Letters Received. The enclosures are *ibid.*

1. Probably an error; on Sept. 3, Governor Robert M. Patton of Ala. had written to USG. "I have recently observed several newspaper reports to the effect that Major General John Pope would probably be removed from command of the Third Military District. As these reports originated in prominent and responsible journals, they cannot but be regarded as entitled to some degree of consideration. In expressing the earnest hope that these rumors are unfounded, I trust that I will not be regarded as wanting in that respect which is due to the high authorities at Washington. My position as Governor of Alabama necessarily places me in close official relations with Gen. Pope. I have had the amplest oppertunities of learning his wishes and his policy in regard to reconstruction. On several occasions he has done me the honor to to invite personal conferences in relation to public affairs in Alabama. These invitations I have gladly accepted. The General has uniformly manifested the most anxious solicitude for the execution of the reconstruction laws in a perfectly fair and impartial manner, with a view of a speedy and satisfactory accomplishment of the objects for which those laws were enacted. To my certain knowledge, he has industriously sought reliable information respecting the temper and disposition of the people. Having ascertained these, he has, as I am thoroughly convinced, endeavored to administer the laws with as much acceptability to the people at large, as their positive requirements would admit of. As to the practical operations of Gen. Pope's orders and regulations concerning civil affairs, I can speak from positive and familiar knowledge, so far as Alabama is concerned; and I have no hesitation in saying that, whether taken separately, or as a whole, their effect has been most salutary. They have been issued from time to time, as circumstances might suggest; and the consequence has been a growing sentiment in favor of reconstruction under the Congressional plan. Gen. Pope's rule has been mild, and free from all semblance of tyranny or even harshness. He has in no way interefered with freedom of speech, or freedom of the press. A large number of newspapers have constantly opposed the pending plan of reconstruction; and animadverted with intemperate severity upon the policy and some of the orders of Gen. Pope. But in this they have reflected the sentiments of only a small number of the people. They have not been able to arrest the swelling tide that was moving on in favor of a settlement of our national troubles upon the basis of the reconstruction laws. On the contrary, as before stated, the sentiment in favor of restoration has constantly increased. If there is a full vote at the ensuing election, the State will go for reconstruction by a majority of more than a hundred thousand. This should certainly be accepted as a conclusive vindication of Gen. Pope's policy. In the State of Alabama, Gen. Wager Swayne has been in command for most of the time since the close of the war. His Head Quarters have been in this city. My relations with him, both personally and officially, have been of the most intimate character. It is but simple justice to say that he is deserving of the very highest commendation for the manner in which he has discharged his onerous and responsible duties. Whatever may be said of the condition of the unreconstructed States, and the temper of their people, I think it may be safely asserted that as little complaint can be urged against Alabama as against any other. In fact I am disposed to claim that she has exhibited a better spirit, and a more correct appreciation of the ligetimate results of the war than most of her southern sisters, if

indeed, she does not in this respect, surpass them all. For this favorable state of things—favorable, at least, when compared to other States—a very large degree of credit is due to Gen. Swayne. I have devoted my utmost exertions in favor of placing this State in harmony with the ruling power of the Federal government. Gen. Swayne has earnestly labored for the same thing. I believe he has accomplished a much good, and given as much satisfaction as any officer could have done in his situation. He enjoys the confidence of the great body of our people of all classes. He has much and deserved influence with the colored population; and that influence has been most wisely exerted for the common good of both blacks and whites. To him the lacks are largely indebted for wholesome advice and instruction as to their true condition as free citizens, and the responsibilities which rest upon them as voters. On all occasions, and in every proper way he has encouraged the freedmen to cultivate relations of amity and good feelings towards the whites amongst whom they were raised, and amongst whom they are to live. For reasons such as these I trust that I will be pardoned for expressing the hope that it may be the pleasure of the authorities at Washington to make no change in the military commander of this District, or of this State. I am only induced to write thus from a thorough conviction that the officers referred to are earnestly laboring for the public good, and that their labors are daily bringing forth good fruit." ALS, *ibid.* An unsigned endorsement of Sept. 9 referring this letter to President Andrew Johnson is *ibid.*

Endorsement

Respectfully forwarded to the Secretary of War.

In my opinion further action in this case is necessary and I respectfully recommend that the Judge Advocate General be directed to prepare charges against Col. H. B. Carrington, 18th US Infantry, based upon the facts herein developed; the same to be sent to the Commanding General Dept. of the Platte, with orders to convene a court martial for the trial of Col. Carrington upon his return from the six months leave of absence granted him in S O. no. 332, Hdqrs. of the Army, June 29 /1867

U. S. GRANT
General

HDQRS. A. U S.
SEPT. 10. '67.

ES, DNA, RG 153, OO-2236. Written on a letter of June 20, 1867, from Judge Advocate Gen. Joseph Holt to USG. "The accompanying record of the proceedings of a Board of Inquiry; Convened by S. O. no. 128, Head Quarters of the Army, at Fort Phillip Kearney, Dakota Terry, for the purpose of inquiring into the facts attending and preceeding the destruction of the party of Officers and Soldiers commanded by Bvt. Lt. Col. W. J. Fetterman, 18th Infy. on the 21st Dec. '66, and to report their opinion of what measures, if any, are necessary by way of punishment; is respectfully submitted. It will be seen that before its investigations were concluded, the Court was adjourned sine die by order of Gen. Sherman, on the ground that the immediate services of the Officers composing it were so necessary, that a longer session of the Court could not be permitted. The Court was ordered by Gen. Sherman to forward the testimony already taken, with its conclusions. This the Court declined to do, for the reason that, without great injustice, the opinion called for by the terms of the order convening it, could not be expressed, until all the testimony should have been taken. Gen. Sherman thereupon sent the following order: 'GEN. JOHN GIBBON President Court of Inquiry GENERAL: Yours of this morning is received. The immediate necessity for the services of the officers composing your Court, demands their presence with their commands. Whatever seeming injustice may result by the present adjournment of the Court, can be rectified at some future more liesure period, and you may therefore adjourn the Court as heretofore ordered, and submit the facts as far as ascertained, and a qualified opinion, or defer any opinion at all; leaving the General-in-chief to form his own, and to apply a remedy, if any is called for, in his own way.' The Court thereupon adjourned *Sine die*, without a statement of the conclusions reached by them. The record of the evidence already taken, together with the papers transmitted to this Bureau in connection with the case, are respectfully transmitted to Gen. Grant for such action as he may deem appropriate." LS, *ibid.* On Sept. 11, Bvt. Maj. Gen. Edmund Schriver, inspector gen., endorsed these papers. "The Secy of War *ad int.* directs these papers to the Judge Advocate Genl to carry out General Grant's recommendation, of Sept. 10. that charges be prepared for the trial of Col. Carrington. When completed to be sent with the papers to the Adjt Genl of the Army." Copy, *ibid.*, RG 107, Orders and Endorsements. On Sept. 26, Holt wrote to USG. ". . . A careful examination of all the testimony has induced me, before drawing formal accusations, to request further instructions in this case: the opinion having been formed that this officer is not chargeable with the main offence which appears to have been imputed to him, but only with some general neglects in his military administration. . . . In view of the conclusion arrived at, that Col. Carrington is not chargeable with the loss of Col. Fetterman's detachment, the question is respectfully submitted to the Secretary of War whether this Bureau shall attempt to prepare charges founded upon the minor neglects of discipline and faults of administration which have been adverted to. The fact that since their occurrence, the Government has granted the accused a six months' leave of absence, is a fact to be considered in connection with this question." Copy, *ibid.*, RG 153, Letters Sent. See *ibid.*, RG 94, Letters Received, 764M 1867; telegrams and letter to Lt. Gen. William T. Sherman, Jan. 14, Feb. 21, May 29, 1867; *SED*, 49-2-97; *ibid.*, 50-1-33.

On June 27, Maj. George K. Leet had favorably endorsed a letter of May 28 from Col. Henry B. Carrington, 18th Inf., Fort McPherson, Neb., to the AG requesting a six-month leave. ES and ALS, DNA, RG 94, ACP, C485 CB 1868. On Nov. 11, Carrington, Wallingford, Conn., wrote to Col. Ely S. Parker. "Will you interest yourself sufficiently in a personal matter of my own to assure Genl Grants direct action upon it. I am still, lame, using a cane & suffer intensely, at times, from exposure of last winter & the effect of the injury of the Ciatic Nerve.

One of my sons has had his leg fractured & while my injury was strictly in line of duty, I had to send to New Haven for surgeon & still have treatment. I asked for 'Allowance of fuel & Quartes,' as Genl *Sickles* has it & *others* have been allowed it. It was 'not favorably considered' I have appealed it to Gen Grant, *It is just*; &, in perfect qui[e]t; with strictest economy, I hardly can meet neccessary expenses—His action, of course, will be accepted as final; but I cannot believe it reached him. & therefore renewed it with reasons given. 'My Military history' on file, at War Dept shows my record & I think never has been seen by him; or it would have been found worthy of recognition—as others, in similar line of duty during the war were honored with Brevets' for less conspicuous & less successful duty of the same kind. I hope to be able to do light duty. office &c by end of my present leave; but it would be signally prejudicial if I must return to the far plains in Jany. My lungs suffer as well as my limb." ALS, *ibid*. On Nov. 15, USG endorsed this letter. "Disapproved." ES, *ibid*. On Nov. 18, USG disapproved another request by Carrington for a commutation allowance for fuel and quarters. ES, *ibid*., Letters Received, 898C 1867. On Dec. 16, USG favorably endorsed a letter of Nov. 29 from Carrington to the AG requesting another six-month leave. AES, Goodspeed's Book Shop, Inc., Boston, Mass. On Dec. 16, 1870, U.S. Senator William Sprague of R. I. wrote to USG. "I recommend Col Henry B Carrington U S A. to be retired. He was an early and efficient teacher of my youth. His wounds & services entittle him to your favor." ALS, DNA, RG 94, ACP, C485 CB 1868. Carrington retired as of Dec. 15.

On Oct. 24, 1872, Carrington, Crawfordsville, Ind., wrote to USG. "It would be highly regarded by me, in my life work, of inaugurating a thoroughly Polytechnic School, in connection with my military chair, if you should deem best to place me among the commissioners to the 'Vienna Exposition.' . . ." ALS, *ibid*., RG 59, Letters of Application and Recommendation. Additional papers are *ibid*.

To Fitz John Porter

Sept. 10th *1867*

General,

Your note of this evening, together with one from Adm.l Porter, asking to see me relative to some business of interest to yourself, is rec'd. I would be pleased to see you at my house this evening but I am just starting out and will not return until late. I will see you however at the War Office at any hour you please to call after 10 a. m. to-morroɣw.

Yours &c.
U. S. Grant

To Gn. F. J. Porter
Willard's Hotel

ALS, DLC-Fitz John Porter. See *PUSG*, 16, 550–51. On Jan. 14, 1867, Fitz John Porter had written to President Andrew Johnson requesting a court to reconsider Porter's 1863 court-martial. ALS, DLC-Andrew Johnson. On Sept. 13, USG endorsed this letter. "Before any consideration should be given to the within application of *Fitz-John Porter* for the reconsideration of the proceedings and sentence of a Court-Martial which convicted him of high crimes against the United States, it is manifestly proper that he should demonstrate to the satisfaction of the authorities his ability to controvert by new evidence the testimony on which he was convicted. If injustice has been done him by the findings of the Court, resulting in a severe sentence damaging to him professionally and otherwise, every opportunity which the law allows should be given to Mr Porter to exculpate himself. But no such testimony is presented with these papers, and until it shall be, and of a satisfactory character—, no action in the case is recommended." ES, *ibid.* Writing on a copy of this endorsement, Porter noted that "Gen Grant especially urged I should take such testimony home with me & assured me I should have the order for a reopening by Tuesday following—the da[y I] recd this." AN (initialed), DLC-Fitz John Porter.

On Sept. 16, Porter, New York City, wrote to USG. "I am to day in receipt of a copy of a report—sent to me by order of the President of the United States, endorsed upon my application of January 14th '67 for a court to re-examine the proceedings in my case. From that Report to the President, I understand you desire I should 'demonstrate to the satisfaction of the authorities my ability to controvert by new evidence the testimony on which I was convicted'. I presume an outline of the testimony I propose to adduce before the court to be appointed is all that you either desire at my hands at this time or your time will permit you to investigate. In this view of the case I respectfully beg leave to submit, that: under the charge of violatingon of the 9th Article of War, in not marching at 1. O'clock, instead of 3. O'clock, on the night of the 27th August 1862, upon which I was adjudged guilty, I propose to show by General Patrick & Col. H. C. Ransom—a member of Genl Pope's staff at the time—& others that it was impossible to have made an effective march that night at an earlier hour, and, that when I moved no delay attributable to me was had. Under the charge of failing on the 29th August 1862 'to push forward my forces on the enemy's flank and rear &c'—as well as that I did retreat from advancing forces of the enemy without any attempt to engage them or to aid the troops already fighting greatly superior numbers &c; and that the other portions of the army were relying on the flank attack I was then ordered to make to secure a decisive victory and to capture the enemy's army, a result which must have followed from said flank attack had it been made &c'—in as much as the possibility of such action by me as he desired at any period within hours of that time which Genl Pope considered available—depend altogether upon the *time* in the afternoon at which the order was received by me, or the *time* when action under that order, or the discretion allowed me, would have been of service.—I propose to show by the testimony of Generals Longstreet, Wilcox & others—whose letters I place in your hands for perusal—that at *no time* for hours anterior to the writing of General Pope's order, was there a possibility of my making the movement directed by him, except with the certainty of annihilation of my command—in as much as by the testimony of these and other Confederate officers, it is shown that the corps of Longstreet, numbering not less than 30.000 men (my own command being less than 11.000 men) was in my front hours before the order of General Pope to me was even penned, and, That the position which was the only tenable one left me under the circumstances, did accomplish all and more than the strict fulfilment of Genl Pope's order contemplated, in that it held (as shown by Generals Longstreet's & Wilcox's letters before referred to) a large body of the enemy in my front, that else would have engaged other portions of our army, already fully employed as has been shown. The reports of the Army of Northern Virginia—since re-published in the Rebellion Records—Vol. 9—all corroborate the position taken by me (upon information had at that time) as not only correct but as General Longstreet now says: 'Had you attacked any time after 12 M (29th August) it seems to me that we surely would have destroyed your army, that is if you had attacked with less than 25000 men.' Making little or no reference to my official conduct during the years preceeding the period immediately under consideration, I also propose to show that my subsequent conduct and that of the troops under my command—that is on the 30th day of August, the day following the one wherin it is alleged General Pope's orders were disobeyed—was of such a character as to prove in the most conclusive manner my energy and fidelity. I am the more anxious to do this as the court did not deem the testimony at the time admissable—the specification having been withdrawn under which I had hoped to do so. I shall have the testimony of Generals Butterfield, Sykes and others in my behalf. I may have occasion to revert to some of the testimony taken before the previous court, in the course of the re-investigation, and with the light thrown upon many matters by the close of the war, thus give an opportunity for those who desire to revise their testimony. Evidence, more or less important, on other points, is at hand, but too tedious to present for your consideration at this time. I propose to bring it forward from time to time before the court as circumstances may require." ALS, DLC-Andrew Johnson. On Sept. 19, USG endorsed this letter. "There is no case like this on record in the War Department. The application calls for a decision which, whatever its nature, will be very important in its effects on the public service. It is therefore recommended that the application be referred to the Attorney-General for his opinion on the following points:—Is there authority to try a second time, by a military court, a person whose case has been regularly and finally disposed of according to law, and after he has been dismissed and been out of the military service for a number of years? If so, what preliminary proceedings are necessary to make such a Court legal? *Especially*, in what mode should the person applying for a second trial be required to demonstrate that he possesses new and additional evidence of a kind which will enable him to prove his innocence of the charges on which he was dismissed? Should not the witnesses on whom he professes to rely be required to make oath that they will, on the trial asked for, give the evidence they now state they can give? In view of his familiarity with the laws and usages which govern the administration of military justice, it is suggested that the views of the Judge Advocate General of the army on the foregoing points be submitted to the Attorney-General." ES, *ibid.*

On the same day, Judge Advocate Gen. Joseph Holt wrote to USG. "In compliance with your verbal request of yesterday, I have the honor to lay before you, informally, the following suggestions upon the point of the legality of allowing a *new trial* to an officer of the army once duly dismissed the service under a sentence of a general court martial. . . . it is held by the unanimous authority of the chief official law officers of the Government; 1. That a new trial can be granted an accused by the President, only in originally passing upon the case as the reviewing officer whose confirmation is necessary to the validity of the proceedings, and in conjunction with a disapproval by him of the same. 2. That upon the formal approval, by the President, of a sentence of dismissal, (pronounced by a court having jurisdiction,) his power to annul, remove or modify it ceases altogether; and that the only relief which can be accorded the accused must be by way of a pardon, exercised in the form of a reappointment to the Senate. 3. That—as a corallary to the above—one President has no power whatever over a sentence once formally executed under the orders of a predecessor in office. 4. That—to merely set forth the principle in a different form—the President has no authority to order a new trial by court martial in the case of an officer whose sentence of dismissal, pronounced by a competent court, has become executed, because it is essential to give such a court jurisdiction that the party *must be in the army*; but he can not be put into the army by means of such order, but only by a new appointment and confirmation. It must thus be seen that for the President to convene a court martial to re-try the case of an officer whose valid sentence of cashiering, (to say nothing of an accompanying disqualification to hold all office under the United States,) was duly confirmed and executed by his predecessor, would be a measure wholly opposed to principle and precedent, and equally so, as it is believed, to a sound public policy. It would be indeed the first instance, within my knowledge, of such a proceeding in our military history, and would be altogether at variance with our present and past system of military administration. Once proceeded with, a sentence of dismissal of an officer of the army—pronounced by a court however eminent and after an investigation however elaborate and complete—would hereafter be deprived of its legal significance and effect; it would lose altogether its character as a finality, since at any time the case might be reopened and retried, without any regard to the existing disability; and the anomaly would result that a cashiered officer, unlike any other convicted official, without any exercise of the pardoning power and wholly independent of it, could be reinstated in his office. This consideration of the subject of *New Trial* having involved a reference to the *pardoning power* as the only agency through which a dismissed officer can be reinstated; allusion may well be made here to a practice, which to some extent prevailed at the period of the recent war—of giving to an executive pardon the effect of restoring a dismissed officer of regulars to his former position, (a vacancy remaining,) *without* a resort to a new appointment. This practice is referred to in the Digest of Opinions of this Bureau, as having grown up during the rebellion and as then acquiesced in, though directly opposed to the former method of proceeding in such cases. I have however myself never held or believed that it was in accordance with law. It is, as has been seen, at variance with the views of the Attorneys General, above quoted, all of whom have been clearly of opinion that a renomination by the President and confirmation by the Senate are essential to the officer's reinstatement. Thus condemned, and in view of the state of peace now existing, the practice in question should, it is submitted, be no longer countenanced. Having its origin in the summary and often irregular proceedings of a time of active hostilities, it was not, as it is understood, founded upon any new examination of the principles involved; but being—unadvisedly as it is conceived—initiated in some single case, (which, on account of peculiar facts, appealed strongly to the clemency of the President,) it came thus to be followed in subsequent instances. As an irregularity which could only have been admitted at a period of war, it should—it is repeated—cease with that period, and not be revived. It is due—it may be added—to the memory of President Lincoln to note, that at the outset of his military administration he strictly observed the rule of law as declared by the Attorneys General. In the files of this office is found a communication, to the President by Major Lee, Judge Advocate, dated June ___ 1862; in which that officer, in discussing the effect and proper form of a pardon in the case of dismissed officers, holds,—that 'the pardoning power does not reach a duly executed sentence,'—and that the restoration of such an officer 'can only be effected by a new appointment emanating from the appointing power.' Following this opinion is an official communication from the President's private secretary in which he states that the President directs him to say that *'the rules of law'* set forth by Major Lee *'are correct and approved by him, and that he desires them to be followed.'* It was not till some time subsequently, and under the pressure of the exigencies of the war, that the President, in a limited number of cases of the character above described, and which at the time of his action were *of most recent occurrence*, was induced to depart from the regular and approved method. It is to these cases that the opinion in the Digest of this Bureau—written before the close of the rebellion—refers, as giving rise to a law of the service, *for that period.* Thus holding, General,—to recur to the main subject—that it is beyond the constitutional power of the Executive to order a *new trial* in the case under consideration, I might close this commumunication, were it not that you desired further to be advised upon the preliminary point, as to the *form* in which an application for such a trial upon the ground of new evidence should be presented, and what *conditions* should be insisted upon before such an application be considered at all. . . . As conditions precedent to the entertaining of the application it should be required not only that this should be sworn to by the party, but that the testimony proposed to be introduced should be verified by the oath of each and every witness; that it should appear that this testimony could not have been procured at the time of the trial by the exercise of reasonable diligence; that it should not be cumulative—should not merely relate to questions upon which evidence was introduced *pro* and *con* on the trial, or be corroborative only of the testimony on the part of the defence as then made, but should pertain to a new defence and one sufficient in law; that the new testimony should be material to the issues of the former trial, constituting an answer to the *specific charges* upon which the accused was convicted; and that it should establish so complete a defence to these charges as properly to induce an acquittal upon another trial. It is only to be added that it must by no means be supposed that a court will entertain *at any period of time*, a motion for a new trial in a case which has been tried before it. On the contrary, such a motion, however strongly presented, must, according to the approved practice, be made *before final judgment.* . . . There may indeed be rare cases where courts for special reasons have allowed the motion to be made shortly after the formal entering of judgment; but certainly no case can, I am convinced, be found where *after a lapse of years* such a motion has been permitted. This practice is in analogy to that of the Government in refusing to reopen a sentence once finally executed; and we are thus brought back to the principle first herein set forth. I conclude therefore General, with the further expression of opinion, that, even if the application for a new trial in the case in question be presented in formal and substantial compliance with all the strict conditions of the law,—to entertain it at the present time, or after an interval of four years since the execution of the sentence, would be, in my opinion, improper, not only for the reasons set forth in the first part of this communication, but because such a measure would be a total departure from the uniform practice of all the courts of law." LS, DNA, RG 94, Letters Received, 316M 1869.

On Sept. 18, Porter, Washington, D. C., wrote to USG. "In my interview this morning I understood that before acting upon my appeal you desired the opinion of the Attorney General upon certain points relating to the power of the President of the United Sta[tes], to grant a re-examination. I infer from this if no such power existed a recommendation would be unnecessary. While I have no reason to believe that the points in question have been presented to the consideration of the Attorney General, I have no doubt of a favorable decision, and that the object of my appeal can be accomplis[h]ed without in any manner compromising the rights of any one or of the Government. That no misunderstanding may exist, I here repeat that my aim and the object of my appeal, are to vidicate my honor and to relieve myself from the burdens of a severe sentence. This I am confident I can acco[m]plish in the most satisfactory manner to the Government and myself, before a Court Martial,—Court of Inquiry—Board, or whatever it may be termed, composed as far as available, of the best talent of the Army, which under rules governing Courts Martial shall decide on the merits of the case by duly considering all the old and new testimony combined—giving to witnesses whom it may be desirable to call, an opportunity to amend or re-affirm their recorded evidence and accepting all other evidence as it stands—The action of the court to be advisory so far as I am concerned. If any such action as is indicated by your questions should be deemed necessary in order to secure the investigation, I desire now, as I did verbally to day, I disclaim all idea present and future of availing my self of any rights which might thus be acquired, other than would be necessary to coduct the re-examination. Cases like mine, on presentation of a just claim, or reasonable grounds to suppose it just, have been re-opened and decided again by the War Department. I could not ask you to devote your time to an examination of the case, nor did I presume, in calling for satisfactory evidence to substantiate my claim, that you desired to judge the; yet as I said to day, if you would be the arbiter, I would be glad of the opportunity to present the whole matter. In order that my wishes may be fully before the President I respectfully request this letter may be forwarded to be placed with the other papers." ALS (2), *ibid.*, RG 60, Letters Received, War Dept. On Sept. 20, USG endorsed this letter. "Respectfully refered to the Atty. Gen. of the U. States as part of the records in the case of F. J. Porter." AES, *ibid.*

On Sept. 13, Bvt. Maj. Gen. John Pope, Atlanta, wrote to USG. "*Confidential . . .* I mail you a letter herewith in the way of remonstrance against the reopening of Fitz John Porter' case or rather it is a letter setting forth the points established in the case which can be verified by the official record of the trial & giving reasons based thereon why neither justice nor military propriety will permit any interference with the Verdict of the Court—Should a Commission be appointed to examine the new testimony which Porter says he has procured since the War I beg that my official communication to you herewith sent may be laid before such Commission as I believe it to be unanswerable against any reopening of the case—Knowing as you do the bitter personal & official controversies which this case occasioned at the time I need hardly ask you, should it be determined to order a Commission to examine Porter' testimony, to detail officers of the highest rank for such Commission who have never had any connection with the Army of the Potomac—I suppose there is no haste about examining into the matter & I hope Genl. Sherman from his rank & character will be placed at the head of the Commission—with other officers above partiality or prejudice & who have never had their opinions prejudiced in the matter—It is a matter of too much consequence to me & many others to permit of haste or an inferior court—" ALS, *ibid.*, RG 108, Letters Received. On Sept. 16, Pope twice telegraphed to USG. "If any commission or Court is ordered to revise the case of Fitz John Porter I trust, for the sake of impartial consideration, that officers of rank will be chosen who have been in no manner connected with the Army of the Potomac. I forward tomorrow an argument in the way of remonstrance against reopening this case for your consideration or that of a commission if one be ordered." "I request respectfully that you make no decision as to reopening Fitz John Porters case until you receive my letter mailed this evening" Telegrams received (at 11:00 A.M. and 4:20 P.M.), DNA, RG 107, Telegrams Collected (Bound); *ibid.*, RG 108, Telegrams Received; copies, DLC-USG, V, 55. On Sept. 18, 11:30 A.M., USG telegraphed to Pope. "Your dispatch in relation to Porter trial received. Your letter will arrive no doubt before final action is taken." ALS (telegram sent), DNA, RG 107, Telegrams Collected (Bound); telegram sent, *ibid.*; copies, *ibid.*, RG 108, Telegrams Sent; DLC-USG, V, 56. On Sept. 16, Pope had written to USG. "As I am one of the principal parties concerned in the case of Fitz John Porter and as I learn that he is in Washington City seeking a reopening of his case on the ground that he has come into possession of testimony since the close of the War which has an important bearing on the subject; and as I suppose it to be not unlikely that a commission may be ordered to examine that testimony and report upon it, I consider it my duty as well as my right respectfully to submit to your attention or that of any Commission that may be ordered the following remarks for such consideration as they merit.—It is unnecessary to set out here in detail the Charges and Specifications on which Fitz John Porter was tried and convicted but I respectfully ask to submit a few remarks upon them merely to call attention to the points of the case established by testimony and uncontested even by the defence.—The only answer made by the defence to the facts established is in the nature of explanation or excuse.—To the first charge and first Specification, (the disobedience of orders being admitted by the defence) the answer is that the night was dark and there was danger of delay and straggling in executing the order for the March, but it will be noticed and I ask especial attention to this fact, that no attempt was even made to obey the order.—It is also established in the testimony on the subject that the whole of McDowell's and Sigel's Corps marched nearly all night that same night on a road but five or six miles north of Porter's Corps and that during the whole night messengers were passing between my Head Quarters to which Porter was ordered and his own and other Corps of the Army—How valid such an excuse as darkness is in the face of a positive order setting forth that the presence of his Corps 'was necessary on all accounts' I leave to your judgement—Especially in the light of the fact that not even an attempt was made under such pressing orders and necessities, to bring the Corps forward. The whole of the circumstances on this point are fully set forth in the testimony. Although the general plea of 'Not Guilty' was made by the defence to all the charges and Specifications, yet it was not disputed that the orders set forth in the Specifications to the Charges were received—Neither (except in the case of the joint order to McDowell and Porter) is it claimed that the orders were obeyed—Substantially the details set forth in all the Specifications except the 4th and 5th Specifications of the 1st charge and the 4th Specification of the 2nd charge remain undisputed, except as to certain phrases and words and the general impression conveyed.—The only defence set up was in the way of excuse and comprised two points.—1st That the ground in front of Porters Corps was difficult and that the road on which he was marching was occupied by the right of the enemy who extended across it.—2nd That the enemy was believed to be in heavy force and that an attack would have been unsuccessful.— To the first of these points it is only necessary to say that difficulty of ground even if it existed is no excuse for failing to obey an order and particularly for failing to *try* to obey it.—The fact established in the testimony that the enemy next day moved over this very ground and attacked our left is sufficient answer as to difficulty of ground, should such a pretext be thought to have any weight.— In relation to the force of the enemy in front of Porter I beg leave respectfully to submit that that question has no bearing whatever on the subject—Whether there were five thousand or fifty thousand of the enemy confronting Porter is a matter not at all affecting the question of his conduct.—A general battle was and had for hours been, raging on Porter's right and almost in his sight; certainly in his hearing.—He had under his Command nearly a third of the whole Union Army.—His Corps had been reenforced by Piatts Brigade and numbered quite twelve thousand men.—One of his Divisions contained nearly the whole of the regular Army.—It was abundantly supplied with Artillery and was altogether the most effective Corps on the field.—It had marched only three or four miles and was therefore by far the freshest Corps in the entire Army—Yet it did not fire a gun during the entire battle of the 29. of August 1862 but lay on the ground with its Arms stacked for seven hours of that battle without an attempt either to attack the enemy in front or to come to the assistance of the other troops elsewhere engaged in deadly conflict and who (as Porter himself says in his dispatch addressed to McDowell and King,) he believed were being overpowered and driven from the field—In the face of a positive order to attack he did not move and when convinced from the sounds of the battle on his right that that portion of the Army was worsted he retired from the field, not *toward* the Army which needed his help but in the opposite direction, although the road was open to him and messengers and orderlies were passing to and fro.—These are facts established by the testimony, and undisputed by the defence.—If in a general battle a Corps or Division Commander receiving a positive order to attack a portion of the enemy's line has the right to disobey this order on the ground that he does not believe the attack would be successful I cannot see how any combinations can be made by the Commanding General or how he can expect that any of his orders will be obeyed.—How can a Corps Commander know that the General in Chief expects his attack to be successful?—How can he know that he is not ordered to attack a particular point of the enemy's line in order that sufficient force to resist his attack may be withdrawn from other points to render an assault elswhere successful? How can he know that his attack is not intended to prevent the enemy's troops in front of him from reenforcing other parts of their line upon which an attack is being made?—The effect of an attack by Porter even had he been repulsed at any time from Midday to Eight O'clock in the evening of the 29th of August 1862 is clearly set forth in General McDowell's testimony in this case.—Had Sherman failed to attack the enemy's right at Chattanooga on the ground that the enemy was in strong force and he would be repulsed (as indeed was the fact) what would have become of Hooker, what indeed of the entire victory at Chattanooga.—In truth I feel ashamed to offer any argument to Military Men on such a matter.—They are patent and as well recognized as the first principles of discipline I say then that whether the enemy's force in front of Porter was great or small it makes not the slightest excuse for his not obeying his orders, nor can any excuse be found, even admitting the above to be one, for an officer who not only disobeys an order to attack, but absolutely keeps a large and effective force out of action any where during a whole day of battle in his presence.—If he was afraid to attack in his front why did he not bring his Corps to the aid of the rest of the Army which he says himself (in his dispatch to McDowell and King) he believes was being worsted? Why above all, did he march *away from*, instead of toward the Union Army?—The amount of the enemy's force in front of him I need not farther say has no bearing upon the subject, since he knew not for what purpose an attack was ordered, but it so happens in this case that testimony on that point unimportant and irrelevant as it is, is at hand.—I presume it will be admitted that the best authority as to the amount of the enemy's force in front of Porter on the 29th of August, 1862, is the report of the Officer in command of the enemy confronting him on that day. This officer was General J. E. B. Stuart of the Rebel Army.— He is now dead but fortunately his report is to be found in the volume of Rebel reports of this Campaign published by the Rebel Congress.—Copies of these published reports are in the hands of the Government and easily accessible.—He (General Stuart) reports that he commanded on Jackson's right on the 29. of August, 1862, with a ridiculously small force of Cavalry and some small guns, that he saw a heavy force which he estimated at twenty thousand men marching upon Jackson's flank, that he was made very uneasy, and sent back word to Jackson, that he disposed of his small Cavalry force so as to make as great a display as possible and made thirty or forty of his men cut brush and gallop up and down the Warrenton turnpike in his rear, so as to make a great dust and give the impression that heavy forces were on that road, that his ruse was successful and that the enemy halted and then fell back.—He further states that this force was Fitz John Porter's Corps.—I do not pretend to quote literally, but this report can easily be had and the exact words ascertained. Farther than this, Longstreet himself reports of his own Corps, the strength of which can be easily ascertained, that he had made forced marches for several days before, and a very long and hard forced march on that day fighting part of the time with Ricketts Division.—It is certain that his Corps was in little condition when it arrived on the field to contend with Porter's which, nearly if not quite of equal strength, was perfectly fresh and contained the best troops of either Army.—To say at this day that Longstreet's wearied and almost broken down Corps was able to overpower the 5th Corps of our Army is the bitterest commentary upon that Corps its worst enemy could make and I have no doubt is utterly groundless.—It would indeed be remarkable if overpowering forces of the enemy were all day in front of Porter that he was not attacked by them.—As astonishing as his own failure to attack.—I cite these facts as to the force of the enemy in front of Porter merely as they seem to be interesting and not because they have any bearing whatever upon Porter's guilt or innocence.—That was determined upon other grounds which no Military man will fail to recognize.—I beg attention however to what will I think very fully explain Porters conduct.—Despatches sent from him to Burnside, sent before and after he joined me and intended as he says himself for McClellan are to be found on the records of the Court Martial.—They indicate a state of mind and a hostility and bitterness I will venture to say unparalleled under such circumstances.—They present the grossest and most outrageous violation of discipline and military propriety—to say nothing of ordinary good manners which can be found on any official record in this country That a subordinate officer in the face of the enemy, without knowledge, of the number or disposition either of the enemy's forces or our own and in the midst of a deadly conflict upon which the very existence of the Government and the lives of thousands of patriotic men were at stake could write such dispatches, almost surpasses belief.—As I said it indicates a state of mind capable of anything and these dispatches themselves furnish the completest explanation of Porters conduct which can ever be given.—I take it for granted, as the general facts set forth in the Specifications of the charges against Porter were and are completely proved, that the testimony he now brings forward upon which to base a reopening of his case is simply testimony as to the amount of the enemy's force in front of him on the 29. of August 1862.—I respectfully submit that such testimony even if strictly true, has no bearing upon the findings and sentence of the Court Martial in his case and furnishes no reason whatever for reopening the case." LS, DNA, RG 60, Letters Received, War Dept. On Sept. 20, USG endorsed this letter. "This communication from Maj. Genl. John Pope, bearing on a subject which is now being investigated by the Attorney-General, is respectfully referred to him by . . ." ES, *ibid.*

On Sept. 21, Porter wrote to [Theodore Randolph]. ". . . Should I see the President this evening—the interview will determine my course. Last night I had a long interview with Genl Townsend—the Adjutant Genl of the army—and I found from—him—the cause of opposition—which he said could not be traced to Holt—but to the principle long established & based on the Constitution that no officer could have a new trial—and that the Prest could not return me to the army & without that, no re-examination could take place &c &c—all of which I fought though some points he was right in—He says Grant will not act until the Attorney General advises that the Prest has the right to give a new trial and to put me back in the army—The Prest has not yet sent the papers to Stansberry unless he did last night—and I learn just that he intends to give the Board without any referance but when—no one can tell—Many influences have been brought to bear on Grant—but without avail—He has taken his stand and though I believe his sympathy is with me—nothing can move or get him to say any thing—Grant sent the papers direct to Stansberry with Pope's letter—which *I* was not to see— but which I will on Monday. . . . I have seen the Presdt & Stansberry and we are now working to remove all legal obstacles & perplexities—All seems on a fair way to success by Wednesday or Friday . . ." ALS, DLC-Fitz John Porter.

On Sept. 21, William B. Franklin, Hartford, wrote to USG. "Fitz John Porter writes me to ask that I will do something to aid him in getting a rehearing of his case. All that I can do is to write you and give you the reasons why I think it will be an act of justice to give him the opportunity to clear himself from the terrible imputation now resting upon him. I saw Porter in Pope's company the day after the latter's defeat at Bull Run, and afterwards until we arrived in front of Washington. I know that they were on very cordial terms, and that Pope on some occasions advised with him confidentially. I talked a good deal myself with Pope, and I think that if he had had at that time any feeling that Porter had acted badly I would have learned it then. But I had no suspicion that he felt aggrieved by anything that Porter or any one who was then near him, had done. At Fairfax C. H., the day that we arrived at Washington I noticed that Pope was particularly in good spirits, and cordial with Porter. I have therefore always thought that the attack upon Porter was the result of an afterthought, and that the charges were not original with Pope. During the trial, I thought it proper to inform Porter that, Gens J. F. Reynolds, Geo H. Thomas & myself would if requested, go before the Court and swear that we would not believe Pope or Roberts under oath. I had consulted Gen. Reynolds before I made the proposition. He consented to go himself, and thought Gen Thomas would have no hesitation in giving such evidence. I was myself well convinced of Gen Thomas's opinion of Pope's veracity from what I had often heard him say, before the war. Porter declined to call us up to give this evidence, on the ground that the Court appeared so well disposed towards him, and his case was going on so well that he did not wish to irritate the Court by an attempt to break down the evidence of the principal prosecutors. The sequel showed that he made a serious mistake. But I think that the most equitable reason for a review of Porter's case is this. The Judge Advocate General, Holt was the Judge Advocate of the Court. That was right enough. But no one will deny that a Judge Advocate of a Military Court, when a prisoner is defended by able Counsel becomes to a great extent a prosecutor, and as such necessarily is biased against the prisoner. To say that Gen. Holt was prejudiced against Porter, is merely to say that he is like other men, and that he was so prejudiced the whole proceeding shows. Whether it is better or worse for the course of justice that the Judge Advocate should be prejudiced has nothing to do with the question. But an abstract of the proceedings and finding and sentence of the Court had to be made by the Judge Advocate General for presentation to the President of the United States, upon which (for he necessarily could not read the evidence) he was to make up his mind as to the guilt or innocence of the accused. Was it right, proper or decent, that this abstract should be made up by the very man who had done his best to convict the prisoner? Did not such a proceeding prevent the President from learning any extenuating circumstance, or finding out anything weak in the evidence; if any such there were? Did it not in fact take away any chance from Porter which he might have had, had a cool, unbiased person of legal knowledge made this abstract instead of Gen Holt. The whole business seems to me like a prosecuting attorney passing sentence upon a prisoner in a civil court immediately after the speeches of Counsel. I think the fact that Mr Lincoln had only Gen. Holt's abstract to guide him in making up an opinion on the proceedings of that Court is enough to invalidate the whole thing. It has been said, and perhaps with truth, that there is no precedent to guide in this matter. It may be said with equal truth that never since the trial of Admiral Byng was injustice so without precedent done. I think that there never was a more appropriate opportunity for going beyond precedent, and establishing the fact that no matter how or by whom flagrant injustice is done, you when the power is in your hands will see the right done. For my part I know that Porter was as loyal as the most loyal soldier now dead, and that no thought of treason or disaffection entered his brain. He was a victim to Pope's failure in Virginia, and it seems to me he has remained a victim long enough. You will in my opinion do an act which will not be the least among those which will make up your fame if you will lend your weight towards giving Porter the opportunity to retrieve his character as a citizen & soldier." ALS, DNA, RG 94, Letters Received, 574R 1867. On Sept. 24, Franklin wrote to Porter. ". . . I am afraid that Grant is not man enough to do what is right in this matter. His reference of any point in the matter to the Atty Genl is simply to shirk a responsibility. . . ." ALS, DLC-Fitz John Porter.

On Sept. 21, Luther Stephenson, Jr., Boston, wrote to USG. "At a meeting of the officers of the 1st Div. 5th Corps called together to give an expression of sympathy at the death of our loved commander Gen Griffen the enclosed petition was presented and signed by all the officers present. The duty of forwarding the document to you was entrusted to me and in so doing I would say that I express the sentiments of most of those who served under General Porter in saying that they most earnestly desire that his request for a new trial be granted. It was my fortune to be in command of a Regiment in General Porter's Corps during that unfortunate campaign which ended in the Battle of Bull Run and having personal knowledge of many of the circumstances connected with his career I have always felt that he was most unjustly dealt with." ALS, DNA, RG 94, Letters Received, 574R 1867. The enclosure is *ibid.*

On Nov. 1, Porter, New York City, wrote to Bvt. Maj. Gen. Edward D. Townsend. "Will you please have sent me a certified copy of a telegraphic despatch from me to General Halleck, dated Williamsburg—Va. Aug 16th 1862, received in Washington and filed in the War Department Aug 17th '62" ALS, *ibid.* On Nov. 5, USG endorsed this letter. "Respectfully forwarded to the Sec. of War. It is recommended that, an official copy of Gen. Porter's dispach be furnished him." ES, *ibid.* On Nov. 7, Bvt. Brig. Gen. Frederick T. Dent approved this endorsement for USG, secretary of war *ad interim.* AES, *ibid.* On Nov. 18, Porter wrote to USG. "I have the honor to enclose for your information a copy of a letter to the President of the United States, in reply to Genl Pope's letter to you of September, relating to my application for a re-examination of my case." ALS (press), DLC-Fitz John Porter. Porter had written to Johnson on Oct. 1. ALS, DLC-Andrew Johnson.

On Dec. 3, USG wrote to U.S. Senator Benjamin F. Wade of Ohio. "In compliance with the Senate's Resolution of the 27th ultimo I have the honor to enclose copies of all papers on file in this Department relating to the case of Fitz-John Porter, late an officer of the Army of the United States—other papers pertaining to the same case have been submitted to the President and not yet returned." LS, DNA, RG 46, Senate 40A–G3, War Dept. Reports. See *CG*, 40-1, p. 802. On Nov. 30, Townsend had written to USG. "In compliance with your instructions I have the honor to transmit herewith copies of all papers on file in this office in relation to the application of Fitz John Porter for a revision of his case, called for by Senate Resolution of the 27th instant." LS, DNA, RG 46, Senate 40A–G3, War Dept. Reports. On Dec. 9, Franklin wrote to USG. "I see by the papers that among the papers which you sent to Congress in the F. J. Porter case was my letter to you on the subject. Now although I do not in the slightest regret that what I said about the case in general should be published, yet I would have prefered that the statement I made as to the fact that c[er]tain officers, myself among the number were willing to testify as to our opinion of the credibility of Pope & Roberts, should have been kept back until the time came to call us to give our evidence. In fact I never for a moment thought the statement would go beyond you, for I considered my letter to you as private. But if you have looked upon it in a different light, is it not possible to obtain my letter from the Senate before it is printed, and change it in this respect, viz: So that it will state that the officers in question were willing to testify that *they would not believe two of the principal witnesses for the Government under oath.* The change would make it just as strong as it is, now that it mentions names, but would suppress names until the time came to tell them names I have understood since I wrote you before that Pope & Thomas are now on friendly terms, so that the publication of their names as I connected them in the letter might make a good deal of trouble. Do not understand me as wishing to withdraw my assertion, I only wish to keep it from the public (with names) until such time as it may be necessary for the public interest to publish the names. I kept a copy of the letter in question, but have looked for it, and have not been able to find it so I cannot refer to it by date, but merely as the letter on this case." ALS, *ibid.*, RG 94, Letters Received, 574R 1867. On Dec. 11, USG wrote to Wade. "In replying to the Senate Resolution of the 27th ultimo, respecting the case of Fitz-John Porter, a copy of a letter addressed to the General of the Army by William B. Franklin, dated September 21st 1867, was sent with the papers called for. I have now the honor to ask at the request of the writer of that letter, that for the words—'we would not believe Pope or Roberts under oath,'—the following be substituted, viz: —'we would not believe two of the principal witnesses for the Government under oath.' " LS, *ibid.*, RG 46, Senate 40A–G3, War Dept. Reports.

On June 15, 1868, Pope, Detroit, wrote to USG. "I have the honor to request that the enclosed extracts from the Testimony of Genl McDowell, & from the official reports of the Rebel Generals, J. E. B. Stuart, Longstreet & Stonewall Jackson be filed with my official letter to you concerning the reopening of the case of Fitz John Porter—They contain the matter referred to in that letter—" ALS, *ibid.*, RG 108, Letters Received. The enclosures are *ibid.* On June 30, Bvt. Brig. Gen. Benjamin S. Roberts, Fort Sumner, New Mexico Territory, wrote to USG. "I had the honor a few days ago to send you a letter from Major General G. H. Thomas, to vindicate myself *first* before my Commander-in-Chief from the secret attack made by General Franklin on my truth and manhood, officially and personally, in a letter to you, intended to be confidential and private. The unequivocal denial of General Thomas of the truth of General Franklin's statement, so far as he was concerned, it was my first duty to place before you. But the covert attack on my character in the letter from General Franklin to you, was by accident sent from your office to the Senate of the United States; presenting me there as an officer unworthy of credit 'on oath or otherwise' and using such matchless names as General G. H. Thomas, and the late General J. F. Reynolds, to accomplish his secret, ignoble, but audacious purpose. It therefore seems to me, General, eminently proper, that you should send the letter of General Thomas to the President of the Senate, with the request that it be filed with the letter of General Franklin for my justification before a Senate that has during 33 years past commissioned me to every grade in the Army from Second Lieutenant to Brigadier General, and to the highest rank and commission in the Volunteer Service. I am too old, General, to submit now, after thirty three years of hard and faithful service in the Army, to be secretly undermined in my reputation, and to be presented to you my Commander-in-Chief and the Senate, as lacking in truth, the very life of an officer and a gentleman. I beg you therefore to transmit to the President of the Senate, the letter of General Thomas, with such remarks as seem befitting and proper in this case." LS, *ibid.*, RG 94, Letters Received, 574R 1867. On Jan. 29, 1869, USG endorsed this letter. "Respectfully forwarded to the Secretary of War with recommendation that Gen. Robert's request be complied with." ES, *ibid.*

To Orville H. Browning

Washington City,
Sept. 11th 1867

HON. O. H. BROWNING, SECRETARY.

SIR,

In reply to your letter of Sept. 10th asking that the necessary order be given for the transfer of the *Navajo Indians* on the Bosque Redondo to the Indian Dept., I have the honor to inform you that your communication of the 8th June on the subject was referred to the Genl of the Army to give the proper instructions to the Comr of the Dist. of New Mexico.[1] On the 19th June Genl Grant referred the papers to Lt. Genl Sherman, Com'dg. the Mil. Div. of the Mo. with orders to give the necessary instructions in the case, which no doubt has been done.

A duplicate of the order however, has this day been sent to General Sherman.

Very respectfully,
Your obt. servant,
U. S. GRANT,
Sec'y. of War ad int.

Df, DNA, RG 94, Letters Received, 86I 1867; copies, *ibid.*, RG 75, Central Office, Letters Received; *ibid.*, RG 107, Letters Sent to the President. On Sept. 10, 1867, Secretary of the Interior Orville H. Browning had written to USG. "Referring to the accompanying copy of a communication dated the 7th inst; from the Act'g Commissioner of Indian Affairs, and to the letter of the Acting Secretary of the Interior of the 8th June last, in reference to the transfer of the Navajo Indians on the 'Bosque Rodondo' Reserve to the care of this Department, I now have the honor to request that the necessary order for such transfer be issued at as early a date as practicable." LS, *ibid.*, RG 94, Letters Received, 86I 1867. The enclosure is *ibid.* On Sept. 14, Act. Secretary of the Interior William T. Otto wrote to USG. "I have the honor to acknowledge the receipt of your letter of the 11th inst; informing the Department that you have issued the necessary

orders for the transfer of the Navajo Indians to the care of the Indian Bureau."
LS, *ibid.*, RG 107, Letters Received from Bureaus.

1. On June 8, Otto had written to Secretary of War Edwin M. Stanton concerning the procedure for transferring control of the Navajos from the War Dept. to the Dept. of the Interior. Copy, *ibid.* On June 13, Stanton endorsed this letter. "Approved, and referred to General Grant to give the proper instructions to the Commander of the District of New Mexico to carry into effect." Copy, *ibid.* On June 19, Maj. George K. Leet endorsed these papers. "Respectfully referred to Lt Genl W. T. Sherman com'd'g Mil Div of the Missouri who will give the necessary instructions in this matter." Copy, DLC-USG, V, 43. See *PUSG*, 16, 332–35.

To Bvt. Maj. Gen. Christopher C. Augur

Sept. 15th *1867.*

DEAR GENERAL,

I am constantly getting letters and appeals to help John C. Dent to one of the "Trade permits" in our Western territory.[1] I would like very much to see him get some good post but regret to have to be appealed to myself on the subject. If you can send him such a permit for some post on the line of the Rail-road, or elsewhere where it will likely pay, I will be obliged to you. Fort David Russell I should think would be a good point.

I have not met any of your family for several days but when I did see them last all were well.

Yours Truly,
U. S. GRANT

ALS, Augur Papers, IHi.

1. On Nov. 11, 1867, William D. W. Barnard, St. Louis, wrote to USG. "Application is respectfully made *to you* for traders permit at Ft Union. Supposing a permit which had been given was valid, we purchased and ship'd some 37.000$ assorted merchandise and now have them within 30 miles of the post. In resent letter from Genl Auger, to John proffering permit at Ft Fetterman he remarks, this is about the only post in my Depart, officers are not in some way or another identified This would seem to hold good at least at Ft Union; the old sutler Moore, has for the last ten years had a complete monopoly there and with regard to trade, appears to be able to dictate what shall be done at that point From my reading of your order and cir[c]ular in reference to same, it is

evident you desire to distroy monopoly and give the soldier all his money will buy. J. E. Barrow, one of our citizens, a highly respectable, worthy and solid gentleman, purchased and forwarded the stock of goods giving me ⅓ interest— our effort has been arrested and are now called on for over 7000$ freight, which might have been realised from sales had we been permitted to sell. He is the gentlemen who furnished the capital for John's store at Ft Fetterman, in which John has half profits and I am convinced from resent interview with Auger, it will prove the best trading post on the plains, the emigration taking that route next season. I dislike exceedingly General, to trouble you, but it is a matter of importance to me and will unquestionably lead to the advantage of the post in distroying the present exorbitant prices by healthy and proper competition. I make this appeal to you direct, if you can not give it, should be most happy to receive such documents as would entitle me, in name of J. E. Barrow, even if it does not procure, the privilage, of subordinate officers and will esteem it a great favour to have an answer as early as your convenience will permit, as we are under heavy expense and the season is advancing. Mrs Barnards health poor, little ones all well—are expecting an addition next week or two. When may we expect to see you out west? With best respects to family and Mr Dent . . ." ALS, DNA, RG 393, Military Div. of the Mo., Letters Received. See *PUSG*, 1, 342. Barnard enclosed a letter of Nov. 11 from John E. Barrow, St. Louis, to USG. "Application is herewith respectfully made for Traders Permit at Fort Union N. Mexico If granted I will in all respects comply with regulations and give any indemnity the Government may require" LS, DNA, RG 393, Military Div. of the Mo., Letters Received. On Nov. 13, USG endorsed these letters. "Refered to Comd.g Officer Dept. of the Mo. There is no objection to competition at Military posts but the question of permiting more than one trader is left to the discretion of commanders." AES, *ibid.* On Nov. 16, Lt. Gen. William T. Sherman, St. Louis, endorsed these letters. "Respectfully referred to Genl. A J Smith Comdg Dept of the Mo, who had better make the decision whether Fort Union New Mexico had not better be made a General Trading Post so that we may in a short time recall all troops." AES, *ibid.* On Nov. 25, Barnard telegraphed to USG. "In answer to letters and telegram to Dr Madison Mills Leavenworth I have just recd following, 'Gen'l Smith is favorable and will give permit for Fort Union if suggested by Genl Grant, Dont hesitate to ask Gen Grant.' Will you please make the suggestion by telegraph" Telegram received (on Nov. 26, 9:00 A.M.), *ibid.*, RG 108, Telegrams Received; copy, DLC-USG, V, 55.

Orders issued on Nov. 4, 1868, at Hd. Qrs., Dept. of the Mo., revoked Barrow's permit to trade at Fort Union and appointed Barnard as post trader. DS, DNA, RG 108, Letters Received. On March 25, 1872, Barrow, New York City, wrote to USG. "*Personal* . . . In January 1859, through the acquaintance of Mr W D W Barnard, and his representations to you, I received a 'Permit' to trade at, Ft Union, New Mexico. Every cent invested in the Enterprize, and all the responsibility rested upon me. In about Eight Months my appointment was revoked; just after I had been to heavy expense in getting the Business in good shape, and every thing fairly under ways without any notice whatever. Through Mr Bs profligacy and the revoking of the 'Permit' ruin followed me—You know the particulars. I have a large family dependent upon me; and believing you to be a just man, I have taken the liberty to ask of you a letter, to Genl Belknap, Secy, reccommending me, as Sutler or Trader, to one of the new Posts, about to be established in Southern Utah. I am familiar both with the country and its Inhabitants." ALS, *ibid.*, RG 94, Applications for Positions in the War Dept. See *HRC*, 44-1-799, pp. 136–44.

To Lt. Gen. William T. Sherman

Private   Washington, D, C, Sept. 18th *1867*.
MY DEAR GENERAL,

I received your very kind letter written from Omaha which gave assurances of your sympathy for me at the very unpleasant position which I am now called on to occupy. It is truly an unenviable one and I wish I had never been in it. All the romance of feeling that men in high places are above personal conciderations and act only from motives of pure patriotism, and for the general good of the public has been destroyed. An inside view proves too truly very much the reverse. I am afraid to say on paper all I fear and apprehend but I assure you that were you present there is no one who I would more fully unburden myself to than yourself, or whos advice I would prise more highly.

I received a letter from Mrs. Sherman yesterday, from New York, which indicates that she will not be in Washington this visit. I answered her letter this morning sending the letter to St. Louis.

Unless great changes take place between this and the 1st of Feb.y I shall not be able to leave Washington this Winter. If I can get off however for a couple of months I shall take about the trip *I refused to take last Winter* and which you had the opportunity of enjoying on that account. If I go I shall not take Campbell with me. I will want you to come to Washington in that case to take my place. I am in hopes of getting the command of the Army back again where it belongs and if I do there should always, for some years at least, be some one present to exercise it lest it revert again to the Sec. of War.

I hope your commission will prove successfull; but my faith is not strong. In the first place Browning would not appoint a man on

it who is not already impregnated with his own views and turn
every thing to confirm them. I do not know any man who contact
with ha~~ds~~ made me think less of, in proportion to his capacity.
That is exceedingly limited.

Yours Truly

U. S. Grant

To Lt. Gn. W. T. Sherman

ALS, DLC-William T. Sherman. On Sept. 7, 1867, Lt. Gen. William T. Sherman, "Steamer St Johns. . . . 10 miles above Yancton," had written to USG.
"There are so many newspaper Reporters with us that I need not give you even
an outline of our progress. We did expect to reach Sioux City today, but a strong
wind prevails, which has pushed the boat to the Bank, and here we must lay till
the wind subsides. At Fort Randall above and at a Dr Burleighs here, we got
newspapers up to August 29, from which I get an outline of the troubles in
Washington. I tender you my sympathies, but I suppose you can weather the
Gale without help, only I shall watch the progress of the game with personal
interest. I regret that the Change of Hancock occurred at this exact moment, as
I fear it will enable those who have the idea that his burning the Cheyenne village was the *Cause* and not one of the Consequences of the present troubles. I
will put myself in his footsteps as far as possible & thereby share the blow. I
suppose Sheridan will be at Leavenworth when we get there about Oct 5, 10—en
route to Fort Larned. I will invite him to go along with us and there he can see
or hear much that will give him an insight to his business—The more I see of
Indians the less inclined I feel to put their treaty and annuity business on the
army.—If we can give these agents & traders 'limits' within which to operate—
and outside of which we the Military can act with vigor, it will be about the
best division of labor I can think of—As to your matters in Washington I wont
venture an opinion unless you ask it, and I feel assured if you want my help you
will command it—I hope by this time Mrs Sherman will have taken Minnie to
the Seminary at Georgetown. If so, and Mrs Grant will drop in to see her I will
consider it a high compliment." ALS, USG 3.
    On Aug. 26, 11:15 A.M., USG had telegraphed to Sherman, St. Louis.
"What is the necessity for keeping up the posts of C. F. Smith Reno Phil Kearney? No emigrants or trains seem to pass over. Let me have your views on this
subject and if you deem it advisable break up these posts and remove the troops
at once." ALS (telegram sent), DNA, RG 107, Telegrams Collected (Bound);
telegram sent, *ibid.*; copies, *ibid.*, RG 108, Telegrams Sent; DLC-USG, V, 56;
DLC-William T. Sherman. On the same day, Bvt. Maj. Gen. William A. Nichols,
St. Louis, telegraphed to USG. "Your telegram of today rec'd   General Sherman
is on the upper Missouri River with the Indian peace commission & is beyond
immediate communication   Gen augur has returned to Omaha in whose Dep't
are the posts of C. F. Smith Phil Kearney & Reno" Telegram received (at 1:45
P.M.), DNA, RG 107, Telegrams Collected (Bound); *ibid.*, RG 108, Telegrams
Received; copies (one sent by mail), *ibid.*, RG 94, Letters Received, 1177M
1867; DLC-USG, V, 55. On Sept. 11, Sherman, Omaha, telegraphed to USG.
"Just arrived will probably start for Laramie tomorrow evening, The Indians

along the Missouri are docile & poverty stricken but of the Sioux I could account only for less than six thousand (6000) leaving the inference that ten thousand (10000) are out at mischief,   Gen Augur is out on the road and I will see him about Fort Reno Phil Kearney & C, F, Smith   That road was opened for the benefit of Montana & if abandoned now the hostile Indians would infer they had compelled their abandonment & they would naturally follow to the Platte where they could do infinite mischief   As soon as I see Augur I will telegraph you again on this point & after you have all the facts we will be ready to do what you order though the season is late to bring in the stores   Will it not be better to leave them till this Commission concludes its work,   For the next month I will be in reach of the Telegraph"   Telegram received (at 7:30 P.M.), DNA, RG 107, Telegrams Collected (Bound); *ibid.*, RG 108, Telegrams Received; copies (incomplete), *ibid.*, RG 393, Dept. of the Platte, Telegrams Sent; DLC-USG, V, 55. On Sept. 13, noon, USG telegraphed to Sherman. "You need not breat up Fort C. F. Smith and other posts mentioned in a previous dispatch from me unless you think it decidedly advisable." ALS (telegram sent), DNA, RG 107, Telegrams Collected (Bound); telegram sent, *ibid.*; copies, *ibid.*, RG 108, Telegrams Sent; DLC-USG, V, 56. On the same day, Sherman telegraphed to USG. "Your two dispatches are rec'd. I will make up a report to Embrace Sept thirtieth 30 as soon as that date is passed. The hostile Sioux cannot meet us at Laramie by the fifteenth 15 inst & the Commission have postponed the meeting till November first. In the meanwhile we will meet some of the friendly bands on the north Platte & then go down to the Arkansas & return to Laramie. I will see Gen Augur further as to the powder River Road & then notify you." Telegram received (on Sept. 14, 8:40 A.M.), DNA, RG 107, Telegrams Collected (Bound); *ibid.*, RG 108, Telegrams Received; copies, *ibid.*, RG 393, Dept. of the Platte, Telegrams Sent; DLC-USG, V, 55.

On Sept. 22, Sherman telegraphed to USG. "Commission has adjourned to Fort Harker October Eighth (8)   Will go to St Louis in the meantime" Telegram received (on Sept. 23, 10:20 A.M.), DNA, RG 107, Telegrams Collected (Bound); *ibid.*, RG 108, Telegrams Received; copies, *ibid.*, RG 393, Dept. of the Platte, Telegrams Sent; DLC-USG, V, 55. On Sept. 25, Sherman, St. Louis, wrote to USG. "I got home yesterday but found that Mrs Sherman, deterred by Reports of Cholera, & heat, had stopped at Lancaster, but she will leave there today and be here by dinner tomorrow. I will remain here till Oct 6, when I am to go to Fort Leavenworth as a Witness for Custar, then up to Harker, Larned &c, for the Indian Council. I had arranged and provided well for the Council on the Arkansas, south side, opposite Fort Larned, but I find that Superintendent Murphy has agreed with the Indians to hold the Council 75 miles further south. I will not increase the escort, and if these Commissioners will trust the Cheyennes I will also. This Change also will make it difficult for us to keep the appointmts Novr 1, at North Platte, and 15, at Fort Laramie. The Missouri River is of course again very low, and the quickest way to go from Leavenworth to Omaha, is to come away round by Chicago. I have now been with these Gentlemen near two months. Commissioner Taylor is a kindhearted well meaning man, full of the stereotyped Indian Talk. Henderson is by far the strongest man with us—Sanborn is clear and sensible enough—Tappan is nobody—Harney even weaker than I had supposed—and Terry improves on close acquaintance. At first they had a strong majority on the Civil side of the question, but at North Platte I carried my address against Taylor, by a vote of 4 to 3—Harney & Tappan going with Taylor & Sanborn & Henderson with me & Terry—Augur was with us and I would make no let up, without his full assent—I think we may do some good, even if we simplify the Case—Henderson admitted to me that the ~~Contrast in the~~ behavior of our officers & soldiers towards the Indians had been to him so wrongly represented, that he had been prejudiced but on contact he saw the great difference between them & the agents. I came home chiefly to make my annual Report as you directed at the end of Septr—Terry & Augur both promised me this, punctually to the day. Hancock & Sheridan are off and I must work up their case, from the letters & despatches I have on hand—My Report shall be mailed you next week. I assure you that I appreciate fully the delicate & responsible position you now have, but believe you will master it. I would be glad to relieve you of some of the details, but this Commission will keep me on the jump till December and it is for Our Common interest that some end be made of this most troublesome business if possible. With you I doubt perfect success, but even partial success will relieve our men to that extent—The marching, escorting &c &c is very laborious, and disorganizing—all the Regimental officers complain that this service ruins their military discipline. If you can possibly put off your proposed Cruize it would be best for you and all concerned. No eventualities down in the Gulf can equal in importance the questions that now disturb us all—I dont think the Country in danger, for the People generally are at work, but Parties are in danger, and that is all. Men always have, and I suppose always will struggle for power, through parties. It would be better if they could substitute the real interests of a whole Country for mere party, but so it was—so is and will be as long as men think and act from common motives. We of the Army can & should keep out, for the reason that we are bound to support the Governmt in existence, and this changes every four years. The next change is near at hand and is the real trouble that agitates the newspapers and to some extent the whole People—John Sherman wrote me a month ago to sound you, saying that if you intended to allow your name to be used by either Party, or even independant of Party without pledge,—he would act on the certainty of your election, but if you took positive grounds not to have your name canvassed then he should support the claims of a person that I am not at liberty to name but one strongly died in the wool as a Republican. Others have asked me similar questions on the supposition that I knew, and I have generally said that I believed that nothing would induce you to change your present Commission for that of the Presidency. I really have not yet seen a name given out that I would support—Chase—Wade—Colfax—&c &c on the one hand—and Pendleton, &c on the other. I suppose with the present strength of Parties we should have a President in accord with Congress, for without some cooperation the Governmt suffers, and most of all the Army, that has to st~p~ep in and get the kicks and cuffs of both parties. Lincoln was a new man at the time of nomination and it may be the wise workers can find another when the time comes, and even with a new and indifferent man, you can be more useful as Comr in Chief than as President. Therefore in no event would I advise you to accept nomination but if you do, let me know, that I may also know what to say and what to do. I now have my house here in first rate order. Minnie is at the Chegasay Institute in New York. By next Monday I will have the rest of the Children at school here— My expenses have been heavy by reason of being compelled to keep servants in the house here, and Mrs Sherman & myself being both apart we have really had the expenses of three establishmts. Still I keep free of debt, and must do it— Mrs Sherman sold one of our carriages & pair of horses at Madison, and I must within a week get her another pair for her close carriage. I will not look out for 2.40 horses, but good heavy stock that will manage to make the trip out home in an hour or so. You must be more careful for the old women shake their heads when they read of your runing over children, paying the fine & making reperation dont satisfy their judgmt in the Case. If you ever want me, give me as much notice as possible for preperation." ALS, DNA, RG 108, Letters Received.

On Sept. 30, USG telegraphed to Sherman. "Forwarded to B̶v̶t̶. M̶a̶j̶. G̶n̶. C̶. C̶. A̶u̶g̶u̶r̶, O̶m̶a̶h̶a̶ N̶. T̶. for such action as he deems proper. By Western Union Telegraph Company Dated 'Fort Laramie, D. T. Sept. 29. 1867. Received at Wash'n Sept. 29: To Hon. O. H. Browning Sec'y Interior Just informed that the General Commanding this Department has ordered his Inspector General to forts Reno, Phil Kearney & Smith on an inspecting tour & know that his escort is to be the celebrated Pawnee Scouts. The Indians inhabiting the part of country to be visited are the bands of hostile Sioux, with whom the Commission are trying to make a treaty of peace. The afore said Pawnees are their hereditary enemies & already even the friendly Indians of the Sioux nation, who are living about this post, are protesting to me against the Pawnees going in that country. My honest opinion is—basing it upon my long acquaintance with the Sioux character—that if the Pawnees go to that country, the present commission may as well cease their labors & go home, as the presence of the Pawnee Scouts in their country will be the signal of hostilities, & every object of the Commission will be defeated. Please have the Honorable Sec'y of War direct that the order sending them into that country be at once countermanded. G. P. Beauvais Sp'l 2d. Comr.' " AES (on a telegram received), *ibid.*, RG 107, Telegrams Collected (Bound); telegram sent, *ibid.*; copy, DLC-USG, V, 56. On the same day, Sherman telegraphed to USG. "Dispatch from Beauvais received. Gen Augur telegraphed me this morning for my opinion on the Same matter & I answered, we had better not send the Pawnees on that duty as the Indians have as many foolish prejudices as an old maid Beauvais knew that Gen Augur would comply with his request & he had no business to magnify so small a matter by telegraphing to Washn—he should pay for the message" Telegram received (at 3:10 p.m.), DNA, RG 107, Telegrams Collected (Bound); *ibid.*, RG 108, Telegrams Received; copies (one sent by mail), *ibid.*, Letters Received; DLC-USG, V, 55. A notation at the foot of a telegram received indicates that a copy was sent to Secretary of the Interior Orville H. Browning. AN, DNA, RG 108, Telegrams Received.

On Oct. 3, Sherman telegraphed to USG. "Construing the Presidents telegram of last night as an order I shall start for Washington at four thirty (4 30) this P m & will come via Indianapolis and the Baltimore & Ohio Road" Telegram received (at 4:10 p.m.), *ibid.*, RG 107, Telegrams Collected (Bound); *ibid.*, RG 108, Telegrams Received; copies (one sent by mail), *ibid.*, RG 94, Letters Received, 1408M 1867; DLC-USG, V, 55. Sherman arrived in Washington, D. C., on Oct. 6, went to USG's office at 9:00 a.m., and, the next day, recorded in his diary. ". . . Saw the President for a long interview—He [shadowed] a wish that I would stay in Washington & Act as Sec of War but made nothing positive, promised to call next day. Dined at Genl Grants & rode out with him" InNd.

On Oct. 4, President Andrew Johnson had written to USG. "Please inform Major Genl C. C. Augur, by telegraph, that he h̶a̶s̶ is authorized and empowered to act as a member of the Indian Peace Commission during the absence of Lieut. General Sherman, and direct him to meet the Commission at Fort Harker on the eighth instant." Copies (3), DLC-Andrew Johnson. On Oct. 5, 11:10 a.m., USG telegraphed to Bvt. Maj. Gen. Christopher C. Augur. "The President directs that you act as a member of the Indian Peace Commission during the absence of Gn. Sherman Meet the Commission at Fort Harker on the 8th inst." ALS (telegram sent), DNA, RG 107, Telegrams Collected (Bound); telegram sent, *ibid.*; copies, *ibid.*, RG 108, Telegrams Sent; *ibid.*, RG 393, Dept. of the Platte, Telegrams Received; DLC-USG, V, 56. On the same day, Augur, Omaha, telegraphed to USG. "Your dispatch of this day received. I leave for Fort Harker in the morning" Telegram received (at 3:30 P.M.), DNA, RG 107, Telegrams Collected (Bound); *ibid.*, RG 108, Telegrams Received; copies, *ibid.*, RG 393, Dept. of the Platte, Telegrams Sent; DLC-USG, V, 55.

To Bvt. Maj. Gen. Joseph A. Mower

Washington, Sept. 18th *1867* [*10:30* A.M.]

MAJ. GEN. MOWER,
NEW ORLEANS, LA.

Your dispatch recommending postponement of election in La. received. This matter is entirely in the controll of District commanders and rests with no one else. If you do postpone I would advise that there be no more opening of registration, it once having been closed, and the time required by law for correcting the lists having been given. A re-opening of registration in my opinion would be much more likely to bring about collission than the holding of an election at the time already ordered.

U. S. GRANT
General.

ALS (telegram sent), DNA, RG 107, Telegrams Collected (Bound); telegram sent, *ibid.*; copies, *ibid.*, RG 108, Telegrams Sent; DLC-USG, V, 56. On Sept. 16, 1867, Bvt. Maj. Gen. Joseph A. Mower had telegraphed to USG. "Telegram from E D Townsend AAG to Genl Hartsuff received, I have assumed Command of the fifth Military District, I earnestly recommend that the elections in this State be postponed, In many parishes both Whites & Negroes are armed & I consider a Collision inevitable should the Election take place as ordered, More troops are needed should they be sent here now they would probably be stricken down with Yellow fever Hence my suggestion that the Elections be delayed" Telegram received (at 4:05 P.M.), DNA, RG 107, Telegrams Collected (Bound); *ibid.*, RG 108, Telegrams Received; copy, DLC-USG, V, 55.

On Sept. 18, 10:30 A.M., USG telegraphed to Mower. "I see it stated that the order releiving Texas Judges has been revoked. If done Please inform me by whos order. ~~if done~~." ALS (telegram sent), DNA, RG 107, Telegrams Collected (Bound); telegram sent, *ibid.*; telegram received (at 11:00 A.M.), *ibid.*, RG 393, 5th Military District, Telegrams Received. On the same day, Mower telegraphed to USG. "Nothing is known at these Head Quarters conserning the order relieving Texas Judges. Will ascertain soon as possibly from Texas whether such an order has been issued" Telegram received (at 3:20 P.M.), *ibid.*, RG 107, Telegrams Collected (Bound); *ibid.*, RG 108, Telegrams Received; copies (one sent by mail), *ibid.*, Letters Received; DLC-USG, V, 55. See letter to Andrew Johnson, Aug. 1, 1867, note 2.

On Sept. 19, Mower telegraphed to USG. "I have seen Gov Flanders this morning he is of opinion that the postponement of the Elections at this late day would result in more evil than good his reasons are sound and I have decided not to postpone the Elections—The Negroes are armed & organized in most if not all of the parishes & I think under the direction of the organization known as the Grand Army of the Republic. I had an interview this morning with Judge Warmouth who is the leader of this organization & desired him to send at once to the Parishes where there is the greatest excitement & counsel the Negroes to conduct themselves with prudence, I endeavored to impress upon him the fact that any overt act of the negroes at this time might result most disastrously to themselves and the Country. The Troops are scattered through the different Parishes but in such small numbers as to be of no use whatever should Collisions occur between the Whites & Blacks, I do not fear any trouble in this City" Telegram received (at 11:15 P.M.), DNA, RG 107, Telegrams Collected (Bound); *ibid.*, RG 108, Telegrams Received; copy, DLC-USG, V, 55. On Sept. 20, 4:00 P.M., USG telegraphed to Mower. "It is wrong that there should be armed organizations in any of the states subject to Military rule except such as is authorized by law and wholly subject to the controll of the District Commander. I do not know how you are to meet the difficulty now better than you have done except to notify the leaders that you will hold them personally responsible for every violations of the law committed by organizations got up under their controll. Also get controll of these organizations yourself as far as you can, by commanding leaders, and deal with the question of disbanding the or retaining them as you may think most conducive to peace and public interest." ALS (telegram sent), DNA, RG 107, Telegrams Collected (Bound); telegram sent, *ibid.*; copies, *ibid.*, RG 108, Telegrams Sent; DLC-USG, V, 56.

On Sept. 23, 11:15 A.M., USG telegraphed to Mower. "Keep me informed by telegraph daily of condition of affairs in La. until after election." ALS (telegram sent), DNA, RG 107, Telegrams Collected (Bound); telegram sent, *ibid.*; copies, *ibid.*, RG 108, Telegrams Sent; DLC-USG, V, 56. On the same day, Mower telegraphed to USG. "There has been no change in the condition of affairs since I last telegraphed, I have issued an order forbidding the meeting of organized armed men" Telegram received (at 5:40 P.M.), DNA, RG 107, Telegrams Collected (Bound); *ibid.*, RG 108, Telegrams Received; copy, DLC-USG, V, 55. On Sept. 24, Mower telegraphed to USG. "The following telegram rec'd this morning 'Shreveport La Sept 23d TO LIEUT N BURBANK AAG Dist of La, I have this day rec'd three petitions from citizens in different portions of Bossier and Caddo parish and the statements of the freedmen representing that the Negroes are drilling and holding secret meetings nightly with guards to prevent whites from coming near, Intending to create a serious disturbance of Insurrectionary character during the present week I am asked for detachment, unable to comply but in one instance on account of strength of command, Please send instructions (signed) C B CLARK Lt 20th Infy Comdg Officer I will take all measures in my power to break up these organizations I cannot spare any troops from this City and I have scarcely any others available, besides it would be inhuman to send out from here troops to die of Yellow fever & at the same

time infect the whole country through which they might pass with that disease"
Telegram received (on Sept. 25, 11:30 P.M.), DNA, RG 107, Telegrams Collected (Bound); *ibid.*, RG 108, Telegrams Received; copy, DLC-USG, V, 55.
On Sept. 25, Mower telegraphed to USG. "Nothing new in the condition of affairs since yesterday" Telegram received (at 7:00 P.M.), DNA, RG 107, Telegrams Collected (Bound); *ibid.*, RG 108, Telegrams Received; copy, DLC-USG,
V, 55. On Sept. 27, 12:30 P.M., Mower telegraphed to USG. "Every thing passing off quietly in the city at the polls." Telegram received (at 2:30 P.M.), DNA,
RG 107, Telegrams Collected (Bound); *ibid.*, RG 108, Telegrams Received;
copy, DLC-USG, V, 55. On Sept. 28, Mower telegraphed to USG. "All quiet at
the Polls and in the City today" Telegram received (at 4:40 P.M.), DNA, RG
107, Telegrams Collected (Bound); *ibid.*, RG 108, Telegrams Received; copies
(one sent by mail), *ibid.*, Letters Received; DLC-USG, V, 55. On Sept. 29,
Mower telegraphed to USG. "The Elections passed quietly in this City. An in-
cipient riot occurred in Jefferson City yesterday Evening but was Quelled by the
energy of the Mayor & the prompt arrival of the Military before it had assumed
formidable proportions" Telegram received (at 3:40 P.M.), DNA, RG 107,
Telegrams Collected (Bound); *ibid.*, RG 108, Telegrams Received; copies (one
sent by mail), *ibid.*, Letters Received; DLC-USG, V, 55.

On Sept. 27, 12:08 P.M., USG had telegraphed to Mower. "I recommend
that election for Texas be ordered to commence first Teusday in November." ALS
(telegram sent), DNA, RG 107, Telegrams Collected (Bound); telegram sent,
ibid.; telegram received, *ibid.*, RG 393, 5th Military District, Telegrams Received. On the same day, Mower telegraphed to USG. "Telegram recommending
postponement of Election in Texas received Orders will be issued accordingly"
Telegram received (at 5:20 P.M.), *ibid.*, RG 107, Telegrams Collected (Bound);
ibid., RG 108, Telegrams Received; copies, *ibid.*, RG 393, 5th Military District,
Telegrams Received; DLC-USG, V, 55. On Oct. 1, Mower telegraphed to USG.
"Registration closed in Texas on twenty eighth (28th) inst Returns will not
be received from Interior for three (3) or four (4) weeks As thirty (30) days
notice is required Election cannot be held until the middle or last of November"
Telegram received (at 12:20 P.M.), DNA, RG 107, Telegrams Collected
(Bound); *ibid.*, RG 108, Telegrams Received; copies, *ibid.*, RG 393, 5th Military District, Telegrams Received; DLC-USG, V, 55; 5th Military District Papers, Duke University, Durham, N. C. At 12:40 P.M., USG telegraphed to
Mower. "Make election order for Texas to suit your receipt of returns" ALS
(telegram sent), DNA, RG 107, Telegrams Collected (Bound); telegram sent,
ibid.; copies, *ibid.*, RG 108, Telegrams Sent; DLC-USG, V, 56.

On Dec. 7, Maj. Gen. Winfield S. Hancock, New Orleans, telegraphed to
USG. "So soon as I receive the rules upon which the apportionment preparatory
to the Election of delegates to the Convention in Texas has been based in the
plan proposed by General Reynolds, (in a very few days) and after necessary
Examination and revision—the Election will be ordered in that state. The matter can be delayed but a few days at furthest unless you have other views" LS
(telegram sent), DNA, RG 107, Telegrams Collected (Bound); telegram received (at 5:10 P.M.), *ibid.*; *ibid.*, RG 108, Telegrams Received. On Dec. 8,
11:00 A.M., USG telegraphed to Hancock. "Order election in Texas soon as
possible" Telegrams sent (2), *ibid.*, RG 107, Telegrams Collected (Bound);
telegram received, *ibid.*, RG 393, 5th Military District, Telegrams Received.
On Dec. 17 or 18, Hancock telegraphed to USG. "The Election in Texas is ordered to commence on the tenth (10) February & continue for five (5) days and

to be held at the County Seats only. Number of whites Registered fifty six thousand, six hundred & seventy eight (56.678) number of Colored Registered forty seven thousand five hundred and eighty one (47581) Total regected about seventy five hundred (7500)" Telegram received (on Dec. 18, 1:30 P.M.), *ibid.*, RG 107, Telegrams Collected (Bound); *ibid.*, RG 108, Telegrams Received; copies (dated Dec. 17), *ibid.*, RG 393, 5th Military District, Telegrams Sent; 5th Military District Papers, Duke University, Durham, N. C.; (dated Dec. 18) DLC-USG, V, 55.

To Andrew Johnson

Washington Sept. 19th 1867

HIS EXCELLENCY A. JOHNSON
PRESIDENT OF THE U. STATES
SIR:

In view of the fact that Yellow Fever has been declared epidemic in New Orleans, and that all officers belonging to the 5th Military District, now absent from it, are authorized to remain absent until the 15th of October, by applying to the Adjt. Gen. of the Army, I would respectfully recommend that Gen. Hancock be notified that the provisions of this authority be extended to him.

General Hancock received orders to proceed immediately to New Orleans, La., when relieved by Gen. Sheridan, after the publication of the circular giving the authority here referred to. This shuts him out from making application for the benefits of it.

I have the honor to be
Very Respectfully
Your obt. servt.
U. S. GRANT
General

Copies, DLC-USG, V, 47, 60; DNA, RG 108, Letters Sent. See telegram to Maj. Gen. Philip H. Sheridan, Aug. 21, 1867; letter to Andrew Johnson, Aug. 26, 1867. On Sept. 19, 1867, Bvt. Maj. Gen. Joseph A. Mower, New Orleans, telegraphed to USG. "I take the liberty of suggesting if Gen Hancock is coming to his command immediately that he should make his Head Qurs temporaily at Amite La a little town about sixty 60 miles from New Orleans & in direct Railroad and telegraphic communication with it. It is in the Pine woods & free from yellow fever." Telegram received (at 2:00 P.M.), DNA, RG 107, Telegrams Collected (Bound); *ibid.*, RG 108, Telegrams Received; copy, DLC-USG, V, 55. On Sept. 21, 3:30 P.M., USG telegraphed to Mower. "Gen. Hancock will not go to New Orleans before the 15th of October." ALS (telegram sent), DNA, RG 107, Telegrams Collected (Bound); telegram sent, *ibid.*; copies, *ibid.*, RG 108, Telegrams Sent; DLC-USG, V, 56.

On Sept. 18, 10:22 A.M., USG had telegraphed to Mower. "Please report condition of officers now down with Yellow Fever." ALS (telegram sent), DNA, RG 107, Telegrams Collected (Bound); telegram sent, *ibid.*; telegram received, *ibid.*, RG 393, 5th Military District, Telegrams Received. On the same day, Mower telegraphed to USG. "General Wheaton Lt Col Wood & Maj Leslie Smith first Infy Col MGonigle A Qm Lt Abbott Sixth Cavalry Surg Clements, Asst Surg Koerper Actg Asst Surgeons Auerbauch & Deal are in favorable condition   Lt Collinan first Inf & Bogle thirty ninth Condition not known   Capt Spangler sixth Cavalry & Lt Rossander ninth Cavy died yesterday" Telegram received (at 4:20 P.M.), *ibid.*, RG 107, Telegrams Collected (Bound); *ibid.*, RG 108, Telegrams Received; copies, *ibid.*, RG 94, ACP, 1118M CB 1867; DLC-USG, V, 55. On Sept. 26, Mower telegraphed to USG. "No change in condition of affairs since yesterday   From what I hear privately I fear that there are no hopes of Gen Wheatons recovery" Telegram received (at 6:00 P.M.), DNA, RG 107, Telegrams Collected (Bound); *ibid.*, RG 108, Telegrams Received; copy, DLC-USG, V, 55. On Oct. 14, 10:00 A.M., USG telegraphed to Mower. "Give Gn. Wheaton leave of absence as soon as he is able to travel." ALS (telegram sent), DNA, RG 107, Telegrams Collected (Bound); telegram sent, *ibid.*; copies, *ibid.*, RG 108, Telegrams Sent; DLC-USG, V, 56.

On Oct. 11, Bvt. Maj. Gen. Samuel P. Heintzelman, New York City, wrote to Bvt. Maj. Gen. Edward D. Townsend. "I last evening received a telegram from Gen. Jno. S. Mason at San Antonio Texas announcing the death from Yellow fever at Victoria Texas, on the 7th Instant of Bvt. Major S. H. Lathrop Captain 35th Infy & that Mrs. Lathrop his wife was convalescing from the same. Her nephew Lt. Henry Norton 17th Infy is convalescing from the same fever in Galveston. Major Lathrop's wife & child are left in straightened circumstances. I have the honor to request that orders may be given to send them North at the expence of the Government & directing Lt. Norton to escort them. She may not be able to travel at present:—can he delay until she can?" ALS, DNA, RG 94, Letters Received, 776H 1867. On Oct. 18, USG endorsed this letter. "Application approved. Transportation will be given to families of Yellow Fever victims whenever applied for." AES, *ibid.*

To William H. Seward

Washington City,
Sept. 19th 1867.

HON. W. H. SEWARD, SECRETARY.
SIR,

I have the honor to acknowledge the receipt of your communications of the 4th & 10th insts., enclosing copies of dispatches from the *Consul of the U. S. at Panama* and the Vice Consul of the U. S. at *Aspinwall*, also copies of a correspondence with the President of the State of Panama, relative to the *disorderly conduct of U. S. troops* who arrived at that port, en route for California, and in reply to inform you that the Adjt. Genl. to whom the papers were referred, reports—"The detachment referred to in the enclosed papers consisted of 452 recruits of the 9th and 14th Inf'y.; and left N. York for San Francisco July 1st 1867, arriving at Aspinwall on the evening of July 9th, Capt. Geo. W. Davis, 14th Inf'y., commanded the Detachment. Under date of July 25 /67 Capt. Davis made the following report.—'Left New York at 10 O'clock P. M. July 1 /67 on Steamship "Ocean Queen", with a detachment of 4 officers and 452 recruits for San Francisco. Arrived at Aspinwall on the evening of the 9th and the troops were immediately landed in consequence of the stm'r. having gotten aground in coming to the wharf. It was therefore impossible to make immediate connection with the Steamer in waiting at Panama at 12 M., and was immediately re-embarked on Steamship "Golden City." While the troops were waiting transportation at Aspinwall a few of the men became intoxicated, but no serious disturbance resulted therefrom.' This report comprises the extent of the information of which this office is possessed relative to this subject. Genl. Butterfield Supt. Genl. Recruiting service has been instructed to caution officers conducting recruits via the Isthmus to prevent such occurrences in future, and to hold such officers to a strict accountability for any violation or neglect of these instructions. Genl. Halleck will be requested to have the matter more fully investigated and offenders properly punished.

> Very respectfully,
> Your obt. servant,
> U. S. GRANT,
> Sec'y. of War, ad. int.

Copies, DNA, RG 94, Letters Sent; *ibid.*, RG 107, Letters Sent to the President. On Sept. 4 and 10, 1867, Secretary of State William H. Seward had written to USG. "I have the honor to transmit herewith for your information and such action as you may deem advisable, a dispatch, No 5, of the 23rd of August last, addressed to this Department by the United States Consul at Panama, relative to the disorderly conduct of U. S. soldiers who landed there on the 9th of July last, from New York, in transit to California. Please return the dispatch after having availed yourself of its contents." "I have the honor to enclose herewith for your perusal a dispatch, No 17, of the 12th of August last, addressed to this Department by the Vice Consul of the United States at Aspinwall communicating copies of a correspondence with the President of the State of Panama, relative to the disorderly conduct of troops of the United States who arrived at that port, en route, for California. Any suggestions which you may have to make, in returning the dispatch, with a view to a reply to Mr Robinson, will be acceptable." LS, *ibid.*, RG 94, Letters Received, 896S 1867. Additional papers are *ibid.*

To Bvt. Maj. Gen. Edward O. C. Ord

Washington, D, C, Sept. 22d *1867.*

MY DEAR GENERAL,

Your letter looking forward to a change of station when the time comes was duly received. I will not forget it. When reconstruction has progressed so far, under the laws of congress, that a change of commanders will not be interpreted as a disapproval of the course of the commander removed I will recommend your transfer to one of the permanent Departments; McDowell's probably.

I am exceedingly anxious to see reconstruction effected and Military rule put an end to. Politicians should be perfectly satisfied with the temperate manner with which the Military have used authority thus far, but if there is a necessity for continuing it too long there is great danger of a reaction against the Army. The best way, I think, to secure a speedy termination of Military rule is to execute all the laws of Congress in the spirit in which they were conceived, firmly but without passion. This I believe has been pretty fully done by all the District commanders.

Please present my kindest regards to Mrs. Ord and the children.

Yours Truly

U. S. GRANT

BVT. MAJ. GN. E. O. C. ORD,
VICKSBURG, MISS.

ALS, James S. Copley Library, La Jolla, Calif. On Sept. 13, 1867, Bvt. Maj. Gen. Edward O. C. Ord had written to USG. "private . . . I am down with rheumatism—pretty bad—Mrs O—is for some months a sufferer from pains in her lungs & has had two Hoemorages—We both want to get out of this climate— but General I shall try and worry thro the election and then I shall ask as a favor some other Dept—You *want one* friend among the Pacific Slope commanders and McDowell will be far more acceptable to the republicans than I am or Terry—please help me in this matter—. . . Genl—you must not think I am unsettled or unreliable in my eh mind—when I asked for Arkansas it was after consulting Genl Sherman & Reynolds who told me the Fort Smith as Head Qurs was high and dry & would suit consumptives—but Genl Little Rock & this bottom are damp and do not suit them or rheumatics—If I thought I could get to Fort Smith I wouldnt ask a change—" ALS, USG 3.

On Sept. 26, 9:35 A.M., USG telegraphed to Ord. "You are authorized to remove your Hd Qrs. to any point within your command you may select during the prevalence of Yellow Fever." ALS (telegram sent), DNA, RG 107, Telegrams Collected (Bound); telegram sent, *ibid.*; copies, *ibid.*, RG 108, Telegrams Sent; DLC-USG, V, 56. On Oct. 8, Ord telegraphed to USG. "Capt Hyatt twenty fourth (24th) Infantry died of fever on the sixth (6th) at Pass Christian Lt Matilde same Company very ill Yellow fever is here since twenty ninth (29th) ulto, Several deaths among Citizens, none among soldiers yet, My staff and self live four (4) miles in the Country, *Ambulance* order compels us to move, I shall move to Holly Springs where cost to Government will be in rents &c one fourth what it is here and as all mails and Troops to or from Arkansas pass via Memphis twill be more central, The order for Gen Kautz Court had better be postponed as Col Gilbert cannot possibly arrive and the fever may Keep others away" Telegram received (at 3:30 P.M.), DNA, RG 94, Letters Received, 1437M 1867; *ibid.*, RG 107, Telegrams Collected (Bound); *ibid.*, RG 108, Telegrams Received; copy, DLC-USG, V, 55. On Oct. 10, 12:40 P.M., USG telegraphed to Ord. "If you move Hd Qrs. you will not be required to return to Vicksburg unless you choose to do so." ALS (telegram sent), DNA, RG 107, Telegrams Collected (Bound); telegram sent, *ibid.*; copies, *ibid.*, RG 108, Telegrams Sent; DLC-USG, V, 56. On Oct. 15, Ord telegraphed to USG. "Head Quarters will leave here for Holly Springs wednesday the sixteenth (16) inst" Telegram received (at 3:40 P.M.), DNA, RG 107, Telegrams Collected (Bound); *ibid.*, RG 108, Telegrams Received; copy, DLC-USG, V, 55.

On Dec. 13, Judge Advocate Gen. Joseph Holt wrote to USG. "Brevet Major Gen. Augustus V. Kautz, Lieut. Col. 34th Infantry, was tried at Vicksburg, Miss., on the 2d instant, by General Court Martial convened by order of General Grant, under the following charge: Conduct to the prejudice of good order and military discipline. In this, that the accused, having had a letter written to him from Head Qrs. 4th Mily District to the following effect:—'Hd Qrs. 4th Mily. Dist. Vicksburg, Miss., Aug. 27th '67 GENERAL: The condition of affairs requires for a time one officer of experience at Columbus, Miss. The General commanding directs you to proceed to, and take command at that post. The General further directs me to say, that as soon as the exigencies of the service will permit, you will be relieved and your leave of absence will be granted. I am, General, Very respectfully, &c. HUGH G. BROWN 1st Lieut. 36th Infy. A. D. C:'—did fail to send his reply through the proper channels, but in a letter addressed to the Bvt. Major Gen. Commanding, did use the following disrespectful & insubordinate language: 'I cannot see anything in your letter except a design to put me off and to procrastinate. I never ask an indulgence except when I feel satisfied it can be granted without injury to the service, and without imposing on any one.

And whilst I am liable to error, I am also open to conviction in this respect; but the exercise of the arbitrary right to refuse or put off does not convince;'—Thereby attributing (in the first extract) motives to his commanding officer other than that of the good of the service, expressing dissatisfaction to his commanding officer with his orders, and intimating that he expected his convictions to be consulted before he should be refused a leave of absence. . . . It is therefore respectfully advised that the sentence be either disapproved or remitted, on the following grounds:—1. That the accused was justified in assuming a right to reply unofficially and through other than the regular channels, to a communication entitled by Gen'l Ord himself a private letter: 2. That while the extracts quoted in the specification, when taken by themselves and apart from their just connection, seem to lack somewhat of the strict courtesy due from Gen. Kautz to his commanding officer, yet the general tenor of the whole letter is so far otherwise as to convince the reviewing authority that Gen. Kautz was not consciously guilty of the disrespect alleged:—and 3. That not only his eminent services and acknowledged value as an officer, but his habitual and well known observance of the rules of official propriety, entitle him to a favorable consideration of his purposes as manifested in his acts." Copy, DNA, RG 153, Letters Sent. See Andrew Wallace, *Gen. August V. Kautz and the Southwestern Frontier* (Tucson, 1967), pp. 64–65.

To Hugh McCulloch

Washington City,
Sept. 23d 1867

Hon. Hugh McCulloch, Secretary.

Sir,

Your letter of the 8th August last, enclosing one from the *Surveyor* of the Port of *Charleston*, South Carolina, relative to certain alleged evils of the military *quarantine* established at that port, has been referred to the Comd'g. Genl. of the Second Military District and returned with the following report, which is furnished for your information, viz;—"The Quarantine on this coast is intended to be effective and to be effective a thorough and searching inspection must be made of all vessels arriving at ports in this District. For this reason the quarantine regulations require that the inspections should be made between sunrise and sunset.

Both of the vessels referred to in this complaint, arrived so late

that the proper inspections could not have been made on the evening of their arrival. The detention over night was unavoidable and
the question of anchoring or standing off and on during the night
was one for the discretion of the master or pilot. If there was any
detention on the succeeding morning by reason of the absence of
the health officer, it furnishes a reasonable ground of complaint.
This however is not shown, and on the contrary the presumptions
are strong that the detention was necessary and for other causes
and that the vessels were released as soon as it was proper and safe
to relieve them. In the case of the Ship 'Amelia', the detention was
clearly the result of her disabled condition, a Providence of God
for which the Quarantine Regulations are in no way answerable.
The case of the Barque 'Annie' will be still further investigated and
if it be found that any evil exists it will be corrected. The station
for the Quarantine vessel was selected after consultation with six
of the harbor pilots—experts—as the best in every particular, most
convenient for vessels coming into port and not in the way. I see
no reason to distrust the correctness of their judgment or the honesty of their recommendation. The quarantine vessel is not 'entirely' or in any degree useless in the judgment of those whose duty
it was to select it. The cost is not $1200. per mo as stated by the
Surveyor, but is $950. per month, and is not unreasonable, and
is not a charge upon the Treas'y. of the U. S."

I am, very respectfully,
Your obt. servant,
U. S. GRANT,
Sec'y. of War, ad int

Copy, DNA, RG 107, Letters Sent to the President.

To Maj. Gen. George H. Thomas

Washington, D, C,
Sept. 23d 1867. [*11:05* A.M.]

MAJ. GN. G. H. THOMAS,

Inform Col. Hamil[1] that Nashville & Chattanooga Rail-road will pay the money due government on the 1st ~~proximo~~ November. Until that time has been given.

U. S. GRANT
sec. of War ad int.

ALS (telegram sent), DNA, RG 107, Telegrams Collected (Bound); copy, *ibid.*, RG 393, Dept. of the Cumberland, Telegrams Received.

On Sept. 27, 1867, Bvt. Col. Samuel R. Hamill, Louisville, wrote to Bvt. Maj. Gen. Daniel H. Rucker, act. q. m. gen. "Presuming that the policy adopted by the Government in the case of the Nashville & Chattanooga Rail Road Co., is intended to govern in similar cases: that Railroad Companies which are indebted to the Government and have not complied with the terms of their original contract with it, must apply all their available means to liquidate their indebtedness and will not be permitted to declare dividends. The Major General Commanding has directed me to invite your attention to the fact that the Memphis & Charleston Rail Road Company propose paying a dividend on the 1st of Jan. 1868. Although in accordance with the terms of the Extension granted them, they will not liquidate their indebtedness within a year thereafter during which time it is proposed to pay two dividends—I enclose herewith a copy of the annual Report of the Compy, of which please see marked paragraphs on pages 7 & 13—" LS, *ibid.*, RG 94, Letters Received, 833C 1867. The enclosure is *ibid.* On Oct. 19, USG endorsed this letter. "Approved" AES, *ibid.*

On Aug. 18, Maj. Gen. George H. Thomas, Louisville, had telegraphed to USG. "I approve & concur in the recommendation of Gen D. H. Rucker A. Q. M. G. regarding case of Memphis & Charleston Railroad referred to me on the sixth (6th) instant." Telegram received (on Aug. 19, 8:45 A.M.), *ibid.*, RG 107, Telegrams Collected (Bound); copy (dated Aug. 17), *ibid.*, RG 393, Dept. of the Tenn., Telegrams Sent. On Oct. 17, Rucker wrote to USG transmitting funds to repay the Memphis and Charleston Railroad debt. LS, *ibid.*, RG 92, Reports to the Secretary of War (Press). On Oct. 18, USG wrote to U.S. Treasurer Francis E. Spinner. "I have the honor to request that you will cause the sum of $127,988.42, deposited by *Winslow, Lamer & Co.* Agents of the *Memphis & Charleston R. Rd.* Co. with the Asst. Treasr. of the U. S. at N. York to the credit of the Treas'y. of the U. S. on account of the Qr. Mrs. Dept., to be placed to the credit of *Bvt. Brig. Genl. J. J. Dana* Qr. Mr. U S. A. to whom previous payments on account of the indebtedness of the Memphis & Charleston R. Rd. Co. have been made." Copy, *ibid.*, RG 107, Letters Sent to the President. On Nov. 9, Rucker wrote to USG concerning this railroad. LS, *ibid.*, RG 92, Reports to the Secretary of War (Press).

On Oct. 15, Rucker wrote to USG. "I have the honor to return herewith the letter of Mr. Sam'l McD. Tate, President of the Western North Carolina Railroad Company, asking that the credit heretofore granted that Company in the payment of its indebtedness to the United States for Railroad property purchased, be extended for a further period of twelve months. Mr. Tate alleges as a reason for this application the want of money and the fact that they are miserably poor. . . . In view of the embarrassment under which the President states the Company to be laboring, I respectfully recommend, that an extension be granted, but upon the following terms, . . ." LS, *ibid.* On Oct. 21, USG endorsed this letter. "The Qr. Mr. Gen. recommendation is approved." Copy, *ibid.*, RG 107, Orders and Endorsements.

On Nov. 22, USG wrote to Attorney Gen. Henry Stanbery. "I have the honor to transmit herewith a com'n from the Qr. Mr. Genl of the Army dated Nov. 21 1867 containing a letter from Judge *Alex M Clayton* respecting a judgment against the *Miss. Central R. R* Co obtained a year before the war of the rebellion, with a request that you will take such action as you may deem necessary for the interests of the U. S. Govmt." Copy, *ibid.*, Letters Sent to the President. Rucker's letter to USG concerning this matter is *ibid.*, RG 92, Reports to the Secretary of War (Press).

1. On Nov. 20, 1866, Thomas wrote to Secretary of War Edwin M. Stanton recommending Hamill for appointment in the U.S. Army. LS, *ibid.*, RG 94, ACP, H823 CB 1867. On Nov. 26, USG endorsed this letter. "Respectfully refered to the Qr. Mr. Gen. I cheerfully endorse whatever recommendation may be made by him on this recommendation." AES, *ibid.* No appointment followed. On Sept. 17, 1867, Thomas wrote to USG. "In consideration of the important services rendered by Capt *S. R. Hamill* a. q. m and Bvt. Lt Col. U. S. vols. in the settlement of the indebtedness of the S. R. R (for the purchase of material Rolling Stock &c from the Government at the close of the war) and of his thorough knowledge of the duties of his office; I respectfully recommend that he be appointed a Capt and a. q. m U. S. a if there be a vacancy in the Q. M. Dept. I also have to request that he be continued on his present duty of attending to the settlement of Southern R. R. indebtedness to the Government. He is thoroughly acquainted with the financial condition of each of the Southern R. Roads now indebted to the Government, and I do not believe that a more competent or zealous officer could be entrusted with their final settlement." Copy, *ibid.*, RG 393, Dept. of the Cumberland, Letters Sent. On Aug. 20, Hamill, Louisville, wrote to USG. "I have the honor to acknowledge the receipt of the notification of my appointment as Colonel of Volunteers by Brevet. The appointment is accepted. As no blank for the required Oath of Office was enclosed I respectfully request that one be furnished me." LS, *ibid.*, RG 94, ACP, H823 CB 1867. On Nov. 21, Thomas wrote to the AG recommending Hamill for additional bvt. promotion. LS, *ibid.* On Dec. 5, USG endorsed this letter. "Disapproved this officer having already received three brevets." ES, *ibid.*

On Dec. 26, Thomas telegraphed to USG. "Bvt Col. S. R. Hamill has been relieved from duty here but has rec'd no order to proceed to Washington City Has such an order been issued?" Telegram received (at 1:40 P.M.), *ibid.*, RG 107, Telegrams Collected (Bound); copy, *ibid.*, RG 393, Dept. of the Cumberland, Telegrams Sent. On Dec. 27, Bvt. Maj. Gen. Edward D. Townsend telegraphed to Thomas. "Order for Colonel Hamill to proceed to Washington issued today. He can retain his chief clerk." ALS (telegram sent), *ibid.*, RG 107, Telegrams Collected (Bound).

To Maj. Gen. George H. Thomas

Washington, D, C, Sept. 24th *1867.* [*3:30* P.M.]

MAJ. GN. G. H. THOMAS,
LOUISVILLE, KY.

The Mayor, City Attorney & President of Common Council of Nashville express great fear of collissions at time of Charter Election on the 28th. Go to Nashville to-morrow to remain until after election to preserve peace. If you think more troops necessary for that pupose order them there from the most convenient points in your command. The Military cannot set up to be the Judge as to which set of Election Judges have the right to controll but must confine their action to preventing or putting down hostile mobs. It is hoped how[ever] by seeing the Governor and city officials here refered to your presence and advice may prevent disturbance. Please keep me advised of condit[ion] of affairs.[1]

U. S. GRANT
General

ALS (telegram sent), DNA, RG 107, Telegrams Collected (Bound); telegram sent, *ibid.*; copies, *ibid.*, RG 108, Telegrams Sent; *ibid.*, RG 393, Dept. of the Cumberland, Telegrams Received; DLC-USG, V, 56; DLC-Andrew Johnson. On Sept. 25, 1867, Maj. Gen. George H. Thomas telegraphed to USG. "Your cipher telegram of 3.30 P. M yesterday received. I forwarded you yesterday a proclamation of the Governor, the Chief Magistrate of the State proclaiming any other election than that held under the franchise law illegal and directing Genl Cooper to take measures to preserve the peace and to protect the judges of election in the discharge of their duties, also a proclamation by the Mayor of the city of Nashville taking adverse grounds to the governor and ordering an extra Police force to be organized to preserve the peace and to protect the judges of election appointed by the city council to hold the election for ~~for~~ city officers under the charter; for your information and instructions. In the endorsement I expressed the belief that under instructions from the War Department I should be compelled to take sides with the Governor, he being the chief civil officer of the State and having proclaimed the law governing elections of the State, should he call upon me for aid. As further expressed in that endorsement I should have used the troops to aid the city authorities to enforce the franchise law and preserve peace at the election had I not received your telegram of 3.30 P. M yesterday. I start for Nashville this afternoon and will do what I can to preserve the peace. Please instruct me whether I am to sustain the Governor or the Mayor." Telegram received (at 3:30 P.M.), DNA, RG 107, Telegrams Collected (Bound); *ibid.*, RG 108, Telegrams Received; DLC-Andrew Johnson; copies, DNA, RG 393, Dept. of the Cumberland, Telegrams Sent; DLC-USG, V, 55. Governor

William G. Brownlow's proclamation of Sept. 18, his instructions of Sept. 22 to Brig. Gen. Joseph A. Cooper, Tenn. State Guards, and the proclamation of Sept. 24 by W. Matt Brown, mayor of Nashville, are printed in *HED*, 40-2-1, II, part 1, pp. 186–88.

On Sept. 25, 6:35 P.M., USG telegraphed to Thomas. "I neither instruct to sustain the Governor nor Mayor but to prevent conflict. The Governor is the only authority that can legally demand the aid of United States troops and that must be by proclamation declairing invasion or insurrection exists beyond the controll of other means at his hands It is hope your presence and good judgement and advice will prevent conflict." ALS (telegram sent), DNA, RG 107, Telegrams Collected (Bound); telegram sent, *ibid.*; copies, *ibid.*, RG 108, Telegrams Sent; *ibid.*, RG 393, Dept. of the Cumberland, Telegrams Received; DLC-USG, V, 56; DLC-Andrew Johnson. On Sept. 26, Thomas, Nashville, telegraphed to USG. "If both parties persist in holding their election there will be great danger of collission. In such contingency am I to interfere and allow both elections to go on? or are my duties simply to prevent mobs from aiding either party?" Telegram received (at 2:00 P.M.), DNA, RG 107, Telegrams Collected (Bound); (at 2:30 P.M.) *ibid.*, RG 108, Telegrams Received; DLC-Andrew Johnson; copies, DNA, RG 393, Dept. of the Cumberland, Telegrams Sent; DLC-USG, V, 55. At 4:00 P.M., USG telegraphed to Thomas. "You are to prevent Conflict. If the Executive of the state issues his proclamation declaring insurrection or invasion to exist too formidable to be put down by force at his own command, and calls upon the United States to aid him, then aid will have to be given. Your mission is to preserve peace and not to take sides in political differences untill called out in accordance with law. You are to prevent mobs from aiding either party ~~unless~~ If called upon legally to interfere, your duty is plain." ALS (telegram sent), DNA, RG 107, Telegrams Collected (Bound); telegram sent, *ibid.*; copies, *ibid.*, RG 108, Telegrams Sent; *ibid.*, RG 393, Dept. of the Cumberland, Telegrams Received; DLC-USG, V, 56; DLC-Andrew Johnson. At 4:00 P.M., Thomas telegraphed to USG. "Gov. Brownlow is in Knoxville. Have seen his instructions to Genl. Cooper not to permit the city authorities to hold their election. The mayor is determined to hold an election in defiance of the State authority. A collision is inevitable. If I command the peace, my action will be a practical decision against State authority & against the franchise law. I cannot preserve the peace without interfering in case of collision." Telegram received (at 7:00 P.M.), DNA, RG 107, Telegrams Collected (Bound); *ibid.*, RG 108, Telegrams Received; DLC-Andrew Johnson; copies, DNA, RG 393, Dept. of the Cumberland, Telegrams Sent; DLC-USG, V, 55. At 9:00 P.M., USG telegraphed to Thomas. "I will send you further instructions to-morrow. Nothing is clearr however than that the Military can not be made use of to defeat the executive of a state in enforcing the laws of the state. You are not to ~~resist the~~ prevent the legal state force from the execution of its orders." ALS (telegram sent), DNA, RG 107, Telegrams Collected (Bound); telegram sent, *ibid.*; copies, *ibid.*, RG 108, Telegrams Sent; *ibid.*, RG 393, Dept. of the Cumberland, Telegrams Received; DLC-USG, V, 56; DLC-Andrew Johnson.

On Sept. 27, 11:15 A.M., USG telegraphed to Thomas. "Untill afternoon I can give you no further instructions than you have already had. Report by telegraph immediately on receipt of this the nature of the difficulty in Nashville and your view of the best way to meet it." ALS (telegram sent), DNA, RG 107, Telegrams Collected (Bound); telegram sent, *ibid.*; copies, *ibid.*, RG 108, Telegrams Sent; *ibid.*, RG 393, Dept. of the Cumberland, Telegrams Received;

(misdated Sept. 30) DLC-USG, V, 56; DLC-Andrew Johnson. On the same day, Thomas telegraphed to USG. "Your telegram of 9 P m yesterday I read to the Mayor this morning and explained to him that under it I should sustain the Governor in case of Collision,   A great many of the City Council being opposed to the strong and defiant attitude of the mayor he has upon reconsideration decided to aquiesce and will not attempt to hold an Election under the City Charter and has this moment so informed me" Telegram received (at 5:30 P.M.), DNA, RG 107, Telegrams Collected (Bound); *ibid.*, RG 108, Telegrams Received; DLC-Andrew Johnson; copies, DNA, RG 393, Dept. of the Cumberland, Telegrams Sent; DLC-USG, V, 55. On Sept. 28, noon, Thomas telegraphed to USG. "The polls were opened this morning at 9. o'clock by the State Authorities. The election has proceeded quietly up to this hour, and I now have no idea there will be any disturbances" Telegram received (at 2:20 P.M.), DNA, RG 108, Telegrams Received; copies, *ibid.*, RG 393, Dept. of the Cumberland, Telegrams Sent; DLC-USG, V, 55. At 5:00 P.M., Thomas telegraphed to USG. "The Election over   All quiet" Telegram received (at 8:30 P.M.), DNA, RG 107, Telegrams Collected (Bound); *ibid.*, RG 108, Telegrams Received; copies, *ibid.*, RG 393, Dept. of the Cumberland, Telegrams Sent; DLC-USG, V, 55.

On Sept. 30, Thomas, Louisville, telegraphed to USG. "Returned here yesterday   Will have to delay my annual report until tomorrow to enable me to embody in it my report on the municipal Election at Nashville" Telegram received (at 4:40 P.M.), DNA, RG 107, Telegrams Collected (Bound); *ibid.*, RG 108, Telegrams Received; copies, *ibid.*, RG 393, Dept. of the Cumberland, Telegrams Sent; DLC-USG, V, 55. On Oct. 1, Thomas wrote to USG. "I have the honor to inform you that I have this day forwarded to you through the Adjutant Generals Office, my report of proceedings connected with the late Municipal Election at Nashville Tennessee. In connection with that I respectfully herein enclose to you a Copy of a proclamation declaring that an insurrection existed in Tennessee, as prepared for issue by his Excellency Governor Brownlow, but happily the necessity for its announcement was avoided by the withdrawal of Mayor Brown from the contest and his cessation of resistance to the State authorities. I send you this that you may know the dangers that threatened the peace of the community and how narrowly they have escaped from a condition of War. There has been so much comment by the Press upon the proceedings at Nashville: all of which are made upon a supposed state of facts, without knowledge of the Orders and instructions in the case, that I respectfully request that my official report of the proceedings be published for the information of the public." LS, DNA, RG 108, Letters Received. The enclosure is *ibid.* Thomas's report (copy, *ibid.*, RG 393, Dept. of the Cumberland, Letters Sent) is printed in *HED*, 40-2-1, II, part 1, pp. 181–237.

1. On Sept. 24, President Andrew Johnson sent a copy of this telegram to Brown. Copy, DLC-Andrew Johnson. On Sept. 25, Brown telegraphed to "President Johnson or Gen Grant." "I am exceedingly pleased with the dispatch rec'd Believing that it will have the effect of preserving peace supposing that it means neither set of Judges peacably holding the election will be interfered with by armed violence from any quarter   Please telegraph me immediately if this construction is correct" Telegram received (at 5:00 P.M.), *ibid.*

To Andrew Johnson

September 25th, *1867*.

SIR:

I have the honor to return herewith the papers in the claim of the Amoskeag Arms Company, referred to me on the 9th instant "for examination and such action as . . . the law and equity of the case will allow."

I deem it proper to report to you that, after examination, my judgment of the law and equities involved will not permit the action, on my part, sought by the claimants, nor would an arbitrary order of the Secretary of War in favor of the claim, in my opinion, protect the officials paying it from future legal responsibility for their action.

A supplemental report of the Chief of Ordnance and an opinion of the Judge-Advocate General accompany the papers returned.

Very respectfully,
your obedient servant,
U. S. GRANT,
Secretary of War, ad interim.

TO THE PRESIDENT

Copies (ellipses in originals), DNA, RG 107, Letters Sent to the President; *ibid.*, RG 156, Letters Received. On Sept. 20, 1867, Bvt. Maj. Gen. Alexander B. Dyer, chief of ordnance, had written to USG. "I have the honor to return herewith the papers, in the case of the claim of the Amoskeag Arms Company, which were referred to me for 're-examination and for report upon the law and equity concerned.' All the facts of the case on which this claim arises are stated in the papers accompanying General Marston's brief; particularly in my reports to the Secretary of War, dated January 24th, February 13th, and May 20th, 1867. My views of the equity of the claim are, also, therein specifically stated. It is my opinion that, as a mere claim under the law, it is not valid; because the contract expired by its own limitation, and because forfeited by non fulfillment, by the Contractor, of its conditions imposed on him, and has been subsequently neither extended, nor renewed. I know of but three ways of obtaining relief in this case; 1st by an Act of Congress—2d by resort to the Court of Claims—3d by the Government's taking the arms, on an executive order to that effect, at such price as may save the contractors from loss. The arms are not fit or suitable for the military service, and it was for that reason that I could not recommend their purchase. They are not superior in fitness for the military service to arms now on hand, which we are trying to dispose of by sale." LS, *ibid.*, Letters to the

Secretary of War (Press). On Sept. 22, Judge Advocate Gen. Joseph Holt wrote to USG. "In compliance with your endorsement of yesterday, referring to this Bureau the claim of the *Amoskeag Arms Co.*, to be paid for 6000 carbines, 'for examination upon the points of Law involved therein and for report,'—I have the honor to report accordingly as follows. . . . The final conclusion is thus reached, that the Secretary of War would not be justified in authorizing the settlement of this claim; that the parties have no legal claim under the original contract; and— inasmuch as since their failure to perform the same, the carbines have been superseded in the service by arms so superior as to be now regarded by the Ordnance Department as 'useless'—that for the Government to take them upon any terms would be contrary to the public interests. Whatever equity there may be in the case in favor of the claimants, there is believed to be none such as should outweigh this last consideration. The opinion of the Chief of Ordnance, that the claimants can properly be relieved only through the Court of Claims or Congress is concurred in" Copy, *ibid.*, RG 153, Letters Sent.

To Hugh McCulloch

Washington, D, C, Sept. 25th *1867*.

HON. H. MCCULLOUGH,
SEC. OF THE TREASURY,
SIR;

Understanding that the office of Assessor of Internal Revenue for the 2d District of Indiana is now vacant I depart from my usual rule of abstaining from making recommendations for Civil office, to recommend James Ferrier, of Jeffersonville, Ia, for the appointment. I make this recommendation with the full belief that, if he is appointed, the office will be efficiently and honestly filled. I am anxious to secure the appointment to Mr. Ferrier becaus[e] I know he has the responsibility and care of a widowed mother and several aunts, now old and destitute, who are and have been my best friends from my childhood.

With great respect,
your obt. svt.
U. S. GRANT
General,

ALS, PHi. After USG nominated James Ferrier as deputy postmaster, Jeffersonville, Ind., on April 14, 1869, both U.S. senators from Ind. opposed him. On Dec. 6, USG renominated Ferrier, who was confirmed on Feb. 18, 1870.

To Bvt. Maj. Gen. John Pope

Washington, D, C, Sept. 25th *1867*, [*2:10* P.M.]
MAJ GN. J. POPE,
ATLANTA GA.

Does order 69 contemplate that all voting in Ga. shall be done at Couty seats? It would seem to be advisable to open the polls at as many points as possible both to insure quiet and full returns.

U. S. GRANT
General,

ALS (telegram sent), DNA, RG 107, Telegrams Collected (Bound); telegram sent, *ibid.*; copies, *ibid.*, RG 46, Senate 40A–F2, Messages; *ibid.*, RG 108, Telegrams Sent; DLC-USG, V, 56. On Sept. 16, 1867, Bvt. Maj. Gen. John Pope had telegraphed to USG. "The registration is completed in Georgia and I shall issue an order for election, day after tomorrow, to take place October 30th unless other arrangements are intended" Telegram received (at 11:00 A.M.), DNA, RG 107, Telegrams Collected (Bound); (at 11:30 A.M.) *ibid.*, RG 108, Telegrams Received; copy, DLC-USG, V, 55. On Sept. 20, Pope had written to USG. "I have the honor to transmit enclosed the order for an election for Convention in Georgia.—I have withheld the order for some days on account of intimations in the papers that some instructions on the subject might be given, but as none have reached me I published the order this morning.—The Registration is very full in Georgia owing to the system I adopted of paying Boards of Registration 'per capita' for the registration of voters—and I think the reopening of the Books of Registration, fourteen days before election, will hardly add many to the lists.— As you will see I have adopted the State Senatorial Districts as established by State Laws—as representative Districts in the Convention—This division of the State is familiar to the people and will obviate any danger of confusion or misunderstanding The assignment of delegates in detail will be forwarded in a few days.—" LS, DNA, RG 108, Letters Received. On Sept. 26, Pope telegraphed to USG. "I have today mailed a letter to you giving my reasons for the provisions of the Election order in Georgia. There will be time enough a week hence to alter the order if you think it desirable after reading my letter" Telegram received (at noon), *ibid.*, RG 107, Telegrams Collected (Bound); (at 12:30 P.M.) *ibid.*, RG 108, Telegrams Received; copies, *ibid.*, RG 46, Senate 40A–F2, Messages; DLC-USG, V, 55. On the same day, Pope wrote to USG. "I have the honor to acknowledge receipt of your telegram of yesterday's date, and in reply to state that the provision of the order for an Election in Georgia, designating the County Seats as the places of voting in the State, was adopted for the following reasons—*First*—At these prominent points every necessary arrangement can be made for a quiet and undisturbed Election—Considering the small Military force in this State, you will I think realize the importance of this reason—*Second*— By holding the Election in such public places, the best men can be had for Judges and Managers of Election, and there will therefore be less danger of fraudulent voting, or of impediments thrown in the way of voting, which would not improbably attend voting at obscure precincts where the polls were in charge of unknown and perhaps irresponsible persons, whose acts could not be under supervision by the authorities and the public—*Third*—The expense to the United States will be but a fraction of what it would be if polls were kept open at all the small precincts in the State—Georgia has about one thousand of these small precincts, which would require three thousand Judges and three thousand Clerks— Under present arrangements only about six hundred and fifty will be needed— The objection, to confining the voting precincts to the County Seats, is simply the distance some of the voters would be obliged to travel to cast their ballots—This objection is admitted to be serious, but not sufficiently so to overcome the very manifest advantage of the plan I have adopted—By keeping the polls open three days, much of this objection is obviated—It is not doubted, under the circumstances and in a crises so important, that a very full vote will be polled—I have advised with prominent citizens of the State on this point, and this arrangement, for voting at the County Seats, is partly due to their suggestions and meets their approval—If, however, you still think that other arrangements would be better, please telegraph me and they will be made—there is plenty of time for any such changes in the Election Order—" LS, DNA, RG 108, Letters Received.

On Sept. 27, 12:05 P.M., USG telegraphed to Pope. "I would recommend that election in Florida be ordered to commence first Teusday in November." ALS (telegram sent), *ibid.*, RG 107, Telegrams Collected (Bound); telegram sent, *ibid.*; copies, *ibid.*, RG 46, Senate 40A–F2, Messages; *ibid.*, RG 108, Telegrams Sent; DLC-USG, V, 56. On Sept. 30, Pope telegraphed to USG. "will endeavor to have Election in Florida as you suggest. There is fear however that the returns of registration from there may not be here in time owing to high water & difficulty of communication. will let you know tomorrow or next day." Telegram received (at 1:20 P.M.), DNA, RG 108, Telegrams Received; copies, *ibid.*, RG 46, Senate 40A–F2, Messages; DLC-USG, V, 55. On Oct. 9, Pope wrote to USG. "The Books and Returns from Florida came in so late, on account of high water all over the State, that I was unable to give the required thirty days notice, and order an Election for November fourth—I have therefore ordered the Election in Florida for the 14th. 15th, and 16th. November—I send the order enclosed. I have also somewhat modified that Paragraph of the order requiring voting to be done only at County Seats—both for Georgia and Florida. I also enclose the order on that point—The Election in Alabama came off without the least disturbance anywhere in the State, and resulted satisfactorily. The full official returns are not yet received, but as far as heard from, the vote is as follows: Whole number of Registered Voters in the State 164.800 No. of voter polled so far 94.500 For a Convention 89.425 Against a Convention 5.075 White vote for Convention 18.000 White vote against Convention 5.075 The final majority for Convention will not vary much from 90.000—I have sent no reports as I could send none that were official—The Election in this State will show similar results, though I think a much larger white vote will be cast—The smallness of the vote in Alabama was due to the fact that there was no opposition—In Georgia it is likely the Anti-Reconstructionists will not vote at all, and thus attempt to defeat a Convention—It is not believed practicable for them to accomplish this purpose." LS, DNA, RG 108, Letters Received. The enclosures are *ibid*.

On Oct. 19, Pope wrote to USG. "I have the honor to transmit herewith an order announcing the result of the late election in Alabama, and the names of the Delegates elected to the Convention—Of these Delegates (one hundred in number) fourteen are colored.—The Convention as you will see is ordered to meet on the 5th day of November, which is about the time recommended by many of its members.—I will in a few days send you a report of the outrageous and indefensible measures resorted to in Alabama to prevent voting on the question of Convention." LS, *ibid.* The enclosures are *ibid.*

On Oct. 24, 1:20 P.M., USG telegraphed to Pope. "Should not Delegates to Convention in Ga. be chosen by Counties instead of by Senatorial Districts to comply fully with the law? Could such change be made in your election order in time for election in that state." ALS (telegram sent), *ibid.*, RG 107, Telegrams Collected (Bound); telegram sent, *ibid.*; copies, *ibid.*, RG 108, Telegrams Sent; DLC-USG, V, 56. On Oct. 18, Governor Charles J. Jenkins of Ga. had written to President Andrew Johnson. "The following analysis of, & commentary upon, the Convention Scheme of Maj. Genl. John Pope, Comdg. 3rd Military District, for the State of Georgia, is respectfully submitted. . . . I proceed to show, that by the selection of these districts, instead of counties, as was clearly intended, in Georgia, an undue advantage is given to the colored race over the white race—. . . I respectfully insist that, considering the unlimited enfranchisement of colored persons over 21 years of age, & the sweeping disfranchisement of Whites—any scheme of representation which still further discriminates against the Whites is grievously oppressive, and tends to make the Government of Georgia a *Negro* Government . . . N. B. in a conversation with Genl Grant to day, I did not call his attention to this matter, because in discussing another subject I understood him to say, that as he construed the reconstruction acts, he had no power to control Genl. Pope's action save in the matter of removals from office" ALS, DLC-Andrew Johnson. On Oct. 24, USG endorsed a copy of the letter from Jenkins to Johnson. "Respectfully returned to the President of the United States. It seems to me it would have been better to have aportioned Delegates to Counties instead of Senatorial Districts, in the State of Ga. but in view of the nearness of the election in that State, (on the 29th inst.) I do not se[e] how the matter can be corrected now. I have however sent the following dispatch to Gn. Pope. . . ." ADfS, DNA, RG 108, Letters Received; ES, DLC-Andrew Johnson.

On Oct. 23, Pope wrote to USG. "The inexpressibly vile newspapers of this State, I doubt not aided & encouraged by the Ben Hill's' of the State are circulating & will doubtless represent to the authorities, that I have as they term it, gerrymandered the State in apportioning Delegates so as to give a majority [of] the Districts to the colored voters or in other words that a majority of the Districts have colored majorities—My order itself is sufficient answer to this base attack yet as assertions may be listened to & the order not examined I enclose a brief extract from a newspaper in this city which States the precise facts—It may be added that these Senatorial Districts were the registration Districts—I need not say to you that no idea of negro or other majorities entered my head in this apportionment—On the contrary I have so far as my personal influence goes, discouraged the negroes from even being candidates for the Convention—The result in Alabama has been that only fourteen negroes are elected to the Convention out of a hundred delegates No larger proportion will be chosen here The fact is that the rebels are desperate—the Convention in this State will be called by a large majority & will contain some of the best men in Georgia—In relation to Senatorial Districts in Georgia the facts are as follows—In order to give control of the state Legislature to the wealthy planters of the State every three Counties, regardless of population were made a Senatorial District—so that Counties having only *1000* white population & sometimes less, had the same representation in the State Senate, that Counties having 10.000 or more white population had—

~~In~~ ~~t~~The wealthy planting counties of the state where a few men owned the whole county, dominated in this manner over the poor whites and the Counties in which there were few or no negroes—The districts I have adopted are of their own making & I have simply allotted delegates to them in proportion to their voting population as you will see from the apportionment I appended to my re- port—I adopted these Districts precisely to avoid any change from the divisions made by the State Laws—I need not enlarge upon the matter & have only written thus much that you might if necessary answer any questions on the subject—" ALS, DNA, RG 108, Letters Received.

On Oct. 25, Pope telegraphed to USG. "If you will examine the returns of Registration sent you for Georgia you will see that the apportionments cannot be made by Counties without giving very unequal Representation. The Counties are small and numerous and in many cases two (2) or three (3) would have to be united to make voters enough for one (1) Delegate, Please try and make the apportionment by Counties and you will see that it is not practicable, I tried it for two (2) days The Districts are precisely as they were established by State Laws & on examination you will find that the apportionment is based precisely in Voters and is in all respects the fairest that could be made on the basis of Registered Voters, It is too late now to change and certainly no man in Georgia can complain because I have taken the Districts established by State Laws. I wrote you fully on the subject day before yesterday, My purpose was to make as little change as possible in Local Divisions in the State Known and recognized by State Laws, You will receive my letter tomorrow I send today a map of Georgia with number of Registered Voters for each County written on face of County Please see if it be possible to make fairer apportionment than we have done" Telegram received (at 11:10 A.M.), *ibid.*, RG 107, Telegrams Collected (Bound); *ibid.*, RG 108, Telegrams Received; copies, *ibid.*, RG 46, Senate 40A– F2, Messages; DLC-USG, V, 55. On the same day, Pope wrote to USG. "I have the honor to transmit herewith a Map of the State of Georgia, with the number of Registered voters written on the face of each county.—The total number of Delegates to a State Convention in Georgia under the reconstruction Acts is *169*— The number entitled to one delegate is therefore *1116.* I would be glad for any one to try and apportion these delegates in any manner which will give a fairer result or more equitable representation than is done in my order, appended to the official report I sent you some weeks since.—Let any one go through the whole apportionment for the State carefully and see if he can do better than I have done, to secure just and equal representation under the Acts of Congress.— The truth is that the State Senatorial Districts of Georgia were purposely ar- ranged in times past so as to give the planting Aristocracy the Control of the State Legislature.—For this purpose every three Counties were made a district entitled to one Senator in the State Legislature so that in the planting Counties a White population however small would have equal representation with a county of five times the White population but in which there were few or no Slaves.— A glance at the enclosed map will make this clear.—If there be anything wrong in this Districting of the State it is the fault of those who now complain of the apportionment.—I have only to say that this apportionment is based strictly upon voting population; that the Senatorial Districts were in the first place adopted as registration Districts and are now adopted as Districts for representation in the State Convention to avoid making any arbitrary divisions not known to the Laws of the State and because they gave a fair and just apportionment.—I need not say that this arrangement is strictly in conformity to the Law.—" LS, DNA, RG

108, Letters Received. The enclosure is *ibid.* On Oct. 28, Pope wrote to USG. "Since I wrote you yesterday I have seen in the papers what purports to be and doubtless *is*, a petition from Governor Jenkins and other citizens of Georgia, of his politics protesting against the Districting of this State for representation in a Convention.—If I had not seen this petition published with such seeming authenticity I could not have believed that any respectable man in this State would have lent himself to such an attempt at misrepresentation and wrong.—My letter of yesterday was based simply upon statements of newspapers which having little respectability and being entitled to little confidence, hardly seemed worthy of notice.—The published petition of Governor Jenkins and others is however of a different character and though equally unfair and so far as I am concerned untrue, demands some official notice.—The reconstruction Acts, clearly indicate two things.—1st That representation in State Conventions called under their provisions shall be based upon voting population.—2nd That both in apportionment of delegates and in elections no discrimination shall be made as 'to color or previous condition of voters.—To charge me therefore with districting this State in the interests of the colored population is to charge me with purposed violation of the Law.—To say that this charge is unfounded is to use very mild words to characterise such an allegation and the proof that it is unfounded is so easy that, if I could be astonished at any thing done or said by the disloyal faction in this District, I certainly should be astonished in this case.—Let us see the facts,—What I state here will be found in the official returns of Registration and apportionment which I have sent you with my official report.—Georgia is divided into One hundred and thirty-two (132) counties.—The aggregate registered vote is 188.671 Under the reconstruction Acts the number of delegates to a State Convention in Georgia is fixed at *169*—This gives *1116* voters as the basis for each delegate.—The problem was to apportion Delegates as nearly as possible to this basis, so that all parts of the State should have as nearly as practicable representation in the Convention, according to the number of registered voters.—To avoid making arbitrary districts in the State unknown to State Laws and unfamiliar to the people I adopted the Senatorial Districts established by State Laws and assigned delegates to those Districts as nearly as possible in exact proportion to the number of registered voters in such Districts.—Be pleased to examine or allow any one to examine this apportionment and it will be seen that all parts of the State are represented with remarkable fairness.—Certainly much more equally than they ever were before Representation in the State Legislature of Georgia has never been based on population at all.—For instance three Counties grouped together make a district entitled to one Senator in the State Legislature without regard to population.—Every County in the State, entirely irrespective of population is entitled to one member of the lower House.—In addition an additional member is allotted to each of the thirty seven counties having the largest population.—It is this rule which the Georgia petitioners insist upon my adopting.—Of course I cannot do so under the Acts of Congress.—Let us see how it would work.—Chatham County has a registered vote of 7142 Under this rule (being one of the populous Counties) it would be entitled to two delegates and no more.—Colquett County has a registered vote of *188*.—It also is entitled by the same rule to one delegate.—That is, one delegate is to be allowed to 3571 voters in Chatham County whilst in Colquitt County only *188* voters have the same representation.—Would such an apportionment be fair or in accordance with the Acts of Congress? I give this merely as one instance out of many in which adherence to the rule advocated by the Georgia petitioners would work the grossest inequalities in representation in a Convention.—To apportion delegates according to popular vote I should have been obliged therefore to group together several counties in many cases to get voting population enough for one delegate.—Such an arrangement would be to district the State anew by arbitrary Military orders and of course would give rise to much more complaint and dissatisfaction than are now represented to exist by the Georgia petitioners.—As I have said it was my wish to avoid making any changes whatever in the existing Sub-divisions of the State and upon careful examination I found that the Senatorial Districts established long since by State Laws would give the fairest apportionment that could be made, and I think you will find upon examination that I am not mistaken.—I never thought for a moment what the results would be as to the number of Districts in which the colored voters had a majority.—If I had it could have made no difference since the Law requires me to make the apportionment without any sort of discrimination against color or previous condition of voters.—I did not at the time dream that the adoption of the State Senatorial Districts, could possibly be complained of.—Since these complaints have been made Known I have learned something of the trouble.—The truth is that the Slave Aristocracy of Georgia arranged representation in the State Legislature so that the planting interests should control it.—Representation in the Georgia Legislature has been by territory and not population.—As an example.—Three counties grouped together make a Senatorial District.—This District however small the white population is entitled to one Senator in the State Legislature.—So also every County regardless of population is entitled to one member of the lower House. Thus in the planting Districts where most of the population were slaves, a few whites had the same representation in the State Legislature that ten times the number of whites had in Counties where there were few or no slaves.—In other words the rich planters dominated over twenty times the number of poor whites.—To effect this very democratic arrangement this System of Representation was adopted in Georgia.—In order that the white planters might farther secure themselves a majority in the State Legislature Counties were multiplied in the Slave Section, so that out of forty-four Senatorial Districts, in the State twenty-three were found in the Slave belt.—The men who perpetrated this wrong on the mass of the whites in Georgia are now very solicitous about the rights of these same whites, doubtless with motives equally calculated for their benefit.— So long as only the whites voted, the planting aristocracy in Georgia took good care that a few of their own faction should have at least the same representation with twenty times the number of non-slaveholding whites; but now that the blacks can vote and are sure to vote against *them* they become extremely solicitous about the rights of these same poor whites.—As I have said before the apportionment I here made is based strictly upon registered voting population, and it was made with care and with every intention to give equitable representation.—I would indeed be glad if you would submit it to any fair man and let him try and make an apportionment more just and equal. If any one can do it I will cheerfully acknowledge that I have been wrong, but I must protest against any such charges as those made by Governor Jenkins and his friends ostensibly in behalf of the poor whites whom they have always wronged on such matters.—I have no right to discriminate against or in favor of registered voters on account of color—Whilst Governor Jenkins and his friends charge me with discriminating in favor of the colored people, their whole petition is an argument in favor of gerrymandering the State in the interests of the Whites, not the mass of the Whites but the aristocratic planting Whites.—Any one who will look into the subject of representation in the State Legislature of Georgia will fully comprehend this Statement.—Governor Jenkins assumes that the Whites in Georgia are going to vote one way and the colored people another.—A most unwarranted assumption and one which implies either great ignorance of the facts or great looseness of Statement.—The fact is that there will be a large white majority in favor of a convention unless I am greatly deceived—The nominating Conventions of Whites and Colored people have been joint Conventions and nearly universally marked by harmony and good feeling.—There will not be one colored man for ten white men in the Convention.—Almost universally white men and men of character and standing have been nominated for the Convention by the Colored people.—The faction to which Governor Jenkins belongs is in despair at these results and seeks to arrest the election in some way.—The objection they make to the apportionment of the State is a pretext merely.—The real object is to obstruct and if possible arrest reconstruction.—Reconstruction accomplished, as there is now every reason to believe it will be in Georgia under the care and control of most respectable and responsible native White Georgians is the death blow to the old slave aristocracy of the State. As I said it is not the apportionment to which this faction really objects, but Reconstruction at all unless they continue to control both whites and blacks.—I rejoice that the President has not gratified them.—" LS, *ibid.*

On Nov. 12, Pope wrote to USG. "As I see that the disloyal papers in Florida are attacking me for the manner of Registration in that State and the apportionment of Delegates made thereon, I conclude (from the Georgia precedent) that a committee will soon wait on the President with a list of grievances on these subjects.—I therefore furnish you briefly with the facts that any representation on the matter may find its answer in your hands.—And first concerning Registration.—I appointed Colonel. O. B. Hart, of Florida Superintendent of Registration for that State. He has lived all his life in Florida and is a Southern man of such high character and standing that I presume no one in that State will be found to assail his integrity.—The only instructions I have ever furnished him are enclosed.—He did his work fairly and honestly there is no doubt.—In relation to apportionments the following are the facts.—Total registered vote of the State 27.244. Number of members of the Lower House in 1860. 46. Making *592* voters entitled to *1* Delegate.—I send you a Map with the number of Registered voters for each County marked on the face of the County—Also the order apportioning Delegates so that you will see the whole matter at a glance.—It is very easy to find fault, but before doing so it would be well for the critics to show that they can do better.—When they have taken the enclosed map and shown that they can make an apportionment fairer or more equitable looking to equal representation all over the State, I shall be prepared to answer their objections.—Until then their complaints have not even the merit of Knowledge of the facts.—It will be noticed that Georgia factionists object because I did *not* do in Georgia precisely what the same faction in Florida objects that I *did* do in Florida. It is not easy to satisfy these Gentlemen who are said 'to have accepted the situation so cheerfully and in such good faith.'—" LS, *ibid.* On Nov. 27, Pope telegraphed to USG. "Election passed off in Florida without disturbance of any kind large majority for Convention. Full returns from all except seven (7) Counties Vote cast already considerably exceeds half of the Registered Vote and nearly all for Convention" Telegram received (on Nov. 28, 9:00 A.M.), *ibid.,* RG 107, Telegrams Collected (Bound); *ibid.,* RG 108, Telegrams Received; copy, DLC-USG, V, 55.

To Hiram Barney

————

WASHINGTON, D. C., Sept. 27, 1867.

MY DEAR SIR: Your polite invitation for me to be present at a dinner to be given to Señor Romero, Mexican Minister, &c., is received. I regret to think it improbable that I will be able to leave this city at the time specified. I regret this because of the high appreciation I have always held the recipient of your compliment in, personally, and the sympathy I have felt for the cause which he has so ably and zealously represented. His cause was our cause, to a greater extent probably than will ever be appreciated, now that success has attended it. Failure would have demonstrated how much we were interested in the success of the Liberals of our Sister Republic. Hoping that you will have a pleasant time, and clearly demonstrate to Señor Romero the heartfelt sympathy of loyal Americans for the the cause of free government in his country. I subscribe myself, respectfully and truly, your friend.

U. S. GRANT, General.

HIRAM BARNEY, ESQ., CHAIRMAN, &C.

New York Tribune, Oct. 3, 1867. On Sept. 18, 1867, Hiram Barney, New York City, had written to USG. "The cause of Mexico will be so greatly served by your presence at the Dinner to her Minister on the 26th instant and she has had so little aid and comfort in all her struggle from our government, that I venture to urge you to accept the invitation and to attend the dinner Let it be seen that our great general and Cabinet minister takes pains to show his sympathy and support ~~of~~ for our sister republic—who has been so badly abused by despotic powers. Hoping to have the pleasure of meeting you here & then . . ." ALS, USG 3. The farewell banquet in honor of Matías Romero was held on Oct. 2. On Sept. 29, Romero wrote to USG transmitting a letter from the wife of Benito Juárez thanking USG for kind treatment when she visited the U.S. Romero, comp., *Correspondencia de la Legacion Mexicana en Washington durante la Intervencion Extranjera 1860–1868* (Mexico, 1870–92), X, 396.

On Nov. 26, Romero, Mexico City, wrote to USG. "I have had the pleasure of receiving your very esteemed favor of the 31st ultimo, the contents of which I communicated to President Juárez. The President was very much pleased with your kind expressions towards him, and he requested me very particularly to thank you in his name both for your kind wishes in regard to our country and to him personally. We thought the publication of extracts of your letter would do great deal of good here, in the present condition of things, and decided to published in the official paper of yesterday what you will find in the enclosed slip from that paper. I hope this publication would not embarrass you in any way.

I have been very much pleased to find political matters looking so well here. I have very little doubt we will enjoy now permanent peace and consolidate our government. Congress will very likely meet on the 1st of December next. There will be some liberal opposition to President Juarez's government, but it will not assume I hope, a factious character. I had the pleasure of making the trip from VeraCruz to this city with Gen. Babcock. We went from Orizaba to Chuacan to see Gen. Diaz and his command. After having expent two days with Gen. Diaz we came to Puebla, where we met the ladies and the other members of our party. I introduced Gen. Babcock to President Juárez and have done what I could to make his trip agreeable. On arriving at VeraCruz I found that President Juarez had given orders to receive Gen Banks and Senator Morton as the guests of the nations Preparations were made at different places to receive them accordingly. Should you come in February next as you desired you will be received in the same manner. I would like very much to be reliably informed about it for the information of the government and my own. Your letters are very acceptable to us and you would confer a great favor on me, if you honored me with them whenever you can find sufficient leisure to write to me. We look upon the events in the United States with great deal of interest and your sound judgement about them will always be quite acceptable to us. Mrs. Juárez and her family are all well and enjoying very much their residence here. They always remember you very kindly. My mother and sister arrived here well after a long unpleasant and dangerous voyage. They as well as Mrs. Juárez and her daughters desire to be very kindly remembered to you Mrs. Grant and your interesting children. With my warmest regards for Mrs. Grant and your children, . . ." ALS, USG 3. See *Calendar*, Jan. 19, 1868.

Calendar

1867, JAN. 2. USG endorsement. "Respectfully forwarded to the Secretary of War. Major Denniston's wounds and services certainly entitle him to consideration and I earnestly recommend him for appointment of Military StoreKeeper."—ES, DNA, RG 94, ACP, D728 CB 1866. Written on a letter of Dec. 21, 1866, from Bvt. Maj. Joseph F. Denniston, commissary of subsistence, Washington, D. C., to Secretary of War Edwin M. Stanton requesting an appointment in the U.S. Army.—ALS, *ibid.* Denniston was mustered out as of Jan. 1, 1867.

1867, JAN. 3. USG endorsement. "Respectfully submitted to His Excellency the President, recommending Bainbridge Reynolds, a son of Gen. Jos. J. Reynolds, for appointment of Cadet at Large to the U S Military Academy."—ES, DNA, RG 94, Correspondence, USMA. Written on an undated letter from Bainbridge Reynolds, Lafayette, Ind., to USG. "I write to ask a favor—I have always wished to go to West Point,—Will you get me an appointment at large? Papa asked for the vacancy for next year in this district for me, & we thought all the summer that I would have it—He applied from Arkansas, also, but there was no vacancy from Little Rock district—So there is no hope for me except through you. They ought to give you whatever you ask for—I heard Mamma tell Papa to ask you to get it for me at large, & he said 'no' that you had enough to do without being bothered with your friends—So I thought I would ask you myself—I have not said a word to Papa because if you do not think proper to get it, he will not be disappointed like he was this summer, & if you do, it will be a pleasant surprise I am going to Texas with Papa tonight—& Mamma will send this to you—Please send your answer to Mamma at this place—She is in my secret—I could wait another year, but then they appoint five & take the best one for West Point, & we Army boys have not had many advantages while our fathers were in the Army, & I am afraid I should not succeed. You will excuse this I am sure—Papa would do anything for Fred if he could & I thought you would for me. Love to Fred—The old poney is all right—"—ALS, *ibid.* Reynolds graduated from USMA in 1873.

1867, JAN. 4. To Bvt. Maj. Gen. Edward D. Townsend. "Please assign Gn. Hunt to duty at any post garrisoned by his regiment that he may select until Spring."—ALS, DNA, RG 94, Letters Received, 21A 1867.

1867, JAN. 4. USG endorsement. "Refered to the Adj. Gn. If there is a vacancy to which Gn. Davidson is entitled he need not be removed ~~this~~ with troops going on the plains this Winter."—AES, DNA, RG 108, Telegrams Received. Written on a telegram of Jan. 3 from Maj. and Bvt. Maj. Gen. John W. Davidson, 2nd Cav., Fort Leavenworth, to USG. "Nothing but the extremity Of the case makes me send this I believe myself to be entitled to the Lieutenant Colonelcy of the tenth (10th) Cavalry Does the order then for the Officers of the second (2nd) cavalry to report to Gen Cooke apply to me? It is only for family reasons I am forced to ask this"—

Telegram received (at 5:00 P.M.), *ibid.*, RG 107, Telegrams Collected (Bound); copies, *ibid.*, RG 94, Letters Received, 1D 1867; DLC-USG, V, 55. On March 16, Maj. Gen. Winfield S. Hancock, Fort Leavenworth, telegraphed to Bvt. Maj. Gen. John A. Rawlins. "I see that Major J. W. Davidson's name has not been sent to the senate for Lt Col of the 10th Cavalry Please inform me if he is to be the Lieut Colonel of that Regiment. Please reply."—Telegram received (at 12:20 P.M.), DNA, RG 107, Telegrams Collected (Bound); *ibid.*, RG 108, Telegrams Received; copy, DLC-USG, V, 55. Davidson was confirmed as lt. col., 10th Cav., on March 28 as of Dec. 1, 1866.

1867, JAN. 4.   To U.S. Representative Elihu B. Washburne. "I have the honor to recommend that Storekeepers of the Medical and Quartermaster's Department of the Army be placed upon the same footing (in regard to rank pay and emoluments) with Ordnance Storekeepers of the Army. The law requires that Medical Storekeepers shall be skilled apothecaries or druggists, & their duties being equally arduous with those of Ordnance Storekeepers, they are in my opinion especially entitled to as high rank and pay as is allowed the latter."—Copies, DLC-USG, V, 47, 60; DNA, RG 108, Letters Sent.

1867, JAN. 5.   To Secretary of War Edwin M. Stanton. "I have the honor to recommend that if any vacancy now exists or should occur among the Captains or Lieutenants of the Vet. Res. Corps, that Major Robert Avery, VRC., receive the appointment."—LS, DNA, RG 94, ACP, M350 CB 1870. On Dec. 3, 1866, Bvt. Maj. Gen. John C. Robinson, Charleston, had written to USG. "I respectfully beg leave to call attention to the application of Major Robert Avery Vet. Res. Corps & Bt. Brig. Genl. Vols. for an appointment in the Regular Army—Genl. Avery has the reputation of a gallant & efficient Officer—he is a gentleman of education, has been twice severely wounded and suffered amputation of the left thigh—I take special pleasure in cordially recommending him to favorable consideration—"—ALS, *ibid.* On Dec. 10, Maj. and Bvt. Brig. Gen. Robert Avery, 7th Veteran, Raleigh, N. C., wrote to USG. "I have the honor to enclose herewith a letter from Bvt. Maj. Gen. Jno. C. Robinson, U. S. A., asking your attention to my application for an appointment in the Regular Army. Nothing that I can say can add any weight to the recommendatory letters of the distinguished officers under whom I have served or those of prominent citizens, United States Senators, Members of Congress and others now on file in the War Department with my application. I can only ask your attention to those papers and submit my case."—LS, *ibid.* On Dec. 24, USG endorsed these letters. "Respectfully forwarded—"—ES, *ibid.* Avery was appointed 1st lt., 44th Inf., as of July 28. On Feb. 3, 1868, President Andrew Johnson wrote to USG. "Please relieve Brevet Major Robert Avery, First Lieutenant Forty-Fourth Infantry, from further duty in the Freedmen's Bureau, and order him to report to his regiment at Washington, giving him thirty days to join his command."—LS, *ibid.*, Letters Received, 47A 1868. On Feb. 25, USG favorably endorsed a letter of the same day from Avery received at USG's hd. qrs. requesting permission to appear before the retirement board.—AES, *ibid.*, ACP, M350 CB 1870. On April 14, Johnson wrote to USG. "Please send to me the application of First Lieutenant Robert Avery, of the 44th Infantry, to be placed on the retired list, together with such report or reports as have been made upon the subject."—LS, *ibid.*, Letters Received, 190P 1868. On April 16, USG wrote to Johnson. "I have the honor to submit, in accordance with your request of 14th inst., application of 1st Lieutenant Robert Avery, 44th U S Infy to be placed on retired list, together with report of retiring board, and other accompanying papers."—LS, *ibid.*, ACP, M350 CB 1870. On March 10, 1869, Avery, Washington, D. C., wrote to USG. "I have the honor to request that I be appointed Major and Judge Advocate United States Army; and to submit herewith letters from Generals Sickles & Robinson recommending me for the office. For my Military history I refer to the records of the War Department and letters on file therein from Officers under whom I have served."—ALS, *ibid.* Three additional communications addressed to USG concerning this appointment are *ibid.* On April 23, U.S. Senator Roscoe Conkling of N. Y. wrote to USG. "Lt Col Robert avery has filed an application to be retired with his Vol. rank at the time he received his disability. He lost his leg in the War. Moved by his disappointments in Some other directions, I meant to ask personally your Consideration of his request, and now compelled to leave Washington without Seeing you, may I ask you to confer with the Sec. of War, and to give the matter such direction as you may feel warranted in doing. . . . P. S. If he can only know that he loses nothing by my failing to see you personally it will console him & me also."—ALS, *ibid.* On May 11, Governor John W. Geary of Pa., Harrisburg, wrote to USG on the same subject.—ALS, *ibid.* On Sept. 3, 1870, Stewart L. Woodford, New York City, wrote to USG. "Permit me to present the case of Brevet Major General Robert Avery, now First Lieutenant, U. S. A., & to respectfully ask that he be *retired*. He was Lieut. Col., 102nd Reg. N. Y. S. V.; commanded his regiment for some time; was wounded at Chancellorsville, May 3/63; shot through neck & face; lower jaw broken; nerves of sensation injured & partial paralysis of left side & arm caused. He returned to his regiment, and while leading his command at Lookout Mountain was shot through the thigh and his right leg was amputated at the groin; stump so short that artificial limb cannot be fitted. I do not know of another officer who has been so wounded and lived. His wounds must materially shorten life. I trust that your Excellency will examine his case & claims, & by retiring him as of the rank to which his record & the law may allow, will serve a brave officer."—ALS, *ibid.* Avery retired as lt. col. as of Dec. 31.

1867, JAN. 5.   USG endorsement. "Respectfully forwarded to the Secretary of War approved."—ES, DNA, RG 94, ACP, 5806 1872. Written on

a letter of Dec. 6, 1866, from Brig. Gen. and Bvt. Maj. Gen. Irvin Mc-
Dowell, San Francisco, to Secretary of War Edwin M. Stanton. "By virtue
of an assignment of the War Department, Brevet Major General *R. Allen.*
Colonel of the Quarter Master's Dept.—*my junior in rank*, both by ordinary
commission and by Brevet—is made to rank me in the Division to which
we belong. As I do not think this was contemplated, I have to ask that I be
assigned to duty according to my Brevet rank. The more so, as I am at this
time—according to the usages and decisions of the Department—in the
exercise of a Command equal to that of a Major General."—ALS, *ibid.* On
March 29, 1867, U.S. Senator John Conness of Calif. wrote to USG. "I
have the honor to request that you will assign or have assigned Bevet
Major General McDowell according to his brevet rank. The propriety of
this I need not argue and hope you will agree with me. I have also to
request that you will order young Coster whom the General wants on his
staff to San Francisco and so that he can accompany Mrs Genl McDowell
who leaves on the 11th of April"—ALS, *ibid.*

1867, JAN. 7.   Bvt. Maj. Gen. Joseph Hooker, Detroit, to USG. "I am in
receipt of Paragraph 3, Special Orders No. 647. of December 31st, 1866,
from the Adjutant General's Office relieving Brevet Brigadier General
C. H. Hoyt, Chief Quartermaster of this Department and directing him to
proceed to his home to report thence by letter to the Adjutant General. I
believe General Hoyt has been transferred to the Quartermaster's Department of the regular Army—If not I think he should be. If he can be thus
commissioned I would especially request that it be done, and that he be
then ordered to report to me for duty as depôt or post quartermaster in this
Department."—Copy, DNA, RG 393, Northern Dept. and Lakes, Letters
Sent.

1867, JAN. 8.   Lt. Gen. William T. Sherman, St. Louis, to USG. "At the
request of Major General Hancock, I have forwarded to you by express, a
roll containing a map of the Department of the Missouri. I am informed
that Bt Brig Gen'l N. Michler, Major of Engineers, will be, in the Spring,
assigned to these Headquarters for duty as Engineer Officer. In the meantime, as I have no copy of this map, I should be glad to have General Michler make a copy of it for me, at your convenience."—LS, DNA, RG 94,
Letters Received, 27M 1867. On Feb. 27, Bvt. Brig. Gen. Cyrus B. Comstock wrote to Sherman. "In accordance with your request of Jany 8th to
be furnished with a copy of the map then forwarded by you, such copy is
sent herewith"—Copies, DLC-USG, V, 47, 60; DNA, RG 108, Letters
Sent.

1867, JAN. 12.   USG endorsement. "Respy. forwarded to the Secretary
of War."—Copy, DNA, RG 108, Register of Letters Received. Written
on a letter of Jan. 3 received at USG's hd. qrs. from Maj. Oliver D.
Greene, Little Rock, Ark., requesting bvt. promotion.—*Ibid.* On Nov. 15,

1866, Bvt. Maj. Gen. John M. Schofield, Richmond, had written to USG. "My attention has been called to the fact that, while nearly every officer of the General Staff of the Army has received several Brevets for service during the war, Whether in the field or not. Major O. D. Greene. A. A. G. has been entirely overlooked; or what is worse has been given the Brevet of *Captain.* As Majr Greene served for a considerable time on my Staff I consider it my duty to do what I can to secure for him the same recognition of services as has been awarded to other officers of his Corps hence I respectfully ask your attention to his case. Maj. Greene had charge of the Adjt Genls Office of the Missouri during the greater portion of the time I was in command of that Department. I was so much pleased with his efficiency and so well convinced of his high capacity that I reccomended his appointment as Brigr Genl of Volunteers and asked that he might be assigned to command of troops under me in the field. I am not personally acquainted with Majr Greenes field service but believe that he has seen more service in the field during the War than the average of Field Officers. I believe Maj Greene is as well worthy of the Brevet of Brigr Genl as the most of the officers who have received that recognition of their services."— Copy, DLC-John M. Schofield. On Feb. 11, 1867, Greene, Washington, D. C., wrote a letter received at USG's hd. qrs. requesting bvt. promotion.—DNA, RG 108, Register of Letters Received. On the same day, USG endorsed this letter. "Respy. forwarded to the Sec of war."—Copy, *ibid.*

1867, JAN. 14. USG endorsement. "Respectfully forwarded to the Secretary of War, with request that this paper be submitted to His Excellency the President. Inasmuch as a long delay would not probably forfeit the right of Gov. Moore to his property, it is respectfully recommended that he be given 'immediate possession of his home place' in accordance with Gen. Sherman's endorsement."—ES, DNA, RG 94, Letters Received, 223M 1867. Written on a letter of Dec. 15, 1866, from Thomas O. Moore, New Orleans, to L. A. Smith concerning his property in La. controlled by the Bureau of Refugees, Freedmen, and Abandoned Lands.— ALS, *ibid.* On Dec. 30, Lt. Gen. William T. Sherman, St. Louis, endorsed this letter to USG. "This letter was given me in NewOrleans, by a particular friend who was associated with me at the College at Alexandria. Govr T. O. Moor, was the Govr of Louisiana, when that state committed the fatal step of attempted secession. He had been a hard working practical Planter: had accumulated much wealth and was regarded universally as a man of marked Character. He did me many acts of personal favor, and I would like to befriend him. I fear his Case however is one of those against which there is such intense feeling at the North. I would not at this time suggest a general pardon, but why cannot an order be given him for the immediate possession of his home place back of Alexandria that he may get to work to support his family—The place is now idle and an industrious man is far better than an idle one. If Govr Moore has given his word, I would trust him absolutely. Please let me know what steps if any you

advise. I fear Gov. Wells is a personal Enemy to Moore"—AES, *ibid.* On
Jan. 17, 1867, Bvt. Lt. Col. Wright Rives, secretary to President Andrew
Johnson, approved USG's endorsement.—AES, *ibid.*

1867, JAN. 14.   USG endorsement. "Respectfully forwarded to the Secretary of War, inviting his attention to the fact that these troops were sent
by the Nicaragua route, which is known to be very unhealthy, and requires
a much greater length of time to cross the Isthmus than by the safe and
certain route via Panama. It is recommended that a thorough investigation
be made to ascertain by whose authority and for what reason these troops
were sent by this unusual route."—ES, DNA, RG 94, Letters Received,
443D 1866. Written on a letter of Dec. 27, 1866, from Lt. Col. Thomas
C. Devin, 8th Cav., Virgin Bay, Lake of Nicaragua, to the AG reporting
twenty-seven deaths from Asiatic cholera while in transit across Nicaragua.—ALS, *ibid.* Additional papers (including a letter of Nov. 21 from
Bvt. Maj. Gen. Montgomery C. Meigs to Bvt. Maj. Gen. Edward D.
Townsend stating that substantial savings could be realized by sending
troops to Calif. via Nicaragua) are *ibid.* On Dec. 20, Secretary of State
William H. Seward wrote to Secretary of War Edwin M. Stanton requesting War Dept. advance notice when troops were to be sent via Nicaragua
so that permission could be secured from the Nicaraguan government.—
LS, *ibid.*, RG 107, Letters Received from Bureaus. On Jan. 22, 1867,
USG endorsed this letter. "Respectfully returned to the Secretary of War,
inviting attention to my endorsement of Jany. 14th inst., upon the report
of Lt Col. Devin, 8th U S. Cavalry, Comdg. the Detachment of troops
which was recently sent by this route."—ES, *ibid.*

    On March 18, William H. Webb, North American Steamship Co., New
York City, wrote to USG. "Learning that a detachment of Troops, for
which Transportation was engaged on our Steamer of January 10th which
order was countermanded—in consequence of Sickness amongst the men—
is soon to be despatched for California I beg herewith to make application for them to go on Steamship—'Santiago de Cuba' hence 30th instant—
and propose to take them—at Seventy five (75) dollars each for privates
and two hundred (200) dollars—for Officers—in first Cabin. Government
to furnish Rations for the men which will be properly cooked & prepared
by the 'Ships Cooks.' Should it meet the views of the Dept—to divide the
detachment—we shall be glad to take one half on this Steamer—and the
other on the succeeding ship—to sail—April 20th—thereby ensuring abun-
dance of space and comfort to officers and men   In this connection—I beg
to call your attention—to the Enclosed copies of letters—from the Commanding officers—of the detatchments—previously sent by this route—and
also—to enclosed copy of a letter we had the honor to address to the Sec—
of War—on the 5th inst—all which are presented as a guarantee that every
effort will be made to make the men as comfortable—as circumstances—
will admit of—The Transit—across Nicaragua is now perfectly healthy—

while the last advices from Panama represent the Yellow fever, as still raging on that Isthmus, and there is a great probability—that Ships from that Port will be quarantined—on arrival at San Francisco—Begging your favorable consideration of—and reply to the above application . . ."—ALS, *ibid.*, RG 108, Letters Received. The enclosures are *ibid.* On March 27, Maj. George K. Leet wrote to Webb. "In reply to your communication of the 16th inst. the General-in-Chief directs me to say that the experience of the last two detachments sent by your Route, convinces him that it is better to send troops by the Panama Route, where they are detained, at the most, but a few hours on land—in a tropical climate—until the other route is fully established and connections more certain."—Copies, DLC-USG, V, 47, 60; DNA, RG 108, Letters Sent.

1867, JAN. 14, 10:00 A.M.   To James F. Casey, Cairo. "You can draw on me for ~~two thous~~ Twenty-nine hundred dollars now but no more. This makes Ninety dollars pr. acre for your place."—ALS (telegram sent), DNA, RG 107, Telegrams Collected (Bound); telegram sent, *ibid.*

1867, JAN. 17.   To Secretary of War Edwin M. Stanton. "If a vacancy to a Lieutenancy still exists in the 'Invalid Corps' I would respectfully recommend Gilbert R. Chandler, of Michagan, to receive such appointment. Capt. G. Chandler served as Capt. of the 16th Michigan Volunteer Infantry, lost an arm in the service, and is now a Capt. in the V. R. C. not yet mustered out of service."—ALS, DNA, RG 94, ACP, C32 CB 1867. On Aug. 24, U.S. Representative John F. Driggs of Mich., East Saginaw, wrote to USG. "You will doubtless remember, that I called on you some time since, at your office in Washington, with Cap't Gilbert R. Chandler, a brave and accomplished one armed soldier, from my state. At that time, he was discharging the duty of Captain in the invalid Corps, at Winchester Va, but had no appointment in the regular army; for which he made application to you, as Captain or Lieutenant. You conversed with him freely, and gave him a letter to Secretary Stanton; asking his appointment if any vacancy existed. I took the letter to the Secretary; but it is not within my knowledge, that the appointment has ever been made. As your present position gives you the full control, of the matter I earnestly hope you will carry out your request then made upon the Secretary, which, I was suprised ~~that~~ Secretary Stanton did not do at the time. His papers are on file."—ALS, *ibid.*, D489 CB 1867. No appointment followed.

1867, JAN. 17.   To Secretary of War Edwin M. Stanton. "I have the honor to recommend that the officers of the regular army in the following list be retired from active service by order of the President, in accordance with Act of July 17 1862. . . ."—LS, DNA, RG 94, Letters Received, 737A 1867. Of the twelve officers listed by USG, four, including Bvt. Maj. Gen. Lorenzo Thomas, were not retired.

1867, Jan. 17. USG endorsement. "Respectfully forwarded to the Secretary of War and the retention of Major Kellogg with Co. "D" 36th Infantry earnestly recommended."—ES, DNA, RG 94, ACP, 1801 1872. Written on a letter of Jan. 6 from Capt. and Bvt. Maj. Lyman M. Kellogg, 18th Inf., Fort Morgan, Colorado Territory, to USG. "I see by G. O. No 92 dated War Dept. Adjt Genl's Office Washington Nov 23rd 1866. that I am transferred from the 3rd Battn 18th Infantry (now 36th Inftry) to the 1st Battn 18th Infantry (now 18th Inftry)—This transfer is bitterly repugnant to my wishes, and I therefore most respectfully request your kind offices to the end that it may be revoked—for the following reasons— Viz. During the existence of the late Rebellion Col. H. B. Carrington (Col of the Regt to which I am now transferred) caused my unjust dismissal (without trial) from the Service, owing however to the strong recommendations of many superior Officers of the Army, Such as General's Sherman, Geo. H. Thomas, Hooker, Howard, Stoneman, Stanley, Granger, J. C. Davis, Baird, R. W. Johnson Ingalls &c. &c. I was re-instated to my original rank and position—Col Carringtons nature will never allow him to forget one he has injured—neither can I forget his unwarranted injury to my reputation and purse—My present Co. "D" 36th Infantry, is one, I have taken particular pains with, and I am confident it will run down should I leave it, My family being with me this transfer will cause much distress to my Wife and great pecuniary loss to myself—Could I remain in Command of my present Company and accompany it and "B" Co 36th Inftry to Fort Sedgwick whither I suppose they will go, I should be highly gratified— The above order transfers me from Co "D" 36th Inftry to Co "A" 18th Inftry—In the 36th Inftry I am 2nd Captain—in the 18th I shall be 1st Captain, but owing to the reasons above stated I greatly prefer a 2nd Captaincy in the 36th I sincerely trust that this earnest appeal may receive your ~~earnest~~ favorable and prompt endorsement, in order that I may retain my present Company. . . . P. S. 'Co' "A" 18th Inf is now at Fort Caspar—owing to present Indian hostilities, it is hardly possible that the transfer can take place for some considerable time, [a]nd not without considerable expense to the Government—Should the transfer be revoked, I would respectfully [s]uggest that I be telegraphed to that effect—"—LS, *ibid.; ibid.*, RG 108, Letters Received. On Feb. 7, USG again endorsed this letter. "Recommendation for this transfer reconsidered and disapproved."— AES, *ibid.*, RG 94, ACP, 1801 1872. On Oct. 17, Kellogg, Fort Fetterman, Dakota Territory, twice wrote to USG. "Beleiving that I am improperly borne on the Army Register to the detriment of my true rank and standing in the Army, and as the matter has been heretofore presented to the War Office and no response received, I now respectfully present the case for your consideration and decision. I graduated, at the United States Military Academy July 1st 1852, and was brevetted 2nd Lieutenant in the 2nd Infantry—March 5th 1855 on the creation of the 10th Infantry I was promoted from junior 2nd Lieutenant in the 2nd Infantry to senior

2nd Lieutenant in the 10th Infantry—Having married, August 16th 1855 I resigned—June 27th 1856 I was re-commissioned as 2nd Lieutenant in 3d Artillery—August. 7th 1860 (the Register says I was 'Out of Service 30th May 1860.) I was dismissed for drunkeness on duty, a false charge, preferred by an Officer whom I had challenged and who failed to accept— The Court refused to send for witnesses necessary for my defence—After dismissal I brought one of these witnesses, Mr Scranton, from the Pacific coast to Washington, General I. I. Stevens then Delegate in Congress was my friend and tried to get my case re-opened, Secretary Floyd refused, but offered me a 2nd Lieutenancy, but this I refused—On the breaking out of the rebellion I raised a Company of Ohio Volunteers and was Commissioned as Captain of Company "A" 24th Ohio Volunteer Infantry and was mustered into the service of the United States by now Bv't. Brig. General James. H. Simpson, Lieut. Colonel Corps of Engineers. . . ." "I respectfully ask your consideration of the enclosed certified copies of letters from Generals Jeff. C. Davis—R. W. Johnson and Col. Edie, my Corps. Division and Brigade Commanders, concerning my services while commanding my Regiment on the Atlanta campaign. . . ."—LS, *ibid.* On Dec. 23, USG endorsed the second letter. "Approved for brevet of Brigr General for the actions mentioned herein, namely: Kenesaw Mount'n, Peach Tree Creek, Utoy Creek."—ES, *ibid.* Bvt. Maj. Gen. Edward D. Townsend noted on additional papers in the case that Kellogg should not be brevetted.

On July 20, 1868, Kellogg, Lodi, N. Y., wrote to Bvt. Maj. Gen. John A. Rawlins. "In December last, General Grant ordered, on the recommendations of Generals Geo. H. Thomas & R. W. Johnson that the Brevet of Major General be conferred on me, that I should be nominated to the Senate for the Brevet of Brigadier General—This order of General Grant, was in the shape of an endorsement on my application for further promotion by Brevet—Genl Comstock A d C to the General gave me an official copy of this order which I gave to the Retiring Board in Jany last, and which is now in the possession of the Adjutant General—On the 11th of January last I was told that further action about the Brevet had been delayed on account of certain reports injuriously affecting me—Accordingly, on this day I applied to the Adjutant General for an official copy of these reports,— (which I have *never* received—) and referred him to those who knew me intimately, during the War, and since. About the middle of March I recd an official communication from the Head Quarters of the Army, dated Jany 25th 1868, signed by Asst Adjt Genl Geo K Leet, stating that 'the General of the Army had authorized me to obtain from Officers, with whom I had been for some time closely associated, during, and since the War, certified statements as to my character, habits and efficiency'—The statements of those who knew me *more* intimately, and *far* longer than most others 'during the War,' have for some time been, and are now, in the War Office— . . . I trust these statements and certificates are satisfactory to the General of the Army, as I deem them conclusive as to my 'character, habits and efficiency, during, and since the War'—stating as they do, that I was 'strictly abstemious, correct in my family relations and general deportment—strictly attentive to my duties—setting a *good*, and *not* a *bad* example to officers and men—faithful and earnest—brave—leading my men into the thickest of the battle, receiving several wounds, from the last of which I am permanently disabled—&c &c'—Accordingly, I herewith respectfully ask to be officially notified whether I stand purged of the injurious reports affecting me at the Head Quarters of the Army in January last, and if so, if further action will be speedily taken on the order of General Grant that I be nominated to the Senate for the Brevet of Brigadier General? For the months of April, May, June & July '68, I have regularly forwarded to the Adjt General, the sworn certificate of Doct Lewis Post of Lodi, Seneca Co, N Y. concerning my health and habits etc—My address is Lodi—Seneca Co, N Y—"—ALS, *ibid.*, RG 108, Letters Received. Numerous enclosures are *ibid.*

1867, JAN. 17. To Henry A. Smythe, collector of customs, New York City, introducing Capt. [George B.] Livingston, ". . . who I have known since the arrival of the Army in the James River in 1864, as one of the most efficient commanders serving in the transportation business for the Government. Capt. L. is well known in the Hudson River where he has commanded river steamers for many years . . . He commanded the Hd. Qrs. boat in the James River . . . which gave me a better opportunity of knowing him than I had of knowing any other Steamer Commander . . ."—Charles Hamilton Auction No. 41, April 23, 1970, p. 27.

1867, JAN. 19, 10:30 A.M. To Maj. Gen. Philip H. Sheridan. "Please come on to Washington as soon as you can be spared from your Dept. long enough. You will not be detained here beyond a few days unless it is your pleasure to remain longer."—ALS (telegram sent), DNA, RG 107, Telegrams Collected (Bound); telegram sent, *ibid.*; copies, *ibid.*, RG 108, Telegrams Sent; DLC-USG, V, 56. On the same day, Sheridan, New Orleans, telegraphed to USG. "Your telegram received. I will start for Washington on or before the first of February"—Telegram received (on Jan. 20, 10:30 A.M.), DNA, RG 107, Telegrams Collected (Bound); *ibid.*, RG 108, Telegrams Received; copies, DLC-USG, V, 55; DLC-Philip H. Sheridan. On Dec. 20, 1866, Sheridan had written to Bvt. Maj. Gen. John A. Rawlins transmitting papers concerning affairs on the northwestern frontier of Tex.—LS and copy, DNA, RG 94, Letters Received, 736A 1866. On Jan. 18, 1867, USG endorsed these papers. "Respectfully forwarded to the Secretary of War for his information."—ES, *ibid.* On Jan. 3, Sheridan had written to Maj. George K. Leet at length concerning the location of permanent posts within the confines of his command and recommending an aggressive policy toward Indians.—Copy, *ibid.*, RG 108, Letters Received. On Jan. 21, USG endorsed this letter. "Respy. forwarded to the Sec of War—with the recommendation that $250.000 be turned over to the Chief Qr. Mr. Dept of the Gulf, for the erection of quarters, storehouses &c., under Genl. Sheridan's Orders."—Copy, *ibid.*, Register of Letters Received.

1867, JAN. 21.   To Secretary of War Edwin M. Stanton. "I have the honor to recommend that Corp'l Albert Leon Matile, Co. A. 33. U. S. Inf now stationed at Mobile, Ala, be ordered examined and if qualified Appointed a 2nd Lt. in the regular army. The enclosed letter from Gen Meade explains more fully the claim of Corporal Matile to this favor"—Copies, DLC-USG, V, 47, 60; DNA, RG 108, Letters Sent. Corporal Leon A. Matile was appointed 2nd lt., 24th Inf., as of March 7.

1867, JAN. 21.   To Isaac Hinckley. "I have the pleasure to acknowledge, with many thanks, your favor of the 1st inst. enclosing me a pass for the year /67 over the Wil. & Balt. R. R."—ALS, War Library and Museum, Military Order of the Loyal Legion, Philadelphia, Pa.

1867, JAN. 22.   To Secretary of War Edwin M. Stanton. "I have the honor to recommend John Davis of Brooklyn N. Y. for the appointment of Military storekeeper in the Regular Army. Mr. Davis has been recommended by the Q. M. Gen. in whose Dept. he has done duty for several years, and by officers under whom he has served more directly."—ALS, DNA, RG 94, ACP, G21 CB 1867.

1867, JAN. 24.   USG endorsement. "Respectfully forwarded to the Secretary of War, inviting attention to the endorsement of Lt-Gen. Sherman hereon."—ES, DNA, RG 94, Letters Received, 61M 1867. Written on a letter of Jan. 13 from Capt. Fall Leaf, Fort Leavenworth, to Maj. Gen. Winfield S. Hancock concerning the removal of the Delaware Indians to the Indian Territory.—LS (by mark witnessed by Hancock), *ibid.* On Jan. 16, Lt. Gen. William T. Sherman endorsed this letter. "This paper is respectfully forwarded to the Hd. Qrs of the Army with a request that it be laid before the proper Bureau of Govt. with the knowledge that it bears Gen Hancock's and my approval."—AES, *ibid.*

1867, JAN. 28.   To Barnas Sears, president, Brown University, Providence, R. I. "Understanding that the institution over which you preside is desirous of obtaining from the Military service of the country an officer to take charge of the instruction of the students in Military Science, under the provisions of Congress already provided, I take pleasure in recommending to you Maj. J. H. Whittlesey. I knew Maj. W. intimately as a Cadet at West Point, and since that as an officer of the Army. As a Cadet he graduated second in his class and is otherwise, in my opinion, eminently qualified for such a position."—ALS, RPB. On Feb. 24, 1868, Maj. Joseph H. Whittlesey (retired), Winchester, Va., wrote to Andrew D. White, president, Cornell University, indicating his interest in an appointment as professor of military science.—ALS, DNA, RG 94, Letters Received, 171W 1868. On March 2, White wrote to President Andrew Johnson requesting that Whittlesey be ordered to Cornell.—LS, *ibid.* On June 19, USG endorsed these letters. "It is respectfully recommended that Major Whittlesey be detailed as requested."—ES, *ibid.* A note on the docket indicates that Whittlesey, detailed to teach at Brown University the preceding year, had been engaged in preparing a report on military education in colleges.—AN, *ibid.*

1867, JAN. 29. USG endorsement. "Respectfully returned to the Secretary of War. I have heretofore approved applications of a similar character to the within because the law and orders upon this subject seem to contemplate the erection of these buildings upon proper application as expedient, although they do not make my approval or disapproval in the premises necessary. It is my opinion however that all posts, garrisons and camps between the Mississippi river and the Pacific coast should be considered and treated, for the present, as temporary posts or camps, and not entitled to the benefits of Sec. 27 of the Act of Congress approved July 28 '66; and that it is wiser and more expedient to expend the moneys, which might be made applicable for these purposes, in providing comfortable quarters for the troops throughout the West, and for more effectually guarding and protecting the public stores transported into and collected in the far West at a great expense."—ES, DNA, RG 92, Consolidated Correspondence, Fort Wadsworth, Dakota Territory. Written on a letter of Jan. 8 from Bvt. Maj. Gen. Daniel H. Rucker, act. q. m. gen., to Secretary of War Edwin M. Stanton forwarding papers recommending the construction of a permanent chapel and schoolhouse at Fort Wadsworth.—LS, *ibid.* On Jan. 28, Rucker wrote a letter received at USG's hd. qrs. submitting plans for a permanent chapel and schoolhouse at Fort McPherson, Nebraska Territory.—*Ibid.*, RG 108, Register of Letters Received. On Jan. 31, USG endorsed these papers. "Respy. returned to the Secretary of War—attention being invited to my endorsement, dated January 29, 1867, on a similar application."—Copy, *ibid.* On Jan. 29, Rucker wrote a letter received at USG's hd. qrs. submitting plans for permanent buildings at Savannah, Ga.—*Ibid.* On Feb. 1, USG endorsed these papers. "Respy. returned, disapproved; in as much as the post at Savannah is only a tempory post and not entitled to the benefits of the law and order referred to."—Copy, *ibid.*

1867, JAN. 29. USG endorsement. "It being impracticable for Col. Bowerman to reach Fort Rice at this se[aso]n of the year his application is approved."—AES, DNA, RG 94, ACP, B677 CB 1867. Written on a letter of Jan. 22 from Lt. Col. Richard N. Bowerman, 31st Inf., Baltimore, to Bvt. Maj. Gen. Lorenzo Thomas requesting a thirty-day delay before reporting to his regt.—ALS, *ibid.* On April 13, Edwin H. Webster, collector of customs, Baltimore, telegraphed to USG. "Lt. Col. Bowleeman of the Thirty first 31 Infantry sent his resignation in. It is at the Adjt. Generals

Office this day. The Causes for same having been removed he desires to with draw it If you will allow this to be done & give him till the April twenty fifth 25 to get ready I will thank you."—Telegram received (at 7:15 P.M.), *ibid.*, RG 107, Telegrams Collected (Bound); *ibid.*, RG 108, Telegrams Received; copy, DLC-USG, V, 55. On April 17, USG favorably endorsed a letter of April 11 from Bowerman to Thomas tendering his resignation.—ES and ALS, DNA, RG 94, ACP, B677 CB 1867. On Nov. 29, 1872, USG pardoned Bowerman who had been convicted on Oct. 19, 1871, of embezzling public funds and sentenced to a four-year imprisonment.—Copy, *ibid.*, RG 59, General Records.

1867, JAN. 29.   To U.S. Senator Henry B. Anthony of R. I., chairman, Committee on Printing. "The Adjutant General of the state of Arkansas informs me that he has presented to your Committee a petition asking for the publication by Congress of his report for the period of the rebellion, the state legislature having refused to make an appropriation for that purpose. I hope the petition may be granted, as I think it due to the troops from that state who served in the Union Army that their services should be placed on record and their history preserved."—Copies, DLC-USG, V, 47, 60; DNA, RG 108, Letters Sent. See *SMD*, 39-2-53.

1867, JAN. 30.   To Secretary of War Edwin M. Stanton. "I have the honor to recommend Zacheriah Taylor, son of the late Gen. J. P. Taylor, Com.y Gen. of the Army, for the appointment of 2d Lt. U. S. Artillery."— ALS, DNA, RG 94, ACP, T51 CB 1869. Zachary Taylor was appointed 2nd lt., 2nd Cav., as of Jan. 22.

1867, JAN. 30.   USG endorsement. "Respectfully forwarded to the Secretary of War. It is such cases as this that in my opinion the Veteran Reserve Corps was intended to provide for—besides, this letter shows a degree of intelligence in the writer that it is especially desirable to get into the service.—I would there fore recommend that the opinion of the examining surgeon in this case that 'he (the applicant) is disabled and disqualified from performing the duties of an officer in the Veteran Reserve Corps' be overruled, and that his appointment remain valid if in other respects he passes a satisfactory examination."—ES, DNA, RG 94, ACP, C59 CB 1868. Written on a letter of Jan. 28 from Jacob F. Chur, former capt., 21st Veteran, Washington, D. C., requesting reconsideration of his appointment as 2nd lt., 43rd Inf., because he had failed the medical examination even though he had performed active duty with his disability for more than two years.—ALS, *ibid.* A notation on the docket indicates that Secretary of War Edwin M. Stanton sustained the medical board's opinion and that the appointment was canceled.—*Ibid.*

   On Jan. 28, Alexander Wishart wrote to President Andrew Johnson concerning his failure to receive an appointment to the U.S. Army.—ALS, *ibid.*, 3546 1874. On Jan. 30, USG endorsed this letter. "Respectfully forwarded with the recommendation that Capt. Wishart be appointed a 2d Lt. in one of the old regiments of Infantry. Capt. W. received an appointment under the 'Act to increase and fix the military peace establishment of the United States', was ordered before a Board for examination, but was rejected because he had not served two years as required by the law.—The reason of his failure to serve two years was in consequence of a severe wound in the face, on account of which the Surgeon gave him a certificate of disability—and he was discharged. Capt. Wishart has now fully recovered, and is competent in every way for field duty"—ES, *ibid.* Wishart was appointed 2nd lt., 27th Inf., as of Jan. 22.

1867, JAN. 30. USG endorsement. "Disapproved"—ES, DNA, RG 94, ACP, B194 CB 1867. Written on papers recommending Henry W. Barry, former col., 8th Colored Heavy Art., for appointment as bvt. maj. gen.—*Ibid.* On July 27, 1866, U.S. Representative William H. Randall of Ky. had written to USG. "As a representative from the State of Kentucky, I have the honor to ask you to approve the papers of Col: H W Barry that he be brevetted a Major General of Volunteers for meritorious Service during the war against the rebellion. Col Barry in 1862, while an officer in the 10th Ky Vol. Infy. was taken prisoner by Genl. Frank C Armstrong C. S. A. who returned to the Col his Sword for conspicuous gallantry displayed on the occasion. He was in 1863 Strongly reccommended by President Lincoln to Genl W S Rosecrans, and has been endorsed by all Officers of prominence with whom he has served including Genl. W T. Sherman and G. H. Thomas He raised the first regiment of Colored troops that was organized in my State, which service was rendered in the face of very fierce opposition from the secessionists and rebels in and about Paducah, and was attended with a Success that of Self, proved his ability. ~~Th~~He afterward Commanded a brigade, and for a time a division, and in recognition of his services and worth I ernestly desire that he receive this promotion. In addition you will pardon me for saying that I with great pleasure bear testimony to his worth as a gentleman in every sense of the word. Hoping that you may find it consistent with your views of right to grant my request, . . ."—Copy, *ibid.* On July 30, Randall wrote to Secretary of War Edwin M. Stanton incorporating USG's favorable endorsement of the same day recommending Barry for the appointment.—ALS, *ibid.* On Feb. 5, 1867, Randall wrote to Stanton calling attention to USG's favorable endorsement.—ALS, *ibid.* On Feb. 8, USG endorsed this letter. "Respectfully returned, approved. In consequence of the foregoing explanation [t]he endorsement of 30th Jan. ['6]7 is recalled."—ES, *ibid.* Barry was confirmed as bvt. maj. gen. on March 28. On March 3, 1868, 2nd Lt. James D. McBride (former lt. col., 8th Colored Heavy Art.), 1st Cav., wrote to Maj. George K. Leet. "I have the honor to comply with your request of the 2d instant. Enclosed please find the autograph letters referred to in my communication of January 13, 1868, to the Hon. Chairman of the Military Committee; also additional documentary evidence which tends to prove the character of the man. If more is required I can refer you to several parties who are victims to a misplaced confidence. I respectfully request that these papers be returned to me."—ALS, *ibid.*, M53 CB 1868. The enclosures demonstrated that Barry had obtained recommendations for bvt. maj. gen. fraudulently.—*Ibid.* On March 5, USG endorsed these papers. "Respectfully forwarded to the Secretary of War with the recommendation that as there appears to have been fraud in obtaining these brevets, steps be taken to have them cancelled."—ES, *ibid.* Barry failed in later attempts to be restored as bvt. maj. gen., but retained the appointment of bvt. brig. gen.—*Ibid.*

1867, JAN. 31. To Bvt. Maj. Gen. Edward D. Townsend. "Extend the time for Capt. & Bvt. Lt. Col. C. G. Bartlett, 30th U. S. Infantry, to rejoin his regiment to such time as his attending physician deems it safe for him to travel. Col. B's address is to the care of Gen. Schofield Richmond, Va."— ALS, DNA, RG 94, Letters Received, 51A 1867.

1867, JAN. 31. USG endorsement. "I take great pleasure in commending the within request for favorable concideration."—AES, DNA, RG 233, 39A–H15.4. Written on a letter of Dec. 26, 1866, from Mrs. William I. Albert *et al.*, Baltimore, to U.S. Representative Nathaniel P. Banks of Mass. requesting an appropriation for the Maryland Disabled Soldiers Home.—LS, *ibid.*

1867, JAN. Anna Ella Carroll, Baltimore, to USG. "Some time between the 20th and 30th of November I drew up the accompanying paper and submitted it on the 30th of November, 1861, to the Assistant Secretary of War, Hon. Thomas A. Scott. At that time the Government at Washington had never thought of the Tennessee River. Two of the cabinet ministers, Mr. Bates and Mr. Smith, told me it was not feasible, from the fact that the depth of that river was not sufficient for the gunboats. Colonel Scott, the Assistant Secretary of War, however, was instantly impressed, and thanked me for the information, and he said to me on his return from Cairo, after the fall of Forts Henry and Donelson and the battle of Pittsburgh Landing, that the paper I submitted had been of the most essential service to the country, and that it entitled me unquestionably to the thanks of Congress. How far this plan influenced military men in turning their attention to the Tennessee River I do not undertake to say; but no paper containing a plan or even a suggestion of the Tennessee River bearing date prior to mine has ever yet been made public, and I do not suppose any can be produced. My reason for this conclusion is, that some friend claimed the suggestion as having originated with General Buell, but no proof whatever was ever adduced to support it. General Frémont put in his claim, yet there was no evidence further than he had suggested the importance of the occupation of Paducah. And at the time I was preparing my paper, Frémont was in command at Saint Louis, and so far as he had a plan, it was to send the gunboats down the Mississippi to New Orleans, with two supporting columns, one east and the other west of the Mississippi. Subsequently, General Sherman claimed this plan for General Halleck; but this, of course, could have no foundation in fact, for General Halleck was not there at that time, and besides, as you told me, he at first opposed your own proposition to go up the Tennessee. Here is one military man of the highest order of genius, to whose mind it had never occurred, and the first time he ever heard it suggested was from General Halleck, several weeks after my paper was in possession of the military authorities at Washington. The suggestion having occurred to your own mind, you think it must naturally have done so to every military mind. Now, in the recital of facts which you are supervising, would it not be well to state the date when you drew up the plan for carrying the expedition into effect, and whether, to your knowledge, it had ever occurred to any other military man? And permit me to suggest the importance of your stating, in the work referred to, the date when the Tennessee became to your mind the plan of conducting the campaign in the Southwest, and to whom you communicated it, verbally or otherwise. You advise me to claim in the history of the rebellion my agency in the adoption of the Tennessee plan in 1862, and hence my desire to have the fact incontestably settled, that I may not infringe upon the rights of any other, and, above all, upon those of yourself, to whom we all owe so much in the preservation of the unity of the United States."—*HMD*, 44-1-179, pp. 120–21. Carroll prepared a memorandum of a conversation with USG in Dec., 1866, that prompted this letter.—Sarah Ellen Blackwell, *A Military Genius: Life of Anna Ella Carroll of Maryland* . . . (Washington, 1891–95), II, 132.

In testifying before the Committee on Military Affairs concerning Carroll's claim for compensation for originating the Tennessee River campaign of 1862, Charles M. Scott submitted three letters allegedly written by USG, the first dated April 16, 1862, addressed to the "Board of Inspectors," St. Louis. "This is to certify that Capt. Charles M. Scott, a pilot on the Mississippi River, has been in Government service, and detained on the Cumberland and Tennessee Rivers until the present time, thereby preventing him from appearing for examination before the local inspectors of Saint Louis at the time required. I will further state that Captain Scott, from his great knowledge of the Tennessee and Mississippi Rivers, and interest felt by him in the Union cause, has been able to give valuable information from time to time, and has done so cheerfully." *HMD*, 44-1-179, p. 27. A letter of March 18, 1865, was addressed to Scott. "I was placed in a position in September, 1861, where I could see the course pursued by you at that stage of the rebellion. It was my understanding that you had been an old Mississippi River pilot, and had left the Lower Mississippi about the last chance that was left for escape. I know nothing about your personal sacrifices further than you have stated them to me, but have no reason to doubt these statements. It gives me pleasure to say that at a time when the great majority of your profession were decidedly disloyal, or at least sympathized with the rebellion, you professed the strongest devotion to the old Union, and as long as I remained in command at Cairo stood always ready to conduct either transports or armed vessels wherever Government authorities wished them to be taken. You also furnished information of the Mississippi River and its defenses, and of the Cumberland, which proved both correct and valuable."—*Ibid.*, pp. 27, 120. A letter of July 30, 1868, was addressed to "Colonel McComb, United States Engineer, Cincinnati, Ohio." "If you can give the bearer of this, Captain C. M. Scott, employment on one of the snag-boats, you will reward a truly patriotic man. Captain S. is one of the very few Union pilots who stood ready in 1861 to help the Government, and to denounce treason. He was with me at Cairo that year, and was always ready to run a boat wherever it was wanted, regardless of danger. I have no doubt but his loyalty to the Government then tells against him in his profession now, and makes the stronger reason why the Government should employ him. I would be well pleased if you could give Captain Scott a good place."—*Ibid.*, p. 30.

On Aug. 29, 1867, U.S. Representative Henry P. H. Bromwell of Ill., Charleston, Ill., wrote to USG. "Capt. Charles M. Scott, long a Pilot on the Mississippi, and who served in the Govt Service during the war, and appears from his papers to be well known to you, desires a position on one of the Govt Snag boats as Master. He is very highly recommended for his firmness and devotion to our cause during the war by officers well known to me, He lost all by being deprived of his property by Genl Pillow and is no doubt a deserving and thoroughly qualified Pilot. He desires from you a recommendation to the proper authorities, which I hope he may receive . . . P. S. Capt Scott will send letter inclosed"—ALS, DNA, RG 77, Explorations and Surveys, Letters Received. Attached is an undated letter from Scott to USG. "The undersigned would most respectfully ask of you to reccomend me to Gen McCombs (who is now engadged at Cincinnatti fitting out Snag Boats for the Mississippi River) for the Position of Master on one of them I feel that it would be useless to state to you either my qualifications for the situation or the servises I have rendered which entitle me to ask this favour but I do not think you are aware of the Ostracism that is exercised on the Southern Rivers against Original Union Men perticularly the Pilots that ~~first~~ stuck by the Goverment Union owners are affraid to hire them as they are unpopular in the South And as I lost all by Rebel confiscation I have nothing to fall back on and must quit the River if not aided by the Goverment in whose behalf I lost the fruits of 30 years labour I ask this favour of you hoping you will grant it and let me know the result at your Earliest convenience"—ALS, *ibid.*

Carroll's letter to USG was not entered in USG's register of letters received, USG's letters to and about Scott do not appear elsewhere, and all alleged documents regarding the Carroll claim must be viewed with suspicion. When Carroll resubmitted her papers two years later, she omitted all USG correspondence.—*HMD*, 45-2-58. See F. Lauriston Bullard, "Anna Ella Carroll and her 'Modest' Claim," *Lincoln Herald*, 50, 3 (Oct., 1948),

2–10, 47; Kenneth P. Williams, "The Tennessee River Campaign and Anna Ella Carroll," *Indiana Magazine of History,* XLVI, 3 (Sept., 1950), 221–48; Williams, *Lincoln Finds a General: A Military Study of the Civil War* (New York, 1949–59), III, 448–52; Janet L. Coryell, *Neither Heroine nor Fool: Anna Ella Carroll of Maryland* (Kent, Ohio, 1990).

On Oct. 26, 1867, Carroll, New York City, wrote to "My dear General," possibly USG. "*Private.* ... I have a claim in the War Dept for certain pamphlets prepared under contract during the War to which I beg leave to ask yr kind attention; feeling assured, that upon ascertaining the facts in its connection, you will at once perceive the justice on which it is founded. The acct with the voucher for the part paid, is in the custody of the Chief Clerk Mr Potts; together with the written opinion of some of the ablest men in the country, as to the reasonableness of the claim. In addition to which, I have letters from other equally distinguished friends, written at the time, I requested a settlement, such as Hon Wm M. Meredith of Pa, the late Hon Edward Everett, &c, and leading Senators such as the late Judge Colamer of Vt Judge Harriss of N. Y Hon Benjamin Wade of Ohio &c, and I think I might safely say, that, there is no one who has read the pamphlets, whether in Congress or out of it, & who know me, but would consider the payment eminently proper. In consequence of the pressure upon Mr Stanton, the case never had any personal attention from him. As the contract was made with Hon Thos. A. Scott, while Asst Sec of War, would it not be well, to have a statement from him—altho, you will find a full endorsement from him upon the acct in the Dpt & had he remained in the Dpt, there would have never been a question as to the payment. I am sorry I cannot see you in person, but I am under medical treatment for my hearing, with a good prospect of recovery & cannot at present return to Maryland."—ALS, DNA, RG 107, Letters Received, C365 1867.

1867, Feb. 1. USG endorsement. "I fully concur with the disable[d] soldiers, holding Government employment, that they should be the elast class discharged, except for incompetency or bad conduct. I can see no reason why there should not be an ~~enactment~~ Act of Congress to that effect."—AES, DNA, RG 233, Committee on Military Affairs, 39–H15.4. Written on an undated petition of William Y. Collins *et al.* to Congress asking ". . . that your Honorable body fix by law, during its present session, the tenure of Offices now held in the civil service by all honorably discharged soldiers and sailors, who were permanently disabled by wounds received or by diseases contracted in the service of our country during the late war, to continue during good behavior. . . ."—DS, *ibid.* On April 1, Paul O'Leary and C. H. [*Chamberlain*], Washington, D. C., wrote to USG. "we the undersigned Sergent Paul oLeary 1st regt. D. C Volls and C. H Chemberlin of the 2nd regt. D. C Volls have been descharge this day from the goverment employment as plasterers and retained five men that never sereved one day the goverment—in which iwill name indevedualy . . . pleas answer for we are at the doore"—ALS, DNA, RG 108, Letters Received. A report of April 3 from 1st Lt. Edward Hunter, 12th Inf., Lincoln Depot, Washington, D. C., to Bvt. Brig. Gen. Charles H. Tompkins, deputy q. m. gen., concludes: "The rule of this Office in reference to discharged soldiers having the preference in the event of their qualifications being equal with others, has not been violated in this case—The best workmen have been retained. Chamberlain was once before discharged from this depot, and for drunkenness and disobedience of orders"—ALS, *ibid.*

1867, FEB. 2. USG endorsement. "Respectfully forwarded to his Excellency the President of the United States,"—AES, DNA, RG 94, Correspondence, USMA. Written on a letter of Jan. 28 from Mrs. John B. Wyman, Chicago, to USG. "Knowing that you are always kindly interested for those who have in any way—suffered by the War, And hearing of several vacancies at the West Point Military Academy—I have been induced to apply to you for one of them, for my Son—Henry S Wyma[n], whose father John B. Wyman, of Amboy Ills—was killed, while in command of a brigade at Vicksburg, Feb 28. 1862—. You will doubtless remember my husband, as he was acting as Adjutant General at Springfield—at the very—commencement of the War—And subsequently took the 16th Ills Regt into the field—but if you do not Hon. E B Washburne, or Ex Gov Yates will give you any information regarding him that you may wish After my husbands death his partner—to whom he had entrusted all his business affairs defrauded myself and four children out of our property— So the placing of my Son at school would be the greatest favor, that could be granted us—, and one never to be forgotten. He is sixteen years of age, and has a fine common school—education. I trust that I shall not be intrusive—if I ask a reply—Which may be addressed to my oldest Son— Osgood. B. Wyman, St Cloud hotel—, 112 Franklin St, Chicago—Hoping that this may meet with your approval—"—ALS, *ibid.* No appointment followed.

1867, FEB. 2. USG endorsement. "Refered to Qr. Mr. Gen. to know if rents are paid in unrepresented states for property occupied by Govt. in which case payment is recommended to Mr. Giers who is and has been undoubted in his loyalty. I rather favor renting to Purchasing for the present."—AES, DNA, RG 108, Letters Received. Written on an unaddressed letter of Oct. 29, 1866, from Charles C. Giers, Nashville, favorably endorsed by Maj. Gen. George H. Thomas on Nov. 1.—AL (incomplete) and AES, *ibid.* On Feb. 5, 1867, Bvt. Maj. Gen. Daniel H. Rucker, act. q. m. gen., wrote to USG. "I have the honor to return herewith the communication of Charles C. Giers. Nashville Tenn. Oct 29th 1866. proposing to sell to the United States certain land in that city now occupied by the U S. military authorities, which was referred by you to the Q. M General to ascertain 'if rents are paid in the unrepresented states for property occupied by the Government', and to report, That rents have been paid for property so occupied in the states referred to since the date of the Presidents

Proclamation of April 2d 1866. except in Texas where no rent has been paid during the rebellion prior to August 20th 1866, the date of the Presidents Proclamation declaring the rebellion at an end in that state—I respectfully recommend that a reasonable rent be paid to Mr C. C. Giers for his property in Nashville, used by the U S military authorities, from April 2d 1866 and continued during such occupancy—"—LS, *ibid*.

1867, FEB. 4. USG endorsement. "Respectfully forwarded to the Secretary of War and appointment as 2d Lt. of Infantry recommended."—ES, DNA, RG 94, ACP, I19 CB 1867. Written on a letter of Jan. 29 from Bvt. Brig. Gen. John C. McFerran, deputy q. m. gen., to USG. "Excuse my calling your attention to the case of Charles H. Ingraham, late captain 14th Infy. You will remember that I brought his name to your notice some time ago. He left the service some time since and is now anxious to return to it—is a graduate of West Point—was in severe action during the late war, and left the service—simply—on account of his love for drink—an appetite—which I feel certain, in saying he has conquered entirely—He is now and has been for some time back, in the employ of the Q Mr Dept under Genl Tompkins who assures me he is and has been perfectly correct in his conduct in all respects. I knew him before the war as a most efficient officer and perfect gentleman, and know he will, do credit to the service, if restored to it—I ask it as a personal favor to myself if you will give his case a favorable, and as early attention as you can, I will try and see you in the morning, in person on this subject."—ALS, *ibid*. On Feb. 8, USG again endorsed this letter. "Respectfully returned to the Secretary of War; previous endorsement of Feby 4th recalled"—ES, *ibid*. On May 3, 1865, Bvt. Col. Theodore S. Bowers had favorably endorsed a letter of April 23 from Capt. Charles H. Ingraham, 14th Inf., Fort Trumbull, Conn., tendering his resignation on account of ill health.—AES and ALS, *ibid*. On Oct. 27, Ingraham, Washington, D. C., wrote to Brig. Gen. John A. Rawlins pledging to abstain from liquor.—ALS, *ibid*. On Nov. 1, USG endorsed this letter. "Respectfully forwarded to the Secretary of War. Reinstatement recommended on the pledge within."—ES, *ibid*. On Feb. 13, 1867, McFerran and two others wrote to USG. "It having been represented to us that Charles H. Ingraham, late Captain 14th U. S. Infantry had failed to keep the good intentions he had formed to refrain from drink, we withdrew the recommendations we had made in his favor.—Upon investigation we ascertain that he was strongly urged by a friend to join him in a glass of liquir which he did, and by which, to a certain extent, he was affected.— This was the extent of his offending. His conduct for several months past has been unexceptionable, and we beg leave to renew our recommendations in his favor. He has taken a pledge to abstain from *all* intoxicating drinks before General Howard, which is enclosed herewith."—LS, *ibid*. On Feb. 14, USG endorsed this letter. "Respectfully forwarded to the Secretary of War. On the statement and recommendations herewith my recommendation for the appointment of Mr. Ingraham as 2d Lt. of Infantry is renewed."—

ES, *ibid.* On April 9, U.S. Senator Henry Wilson of Mass. wrote a letter to "Dear General," probably USG. "The writer of the enclosed note is desirous of again entering the army, and I am informed that there is some disposition to reinstate him Will you please see if any thing can be done for him"—LS, *ibid.* On April 12, USG endorsed this letter. "Respectfully forwarded to the Secretary of War in connection with previous papers."— ES, *ibid.* Ingraham was appointed 1st lt., 41st Inf., as of March 7 and died on Sept. 20.

1867, FEB. 4.   Jesse Root Grant, Covington, Ky., to USG. "Allow me the pleasure of introducing the Bearer Miss Laura Bradford—daughter of Dr Bradford of Augusta. The Dr has been an unconditional Union man, & a warm admirer of yours during the whol[e] of our late civil war—When you wer[e] at Georgetown he came there to meet you—You may remember of me introducing him to you on the stand   It is suggested that Miss Brad-ford will be at the Worlds Fair at Paris. And I have heard it rumored that you would be there also. As Miss B & you were born & brought up within a dozen miles of each other, to meet there would be like the meeting of Old Friends   Miss B. is now in Philadelphia and learning the above facts I forward this letter to her through her Corrispondent here"—ALS, George C. Marshall Research Foundation, Lexington, Va.

1867, FEB. 5.   USG endorsement. "Refered to the Sec. of War for his information."—AES, DNA, RG 108, Telegrams Received. Written on a telegram of Feb. 4 from Maj. Gen. Winfield S. Hancock, Norristown, Pa., to USG. "Gen A J Smith telegraphs today that he does not beleive the rumor of the massacre of the fifty nine men near the head of the smoky Hill a few days since by the Cheyennes and that he has had no report yet what-ever"—Telegram received (at 9:15 P.M.), *ibid.*, RG 107, Telegrams Col-lected (Bound); *ibid.*, RG 108, Telegrams Received; copies, *ibid.*, Letters Received; DLC-USG, V, 55.

1867, FEB. 5.   To O. D. Barrett. "I regret that we have no cards for to-morrow evening['s] reception at the house. Mrs. Grant & myself will be pleased however to see Dr. Graham & Abbot at their reception and will send cards to-morrow."—James Lowe Autographs Ltd., Catalogue 44 [1989], no. 44.

1867, FEB. 6.   To Secretary of War Edwin M. Stanton. "I have the honor to return herewith Senate Resolution of Feb. 5th inst. asking whether any order has been issued by Lt. Gen. Sherman in regard to the protection of trains on the overland route so-called and if so what' referred to me for report. In reply I would respectfully state that no order of the character mentioned has been received at these Headquarters."—Copies, DLC-USG, V, 47, 60; DNA, RG 108, Letters Sent. Variant text in *SED*, 39-2-23. On Feb. 16, Lt. Gen. William T. Sherman, St. Louis, wrote to Maj. George

K. Leet. "In compliance with the provisions of the Resolution made in the Senate of the US under date of February 5, 1867, & transmitted from your Headquarters, I have the honor to enclose herewith copies of my General Orders No. 2, of March 26th 1866, ratifying and approving those of Major General Pope, No. 27. of February 28, 1866, 'regulating travel across the Plains.' These Orders were in force during the past year, and, with some modifications, will be enforced for the present year, (1867). Under the provisions of these Orders, a vast amount of merchandize and great numbers of people passed safely to their destinations in our remote and exposed Territories   For the general safety it is deemed best to define and limit the roads by which this overland commerce is carried on, as it enables us to collect our military forces along them   For the year 1867, I propose to apply the general rules laid down in General Pope's General Orders No 27, to four principal routes. 1 From Minnesota to Montana, via Forts Abercrombie, Wadsworth, Rice, Berthold, Buford, and Judith and Sun Rivers, with a couple of new stations between Wadsworth and Rice. 2. The great Platte route, by which full 90 per cent of the travel to Montana, Utah California and Colorado have hitherto gone   In this connection I also propose to give increased force and protection to the shorter line to Virginia City from Laramie, via Forts Reno, Philip Kearney and C. F. Smith. 3 The Smoky Hill route to Colorado, via Forts Riley Harker, Hays, Wallace. &c, to Denver City   4. The Arkansas route from Kansas and Arkansas, via Forts Zara, Larned, Dodge, Lyon, the Purgatoire, &c., to Fort Union and New Mexico. I also propose to leave the Post Commanders along the routes a little more latitude of judgment as to the strength of trains passing out, as sometimes cost and delay have resulted, from holding trains until the requisite number had accumulated"—LS, DNA, RG 94, Letters Received, 186M 1867. On March 1, USG endorsed this letter. "Respectfully forwarded to the Secretary of War."—ES, *ibid.*

1867, FEB. 6.   George O. Glavis, "Tribune Office," New York City, to USG. "On the 12. day of December 1866. I had the honor to address you regarding a suit brought against me in Goldsboro, N. C., while on duty there as Chaplain, in the freedman's Bureau. So far I have received no reply;—while the Courts there have brought judgment against me, and fined me to the sum of 400 Dols., 475 dols,—including lawyer's fees. I can ill afford to loose this money—and as my action came, I honestly believe and feel, under your order, I would once more beg of you, to have this case investigated, so that I may be freed from this odious and unjust judgment."—ALS, DNA, RG 108, Letters Received. Glavis had been dismissed as hospital chaplain and asst. commissioner, Bureau of Refugees, Freedmen, and Abandoned Lands, as of Nov. 17, 1866. On Dec. 6, 1870, Glavis wrote to USG. "In the Summer of 1864. I was tried by a General Court Martial in Raleigh N. C. together with General E. Whittlesey & others. The findings of this Court were never transmitted to me & are even now refused—all I know of the facts is by Newspaper reports, & from these I learned that I had been dismissed the service. I was charged (1) that I had an interest as partner in a plantation, on which I employed freedmen who were under my official care; that I gave them (Government) rations; that I did not pay them equitably. (2) That I swore falsely that I had no other interest in the said plantation than a loan of money to its proprietors. (3) That I sold to others than refugees & freedmen 'a large quantity of men's & women's clothing, blankets & shoes,' U. S. property, to the value of $400.—for at least $260.—of which no account was made to the Government. Incredible as it may appear, the Court decided that I *had* a pecuniary interest in the plantation *as alleged*; that I did *not* swear falsely concerning my interest in it; that I *gave* the laborers rations ('guilty') but— *they were not Government rations*; that I did *not* pay the freedmen unfairly; that I did *not* dispose of men's or women's clothing, or shoes, but blankets only, & these, twenty eight, worth not $400.—but $196.—, & netting me not 'at least $260.—' but $42—! *Ad No. 1.* I beg to say that I *did* interest myself as a partner on a plantation, as indeed did all the Officers tried at the time & acquitted, but I did this at the special solicitation of my superior officers, who where encouraged to do so by Genl. O. O. Howard, the Commissioner of the Freedmen's Bureau. *Ad No. 2.* nothing need be said as I was acquitted of that charge. *Ad No. 3.* I beg to state that the said blankets were sent over from England with the mark 'U. S.,' by the friends of the freedmen in that country, to the American Freedmen's union Commission; that the Commission sent them to me to distribute gratuitously or for some price, according to my best judgment; that I received in this way $41.89 (not $42), which had no more place in my accounts with the Government than the receipts of the Atlantic cable, but which I duly paid over to the Commission to whom it belonged. The enclosed Certificate from the Quarter-Master's Department, G̶ which at the time of my trial was denied to me, further shows that I never was indebted to the United States for any clothing or blankets whatever. Trusting that upon examining this case fully you will find the gross injustice done to me & revoke the sentence of the Court which rests upon me with peculiar hardship"—ALS, *ibid.*, RG 94, ACP, G495 CB 1865. See *HED*, 39-1-120; *ibid.*, 39-1-123; George R. Bentley, *A History of the Freedmen's Bureau* (Philadelphia, 1955), pp. 128, 132–33.

1867, FEB. 7.   To Secretary of War Edwin M. Stanton. "I have the honor to recommend the following brevets be conferred upon 1st Lt. Albert M. Murry, 2d U S Artillery who died a prisoner of war in a rebel prison at Macon, Ga. viz. brevet of Captain for gallant and meritorious services at the battle of Antietam, Sept. 16–18, 1862 and brevet of major for gallant and meritorious conduct before Atlanta, July 22d 1864."—LS, DNA, RG 94, ACP, 87M CB 1867.

1867, FEB. 7.   USG endorsement. "Respectfully forwarded."—ES, DNA, RG 107, Letters Received from Bureaus. Written on a letter of Jan. 15

from John C. Palmer, Helena, Ark., to USG. "Upon the arrival at this place, in November last, of Mrs. Gen. T. C. Hindman, she brought me a letter from her husband, who has long been my intimate friend, and upon whose staff I served during the war, in which he stated his earnest desire to return to the United States. And requested me to apply to the proper authorities, in his name, asking a parol, upon the same terms as those granted to the Officers of Lee's and Johnston's armies by yourself. I immediately prepared a Memorial to that effect, and forwarded it to President Johnson, through Gov. Murphy of this State. Up to this time I have heard nothing from it; And I have thought that perhaps I should have addressed myself to you upon the subject. I profess to be thoroughly reconstructed. As much so as any true confederate can be at this day. And as evidence of it, I forward herewith some communications that I have been publishing in the 'Shield' of this City, upon the subject of the 'Constitutional Amendment.' I have every reason to believe that Gen. Hindman, if allowed to return, would make a good and peaceful citizen. And I pledge myself, for him, to that effect. If any more formal application than this is necessary, please to inform me in regard to it, that I may make it."—ALS, *ibid.* Additional papers indicated that Thomas C. Hindman no longer needed a parole to return to the U.S.—*Ibid.*

1867, FEB. 8.   To Secretary of War Edwin M. Stanton. "I have the honor to recommend that Bvt Col. W. F. Raynolds, U. S. Engineers, be promoted by brevet, to the rank of Brigadier General for meritorious services, in the field, during the rebellion, to take rank from the 13th of March 1865."—Copies, DLC-USG, V, 47, 60; DNA, RG 108, Letters Sent.

1867, FEB. 8.   To Comptroller of the Currency Hiland R. Hulburd.— Parke-Bernet Sale No. 1825, April 29–30, 1958, no. 338.

1867, FEB. 9.   To Secretary of War Edwin M. Stanton. "I have the honor to make requisition for Five Thousand Dollars, ($5,000) of the appropriation for 'Expenses of Commanding General's Office' and request that it be drawn in favor of Major Geo. K. Leet, Assistant Adjutant General, of my staff."—Copies, DLC-USG, V, 47, 60; DNA, RG 108, Letters Sent.

1867, FEB. 9.   USG endorsement. "Respectfully forwarded to the Secretary of War. I know personally of the good record of Col. Sibley whilst in the service. Of his reasons for resigning I know nothing beyond his statement in the within application for restoration. If he can be authorized to withdraw his resignation, without affecting the claims of officers who were promoted by such resignation, and without affecting the order of promotion of officers who served throughout the rebellion, (in the Qr. Mr. Dept.,) under existing laws for the reorganization of the Army, I would be pleased to see his long and faithful services rewarded by restoration, provided he be placed on the *retired list*"—ES, DNA, RG 94, ACP, S1749 CB 1866.

Written on a letter of Nov. 13, 1866, from Ebenezer S. Sibley, New York City, to Secretary of War Edwin M. Stanton requesting reinstatement in the U.S. Army.—ALS, *ibid.* On the same day, Sibley wrote to USG. "My object in now addressing you is to bespeak your influence & assistance in having me restored to the position I formerly held in the Army—I feel after a connection with it of nearly thirty seven years, that I am wholly out of my element in civil life, & I am anxious to renew the connexion which ill health forced me to sever three years since—My record while in the Army is, as you well know, beyond reproach—I have served the United States faithfully & zealously in the field, on the remote frontier & as acting Q. Mr General, & in view of my services I think the application to the Secretary of War to be reinstated in my former position in the Qr. Mr Department, which I now enclose & on which I not only ask your favorable endorsement, but, on its presentation, your active interest, I hope will command a favorable consideration. The ill health that compelled me most reluctantly to resign was caused by laborious duties performed in the Q M Genls office continuously for a period of seven years, & from which I could not obtain relief altho' frequently asked. To my repeated applications the Q M General always turned a deaf ear & I resigned to save my life—If objections are made to my being reinstated & placed in the line of promotion, I am willing to be retired, & as a retired officer perform the duties that may be required of me—In that event, however, I trust the importance of the services I have rendered, especially during the rebellion, may not be overlooked & that I may receive the brevet of a Brig. General & be retired with that rank & the pay & emoluments thereto, under the law, pertaining—I have been so long in the Army that I am anxious, very anxious to get back into it again, there to die, & if you can by your influence get me reinstated I shall, I assure you, properly appreciate the friendly act—"—ALS, *ibid.*, RG 108, Letters Received. On Nov. 26, Bvt. Maj. Gen. Montgomery C. Meigs wrote to USG. "I have the honor to return the letters of E. S. Sibley Esq. late Lieut Col. and Deputy Quartermaster General and Brevet Colonel USA, asking that he be restored to the position he formerly held in the army, or that he be placed on the retired list with the Brevet rank of Brig General and the pay and emoluments thereto under the law pertaining. Colonel Sibley was a most faithful and useful officer.—He was on duty in this Office until the Spring of 1864. when he resigned as stated in his letter of resignation, (copy of which, I enclose) to pass the remainder of his life with his family in the enjoyment of the comforts of a quiet home and to endeavor, free from official cares, to recover his failing health. Colonel Sibley in his letter to the General of the Armies, states that to his applications for relief from laborious duty in this Office which was injuring his health, the Quartermaster General turned a deaf ear and that he finally resigned to save his life. While acknowledging the faithful services of Colonel Sibley and valuing his friendship, the Quartermaster General must in self defence, say that he always understood these intimations of a desire to be relieved, to be coupled with a desire to be stationed at New York in

charge of the duties of the Quartermaster's Department at that Post;—
That in his opinion the successful performance of those duties would have
proved no relief from labor or responsibility, and that he did not feel justified in recommending to the Secretary of War at that time, to make such
a change ~~as that~~ Either in the interest of the public service, or in the interest of Colonel Sibley's health. To replace him now in the position which he
resigned would be unjust to Officers who have served through the war, and
who are entitled to hope for promotion under the increase of the Corps
authorized by Congress. To reappoint him and place him on the retired
list would affect the course of promotion and the interests of candidates
entitled to consideration, and the legality of such a course is at least doubtful. When Col Sibley resigned, I expressed my regret and my appreciation
of his past services, in a letter of which I enclose a copy for the record, and
I then, I think, verbally advised him, that however flattering the prospects
opened to him in New York, experience convinced me that he would soon
regret the step he had taken. Failing health would then have enabled him
to take advantage of the provisions for the retirement of disabled Officers,
if retirement on that account was necessary."—LS, *ibid.* On Oct. 28, 1867,
Sibley again wrote to USG requesting reinstatement.—ALS, *ibid.*, RG 94,
ACP, S1560 CB 1867. No action followed.

1867, FEB. 9. USG endorsement. "The appointment of Wm S. Alexander to West Point is respectfully recommended. His father is now an
officer of the Army and has been for over forty years and could procure this
appointment no way except 'at large' or from one of the Territories. I would
respectfully recommend the appointment 'at large.' "—AES, DNA, RG 94,
Correspondence, USMA. Written on a letter of Feb. 1 from Col. and Bvt.
Brig. Gen. Edmund B. Alexander, 10th Inf., Fort Snelling, Minn., to USG.
"My son who hands you this is extremely anxious to return to the Military
Academy having been withdrawn from there by me in consequence of
being too young to compete successfully with young men of 18 and 20—
being just over 16. when he entered much the junior of the Class—Is now
18 and more able to bear the rough usage a Cadet has to undergo as you
and myself have experienced—He entered in June 1865 from Dacotas in
which part of the country I was then serving—would wish to return if possible under his first appointment (or warrant) considering his absence
temporary if possible, if not, at large, or in any way thought advisable—
He is at College in Georgetown D. C. and in recommending him to you I
feel thoroughly convinced of his fitness & ability in every respect—With a
hope that you will aid him in his wishes—My length of service may be a
recommendation in his favor,"—ALS, *ibid.* On Oct. 3, John B. S. Todd,
Washington, D. C., wrote to USG, secretary of war *ad interim.* "I have
the honor to present to you the name William S. Alexander for an appointment as 2d Lieut in the army of the United States. He is a very promising
young man of Eighteen years of age, and the Son of an old officer of the
army, Genl E. B. Alexander, Colonel of the 10th Regt of Infy—I feel a

warm personal feeling in the Success of this gentleman and will esteem it a personal favor if the appointmt can be made."—ALS, *ibid.*, ACP, A116 CB 1868. On the same day, USG endorsed this letter. "Respectfully recommended."—AES, *ibid.* William S. Alexander was appointed 2nd lt., 8th Inf., as of Oct. 9. On Oct. 17, Alexander wrote to USG acknowledging receipt of his commission.—ALS, *ibid.*

1867, FEB. 10. Nelson Cole, former col., 2nd Mo. Light Art., St. Louis, to USG. "Herewith inclosed I have the honor to forward a copy of my report of the operations of the Eastern Division, Indian Expedition, for July, August, September, and October, 1865. This report was made shortly after the return of the Eastern Division, Indian Expedition, but after Brigadier-General Connor had forwarded his report, and on the supposition that it was never forwarded, I sent this copy, revised, as it is more in detail than the first report made to General Connor and upon which he made his official report, and presuming that it may contain information that may be of some value to the Government."—*O.R.*, I, xlviii, part 1, 366. Cole's undated report addressed to USG is *ibid.*, pp. 366–80.

1867, FEB. 13. USG endorsement. "Respectfully refered to His Excellency, the President of the United States. I know the writer of the within recommendation for amnesty to be a strictly loyal supporter of the war against rebellion and worthy of consideration in a recommendation of this kind. I respectfully endorse his recommendation."—AES, DNA, RG 94, Amnesty Papers, Ga. Written on a letter of Jan. 28 from Jesse K. Dubois, Springfield, Ill., to USG. "Genl. Alfred H Colquitt of Georgia has made application to the President for an unconditional pardon & I learn both from officers of our Army & other gentlemen here in whom I have full confidence that Genl Colquitt treated with humanity & kindness our prisoners who by the fortunes of war were under his control & also that he accepts cheerfully the results of the war. I would therefore ask your kind interposition in his behalf & trust that he may be Successful in his application"— ALS, *ibid.* Docketing indicates that Alfred H. Colquitt, former C.S.A. brig. gen., was pardoned as of Feb. 7.—*Ibid.*

1867, FEB. 14. To U.S. Senator James W. Nesmith of Ore. "Enclosed please find 'my Valentine.' This is the day for distributing such things. It is worth about $10 00 to be forced to take an article like the one enclosed so I send you that amt. in concideration of the infliction."—ANS, OrHi. A notation on the docket reads: "From U S Grant the 10$ was a little balanc on a poker transaction"—AN, *ibid.*

1867, FEB. 15. To Bvt. Maj. Gen. Montgomery C. Meigs. "Seeing a joint resolution, introduced in the Senate, by Mr. Wilson of Mass, appointing Commissions for the settlement of Claims for quartermaster's stores, &c. furnished by loyal persons during the rebellion, I take the liberty of suggesting to you the name of Gn. J. McArthur, of Ill. for one of such Commissions. Gn. McA. served during the entire rebellion as Colonel and Brig. Gn. the first two years directly with me. I believe he would prove well qualified for such Commission."—ALS, IC.

1867, FEB. 15. USG endorsement. "The recommendation of Gn. Griffin is approved and the appointment of Col. Warren to the rank of Bvt. Brig. Gen. of Vols. is recommended."—AES, DNA, RG 94, ACP, W21 CB 1867. Written on a letter of Jan. 27 from Lt. Col. and Bvt. Col. Lucius H. Warren, 38th Colored, Indianola, Tex., to U.S. Representative Nathaniel P. Banks of Mass. requesting assistance in obtaining an appointment as bvt. brig. gen.—ALS, *ibid.* On Jan. 15, 1866, Warren, Camp Sumner, White Ranch, Tex., had written to U.S. Senator Charles Sumner of Mass. concerning promotion.—ALS, *ibid.* On April 4, 1867, USG endorsed this letter. "Respectfully forwarded to the Secretary of War, not approved for any higher brevet rank than has been already given."—ES, *ibid.* Additional correspondence addressed to USG is *ibid.* On Nov. 26, U.S. Senator Henry Wilson of Mass. wrote to USG. "I have the honor to request that Capt _____ Warren 39th US Infantry may be brevetted Lieut. Col, for distinguished services during the War."—ALS, *ibid.*, 1125W 1867. On Dec. 20, USG endorsed this letter. "Approved for brevet of Lieutenant Colonel, for siege of Petersburg."—ES, *ibid.*

1867, FEB. 16. To Secretary of War Edwin M. Stanton. "I have the honor to respectfully recommend that Brevet Brigr General Albion P. Howe, Major 4th U S Artillery, be appointed a Major General in the U S. Army by brevet for gallant and meritorious services during the war, to date from March 13th 1865, and that Brevet Colonel Joseph Roberts, Lieutenant Colonel 4th U S Artillery be appointed a Brigadier General by brevet in the U S Army, for 'meritorious and distinguished services during the war' to date from March 13th 1865"—LS, DNA, RG 94, ACP, G42 CB 1867.

1867, FEB. 18. USG endorsement. "Respy. returned to the Q. M. G. The boundaries of the Reservation of Fort Boise as defined in the accompanying map are approved; and I recommend that it be declared a Military Reservation."—Copy, DNA, RG 108, Register of Letters Received. Written on a letter of Feb. 13 from Bvt. Maj. Gen. Daniel H. Rucker, act. q. m. gen., to USG. "I have the honor to state that a letter from the Commissioner of the General Land Office of the 5th inst, addressed to the Honorable Secretary of War relative to the Reservation at Fort Boise, Idaho Territory, has been referred to the Quarter Master General for report. In this letter the Commissioner states that 'the initiatory steps having been taken for the survey of the public lands in Idaho Territory I have the honor to request that information be furnished this office, as to what action has been taken in regard to the reservation at Fort Boise and the farming lands six miles below Boise City in order that the Surveyor General may receive instructions in accordance therewith If the Reservation has been made by the President, I would request a copy of the Order, with the necessary diagram If it has not been made and the lands are required for military purposes, I would respectfully suggest that the Order of the President be obtained and transmitted to this Office.' The enclosed tracing of the Reservation as surveyed is respectfully transmitted. It does not appear from any records in this office, that this Reservation has ever been declared such by the President. From the following extract from a report of Bt. Maj. Gen. Robert Allen, Chief Quarter Master of the Military Division of the Pacific, dated January 17th 1867, it appears that a removal of the troops from Fort Boise, and the establishment of a post elsewhere, are contemplated. . . . 'I observe that General Rusling in his inspecting report, (from which he has obligingly furnished me extracts,) recommends the breaking up the depot at Fort Boise' 'The Depot there never had any existence, separate from the post, *and as the command is soon to be removed,* the depot will go with it as a matter of course, but it is not probable that *the new position which the troops will take up* will be easier of access or any less expensive in its support than Boise itself.' I have the honor to request to be informed, if the abandonment of the present post of Fort Boise, has been decided upon, and if so, whether the proposed new site, will render necessary a change in the limits of the Reservation as surveyed. In case no change of these boundaries will be requisite the Acting Quarter Master General proposes to submit the maps to the Secretary of War, recommending that the Reservation of Fort Boise as surveyed, be declared a Military Reservation by the President."—LS (ellipses in original), *ibid.*, RG 92, Miscellaneous Letters Sent (Press).

1867, FEB. 19.   Maj. George K. Leet endorsement. "Respectfully referred to the Chief of Engineers for remark."—ES, DNA, RG 94, Letters Received, 145M 1867. Written on a letter of Jan. 24 from Capt. Anson Mills, 18th Inf., Fort Bridger, Utah Territory, to Secretary of War Edwin M. Stanton requesting authority to organize an expedition to explore portions of the Colorado River.—LS, *ibid.* On March 7, Brig. Gen. Andrew A. Humphreys, chief of engineers, wrote to USG. ". . . An examination should be made of the Colorado and also to ascertain the best route from the head of permanent navigation on the Colorado to the Utah settlements, but as no representation has been made to the Engr. Department showing any immediate necessity for the use of these routes for the transportation of military supplies, &c, there seems to be no urgent need for organizing a party specially for the purpose at this time."—LS, *ibid.* On April 13, William Gilpin, former governor of Colorado Territory, Washington, D. C., wrote to USG. "It is desirable to accomplish during the present Summer Season, a recognizance and exploration of the middle region of the Rio Colorado. This great river traverses a cañon, estimated to be 557 miles in length, in its longitudinal course through Utah and Arizona. The rugged character of the mountains, which it tunnels through and through, have heretofore proved insuperable by the unassisted resources and energies of the pioneers. The aid of the army is asked and needed. A correct inference, from all collected facts, suggests a navigable channel throughout this gorge, whereby the interior region of the mountains may be reached from the ocean. I would suggest, this exploration may be accomplished by a picked command of fifty men, thoroughly equipped and provided with pack trains, canoes and knapsacks. Possibly ninety days would be sufficient time to make the ascent from the southern to the upper mouth of the Cañon. Such a party, departing from Fort Garland ~~and~~ in June, might reach the southern mouth of the Cañon at the season of low waters. It is not supposed that any insuperable difficulties will be encountered by a party *ascending* against the current, or that this chasm differs essentially in its structure from those elsewhere known. The great length and obscurity of the country along the flanks dictate ample provisions for the *whole trip*, for as yet there is no known place of entrance or exit, except at the two extremities. No government explorations have penetrated this region of country Since those of Lt Ives and Captn Macomb in 1858, both of which were ineffectual in unveiling the mystery of the *great Cañon*. The pressure of the two advancing lines of population, advancing simultaneously from the Atlantic and Pacific seas, has uninterruptedly increased and their fusion both to the north and the south is now very complete. Both, are here checked by this disc which postpones their junction along a line of latitude both favorable and important to the general harmony. I enclose herewith some printed memoranda which may be useful. When heretofore engaged in the performance of military and civil duties, I have closely approached this region at several points, especially in the Summer of 1844 and the winter of 1846 & 47. As it is my wish to explore the Parks and San Juan and La Plata mountains during the coming Summer, which lie upon the eastern approach and within the boundaries of Colorado, will it not be agreable to you to instruct the officers in charge in that military department to give such assistance as may be entirely consistent with the policy of the government and the military Service?"—ALS, *ibid.*, RG 108, Letters Received.

On April 29, John W. Powell, former maj., 2nd Ill. Art., Illinois Normal University, Washington, D. C., wrote to USG. "A party of Naturalists, under the auspices of the State Normal University of Illinois, will visit the Mauvaises Terres of Southwestern Dakotah for the purpose of making a more thorough geological survey of that region. From thence the party will proceed to explore the 'Parks' in the Rocky Mountains. An appropriation was made by the Legislature of Illinois, which will in part defray the expenses of the expedition. Two or three other scientific societies will lend their assistance. The aid of the War Department is also needed in order that the expedition may succeed. I therefore respectfully request that the commanding officer of the Department of the Platte may be instructed to furnish the party with an escort from Fort Laramie to the Mauvaises Terres and return, of as many men as he may think necessary, and the exigencies of the service may permit. And I further request that he may be instructed to render such assistance as he may be able, in transporting the collections made by the party to Fort Laramie. And I also request that the officers of the Commissary Department, on the route traveled by the party, may be instructed to sell supplies to it at government rates."—Copy (printed), *ibid.,* RG 107, Letters Received from Bureaus. On the same day, Leet favorably endorsed this letter.—Copy (printed), *ibid.*; (attributed to Bvt. Maj. Gen. John A. Rawlins) *ibid.,* RG 108, Register of Letters Received. Also on April 29, Leet wrote to Maj. Gen. Winfield S. Hancock repeating the endorsement.—Copies, DLC-USG, V, 47, 60; DNA, RG 108, Letters Sent. On April 2, 1868, Powell, Normal, Ill., wrote to USG. "A party of Naturalists under the auspices of the State Normal University of Illinois wishes to make a scientific Survey of the Colorado River of the West This work is to be a continuation of work done last year in North Middle and South Parks It is hoped that a survey of that river can be made from its source to the point where the survey made by Lieutenant Ives was stopped In addition to the general scientific survey a topographical survey of the region visited will be made. The services of two civil engineers have been secured for this purpose I most respectfully request that the proper Officers be instructed to issue rations to this party while thus engaged The party to consist of not more than twenty five persons I need not urge upon your attention the importance of the general scientific survey to the increase of knowledge It is believed that the grand Canon of the Colorado will give the best geological section on the Continent Nor is it necessary to plead the value to the War Department of a topographical survey of that wonderful region inhabited as it is by powerful tribes of Indians that will doubtless become hostile as the prospector and pioneer encroach upon their hunting grounds You will also observe that the aid asked of the government is trivial in comparison with what such expeditions have usually cost it The usual appropriation for such an exploration has been many thousands of Dollars I transmit herewith a copy of my 'Preliminary Report' to the Board of Education of the State of Illinois on last years work"—ALS, *ibid.,* RG 107, Letters Received from Bureaus. On April 3, USG endorsed this letter. "I respectfully recommend that rations be ordered to be issued to Maj. Powell, and his party of twenty-five men by Army Commissaries wherever he may call for them whilst engaged in the exploration of the Colorado of the West. The work is one of [nat]ional interest."—AES, *ibid.* See Wallace Stegner, *Beyond the Hundredth Meridian . . .* (Boston, 1954); William Culp Darrah, *Powell of the Colorado* (Princeton, 1951); *PUSG*, 3, 31.

1867, FEB. 20.   To Secretary of War Edwin M. Stanton. "I have the honor to invite attention to the enclosed communication of L. H. Morgan, Esq., of Rochester, N. Y., and to recommend that Isaac N. Parker, late of the Volunteer Service, to whom it relates, be appointed a Second Lieutenant of Infantry in the USA., and that he be assigned to one of the regim'ts serving with Lieut Gen'l. Sherman"—LS, DNA, RG 94, ACP, P743 CB 1867. On Dec. 31, 1866, Lewis H. Morgan, Rochester, N. Y., had written to U.S. Representative Burton C. Cook of Ill. "In October last I wrote to Lieut Gen Sherman, asking him if he would take Isaac N. Parker into the Military Service, in his District, and in due time have him promoted with a commission in the regular Army if he deserved it. Mr Parker is a Seneca Indian the youngest brother of Col. Ely S. Parker of Genl Grants staff, and the equal of his brother in capacity . . ."—ALS, *ibid.* On Nov. 3, Morgan had written to Stanton requesting the appointment of Isaac N. Parker, former sgt., 182nd N. Y., to the U.S. Army.—ALS, *ibid.* On Sept. 18, 1867, USG, secretary of war *ad interim*, endorsed this letter. "Respectfully referd to the President with the recomendtn that this appointment be made"—ES, *ibid.* On the same day, President Andrew Johnson endorsed his approval on this letter.—AES, *ibid.* Parker was appointed 2nd lt., 36th Inf., but failed the physical examination because of poor eyesight.—*Ibid.*

1867, FEB. 20.   USG endorsement. "Respectfully forwarded to the Secretary of War."—ES, DNA, RG 94, Correspondence, USMA. Written on a letter of Feb. 16 from Mrs. M. C. Washington, Chambersburg, Pa., to USG. "When I wrote to you two years ago, it was to ask a favor—which was granted. My boy Reade M Washington entered Wst Pt. & I was content. But he has abused his opportunities & been put back & in Jany was dismissed. His demerits were 118. Can any thing be said for a boy under these circumstances? General Pitcher in a letter to Genrl Crawford says 'I think if the boy was re-instated he would do better' & 'if he should come back any time during Feb he ought to be able to get through his course' &c   I entreat you to allow him to be re-instated. One more trial I beg of you. A claim to favor he has not—I only come in a mothers despair hoping to gain favor from you. The dismissal was a great surprise to the boy—for he assures me his studies were not neglected. General Grant can you pass over this offense & give him one more chance? The battle of life is a hard one, fought single handed, & my hopes hang on that boys success—Judge him I pray you, kindly & give the order for his re-instatement"—ALS, *ibid.* See *PUSG*, 13, 435–36. On June 7, 1869, Charles Ewing, Washington, D. C., wrote to USG. "I have the honor to ask that Reade M. Washington, a son of Capt: Washington late of the 13 U. S. Infantry, be appointed a 2d Lieutenant in the Army of the United States to take rank next after the last man of his Class at West Point who graduates on the 15th of this month"—ALS, DNA, RG 94, ACP, W147 CB 1869. USG noted on the docket. "Let this be brought up when apts. of graduating class at West Point are being made."—AN (undated), *ibid.* On June 16, the USMA class of 1869 petitioned USG. "The Graduating Class of '69 respectfully request the President that he appoint Reed Washington,—late of our class a lieutenant in the Army with us."—DS (thirty-nine signatures), DLC-Charles Ewing. On Dec. 6, USG nominated Reade M. Washington for 2nd lt., 9th Cav., as of June 24.

1867, FEB. 20.　To Bvt. Maj. Gen. Edward D. Townsend. "Please see the Sec. of War and ask if it would not be well, in view of the relations necessarily existing between the Army and the Coast Survey, as well as in view of the personal relations that always existed between Prof. Bache and the Officers with whom he was brought in contact, that notice should be taken of his death by the Dept."—ALS, DNA, RG 94, Letters Received, 96A 1867. On the same day, Townsend noted on the docket. "Submitted to the Secretary of War, who does not think there is sufficient reason for issuing such notice"—ANS, *ibid.* Alexander M. Bache, USMA 1825, headed the U.S. Coast Survey from 1843 until his death on Feb. 17, 1867.

1867, FEB. 21.　USG endorsement. "Respectfully forwarded to the Secy of War　From the statement of Major Atherton & the evidence submitted therewith I am satisfied that great injustice was done him in the revocation of the orders accepting his resignation & would therefore recommend that Par 24 S. O. 186 War Dept A. G. O. Apr 25, '65 be revoked & the order accepting his resignation remain as originally given."—Copy, DLC-USG, V, 43. See *PUSG*, 14, 488.

1867, FEB. 22.　To Secretary of War Edwin M. Stanton. "I have the honor to recommend that so much of par. 1111, Revised Regulations of the Army, as provides that 'mileage is computed by the shortest mail route, and the distance by the General Post Office book', be modified so as to read as follows: mileage is computed by the route usually travelled, and when the distance cannot be ascertained with certainty it shall be reckoned subject to the decision of the QuartermasterGeneral."—LS, DNA, RG 94, Letters Received, 108A 1867. Additional papers are *ibid.*

1867, FEB. 22.　Lt. Gen. William T. Sherman, St. Louis, to USG. "Last summer when in Vermont I called to see the mother & sister of General Ransom, who were still in deep mourning & affliction for him—I offered to do any thing in my power to alleviate their situation. They now Call on me, and of course I want to do all that is possible. You knew Ransom as well as I, & are equally interested in his family. I suppose the only difficulty is in a *double* Pension, and our Congress may by Law have specially guarded against any single person getting two pensions. Then this one might go to the sister. I think if you write some thing handsome in addition to what I have done, the Commissioner of Pensions can manage the Case—I have written to Miss Kate, a very interesting young miss, not over 16 or 17 what I have done, and if you can give her hope you might drop her a short & kind note which the family will prize beyond anything. We had a Grand Party at John How's last night and generally social matters here are prosperous. I think the Bill for the Better Gov of the South will force you to ask for *more* troops—Better do it when Congress has its blood up—the Increase might be provisional—The Districts too should be by states, Arkansas & Mississipi dont fit at all. Arkansas might be grouped with Louisiana.—If Each State constituted a seperate Mil Dept. the Commander could use the state machinery & courts as much as possible to save the labor of Military courts. The practical working of the Law is going to breed immense labor & trouble, unless you can use local courts, sheriffs constabls &c subordinate to the Military—Also is Uncle Sam to be charged with all the Expense? If you have a chance to put in a word, it might be well to do so."—ALS, USG 3. On March 7, USG favorably endorsed a letter of Feb. 14 from Mrs. Margaret M. Ransom, Eastport, Maine, requesting a pension.—Copy, DNA, RG 108, Register of Letters Received. On March 23, USG favorably endorsed a letter of March 4 from 2nd Lt. James O'Hara, 3rd Art., Eastport, to Sherman requesting an Army appointment for Frederick E. Ransom.—ES, *ibid.,* RG 94, ACP, R96 CB 1867.

1867, FEB. 22.   B. W. Hunter, Alexandria, Va., to USG. "The municipal election of this city, takes place on the first Tuesday in March. There are several rebel candidates for each office; and six or seven for Mayor. We have a Loyal Association, and at the last meeting I introduced a resolution to the effect that we would run no loyal candidates on account of our small minority, intending in this way to prevent the rebels from calling a convention, in which event, they would adhere to their particular candidate, and put him in office by an overwhelming majority. I proposed we should thus give them to understand we would run no candidate, and let them run as many as they saw fit, and then, on the eve of election call our union men together, make nominations after recinding or re-considering the resolution, and thus make the last attempt to run ahead on their division. We are like men, or were, without hope in the political world, and such strategy is allowable. But a new face is put upon things, and now, I desire to know for myself and others, at whose suggestion I write, if things cannot be so arranged for the benefit of the loyal people of this town, as to have the colored people vote on the fifth of March, and the rebels disfranchised who have violated their previous oaths, and those who voluntarily gave aid &c., to rebels, according to third section of the fourteenth article of the Constitution, or rather the proposed amendment. If we could now commence right, we could move forward in a streight line, but I see no way to so do, unless you or your *Brigadier* immediately intercedes after Congress has re-passed the reconstruction bill, and appoint *commissioners* to do the work understandingly. I should like you to understand that many rebels in this town are in favor of the bill just posted because Reverdy Johnson voted for it, and some union men against it, because of *this* vote. Such is the state of ignorance. The result of the coming election will greatly influence elections elsewhere, of a local character throughout the State. Pardon my apparent obtrusiveness, but you must feel an interest in the country you once saved." —ALS, DNA, RG 108, Letters Received.

1867, FEB. 25.   USG endorsement. "Respectfully forwarded to the Secretary of War. As Gen. Rosecrans' resignation has not been received, I respectfully recommend that this communication be regarded as a tender of resignation, and that it be accepted to date from the expiration of his leave of absence."—ES, DNA, RG 94, ACP, R160 CB 1867. Written on a letter of the same day from Bvt. Maj. Gen. Edward D. Townsend to USG. "By paragraph 10, Special Orders, No, 278, of June 13, 1866, the leave of General Rosecrans was extended until January 1, 1867. His last report dated Jamestown California, Decr 31, 1866, says he has forwarded his resignation as Brigadier General, & that report would be his last communication—His resignation has not, however, been received."—ALS, *ibid.* Brig. Gen. William S. Rosecrans resigned as of March 28.

1867, FEB. 26. USG endorsement. "Since this officer entered the service his regiment has been through three wars. In no one of them has he been in battle. I cannot therefore recommend him for a brevet."—ES, DNA, RG 94, ACP, S53 CB 1869. Written on a letter of Feb. 16 from U.S. Senator Edwin D. Morgan of N. Y. to Secretary of War Edwin M. Stanton recommending Col. John T. Sprague, 7th Inf., for appointment as bvt. brig. gen.— ALS, *ibid.*

1867, FEB. 26. Maj. Gen. Oliver O. Howard, Bureau of Refugees, Freedmen, and Abandoned Lands, to USG. "Allow me to introduce [t]o you Lt. O. M. Mitchell of the 17th Infty., who is a son of General Mitchell deceased. Prof. Church proposes to ask for him in his department about the 1st of June and the interim is so short it would be a great favor to Mr. Mitchell if he could be placed on recruiting or other duty at the North till that time."—ALS (press), Howard Papers, MeB. On April 9, Maj. George K. Leet favorably endorsed a letter of April 8 from Bvt. Maj. Gen. Edward R. S. Canby, Washington, D. C., to Bvt. Maj. Gen. John A. Rawlins requesting that 1st Lt. Ormsby M. Mitchel, 17th Inf., USMA 1865, be assigned as his aide.—ES and ALS, DNA, RG 94, Letters Received, 229½W 1867. On July 13, USG approved Mitchel's transfer to the 4th Art.—ES, *ibid.*, ACP, 2682 1871.

1867, FEB. 27. William Gray, Boston, to USG. "As chairman of an Executive Committee to collect subscriptions and purchase and forward food to relieve the destitution now existing at the South, I am anxious to procure information to enable the Committee to discharge the trust confided to them. We shall feel greatly obliged to you for any information which you can give us in regard to the localities of the greatest need, as to the best mode of forwarding food to them, and the agency of distribution which will be most efficient and useful, with any suggestions which may occur to you, on the whole subject."—ALS, DNA, RG 108, Letters Received. On March 4, Maj. Gen. Oliver O. Howard wrote to Gray providing the information and on March 6 forwarded a copy of this letter to USG.—Copy and ES, *ibid.*

1867, FEB. 28. To F. W. Owen *et al.* "Your kind invitation of this date, for me to be present at the Eighteenth Annual Commencement, Medical Dept. Georgetown College, in the 5th of March proximo is received. It affords me pleasure to accept your kind invitation and unless something unforseen occurs to prevent it I will be present on that occasion."—Joseph M. Maddalena, Catalog 7 [1989], no. 57.

1867, MARCH 1. Bvt. Maj. Gen. John M. Schofield, Richmond, to USG. "I propose, if you have no objection, to replace the cavalry company now at Winchester by a company of Infantry, and bring the cavalry to Richmond, where it will be available for general service throughout the state. Will you please inform me if you object to the proposed change?"—ALS, DNA, RG 393, Dept. of the Potomac, Letters Received. On March 2, Maj. George K. Leet favorably endorsed this letter.—ES, *ibid.*

1867, MARCH 5. Theodore C. Peters, former president, New York State Agricultural Society, Washington, D. C., to USG. "Private . . . I was so jeered at yesterday by my Radical friends because I called the Southern people *Loyal* that I almost doubted my identity. I understand loyalty to mean a disposition to faithfully support the government, and obey and uphold its laws. Such I believe is the Southern definition. But our friends here seem to think the dominant party is the government. In that view the people are not loyal, for no amount of *pounding*, will make them love the Radical, or the Democratic parties, you have not bayonets enough in all the arsenals of the union to overcome their aversion to the Radical party. They are *loyal* but not *cordial.* If you will pardon me I will illustrate my meaning by giving you a little of my own experience. About a year ago I sold my farm in Western NewYork, came down into Maryland near the Carrol Manor in Howard Co. and bought a farm. It was in a region which had been intensely rebel, but which seemed orderly, and quiet. I found arround me many blacks who were most anxious to study the bible, but their old masters, and the whites generally though members of the church would do nothing for them. I thought there could be no harm in helping the poor things. So I told them to come to me and I would help them orga- nise a Sunday school. I have always felt it a duty to aid the poor and lowly to become familliar with the word of God. The only building to be had was a part of shop on my farm. I rented it to them helped them organize their school. They had their own superintendnt and teachers, for my health would not permit me to assist them. The school was most orderly, and pro- ductive of much good to the poor things. I was denounced at once by my neighbors, threats of violence, and to destro[y] the building were freely made. But as I never shrink from doing what I consider my duty I paid no attention to them. The social position of my family for the past year can be infered from the fact that not a single neighbor of the old residents have called upon them yet. But that was not all. On the property was a good mill which I repaired and put in good order, but they gave out that if I staid there one hundred years they would not patronize it, and actually went miles out of their way to avoid it. I have been compelled to leave the place, sacrificing most of my rather slender means, and yet sir, I believe those people are truly loyal. If these things should happen in a community 20 miles from a city like Baltimore and 30 from the capitol of a great nation, what wonder that the prejudices of the people whould be great in the rural regions of the South. But I do not mention these things to make myself a matyr, nor shall I ask congress for an office because of my losses. I might have made a great ruin by simply narating the truth. But would it be right? We are taught by One who never errs, 'to forgive our enemies, and to pray for them who dispitefully use us.' At this time kind words are most important to heal the troubles of this most unhappy country—I think if the South is made to understand that the Military Bill will be firmly and surely enforced, they will soon come into *line.* They want now firmness, and kindness blended. If the Pesident can give me some appointment that would enable me to go quietly among them much good could be affected, perhaps the best would be to go from the Aggricultural department—I am free to say General that something of that kind in my present condition would be most gratefully appreciated— . . . P. S. After this week if you have a kind word for me I shall probably be at the Ebbetts House"—ALS, DNA, RG 108, Letters Received. Peters enclosed a lengthy letter of March 1 addressed to USG reporting conditions in the South.—LS, *ibid.* Printed in *National Intelligencer*, March 8, 1867.

1867, MARCH 8. To Secretary of War Edwin M. Stanton. "I have the honor to recommend, that the following named officers of my staff, viz:—Brevet Colonel *Eli S. Parker*, late Captain and Asst. Adjt. General U. S. Vols, and Brevet Colonel *Adam Badeau*, late Captain & Addl. A. D. C. U. S. Vols, be appointed Brigadier Generals by brevet of U. S. Vols, 'for gallant and meritorious services during the campaign terminating with the surrender of the insurgent army under General Robert E. Lee; to date from April 9th, 1865.'"—LS, DNA, RG 94, ACP, G103 CB 1867.

1867, MARCH 8. To Secretary of War Edwin M. Stanton. "I have the honor to recommend, that Brevet Colonel Michael R. Morgan, Major and Commissary of Subsistence, be appointed a Brigadier General by brevet in the United States Army 'for gallant and meritorious services during the campaign terminating with the surrender of the insurgent army under General Robert E. Lee; to date from April 9th, 1865.' Colonel Morgan is one of our best officers. He was Chief Commissary of Subsistence for the Armies operating against Richmond from June 16th, 1864, until after the surrender of General Lee, and discharged his duties to my entire satisfaction"—LS, DNA, RG 94, ACP, 1330 1882.

1867, MARCH 8. Lt. Gen. William T. Sherman, St. Louis, endorsement. "Respectfully forwarded to the General Commanding the Armies of the

U. S. Gen Hancock has now all the troops that can be given him, and will do his best to protect infant settlements. But I do not deem it wise to encourage too much dispersions. The People should not be encouraged to scatter too much especially in this case when old settlements demand so many troops as they do in NewMexico."—AES, DNA, RG 94, Letters Received, 269M 1867. Written on papers concerning the need for troops to protect a new settlement in New Mexico Territory.—*Ibid.* On March 16, Bvt. Maj. Gen. Edward D. Townsend noted on the docket that USG approved Sherman's views.—ANS, *ibid.*

1867, MARCH 9.   To Secretary of the Navy Gideon Welles. ". . . Young Johnston is the grandson of Gen. T L. Harmer [*Hamer*] of Ohio, who died in the service of his country during the Mexican War. He was a man of national reputation and as he has no son to represent him in the national service I think it would be an appointment well bestowed . . ."—Charles Hamilton Auction No. 33, March 20, 1969, p. 39.

1867, MARCH 9.   U.S. Senator Richard Yates of Ill. to USG. "Dr D K Green the bearer visits your office for the purpose of asking Sixty days leave of absence from his command, for his son who is a Lieutenant in the Army, Stationed in Minnesota. I shall feel personally obliged by any favor you may show him in the matter."—ALS, OCIWHi.

1867, MARCH 10.   Addressee unknown. "Brevet Major de Kay. late of the Volunteer Army Served during the Rebellion with credit to himself and to the Satisfaction of the General Officers immediately over him, two at least of whom selected him to Serve on their staffs during portions of the war. Major deKay is a gentleman who can be recommended to the confidence of those who he may meet whilst traveling abroad."—Copy, DNA, RG 59, Letters of Application and Recommendation. Enclosed in a letter of March 23, 1869, from Sidney B. De Kay, Washington, D. C., to Secretary of State Hamilton Fish applying for the position of legation secretary, Constantinople.—ALS, *ibid.* No appointment followed. De Kay, born in New York City in 1845, enlisted as a private and was promoted to 1st lt., 8th Conn. De Kay was badly wounded in 1867 fighting against the Turks in Crete. See *New York Times*, Dec. 4, 1867. On May 12, 1871, De Kay, asst. U.S. district attorney, New York City, wrote to USG. "I have the honor to offer my services as one of the assistants or other 'officers' in the Commission to be appointed for the fulfilment of the Anglo-American Treaty. A knowledge of the French and German languages (acquired in a residence of five years in Europe); a fair war-record—and a strict application during the past two years to the study and practice of Law—lead me to hope that my offer may be favourably considered—"—LS, DNA, RG 59, Letters of Application and Recommendation. No action followed.

1867, MARCH 11.   USG endorsement. "The appointment of Lucien How to the Military Academy at West Point is respectfully recommended. His father, Col. How, is an old Army officer who has not the same opportunity of securing this appointment through Congressional recommendation that a private Citizen has therefore the appointment 'at large is recommended." —AES, DNA, RG 94, Correspondence, USMA. Written on a letter of the same day from retired Col. Marshall S. Howe, 3rd Cav., to Secretary of War Edwin M. Stanton requesting an appointment to USMA for his son Lucien.—ALS, *ibid.* No appointment followed.

1867, MARCH 12.   USG endorsement. "Respectfully returned to the Secy of War—not approved, there being no sufficient military recommendations in this case."—ES, DNA, RG 94, ACP, H1381 CB 1866. Written on an undated letter from U.S. Delegate José Francisco Cháves of New Mexico Territory to Secretary of War Edwin M. Stanton recommending 1st Lt. Mason Howard, 5th Inf., for bvt. promotion.—ALS, *ibid.* On Oct. 10, Lt. Col. and Bvt. Maj. Gen. George Sykes, 5th Inf., New York City, wrote to Bvt. Maj. Gen. Edward D. Townsend recommending Howard for bvt. promotion for bravery near Fort Harker, Kan.—ALS, *ibid.* On Oct. 18, USG endorsed this letter. "Lieut. Howard is recommended for one brevet."—ES, *ibid.* On Sept. 9, 1868, U.S. Senator Samuel C. Pomeroy of Kan., Topeka, wrote to USG. "I have the honor to State that it has come to my knowledge—That the most deserving young man, that I have met, in the Army in this State, is *Lieut. Mason Howard*, of the 5th Infantry now Stationed at Fort Riley. Lieut. Howard, is deserving of a *brevet. Majority*; for his galantry at Wilsons Creek in Aug. 1861—And his general good conduct as an officer at the Post—If you will recommend him to the President, I Shall be greatly obliged—And one of our very best officers, will have had a suitable recognition—"—ALS, *ibid.* On Dec. 6, 1869, USG wrote to the U.S. Senate. "I desire the consent of the Senate to the appointment, under his true name of *Mason Carter*, 1st Lieutenant 5th U. S. Infantry, and Brevet Captain U. S. Army. . . . *Statement.* A short time prior to the breaking out of the rebellion, this officer enlisted, as a private in the Regular Army, under the assumed name of Howard. A Southerner by birth, he resisted the appeals of his friends to desert the union. He rose to the grade of Corporal. Without his knowledge and for gallant conduct at the battle of Springfield, Mo., where he was wounded, he was commissioned (under the name he then bore) a 2d Lieutenant in the 5th U. S. Infantry, 12 May, 1862; was promoted 1st Lieutenant 14 May, 1864, and was brevetted Captain 18 October, 1867."—LS, DNA, RG 46, Executive Nominations, 41–2. Carter was confirmed on Dec. 22.

1867, MARCH 13, Wednesday.   To John W. Garrett, president, Baltimore and Ohio Railroad. "On Monday evening next I propose, with a portion of my family and one or two staff Officers, to go to New York. Will it be too much to ask you for a special Car, to the regular train, for that occasion?"—ALS, DLC-Garrett Family Papers.

1867, MARCH 13. To N. and N. G. Whitmore. "I have the pleasure to acknowledge receipt of the beautiful rifle of your manufacture entirely from American material presented to me by the citizens of Providence, R. I. I scarcely know how to thank the citizens of Providence, yourself included, for this token of their esteem. Through you, however, I do extend my sincere thanks for this testimonial which will ever be appreciated."—Philip B. Sharpe, *The Rifle in America* (New York, 1938), p. 90. See W. C. Overstreet, "A President's Rifle . . . ," *Muzzle Blasts* (March, 1948). U.S. Senator William Sprague of R. I. and eight others joined the manufacturers in presenting the rifle.—DS, USG 3. On Dec. 2, Nathaniel G. Whitmore, Mansfield, Mass., wrote to USG. "I have the honor to apply for the appointment of Master Armorer of the U. S. Armory at Springfield Mass. I have also the honor to call your attention to the following statement   I have been for the past twenty years a constructor of all kinds of rifles—I have also had large experience in constructing machinery for making rifles— and also in the superintending of the Manufacture of Fire Arms—I would also inform you that I have made the principles of Gunnery and Ordnance large and small my sole and entire study—for the past twenty years—And understand I believe thoroughly every branch of the business of Manufacturing and Inspecting Fire Arms—And as a specimen of my work I would very respectfully call your attention to the Rifle Manfactured for the Citizens of Providence R. I. for presentation to you—And I would also refer your honor to the following Gentlemen—they being familiar with my qualifications as a Machanic and Rifle Maker—viz Hon. William. Sprague, Hon. Oakes. Ames and Hon. Henry. Wilson,—and would also refer you to testimonials as to my fitness for the position—now on file in your Department.—And if in your judgment after Examination as to my ability to fill acceptably the position asked for you should deem me competent to discharge the duties thereof.—I would be very happy to receive the appointment"—ALS, DNA, RG 156, Letters Received.

1867, MARCH 14. To Bvt. Maj. Gen. Edward D. Townsend. "Please give fifteen days leave of absence to Capt. Corbin, 38th Inf.y."—ALS, DNA, RG 94, Letters Received, 143A 1867.

1867, MARCH 15. Addressee unknown. "I have the honor to acknowledge the receipt of the medal, (fac-simile of the gold medal presented to Mrs. President Lincoln by 40 000 French Republicans) which the *Committee* of *Subscribers* desire to present to me as one of the supporters of Mr. Lincoln's Administration. I feel proud to be recognized as one of the supporters of that great and good man in his efforts to suppress rebellion and to maintain freedom and equality, and through you, desire to return my thanks to the committee for the compliment they thus pay me."—Copy,

NN. See Justin G. Turner and Linda Levitt Turner, *Mary Todd Lincoln: Her Life and Letters* (New York, 1972), pp. 376, 404; William H. Allen, *The American Civil War Book and Grant Album* . . . (Boston and New York, 1894), p. [43].

1867, MARCH 16. USG endorsement. "Respectfully forwarded to the Secretary of War."—ES, DNA, RG 108, Letters Received. Written on a letter of March 4 from Bvt. Maj. Gen. Alfred H. Terry, Fort Snelling, Minn., to Lt. Gen. William T. Sherman's adjt.—ALS, *ibid.* On March 8, Sherman, St. Louis, endorsed this letter. "Respectfully referred to the General Commanding the Armies of the U. S. and his attention invited to that part of Gen Terrys letter which refers to the habit of hostile indians taking refuge within British Territory when pursued. This actually occurred in the expeditions of Generals Sully and Sibley, and will occur again. Inasmuch as no part of the British Territory West of the Red River of the north is occupied by a civilised People, I have reason to believe on a proper representation that Her Britannic Majestys Govt will consent to a pursuit to a reasonable extent say a hundred miles. If the Indians learn that this line does not afford them protection they will be deterred from the commission of crime. No damage can possibly arise to British property or nationality as our troops are regulars, governed by the same General laws as prevail in the English army."—AES, *ibid.* On March 26, Bvt. Maj. Gen. Edmund Schriver, inspector gen., wrote to USG. "The Secretary of War directs me to acquaint you that Genl Terry's communication respecting the pursuit of hostile Indians within Her Britannic Majesty's dominions, forwarded by you to this Department has been sent to the Department of the State, and the Secretary replies that the subject will promptly receive attention."—ALS, PHi; ADfS, DNA, RG 107, Letters Received from Bureaus. See *HED*, 40-2-1, I, part 1, pp. 68–70, 79.

1867, MARCH 16. To Bvt. Lt. Col. James B. M. Potter. "For guidance to the Pay department in making up my pay accounts, under the law giving 'Ffogy rations' to general officers, I have the honor to state that I was commissioned in the regular army, to date from July 1st 1843. I served continuously until the 31st of July 1854, a period of Eleven years and one month. Re-entered the military service, as Col. of Volunteers, June 15th 1861, but about two months & a half after I was promoted to Brig. Gen. to rank from the 17th of May 1861."—ALS, deCoppet Collection, NjP. On March 31, USG wrote a detailed statement of his military appointments, perhaps to supplement this letter.—ADS (facsimile), IHi.

On Dec. 19, 1866, USG *et al.* had petitioned Congress. "The undersigned memorialists, confidently relying upon the disposition of your Honorable Bodies to do justice to the old officers of the army, who have honestly and faithfully served their country, respectfully pray that, when such officers are withdrawn from active service and placed on the retired list, under existing laws—except upon their own request—they may, in addition to the ~~mere pittance~~ of pay now granted to them, be allowed ~~to retain~~ their service or longevity rations; which is one ration per day for every five years service, as now provided by law, for all officers on the active list."—LS (printed text), DNA, RG 46, Senate 39H–10.1, Petitions and Memorials, Military Affairs; *ibid.*, RG 233, 39A–H15.4. See *U.S. Statutes at Large*, XIV, 423.

1867, MARCH 18. USG endorsement. "Respectfully forwarded to the Secretary of War for his information."—ES, DNA, RG 94, Letters Received, 119T 1867. Written on a letter of March 12 from Maj. Gen. George H. Thomas, Louisville, to USG's hd. qrs. "I have the honor to forward the enclosed Joint Resolution of the State of Tennessee, applying for the assistance of the United States in quelling violence in certain counties in that State, with my reply thereto for the information of the General-in-Chief."—LS, *ibid.* The enclosures include a letter of March 7 from Thomas to Governor William G. Brownlow of Tenn. ". . . The troops under my command are available for assistance to the civil authorities in enforcing the laws and preserving order, and upon the application of Your Excellency a sufficient force for that purpose will be sent to any locality in the State of Tennessee that may be designated, but the troops will act as aids only to the properly constituted civil authorities and not assume control of the citizens by virtue of Military orders. . . ."—Copy, *ibid.*

1867, MARCH 19. Isaac F. Quinby, Rochester, N. Y., to USG. "Has Dr Harts nomination been confirmed or will it be? Answer"—Telegram received (at 7:25 P.M.), DNA, RG 107, Telegrams Collected (Bound).

1867, MARCH 24. To William W. Smith. "Mrs. Grant and myself will leave here on Tuesday evening next, the 26th inst. to accompany my sister as far as the Ohio river on her way home, going by the B & O road. If you will meet us there, or let me know that you will be at home, we will go up to Washington and spend a day with you."—ALS, Washington County Historical Society, Washington, Pa. On April 1, USG telegraphed to Jesse Root Grant, Covington, Ky. "Jennie has not yet left here. ~~I~~Will telegraph when she starts."—ALS (telegram sent), DNA, RG 107, Telegrams Collected (Bound).

1867, MARCH 25. USG endorsement. "Respectfully forwarded to the Secretary of War; recommended for a 2d Ltcy of Colored Infantry."—ES, DNA, RG 94, ACP, T82 CB 1867. Written on a letter of March 18 from George Arthur Tappan, Lowell, Mass., to the AG requesting an appointment in the U.S. Army.—ALS, *ibid.* On July 11, Tappan wrote to USG. "Pardon me for taking the liberty of writing to you, but I feel that you are the only one I can make known my wishes to with any chance of success for I have exausted every means in my power to obtain a commission as 2d Lieut. in the Regular Army. In September 1865 I was stationed at Fort

Jefferson Tortugas Fla. and was the officer who discovered and arrested Dr. Mudd in his attempt to escape. soon after that I was appointed Provost Marshal by Bvt. Brig. Genl B. H. Hill 5th U. S. Arty. In Decr /65. Gen. Hill requested me to make an application for a commission in the U. S. Army. I done so and it was favorably endorsed by my commanding officer, Gen. Hill. Gen. Newton and Maj. Genl J G. Foster. but I never heard from it. . . ."—ALS, *ibid.*, T345 CB 1867. No action followed.

1867, MARCH 25, 1:15 P.M. To Bvt. Maj. Gen. John M. Schofield. "Can you not spare one regiment from your command? If so please designate which one."—ALS (telegram sent—misdated March 26), DNA, RG 107, Telegrams Collected (Bound); telegram sent, *ibid.*; telegram received (on March 25), *ibid.*, RG 393, 1st Military District, Telegrams Received. On March 25, Schofield, Richmond, telegraphed to USG. "I do not think I aught to spare any troops from my command   I shall greatly need all the Officers I have from this time forward and if troops become necessary at any time Even what I now have will be insufficient"—Telegram received (at 8:20 P.M.), *ibid.*, RG 107, Telegrams Collected (Bound); *ibid.*, RG 108, Telegrams Received; copies, *ibid.*, RG 393, 1st Military District, Telegrams Sent; DLC-USG, V, 55.

1867, MARCH 26. To Bvt. Maj. Gen. John Pope. "This will introdu[ce] to you J. J. Giers, of Alabama, a man who was entirely loyal to the Government during the entire rebellion. During the war Mr. Giers was a refugee from his home, on account of his loyalty, a great part of the time. He then voluntarily gave all the aid he could to the Union cause. I placed great reliance, during the rebellion, and since, upon the statements of Mr. Gier and I think you can safely do the same."—ALS, CtY. On Feb. 18, 1866, USG had written: "I know Mr. Giers well, and I always found him ready to aid the government in every way possible. He is competent and reliable."— *HRC*, 39-1-51, p. 9. See *PUSG*, 13, 17–18.

1867, MARCH 26, 10:45 P.M. To Halliday and brother, Cairo. "Can you tell me [w]here J. F. Casey's is, and condition of affairs at Friar's Point."— ALS (telegram sent), DNA, RG 107, Telegrams Collected (Bound); telegram sent, *ibid.*

1867, MARCH 27. Col. and Bvt. Maj. Gen. Edward Hatch, 9th Cav., New Orleans, to USG. "When calling upon you last Summer you very generously allowed me to look at a letter from Holly Springs written by Mrs Govan, who was complaining seriously of ill-treatment from myself, I at once wrote for a copy of my report at the time, and any orders, & papers to which her name was attached, in the records of my Division, and have but recently received the enclosed report, and request for a guard to protect Mrs Govans house. I forward them merely in justice to myself, to show that she must have made an erroneous statement"—ALS, PHi. On Sept. 9,

1864, Hatch, White's Station, Tenn., had written to Maj. Gen. Cadwallader C. Washburn concerning his efforts to protect the property of Mrs. Pugh Govan in 1862.—Copy, DNA, RG 108, Letters Received. See John Y. Simon, ed., *The Personal Memoirs of Julia Dent Grant* (New York, 1975), p. 117.

1867, MARCH 29. To Secretary of War Edwin M. Stanton. "I would respectfully recommend that Gen. M. C. Meigs, Qr. Mr. Gen. U. S. army, be appointed a Commissioner to the Worlds Fair, Paris France. Gen. Meigs, by his zeal and indefatigable attention to his public duties, during the War, and since, has so far prostrated his constitution as to make rest, and freedom from care, necessary to his recovery, as I am informed."— ALS, DNA, RG 59, Applications and Recommendations, Lincoln and Johnson.

1867, MARCH 29. To Secretary of War Edwin M. Stanton. "I have the honor to make requisition for Nine Hundred and Sixty Nine Dollars. ($969.00) to be used in payment of the twenty per cent additional compensation allowed by Joint Resolution of Congress approved Feb 28th 1867. to Civilian Clerks employed at these Headquarters.—I respectfully request that the Warrant be drawn in favor of Major Geo. K. Leet. A. A. G. of my Staff."—Copies, DLC-USG, V, 47, 60; DNA, RG 108, Letters Sent.

1867, MARCH 30. USG endorsement. "Respectfully forwarded to the Secretary of War for instructions. Major General Meade has been directed to act under the President's Proclamation of June 7. 1866, until orders are received countermanding it."—Copy, DLC-Andrew Johnson. Written on a letter of March 28 from Maj. Gen. George G. Meade, Philadelphia, to the AG concerning the renewal of Fenian activities.—Copy, *ibid.* Additional papers are *ibid.* See *PUSG*, 16, 215–20.

1867, MARCH 30. USG endorsement. "Respectfully forwarded to the Secretary of War. I recommend that copies of these papers be submitted to the Secretary of the Interior, with the request that he will give orders to discontinue the issue of these permits."—ES, DNA, RG 107, Letters Received from Bureaus. Written on a letter of March 8 from Maj. and Bvt. Col. Andrew J. Alexander, 8th Cav., Santa Fé, New Mexico Territory, to Bvt. Brig. Gen. Cyrus B. Comstock. "During the time, I was in command of Fort Bascom, N. M., my attention was called to the large number of persons, passing East, with trains and pack animals for the purpose of trading with the Kiowa and Camanche Indians, who have been wintering in the vicinity of the Antelope Butts on the Canadian River. I immediately reported this fact to the Comd'g General of the District and requested his instructions in regard to putting a stop to it. He, having no orders covering the case, forwarded the matter to Superior Head Quarters. No answer has as yet been received. Very large numbers of wagons have gone down into the Indian Country, and large numbers of Cattle, Horses &c have been brought back to this Territory by these Traders. The Indians obtain their horses and cattle by plunder from the people of Texas, and dispose of them by trade to the people of New Mexico. Of course the traders take the most profitable goods which are arms and ammunition, and the result is a few selfish and interested parties furnish means to these Indians of inflicting great injury upon not only the citizens of Texas, but emigrants to the Gold fields of the West It is announced and I fear with truth, that the Kiowas and Camanches contemplate hostilities in the Spring and the unusually brisk trade from this country would seem to indicate this. Now if this is so irreparable mischief may ensue from this traffic which the military commander under existing orders is utterly powerless to suppress. Permits are freely given by a man by the name of Henderson, who represents himself as the Agent of the Pueblo Indians, but I do not understand, what authority he has to give persons permission to trade with the Kiowas and Camanches, who are Indians not belonging to this Superintendency. I would most respectfully suggest that authority be given as soon as possible to the Commander of the District, to stop this contraband trade, although I fear they have already obtained supplies enough to make a war with them the coming summer a very serious matter . . . P. S. I enclose a copy of Genl. Carleton's Letter to Department Head Quarters."—ALS, *ibid.* On April 10, Secretary of the Interior Orville H. Browning wrote to Secretary of War Edwin M. Stanton. ". . . Prior to the receipt of your letter information had reached this Department, touching the irregular practices of Agent Henderson, and orders have been given that he be instructed to recall all licenses issued by him for trading with the tribes above named, and, on no pretext, to issue another."—LS, *ibid.*

1867, APRIL 2. To President Andrew Johnson. "I would respectfully recommend that the name of Capt. & Bvt. Brig. Gen. Wm. Myers, be sent in for the vacant Majority in the Quartermaster's Dept. I was under the impression that his name had been sent in, and that he had been rejected by the Senate. He is well known as one of our most efficient Quartermasters, and I now learn that he has never been rejected, but would be confirmed without hesitation."—Copies, DLC-USG, V, 47, 60; DNA, RG 108, Letters Sent. On April 12, Charles W. Ford, St. Louis, telegraphed to USG. "March 20th Mr Stanton sent Wm Myers name to the President to be promoted a major—What can be done to have him confirmed."— Telegram received (at 6:10 P.M.), *ibid.*, RG 107, Telegrams Collected (Bound). William Myers, nominated on Feb. 16 as maj. and q. m., had been confirmed on March 2. On May 30, 1865, Ford *et al.* had written to USG. "Yesterday, I accidentally met some of the friends of Col Myers, our Quarter Master, when the subject of some recognition of his services, by the Government, was discussed by those present—Each answered as to what he had done, and in my turn, said, I had written you on the subject— telling you the services performed by Myers,—the sacrifices he had made by the chances of promotion he might have had in the field &c. and asked you—if not inconsistent with the interest of the service,—that you would endorse your approval, in an Effort to make him a Brigadier. Readily accounting, in my own mind, why you did not answer by the overwhelming public duties devolving upon you. I thought when the time came you would do what you thought would be right & just in the premises—and knowing that others of your personal friends here, had written you similar letters, I rested content—'Hope defered', it is said, 'maketh the heart sick'—and the friends of Col Myers feel that in the general scramble for services to be recognized by way of promotions and otherwise, that his claims may be forgotten or overlooked. In urging his claims—you know I do it as his neighbor & friend—and as a *citizen*, with no knowledge of what may be best for the Service or the country—but I do know his personal worth as a man and an officer and have no hesitation in saying—that whatever may be the upshot of the applications of his friends for his promotion—he has earned it as fairly as any man could have done—Pardon this long letter—and I will close— . . . The undersigned friends of Yours & Col Wm Meyers & thro those have been in a position to observe the labor of the Col, since the rebellion broke out, heartily concur in the request of Mr Ford & believe that in promoting Col. Meyers to the rank of Brig, Genl. an act of justice will be done to a meritorious Officer who has performed his arduous & exceedingly responsible duties in a manner which has made in deserving of all the honors which his Govt, may see fit to bestow on him   Hoping You will interest Yourself in this matter . . ."—ALS and LS (eight signatures), *ibid.*, RG 108, Letters Received.

1867, APRIL 2.   USG endorsement. "Respectfully forwardd to the Sec- retary of War"—ES, DNA, RG 94, Letters Received, 148Q 1867. Written on papers endorsed on March 17 by Bvt. Maj. Gen. Edward O. C. Ord and on March 27 by Lt. Gen. William T. Sherman. "The within application is respectfully forwarded to Hd Qurs Mil Div Mo Approved for the reasons here referred to—the Indians furnish much finer horses than the govt and can render better service on them, besides it is an inducement for them to secure horses from the wild indians against whom they are to operate   they will take better care of their own horses   it should be stipulated that the 40 cents a day should be in full for all losses and damages—"   "There was a Law, that volunteers should receive a pr. diem, 75 cents I think for the use of their private horses—but I think that Law is not applicable to the present time.   officers should be most careful in making Stipulations to Indians which they are not absolutely certain of being able to fulfil as it produces the very worst effect on ignorant Indians, who charge it to bad faith. Respectfully referred to the Genl in Chief as I am in doubt myself whether the War Dept may not have the power to sanction such an ar- rangemt, in which case I approve for the reasons given by Genl Ord."— ES and AES, *ibid.*

1867, APRIL 2. Franz Schumann, Williamstown, N. J., to USG. "I hope you will pardon my liberty of addressing you, and to lay before you a statement of my circumstances, in which I am soliciting your kind assistance and influence   I am an old soldier, who has fought in the Mexican as well as in the late war against the rebellion. In the Mexican war I fought as Dragoon of the 2d Regmt Comp F Capt Thornton, Col Kearny commanding the Regiment. Our Regiment was first under General Taylor, and afterwards under General Scott with the exception of Comp H. On our march from Vera Cruz to the national Bridge, I had the misfortune to be kidnapped by Mexican Rancheros or Guerillas near Passo Obejas, and kept in captivity during the remainder of the war. The particulars of my captivation I have stated in a letter to Adjutant General Jones deceased after my return from captivity in Washington in Decbr 1848, which letter may be found on file at the war department with the certificate of the Mexican authority the Brigade General and Governor of the State of Vera Cruz Don Juan Soto, who kept me prisoner of war until peace was made. The sufferings and privations we few prisoners had to undergo during our captivity will any one appreciate, who knows something about the hatred of the Mexican Guerillas at that time against their victims, particularly of those under command of the famous padre Guarante. My health had suffered a great deal during that campaign and captivity, but the worst of it, after my return to this country, was, that I had sacrafized by that war my former carreer in the mercantile line as Bookkeeper &c. Who would then take an old Dragoon as Bookkeeper to the prevalent prejudice against soldiers? No body. Thus I was compelled to change in my 50 years of age my former occupation and turn to hard labour in order to make a living. I did so, learned plowing cradeling, chopping woodde, and have since the Mexican war supported myself in this way. The last 10 years I have chopped wood here in the State of New Jersey, chiefly for the Glassfactories. My health had improved by this rustic life, and I was strong and robust for my age, when the rebellion broke out   As great many of the young men rushed to arms under the call of the late President A. Lincoln, the soldiers' spirit took hold of me, and I also went, and enlisted on the 4th September 1861 in the 74th Regiment Penna Vol Infantry for the term of three years or during the war. I was then 61 years of age; but no one found fault with my age, and the recruiting Officer was glad to have an old Veteran amongst the young crowd. The 74th belonged to the Division of General Blenker and was included in the Potomac Army under Maj Genl McClellan. But the next spring when the campaign opened, Blenker's Division was sent to Western Virginia to join General Fremonts Army corps. Under General Fremont we had the first battle at Crosskey on the 8th June 1862, to crush the rebel General Stonewall Jackson (who had chased General Banks to Winchester) and to prevent him from crossing the Rapidan Shenandoah on his return to join General Lee at Richmond. We failed in that attempt, as we lay idle the next day to let him unmolested cross the river, and to drive away Genl Shields, who opposed his crossing on the other side of the river. After this affair Genl Fremont and Genl Blenker retired from command: Our Division came then under Brigade General C Schurtz, under Maj General Sigel as corps commander, and Maj Genl Pope as commander in chief. After sundry battles and fights, at freman's ford, where our Regmt lost heavily, we fought at sulphur spring, waterlobridge and 2 days at Manasses or Bullrun, and our army corps covered the retreat, and protected the capital of Washington. We encamped then in the vicinity of Fairfax CourtHouse, Centerville &c, and it appeared we might go there into winter quarters. Under these impression, and that the war would soon be settled, and hating an inactive camplife with its usual bothersome nicknacks, and being superceeded and overlooked by my superiors (most likely on a/c of my age) by young favorite Sergeants (though I was Sergeant Major that time) and having one of them over me as Adjutant, who, as Orderly scarcely could make a correct morning report, and all the bureaux business was put on my shoulders, I got tired of the service, and came in for my discharge under the plea of high age. I obtained such by Maj Genl Sigel, and enclose a copy of the same, and also one of my testimonial with regard to my conduct for your perusal. Had I known that the Potomac Army would follow up a winter campaign I would not have left the Regiment. But when I returned to the NewJersey woods to follow my former occupation as woodchopper, I heard of the unlucky battles at fredericksburg and Chancelorsville, and I saw then the war would not be so soon over as I had anticipated. The President of the U. S. ordered new levies; the conscription law was passed by congress, and soldiers, who had been discharged on a/c of disability, might, if well, be accepted as Veterans, to fill up the Skeletons of the old Regmts. Feeling myself robust and healthy as before, I started for Philade to reenlist. The commander of the 75th Rgt Pa V. I accepted me willingly; but when I came to the Provost Marshalls to be examined and sworn in, and they saw my discharge with my real age, I was refused, stating, they had to stick stricktly to the formality of the army regulations with regard to age, no matter how fit I might be for soldiership. Thus I had to return to the woods, and to leave it to the other Veterans, and not to the bounty jumpers to finish the job with the already half broken rebellion. I cannot deny it, it grieves me, if I see these young fellows, have served 8 or 9 months, stayed at home to the last, and only enlisted to get the heavy bounty of 600—800$, and to avoid the draft, and if they got a scratch of a wound, sometimes inflicted by themselves most likely to save their lives to get out of the battlescrape, can still do their work, some well of, get besides pensions, I and I shall now beg my bread in my old age of 67 years, sick and consumptive, now unable to support myself longer by hard labour, have fought for the country and Goverment in two wars; 2½ year in Mexico and 14 months in this war, for which I have received not not a cent bounty nor pension, except my pay during the service. I therefore appeal to your sympathy, General, that you might cause by your influence, that the Government may grant me likewise a small pension as an invalid to save me from starvation. The few years I have to live what a trifle of expence is it to the Govrment to grant me a pension to those, who may live 30—40 years yet. In hopes, that you may have the kindness to use your influence in my behalf, . . ."—ALS, DNA, RG 108, Letters Received.

1867, April 4. USG endorsement. "I would respectfully recommend that the Chief Engineer be directed to detail an officer from his Corps to take charge of the construction of the wagon road refered to within. More and better work will probably be obtained, with the amount appropriated, in this way than in any other."—AES, DNA, RG 108, Letters Received. Written on a letter of the same day from U.S. Delegate Walter A. Burleigh of Dakota Territory to USG. "At the close of the 38th Congress (March 3d 65) an appropriation was made for ~~the~~ the construction of certain 'Wagon Roads' in the Territory of Dakota—The work was commenced and partially completed—What is known as the 'Shyenne Road' is incomplete—The appropriation has been exhausted except some twelve or fifteen thousand dollars—With strict economy—I think the unexpended funds now applicable to this object—will in the hands of an experienced man be suffient to complete the work—I therefore, respectfully request, that if practicable, you will detail a competent Engineer, from the regular Army—and give him a suffient Escort to protect the party—and I will have him appointed by the Interior Dept. to take charge of the work—"—ALS, *ibid.* On May 1, Burleigh, Yankton, wrote a letter received at USG's hd. qrs., docketed as stating "that the people of Dakota have prevailed upon Gen. J. B. S. Todd to accept superintendency of the 'Cheyenne wagon road' if Secretary of the Interior will give him the appointment. Requests military escort and facilities for him in his work."—*Ibid.*, RG 48, Lands and Railroads Div., Wagon Roads; *ibid.*, RG 108, Register of Letters Received. On May 21, USG endorsed this letter. "Referred to Commander Dept. of Dakota who will give protection as asked within if consistent with the pressing demand for troops elsewhere. Report action to Governor of Dakota and to these Headqrs."—Copies, *ibid.* On June 6, Bvt. Maj. Gen. Edward D. Townsend referred to USG a letter of May 29 from Bvt. Maj. Gen. Alfred H. Terry, St. Paul, Minn., to Townsend recommending against the escort because of Indian difficulties.—ES and LS, *ibid.*, RG 94, Letters Received, 660M 1867.

1867, April 4. USG endorsement. "The order will be given immediately to have the escort furnished as requested within."—AES, DNA, RG 107, Letters Received from Bureaus. Written on a letter of April 1 from Secretary of the Treasury Hugh McCulloch to Secretary of War Edwin M. Stanton requesting a military escort for "treasure" en route from Batesville, Ark., to Cincinnati.—LS, *ibid.*

1867, April 4.   USG endorsement. "I cordially recommend that Lt. Col. & Bvt. Brig. Gn. Eastman be assigned to duty, in this City, and directed to aid in the work on the Capitol for which he is so well qualified. Gen. Eastman is an Artist of great merit and could do the government good service as such."—AES, DNA, RG 94, Letters Received, 53I 1867. Written on papers favorably endorsed to USG on April 3 by U.S. Representative Robert C. Schenck of Ohio.—AES, *ibid.* On Sept. 2, Act. Secretary of the Interior William T. Otto wrote to USG, secretary of war *ad interim.* "I have the honor to acknowledge the receipt of your communication of the 29th ult enclosing a printed copy of Special Orders No 427. dated, August 28th 1867. detailing Brevet Brig: General Seth Eastman, Lieut Colonel U S Army to report for duty to this Department."—LS, *ibid.* See *Art in the United States Capitol* (Washington, D. C., 1978), pp. 184–93; Charles E. Fairman, *Art and Artists of the Capitol . . .* (Washington, D. C., 1927), pp. 235, 237–40.

1867, April 5.   U.S. Senator Alexander Ramsey of Minn. endorsement. "Respectfully referred to Genl. Grant. At this frontier post there is a U. States Custom House office—this correspondent—Indians of the Sioux & Chippeway tribes meet here frequently in battle to the great dread & annoyance of the setters. In view of this & other consideratns I deem it proper that some mility force be stationed here."—AES, DNA, RG 108, Letters Received. Written on a letter requesting protection at Pembina, Minn.— ALS, *ibid.* On April 26, Bvt. Maj. Gen. Alfred H. Terry endorsed this letter. "Respectfully returned to the Head Quarters of the Mil. Div. of the Missouri. The pressing necessity for troops at other points in this department will in my judgemt forbid the sending of any force to Pembina this year"—AES, *ibid.*

1867, April 6.   USG endorsement. "There is not now Military force enough in the West to give adequate protection to settlements and travel. It would not therefore be expedient to promise contractors escorts for their trains & droves to enable them to carry out their contracts. If this were done they, the contractors, would regard governmt has having become insurers against losses, by hostile Indians and also responsible for any failure to carry out their contract. It is quite likely the Indians can be fed cheaper by the Interior Dept. than they have been fed by the Army, if the latter will assume all the costly part of the enterprise."—AES, DNA, RG 94, Letters Received, 283B 1867. Written on a letter of April 5 from John B. Brown of San Antonio, Tex., Washington, D. C., to Secretary of War Edwin M. Stanton concerning beef contracts.—ALS, *ibid.*

1867, April 8.   Pussie Walker Gibbs, St. Louis, to USG. "Please do me the favor to grant a leave of thirty (30) days by telegraph to Capt. H. C. Robinett 1st Infantry at NewOrleans to visit a dying sister in Wilmington Del."—Telegram received (at 1:00 P.M.), DNA, RG 107, Telegrams Collected (Bound); *ibid.*, RG 108, Telegrams Received.

1867, April 10. To Secretary of War Edwin M. Stanton. "I have the honor to recommend that the brevet rank of Major General of Vols. be conferred upon the late Bvt Brig Gen. Fred Winthrop, Col. 5th N. Y. Vols & Capt 12th U S Inftry, for gallant conduct at the battle of Five Forks, Va., April 1st 1865."—LS, DNA, RG 94, ACP, W302 CB 1867.

1867, April 12. USG endorsement. "Respectfully forwarded to the Secretary of War, with recommendation that the Secretary of State be requested to ask the *Liberal* Government of Mexico, for permission to pursue hostile Indians into Mexican Territory, when necessary."—ES, DNA, RG 108, Letters Received. Written on papers endorsed on April 2 by Maj. Gen. Philip H. Sheridan, New Orleans. "Respectfully referred to General U. S. Grant with the request, that some arrangement may be made with the Mexican Authorities, which will prevent the evils complained of in the endorsement by Bvt Maj. Gen'l Chas Griffin, Com'dg Dist. of Texas. It is impossible to protect the Rio Grande frontier effectually against the small bands of Indians who infest certain portions of it, so long as they are permitted to obtain complete safety by crossing the river;—and so long as bands permanently residing in Mexico may cross the river and commit depredations in Texas with impunity."—ES, *ibid.*

1867, April 12. USG endorsement. "In June 1864 Lieut E. P. Brooks, Adjutant 6th Wisconsin Infantry left City Point, Va. under my orders with a detachment of 30 men for the purpose of cutting the telegraph lines and destroying R. R. bridges in the rear of the enemy. The Q. M. Dept. was ordered to issue horses to mount Lt. Brooks and 30 men, and the Ordnance Dept. to issue the necessary number of carbines and equipments. The whole command together with the Government property was captured by the rebels."—Copy, DNA, RG 108, Register of Letters Received. Written on a letter of March 19 received at USG's hd. qrs. from Edward P. Brooks. See *PUSG*, 11, 96–97.

1867, April 13, 1:30 P.M. To Maj. Gen. Philip H. Sheridan. "Give Gen. Heintzelman three months leave, without forfeiture of pay, he not having had that time previously, in accordance with the rule adopted towards officers of the regular army when mustered out of the volunteer service."—ALS (telegram sent), DNA, RG 107, Telegrams Collected (Bound); telegram sent, *ibid.*; telegram received, *ibid.*, RG 393, 5th Military District, Telegrams Received.

1867, April 13. USG endorsement. "Mr. Woodbridge's loyalty I have never heard questioned. If there is any claimant for the cotton captured at

Savannah, Ga. entitled to investigation, and return of proceeds in case the claim is properly proven, his is one. I concur with Gn. Howard in recommending an early investigation."—AES, Mrs. Arthur Loeb, Philadelphia, Pa. On April 30, Secretary of the Treasury Hugh McCulloch wrote to President Andrew Johnson acknowledging receipt of papers concerning the claim of Wylly Woodbridge, including a letter from Maj. Gen. Oliver O. Howard to Johnson endorsed by USG and others, and concluding: "I cannot take jurisdiction of the case under notice; and I see no remedy for Mr. Woodbridge except in the Court of Claims or before Congress. . . ."— Copy, DNA, RG 56, Letters Sent Relating to Restricted Commercial Intercourse. See *SRC,* 40-2-70.

1867, APRIL 13.   Maj. George K. Leet to William P. Ross, principal chief, Cherokee Nation, and others. "Referring to your communication of Feby. 1st 1867, relative to payment for horses belonging to the Indian Home Guards which, it is alleged, were used and destroyed in the Govt. service during 1862, 3, 4, the General in Chief directs me to say that a full investigation of the subject fails to show that authority was ever given for the mounting of said Home Guards, and therefore, under existing orders, they are not entitled to compensation for the horses so claimed to have been used and destroyed. In the event of an appeal to Congress the recommendation of the General-in-Chief would depend entirely upon the facts presented."—Copies, DLC-USG, V, 47, 60; DNA, RG 108, Letters Sent. On Feb. 1, Ross and two others, Washington, D. C., had written to USG. "We desire to call to your attention and ask your aid in a matter concerning the interests of our people—The 1st 2nd and 3rd regiments of Indian Soldiers in the United States service during the late war were, when they entered the Service, mounted on their own horses, and were used as mounted men under orders during the war   The horses thus brought to and used in the Service were never purchased by the United States and no amount was ever received by these men for the use of horses they being paid as infantry   Having thus furnished horses to the goverment during the years 1862, 1863 and 1864 and these horses having been used and destroyed in the goverment Service an order was issued by you, through General Halleck in 1864 to the commanding officer of the indian troops on the at Ft Gibson to mount as many of the indian troops as he deemed necessary   Owing to the impossibility of obtaining fresh horses this was not carried out but as stated a large amount of useful and active Service was performed by these troops on their own Stock   As the 2nd and 3rd Regiments of Indian troops were of the Cherokee Nation and as these portions of our people have become impoverished by the war and have thus lost much of their valuable and necessary Stock our authorities have felt it incumbent on them to secure a fair compensation for the horses thus used in the goverment service, no extravagant price being Sought. We desire to ascertain of you if there is any way under existing orders for the payment of horses which can be proven to have been thus used and destroyed in the federal Service without pay   If so what means can be taken thus to audit the claims of these our people—If it cannot be done without legislation from Congress would you recommend Such legislation   Beleiving that the goverment desires to liquidate every honest claim against it and [—] all to meet the just expenses of the w[ar] part of which has thus been borne by our people to there great loss. . . ."—LS, *ibid.*, Letters Received.

1867, APRIL 16.   To Bvt. Maj. Gen. Edward D. Townsend. "Order Capt. G. B. Russell, 44th U. S. Inf.y to report to Gn. Augur for duty. . . . Give Capt. Russell Twenty days to report at Omaha."—ALS, DNA, RG 94, ACP, R15 CB 1868. On July 29, 1866, U.S. Senator Henry Wilson of Mass. had written to USG. "I desire to urgently recommend for a Captaincy of infantry in one of the new 54 companies under the army bill, Captain George B. Russell, Bvt Lieut Colonel USV. He has served with distinction in the war, and is now serving on the staff of General Augur, He has endorsements and testimonials of the highest character and I have no doubt would make a fine officer. May I beg of you to aid him so far as lies in your power, as I am very desirous he should receive the appointment he desires."—LS, *ibid.* George B. Russell was appointed capt., 44th Inf., as of July 28. On April 16, 1867, Russell, Washington, D. C., wrote to Townsend requesting the appointment of bvt. maj.—ALS, *ibid.* On April 29, USG endorsed this letter. "Respectfully forwarded to the Secretary of War, approved for a brevet majority for gallant and meritorious conduct in the assault on Port Hudson to date March 2d 1867."—ES, *ibid.*

1867, APRIL 18.   To President Andrew Johnson. "I have the honor to recommend Col. Jas. A. Mulligan, 23d Illinois Volunteer Inf.y, for promotion to the rank of Brigadier General of Volunteers, to date from September 1st 1861. From the above date to the date of his death Col. Mulligan exercised a command at all times, I believe, equal to that of a Brigadier General. In August 1864 he was killed, leaving a widow & several children to mourn his loss, and who will be much benefited by this recognition of the services of Col. Mulligan."—ALS, DNA, RG 94, Vol. Service Div., Letters Received, A626 (VS) 1863. Secretary of War Edwin M. Stanton endorsed this letter. "Respectfully returned to the President with report that in the opinion of the Secretary of War the within application cannot be complied with under existing laws because 1st The power to appoint General officers in the volunteer service has expired. 2d A person not in being cannot receive or accept an office   3d Brevet appointments being an acknowledgement of meritorious service during life have been sanctioned but they are the only exceptions   4—The meritorious services of Col Mulligan however deserving can only be rewarded [necessarily] by Act of Congress"—AES (undated), *ibid.* On April 9, Reverend Dennis Dunne, Chicago, had written to USG. "The bearer—Mrs Mulligan—is the widow of the lamented Col. James A. Mulligan. She will explain to you the object of her visit, & I sincerely hope you will aid her in acomplishing it. Not having the pleasure of a personal acquaintance with you, I beg leave to state that I raised the Chicago Irish Legion (90 Ill). of which Col. O'Meara, who was killed at Mission-ridge, was commander, As I have done some little service for my Country, I will consider myself amply compensated if the petition of Mrs Mulligan be granted. Her husban was my dear friend & the Country owes something to widow & children & to his memory."— ALS, *ibid.* On the same day, Bishop James Duggan, Chicago, wrote to USG. "I venture to commend to your kind attentions the Lady presenting this note, Mrs Marian Mulligan. She will explain to you the reasons of her visit to you. Her husband fell at the head of his small force, doing battle bravely for his Country, and her brother was likewise lost to her on the same fatal day. She and her children are now poor, and appeal to the justice and generosity of their Country."—ALS, *ibid.* On Dec. 12, 1864, President Abraham Lincoln had nominated Col. James A. Mulligan for promotion to bvt. brig. gen. as of July 23, the date of his mortal wound. Congress confirmed this promotion but took no later action in behalf of Mulligan.

1867, APRIL 20. To Secretary of War Edwin M. Stanton. "I have the honor to recommend Brevet Colonel Elisha G. Marshall, Major 5th U. S. Infantry, for promotion, by brevet to the rank of Brigadier General U. S. A., for gallant and meritorious services during the war, to date from March 13th, 1865."—Copies, DLC-USG, V, 47, 60; DNA, RG 108, Letters Sent.

1867, APRIL 22. Maj. Gen. Philip H. Sheridan, New Orleans, to USG. "I find that Brevet Major. Thomas C Sullivan of the subsistence department now stationed here is ordered to the Third 3 Military district His services here are very much required we supply to all of Florida Portions of Alabama also sometimes Arkansas making a large depot here. I also desire to send brevet Maj. General Beckwith to Northern Texas to make arrangements for the supply of flour by purchase for the troops there & would like Sullivan if not injurious to service."—Telegram received (at 12:30 P.M.), DNA, RG 108, Telegrams Received; copies, DLC-USG, V, 10, 55; DLC-Philip H. Sheridan. On April 23, Bvt. Maj. Gen. Amos B. Eaton, commissary gen., endorsed a copy of this telegram with a justification of his policy.—Copy, *ibid.*, RG 192, Register of Letters Referred.

1867, APRIL 23. Col. Adam Badeau to USG, care of Aubrey H. Smith, Philadelphia. "The staff congratulates you on being thirty eight years old today."—ALS (telegram sent), DNA, RG 107, Telegrams Collected (Bound). See *PUSG*, 16, 263, for a letter in which USG inadvertently misstated his date of birth; presumably the subject provoked teasing. USG celebrated his forty-fifth birthday on April 27.

1867, APRIL 27. George Clendenin, Washington, D. C., to USG. "My Son Geo Clendenin Jnr is the commissioned Sutler at Fort Benton Mon-

tana   In consideration of the distance betwen us I take the liberty of
Making application for his appointment as Trader under the late resolution
of Congress   He has a large amount of Merchandize on the Steamer Wa-
verly which Vessel was reported at Omaha on the 15th Inst consequently
will not reach him much before his commission expires July 1st   During
the Rebellion he was on Gen'l Wheatons Staff and if here could furnish
abundant evidence of his qualification for the appointment   your favourable consideration of his petition will be duly appreciated by him & myself"—ALS, DNA, RG 108, Letters Received. On May 24, Bvt. Maj. Gen.
Horatio G. Wright, Washington, D. C., wrote to Bvt. Maj. Gen. John A.
Rawlins. "I have the honor to enclose a note recd from Genl Wheaton in
relation to Col Geo Clendenin, now the Sutler at Fort Benton, and whom
the General recommends for appointment as a trader at that post on the
expiration of his term as sutler. . . ."—ALS, *ibid.* The enclosure is *ibid.*

1867, APRIL 29.   USG endorsement. "Respy. submitted to the P. M. General"—Copy, DNA, RG 108, Register of Letters Received. Written on a
letter of April 20 from James W. Hale received at USG's hd. qrs.—*Ibid.*
On May 1, Postmaster Gen. Alexander W. Randall wrote to USG. "I have
the honor to acknowledge the receipt of a communication addressed to you
by *James W. Hale* Esqr of 54 Wall St New York on the 20th ultimo, and
referred by you to this Department, in which complaint is made of the
order issued by this Department on the 8th of May 1864. directing that
'all transient printed matter' conveyed by mail westward from Kansas and
eastward from the Eastern boundary of California be charged with letter
rate of postage. In reply thereto I have to state that the order referred to,
is not, as the writer supposes; *a regulation* of this Department; which the
Postmaster General, can, in his discretion, modify or change, but was issued
to carry into effect a law of Congress; (Act of 25th March. 1864, Section
4) requiring the *prepayment of letter postage rates* on 'all Mailable matter
which may be conveyed by mail westward beyond the western boundary of
Kansas; and Eastward from the Eastern boundary of California,' excepting
only 'Newspapers from a Known office of publication to bona fide subscribers. Not exceeding one copy to each subscriber,' and 'franked matter' "—Copy, *ibid.*, RG 28, Letters Sent by the Postmaster Gen.

1867, APRIL 30.   Maj. George K. Leet endorsement. "Respectfully referred to the Adjutant General for file."—ES, DNA, RG 94, ACP, 860
1875. Written on a letter of April 20 from Maj. Gen. Oliver O. Howard to
USG. "I desire to recommend, earnestly, for promotion by brevet, to the
grade of Brig. General, *C. C. Sibley,* Col 16th Infantry, *for long and faithful Services.* Col. Sibley has been Asst. Commissioner of Georgia for several months past, and has labored in this work faithfully and efficiently.
He is one of the few Colonels of the old regiments who have no brevet
rank."—LS, *ibid.*; (press) Howard Papers, MeB.

1867, [APRIL?].   George Trask, Fitchburg, Mass., to USG. "Public men
we regard as public property; hence their public acts are legitimate subjects
of public animadversion. Newspaper reporters, who chronicle your movements from Dan to Beersheba, identify you with your cigar, and find pleasure in proclaiming, far and near, that you are a great smoker as well as a
great general. Whether they report you in one battle or another, in the
siege of Richmond or the capitulation of Lee, receiving the homage of fair
women or the noisy applause of men, they 'ring the changes' on 'Grant and
the inevitable cigar.' You conquered, general, in spite of your cigar; but
had you conquered by its virtues, as Constantine by the sign of the cross,
they could have given it little or no more prominence. We addres you,
general, with sincere respect and gratitude; still, be it understood that,
while we meddle not with your private habits, we make no apologies for
assaulting a vice which you persistently obtrube upon public notice. The
war we wage is simply defensive. Your habit is contagious, and, associated
with your powerful name, is doing irreparable mischief in the great community. . . . You, general, and the sturdy portions of your staff, may stand
the insidious assaults of this poison for years; but how attenuated lilliputian
cadets, how our pale, furloughed lieutenants, who, in the guise of officers
and disguise of gentlemen, meet us at eveyy corner and in every omnibus
and puff their fowl smoke in our faces, are to withstand it, become men
and ably head an army, is a problem which no sagacity can solvo. Dear
general, we ask you to set a better example to our military and naval schools,
to our army and nation. You have conquered a city; the world calls it a
great achievement. We ask you to conquer a despotic habit, perhaps as
invincible as Richmond, and God's Word will justify us in calling it a great
achievement."—*Chicago Times*, April 9, 1867. The letter may have been
prepared solely for newspaper publication. Trask, born in Mass. in 1798,
ordained in 1830, a temperance agent in Fitchburg after 1850, lectured
often on the evils of tobacco and liquor.

1867, MAY 2.   USG endorsement. "Respectfully referred to the Sec'y of
War   I would recommend the referrence of this to General Thomas with
authority for him to give up the property referred to if other suitable prop-
erty can be leased without detriment to the Government."—Copy, DNA,
RG 108, Register of Letters Received. Written on a letter of Feb. 25 from
Bvt. Maj. Gen. Daniel H. Rucker, act. q. m. gen., to USG. "I respectfully
submit herewith for your opinion, as to the propriety and desirability of a
purchase of the property in Nashville, Tenn, proposed to be sold to the
United States, for Military purposes, the enclosed communications of Mrs
Rachel D. Foote, favorably endorsed by the Commander of the Department
of the Tennessee, requesting a return of these enclosures."—LS, *ibid.*, RG
92, Miscellaneous Letters Sent (Press).

1867, MAY 2.   Maj. George K. Leet endorsement. "Respectfully referred
to the Adjt. General for file."—ES, DNA, RG 94, ACP, B870 CB 1867.

Written on a letter of April 29 from G. M. Bridge, St. Johnsbury, Vt., to USG. "for reasons known to myself I Wish to Join the army, and if you Will give me a Comission if nothing more than Lieut. I Will give you ($500.). five Hundred Dollars. I Want a Chance Where there is fighting if possible. I am 23 years of age 5 feet 11 inches in height and have Been in the Army 3 years. Was Wounded in the fight of the Wilderness also at Petersburg, and if you Will give me a Comission it Will Be a favor I never shall foget. . . . P. S. Please answer imediately."—ALS, *ibid.*

1867, MAY 3, 11:20 A.M.   To Maj. Gen. George G. Meade. "You are authorized to detain Col. Pennypacker as requested"—Telegrams sent (2), DNA, RG 107, Telegrams Collected (Bound); telegram received, *ibid.*, RG 393, Dept. of the East, Letters Received. On May 2, Meade, Philadelphia, had telegraphed to USG. "Considerations of public interest require the presence of Colonel Pennypacker here till the tenth 10 Instant   Can I be authorized to detain him   His orders require him to leave on the sixth 6."—Telegram received (at 6:40 P.M.), *ibid.*, RG 108, Telegrams Received; copies, *ibid.*, RG 393, Dept. of the East, Letters Sent; DLC-USG, V, 55.

1867, MAY 3.   USG endorsement. "The writer of this letter is well known to me. He was a good soldier during the entire rebellion and his recommendation is entitled to the highest consideration. If a vacancy still exists in the Veteran regiments I recommend the appointment of John U. Hitz."— AES, DNA, RG 94, ACP, H424 CB 1867. Written on papers submitted from Georgetown, Ohio, on April 27 concerning John U. Hiltz, former capt., 23rd Ohio; docketing indicates that the papers were returned in Feb., 1869.—*Ibid.*

1867, MAY 4.   Governor Richard J. Oglesby of Ill., Springfield, to USG. "I take the liberty to re-call to your notice Brevet Brig Gen Herman Lieb and to request your favorable consideration of his wishes upon a subject of some interest to him. General Lieb you will remember as having been one of your best soldiers; he was long in the service and always served well. I served with him a long time and know him to be not only a good soldier but a worthy and intelligent citizen. I would like very much to see him selected and appointed to some position in the army or in some place in connection with the army. He will state to you or to Gen John A Rawlings his wishes. There is no place to which you can appoint him that he will not fill creditably. He has for sometime been employed here in editing and publishing a german newspapr but there are so few germans in our community that he has not been able to make it remunerative   I shall be much pleased to hear you have been able to confer upon him some suitable appointment"— LS, DNA, RG 108, Letters Received. On May 28, Herman Lieb, Springfield, wrote a letter received at USG's hd. qrs. requesting an appointment as "Storekeeper (presumed Trader)."—*Ibid.*, Register of Letters Received.

1867, MAY 6.   USG endorsement. "Respectfully forwarded to the Secretary of War for his information. The necessity for more officers with the 9th U S Cavalry is urgent and demands attention. I respectfully recommend that all vacancies in that regiment be filled as soon as possible."—ES, DNA, RG 94, ACP, M991 CB 1863. Written on papers concerning a mutiny in Co. E, 9th Cav., at San Pedro Springs, Tex.—*Ibid.* On May 4, Maj. Gen. Oliver O. Howard had written to USG. "I have the honor to apply for Captain J. S. Brisbin, 9th U. S. Cavalry, for duty in Alabama, in the Freedmen's Bureau. I believe he is now off duty at Lexington, Ky."—Copies, *ibid.*, RG 105, Letters Sent; (2) Howard Papers, MeB. On May 6, Maj. George K. Leet unfavorably endorsed this letter.—Copy, DNA, RG 108, Register of Letters Received. On March 30, Maj. Gen. Philip H. Sheridan, New Orleans, had telegraphed to Bvt. Maj. Gen. John A. Rawlins. "The ninth 9 Cavalry is now Enroute to occupy the frontier posts of Davis & Stockton on the line from San Antonio to El Paso   It has only Eleven 11 line officers with it. It is very important that all officers be compelled to join quickly   the public service is suffering from their absence."—Telegram received (at 3:00 P.M.), *ibid.*, RG 107, Telegrams Collected (Bound); *ibid.*, RG 108, Telegrams Received; copies, *ibid.*, RG 94, Letters Received, 164G 1867; (sent by mail) *ibid.*, RG 108, Letters Received; DLC-USG, V, 55; (2) DLC-Philip H. Sheridan; DLC-Edwin M. Stanton. See *Calendar*, Oct. 2, 1867.

1867, MAY 6.   Bvt. Maj. Gen. Edward D. Townsend endorsement to USG stating that current law prohibited continuance of a trading post at the Presidio of San Francisco.—ES, DNA, RG 94, Letters Received, 276P 1867. Written on an undated letter from Jonathan D. Stevenson, San Francisco, to USG. "The undersigned would respectfully represent that he received the appointment of Sutler at Presidio Barracks San Francisco California on the 25th Feby: 1865 for the term of three years. At the time of my nomination by the Post Council of Administration, to the nomination was attached a condition that I should purchase the Store House and fixtures belonging to my predecesor, the cost of which with some improvements made by myself was Three Thousand dollars and upwards, all of which is now valueless owing to the repeal of the Law authorising the appointment of Sutlers and the instructions contained in General Orders No 6 issued from the War Department Jany 26th 1867 in relation to Sutlers. This order renders my property valueless; for my Store and fixtures are upon the Government reserve and of no use to me except for the purpose they were originally intended, and could not be sold for an amount beyond the price of old lumber as the building would have to be torn down and removed. Under these circumstances I most respectfully solicit permission to establish on the Presidio Reservation a trading Post or Store. The Reservation is some two miles in length and is a distance of two miles from the populated portion of the City of San Francisco and supplies could only be obtained from Sutler Stores for the laborers mechanics and other employees up[o]n the public works within the limits of the Reserve as well as upward of Four Hundred soldiers Rank & file quartered within the said limits; besides which a large number of citizens and travellers daily visit and pass over the reserve for health and recreation to nearly all of whom refreshments would be most agreeable if not absolutely necessary. I therefore most respectfully solicit permission to open a trading store at such point on the Reserve as the Commanding General of this Military Department or reserve may direct and for the sale of such stores and articles only as may be authorised and under such restrictions as the commanding officer of the Department or reserve may direct. It may not be improper for me to remark here that I have been a resident of California for Twenty years and upwards having come to California during the War with Mexico in command of the First Regiment of New York Volunteers raised and organized for service in California and have remained here ever since without a single visit to the Atlantic States."—ALS, *ibid.* An undated petition of officers of the post to USG recommending Stevenson is *ibid.*

1867, MAY 7. USG endorsement. "Respectfully forwarded to the Secretary of War. The findings of the Court of Inquiry are approved and I recommend that they be given to the press for publication, in vindication of the military force at Carlisle Barracks."—ES, DNA, RG 94, Letters Received, 525M 1867. Written on a report of April 19 from Judge Advocate Gen. Joseph Holt. "The accompanying report of a Court of Inquiry convened to investigate the circumstances connected with the riot which occurred at Carlisle, Pa. between certain enlisted men and citizens, is respectfy. referred to Gen. Grant. The Conclusions reached by the Court are believed to be fully justified by the testimony. The general good conduct and peaceable character of the troops at Carlisle Barracks are sworn to by many citizens of the town of respectability and station. The riot appears to be attributable to the drunkenness of certain violent citizens of the place, inflamed by drink and the excitement of a contested election, who attacked without provocation a few soldiers belonging to the garrison on their way to or from the Post office. The animus of these citizen rioters, the four most prominent and most lawless of whom are named Hamwell (since dead) Hollenbaugh, Gilmore (who appears to have fired the shot which killed Sergt. Bergman) and Green, is shown by their cheering for Wilkes Booth, on the evening of the riot. From the testimony given both by soldiers and citizens, it is evident that the riot was commenced by certain people of the town, in gratification of an disloyal animosity towards Federal troops. The conduct of the soldiers seems to have been remarkable for forbearance, even under circumstances of the most irritating character. Very few shots were fired by the military, and those few strictly in self defence. The conduct of the officers without exception, seems to have been discreet and moderate."—DS, *ibid.*

1867, MAY 8.   To Secretary of War Edwin M. Stanton. "I have the honor
to recommend the promotion of the following officers of the Army to fill
original vacancies, in the grade of captains of Infantry which may now or
hereafter exist. 1st Lt. B. Langdon. 35th Infty. (Lt. Col. 1st Ohio Vols.)
[1st Lt.] A. P. Bonnafore 35th Infty (Col. 78th Penna Vols)   [1st Lt.]
W. W. Barrett 34th [Infty] (Bvt. Brig. Gen. Vols)   [1st Lt.] Lewis
Johnson 41st [Infty] (Col. Vols)"—Copies (in tabular form), DLC-USG,
V, 47, 60; DNA, RG 108, Letters Sent.

1867, MAY 9.   USG note. "Will the Sec. of War please see Mrs. Boyd &
Mrs. Day, old acquaintances of mine of years ago. They wish to ask for the
appointment of their brother, Maj. E. M Camp, to the regular Army. Maj.
Camp has military recommendations on file with *my recommendation*
also."—ANS, DNA, RG 94 ACP, C598 CB 1867. Written to accompany
the printed card of Mrs. Edgar B. Day with Mrs. James R. Boyd's name
added.—*Ibid.* On Feb. 20, USG had favorably endorsed three letters recommending Erskine M. Camp for appointment in the U.S. Army.—ES
(undated), *ibid.*, 2810 1874; copy (dated Feb. 20), *ibid.*, RG 108, Register of Letters Received. On April 10, Camp, Washington, D. C., wrote to
USG. "Pardon the liberty I take in addressing you, but the necessity of the
case I hope may plead my excuse   Upon being mustered out of the United
States Service last August, I received employment in the Burial Corps, my
services in that Corps are no longer required, and now I am out of Work. I
served my country faithfully six years, and nearly all my early associations
are connected with the Regular Army. I have been an applicant for a Commission in the Infantry Line over two years, and my reccomendations on
File testify to my ability and services. But my prospects seem as dim as
when I first applied. General, may I hope in your kind intercession in my
behalf"—ALS, *ibid.*, RG 94, ACP, 2810 1874. On April 11, USG favorably endorsed this letter.—ES, *ibid.* Camp was appointed 1st lt., 40th Inf.,
as of June 10. On Dec. 19, U.S. Senator Roscoe Conkling of N. Y. wrote
to USG, secretary of war *ad interim.* "I have the honor to commend to your
consideration the name of Erskine M. Camp—1st Lieu't. 40th U. S. Infantry, Comd'g Co. H.—for the rank of *Major* by *Brevet.*"—ALS, *ibid.* On
Dec. 27, USG endorsed this letter. "Approved for brevet of Captain for
battle of Cedar Mountain."—ES, *ibid.*

1867, MAY 9.   To AG. "Please telegraph Gen. L. C. Hunt, Fort Gratiot,
Mich. authority to delay joining his regiment for thirty days."—ALS,
DNA, RG 94, Letters Received, 282A 1867.

1867, MAY 10.   U.S. Senator Oliver P. Morton of Ind., Indianapolis, to
USG. "While at Washington I earnestly recommended the appointment of
Jas Nathaniel Kimball as a cadet at West Point   He is a most worthy son
of your old friend Brevet Maj. Gen Nathan Kimball this state   anything
you may be able to do in his behalf will be appreciated by . . ."—Telegram

received (at 9:40 P.M.), DNA, RG 107, Telegrams Collected (Bound); *ibid.*, RG 108, Telegrams Received; copy, DLC-USG, V, 55. On Jan. 5, 1870, Nathan Kimball, Indianapolis, wrote to USG. "During the administration of Andrew Johnson, Senator Morton made application for appointment as Cadet to West Point—for my son—and you were kind enough to give it your recommendation but it failed. Remembering your kindness I again presume to ask you to favor me & my son by appointing him and I am sure you cannot confer a favor of the kind upon one who will be more thankful. My son will be Sixteen years old in March next, and is well advanced in his studies. I am sure he will do honor to himself & prove himself worthy the honor & favor you may do him. His name is William A. Kimball and is of fine development physically and mentaly and is all that could be desired morrally. Hoping that you will give this my only application for Executive favor a favorable consideration . . ."—ALS, DNA, RG 94, Correspondence, USMA. Three additional letters to USG recommending William A. Kimball are *ibid.* Kimball entered USMA in July, 1872, failed to graduate, and was appointed 2nd lt., 13th Inf., as of Aug. 31, 1876.

1867, MAY 11.   USG endorsement. "Respectfully forwarded to the Sec'y of War. I approve Genl Ord's order and recommend that the issues of potatoes under it, to the troops at Fort Smith, Ark. be allowed."—Copy, DNA, RG 108, Register of Letters Received. Written on a letter of April 11 from Bvt. Maj. Gen. Edward O. C. Ord received at USG's hd. qrs. complaining that Bvt. Maj. Gen. Amos B. Eaton, commissary gen., had charged him $16.95 for issuing an extra ration of potatoes to troops for medical reasons.—*Ibid.* On May 8, Eaton wrote to Ord billing him $2.64 for another extra ration of potatoes.—LS, *ibid.*, RG 192, Letters Received by Referral. On May 31, USG endorsed this letter. "Respectfully forwarded to the Secretary of War in connection with similar papers forwarded May 11th 1867."—ES, *ibid.* Docketing indicates that Eaton was directed to approve Ord's orders.—*Ibid.*

1867, MAY 11.   USG endorsement. "Respectfully forwarded to the Secretary of War. I concur in the recommendation of the Board of Engineers."—ES, DNA, RG 153, Military Reservation Files, Calif. Written on papers concerning the status of military reservation land near Mare Island, San Francisco.—*Ibid.* See *HED*, 42-3-99.

1867, MAY 13.   Edwin D. L. Wickes, San Antonio, Tex., to USG. "The undersigned begs leave to represent, that the 9th U. S. C. Cavy of which he is now acting as Sutler, being about to move to the frontier, he would most respectfully ask the permission and authority of the Commanding General, to enable him to conduct a 'trading establishment' at Fort Davis. Texas, agreeably to Resolution No 33, passed at the second session of the Thirty ninth Congress Approved March 30. 1867. entitled: 'A Resolution to authorize the Commanding General of the Army to permit traders to remain at certain Military Posts.' "—ALS, DNA, RG 108, Letters Received. On June 22, 1866, USG had favorably endorsed a letter of March 25 from Maj. and Bvt. Col. John P. Hatch, 4th Cav., San Antonio, to Secretary of War Edwin M. Stanton recommending Wickes for appointment as sutler at Fort Davis, Tex.—AES and ALS, *ibid.*, RG 94, ACP, W588 CB 1866.

1867, MAY 14. USG endorsement. "Respectfully forwarded to the Secretary of War. Captain Barstow is recommended for brevet majority for gallant and meritorious services at battle of Gettysburg and for brevet Lieut Colcy for gallant and meritorious services at fall of Petersb'g. Captain Meade is recommended for brevet majority for gallant and meritorious services at battle of Gettysburg and for brevet Lt Colcy for gallant and meritorious services in campaign ending in surrender of Army of Northern Virginia."—ES, DNA, RG 94, ACP, 544M CB 1867. Written on a letter of May 4 from Maj. Gen. George G. Meade, Philadelphia, to Secretary of War Edwin M. Stanton. "In conformity with the authority granted in the Act approved March 2nd 1867, authorizing 'The President to confer on officers of the Army of the United States brevet rank on account of gallant, meritorious or faithful conduct in the Volunteer Service prior to appointment in said Army of the United States,' I have the honor to make the following recommendations: . . ."—LS, *ibid.* On May 24, John A. Andrew, Boston, wrote to USG. "I learn that Genl Meade has recommended for the brevets of Maj., Lt. Col., & Col. in the regular army, my friend & relative, Simon F. Barstow, now Capt. by commn, in the Quarter Master Genls Dept. of the regular army, formerly a Major, A. A. G. of Vols, & Bt. Brig. Genl of Vols.—This recommendation, coming as it does from a source so distinguished, & in the proper & regular method brought to yr notice, may almost render it impertinent in me to allude to the subject, lest I might seem to doubt its influence. But, my own long & intimate knowledge of Genl Barstow, my information as to his specific services & abilities as a staff officer, & his long & ample experience during the rebellion, & always in the most active service, prompt me, (rather as a matter of duty & fidelity than otherwise), not to omit adding my own assurance that his friends in Massachusetts & in civil life, will appreciate his just recognition, with grateful remembrance. I trust, Genl, that if you fulfil yr expectation of an Eastern trip this summer—and I hope you will do so—that I may have an opportunity of meeting you in Boston."—ALS, *ibid.*, RG 108, Letters Received.

1867, MAY 15. To President Andrew Johnson. "I most cordially unite in recommending James Warden for Executive Clemency"—DS (also signed by Bvt. Brig. Gen. Frederick T. Dent and Mayor Richard Wallach of Washington, D. C.), DNA, RG 204, Records of Pardon Attorney, Case B-350. Docketing indicates that the pardon was granted on July 8.—*Ibid.*

1867, MAY 15. Maj. George K. Leet to Bvt. Maj. Gen. Montgomery C. Meigs, Bvt. Maj. Gen. Joseph K. Barnes, surgeon gen., Bvt. Maj. Gen. Alexander B. Dyer, chief of ordnance, and Brig. Gen. Andrew A. Humphreys, chief of engineers. "General Grant directs me to notify you that the Board of Officers convened by Special Orders, No 235, War Dept. A. G. O., May 7th 1867, will be recommendnvened tomorrow morning, Thursday, 16th inst, at ten oclock in pursuance of orders from the Sec of War."—Copies, DLC-USG, V, 47, 60; DNA, RG 108, Letters Sent. On May 7, Bvt. Maj. Gen. Edward D. Townsend had issued Special Orders No. 235. "A Board will assemble in the City of Washington at 11 o'clock A. m. May 9th 1867, to consider the subject of headstones, or blocks, by which, under section 1, Act '*To establish and to protect national cemeteries,*' approved February 22, 1867, the graves in national cemeteries are to be marked. The Board will report upon the following points: 1st: The best, most durable, and most economical material. 2d—The most appropriate form of headstone, or block. 3d. The estimated cost of each stone; and the aggregate cost of the number required for all the national cemeteries. *Detail for the Board.* General U. S. Grant, Bvt. Major General M. C. Meigs, QrMrGenl, Bvt. Major General J. K. Barnes, Surgeon Genl, Bvt. Major General A. B. Dyer, Chief of Ordnance, Bvt. Major General A. A. Humphreys Chf. of Engrs."—ADfS (unnumbered), *ibid.,* RG 94, Letters Received, 278A 1867.

On June 10, Bvt. Maj. Gen. Lorenzo Thomas, Washington, D. C., wrote at length to Secretary of War Edwin M. Stanton reporting his inspection of nineteen national cemeteries in Va.—LS, *ibid.,* 736A 1867. On May 23, USG had endorsed papers concerning the national cemetery at Winchester, Va. "Respectfully refered to the Sec. of War with recommendation that the Qr. Mr. Gn. be directed to investigate as to the correctness of charges here made."—AES, *ibid.,* 428A 1867. On July 13, Thomas, Galveston, Tex., wrote to Stanton concerning the case. ". . . The investigation to my judgement shows that the charges against Lieut Col. Moore A. Q. M. and Superintendant R. R. Brown are entirely without foundation; that they were preferred in a spirit of malice and revenge especially by William W. Allen, in consequence of his having been discharged as an employee at the National Cemetary at Winchester."—LS, *ibid.* On Sept. 27, Thomas, Corinth, Miss., telegraphed to USG, secretary of war *ad interim.* "My inspection of the Cemeteries at this place and Shiloh Pittsburg Landing Tenn cannot be completed before three (3) and two (2) months Respectfully I request that Bvt Lt Col A. W. Mills A Q M who has them in charge and doing so well may not be mustered out of service until December thirty first (31st)"—Telegram received, *ibid.,* ACP, T445 CB 1867; (2) *ibid.,* RG 107, Telegrams Collected (Bound). On Oct. 8, Thomas, Louisville, wrote to USG. "I have completed the inspection of the Cemeteries in the State of Tennessee, and also those at this place and Camp Nelson Kentucky. I am perfectly satisfied with those at Chattanooga, Knoxville, Nashville and Stone River and Shiloh, also at Corinth Mississippi. As previously reported the position of the Cemetery at Memphis is not a good one, and to give a proper drainage involves a heavy expense. The site at Fort Donaldson is not the best that could have been selected in that immediate locality and when the Officer placed in charge, Lieut. Rosencrantz, 34th Infantry, commenced, the work, he first destroyed a very handsome field work constructed of Stone and earth, on the crest of the eminece, and then cut the crest some six or seven feet and carted the earth to a ravine, only to be washed into the Cumberland River. The beauty of the place was thus destroyed, and at a heavy expense. This Officer has been relieved, but he should be made to account for his extravagant useless expenditure of the public money. After a full consultation with Major General Geo. H. Thomas Commanding the Department of the Cumberland, we have arrived at the conclusion, that but two Cemeteries should be established in Kentucky, One at Cav Hill Cemetery near this City, where a large number of Union Soldiers have been interred, and where ample ground can be obtained, for additional interments, and the other at Camp Nelson. The bodies at the other little Cemeteries to be removed to these, and to Nashville. The expense of maintaing the two will be far less than the cost of removal and keeping up a number. The bodies at Cumberland Gap should be taken to Knoxville, and this can be done at the present time at little cost, as the Government transportation and employees at Chattanooga can be used for that purpose. I shall request General Thomas to carry out these views, If not approved by you, countermanding Orders can be received by him before the work of removal commences, I leave to day for Mound City Illinois where I learn there is a Cemetery, and shall then Inspect the one at Indianapolis Indiana and then return to Washington to make my report of the inspections thus far made, and to receive your further instructions."—Copy, DLC-U.S. Civil War National Cemeteries. On Nov. 2, Thomas, Charleston, telegraphed to USG. "In my report of the Cemeteries in North Carolina I may have done Col Stubbs injustice and I request that no action be taken on it in reference to him as Gen Tyler will make a full investigation of the case. I will be satisfied with his decision, I think that the administration of affairs at Salisbury was beyond the control of the officer here"—Telegram received (on Nov. 3, 10:00 A.M.), DNA, RG 94, Letters Received, A116 1867; *ibid.*, RG 107, Telegrams Collected (Bound). On June 1, 1868, Thomas wrote at length to Secretary of War John M. Schofield. "I respectfully submit the following report of my inspections of the National Cemeteries under the instructions, dated Adjutant General's Office May 6th and June 14th, 1867— . . ."—LS, *ibid.*, RG 94, Letters Received, 736A 1867.

1867, May 16. USG endorsement. "Respectfully returned to the Secretary of War, with recommendation that these papers be referred to Lt. Gen. W. T Sherman, Command'g Military Division of the Missouri, with authority to issue the arms and ammunition, if upon investigation he deems it advisable."—ES, DNA, RG 107, Letters Received from Bureaus. Written on a letter of May 8 from Act. Secretary of the Interior William T. Otto to Secretary of War Edwin M. Stanton forwarding two letters requesting that arms be supplied to Pueblo Indians in New Mexico Territory to defend themselves against hostile Indians and Mexicans.—LS and copies, *ibid.*

1867, MAY 17. USG endorsement. "Approved."—ES, DNA, RG 94, ACP, S77 CB 1868. Written on a letter of April 26 from Bvt. Brig. Gen. Orlando Brown, Richmond, to Secretary of War Edwin M. Stanton recommending Capt. Joshua W. Sharp, 22nd Veteran, for bvt. promotion.— LS, *ibid.* On Dec. 18, Bvt. Lt. Col. Wright Rives, military secretary for President Andrew Johnson, wrote to USG. "I am directed by the President to request that you will please to forward to this office the application and accompaning papers of Capt. J. W. Sharp Veteran Reserve Corps (old organization) for a commission in the Regular Army."—ALS, *ibid.* On the same day, USG endorsed this letter. "The application referred to within is herewith respectfully forwarded to the President   There are at present no vacancies in the V. R. Corps regiments   The last vacancy was filled July 2d"—ES, *ibid.* Johnson also endorsed this letter. "Let the appointment be made—"—AES (undated), *ibid.* Sharp, however, was mustered out as of Jan. 1, 1868. See *PUSG*, 2, 140, 142; *ibid.*, 6, 187–88.

1867, MAY 17. USG endorsement. "Forwarded to Com Officer Ft. Sedgwick for remarks as to the necessity for having Trader at his post"—Copy, DNA, RG 108, Register of Letters Received. Written on a letter of May 11 from Wallace Macrae, Fort Gratiot, Mich., received at USG's hd. qrs. requesting an appointment as trader.—*Ibid.* On May 9, Macrae, Cincinnati, had written a similar letter received at USG's hd. qrs., and on June 10 Maj. George K. Leet endorsed this letter. "Respy. referred to the A G. who will issue an order directing Wallace Macrae to open a Trading Establishment at Camp Douglass, U. T., under the resolution of Congress, entitled— 'A Resolution to authorize the Commanding General of the Army to permit Traders to remain at certain Military Posts. Mr. Macraes address (P. O) is Detroit, Michigan, care Mrs Eunice Tripler."—Copy, *ibid.* On May 28, USG had written to Mrs. Tripler concerning "the subject of . . . continuing old Sutlers as traders . . ."—*ABPC*, 1974, 1031.

1867, MAY 18. Postmaster Gen. Alexander W. Randall to USG. "The Indian troubles on the plains are very mischievous to our mail service, and the obstructions are very serious. The inclosed dispatches indicate the general character of our troubles. Unless there can be found some way of relief, I fear a total suspension of the mails over the routes mentioned in these dispatches. I hope the government may be able soon to relieve the mail service of such unfortunate obstructions."—*HED*, 41-2-240, p. 56. The enclosures are *ibid.*, p. 57. On May 30, USG endorsed to Lt. Gen. William T. Sherman a letter of the same day from Wells Fargo and Co. concerning the disruption of overland mail routes.—Copy, DNA, RG 108, Register of Letters Received. On July 3, Sherman wrote a letter received at USG's hd. qrs. "General Augar has charge of that particular part of the Overland Route, and is now there on the spot to give it his personal attention, It is fair question if it would not be more economical for the Military to under take to do the Mail Service, and avoid the necessity of turning over the command of our army to any driver and agent along the road, who knows more about Military affairs than we pretend to do."—DLC-USG, V, 43. On July 18, USG endorsed this letter to Secretary of War Edwin M. Stanton.—Copy, *ibid.*

1867, MAY 18.   Secretary of War Edwin M. Stanton to USG. "Recent occurrences in some of the Military Districts indicate a necessity of great vigilance, on the part of Military Commanders, to be prepared for the prevention and prompt suppression of riots and breaches of the public peace, especially in towns and cities, and that they should have their forces in hand and so posted, on all occasions where disturbances may be apprehended, as to promptly check, and, if possible, to prevent outbreaks and violence endangering public or individual safety. You will please, therefore, call the attention of the Commanders of Military Districts to this subject and issue such precautionary orders, as may be found necessary, for the purpose indicated."—LS, DNA, RG 108, Letters Received; copies (misdated May 20), *ibid.*, RG 107, Letters Received; *ibid.*, Letters Sent to Bureaus. On May 22, Maj. George K. Leet issued a circular to the five military district commanders, incorporating Stanton's letter to USG. ". . . The above conveys all the instructions deemed necessary, and District Commanders will act in accordance therewith, making special reports of the precautionary orders issued by them to prevent a recurrence of mobs or other unlawful violence."—DS (addressed to Maj. Gen. Philip H. Sheridan), *ibid.*, RG 393, 5th Military District, Letters Received; copies (2), *ibid.*, RG 46, Senate 40A–F5, War Dept. Messages; *ibid.*, RG 108, Letters Sent; DLC-USG, V, 47, 60.

A riot broke out in Mobile during a speech by U.S. Representative William D. Kelley of Pa. who had been touring the South to encourage the organization of the Republican Party. See Sarah Woolfolk Wiggins, "The 'Pig Iron' Kelley Riot in Mobile, May 14, 1867," *The Alabama Review*, XXIII, 1 (Jan., 1970), 45–55; William D. Kelley, *Speeches, Addresses and Letters on Industrial and Financial Questions* (Philadelphia, 1872), pp. 171–73. On May 22, Bvt. Maj. Gen. John Pope, Atlanta, telegraphed to USG. "Official reports of the late riot at Mobile received and transmitted to you today by mail I have deposed the mayor and Chief of Police and replaced them by efficient union men. The whole city government will be remodelled in a day or two. The military force exercise, & will continue to do so, general supervision over the municipial government The Principal instigator of the riot is in confinement at Fort Gaines & will be tried by military commission. Active exertions are being made to apprehend other riotous parties. Full details by mail"—Telegram received (at 11:40 A.M.), DNA, RG 107, Telegrams Collected (Bound); *ibid.*, RG 108, Telegrams

Received; copies, *ibid.*, RG 46, Senate 40A–F5, War Dept. Messages; *ibid.*, RG 94, Letters Received, 977M 1867; DLC-USG, V, 55. On the same day, USG forwarded a copy of this telegram to Stanton.—ES, DNA, RG 94, Letters Received, 977M 1867. On May 23, Pope wrote to USG. "I have the honor to transmit enclosed the Report of Generals' Swayne and Dunn concerning the late riot in Mobile, Ala, as also the report of Colonel Shepherd, 15th Infantry, Commanding the Post. You will not fail to notice some (though not important) discrepancies in these two reports. One thing is manifest, and that is that the Mayor Jones M. Withers though everybody (and no doubt himself included) apprehended disturbance during Judge Kelley's speech, instead of being present with the necessary police force and arrangements to keep the peace, went off to his house a mile and a half distant, because probably he supposed the sentiments of the Speaker would not be pleasant to him, and left the peace of the City in the hands of a Chief of Police, who either sympathized with the rioters or was wholly inefficient. It certainly is not to be attributed to the zeal or conduct of either of these functionaries that the riot did not assume formidable proportions. I have therefore removed both; not only because of their criminal misconduct on this occasion but because there is not likely to be confidence of any security whatever hereafter whilst they retain their Offices I have appointed Mr Horton, a much respected Union man of Mobile, Mayor, and Colonel Dimon formerly of the Army but for the last year a citizen of Mobile, Chief of Police. I will remodel the entire Police Force and probably change the Board of Alderman in a few days. Colonel Dimon I know well personally as he served for a long time under my command, and whilst he is Chief of Police, I will guarantee that there will not be another riot in Mobile. The instigator of the late riot or rather the most conspicuous actor in it, is in confinement at Fort Gaines, and will be tried by Military Commission. The Civil Authorities released him on bail. Active measures are being taken to arrest the other parties concerned. Until the new City Government is fully installed and in successful operation the military authorities will control the police of the City."—LS, *ibid.* The enclosures are *ibid.* On May 26, USG forwarded these papers to Stanton.—AES, *ibid.* On May 29, President Andrew Johnson endorsed these papers. "The reports of Genl. Pope, Genl Swayne, and Col Shepherd have been read with care, and are returned to the secretary of War, for comment."—ES, *ibid.* On May 30, Pope wrote to USG. "I have the honor to enclose herewith copy of General Orders No 25 c. s from these Head Quarters which I think will render riots or riotous proceedings in this District so dangerous to the Civil Officials whose friends are generally the instigators of riots at political meetings that there is good ground for belief that there will be no more disturbances such as occurred at Mobile.—I have provided in this Order mainly for public political meetings as they are generally if not entirely the occasions used to get up riots.—This Order although prepared before the receipt of your Circular of May 22nd will I think cover the purpose of that Circular.—"— LS, *ibid.*, RG 108, Letters Received. The enclosure is *ibid.* On June 1, Pope wrote to USG. "I notice in the papers that the summary given of the reports of Colonel Shepherd and General Swayne, of the Riot at Mobile and in my letter transmitting them, indicates that there is an absolute difference of opinion between General Swayne and myself in relation to the apprehensions entertained of a riot upon that and similar occasions. This difference of opinion is more in seeming than in reality and arises entirely from the fact that neither in General Swayne's report nor my letter, were sufficient details given. The enclosed report from General Dunn will make clear wherein lies the misunderstanding. There was no apprehension at the moment of any disturbance at the meeting, because the Mayor had assured the parties that he would take efficient measures to prevent disturbance;— On this assurance the meeting was held without apprehension. The fact that such apprehensions were generally entertained is not only found in this application to the Mayor for protection, but in the general uneasiness in Mobile for a long time previous. Adherents of both political parties have again and again addressed me on the subject of apprehended disturbances, and whilst on the one hand, I have been applied to on several occasions both by letter and by committees to remove the Mayor and Chief of Police in Mobile, on the other hand I have been requested or advised to prevent public meetings of Freedmen. Both of these applications were made on the ground of apprehended disturbance or danger, and I look upon the late riot as a mere outcropping of the feeling and animosities which have long been prevalent in the City. From what I can learn I doubt if the removal of the Mayor and Chief of Police has been most satisfactory to the Union men, or the respectable rebels in Mobile. If you think it advisable to publish this letter and the appended report of General Dunn please do so."—LS, *ibid.*, RG 94, Letters Received, 977M 1867. The enclosure is *ibid.* On June 6, USG endorsed these papers. "Respectfully forwarded to the Secretary of War, for his information and with recommendation that these communications, with the exception of the last paragraph of Gen. Pope's letter be given to the press for publication."—ES, *ibid.*; copy (attributed to Leet), *ibid.*, RG 108, Register of Letters Received. On June 5, Pope wrote to USG. "The City Government of Mobile is now remodeled as far as is essential to the smooth working of the new authorities. The appointees were very carefully selected by General Swayne after a full conference with responsible citizens of Mobile, and it is believed that they give very general satisfaction. I feel satisfied that the change of authority in Mobile was essential to the peace of the city in the future, and to the best interests otherwise of the people. It had been plain ever since I arrived here, that the City Government of Mobile was inefficient, and unsatisfactory to the citizens. The disturbance which was the immediate occasion of the removal of the municipal authorities was only the natural result of long continued bad management.—Something of the kind had been expected for some time. I think it safe to say that the peace and quiet of the city for the three months during which registration is progressing, and during which the excitement of political discussion will be at its height, will be far more secure in the hands of the present municipal authorities, than in those of their predecessors in office. As soon as Registration is completed, the usual elections will be held for these and other civil offices temporarily filled by appointment. I trust on all accounts that these changes in Mobile, will not be interfered with. Aside from the want of confidence in the deposed officials, the very fact of the interposition of the President in the affairs of so unsettled a place as Mobile, and the re-instatement of these deposed officials would create so much excitement and alarm, that I should feel bound at once to declare Martial Law in that City, and entirely set aside the civil authorities. I think, you know General, that I desire to act judiciously and carefully in these matters, and not to interfere with existing civil authorities at all if I can help it, and certainly no farther than the peace and security of the people absolutely demand. What I have done in Mobile, I consider absolutely necessary for the protection of life and property in that city, and I trust that the Authorities in Washington, acting at such a distance from the scene, and of course much less able to understand the necessities of the case, will be very careful in taking any action which will set aside so deliberate and well-considered an act, as the removal of the municipal officers in Mobile. The fact, that I have made no removals elsewhere, and have interfered not at all with the civil administration in any other place, ought to be good evidence that I am not disposed to act hastily, and that when I interpose, I do so reluctantly and only because I think it cannot be avoided, in view of the security of property and person, to citizens, for whose safety I am held responsible by the Law."—LS, *ibid.*, RG 94, Letters Received, 864M 1867. The enclosure is *ibid.* On June 8, USG forwarded these papers to Stanton.—ES, *ibid.* On the same day, Pope telegraphed to USG. "I learn that influences are on foot to procure the removal of Gen Swayne, He is a most admirable Officer thoroughly posted about affairs in Alabama and I beg that you will not think of his removal   I have written you important letters which I hope you will be in Washington to receive by this time"—Telegram received (at 5:00 P.M.), *ibid.*, RG 107, Telegrams Collected (Bound); *ibid.*, RG 108, Telegrams Received; copy, DLC-USG, V, 55. On June 10, 9:30 A.M., USG telegraphed to Pope. "I have heard of no move or desire to relieve Gen. Swayne from command in Ala."—ALS (telegram sent), DNA, RG 107, Telegrams Collected (Bound); telegram sent, *ibid.*; copies, *ibid.*, RG 108, Telegrams Sent; DLC-USG, V, 56. On June 17, Pope telegraphed to USG. "It is untrue that negroes have been appointed in the Municipal Gov't of Mobile. The city Government is complete and of the best men in the city. The following is an extract from a letter of Gen'l Swayne—'Governor Parsons leaves for Washington tonight and informs me that he will probably take with him the spontaneous expression of the best public men in this state against the restoration of any of the persons removed' "—Telegram received (at 2:30 P.M.), DNA, RG 107, Telegrams Collected (Bound); *ibid.*, RG 108, Telegrams Received; copies, *ibid.*, RG 46, Senate 40A–F5, War Dept. Messages; DLC-USG, V, 55; DLC-Andrew Johnson.

On May 23, Bvt. Maj. Gen. John M. Schofield, Richmond, wrote to USG. "I have the honor to acknowledge the receipt of your communication of the 22nd instant, embodying instructions from the War Department, dated the 18th instant, in relation to the prevention and suppression of riots and breaches of the peace, and calling for special reports of the precautionary measures taken to guard against the recurrence of mobs or other unlawful violence. I have to report that I have had no cause to apprehend any disturbance of the peace, in this Military District, except in this City; and that troops were so stationed that the disturbances was easily and promptly suppressed. To prevent a recurrence of mobs, I have directed one of the Companies on duty at Libby Prison, to be posted on the north side of the city, and have caused the city to be patroled, night and day, by a portion of the Cavalry Company stationed in the vicinity. Before the arrival of that Company, I had used the Artillery Company, as Cavalry, for the Same purpose. In the other principal towns and cities, in this District, troops are posted at convenient points, prepared to suppress any disturbance that may arise."—LS, DNA, RG 108, Letters Received.

On June 18, Maj. Gen. Daniel E. Sickles, Charleston, wrote to USG's adjt. "I have the honor to report in compliance with Orders Headquarters of the Army, 22d May 1867, that no riots or tumultuous disturbances of the peace have occurred in this Military District. The precautionary measures adopted are substantially as follows: . . ."—LS, *ibid.*

1867, MAY 20.   Col. Benjamin H. Grierson, 10th Cav., Jacksonville, Ill., to USG. "My father dead   Please telegraph Capt. John C. Grierson Moline Thirty 30 days leave"—Telegram received (at 4:30 P.M.), DNA, RG 107, Telegrams Collected (Bound); *ibid.*, RG 108, Telegrams Received; copies, *ibid.*, RG 94, Letters Received, 250G 1867; *ibid.*, 304G 1867; DLC-USG, V, 55.

1867, MAY 21, 1:00 P.M.   To Bvt. Maj. Gen. Alfred H. Terry. "You may retain Capt. Graves 34th Infty. until your return from inspection of Dept. Dakota, if you desire"—Telegrams sent (2), DNA, RG 107, Telegrams Collected (Bound); copies, *ibid.*, RG 94, Letters Received, 246G 1867; *ibid.*, RG 108, Telegrams Sent; DLC-USG, V, 56. On May 22, Terry telegraphed to USG. "Your telegram received. I much desire to retain Capt Graves and am very grateful for permission to do so"—Telegram received (marked as sent from St. Louis, received at 3:00 P.M.), DNA, RG 107, Telegrams Collected (Bound); copy (sent by mail from St. Paul, Minn.), *ibid.*, RG 108, Letters Received.

1867, MAY 21.   Maj. George K. Leet endorsement. "Respectfully returned to the AdjutantGen'l, application of Major General Sheridan appr'd."—ES, DNA, RG 94, Letters Received, 242G 1867. Written on a letter of May 11 from Maj. Gen. Philip H. Sheridan to USG. "I have a vacancy on my staff of the position of Aide-de-Camp, which I kept open for my brother, Captain

M. V. Sheridan, of the 7th Cavalry. When he was appointed to that regiment he preferred joining it and I let him go, very much to my inconvenience. He now wants to come back, having seen the 'elephant' in Colorado last winter to his heart's content. If the interests of the service will permit, I would be greatly obliged to you if you can let him join me."—LS, *ibid.*

1867, MAY 22, 9:45 A.M. To Phelan and Callender, New York City. "Billiard table has arrived."—ALS (telegram sent), DNA, RG 107, Telegrams Collected (Bound).

1867, MAY 23. USG endorsement. "Respectfully forwarded to the Secretary of War—not approved."—ES, DNA, RG 94, ACP, J26 CB 1868. Written on a letter of May 3 from John Jackson to the AG requesting revocation of the order accepting his resignation from the U.S. Army.— *Ibid.* On Oct. 18, Jackson wrote to USG, secretary of war *ad interim.* "I have the honor to state that in 1864—I filed several recommedations for an appointment as Quartermaster U. S. Army, but never heard from said application—In June 1866, I resigned my commission as Captain 7th U. S. Inf. and Brevet Major U. S. Army—Through misfortunes I lost everything I posessed and returned here to Washington—In May 1867. I made an application for Re-appointment in the Army, and filed several recommendations, but have never heard from the same—I now respectfully request that I may receive an answer, and if unfavorable, that all of my papers may be returned to me—as they are very valuable to me—"—LS, *ibid.* On March 7, 1873, two U.S. senators and two U.S. representatives signed a letter to USG, favorably endorsed by Vice President Henry Wilson, requesting Jackson's reappointment.—LS and AES, *ibid.* No action followed.

1867, MAY 23. USG endorsement. "Respectfully forwarded to the Sec. of War. In my opinion brevet rank falls with the real rank on which it is based, except in the case of promotion, and I am therefore of the opinion that Lt. Col. Fry's brevet rank is only that of Col. In view of Col. F's valuable services during the War, I would recommend him for the brevets of Brig and Maj. Genl. to date Mc'h. 13, '65."—Copies, DLC-USG, V, 43; DNA, RG 94, ACP, 2910 1871. Written on a letter of March 26 from Lt. Col. James B. Fry, San Francisco, concerning the Senate's failure to confirm his appointment as bvt. brig. gen.—DLC-USG, V, 43. On June 24, 1869, Horace Porter wrote to Secretary of War John A. Rawlins. "The President directs me to inform you that he wishes to withdraw the endorsement made by him when General of the Army upon a letter written by Gen'l James B. Fry to Genl. J. C. Kelton May 17th 1867. The date of the endorsement is May 23d 1867. The above letter is believed to be in the hands of the Attorney General to whom the question of Genl Fry's brevet rank has been referred."—LS, DNA, RG 94, ACP, 2910 1871.

1867, MAY 23. To Bvt. Maj. Gen. Edward D. Townsend. "If a detachment of recruits are going to the Pacific Coast about the 1st of June order Gn. Jeff. C. Davis to take charge of them."—ALS, DNA, RG 94, Letters Received, 319A 1867.

1867, MAY 23, 9:45 P.M. To Maj. Gen. George H. Thomas, Louisville. "Come to Washington as soon as you can after receipt of this. Answer"—ALS (telegram sent), DNA, RG 107, Telegrams Collected (Bound); telegram sent, *ibid.*; copies, *ibid.*, RG 108, Telegrams Sent; *ibid.*, RG 393, Dept. of the Cumberland, Telegrams Received; DLC-USG, V, 56.

1867, MAY 28. To Secretary of War Edwin M. Stanton. "I have the honor to recommend Lt. Col. C. B. Rassander, late of R. I. Vol. Artillery, for the appointment of Lieut. of Cavalry. Col. Rassander is not elegible for an original vacancy in the Cavalry, not having served in that arm of the service during the rebellion, but he can be appointed at the foot of the list of Lieutenants. My object in recommending him for the Cavalry branch of the service is because he is represented as an excellent instructor in 'Brod Sword Exercises,' a branch of instruction which but few of the Cavalry officers now in service are capable of giving."—ALS, DNA, RG 94, ACP, R567 CB 1867. Charles A. Rossander was appointed 2nd lt., 6th Cav., as of June 5 and died on Sept. 17.

1867, MAY 30. USG endorsement. "Respectfully refered to the Sec. of War. I have no recommendation to make on either of the within applications, or recommendations."—AES, DNA, RG 94, ACP, L297 CB 1867. Written on two letters of the same day from U.S. Representative William Lawrence of Ohio to USG. "I filed an applicatn for appointmt of Geo S Hardenbrook as 2d Lieut in Reg Army You retund it not recommded I assure you he is worthy & well qualified & if you can order the appointmt I would feel grateful . . . Advise me at House Reps" "I have filed application for brevet of Brig. Gen for Regular Army under Act of March 1867 for Ben P Runkle a brevet Major Genl of Vols. He is now at Louisville in Freedm Bureau—I hope you can concur in the desired brevet for gallantry at Shiloh."—ALS, *ibid.* On Aug. 19 and Oct. 19, Lawrence wrote to USG, secretary of war *ad interim*, recommending Maj. Benjamin P. Runkle, 45th Inf., for bvt. promotion.—ALS, *ibid.*, 4408 1872. On Sept. 7, Governor Ambrose E. Burnside of R. I. wrote to USG recommending Runkle for bvt. promotion.—ALS, *ibid.* On July 26, Maj. Gen. George H. Thomas, Louisville, wrote to the AG recommending Runkle for bvt. promotion.—LS, *ibid.* On Oct. 12, USG endorsed this letter. "Approved for brevet of Lieut. Col. for battle of Shiloh, and brevet of Colonel, for gallant and meritorious services during war—to date 2d Mch. 1867."—ES, *ibid.* On Jan. 8, 1873, Lawrence, Bellefontaine, Ohio, wrote to USG. "I am just informed that Major Ben—P—Runkle has been fined & dismissed by sentence of Court Martial approved by Judge Holt—When I was in Washington as you will remember three weeks ago I called your attention to this & asked for Runkle such favorable consideration as you could properly give—I beg again to invoke for him all the clemency you can give   He was a brave soldier—desabled by wounds for life—He is my friend   His father is one of our good & best citizens in this County—I earnestly invoke for Major Runkle your kindliest consideration and clemency"—ALS, *ibid.* On Nov. 30, 1875, Runkle submitted a lengthy petition to USG requesting reappointment to the U.S. Army.—(Printed) *ibid.* Additional letters addressed to USG on the subject are *ibid.* See Ross A. Webb, " 'The Past Is Never Dead, It's Not Even Past': Benjamin P. Runkle and the Freedmen's Bureau in Kentucky, 1866–1870," *Register of the Kentucky Historical Society,* 84, 4 (Autumn, 1986), 343–60.

1867, MAY 31.   USG endorsement. "Military Commanders serving in the west will give Prof Hayden such facilities as they can without manifest injury to the service, to aid him in carrying out the object of his Explorations. Dept Commanders may give the necessary orders for carrying out this design, in accordance with the within application"—Copy, DNA, RG 57, Hayden Material, Letters Received from the War Dept. Written on a letter of May 27 from Ferdinand V. Hayden, Philadelphia, received at USG's hd. qrs., requesting War Dept. support for scientific explorations of the territories.—*Ibid.*, RG 108, Register of Letters Received. On July 5, 1866, USG had favorably endorsed a letter of the same day from Joseph Henry, Smithsonian Institution, received at USG's hd. qrs., making a similar request for Hayden.—Copy, *ibid.* On July 17, 1868, Hayden, Washington, D. C., wrote to USG. "For two years past I have been Exploring the geology of various parts of the public domain west of the Mississippi, with very limited appropriations. With the kind Endorsements you have placed on my letters of application for facilities from Military Officers at the different posts I have been able to succeed Even beyond my Expectations. The present Congress has granted me only $5.000 to continue these Explorations. I venture again to ask your sanction to such facilities as the Military Commanders of the west can afford me without manifest injury to the public service. In addition to aid from the Quartermasters Department I desire to purchase such subsistence stores from the Commissary Department as I may need for my party at Officer's prices,   My party will not Exceed six persons and probably not more than three or four. I would say here that for two years past I have received from different Military Officers every facility desired without which I could not have succeeded, and I know they are now ready to extend all needed facilities to me if the responsibility can be removed from them. Hitherto I have been so fortunate as to be able to return every article of property which I have been permitted to use in good order. Earnestly hoping you may be able to grant my request . . ."— ALS, *ibid.*, RG 57, Hayden Material, Letters Received from the War Dept. On July 27, Bvt. Maj. Gen. John A. Rawlins endorsed this letter, repeating USG's endorsement of May 31, 1867.—ES, *ibid.*

1867, MAY 31. Arthur S. Colyar, Nashville, to USG. "Allow me, though a stranger, to Call your attention to the enclosed printed slip Cut from the Nashville Banner. All our Complaints so far, have been drowned in the Cry of 'rebel' We were once rebels—we are not now, but the Cry of our present persecutors—generally men who were on both sides during the war—but fought on neither—is so loud and Constant that we Cannot be heard. Offering an Apology for addressing you . . ."—ALS, DNA, RG 108, Letters Received. The enclosure is *ibid.*

1867, JUNE 3. USG endorsement. "Acceptance of resignation is recommended."—ES, DNA, RG 94, ACP, D632 CB 1865. Written on a letter of May 19 from 2nd Lt. Benjamin K. Davidson, 30th Inf., to the AG tendering his resignation.—ALS, *ibid.* On Aug. 12, Bvt. Col. William Winthrop, act. judge advocate gen., wrote to USG, secretary of war *ad interim.* "2d Lieut. B. K. Davidson, 30th Infy, was tried June 1st 1867, by General Court Martial convened at Fort Sedgewick, C. T. under the following charge: Violation of the 45th article of War. In that accused, while on duty as Officer of the Day at Fort Sedgewick, was in such a state of intoxication as to be unable to perform his duties. This May 10. 1867. The Court find him guilty of the charge; and sentence him to be cashiered. The sentence was pronounced on the 6th of June. . . . It is for the Executive to determine whether the case is of such a character as to call for the revocation of the order accepting his resignation and the enforcement of the sentence."—Copy, *ibid.*, RG 153, Letters Sent.

1867, JUNE 4. U.S. Senator Reverdy Johnson of Md., Baltimore, to USG. "private . . . I am glad to see by the papers, that you will be willing to accept a nomination for the presidency, at the next Election. I write thus early to say, that you will have all the support I may be able to give—The Country is now in a condition which must cause with all reflecting men, great solicitude—I know no one, who would be more likely than yourself, who as President, to rescue it from whatever may be its present or future danger—Nor do I know any one, who could more certainly receive the support of the people—Why I so think, in addressing you, delicacy restrains me from saying—"—ALS, USG 3.

1867, JUNE 5. Act. Postmaster Gen. St. John B. L. Skinner to USG. "I have the honor to enclose herewith as required by the P. M. at Memphis, Tenn. copies of letters received from him in reference to the unfortunate condition of. Mr O. H. Ross who is represented as a person in whom you may probably have some interest"—Copy, DNA, RG 28, Letters Sent by the Postmaster Gen.

1867, JUNE 7. To Secretary of War Edwin M. Stanton. "I have the honor to recommend the appointment as Captain of Cavalry of 2d Lieutenant Charles G. Cox, 7th U S. Cavalry."—LS, DNA, RG 94, ACP, C732

CB 1867. 2nd Lt. Charles G. Cox, 7th Cav., was appointed capt., 10th Cav., as of June 12. President Andrew Johnson endorsed a paper of Dec. 23, datelined "Executive Mansion," recommending Cox for appointment as bvt. col. "Let the Brevet be granted if there is no good reason why it shall not be done"—AES (undated), *ibid.* On Dec. 27, USG endorsed this paper. "Capt. Cox's highest volunteer rank was that of Major, and it is unjust to others to brevet him Colonel. Approved for brevet of Major for Cold Harbor."—ES, *ibid.* Cox received a bvt. as maj. as of June 12.

1867, June 7. To Lt. Gen. William T. Sherman. "J. W. Wright formerly of Ohio, who has been much among the Indians, West of Ark. proposes to interest himself in inducing the Indians on the plains to keep the peace. He will write to you today his plans. You make use of his services so far as you think proper."—Copies, DLC-USG, V, 47, 60; DNA, RG 108, Letters Sent.

1867, June 7, 12:30 p.m. To Maj. Gen. George H. Thomas. "Release from confinement and restore to duty, (awaiting final action here) Selwin T. Nye, Co. "H" 25th U. S. Inf.y."—ALS (telegram sent), DNA, RG 107, Telegrams Collected (Bound); telegram sent, *ibid.*; copies, *ibid.*, RG 108, Telegrams Sent; (misdated June 6) *ibid.*, RG 393, Dept. of the Tenn., Telegrams Received; DLC-USG, V, 56. On June 1, H. R. Nye, Springfield, Ill., had written a letter received at USG's hd. qrs. requesting reinstatement of his son Selwin T. Nye in the U.S. Army.—DNA, RG 108, Register of Letters Received. On June 6 or 7, USG endorsed this letter. "Respy. referred to the Sec of War—with recommendation that this letter be referred to Gen Thomas with the instructions to examine into the case of the prisoner Nye and with authority to discharge him if the circumstances warrant that leniency."—Copies (dated June 6), *ibid.*; (dated June 7) *ibid.*, RG 393, Military Installations: Union City, Tenn., Register of Letters Received. Nye had allowed a prisoner to escape, then himself deserted, and was convicted by court-martial.—*Ibid.*, RG 108, Letters Received.

1867, June 8. Maj. George K. Leet endorsement. "Respectfully returned to Major Gen'l O. O. Howard, Com'r Bureau R. F. and A. L. So many officers are required for duty under the reconstruction laws in the Southern States that none are available for duty in the Freedmen's Bureau at present."—ES, DNA, RG 105, Letters Received. Written on a letter of June 3 from Maj. Gen. Oliver O. Howard to USG. "I have the honor to apply for the detail of twenty officers, ten for Mississippi, five for Arkansas, and five for Alabama. These officers are solicited by the Assistant Commissioners of those states respectively, in addition to their present force, for duty in the Bureau of Refugees, Freedmen and Abandoned Lands. General Ord presses me very much for the detail for Mississippi and Arkansas. The means of this Bureau are not adequate to the payment of so many civil agents in addition to those already employed. It is also difficult to procure the services of citizens suitable for the duties required. If the whole number asked for cannot be supplied I would be glad to have as many as can possibly be spared."—LS, *ibid.*

1867, June 11. Maj. Gen. Philip H. Sheridan, New Orleans, to USG. "Forts Jackson and St Phillip on the Mississippi River, about 70 miles below New Orleans are now garrisoned each by a company of the 39th Infantry. The quarters for these troops are of the worst character consisting of old frame sheds put up during the Rebellion by the rebels. I think I could make comfortable quarters for the present garrison by tearing down these old buildings and making use of the lumber in the erection of a new set of quarters and would do so at once but I am not fully advised of the claims of the Engineer Department in reference to these sheds. I consider them of no value as they stand and respectfully refer you to Generals Babcock and Porter for a full explanation. Perhaps by refering this communication to the Engineer Department, if the sheds can be claimed as its property some arrangements can be made to enable me to make the men more comfortable than they now are"—Copy, DLC-Philip H. Sheridan.

1867, June 14, Friday. To Secretary of War Edwin M. Stanton from Baltimore. "Is it necessary that I should be in Washington before next tuesday morning? If so I can go there tonight but would prefer going north"—Telegram received (at 6:30 P.M.), DNA, RG 107, Telegrams Collected (Bound). At 8:30 P.M., Stanton telegraphed to USG. "Your presence before Tuesday morning not needed"—ALS (telegram sent), *ibid.* On June 10, the *New York Times* reported that USG, accompanied by Julia Dent Grant, and Bvt. Brig. Gen. and Mrs. Frederick T. Dent, planned to go to Washington, Pa., on Tuesday to attend a wedding, and that USG then planned to go to USMA. On June 11, Bvt. Brig. Gen. Thomas G. Pitcher, superintendent, USMA, had telegraphed to USG. "We want to deliver Diplomas to first (1st) class Monday next Can you be with us? Can be ready Friday or Saturday if will suit you better—Please answer and name day."—Telegram received (at 9:00 A.M.), DNA, RG 108, Telegrams Received; copy, DLC-USG, V, 55. On June 13, Pitcher telegraphed to USG. "Yours received Can you stay over Monday Please answer"—Telegram received (at 12:40 P.M. at Wheeling), DNA, RG 108, Telegrams Received; copy, DLC-USG, V, 55. USG presented diplomas at USMA on June 17, remarking to the top cadet: "I am very glad to know that you are a smart boy, and at the head of your class. Pay attention to your studies, and there is no goal you may not hope to reach in this country."—*New York Times*, June 18, 1867.

1867, June 14. Bvt. Maj. Gen. John Pope, Atlanta, to USG. "I have the honor to enclose herewith extracts from letters of Col. J. T. Sprague, Comd'g in Florida, in relation to Indian affairs in that State.—He has made requisitions for horses to mount Infantry but I have disapproved them. If you think the facts warrant it I would suggest that a Cavalry company be ordered to report to him in Jacksonville   I have waited to see if I could not learn something more on the subject but communication with Florida is so slow and uncertain that I have not been able to ascertain more than is stated by Colonel Sprague"—LS, DNA, RG 108, Letters Received. The enclosures discuss problems concerning the Miccosukkee.

1867, JUNE [16].   U.S. Senator John M. Thayer of Neb. to USG and Secretary of the Interior Orville H. Browning. "If Gen. Buford has reported what the telegraph attributed to him in regard to Indian matters, he is guilty of reckless misrepresentation or criminal stupidity. A barbarous and unparalleled warfare is now being carried on upon the plains by savage Indians upon small parties of defenceless settlers, and upon the railroad surveying parties and laborers. The government must not be deluded by any such reports as Buford's."—*Chicago Times*, June 18, 1867; (dated June 16) DNA, RG 108, Register of Letters Received.

1867, JUNE 18, 3:00 P.M.   To George G. Pride, Fifth Avenue Hotel, New York City. "Yes."—Telegrams sent (2—one misdated July 18), DNA, RG 107, Telegrams Collected (Bound).

1867, JUNE 18.   Governor Ambrose E. Burnside of R. I., Providence, to USG. "I write to recommend to your favorable notice for the appointment of Trader at the newpost in Colorado Ter. 'New Fort Lyon' by name— Colonel William C. Rawolle, formerly of General Sturgis staff and one of the most gallant and dashing officers of the 9th Corps—A better appointment for the position in my opinion could not be made and I heartily endorse the application"—ALS, DNA, RG 108, Letters Received.

1867, JUNE 19.   USG endorsement. "Respectfully forwarded to the Secretary of War. I concur in the recommendation of the Chief of Ordnance." —AES, DNA, RG 94, Letters Received, 572M 1867. Written on a letter of May 10 from John E. Reeside, Leavenworth, to Maj. Gen. Winfield S. Hancock. "We beg to advise that a contract was entered into on the 4th day of April 1867. between Brevet Col. Alexander Bliss A. Q M U. S and John E Reeside, in which the said Reeside had agreed to transport 20.000.000 pounds in Military Stores and supplies, on Route No 2. For the better security in the fulfillment of this contract and the protection of the public property, we solicit the Government to supply the Contractor with sufficient arms and ammunition to arm the persons accompanying the trains on said Route No 2.—The Contractor agreeing to return said arms when the necessity for their use in that service shall cease, or a demand for them by the Gov't shall be made: Say 300 Spencer Carbines 300 Army Size 6 Shooters"—ALS, *ibid.* On June 6, Bvt. Maj. Gen. Alexander B. Dyer, chief of ordnance, favorably endorsed Reeside's request.—AES, *ibid.* On Nov. 9, Bvt. Maj. Gen. Daniel H. Rucker, act. q. m. gen., wrote to USG.

"I have the honor to transmit herewith application of Mr. J. E. Reeside for payment of accounts for transportation service performed by him under Contract with the Government on Route No 2. . . ."—LS, *ibid.*, RG 92, Reports to the Secretary of War (Press). On Nov. 23, Judge Advocate Gen. Joseph Holt wrote to USG recommending that the q. m. gen. prepare an estimate of the amount due Reeside.—Copy, *ibid.*, RG 153, Letters Sent. On Jan. 8, 1868, Rucker wrote to USG concerning this matter.—Copy, *ibid.*, RG 92, Reports to the Secretary of War (Press). On Feb. 1, 1870, Congress authorized payment of Reeside's claim.—*CG*, 41-2, 947, 960.

1867, JUNE 20.   Charles A. Cook, Denver, to USG. "I have the honor to apply for the position of Trader at the Military Post about to be established near Pueblo, in this Territory, under the provision of the resolution of Congress approved March 30th 1867. I also have the honor to refer you to Bvt. Maj. Gen. Rufus Ingalls, and Bvt. Brig. Gen. O. E. Babcock U. S. A. for a more intimate Knowledge of my capacity and character.—"—ALS, DNA, RG 108, Letters Received.

1867, JUNE 24.   To Dr. Alexander Sharp, Richmond. "Send Fred home this evening."—ALS (telegram sent), DNA, RG 107, Telegrams Collected (Bound).

1867, JUNE 25.   Col. Adam Badeau to Bvt. Maj. Gen. George W. Cullum. "General Grant directs me to forward you the following memoranda, in reply to your communication of June 1st enclosing for correction his Etat de Service. General Grant was not Adjutant Gen'l of the State of Illinois, but *assisted* 'in organizing' &c; instead of 'July 15th' this date should read 'June 17th'   He was in command at Ironton from Aug. 7 to Aug. 17 and at Jefferson City from Aug. 17 to Aug. 29th also of District of S. E Missouri from Sept 1 1861 to Feby 17, 1862   General Grant had nothing to do with the seizure of Smithland; that place was seized by Gen. C. F. Smith (not then under General Grant's command), by order of Gen. Fremont. At Fort Donelson the number of captives was 14,623, not 13,500. In the advance upon and siege of Corinth, General Grant was *second in command* of Gen. Halleck's army, as well as in immediate command of the Right Wing and Reserve. After the battle of Iuka, Gen'l. Grant planned and directed all the preliminary operations of the battle of Corinth, Oct. 3d & 4th 3d and 4th 1862, and of the battle of the Hatchie, Oct. 5th 1862. After the battle of Raymond, May 12 1863 should be inserted 'Battle and Capture of Jackson, May 14 1862.' At capture of Vicksburg, Gen. Grant received the surrender of 31,500 prisoners—*not* 37,000. About five or six thousand had previously been captured during the campaign. The statement of 'operations against the relieving forces' should read 'resulting in the *reoccupation* of Jackson' &c not 'capture.' Tour of inspection in 1863 was from Cairo to Natchez, *not* 'Memphis to New Orleans,' the latter place not then being in Gen. Grant's command; dates of tour are from Aug. 23d to Sept. 2d   Battle of Missionary Ridge should read: 'Battle of Chattanooga'—Missionary Ridge being only one part of the battle-field. 'In command as General-in-Chief' &c should read 'In command of the Armies of the United States, planning and directing all their movements and operations since March 17th 1864, and directing in person the armies operating against Richmond from May 4, 1864—Battle of the Wilderness' &c   Operations about Petersburg terminated April 3d—*not* April 8th   'General U S Army July 25 1866' should be inserted. The above changes are regarded by General Grant indispensable to render his Etat de Service, as furnished by you, correct."—LS, USMA; ADfS, USG 3. On June 1, Cullum, New York City, sent a printed form letter received by USG. "Herewith is enclosed your Etat-de-Service as prepared for the new edition of my Register of Graduates of the United States Military Academy. . . ."—Copy, *ibid.* On Jan. 14, 1866, Bvt. Brig. Gen. Cyrus B. Comstock had written to Cullum. "Gen Grant requests me to enclose the following datesa for use in the Register, in reply to your letter of the 12th inst. U. S. Grant, farmer, Missouri 1854–1859   Real Estate Agent St. Louis 1859–1860   Merchant ~~St Louis Mo~~. Galena Ill. 1860–1861   Col 21st Ill. Vols. 15 June 1861   Brg Gen Vols July 31/61 to date 17 May 1861   Maj Gen Vols 16 Feb 1862   Maj Gen U. S. A 4 July 1863   Lt-Gen USA 9 2 March 1864"—ALS (in tabular form), USMA. Comstock also enclosed a more complete sketch. "*Lt. Gen. Grant*   Farmer in Mo 1854–1859   Real Estate Ag.'t St Louis 1859–60   Merchant Galena Ill. 1860–61   Com'd Company organized at Galena in april/61 till it was assigned to 12th Ill. Vols.   Assisted Gov. of Ill. in organizing troops till July 15/61   Then appointed Col. 21 Ill. Vols. & commanded it till Aug 7/61 in Ill. & Mo.   July 31 appt'd B. G. Vols. to date May 17. and in command at Ironton Mo.   Aug 24 ordered to Cape Girardeau to command district of S. E. Missouri. In September command extended to embrace Southern Ill. & western Ky. Seized Paducah Sept 6. Fought battle of Belmont Nov 7   In command of expedition against Ft. Henry Feb 2 1862. Ft Henry captured Feb 6. Moved command toward Ft Donelson, Feb 12 and captured it Feb 16. Appt'd Maj. Gen. Vols Feb 16 1862. Commanded US forces at battle of Pittsburg Landing Apr 6 & 7. Commanded District West Tenn. and right wing and reserve of army under Gen Halleck in advance on Corinth & at its capture May 30/62   Commanded at battle of Iuka Sept 19/62. Assigned to command of Dept of Tenn. Oct 6. Commanded Army of Tenn. in the move to Oxford Miss & its subsequent movement via Memphis down the Miss. to Youngs Point opposite Vicksburg. April 30 crossed Miss. at Bruinsburg fighting battle of Port Gibson May 1, Raymond May 12, Jackson May 14, Champion Hill May 16, Big Black May 17 & investing Vicksburg May 18. Received surrender of Vicksburg July 4/63   Apptd Maj. Gen USA July 4/63   Ass'd to command of Mil. Div. of the Miss. Oct 16, fought battle of Chattanooga Nov 24 & 25. Apptd Lt. Gen. & assigned to command of armies U. S. March 9 1864 In command of armies U. S. till the close of the rebellion, & present in command at battles of Wilderness May 5 & 6 Spottsylvania May 12 Coal Harbor June 3 Petersburg June 16 Petersburg June 18 New Market Heights Sept 29, Petersburg April 2/65 Surrender of Lee at Appomattox C. H. Apr 9 1865."—AD (in tabular form), *ibid.*

1867, JUNE 28, 10:30 A.M. To Maj. Gen. Daniel E. Sickles. "Where is Gen. Burton now? and whatere will be his station?"—ALS (telegram sent), DNA, RG 107, Telegrams Collected (Bound); telegram sent, *ibid.*; telegram received, *ibid.*, Telegrams Collected (Unbound); (at 11:55 A.M.) *ibid.*, RG 393, Dept. of the South, Telegrams Received. At 1:25 P.M., Sickles, Charleston, telegraphed to USG. "Telegram received. I respectfully report that General Burton is stationed at Columbia, S. C. commanding that post. ~~which is one of the most important within my command~~ —see paragraph II. of my S. O. No 69. of ~~June~~ 12. inst."—LS (telegram sent), *ibid.*, RG 107, Telegrams Collected (Unbound); telegrams received (2—one at 3:10 P.M.), *ibid.*, Telegrams Collected (Bound).

1867, JUNE 28. Maj. George K. Leet endorsement. "Respectfully referred to Major General W. S. Hancock, Comdg Dept. Missouri, for remark."—ES, DNA, RG 94, Correspondence, USMA. Written on a letter of June 14 from William Heimke (alias of Charles V. de la Mare), 3rd Inf., Fort Dodge, Kan., to USG. "Pardon the liberty I thus assume in writing to you: being an entire stranger; but ambition has prompted me to seek your aid, and to humbly and respectfully ask you, to use your influence to have me appointed to the Military Acadamy at West Point. I hold the humble position of Fifer in the Army; am poor, but honorable, and ambitious, and have a great desire to become an Officer of the Army; I have no one on earth to give me a helping hand; having lost my father and four brothers in defence of their country during the late rebellion; and I think that if I had a start in life, I might be of great value and interest to the Goverment of the United States. I have served three years in the 17th U. S. Infantry during the late rebellion, and participated in some of the most prominent battles before Richmond:—two years of which enlistment I served as Musician, and the last year as Acting Regimental Quartermaster Sergeant. In my second enlistment I have served eighteen months and for upwards of fourteen months have been on detached service, in 'charge of the Bureau of U. S. Military Telegraph, Headquarters Department of the Missouri,' and four months as Chief Clerk at same Headquarters. I have been relieved from duty there, because my services were required with my Company. I am well versed in Military papers of every description and understand them in every branch   I have permission from Major General Hancock, Brig: General Pope. Bv't Brig: General Chauncey McKeever; Major J. P. Sherburne Ass't Adj'ts General U. S. A. Bvt Maj Gen'l Wm Hoffman, Col 3rd Inf'y, my Company Com'd'r and many others, to refer to them as to my character. I have excellent recommendations from the Officers above enumerated. I have seventeen months more to serve, which I will willingly serve, and forfeit to the United States all money's that are now, or may become due, for the same period, if I could but enter the Acadamy, or receive an appointment at the expiration of my term of enlistment. Please, General, consider my case well, before laying this aside. If I am not successful in this undertaking, I have but one thing left: which will be: to again re-enlist and study—study hard and work my way up;—but it will be hard indeed, as I am only, 18 years of age and have no one on whom to lean and depend. I will thank you, General, from the depth of my heart, if you will kindly aid me; and please pardon me if I use an hackneyed phrase, save the simple—'I thank you!' Please answer and give this your immediate action if favorable: though it *does* come from only a Musician, and that I may know what course to pursue."—ALS, *ibid.* On June 27, Col. Adam Badeau wrote to Heimke. "General Grant directs me to inform you that he has recommended you to the President for appointment to the Military Academy at West Point. There are several vacancies now existing, for the present year, and you have been recommended to fill one of these, and if this is not approved, to an appointment for next year."—ALS, *ibid.* No appointment followed. On July 20, 1869, Heimke wrote to Badeau, London, requesting return of the papers relating to his appointment to USMA. —ALS, *ibid.*, RG 107, Letters Received from Bureaus. On Aug. 31, an endorsement was prepared for Secretary of War John A. Rawlins. "Respectfully returned to the President—It does not appear that the application herein referred to was ever received at this Department."—Df, *ibid.* On July 23, 1876, Bvt. Maj. Gen. John Pope, Fort Leavenworth, forwarded to USG papers recommending Heimke for appointment as 2nd lt. in the U.S. Army.—AES, *ibid.*, RG 94, Applications for Positions in War Dept. No action followed.

1867, JUNE 29. To Secretary of the Treasury Hugh McCulloch. "The bearer of this, Mrs. Booth, is the widow of the Officer who commanded at Fort Pillow, Ten. at the time of the massacre in Apl. 1864. She is now desirous of getting a position in the Treasury which will support her and which I hope you can give without displacing any worthy person."—ALS, DLC-Miscellaneous Manuscripts. See Roy P. Basler, "And for His Widow and His Orphan," *Quarterly Journal of the Library of Congress*, 27, 4 (Oct., 1970), 291–94.

1867, JUNE 29, 9:50 A.M. To commanding officer, Fort Wallace, Kan., care of Bvt. Maj. Gen. Christopher C. Augur. "Has body of Geo. W. Brownell, killed by Indians June 15th, been recovered? Have it buried where friends can recover it and report action."—ALS (telegram sent), DNA, RG 107, Telegrams Collected (Bound); telegram sent, *ibid.*; telegram received, *ibid.*, RG 393, Dept. of the Platte, Telegrams Received; *ibid.*, Dept. of the South, Telegrams Received. On June 28, Mrs. George W. Brownell, Galena, had telegraphed to USG. "Will you telegraph Comdg Officer at Fort Wallace Nebraska or Colorado and ascertain if body

of Geo W Brownell Killed in fight near Big Timber June fifteenth was recovered identified & where buried. Cannot learn from here—Answer"—
Telegram received (at 7:00 P.M.), *ibid.*, RG 107, Telegrams Collected
(Bound). On June 29, 9:50 A.M., USG telegraphed to Mrs. Brownell.
"Your dispatch received and directions given to bury Mr. Brownell where
friends can give such directions as they like hereafter about his body. I
deeply sympathize with you in your berievement."—ALS (telegram sent),
ibid.; telegram sent, *ibid.*; copies, *ibid.*, RG 108, Telegrams Sent; DLC-
USG, V, 56. On July 1, Bvt. Brig. Gen. Chauncey McKeever, adjt. for
Maj. Gen. Winfield S. Hancock, Fort Leavenworth, telegraphed to USG.
"General A. J. Smith telegraphs me from Fort Harker that it is reported a
detachment was sent out from Fort Wallace on the sixteenth (16th) to remove the body of George W. Brownell, killed by Indians. I will give full
particulars when received."—Copy (sent by mail), DNA, RG 108, Letters
Received. On July 26, Hancock, Fort Leavenworth, wrote to USG. "Referring to a despatch from you of June 29th, to the Commanding Officer at
Fort Wallace, Kansas, transmitted through these Headquarters, concerning the body of Mr. George W. Brownell, who was killed by Indians near
'Big Timbers' mail station on the Smoky Hill, June 16th, 1867, I have the
honor to furnish the following information: During my recent march to
Denver City, C. T., I left Fort Wallace on the 18th of June, and upon
reaching a point the same day within three and one half (3½) miles of Big
Timbers mail station, discovered the bodies of two men lying in the road,
who had been killed during an attack made by Indians at that point on the
16th of June upon two stages coaches on their way to Denver City. One of
the bodies was that of a soldier who was on duty with the escort to the
coaches—the other was reported to me by the Agent of the Overland Mail
Company, to be that of Mr. G. W. Brownell, a citizen of Galena, Ills., who
was en route to Denver City, when he was killed. The body of Mr. Brownell had been stripped of all clothing, was scalped, and otherwise mutilated. They had lain so long exposed to the sun that it was impossible at
that time to remove the bodies to the station at Big Timbers for burial, as I
wished to have done. I therefore directed them to be interred at once in the
same grave, on a small mound near where they were lying—the mound in
question being on the South side of the road and but a few yards from it.
The remains of Mr Brownell were laid on the South side of the grave—
those of the soldier on the North side. I was careful to have them buried at
a conspicuous point, so that the locality of the grave could not be mistaken
in case his relatives should desire to remove the remains of Mr. Brownell.
Instructions were given the Commanding Officer at Fort Wallace to remove
the remains of the soldier (with those of Mr. Brownell also, in case they
were not recovered by his friends in the meantime), for burial at Fort Wallace, as soon as it became practicable to do so. On my return from Denver
City. (July 3d), I discovered that the Indians had violated the graves,—
had severed the heads from their bodies and thrown them aside on the
prairies, where they had been so torn by the wolves, that it was impossible

to distinguish to which they each belonged. I directed the bones of the heads to be placed in the grave, and directed it to be filled up as before. Since the latter mutilation by the Indians, I do not conceive that the remains of Mr Brownell could, with any certainty, be distinguished from those of the soldier with whom he was buried, and I am of the opinion that it would be injudicious to attempt to remove them from the spot where they now lie."—Copy, *ibid.*, RG 393, Military Div. of the Mo., Letters Sent.

1867, JUNE 29. Maj. George K. Leet to Maj. Gen. Daniel E. Sickles. "By direction of Gen. Grant I enclose herewith an extract from a private letter to General Dyer, Chief of Ordnance, who is personally acquainted with the writer, & the person referred to therein and before the war he knew them to be good & reliable citizens. The General requests that a speedy trial be granted Mr. McRea if there is no good reason against it."— ALS, DNA, RG 393, 2nd Military District, Letters Received. On June 25, T. D. Haight, Fayetteville, N. C., had written to "My Dear Sir," presumably Bvt. Maj. Gen. Alexander B. Dyer, chief of ordnance. ". . . The case is as follows:—Arch Beebe (colored boy) made a desperate attempt to commit a rape on a white girl of respectable parents: this occurred on Sunday (in February or January I think). On Monday the boy was brought before D. G. McRae & J W Lett for examination. In deference to the young lady the doors were closed & no outsiders were permitted to enter the room. When the girl came out and some one told her to show the marks on her throat the crowd outside was very much excited. The boy was fully committed and given into the custody of Robt. Hardie, Sheriff, who had a posse of Town guards & constables with him. Our Jail had been burned & the boy had to be sent from the market to the Gaurd House (just below A. W. Steel's Store). As soon as the boy reached the bottom of the stairs a rush was made at him by a crowd and they were repulsed and driven before the officers until they reached the south-east corner of the market—there the boy became very much alarmed & attempted to get away & while he was making this attempt he was shot in the head by one of the crowd & fell while Hardie still had him by the arm—& died in five minutes. It is charged upon D. G. McRae upon the affidavit of a woman named Elliott—a vile strumpet of the lowest order, that she saw Maj. McRae come out on the Balcony of the market & leaning over call out to some one in the crowd to 'shoot the damn scoundrel,' & this is the only evidence. We have proved that Maj. McRae knew nothing of the excitement below—never left his seat at the table until some one came running up & said the boy was killed & that when he heard it he said it was 'an outrage and would bring trouble—' This we prove by Lett the associate Justice. French Strang Prosecuting att'y, H H Howe Att'y for boy & Dennis McIvor uncle of the boy: There is not a man in the town that believes Maj. McRae guilty in thought even. He has filled his office acceptably to black and white since the war. All we ask now (since all trials to effect his release have failed) is a speedy trial."—Copy (incomplete), *ibid.*

1867, JUNE 30. Edmund N. Lewis, Fort Sanders, Dakota Territory, to USG. "I have the honor to request to be appointed Post Trader at the new Post to be built on Crow Creek   I have respectfully to state that I was in the service from the first call for troops in 1861 until the end of February last."—LS, DNA, RG 108, Letters Received. On July 16, U.S. Representative Rutherford B. Hayes of Ohio wrote to USG. "The bearer of this, Dr J. H. Finfrock is introduced to me in such a way that I feel authorised to say that he is a perfectly trustworthy gentleman, and I hope he will be able to secure the place for Edmund H. Lewis of the regular army for which he calls on you."—ALS, *ibid.*

1867, JULY 2. Charles F. Tracy, Junction City, Kan., to USG. "Some time since I forwarded through the proper channels an application for Sutlership at Fort Larned. I have heard since that there will be no changes at the posts where sutlers now are. My application does not contemplate a change. The facts are that the present acting Sutlers at this post are not *the Sutlers in fact* but merely the agents (for a consideration) of one S D R Stewart, whose time expires July 1/ & who disposed of his right to the post to the present sutlers & has never been *at the Post at all*. I respectfully ask then your favorable consideration to my application, falling as it does outside of the decision arrived at by the Secty of War & yourself on this Subject. The application has been favorably endorsed by the Commander of Post of Fort Larned & also Genls Smith & Hancock & is now at Genl Sherman's Hd Quarters awaiting his official sanction. With my Kind regards to Mrs Grant & my young friend Fred & to Brig Genl F. T Dent & family . . . My Post Office address is St Louis."—ALS, DNA, RG 108, Letters Received.

1867, JULY 5. USG endorsement. "Respectfully forwarded to the Secy of War, for his information."—ES, DNA, RG 94, Letters Received, 915M 1867. Written on a telegram of July 4 from Maj. Gen. Daniel E. Sickles, Charleston, to USG's adjt. "I have the honor to report that this day has been duly observed throughout the Carolinas   Salutes have been fired at Sunrise Meridian & sunset, business places closed and at Charleston the time honored chimes of St Michaels Church—so long the target of gilmore during the dark years of rebelion rang out the national airs, public buildings streets hotels & ships decorated with the American flag   The Colored people have been enmasse parading the streets displaying flags in profusion. Bunting in great demand   Reports received from principal points throughout the Carolinas of appropriate observance of this day   All quiet & orderly   Promenade concert Illumination & fireworks at the Citadel attended by the principal citizens tonight"—Telegram received (on July 5, 8:30 A.M.), *ibid.*; *ibid.*, RG 108, Telegrams Received; copy, DLC-USG, V, 55.

1867, JULY 6. To Bvt. Maj. Gen. Daniel H. Rucker, act. q. m. gen. "Understanding that a decision has been made against officers on duty at Camp Grant, near Richmond, Va., receiving the fifty cent commutation, allowed officers serving in the field, I take the liberty of saying that if such allowance is due to any officers serving in the unreconstructed States it is also due to the officers at that camp. The same construction that puts them in Public Quarters would put all other officers in Public Quarters. If they are more comfortable than many others it is because they have made themselves so and reflects credit upon them."—Copies, DLC-USG, V, 47, 60; DNA, RG 108, Letters Sent.

1867, JULY 6. U.S. Representative Kellian V. Whaley of West Va. *et al.*, Washington, D. C., to USG. "We take the liberty to most respectfully recommend M. Stewart, late Lieut. Col. 13th West Va. Inf Vols for the appointment to the position of Trader at the Post of Puebla, Colorado Ty. or if that Post be alrady filled, that he may be appointed to and assigned to such other post in that Territory as to you shall seem best. Col. Stewart has, we think, well merited, the appointment asked for him by his very gallant and meritorious services throughout the late war; and in addition to this we can say that he is a gentleman of undoubted integrity and possesses good business qualifications, and we are satisfied that, if appointed he will fulfill the duties of the position to the entire satisfaction of all concerned. The appointment would be an act of justice to him and a matter of personal gratification to us—"—LS, DNA, RG 108, Letters Received.

1867, JULY 7. USG endorsement. "This appointment is specially recommended. Gen. Rucker, the father of the applicant, has devoted his life to the service and during the late rebellion proved himself one of the most efficient as well as one of the most faithful officers of the Army."—AES, DNA, RG 94, Correspondence, USMA. On July 8, Bvt. Maj. Gen. Daniel H. Rucker, act. q. m. gen., wrote to Secretary of War Edwin M. Stanton requesting a USMA appointment for his son.—ALS, *ibid.* John A. Rucker left USMA in 1870 and was appointed 2nd lt., 6th Cav., as of July 27, 1872.

1867, JULY 7. USG endorsement. "Col. Townsends resignation is not approved. of. It appears to have been tendered immediately after enjoying a years leave of absence and before resuming his appropriate duties. I recommend that Col. Townsend be ordered immediately to his regiment."— AES, DNA, RG 94, ACP, T59 CB 1868. Written on a letter of June 28 from Lt. Col. Frederick Townsend, 9th Inf., Albany, N. Y., to the AG tendering his resignation.—LS, *ibid.* An endorsement of July 5 by USG approving the resignation is cancelled.—ES, *ibid.* On March 21, 1868, USG approved Townsend's resignation.—ES, *ibid.*

1867, JULY 8.   USG endorsement. "Respectfully returned to the Sec. of War. No official information of the flogging of a civilian at Ft. Sedgwick, by order of Col. Dodge, has been received at these Hd. qrs. On the 28th of June 1867, a newspaper slip containing an account of the affair was sent to Bv't. Maj. Genl. C. C. Augur Comd'g Dept. of the Platte, endorsed as follows: Respectfully referred to Bvt. Maj. Genl. C. C. Augur, Comd'g Dept. of the Platte for investigation. If the newspaper statement is found to be correct Genl. Augur will order the trial by G. Court Martial of the offender, otherwise the statement will be contradicted. Immediately upon its receipt the report of Genl. Augur will be transmitted to the Sec. of War."—Copy, DLC-USG, V, 43. Written on papers received at USG's hd. qrs. "Refers for report, House Resolution of July 3rd requesting information relative to the whipping of a citizen by order of Col. Dodge at Ft. Sedgwick for the alleged offence of furnishing a bottle of whiskey to two soldiers."—*Ibid.* See *HED,* 40-1-24. On Aug. 2, Bvt. Maj. Gen. Christopher C. Augur, Omaha, referred papers to USG's hd. qrs. indicating that a sgt., acting without authority, had flogged a civilian for selling liquor to soldiers in exchange for their weapons.—ES and copies (newspaper clippings), DNA, RG 94, Letters Received, 1150 1867. On Aug. 9, USG endorsed these papers. "Respectfully forwarded to the Secretary of War for his information."—ES, *ibid.*

1867, JULY 8.   Charles W. Denison, Paris, to USG. "Your friends on this side, in England as well as France, are all right."—ALS, USG 3.

1867, JULY 10.   Bvt. Maj. Gen. John A. Rawlins, Fort Sanders, Dakota Territory, to USG. "Capt Lewis Lowry has been nominated for Trader by Gibbon at his new post *Fort John F. Reynolds* beyond old Fort Halleck, and Augur requests his appointment, Papers have gone to Sherman I think he should be appointed"—Telegram received (on July 12, 8:08 P.M.), DNA, RG 107, Telegrams Collected (Bound); *ibid.,* RG 108, Telegrams Received; copy, DLC-USG, V, 55. On July 11, John Wanless, Fort Sanders, telegraphed to USG. "I respectfully protest against appointment of Lewis Lowry Trader at Fort Reynolds, The troops at this place go there and I respectfully claim position as matter of right and justice"—Telegram received (on July 12, 8:10 P.M.), DNA, RG 107, Telegrams Collected (Bound); *ibid.,* RG 108, Telegrams Received; copy, DLC-USG, V, 55. On May 24, Capt. and Bvt. Lt. Col. Henry R. Mizner, Fort Sanders, had written to USG. "I have the honor to introduce to your favorable consideration Col John Wanless, late Lieut Col 5th U S Vols, Sutler at this Post since 15th January 1867. During the year 1866 Geo Wilson Jr was Sutler here, but having rendered himself so obnoxious to the entire Command (by extortionate charges, disregard of orders and selling Three cent postages stamps for Five cents each), as to drive his trade from him, Col Wanless purchased his entire stock and building and has since given general satisfaction to Officers and men. Col Wanless keeps a large and well assorted stock, sells at fair prices and has been recommended by Council of Administration for position of Post Trader with reference to Joint Resolution of Congress March 30th 1867."—ALS, DNA, RG 94, Letters Received, 397W 1867. On June 10, Wanless wrote to USG requesting appointment as post trader.—ALS, *ibid.*

1867, July 11. To Bvt. Maj. Gen. Edward D. Townsend from West Point, N. Y. "Grant Gen Hazen authority to leave the United States during his leave of absence. Send notice to him to St James Hotel N. York."— Telegram received (at 12:30 P.M.), DNA, RG 94, Letters Received, 542H 1867; (press) *ibid.*, RG 107, Telegrams Collected (Bound).

1867, July 11. Bvt. Maj. Gen. John A. Rawlins, Crow Creek Crossing, Dakota Territory, to USG. "Train attacked near here last night. One man killed"—Telegram received (on July 13, 9:45 A.M.), DNA, RG 108, Telegrams Received; copy, DLC-USG, V, 55.

1867, July 12. Anthony M. Dignowity of San Antonio, Tex., Washington, D. C., to USG. "Inclosed I take the liberty to submit to you, duplicates of Papers; such as I forwarded to Gen: Sheridan one month back— and inclose his acknowledgement; except an explanatory letter similar to this, and a letter addressed to me last Feb: by the Hon: James Harlan, assuring me of his assistance, all in his Power, to bring back the Government of Texas from the Rebel, into Loyal hands &. &—The inclosed copy of an address, that was presented to President Johnson in May 1865—will give you a sinopsis of my struggle for more then Thirty years for freedom in Texas—The printed Address, will convey to you my idias as entertained by me on the subject of Reconstruction of the Rebel States—I must also add some explanation why I have thus far been unsucesful, in my effords in Regard to Texas. In spring of 1862. Gen: Casius M. Clay arived in this City from his Mission in Russia, he obtained a promise before leaving Russia, that he shall have comand of the Military Dept west of the Miss: River, &. east of the Mountains including Texas, Gen: Clay and myself came to an understanding, that he would addopt, and carry out my Plan in regard to Texas, and I was to be made Military Gov: of Texas, as he said he mainly depended on me to carry out said Plan—we found great obstacles unexpectedly in the Pro: Slavery, and Pedantic Antagonisim of Gen: Halleck—assisted by the Machinations of the Blairs, President Lincoln, vasciliating Nature was agains us—he wished to conciliate matters, so he proposed, and divided said comand, giving, or assigning Gen: Curtis Misury and Ark: with Kansas, and the Indian Teritory—and proposed to Gen: Clay to take the Comand of Texas, I was sent for and consulted by Gen: Clay—also Secretary Chase, a personal and Political Friend of the Gen: and it was agreed that the Gen: take said offer, who agreed that he will only with the proviso that I shall be made Military Gov: of Texas—as he considered me his right hand in this meditated great work   the following day Gen: Clay called on the President and stated his acceptance and his terms—President Lincoln said that he cannot make that concession, that Mr: F. P. Blair Jr: made applycation for said Governorship—and he told him that he shall have it—under this circumstances Gen: Clay declained the comand of Texas—and a coldniss between him and President Lincoln was the consequence—which lasted all sumer until durring the Fall election 1862 the Gen: made some telling speaches—and finding Halleck as antagonistic as ever—*and all Powerfull*—Gen: Clay applayed and obtained his former Mission, and returned to Russia—thus all my Plans in behalf of Texas miscarried in 1862. Now it was at this time that A. J. Hamilton arrived in this City—I called upon him immediately—and laid my Plan before him, and appealed to his patriotisim to unite with me and trow his influence in the Scale—and help me to do the work—but I was disapointed—Why! said Hamilton Doctor Your Plan of Reconstruction contemplate the controuling Power of the Military over the Civil—let me say to you—you have to destroy the constitution first—Why! the American People will not stand it one hour—I replayed that he was wrong—that the whole subject comes within the War Powers of Congress, all that is needed was proper legislation—Again said Hamilton Doctor you wish to confiscate the Public Lands of Texas—and distribute them to Soldiers for settlement—let me tell you the Public lands of Texas belong to the Loyal men of Texas—I replayd if his assession was true—and him and I, shall prove the only Loyal men in Texas—we will be the richest men in the World— now the fact was Hamilton wanted all the Power in his hand—*and he got it*—his Political Speaches—'which is all his forte' assisted him to get it—he was made Military Gov: as he took the wind of the Sails of all opoments F. P. Blair included—he held it four Years—and he left Texas in worst condition then he found it—in July 1865 when President Johnson—was about reapoint Hamilton—I went to the President with a protest—I found Hamilton there, and had more then one hours argument with him—I told him his and the Presidents Plan will be a failure—I told him that he cannot Reconstruct one single County—that he will meet the most Rabbit sessesh Element in Texas that could be found outside of H—ll—I told him that any Mechanic who would undertake to overcome Thousand lbs of Resistance— with 100 lbs of Force will pruve himself a fool—Hamilton is found of strong languidge and I treeted him with it—my predictions pruved all correct—Now I hope and trust he is plaid out—he is not a Political economist— he is patriotic and earnest howsoever—but was formerly connected with the Know-Nothing Party—it was a Part of his argument against my being apointed Military Gov: in 1862—that I was born on forighn soil—although I was on the soil of Texas 13 years before he put his foot on it—and at a time when Texas was still an integral part of Mexico—and all citizens of the U. S. were forighners there   Now my dear General, excuse my long letter, which is of neseasity personal subjects which may be of little interest to you, accupaying your high position—but it is mach to me—I see that the

New Bill, place it in your hand, and in the Hand of General Sheridan—to restore the Government of Texas into Loyal hands—*I know the Work that it to be done—and I know how to do it*—with my experience—my Knowledge of the Country and the People—I beleave firmly that the time has arrived, when I shall be able to do my country great and valuable service— excuse my long communication but the subject is of great and immence importance—and will affect generations still unborn—With great essteeme for you personally . . ."—ALS, DNA, RG 108, Letters Received. The enclosures are *ibid.* On Nov. 25, Dignowity wrote to USG. "Inclosed I take the liberty, to lay before you the letter of Resignation of the Attorney General of Texas—it will show that a serious difference has arised between Gov: E. M. Pease, and the Radical part of the Loyalist of Texas, that may result in serious difficulties, and grave obstructions to the Reconstruction of that State—in the later part of July, when it was apprehended, that a change in the Government of Texas, would be made, I was urged by Radical friends, to send papers to Gen: Sheridan, drawing his Attention to my effords for many Years, in urging a Plan on the government, which I am more and more convinced, is the true Plan for the Reconstruction of Texas; about the 10th of August I forwarded to your Address Copyes of said papers, with a leter of acknowlegement from headquarters of the fifth Dist. I would take the liberty again to draw your attention to said papers—in Sumer of 1862 when Genl A. J. Hamilton came to this city—I laid my Plan before him, and urged him to unite with me, and help me to carry out my Plan for the Reconstruction of Texas—His Reply was—Doctor before your Plan can be addopted—you must first abolish the U. S. Constitution, your Plan contemplates the Supremacy of the Military over the Civil Power —our People would not stand this one hour &. &. &. Gen: H. had to live five Year longer, to see this addopted by Congress—allthough he did opose the Military Bill with all his Powers of elequence—it was addopted—I wished and hoped that Congress would discover the great difference, between the existing conditions of Texas, and the other States of the late Rebelion—while large portions of the later was devastated—Texas was not affected—in fact by its proximity to Mexico—it was made rich by the Rebelion—and was reenforced from other locallities, with the most infernal, and blatant Rebel element, that can be found outside of Hell—Rebels in other localities will accept the situation—in Texas—it will again end in Bloodshead—and as my Plan is a measure easyly carried out durring the War—I hope and pray that our men in Power will see the Wisdom of its adoption—it is the greatest Plan of Political Economy of the day—Texas shuld be made a seperate Military Dept and the nescassary legislation should be made so as to carry my Plan into practice—a streem of Farmers and Artisans—Native and forighn—would be turned towards Texas— which will soon become the preponderating element—but my dear Sir— your comprehensive mind is well able to understand the practicability of my Plan—excuse my long letter, . . ."—ALS, *ibid.* The enclosure is *ibid.*

1867, JULY 13. USG endorsement. "I am opposed to all collections of funds by the Army where the method of doing so, and the system of accountability, are is not fixed by law. Such collections, without proper accountability corrupt too many officers for all the benefit derived. This order however is published under the authority of the reconstruction act which I think gives me no power over District Commanders so far as their civil duties are concerned."—AES, DNA, RG 94, Letters Received, 403A 1867. Written on a circular of June 28 issued by Capt. John W. Clous, 38th Inf., adjt. for Maj. Gen. Daniel E. Sickles, concerning the collection of fines by post commanders.—(Printed) *ibid.*

1867, JULY 17. To Bvt. Maj. Gen. Edward D. Townsend. "Direct Gn. Crawford to proceed to Louisville Ky. in arrest, to report himself to Gn. Thomas, in Arrest; also to report to the Adj. Gn. of the Army, by telegraph, his compliance with the order."—ALS, DNA, RG 94, Letters Received, 415A 1867. On July 13, Townsend had drawn up a charge against Lt. Col. and Bvt. Maj. Gen. Samuel W. Crawford, 2nd Inf., for being in Washington, D. C., despite orders to join his regt.—ADf, *ibid.* On June 27, Maj. George K. Leet had written to the AG. "The Adjutant General will issue an order directing Brevet Major General S. W. Crawford, Lieut. Colonel 2d Infantry, to join his regiment at once."—LS, *ibid.*, 380A 1867.

1867, JULY 17. Writer unknown, Red River, to USG. "Private—Please Read— . . . To write politics to you would be absurd—To dictate would be presumptuous—We of the South are gone, Status liberty, property, hopes &c all gone, our children and our children's children have nothing to hope for, In rebellion admitting we did sin, in sack cloth and ashes we have felt the result, There is no hope nor charity for us in the U. S. The last plank of civil liberty was wrenched from the old ship in the supplementary act passed a few days ago. The president is powerless—The power has been placed in your hands—If in your hands rested the entire power we would have nothing to fear—In your ability and magnanimity the South has every confidence, You do see and know the whirlpools ahead over which this country is bound to drift It is a problem far easier of solution than was the condition of Genl Lee's army on the James, Cannot you in this hour of Frenzy declare your power and put to flight the Seeming shadow of civil liberty and save this country, Happy would the South be to know you were the Dictator, Surfdom would be a contented situation under such rules as would treat all classes of surfs alike, . . ."—AL (torn), USG 3.

1867, JULY 18. E. G. Barney, Selma, Ala., to USG. "Please secure the confirmation of Chas. B. Andrews for Collector of Second 2nd Dist of Alabama—his nomination has been sent to the Senate—he is a reliable & influential man & deserving for his faithful adherence to the Union."— Telegram received (at 10:00 A.M.), DNA, RG 107, Telegrams Collected

(Bound); *ibid.*, RG 108, Telegrams Received; copy, DLC-USG, V, 55. An endorsement of the same day was drafted for USG's signature. "Respy. referred to Hon. Henry Wilson, U. S. S. I know Mr Barney to have been a Union Man, living in Mississippi, during the War, but I know nothing of Mr. Andrews"—Copy (unsigned), DNA, RG 108, Telegrams Received. Charles B. Andrews was confirmed as collector of internal revenue, 2nd district of Ala., on July 19.

1867, JULY 18. Thomas R. Jennings and W. Matt Brown, Nashville, to USG. "We have the honor herewith to transmit to you, through General Duncan, Commandant of this Military post, a a printed coppy of certain resolutions recently adopted by a verry numerous assemblage of our fellow citizens of this vicinage, in which you are verry distinctly, and, at the same time, most respectfully and gratefully referred to, in your official character, though for reasons sufficiently obvious it was deemed most delicate and propper, in drawing them up, to refrain from any formal mention of your name, Had these resolutions originated in a mere political or party meeting, or been in the least degree marked with a partisan or controversional spirit, we should have been verry far indeed from calling your special attention to them in the maner we now presume to do; feeling the fullest assurance, that in the exercise of the verry delicate and important powers entrusted to you as the Chief Military Commander of this District, you have no objects desires incompatibbe with the welfare and happiness of evry class of your fellow citizens who have been committed to your protecting care, and that you are annimated with an inflexible determination to maintain justice, support law and order, and suppress all movements calculated to generate needless strife, and rekindle the flames of civil contention and violence in our midst, That there a few excited and imprudent persons to be found in various parts of the State of Tennessee, who, in the abscence of the restraining influence which it is in your power to bring into action, might more or less put the public peace in danger, we are not at all disposed to deny; but, that a verry large majority of our citizens, of all classes and conditions, are at this moment intensely solicitious of contributing, as far as they may be able, to the mentainance of civil repose and to the avoidance of all discord and collisions, we do not entertain the smallest doubt, Some verry disagreable occurrences, togather which have taken place in this neighborhood a few days since, togather with the excitement naturally incident to the political election which now nearly approaching, have induced us, and those whom we represent on this occasion to feel excedeingly desirous that you should, so far as you may deem it wise and proper to do so, strengthen the military force of the Federal Government under your command in different parts of our State, for the purpose of guarding against mischief which it is to be seriously feared might otherwise ensue, We are excedeingly anxious to aid to the extent of our ability in the prevention of evils to which we cannot but believe that our community is to some extent now liable, and feel assured that you will pardon the liberty that we take of asking at your hands such present interposition in behalf of law-abiding and order-respecting citizens, as your own high sense of propriety shall prompt you to supply,   With sentiments of cordial respect and Kindness we have the honor to be your friends and fellow citizens"—LS, DNA, RG 108, Letters Received.

1867, July 19.   To Secretary of War Edwin M. Stanton. "I have the honor very respectfully to request the appointment of Lieutenant of cavalry for Oscar Elting. The applicant served during the entire rebellion in the volunteer cavalry service. An appointment sent to my office, for Mr. Elting, will reach him without delay."—Copies, DLC-USG, V, 47, 60; DNA, RG 108, Letters Sent. Oscar Elting was appointed 2nd lt., 3rd Cav., as of July 22.

1867, July 19.   USG endorsement. "Respectfully forwarded to the Secretary of War."—ES, DNA, RG 107, Letters Received from Bureaus. Written on papers concerning the repair of levees in La. endorsed on July 10 by Maj. Gen. Philip H. Sheridan. "Respectfully forwarded to the Headquarters of the Army with the endorsement: that in my opinion Congressional action is necessary to save a large portion of the inhabitants of Louisiana from ruin; but, inviting attention to accompanying letter from the undersigned"—ES, *ibid.* Sheridan enclosed his letter of July 2 to Judge R. C. Downes, Richmond, La. ". . . I will most cordially cooperate with the citizens of this State in obtaining this Congressional assistance; but, my influence would be of no avail until the State is admitted to representation. To push the matter now, when nearly every newspaper in the State, and a considerable portion of the people, are abusive of Congress, would be, I fear, without results, and I feel a delicacy in taking any steps at the present time: it is too much like abusing a man bitterly and at the same time asking him to loan you money. . . ."—LS, *ibid.*

On July 18, E. H. Angamar, special levee commissioner of La., Washington, D. C., wrote to USG. "In the name of the people of Louisiana, I beg leave respectfully to represent to you that unless the Levees that protect the alluvial Lands of Louisiana be repaired *this year*, there will not be any crops raised on those Lands in *1868*, which would subject the inhabitants of that section of Country (about 700,000 in number) to a great deal of suffering and perhaps to the danger of starvation, besides depriving the general wealth of the United ~~crops~~ States of crops, the value of which would be about One Hundred Million Dollars, and the Internal Revenue taxes on which would yield to the United States Treasury about Ten Million Dollars. The above said Levees could be repaired, if Louisiana was enabled to negotiate the sale of four Million Dollars of Levee Bonds authorized to be issued by the Legislature of said State: and that negotiation can be effected only if said Bonds are officially signed and negotiated by Governor Wells and the Board of Levee Commissioners appointed by him. I, therefore, in the name of a suffering people, beg of you, General, to reinstate in office Governor Wells and said Board of Levee Commissioners, for the purpose of legalizing the issue and negotiation of the aforesaid Bonds, which being accomplished, you might Keep in office or remove said officials, whenever you may think fit."—ALS, *ibid.*, RG 108, Letters Received. On July 19, U.S. Senator Reverdy Johnson of Md. endorsed this letter. "From the statement in the within letter, it seems to me that the request it contains, is a reasonable one—The interests depending upon this, or some measure, the restoring of the Levees in La are so great & vital to many American Citizens, that I hope some step may be taken, calculated to save them from destruction"—AES, *ibid.* Angamar made the same point at greater length in an undated letter addressed to USG.—LS, *ibid.*

On July 20, U.S. Senator John B. Henderson of Mo. wrote to USG. "I am informed that previous to the removal of Govr Wells by Genl Sheridan, some steps had been taken for the negotiation of the bonds of the state of Louisiana for the repair of the Levees of said state, but that the Capitalists who had agreed to take the bonds now refuse to do so, because of the want of Govr Wells signature, whom they regard as the proper person to sign them to give them legal validity. I make no inquiry into the controversy in regard to Levee Commissioners in Louisiana, nor the legality or illegality of such appointment coming from any source, nor have I inquired into the probability of sale of bonds under any circumstances, but I write this to express my convictions of the great importance of Levee improvement, in that state, during the coming autumn and winter, that a crop of sugar and cotton may be grown next summer. It is not only important to the people who will be thus saved from continued suffering and almost starvation, but it is very important to the interests of the national revenues. Now if anything can be done to secure the sale of these bonds and the progress of work on the levees this fall, by the use of the power given you by the late reconstruction amendatory ~~bill~~ act, I hope you will not hesitate to use them in a direction so beneficial to the people of that state and so obviously advantageous to the public weal"—ALS, *ibid.* Thirteen additional senators favorably endorsed this letter.—ES, *ibid.* Three copies of Henderson's letter with numerous signatures of La. residents are *ibid.* On the same day, U.S. Senator Timothy O. Howe of Wis. wrote to USG. "I do not quite like to add my signature to the letter of this date addressed to you by Hon J. B. Henderson & others for fear it might be construed into the Expression of a wish for the restoration of Gov Wells whose signature is said to be required by Capitalists to the bonds issued by Louisianna in aid of the Levees of the Mississippi—But I cordially join in the wish that in the Execution of the several reconstruction Acts you will afford every facility to the negotiation of those bonds & the restoration of those Levees, that you can afford consistently with a faithful Execution of the laws themselves"—ALS, *ibid.* See letter to Maj. Gen. Philip H. Sheridan, June 7, 1867.

1867, [JULY 19]. USG note. "Issue order permitting free trade at all Military posts West of 100° W. Longitude & eastern boundary of California subject only to such regulations & restrictions as may be imposed by Dept. Comdrs."—AN, DNA, RG 94, Letters Received, 414A 1867. On the same day, Bvt. Maj. Gen. Edward D. Townsend issued General Orders No. 68 promulgating these instructions.—ADfS, *ibid.* On May 23, Maj. George K. Leet had written to Bvt. Maj. Gen. Amos B. Eaton, commissary gen. "General Grant directs me to inform you that an order is prepared, and will be issued at once, retaining as Traders, after the 1st of July 1867, under the Resolution of Congress approved March 30 1867, the present Sutlers at Military Posts between the 100th meridian of west longitude and the eastern boundary of California."—ALS, *ibid.*, RG 192, Special Orders. See General Orders No. 58, May 24.—ADfS, *ibid.*, RG 94, Letters Received, 321A 1867.

1867, JULY 19. Maj. George K. Leet endorsement. "Respectfully referred to the Adjutant General, who will ~~either~~ order either the band at Ft. Monroe or the one at Richmond at the option of Gen. Schofield, to Atlanta. The band now stationed at Louisville will be ordered to Vicksburg"—ES, DNA, RG 94, Letters Received, 943M 1867. Written on a letter of July 16 from Bvt. Maj. Gen. John Pope, Atlanta, to USG. "As there are two Post Bands (indeed three) in the Department of the Cumberland—viz— one at Louisville, one at Nashville, and one at Newport, and none at all in this Department, I have the honor to request that Atlanta be designated as a post entitled to a Band, and that *one* of those now in the Department of the Cumberland be ordered here."—LS, *ibid.*

1867, JULY 19. Maj. George K. Leet endorsement. "Respectfully referred to Bt. Maj. Genl. E. Schriver, Insp'r General."—ES, DNA, RG 94, Correspondence, USMA. Written on a letter of July 14 from Sherman Armsby, Beloit, Wis., to USG. "I beg a thousand pardon for the liberty I take in writing to you, but if you felt so utterly miserable as I do, I dont think you could blame me at all. Last January I was 'found deficient' in Mathematics at West Point N. Y. & I am going to ask a great favor of you, not so much because I think I deserve it, but because I am so repentant of past sins. The only excuse I can give is that being in the army unfitted me for such close application as was required at W. P. I am naturally easy to learn, but the peculiar style of recitation at the Mil—Academy, I could not get used to in time to keep me from being 'found.' I think I *knew* my course well enough to pass examination, but I was so embarrased I could not do justice to my self. If you will speak a word for me and get me reappointed I solemnly promise on the honor of a *Gentleman* I will, if it is in the limits of possibility, not to do *any thing* you or I would be ashamed of, and do my duty in every respect. I was a soldier in the late war. I served as a private in the 11th Minnesota Vol. Ifty. for one year. I should have enlisted long before, but I was not old enough. I was 17 when I entered the army. My Father was Chaplain in the 8th Min—for three years. I entered West Point in June 1866 (in the same class with your son) through the influence of Hon Wm Windom. I have many friends among the cadets at W. P. & I trust your son is among the best of them. I know they are anxious to have me come back, and if you can consent to use your influence in my be half I assure you you will not regret it. I am not sure that I do right to ask this of you, but I am getting more & more anxious every day th to show the world I can graduate at W. P. At times it seems as if I wanted to kill my self for being so foolish   If you will be so kind as to use your influence in this matter, I will do my whole duty & bless you for it. Please write to me when you receive this, for I shall anxiously look for an answer. Hoping you are well . . ."—ALS, *ibid.*

1867, JULY 20.   USG endorsement. "Respy. forwarded to the Sec of War. In view of the evidence furnished by Dr. Hall of his uniform honesty and good conduct through life, and the partial evidence of his innocence of the charges on which he was dismissed, and the record, or the evidence on which the order summarily dismissing him was based, having been lost—I would respectfully recommend the revocation of Par. 29. Sp. Or. No. 58. Headqrs. 13th Army Corps, Tenn. Dept., and the acceptance of Dr. Hall's resignation as of same date of the order of dismissal, provided that the order accepting his resignation should not give him back pay and allowance"—Copy, DNA, RG 108, Register of Letters Received. Written on papers received at USG's hd. qrs. concerning Lyman Hall, dismissed as asst. surgeon, 63rd Ill., as of Dec. 31, 1862.—*Ibid.*

1867, JULY 20.   George C. Bates, Chicago, to USG. " 'I am not a Prophet, nor yet the son of a prophet,' yet I saw clearly that during that fearful war 'God alone sustained and upheld, us; and that a part of his special Providence was to select you finally: as he had done Washington in the Revolution; to lead us to victory and to save our Union—So I see clearly now that that same God, has and will preserve you to End this great Rebellion and to give us final and perfect peace—No other man but you this day Commands any Confidence of any *Considerable proportion* of our people; and while Candidates for the Presidency can be numbered by *hundreds* if not thousands, yet no man save yourself has the support of any but mere fragments of the people,—I saw the hand of God Clearly in all the great Events of the War, and I see as clearly now, that under his providence you are the only man in this Union to bind up its bleeding wounds, to give peace and unity and happiness, and more to our beloved Country;—I shall therefore not merely as a political but a *Religious* duty, talk for you, write for you, speak for you, and pray for you as our next President, to Complete the parallell between the Father and the Saviour of our Country."—ALS, USG 3.

1867, JULY 20.   Joseph J. Hendley, president, Houston, Trinity, and Tyler Railroad Co., to Lorenzo Sherwood, vice president. "I have to-day had a conference with General Grant respecting our Railroad Iron. After looking over the subject he expressed surprise that the company had not been permitted to take the Iron—Railroad property not having been taken in any instance except for temporary accommodation—Upon being informed that the War and Treasury Departments laid no claim to the Iron, and declined to take any cognizance of the matter, he inquired Very emphatically—'Why dont the company go and take the Iron'? I showed him Genl Wrights printed order which I had incorporated into the statement of the case—He answered by saying that 'if neither the Treasury nor War department claimed the property he did not know what right any one had to interfere.' I asked him to give an order or permit for the company to take the property—he declined by saying that 'he had nothing to do with it, and had no right to give any order, and repeated that 'if the company owned the property they might as well go and take it'—This is all I could get—I inclose to you the statement and accompanying papers which I presented to Genl Grant, and advise that the company go and collect the Iron and put it in their yard unless prohibited by military force. I do not think, after what has transpired here, that any one will attempt to prevent it—"—ALS, DNA, RG 107, Letters Received from Bureaus. Hendley and Sherwood had signed an undated petition concerning their claim addressed to USG.—LS (undated), *ibid.*

1867, July 22.   Louis J. DuPré, Memphis, to USG. "I enclose a pamphlet to at least one page of which I ask yr attention. I am as bitterly hostile to Democracy of the Brick Pomeroy, Avalanche sort as to insane Radicalism of which Mr Stevens is an exponent—Between these two parties, as an upper & nether millstone my people, are ground to powder—I think you the only man that can save the country. The President lost his opportunity. He is impotent; you, potent; & for the reason that y'r partizan programme is unknown—You will live in history immortal, because you will twice save y'r country; once, in the field; and again in the council chamber of empire— I met you just after Belmont with Genl (Capt) McCown formerly of U. S. A. There will be a Grant paper here at an early day—Refer to J. M. Tomeny U. S. Marshal—under arrest I beleive . . . I was a *rebel* & Douglas Democrat"—ALS, USG 3.

1867, July 23.   Governor Marcus L. Ward of N. J., Trenton, to USG. "You will perhaps see in the journals a report of the introduction of a resolution into our Convention of to day and the action upon it which needs explanation. We had at Trenton an Impartial Manhood Suffrage Convention largely attended, the simple object of which was to strike the word 'white' out of our State Constitution. We desired to keep out of it all extraneous questions whatever. A very injudicious but perhaps well meaning member of the Convention, placed on the Committee on Resolutions, desired the introduction of a resolution naming you for the Presidency. The majority of the Committee expressed their high admiration of your character and your services, but opposed the introduction of the question into such a Convention. It was not accordingly embraced in the report, but subsequently the gentleman referred to introduced the resolution into the Convention. Upon its introduction it was opposed upon the ground that it was entirely foreign to the object of the Convention. Almost the whole convention were of this opinion and it was laid upon the table. I write to say that this action was based upon the reasons stated, and that you are in my opinion, the choice of nearly all our Republicans for President. They regard your name, fame and patriotic services as a tower of strength, and will be among the first and foremost to place you in the seat of Abraham Lincoln There may be some who will endeavor to misrepresent the action of the Convention, but you may rely implicitly upon the statement I have given you. I am sorry for the ill-timed and injudicious movement, but you have not now to learn that such friends are sometimes worse than enemies."—ALS, USG 3.

1867, JULY 24. Ludwig Horneburg, Hamburg, to USG. "In December 1860 after the election of President Abraham Lincoln four Germans, named Mr. Wenmerskisch, Mr Sixtus Kapf, Mr Goebel and I created a Volunteer Company for the protection of Mr Lincoln, if he should come by his Inauguration tour at New York. We paid by our own means the muskets, and I drilled myself the men at Harmony Hall Hester Street, New-York City: Afterwards we called together a Mass Meeting, and created the 7th Steuben Regiment. My Company elected by Acclamation Mr Goebel for Captain, I was elected First Lieutenant, and Mr Dupré Second Lieutenant. In the night of the 13th April 1861 the message came to New York, that there was fired at Fort Sumter, in the same night we sent a Telegramm to Governor John Morgan, now Senator in the Congress for the State of New-York, offered him our Regiment, which he accepted and were all the elections of officers authorized by him. On the 19th we left New-York, together with the 6th State Militia Regiment, and after my return I was in the Battle of Bull's Run, Manassee Junction etc. Things went on so quick, that I could not get my Commission as Officer. Now I would ask you, honorable Sir, if you are willing, to procure me the same, not so much for my own use, but for the honor of it, and am I willing, to give to the American Museum, a Color, of Virginia from 1728, which was taken from a Minute Man at the Battle of Bull's Run, which is now in my posession. Hoping you will agree with my wishes, . . ."—ALS, DNA, RG 94, ACP, H80 CB 1869. On March 4, 1869, Horneburg wrote again to USG on this subject.—ALS, *ibid.*

1867, JULY 25. Judge Advocate Gen. Joseph Holt to USG. "John F. Lukins, 2d Lieut. 30th Regt. U. S. C. T. and Depot Ordnance Officer, was convicted May 14. 1866, by a General Court Martial sitting at Wilmington N. C., of the following charges and specifications: Charge 1st Wrongfully and knowingly selling ordnance stores, the property of the U. S. To this charge were nine specifications, alleging that the accused sold to the Wilmington and Weldon R. R. Co. 2522 pounds of block tin for $822.70—; that he sold to the same Company a quantity of zinc for $61—; 22 boxes of tin for $220—; 3054 pounds of block tin for $1068.90—: 500 pounds of block tin for $175—: 7 boxes of plate tin for $70—: 2 tarpaulins for $40—; 1 portable forge for $15—. 3000 pounds of potash for $90—;— and that the accused appropriated the proceeds of all these sales to his own use. Charge 2d Misapplication and embezzlement of public money entrusted to him. In this—that he embezzled the sum of $1334.59, public money of the United States to his own use. He was sentenced to be cashiered, with loss of all pay and allowances; to refund to the Government $3957.15, being the amount due from him, and to be imprisoned until payment, said imprisonment not to exceed two years. The prisoner is now undergoing confinement at Fort Macon, from whence he addresses an application to the General comm'd'g. the army, for intercession with the Executive in his behalf. His wife makes an earnest appeal for his pardon, and pleads destitution. The Judge Advocate of the court before which he was tried, states as his opinion, that the prisoner was led away by young men of the South, with whom he associated. A careful examination of the record of his trial has been made by this Bureau, and shows, conclusively, that the accused misapplied the different sums alleged, to his own use, amounting in the aggregate to the sum named in the sentence. His claim that the trial was not fairly conducted, does not appear to be true. He now charges that three of the officers composing the Court were prejudiced against him. When he was arraigned, he stated that he had no objection to any member of the court. He was permitted the aid of counsel in his defence. In view of the certainty of the prisoner's guilt, this Bureau does not feel justified in making any recommendation in his favor; and it is advised that when a term of imprisonment is limited to a definite period, unless restitution of embezzled funds shall be sooner made, the full sentence of the court should be enforced."—Copy, DNA, RG 153, Letters Sent.

1867, July 25. George E. Cole, Portland, Ore., to USG. "*Private . . .* Pardon the liberty I take in addressing you at this time upon a matter that deeply interests every lover of his country. It is apparent to thinking men everywhere that the extreme lengths to which party politics are being carried in the United States is seriously endangering, and if not checked, will eventually overthrow our Republican System of Government. I know of no means of checking this spirit, but by the united action of men of all parties in every section, and the election of a President in whom the people have implicit confidence—You happen to occupy in the hearts of the people the position that makes you *the man who as President can restore this Union, and give peace to this distracted country. Is it not your* DUTY *to do it?* You would be elected by the spontaneous voice of the entire people. I do not ask you to commit yourself, or even to reply to this note, but as a friend of my country, and as one who knows something of the pulse of the people, I assure you, I but express their sentiments. Our mutual friend Nesmith is hard at work on his farm and enjoys it better than the Senate Chamber. Saml. D. Smith has had one foot amputated, but is doing well."—ALS, USG 3.

1867, JULY 25.   Samuel R. Wells, editor, *The Phrenological Journal*, New York City, to USG. "You are now Your Nations Idol—All take off their hats to you. I would have You *retain* this *more* than respect, and trust. You will be teased, if not dragooned into politics—Will You, *can* you resist? I hope You will do that, which may be best for the nation. Should You be nominated for the presidency by the Republicans You can be elected. But is it best? If nominated by the Democrats I do not see You rising, and it would reverse the feelings of thousands who now *boom* you—to know that You could be used by the Dem. party—I hope You may be guided by true inspiration in whatever you may do—and that You may retain the gratitude of the nation as You now have the gratitude of Yours Truly—"—ALS, USG 3.

1867, JULY 28.   W. J. Neff, Cincinnati, to USG. "For Heaven's sake do not let political parties use you as a candidate for Presidency. You have now the hearts of the people; you hold an office equally as honorable as that of President, and it is a permanent one, with a good salary. If you accept and are elected to the Presidency, it will only be for four years, and then you do not know how you will stand in the hearts of the people afterwards. Besides it will be impossible for you to be replaced afterward in your present position; for when you resign, Genls Sherman, Sheridan and others will be advanced. I would really be happy to see you president, but I do not believe you will be in any way a gainer by it. Refuse, refuse, refuse, and you will never regret it. When the political leaders try to entrap you into an acceptance of the nomination for Presidency, (for all they care for you is to have the winning man for the party) refer them to Sherman, to Sheridan, to the patriotic Stanton, or to Genl O. P. Morton, Gov. of Ind., and many others,—but do not let them budge you. Pardon this bold intrusion; I could not, however, feel that I had done my duty to my country and to you, had I passed by the present crisis without writing these remarks for your most serious consideration."—ALS, USG 3.

1867, JULY 29.   Mary E. Sternburg, Joliet, Ill., to USG. "Will you give me protection? Life and property is in danger. In the name of God protect a soldiers widow   Answer yes, or no."—Telegram received (at 11:45 A.M.), DNA, RG 107, Telegrams Collected (Bound).

1867, JULY 30.   To Secretary of War Edwin M. Stanton. "I would respectfully recommend that a Board to consist of the Surgeon General, Act. Qr. Mr. Gen. & Chief of Ordnance & Gen. Canby be ordered to convene in this city from time to time until the 1st of Nov. next for the purpose of examining the various patterns of Knapsack & accoutrements that may be presented to them, and to report recommending for adoption by the Army of the best pattern in their judgement. I would also recommend the appointment of Bvt. Maj. J. B. Campbell, 4th Art as recorder of the Board." —ALS, DNA, RG 94, Letters Received, 446A 1867.

1867, July 30.   USG endorsement. "Approved for Brevet Brigadier General of Volunteers"—ES, DNA, RG 94, ACP, B278 CB 1868. Written on a letter of May 24 from William Barney, New York City, to Secretary of War Edwin M. Stanton requesting an additional bvt. for his brother Lewis Barney.—ALS, *ibid.* On Sept. 16, Bvt. Brig. Gen. Rufus Saxton, Atlanta, wrote to USG. "I have the honor to recommend Brevet Brigadier Genl Lewis T. Barney late Colonel of the 106th New York Volunteers for the brevet of Major General of Volunteers, for *gallant* and *meritorious* service during the late war—General Barney entered the service at the commencemt of the war and served with great gallantry until its close. He was on my staff until he was appointed Colonel of Volunteers when with his regiment he joined the Army of the Potomac—He served on my staff in South Carolina—I always found him brave, and ready in action, and for any service he was called upon to perform—never shunning danger or exposure where duty called—In my judgemt General Barney is fairly entitled to this slight recognition for gallant and meritorious service and duty well performed, and I earnestly commend him to your favorable consideration"— ALS, *ibid.* USG wrote on a card. "Gen. Kelton will please make this Bvt. unless there is good reason for with holding it."—AE (initialed and undated), *ibid.*

1867, July 31, 2:20 p.m.   To U.S. Senator William Sprague of R. I. "It will be impossible for me [to] go to Providence this week"—ALS (telegram sent), DNA, RG 107, Telegrams Collected (Bound); telegram sent, *ibid.* On July 30, Sprague, Providence, had telegraphed to USG. "[The] races mentioned to you come off Wednesday. Thursday & Friday. Can I Expect you."—Telegram received (at 1:30 p.m.), *ibid.*; *ibid.*, RG 108, Telegrams Received.

1867, Aug. 1.   To Secretary of War Edwin M. Stanton. "I have the honor to forward herewith a list of recommendations of applicants for appointment in the Army. The number recommended is equal to the whole number of existing vacancies."—LS, DNA, RG 94, ACP, W813 CB 1867. The enclosure is *ibid.* See *ibid.*, 84W CB 1867. On Aug. 16, USG wrote to the secretary of war (a position he held *ad interim*). "I have the honor to forward herewith a list of recommendations of applicants for appointment in the Army. The number recommended is equal to the number of existing vacancies."—LS, *ibid.*, G485 CB 1867. The enclosure is *ibid.*

1867, Aug. 3, 10:00 a.m.   To Maj. Gen. Daniel E. Sickles. "Suspend ~~further~~ proceedings in case of Lt. Jno. T. Deweese, 8th Infantry, until

further orders"—Telegrams sent (2), DNA, RG 107, Telegrams Collected (Bound); telegram received, *ibid.*, Telegrams Collected (Unbound);
ibid., RG 393, Dept. of the South, Telegrams Received. On July 29,
Sickles, Charleston, had written a letter received at USG's hd. qrs. "Returns tender of resignation of Lt. John T. Deweese, 8th US Inft. of date
8th June 1867. Enclosing charges and specifications preferred against said
Deweese for making a public speech at Raleigh, N. C. in July rather de-
rogatory of His Excellency President Johnson. The law firm of McAllister
and Henderson of Washington, D. C. urge and recommend the acceptance
of Deweeses resignation."—*Ibid.*, RG 108, Register of Letters Received.
On Aug. 3, USG endorsed this letter. "Respy. forwarded to the Sec of
War, recommending the acceptance of Lieut Deweeses resignation."—
Copy, *ibid.* On Aug. 7, 3:10 P.M., USG telegraphed to Sickles. "Dismiss
the court convened for trial of Lt. Deweese, 8th Infantry, & release him
from arrest. Answer"—Telegrams sent (2), *ibid.*, RG 107, Telegrams
Collected (Bound); telegram received, *ibid.*, RG 393, Dept. of the South,
Telegrams Received. On the same day, Sickles telegraphed to USG. "Your
telegram recd. In obedience to your orders the charges against Lieut Deweese were withdrawn from the General Court Martial   He is at present
at Salisbury North Carolina. Orders have been sent to the Comdg Officer
of that Post to release Lt Deweese from arrest"—Telegram received (at
10:30 P.M.), *ibid.*, RG 107, Telegrams Collected (Bound); *ibid.*, RG
108, Telegrams Received; copies, *ibid.*, RG 393, 2nd Military District,
Telegrams Sent; DLC-USG, V, 55. See DNA, RG 94, Letters Received,
294D 1867.

1867, AUG. 3.   Charles F. Morris, Pacific Place, Ark., to USG. "I have
taken the liberty, to address you, as the personal friend of *Mr James
Cacey*—who has frequently told me—that you would find time to answer
all letters—from his friends on business, I write you to state that at the
time the U S Forces. occupied 'Fort Pickering' my mother was a property
holder at the time & by order of Genl W T Sherman let her 'home—' represented as 'Block 3' on the plot of the town also—Blocks "F" & "G—,"
The entrenchments runs through the two last Blocks, which are located at
the Southern Boundry—or 'Mounds'   The homestead is a wreck and nothing is left to mark the spot   My mother Mrs Cynthia E Morris, has a
receipt from the assessors orderd by Genl Sherman for the small sum of
Fourteen Hundred dollars; which would not pay for the 'Fensing'   The
property would bring to day if put in order—as it originally was 75.000$.
Dollars: I write you—prompted by a hope; that through you—I have redress. and remuneration—I am willing to put the claims in your hands or
any friends—you may kindly sugest at *Washington*, City. I have the pleasure of writing you, that my mother *asks* this at *your hands*, having the
honor knowing you—when in Command at Memphis—'Head Quartes' at
Col W R Hunts   She is the only living daughter of the late Col George
Elliott of Sumner Co—Middle Tennessee; one of the Vetrans of '1812'—

with Genl Jackson—at N Orleans Emuckfaw. Taladega & Pensacola,' and who gave her onley brother at the Gates of Monteray   I metion this, as a record of the past, her farther was a personal friend of the president This matter was once, referd to him, and the Commissioners at the request of Mr Johnson awarded her damages at $8.000 dollars; and the matter thus stands, unfixed,   in 'war the innocent' must suffer with the guilty,   But to you I appeal as the General and 'true soldier' in behalf of an old soldiers daughter, and if the 'grave of the Hermitage could speak' I would need no appeal—in her behalf   You have fought that our 'Fedral Union should be preserved' so did he, 'victory was his' and may the future verdict of his people—transfer it to you, if the *laurels* he wore, you would wear,   In writing you General—it is due my humble self, to say,—that I took no part in the war,—and would most respectfully refer you—to Govr Jno S Phelps —and to Genl S A Hulbert   You will pardon—*my long letter* knowing. your admiration for *brevity* & nothing extended save a '*seige*'   Your kind attention & *advise* at your earliest Convenience . . . P S Please address me Care Capt Dan Able Memphis"—ALS, DNA, RG 94, Letters Received, 1124M 1867.

1867, AUG. 4.   Maj. Gen. George G. Meade, Long Branch, N. J., to USG. "This letter will be handed to you by my friend Capt. Scott of the Navy, who has a favor to ask at your hands which if you can grant I shall feel much obliged—It is briefly this—His son Douglas Scott has been appointed a 2d Lieut in in the 4th Cavalry—has passed his examination has been ~~as~~ assigned to a company at Camp Verde in Texas, and has been authorised to delay joining for 30 days, his time being up on the 10th inst.—To join his regiment he will have to pass through both New Orleans & Galveston where as you are doubtless aware the yellow fever is at present prevailing   Being young & unaclimated his parents are naturally anxious, and I think myself it will be running a great risk for him to go to these places at the present time—Under these circumstances, it has occurred to me that perhaps he might be ordered to report to Grier at Carlisle where whilst awaiting the abatement of the epidemic, he could be instructed in his duties as a cavalry officer—If this could be done it would relieve his Mother & be a benefit not only to the young man but to the service—If this is not practicable, would it be, to authorise his delaying reporting till November when the frost appears—Hoping you may be able to do some thing for him . . ."—ALS, OClWHi. USG noted on this letter. "Address 22d S Broad St Phila"—AN, *ibid.*

1867, AUG. 5.   USG endorsement. "Respectfully forwarded to the Secretary of War with recommendation that authority be given for the issue of rations to the Indians within mentioned."—ES, DNA, RG 94, Letters Received, 949M 1867. Written on a letter of June 30 from Bvt. Brig. Gen. Alfred Sully, Fort Buford, Dakota Territory, to Lt. Gen. William T. Sherman requesting that rations be issued to four Sioux for services as scouts in 1863–64.—ALS, *ibid.* On July 18, Sherman, St. Louis, had endorsed this letter. "I feel inclined to make an order such as Gen Sully asks for and think a Post Commander could easily make such provision for special cases. Yet as a principle is involved, it is best to have some General Rule, prescribed for all like cases. Referred to the Adjt Genl."—AES, *ibid.*

1867, Aug. 6. Lt. Gen. William T. Sherman, St. Louis, endorsement. "Respectfully submitted to Genl Grant—If other Military Academies at the South are allowed arms there is a seeming injustice in denying them in Louisiana. I know Boyd well and though he was a Rebel I would trust him as far as Frank Smith at Lexington Va—If you will put a few words on this to show there are precedents & send it to me again I will forward with a note to Sheridan—"—AES, DNA, RG 108, Letters Received. Written on a letter of July 29 from David F. Boyd, Louisiana State Seminary and Military Academy, to Sherman. "I wish you would ask Genl Sheridan to give the Seminary the priviledge of having *arms, uniform & drill,* as has been granted by other commanders or the War Dep't to the Va Mil. Institute, the Ky Mil. Institute & the N. C. Military Academy, all superintended by *late* confederate officers, . . . Sent your letter to Gen. Grant, which he kindly laid before the Peabody Agent, Dr Sears. From what the Dr says, I fear we will not get much aid from Mr Peabody. . . ."—ALS, *ibid.*

1867, Aug. 6. P. B. Blow, Washington, D. C., to USG. "I beg to submit for such consideration & action as you may see fit to give it, the following statement: Some 3 weeks ago I was summoned before a committee of congress to testify as to my knowledge concerning the 'Loewenthal swindles. As my connection with that case is a matter of public knowledge, I will refrain from giving details. Yesterday morning I recvd a Note from Gen. Tompkins, (in whose employ I have lately been) that he was unwilling to retain in his employ 'any person who occupied the position of a detective' and consequently that 'my services were no longer required'. As I have every reason to believe that this course was prompted by Gen B. W. Brice Pay Mr. Gen. in view of my having made certain statements before the committe above referred to, which possibly were unpalatable to him. As I acted entirely under the orders and by the consent and advice of Gen Sheridan in all my operations in connection with the Loewenthal case, I beg respectfully, as an act of justice that you will cause an investigation to be made of the facts concerning my summary dismissal from Govt. employ."—ALS, DNA, RG 108, Letters Received. On Oct. 8, 1866, Maj. George K. Leet had referred papers received at USG's hd. qrs. to Maj. Gen. Philip H. Sheridan concerning J. Loewenthal (or Lowenthal) and Co., claim agents.—*Ibid.*, Register of Letters Received. On Oct. 17, Sheridan, New Orleans, endorsed these papers. "Prior to reciept of this communication measures were taken to cause the arrest of J. Lewenthal in New Orleans, La. but, he eluded the officers—the papers in the matter have been sent to War Dept."—Copy, *ibid.* See *New York Times,* Dec. 24, 1866, Jan. 5, 1867; *New York Tribune,* July 24, 1867; *CG,* 40-1, pp. 736–37.

1867, AUG. 8. USG endorsement. "Respectfully forwarded to the Secretary of War with recommendation that Bvt. Major General Eli Long, Captain 4th Cavalry, be retired upon his present rank."—ES, DNA, RG 94, Letters Received, 339R 1867. Written on papers concerning the retirement of Capt. and Bvt. Maj. Gen. Eli Long, 4th Cav., endorsed on Aug. 2 by Bvt. Maj. Gen. Edward D. Townsend. ". . . The records of this Office show that when wounded General Long was Commanding 2d Division, Cavalry Corps, Military Division of the Mississippi at Selma, Alabama. Attention is respectfully invited, in this case, to Section 32 of the Act approved July 28th 1866, which provides that 'Officers of the Regular Army entitled to be retired on account of disability occasioned by wounds received in battle *may* be retired upon the full rank of the command held by them, whether in the Regular or Volunteer service, at the time such wounds were received. When wounded Gen. Long was Brig. and Bt Maj. Gen. of Vols."—ES, *ibid.* On Sept. 2, Long, Louisville, wrote to Lt. Gen. William T. Sherman. "In looking over some old papers I find two letters from you to me, in which you express kind sentiments towards me, and a willingness to assist me. I have no doubt but that you recommended me for promotion, that Genl Grant is down on me hard and heavy for some reason unknown to me. He told me that he did not recommend me for any promotion when the new Regiments were raised, and he, as I think, carries his dislike of me so far as to do me injustice. In July I was retired by the Board of which Genl Mead is President on account of a wound in the head which fractured the scull at Selma Alabama. Under the law of Congress I am clearly entitled as was Ricketts and Fessenden to be retired on the rank of the command I held at the time, which was that of Maj Genl Cm'g a Division. Genl Grant has retired me as Captain. I start to Washington tomorrow with but little hope of changing the decree. As I want all the help I can get I wish you would send me a letter to Genl Grant on receipt of this, directed to me at the Ebbit House Washington City, or if you think better telegraph to Genl Grant, or write to him direct. Hoping that you will aid me in this matter, and that you will see as I do that all I ask is simple justice, . . ."—ALS, DLC-William T. Sherman. On Sept. 9, USG, secretary of war *ad interim,* again endorsed Long's retirement papers. "As it appears that Bvt. Major General Long was in command of a Division at the time he received the wounds which the Board find incapacitate him for active duty, the former Orders in his case will be revoked, and he will be retired on his Brevet rank of Major General under Section 32, act approved July 28, 1866."—ES, DNA, RG 94, Letters Received, 339R 1867.

1867, AUG. 8. To B. D. Palmer, 9th Kan. Cav. "It affords me pleasure to inform you, that I have selected your manuscript for the 'Grant Pre-

mium,' offered by Mr Wm Oland Bourne, Editor of the 'Soldier's Friend.'
I wish you prosperity and success in all your honorable undertakings."—
Copy, DLC-William O. Bourne. On the same day, USG and Admiral David
G. Farragut wrote to Selden C. Clobridge. "I have the pleasure of informing you that your manuscript has been selected for the Farragut Premium
for Left Hand Penmanship, offered by Wm Oland Bourne, Editor of the
Soldier's Friend. The voyager on the sea of life has storms to meet, and in
some of his experiences he may find that the Conflict of winds, and waves,
and of enemies has disabled his Craft, and he must reach the haven of rest
under clearer skies and favoring winds, with his eye steadily turned to the
true point. I Congratulate You on your skill in the use of the pen, and hope
you will be rewarded by success and prosperity."—LS, *ibid.* On June 12,
Louis E. Kline, St. Louis, had written to USG and others to explain his
contribution of money to the penmanship fund.—ALS, *ibid.*

1867, AUG. 9. USG endorsement. "The ruling in this case seems to me
to be very unjust, if not altogether illegal. I do not see that Lieut. A. Thieman ever was Captain of the 33d Infantry. The law requires that officers
appointed to fill original vacancies in the army shall pass an examination,
which this officer seems to have failed in. He certainly cannot be considered
as having vacated his commission as 1st Lieut. 12th Infantry, and I
recommend that such decision be made in his case"—ES, DNA, RG 94,
Letters Received, 222T 1869. Written on papers concerning August Thieman.—*Ibid.* On Aug. 22, Thieman, Washington, D. C., wrote to USG,
secretary of war *ad interim.* "I have the honor to request to be ordered
before a retiring Board of officers of the army and should their report be
favorable that my name may be placed on the retired list to take effect
from a date when I was in the service. While holding the commission of
1st Lieutenant & Brevet Major 12 US Inf'y I received on the 20 Nov
1866 the appointment of Captain 33d Inf'y, which I accepted. I was at
that time in Hospital in New York Harbor, on account of wounds, and
when ordered before the Examining Board failed to pass the examination
both physically (the disability caused by wounds being the cause) and
mentally. At the battle of Wilderness May '64 I received a wound in head—
the ball has not yet been extracted—and this wound has I feel convinced
affected my mind to a certain extent. Besides this wound at the battle of
the Weldon Rail Road on the 18th August '64 while acting as Inspector of
the regular brigade, Army of the Potomac, and in recapturing the national
colors of the 12th Inf'y I received a wound in my right thigh and one in
the groin—thus disabling me entirely for service. I am without *any* means
of support and it is on the strength of the wounds (and a severe injury received in December 1864) contracted in the service of the government,
that I ask the above indulgence. By letter received from the Adjutant General it was decided that by accepting the appointment of Captain 33d Infy
I vacated my former appointment in the 12th Infy and the senior 2d Lieutenant was promoted in my place. By not passing the examination before

the New York Board my appointment as Captain expired. I am thus thrown entirely out of the service and on account of my wounds it is *impossible* for me to gain a livelihood   My being retired (should the Board so recommend) would not be to the prejudice of any officer of the army and I would respectfully ask the same indulgence as that granted Major Linde. In 1861 or '62 Maj Linde was dismissed the service and I believe, General, was on your recommendation restored to *his commission as Major and retired from the same date*   The total disability under which I labor forces me, General, to ask of the government this indulgence. I would respectfully refer you to General Meade who is well acquainted with my services"—ALS, *ibid*. On Oct. 12, Bvt. Maj. Gen. Edward D. Townsend endorsed papers concerning Thieman. ". . . Major Thieman was examined on the 8th & 9th of October, and found by [t]he Board to be incapacitated for a[ct]ive service and that said inca[pa]city resulted from his own ne[gle]ct to use the means prescribed f[or] him in the earlier stage of [the] disease, which disease originated in the line of his duty. Although the disease 'originated in the line of his duty,' it does not appear to have been caused by performance of any duty. It is respectfully recommended that Bvt. Major Thieman be wholly retired with one year's pay, and dropped from the rolls of the Army."—ES, *ibid*. On Dec. 23, President Andrew Johnson asked USG "what relief can be granted in this case."—ES, *ibid*. On Jan. 9, 1868, USG forwarded to Johnson an AGO memorandum explaining what action had been taken.—ES, *ibid*. On April 21 and 26, 1869, Thieman wrote to USG asking to be placed on the regular retired list.—ALS, *ibid*. On May 10, Thieman wrote to USG. "I have the honor to Submit my case to your Excellency's favorable consideration and high sense of justice, hoping that it will be favourably considered. I have been a Soldier in the United States Army for upwards of sixteen years as a Non-Commissioned and Commissioned Officer, been on active service all through the war and so severely wounded as to incapacitate me from getting my living by labor, and at present without money or friends in the City of Washington. I stand in a fair way of perishing of hunger and want. If this be the reward of a grateful Country to its heroes it seems poor encouragement to the patriotism of the future Generation. If your Excellency would but appoint me to some one of the many positions (I dont care how humble it may be) in the gift of the Executive for the present. Trusting your Excellency will take this my application into your favorable consideration . . ."—ALS, *ibid*., RG 107, Applications. No action followed; Thieman later served three enlistments in the U.S. Army.

1867, AUG. 10.   Lt. Gen. William T. Sherman, St. Louis, to USG. "A Friend of yours and mine Dr Linton of this city, has made a singular request of me which I could not well refuse and therefore must fulfill—He says last summer he dined with you at Dr Pope's when the conversation turned on the War between Prussia & Austria, and you expressed a satisfaction that the Prussians were victorious, because they were Protestant and the Austrians were Catholic.—The Dr thinks you will be the next President, and being a Catholic he asked me to get for you a certain book, which he cannot find here, but which I will procure East & have laid on your table 'Millners End of Controversy', which the Doctor wants you to read, or if you do not care about reading it he wants you not to express so emphatic an opinion about Catholics where it might be repeated. That is about the substance of his request of me and is now fulfilled. You know I suppose that I am not a Catholic, but that my family (wife & children) are—strong, and the only thing 'that occurs to me to say in this connexion is, that whether Catholicism be right or wrong—it has a terrible hold on large masses of people, who cannot be called Ignorant, and whose Faith is so strong that all other considerations yield to it, so that their Religion is entitled to respect. I read Millners End of Controversy twenty years ago, and cannot say it made much impression, nor do I think that it will shake any convictions you may have on the matters discussed, but it, coupled with the request of Dr Linton may make you as cautious on that point as you are on all others. I start tomorrow for Leavenworth & beyond on the Indian Commission to be absent, till the meeting of Congress compels the members to go to Washington. I propose to lay low, and let the civil members try their hand—at all events will throw no obstacles in the way of their adjusting this troublesome business, although I have little faith in the result of talking conferences with hostile Indians. I have heard from Genl Terry in Montana. We will probably meet him & take him on board between Omaha & Fort Sully. We ascend the Missouri in the steamboat St Johns.—"—ALS, USG 3.

1867, AUG. 10.   Matías Romero, Mexican minister, New York City, to USG. "At Gen. Badeau's request I called yesterday at Messrs. Appleton & Co, and agreed with them to furnish without any charge or terms a translation into Spanish of Gen. Badeau's book on you, with the only condition that it should be published by them, with the maps, engravings and portraits of the English edition. In this way the edition will be more complete than if made in Mexico, and it will have a wider circulation in all South America. It is with great pleasure that I have made these arrangements in deference to you. I have heard some important things here which I will communicate to you when I return to Washing. I expect to leave here tomorrow evening."—ALS, MH.

1867, AUG. 13.   Bvt. Maj. Gen. Daniel H. Rucker, act. q. m. gen., to USG. "I have the honor to submit herewith a copy of my report to the Secretary of War, dated June 10th 1867, with reference to the proposed purchase of the Sutler's buildings at Fort Riley, Kansas, in which was stated that there appeared no probability that the rival claimants would execute a joint deed, or separate deeds conveying their respective interests in the property, and, that, in view of the opinion of Bt. Major Genl. L C. Easton, Depy. Qr. Mr. General, Chief Qr. Mr. Dept. of the Missouri, that the necessity for the proposed purchase would not much longer exist owing to the fact that Fort Riley would soon cease to be of any importance as a Depot, and that the buildings would be of no further use for Govts purposes, I had the honor to recommend that the order for the purchase of the buildings be rescinded, and that the rival claimants be so advised. This office is not aware that any action has been taken on that communication, nothing, since that date, having been received from the War Dept, on the subject. Since the submission of that report, and on the 26th. of July last, this office received a communication, dated St. Louis Mo. July 10th 1867, from R. McBratney, attorney for Henry F. Mayer, and S. S. Ludlum, attorney for Julia A. Rich, (said Mayer and Rich being the rival claimants to the ownership of the property in question) covering separate deeds from said Mayer and Rich transferring their various and respective titles to, and interest in, the property proposed to be purchased, to the United States, wherein, it is respectively stated that for the sum of $8000. said Mayer will convey all his right, title, and interest in the property to the U. S., and, that for the sum of $2000. said Julia A. Rich will transfer her right, title and interest in the property to the U. S., which sums together make to the amount of $10,000., for which they severally and separately agree to convey the property, which sum, is the amount of the appraisal of the Military Board, convened in the premises, and which appraisal has been approved by the Secretary of War. They ask that the warrants for the purchase money be transmitted to a third party in St. Louis, for equitable division, together with the note of Robert Wilson, filed in this office with the papers in the case. The delay in furnishing these deeds having been so prolonged by the nonagreement of the parties claiming the ownership of the property, and, the necessity for the retention of Fort Riley being rapidly diminishing, I see no reason for changing my recommendation in the premises, contained in my report, dated June 10 1867, before referred to herein, and which reads as follows, viz:—'that the order for the purchase of these buildings be rescinded, and that the rival claimants to the property be so advised.' The communication of the attorneys with its enclosures—the deeds and agreement—are herewith respectfully transmitted."—LS, DNA, RG 92, Reports to the Secretary of War (Press). On Aug. 20, Bvt. Maj. Gen. Edmund Schriver, inspector gen., endorsed this letter. "Q. Mr. Gen's. recommendation approved by the Actg Secy of War,"—Copies, *ibid.*, Decision Books; *ibid.*, RG 107, Orders and Endorsements. See *PUSG*, 15, 417–18.

1867, AUG. 13.   John W. Osborn, hospital steward, Washington, D. C., to USG. "(Unofficial.) . . . I have the honor herewith to solicit *your opinion* in regard to Extra Duty payments. I am a Hospital Steward U. S. A. on clerical duty in the Surg Genl's Office, and respectfully beg leave to inquire whether I am not entitled, as an *enlisted man*, to the extra duty pay allowed *other* classes of enlisted men doing *similar* service in the War Department, submitting for your kind consideration the following reasons: 1st According to Army Regulations, the rank and pay of a Hosp'l Steward is *higher* than that of an Orderly Sergeant, or *Sergeant-Major*; Yet, *all Sergeants*, now doing duty in the Departments, *receive more pay* than Hospital Stewards doing the same duty. 2d The pay of Hosp'l Stewards doing clerical duty is much *less* than that of *first-class* citizen clerks engaged in *like duties*. 3d Extra duty pay *was allowed Hosp'l Stewards* in the Surg. Gen'l's Office until the Spring of *1863*, and *is still allowed to all other enlisted men* on duty in said office,—making the pay of a *private* soldier nearly *equal*, and that of a Sergeant *superior* to the pay of a Hosp'l Steward—contrary to the expressed regulations of the Army. Respectfully tendered, with the earnest assurance of the esteem and gratitude of a soldier who shared in your battles, and sprinkled his blood in the glorious libations of your Vicksburg triumph"—ALS, DNA, RG 99, Letters Received. On Aug. 19, Bvt. Maj. Gen. Benjamin W. Brice, paymaster gen., endorsed this letter. "Respectfully returned to the Secretary of War, and attention invited to the foregoing remarks of the Surgeon General. Reference to the Surgeon General was made only to invite his attention to the fact that this communication had been sent direct to the Secretary of War without being passed through the proper chief. The remarks of the Surgeon General are fully concurred in by this Office"—ES, *ibid.* On Aug. 21, Bvt. Maj. Gen. Edmund Schriver, inspector gen., endorsed this letter. "Approved by the Actg Secy of War."—AES, *ibid.* On Aug. 31, Bvt. Maj. Gen. Edward D. Townsend issued Special Orders No. 431. "9. Hospital Steward, *J. W. Osborn*, U. S. Army, is hereby relieved from duty in the office of the Surgeon General, U. S. Army, and will report to the Commanding Officer and Medical Director, Department of Dakota, for assignment to duty. . . ."—DS (printed), *ibid.*, RG 192, Special Orders.

1867, AUG. 13.   Chipman, Hosmer, & Co., Washington, D. C., to USG. "Enclosed we have the honor to transmit a Statement made by a citizen, alleging cruel and unwarranted treatment at the hands of officers in the U. S. Army. Of the truth or falsity of the Statement we are ignorant, but, deeming it of sufficient importance to be brought to your official notice, we transmit the statement just as recd, asking that you take such action as in your judgment the premises warrant."—LS, DNA, RG 94, Letters Received, 1811M 1867. A statement concerning two brothers apprehended while selling whiskey to Indians near Fort Laramie, Dakota Territory, is *ibid.*

1867, AUG. 13.   Governor Jacob D. Cox of Ohio, Columbus, to USG. "I desire to present as urgently as may be, the request that Brevet be granted to G. M. Bascom 1st Lieut. 17th U. S. Infty. for gallant and meritorious services in the Volunteers during the War. He was mustered out with full rank as Major & Asst. Adjt Genl and Brevet rank of Colonel of Vols. I think he should have equal brevet rank in the regular service, the brevets being specially for the following services   1st For meritorious services in the Campaign of 1861 in the Kanawha Valley. 2d For distinguished gallantry in the battle of South Mountain. Sept. 14th. 1862. 3d For distinguished gallantry and meritorious service in the battle of Antietam Sept. 17. 1862   4th For meritorious service in the winter Campaign of East Tennessee and Knoxville 1863. 5th For gallant and meritorious services in the Campaign of Atlanta. 6th For faithful and meritorious services in Department staff duty in Tennessee 1865. Down to the spring of 1864 his services were upon my own staff. During 1864 he was on Genl Schofields staff and in 1865 on Genl Stonemans and General Gillems   Sincerely hoping his claim to such recognition may be found conclusive . . ."—Copy, DLC-John Sherman.

1867, AUG. 13.   W. M. Hunter, Alexandria, Va., to USG. "I have the honor to submit that, during the month of January last, I filed in your office an application for the position of compiler of the 'Official History of the War,' together with testimonials, &c., and enclosing therewith a request that the said papers should be returned to my address, in the event of the rejection of the application. I have thus far heard nothing farther from them, and would respectfully make application for the papers, desiring to use them otherwise."—ALS, DNA, RG 94, Letters Received, 620H 1867. The papers were returned on Aug. 14.—*Ibid.*

1867, AUG. 13.   Anonymous, Augusta, Ga., to USG. "Twas with profound pleasure, we heard yesterday—that you had accepted & entered upon —the duties of Secty of War—Believe me Sir—tis the sentiment of the Ten states—whose soldiers, surrendered their arms to you—There is no man now living—who has it in his power to do the service to his Country, you have—You do not know the writer & he wants *no office*—he speaks *only* what he feels to be truth—The Liberties of the People are in *great danger* & The Constitution has been trampled upon—You Sir—can rescue both— do it & yr Countrymen will hand down yr name in connection with Washington—what greater glory could mortal wish—You only have to accept the nomination which will be tendered to you—Let the Platform be; Liberty & the Constitution and you can sweep the *entire* Country—an effort will be made—(tis at work now)—to force a Negro on the Presidential Ticket with you—One word against it from you & they dare not do it—You can go so far as to say, who you wish & you will get him *Terrible power* for One Man to possess—but *truth* compels me to say it—Use the power for the good of yr Country & your children's children & those of *all* yr Countrymen will rise up & bless you—Think of what has been said & believe at least—you have the Esteem of—~~at least~~—One 'reconstructed' Georgia—*Rebel*"—AL, USG 3.

1867, AUG. 14.   To Secretary of the Interior Orville H. Browning. "I have the honor to transmit herewith a copy of a letter dated the 9th inst. from Lieut. Genl. Sherman, commanding Division of the Missouri, in which he states his opinion that it would be unsafe to prosecute surveys of the ceded lands of the Osages in Kansas, south and west of the Arkansas; being a reply to your request for military protection for the party of surveyors under Samuel S. Smoot, esquire."—Copies, DNA, RG 94, Letters Received, 1080M 1867; *ibid.*, RG 107, Letters Received from Bureaus; *ibid.*, Letters Sent to the President. On Aug. 9, Lt. Gen. William T. Sherman, St. Louis, had written to Maj. George K. Leet. "I have the honor to acknowledge the receipt of the communication of the Honorable O. H Browning, Secretary of the Interior, asking military protection for the party of surveyors under Saml S. Smoot engaged in laying off the ceded lands of the Osages in Kansas south and west of the Arkansas. I regret to say that in the present condition of hostilities of all the Indians in that quarter, in my opinion it would be folly to undertake to protect a party of surveyors and it is better to admit that fact at once, before it is attended with murder and disaster. All such surveys should of necessity be discontinued until something like peace is restored on that frontier. I think the Indians south and west of the Arkansas below Forts Zarah and Larned are hostile. I understand that the Secretary of the Interior thinks they are friendly: then why ask for military guards? I know that General Hancock has every soldier subject to his orders hard at work and has none to spare this season; and therefore I return this answer without reference to him."— LS, *ibid.*, RG 94, Letters Received, 1080M 1867.

On Sept. 11, Browning wrote to USG. "For the reasons mentioned in the accompanying copy of a letter of the 3rd ult; from U. S. Surveyor S. S. Smoot, I have the honor to request your favorable action upon his application to purchase Commissary Stores from the proper Officers at Forts, Zarah Larned and Dodge."—LS, *ibid.*, RG 192, Letters Received by Referral. On Sept. 14, USG wrote to Browning. "I have the honor to inform you that the requisite instructions have been given for a compliance with the request contained in your communication of the 11th instant, that Mr. S. S. Smoot U. S. Surveyor be permitted to purchase Commissary Stores from the proper officers at Forts Zarah, Larned and Dodge."—Copies, *ibid.*, RG 107, Letters Sent to the President; *ibid.*, RG 192, Letters Received by Referral. At 10:40 A.M., USG telegraphed to Maj. Gen. Philip H. Sheridan, Fort Leavenworth. "Let Mr. Smoot, U. S. Surveyor have Forty stand of Arms with ammunition."—ALS (telegram sent), *ibid.*, RG 107, Telegrams Collected (Bound); telegram sent, *ibid.*; telegram received (at 10:35 A.M.), *ibid.*, RG 393, Dept. of the Mo., Telegrams Received.

1867, AUG. 14. To Secretary of the Interior Orville H. Browning. "I have the honor to send herewith for your consideration a copy of a communication from General Comstock, Aid-de-Camp, respecting the issue of damaged subsistence stores to destitute Indians."—Copies, DNA, RG 75, Central Office, Letters Received, Miscellaneous; *ibid.*, RG 107, Letters Sent to the President; *ibid.*, RG 192, Letters Received, 4606A 1874. USG enclosed an extract from a report of July 20 from Bvt. Brig. Gen. Cyrus B. Comstock, Missouri River, to Bvt. Maj. Gen. John A. Rawlins. "As

Posts in progress of construction, commissary stores are inevitably, to some extent, damaged by exposure so as to be unfit for issue. During Sully's Ind. Campaigns large quantities of stores were accumulated at certain points on the river, which have been damaged in this way: such stores unfit for issue have accumulated at Fort Rice and this point. They can be and have been well used, in issueing them to starving Indians, who are very glad to get them during the winter, and who will live on [what no] white man could. Such issue tends far more strongly than treaties, which are rarely kept, to make the Indians friendly."—Copies, *ibid.*, RG 75, Central Office, Letters Received, Miscellaneous; *ibid.*, RG 192, Letters Received by Referral. On Aug. 7, USG had endorsed this extract. "Respectfully forwarded to the Secretary of War for his information, and recommending that a copy be furnished to the Sec. of the Interior"—ES, *ibid.*

1867, Aug. 14.   To Secretary of the Navy Gideon Welles. "The Third Auditor of the Treasury wishes to be informed, for the adjustment of a case now pending in his office, whether the United States had control of the navigable waters at Roanoke Island, Head Quarters of the Sub-district of the Albemarle, Norfolk, Va., and Newberne, N. C., from September 1st, 1864 to March 18th 1865. Will you please furnish the information."—LS, DNA, RG 45, Letters Received from the President. On Aug. 19, Welles wrote to USG. "I have the honor to inform you, in reply to your letter of the 14th inst, that the Navy had general control of the navigable waters of the Sounds of North Carolina at the dates mentioned; but it is believed that the Army at the same time had vessels in those waters—some of them being gun boats."—LS, *ibid.*, RG 92, 4th Div., Letters Received.

1867, Aug. 14.   USG endorsement. "The recommendation of MajorGeneral Thomas is approved."—ES, DNA, RG 94, ACP, 238N CB 1867. Written on papers charging 1st Lt. Charles L. Noggle, 2nd Inf., with embezzlement, endorsed on Aug. 7 by Maj. Gen. George H. Thomas, recommending that Noggle's resignation be accepted in lieu of a court-martial.—ES, *ibid.* On Sept. 16, Mrs. James R. Doolittle, Racine, Wis., wrote to USG, forwarding a letter from Noggle. "The enclosed papers were sent to Mr Doolittle, but as he is absent in Europe I take the liberty of forwarding them to the War Department, and in consideration of the young man being the Son of a personal friend, I would most respectfully ask the Department to exercise as much leniency in the case, as duty to the Government will permit."—ALS, *ibid.* Noggle resigned as of Aug. 15.

1867, Aug. 14.   Bvt. Maj. Gen. Daniel H. Rucker, act. q. m. gen., to USG. "I have the honor to return herewith papers in the claim of Mr C. D. Spaids, for value of the steamers 'Mussleman' and 'Minnesota', . . ."—Copy, DNA, RG 92, Reports to the Secretary of War (Press). On Sept. 18, Nov. 27, 29, and Dec. 2, Rucker wrote to USG concerning this case.—LS, *ibid.*

1867, AUG. 14. Vice Admiral David D. Porter, Annapolis, to USG. "If in your opinion he ought to resign to allow him to do so. I have done for him all that I can do consistently."—Stan. V. Henkels, Catalogue No. 1194, June 8, 1917, pp. 92–93. Porter's son, 1st Lt. David Essex Porter, 28th Inf., resigned as of Aug. 20.

1867, AUG. 14. Bvt. Maj. Gen. Frederick Steele, Portland, Ore., to USG. "Reccommended Chaplain Raynor be ordered to Sitka instead of Arizona"—Telegram received (at 8:20 P.M.), DNA, RG 94, ACP, R441 CB 1867; *ibid.*, RG 107, Telegrams Collected (Bound); *ibid.*, RG 108, Telegrams Received; copy, DLC-USG, V, 55.

1867, AUG. 14. Logan U. Reavis, St. Louis, to USG. "I am an humble citizen of the Republic but feel deeply interested in his welfare. The great Napolean said at one time to his army—that forty Centuries looked down upon them and asked them to duty. Thirty millions of the American people look down upon you in this perilous moment, and pray for you to save the Republic, You who started from that noble state of Illinois C̶a̶i̶r̶o̶ in the great Contest Cannot be expected to shrink from duty now, You must stand on the side of the school houses—the steam engines, and the great free north, This perils of our Country are great now, Johnson is worse than Cataline or Coligula, He is a traitor to the human race, a traitor to the american people He surely is the Moses that has led the nation into the 'Wilderness,' The great free people expect you to do your duty—A single word from you to the north will settle Johnson forever—You must be on your g̶a̶r̶d̶ guard, he is looking to military power, and military force, *These are no idle words You must Save the Republic* With Sentiments of high Consideration from one who loves his native Country . . ."—ALS, USG 3.

1867, AUG. 14. U.S. Senator Benjamin F. Wade of Ohio, Jefferson, to USG. "My son Capt H. P. Wade of the 8th U. S. Cavalry, is here now on an order to report to Gen Butterfield on the 21st inst. with a view to be ordered to his regt. in California. Now there is so much sickness prevailing on the Isthmus and along the route of a highly dangerous character, that if you can allow him to delay joining his regiment, without detriment to the public service until some time in October, I would esteem it a great favor. My other son Major Wade was ordered on the 9th of June to Stocton Texas, via New Orleans Galveston, Indianola & San Antonio. While at Indianola, Lt. Blackaller who accompanied him was taken with yellow fever and died at San Antonio the day after his arrival there. My son attended him during his illness and had an attack of the same disease from which he recovered. Please answer by telegraph—as his time is short."— ALS, DNA, RG 94, Letters Received, 592W 1867. On Aug. 17, Maj. George K. Leet endorsed this letter favorably.—ES, *ibid.*

On June 16, 1868, USG endorsed papers concerning Capt. Henry P. Wade, 8th Cav. "Approved for brevet of Major, for action at Saltville"— ES, *ibid.*, ACP, W168 CB 1869. On March 11, 1872, Wade, Jefferson, wrote to USG. "I have the honor to request an appointment as Paymaster in the U. S. Army should Congress authorize appointments to be made to fill the vacancies now existing in the Pay Department. I served as an officer in the volunteer service during the war and in the regular Army up to August 1869 when I resigned my Commission as Capt 8th U. Cavalry & B'v't Major U. S. A."—ALS, *ibid.*; (press—incomplete) DLC-Benjamin F. Wade. No appointment followed.

On Jan. 9, 1868, USG wrote to the AG. "The Adj. Gen. will please give leave of absence untill mMay next to Maj. Jas. F. Wade, 9th U. S. Cavalry"—ANS, DNA, RG 94, Letters Received, 19W 1868.

1867, AUG. 15. To Secretary of the Treasury Hugh McCulloch. "Upon the recommendation of the Chief of Engineers I respectfully request that $25.346.48, standing on the books of the Assistant Treasurer at New York, to the credit of Major E. B. Hunt, late of the Corps of Engineers, deceased, may be repaid into the U. S. Treasury, and that the usual evidence of such repayment may be transmitted to me."—LS, DNA, RG 56, Letters Received from the War Dept. On Aug. 16, Asst. Secretary of the Treasury John F. Hartley wrote to USG. "In answer to your letter of the 15th inst. I have directed the sum of $25.346.48. now standing on the books of the Assistant Treasurer at Newyork, to the credit of Major E. B. Hunt, late of the Corps of Engineers, deceased, to be placed to the credit of the Treasurer U. S. The Original Certificate of Deposit, I have directed to be sent to you."—LS, *ibid.*, RG 107, Letters Received from Bureaus.

1867, AUG. 15. To Secretary of the Treasury Hugh McCulloch. "In reply to your letter of the 14th instant I have the honor to state that the following mentioned balances should be carried to the surplus fund, viz For clerks, messenger and laborer in the office of the Colonel of Topographical Engineers, per Act of 25th February, 1863—$5,069.55 For compensation of additional clerks in offices of Surgeon General, Paymaster General and Adjutant General, per Act of 5th July 1862—$15,120.87"— Copy, DNA, RG 107, Letters Received from Bureaus.

1867, AUG. 15. To Attorney Gen. Henry Stanbery. "I have the honor to forward herewith copies of certain papers relating to a supposed conspiracy to defraud the Government at Indianapolis, Indiana, and to request that instructions be given to the U. S. District Attorney at that place to investigate the matter with the view of protecting the Government and punishing the offenders."—LS, DNA, RG 60, Letters Received, War Dept. See *ibid.*, RG 94, Letters Received, 285Q 1867. On Aug. 17, Act. Attorney Gen. John M. Binckley wrote to USG. "I have the honor to acknowledge the receipt of your letter of the 15th instant, enclosing copies of certain papers relating to a supposed conspiracy to defraud the Government, at Indianapolis, Indiana; and to say that I have transmitted the same to the U. S. Attorney for Indiana, with instructions to take such action in the matter as may be necessary to protect the Government and punish the offenders."—LS, *ibid.*, RG 107, Letters Received from Bureaus.

1867, AUG. 15. Act. Attorney Gen. John M. Binckley to USG. "I have the honor to lay before you copies of a report just received at this Office from George H. Hand, Esq. U. S. Attorney for the District of Dakota Territory, and of affidavits accompanying the same, from all which it appears that an officer of the army has obstructed the judicial process of the United States, in the territory of Dakota, near Fort Union. It is rendered probable that the officer did not contemplate an unlawful interference, but acted under the impression that he was at the time without the District in which the process would run, and consequently, that the United States Marshal had not adequate authority to hold the prisoner, who was thus taken from his custody. I would, in this view, respectfully recommend that the officer in question be instructed to reärrest and deliver to the proper civil officer, the person named in the warrant of arrest issued as reported, under the authority of the court, by U. S. Commissioner Bradford, to await prosecution according to law, unless the fact should turn out to be that the prisoner was not, at the time of rescue, in the lawful custody of the deputy marshal. It may not be inopportune to suggest for your attention the law as it now stands touching the obstruction of process of the courts of the United States. I therefore subjoin to this communication, from the 1st volume of the U. S. Statutes at Large, page 117, Sections 22 and 23 of the act of Congress of the 30th April 1790. for your convenience."—LS, DNA, RG 94, Letters Received, 476A 1867. On Nov. 12, Capt. and Bvt. Lt. Col. William G. Rankin, 31st Inf., Fort Buford, Dakota Territory, endorsed these papers. "Respectfully returned with the Information that on th 19th day of June last, Deputy United States Marshal for Dakota, A. B Griffin, arrested Thomas Campbell on board the Steamer 'Jennie Brown', at Fort Union which is in Montana Territory. At the time Campbell was arrested he was proceeding up the River to the Crow Country, with presents to the Crow Indians. I having a few days before received from General Sully (a Commissioner sent out by the government to see the Indians in this vicinity) a request that I would send some trusty person to the Crows to have them come down to this post to meet him and the rest of the Commissioners. Campbell was the person I selected for this duty; when he was going aboard the boat he was arrested and carried up the River for the purpose of being taken out of the country. I, hearing that he was being kidnapped, rode into Montana, about ten miles from this post, stopped the boat, and asked the persons who held Campbell in custody, for their authority. A writ was produced for the territory of Dakota, but none for the territory of Montana. Knowing the arrest was made at Fort Union, which is in the latter territory, I told the Marshal if he produced a warrant for the territory he was then in for the arrest of Campbell, I should not interfere but on the contrary should aid him in making the arrest, it was not my desire or wish to interfere with, or interrupt a civil process, but on the contrary would do all in my power to aid the civil authorities even in this case, but I thought it of vital importance at the time, for the country, to get the Crow Chiefs to see the commissioners, and had no other trusty person to send for them."—ES, *ibid.* On Feb. 24, 1868, Judge Advocate Gen. Joseph Holt endorsed these papers. "Respectfully returned to General Grant, Commanding U. S. Army, with opinion as follows: 1. The act of Capt. Rankin, in rescuing the prisoner named from the U. S. Marshal, is believed to have been unauthorized and highly reprehensible. Whether or not the arrest of Campbell was strictly regular—was made to the east or to the west of the line separating Montana from Dakota—is not regarded as material. It is deemed to have been made in good faith; under color of a formal warrant setting forth a specific offence; and to have been clearly in the interests of public justice. That such a warrant was held, and such an arrest had been made, by an authorized officer of the United States—should have been sufficient under the circumstances of this case to have deterred any other officer of the same sovreignty from interfering with the former in the execution of his duty. Had the arrest been made in a time of war, or had the party arrested been in the military service, there might perhaps have existed some excuse for such an interference; but Campbell was a citizen and was apprehended in time of peace. As a formal indictment—of which a copy is enclosed—has been duly found against Capt. Rankin, it is recommended that he be ordered forthwith to surrender himself for trial upon the same, to the United States District Attorney or Marshal of Dakota Territory. As it is understood that no charge has yet been preferred against him for the military offence involved, and that he is not now under arrest for other charges, it is advised that his trial under the indictment should properly take precedence of any proceedings which may hereafter be instituted against him before a court martial. 2. Campbell, being a civilian and not—as it is understood—in any manner under military control; his arrest cannot of course be legally made or ordered by the military authorities. The military department of the government is not authorized in time of peace, to apprehend a citizen for a civil offence for which he is amenable to a civil tribunal only—unless upon some emergency which has not arisen in this case."—ES, *ibid.* On March 2, Bvt. Lt. Col. George K. Leet endorsed these papers. "The recommendation of the Judge Advocate General is approved. The Adjutant General will order Bt. Lt. Col. Rankin to surrender himself for trial to the US. Dist. Attorney, or Marshal, of Dakota Territory."—ES, *ibid.*

1867, AUG. 15.   Bvt. Maj. Gen. Daniel H. Rucker, act. q. m. gen., to USG. "I have the honor to return herewith communication of E. Pearson Esq, dated August 6th 1867, making enquiries relative to the claim of Wm M. Stevens, for the steamer 'Grey Cloud,' alleged to have been taken by

United States forces and converted into the Gunboat 'Kinsman.' On the 16th of July last a communication was received at this office from the War Department from Mr W. M. Stevens, making enquiries relative to this claim. This letter was returned on the 22d ultimo to the War Department with report, a copy of which is herewith enclosed, together with a copy of report dated October 16th 1866. The records of this office do not show that the claim referred to by Mr Pearson, has ever been received."—Copy, DNA, RG 92, Reports to the Secretary of War. On Aug. 17, Bvt. Brig. Gen. Horace Porter wrote to E. Pearson. "I am directed to inform you that in reply to your inquiry of the 6th instant, in relation to the claim of *William H. Stevens* for payment for the destruction of the steamer 'Grey Cloud,' that the records of this Dept. do not show that the claim referred to has ever been received."—Copy, *ibid.*, RG 107, Letters Sent. On Aug. 20, Pearson, New Orleans, wrote to USG. "Mr. Wm. M. Stevens by his Attorneys 2 years ago this month filed his claim in your office (Sec. of War) for the Value of the Steamboat 'Grey Cloud' afterwards changed by the Govt to the gunboat 'Kinsman'—Mr. S. has never heard from his claim since—his Attys having left this city he concluded they had abandoned his claim. He therefore requested me to enclose a letter over his own signature to the War Office for information respecting said claim—which I did on the 3d day of July last—I have also written a letter since then to know why no answer came &c—Now if such information can be furnished Mr. S. would esteem it a great favor to have it or at least he would be glad to know how he can obtain such information—Mr. Stevens desire the reply to be sent to me or to my care as he resides in the country—I trust an early mail will bring the desired reply—"—ALS, *ibid.*, Letters Received, P231 1867.

On April 22, 1869, Pearson wrote to USG. "I confess that I have coveted & still do covet the office of judge—As one or more are to be appointed for this state or Vicinity I beg to present my name for that high station—without pretending to be the fittest man for such a place I can promise that integrity, impartiality & untiring industry in the discharge of the duties of the office—I am sure the now overcrowded docket would disappear—I have written to Ch. J. Chase as I understand you would consult him & other judges—aAtty. Gen & Judge Nelson know me having argued cases before each of them—I can procure recommendations in almost any part of the land—I am & have never been an office holder or office seeker   I will comply with any demand proper or requisite—I am no politician—I did not vote for you—I regard my political opinions as sacred, I regard my duty of supporting the present administration as sacred as far as right—and now should you select my name for that high office my lasting gratitude would be your due & I ~~will~~ will omit no effort to justify the selection—"—ALS, *ibid.*, RG 60, Records Relating to Appointments. No appointment followed.

1867, AUG. 15.   C. H. Lyon, New York City, to USG. "I am a friend—an earnest admirer of your character as shown, both in war and peace. You have won a reputation I had rather have than that of any man living

in America to-day. To your military record which is glorious and untar-
nished is added the sterling Common Sense which has sustained you under
all circumstances   The admiration or the criticism of an humble citizen
like myselsf may be nothing to you Sir, but I cannot help thinking that it
would have been better if you had declined the office of Secretary of War.
I hope you may not—consider it your duty to identify yourself with the
Policy of Andrew Johnson, our unfortunate President, and in opposition to
the Congress of the United States,   As a citizen of NewYork proud of your
fame I take the liberty to address you   It may be deemed impertinence
but my only motive is an earnest wish to see your name go down to posterity
just as unblemished as it is now. In God's name then, act with the men
who go with the Spirit of the Age and not against it. If you go with Johnson
you will destroy the fairest name in the world—if with the country you will
preserve it, and it will grow brighter with time"—ALS, USG 3.

1867, AUG. 16.   To President Andrew Johnson. "I have the honor to send
herewith the papers in the claim of Wm E. Taylor, referred to this Dept
for report, with a statement on the case from the Commissioner of the
Bureau of Refugees Freedmen & Abandoned Lands—"—Copies, DNA, RG
107, Letters Sent to the President; *ibid.*, Letters Received, N93 1867. On
Nov. 26, W. E. Taylor, Norfolk, Va., wrote to USG. "I have to ask your
attention to a case of great oppression and injustice on the part of the
Freedmen's Bureau. I have been, for more than 2 years urging on the FB—
the restoration of my farm in Norfolk County, called the 'Taylor Farm.'—
Originally siezed without legal process, it has been held by force without
colour of law. On 10th September 1865 I received the signature of the
President to a paper purporting to be a pardon, yet to this time it has
proved useless to restore my property and all my efforts have been made in
vain; Subterfuge of all kinds has been used by the FB to defeat my possession. . . . In few words the case is this—The FB holds my property; the
pardon of the Prest professes to restore it, but the FB undertakes to set
that aside & to confiscate my farm against all law & justice & to do so has
violated its pledges & broken its promises & now claims that by simply
'dropping from its returns' it escapes all responsibility—I assert boldly that
in this case the Bureau has consulted neither justice nor truth—The buildings now occupied by these negroes were erected from timber cut from my
own land;—in the allowance made me for rent, they were assessed greatly
beyond their value & I was compelled to accept them at the valuation, as so
much of the amount to be paid me—the FB now refuses to give me possession of the very houses I was forced to *purchase from the US.* Genl Howe
admitted to me that secret influence had been at work in FB against me. In
all other cases of restoration the removal has been made & I wish to know
on what grounds Genl Howard bases his confiscation of my farm & his
variation from the practice of his own Bureau. I enclosed copies of Letters
of 26th & 28th Oct 1867 to Prest Johnson & of a Protest sent Gen Howard

on 25th Oct 1867. and respectfully ask of your justice an Order for the speedy & actual possession of my farm."—ALS, *ibid.*, RG 105, Land Div., Letters Received. The enclosures are *ibid.*

1867, AUG. 16. To Secretary of the Treasury Hugh McCulloch. "In reply to your letter of the 7th Augt 1866, enclosing a comn from the Prest of the Memphis & Little Rock RR Co respecting payment of duties on certain rail road iron imported in March '61 & said to have been appropriated by the US for military purposes, I have the honor to send herewith a report from Genl Sherman of Augt 8th on the subject, in wh. this Dept concurs."—Df, DNA, RG 107, Letters Received from Bureaus; copy, *ibid.*, Letters Sent to the President. On Aug. 7, 1866, Act. Secretary of the Treasury William E. Chandler had written to Secretary of War Edwin M. Stanton concerning the Memphis and Little Rock Railroad Co.—LS, *ibid.*, Letters Received from Bureaus. Additional papers are *ibid.* On Aug. 24, 1867, USG wrote to McCulloch. "In reply to your communication of the 7th instant, enclosing a letter from R. C. Brinkley, Esq., President of the Memphis and Little Rock Railroad, in relation to the payment of duties on certain railroad iron imported by that Company in March, 1861 into the port of New Orleans and sent thence to Memphis, I have the honor to enclose herewith a copy of a communication from Lieutenant General Sherman of the 8th instant, which contains all the information on the subject which is possessed by this Department."—LS, *ibid.*, RG 56, Letters Received from the War Dept. On Aug. 29, McCulloch wrote to USG. "Respectfully referring to your communication of the 24th instant, in reply to Departments letter of August 7th 1866, transmitting a communication from R. C. Bruckley Esq. President of the Memphis and Little Rock Railroad, in relation to the payment of duties on certain railroad iron imported by that company in 1861; I have the honor to request the return of the said communication, if you have fully availed yourself of its contents."—LS, *ibid.*, RG 107, Letters Received from Bureaus. On Aug. 8, Lt. Gen. William T. Sherman, St. Louis, had written to Bvt. Maj. Gen. Edward D. Townsend. "Your letter of July 26th is received, and I herewith return you the letter of Mr. R. C. Brinkley, of Memphis, with this reply. I reached Memphis, July 21, 1863 [*1862*], and assumed command. The place had been occupied for about a month by our troops, first under General Lew. Wallace, then General Grant, and I relieved General Alvin P. Hovey. At the time there was a lot of railroad iron, lying on the west bank of the Mississippi, a little above Memphis, which I understood belonged to the Memphis and Little Rock Railroad, which was being used to repair the captured roads back of Memphis (Memphis and Charleston), but chiefly was shipped to Columbus, Kentucky, by General Halleck's or General Grant's orders, and used in repairing the road from Columbus to Corinth, then in charge of General McPherson. I took no accout of the quantity nor gave any orders about it, but I am certain that a large lot of iron was used in the manner I have stated, and no particular person kept account of it. At that time, Mr. Brinkley was not in Memphis, and an old man whose name I have forgotten who lived at Mound City, six miles above Memphis, on the west bank, seemed to exercise control over the iron, and applied to me to spare it from seizure, but I paid no attention to his remonstrances, but permitted the iron to be freely used as 'public property captured in war.' At that time the Railroad Company to which this iron belonged seemed to be in open hostility to us, and their road as far as finished, viz., from Devall's Bluff to Little Rock, was in use by the Confederates then commanded by General T. Holmes at Little Rock. As Mr. Brinkley's letter goes simply to the question of duties, I agree with him that it would be a little hard to appropriate his iron by the rules of war, and make him pay duties on the theory of peace."—LS, *ibid.*

On Aug. 20, R. C. Brinkley, Memphis, wrote to Sherman. "My pet Road is in trouble again and I write to ask you to assist me in releaving it. . . . Now that Gen. Grant is acting sec of War, and a man free from the prejudices of his predicessor, (for Mr Stanton seemed to take pleasure in oppressing this little road) can you not take the trouble upon yourself to speak a word in my behalf and in behalf of this strugling enterprise. To destroy it would not benefit the Government and greatly damage an entire community."—ALS, *ibid.*, Letters Received, S352 1867. On Sept. 12, Sherman, Omaha, endorsed this letter. "Respectfully forwarded to Genl Grant,—I was present at Little Rock at the time Gen Reynolds made the first Bond to secure paym't of the interests of the U. S. in Said Road—For Reasons then given by Gen Reynolds I approved his action and do not know why the Secretary of War, Mr Stanton leaned so heavily against this Road—It is at best a poor Concern & Entitled to sympathy. For it & Mr Brinkley I ask Gn Grant to revise the decision of his predecessor in this Case."—AES, *ibid.* See *SED*, 39-1-20.

On Sept. 11, Bvt. Maj. Gen. Daniel H. Rucker, act. q. m. gen., wrote to USG. "I have the honor to forward the letter of R. C. Brinkley, Esq President of the Memphis and Little Rock Rail Road Company dated August 20th 1867. referred to this Office by Brig. and Brevet Major General. E. O. C. Ord, Commanding 4th Military District Vicksburg Miss: August 29th 1867. requesting that the order for the sale of the railroad material received from this road, and advertised to be sold at auction by Bvt: Major. L. Cass. Forsyth under orders from this Department October 1st 1867 may be suspended or postponed; also to return the protest of Mr Brinkley of Sept 9th and his letter of Sept 10th 1867 upon the same subject, and to make the following report in relation thereto. . . . Under instructions from this Department Bvt. Major. L. C. Forsyth. A. Q. M. Little. Rock Ark took possession of the property remaining in the hands of the Company, and has advertised it to be sold at public auction the 1st day of October 1867. In view of the circumstances connected with the indebtedness of this road to the Government, it is respectfully recommended that if the Company will furnish a new bond, in conformity to the requirements of this Dept & with two or more good and sufficient sureties in the sum of two hundred thousand Dollars, approved by the United States District Judge for the State of Arkansas, conditioned to pay to the United States the amount due in the following manner, . . ."—LS, DNA, RG 92, Reports to the Secretary of War (Press). On Sept. 18, Rucker wrote to USG. "Mr. R. C. Brinckley President of the Memphis & Little Rock Railroad Company. having requested that a copy of the enclosed letter from this office to the Secretary of War. dated Sept 13. 1867. and containing his acceptance of the terms & conditions upon which the Railroad Property upon that road. & now offered for sale would be restored to that Company, be furnished him, I respectfully recommend that authority to furnish the same be granted."—LS, *ibid.* On Oct. 29, Rucker wrote to USG. "I have the honor to return herewith the letter of Saml V. Niles Esq., enclosing Power of Attorney authorizing Willis Gaylord Esq., to represent the claim of the Memphis and Little Rock Railroad Company for iron alleged to have been taken from that road by the United States. . . ."—LS, *ibid.*

1867, AUG. 16. To Secretary of the Navy Gideon Welles. "It having been reported to this Office by Brevet Major-General A B Dyer, Chief of Ordnance, that one Thomas J. Burke, who has twice deserted from the Ordnance Detachment at Watertown Arsenal, has enlisted in the U. S. Navy and is now serving at the Charlestown Navy Yard, I have the honor to request that you will issue such instructions as will ensure the delivery of the man to the Commanding Officer Watertown Arsenal, or such other officer as may be designated to receive him that he may be brought to trial for his offenses."—LS, DNA, RG 45, Letters Received from the President. On Aug. 21, Welles wrote to USG. "Your communication of the 16th inst. has been received. The Commandant of the Charlestown Navy Yard has been directed to hold Thomas J. Burke, an alleged deserter from the army subject to your order and to deliver him to such officer as may be designated to receive him."—Copy, *ibid.*, Letters Sent to the President.

1867, AUG. 16. To Bvt. Maj. Gen. Edward D. Townsend. "Issue order assigning Gen. Ingalls to duty ~~with~~ on his Bvt. rank of Maj. Gn."—ANS, DNA, RG 94, ACP, I77 CB 1867.

1867, AUG. 16. Joseph Carroll, Fort Whipple, Va., to USG. "I have the honor to state that I loaned 1st Lt: J, M, Stephenson, 4th u. s. arty, one hundred and twenty five Dolls (including principal & interest) last spring one year ago, since which time I have been unable to obtain even a reply to my communications so indifferent does he appear about the matter. As security for the above amount this officer gave me his pay accounts for the Month of May, last, one year ago, which I presented then for payment, but, Col. Potter, Paymaster, u. s. a., informed me that they could not be settled inasmuch as that Lt: Stephenson's pay had been stopped by an order from the Treasury Dep't. I came to Washington a few days with the hope of getting the matter settled at once, and for that purpose presented the papers to the Paymaster General, who informed me that the officer had drawn his pay for the month for which he had given me his accounts. I am in poor circumstances, and most respectfully ask your influence in my case so that I may return soon as possible to the bosom of my family, Waiting your reply . . ."—ALS, DNA, RG 94, Letters Received, 696C 1867.

1867, AUG. 16.   Bernard H. Nadal, Philadelphia, to USG. "*Private* & *confidential* . . . You may remember my name, I am a Methodist Minister, one of the Editors of the *N. Y. Methodist*, & was lately stationed at Wesley Chapel, Washington. My love of country, & my affection & gratitude to yourself as the chief among her earthly deliverers, must be my apology for this intrusion. My confidence in your integrity is unshaken & perfect. But you now occupy a peculiar position. The loyal people of the country are opposed, almost *en masse*, to President Johnson & his policy. The Methodist Episcopal church shares that opposition *most intensely* and nearly *universally*. I find almost all with whom I am in intercourse reluctantly, expressing fears, dim & undefined, as to your relations to the President and his policy. I am deeply anxious to relieve their fears. Any thing you may say in reply to this will be used precisely as you may direct I write as a lover of my country & of General Grant. I know you will respect my motives."—ALS, USG 3.

1867, AUG. 16.   "A Radical Republican," Newark, to USG. "I am so out of patience this morning after reading the papers and their comments upon Your acceptance of the position of Sec of War, that I can hardly contain myself. Why in the name of manhood do You not let the people know what Your political opinions are? Your have been claimed as a Republican and You are now claimed as a Copperhead. Every Copperhead and Rebel paper in the land are applauding You, while the Republicans are holding their breath, and restraining their indignation in hopes that You will still prove true to You Country and humanity. Generel be honest, and have the courage to let the country know where You Stand. If You are a Copperhead frankly avow it and let all the demons in hell and devils on earth have a glorification over it. If You are a Republican (not of the conservative Stripe) let us know it and we will Stand by You till the Judment trump shall call us before its [—] I do not think I am [so] foolish as to Suppose that these few lines will cause You to open Your lips, but I do hope that You will Show Yourself a man, and let the country know where You Stand. . . My name is of no consequence or I would give to to You."—AL, USG 3.

1867, AUG. 16.   "Many Union Citizens," Baltimore, to USG. "In the presss of business that must of necessity be at present upon you any additional tresspass may seem but ill timed, but my object is simply to *ask your attention* to the manner in which matters are managed at the *Freedman's bureau* in this city   It is controlled by Genl Greogory, aided by a Number of Salelites, among whom, is Col Weigle who has been twice, put out of Service, but has been put back by influnce—The whol arrangement is of the ~~Beaure~~ Bureau is on the most extravagant plan,   They drive a splendid equipage and fare sumptuously, while the poor Negroes are being swindled, and are kept waiting day after day for the pittance due them, wilst the whole is consumed by expenses of board &c &c   Thorough reformation is required, and a discreet conscientius officer placed in charge   There is an old Army officer here without employment who would make an excellent head of this Bureau, this person is a Col Hendrickson. he is a conscentius loyal safe man, and his appntment to the place would give great satisfactn" —AL, DNA, RG 105, Letters Received.

1867, AUG. 17.   President Andrew Johnson to USG. "If there is a vacancy in the 2d Regiment Artillery, as Lieutenant let Edwards G. Fast of District Columbia be appointed to fill it."—Copies (2), DLC-Andrew Johnson. See DNA, RG 94, ACP, F64 CB 1869.

1867, AUG. 17.   George S. Boutwell, Boston, to USG. "I very well know that our personal acquaintance is too slight to warrant me in troubling you with a letter, but the gravity of public affairs compels me to depart from the routine of private life. Your assignment to the War Department does not as an isolated fact disturb the public mind in the least; but the suspension of Mr. Stanton has awakened the most serious apprehensions. For myself I regard the act as the first of a series not unlike those which preceded the civil war of 1861. I will not trouble you with the facts or theories on which I proceed, and I shall be much rejoiced if my apprehensions prove to be unfounded. The purpose of this letter is to implore you to adhere rigidly under all circumstances, to the plan of reconstruction prescribed in the acts of Congress, and to avoid, especially, all commitments to or complications in any antagonistic schemes. Adhering to thats plan you can rely upon a support among the people and in Congress which will enable you to overcome all obstacles; but no man or set of man can sustain successfully any hostile, or different, policy. I do not write because I am in doubt concerning your intentions, but rather that I may pledge you my support in the discharge of the difficult duties that are before you."—ALS, USG 3.

1867, AUG. 17.   Governor Jacob D. Cox of Ohio, Columbus, to USG. "I have the honor to call your attention to the enclosed communication from the Adjutant General of this State to me, covering copy of a letter from him to the Pay Master General U. S. A. and to ask that the Pay Department be instructed ~~to settle~~ that all claims against that department which were prior to July 1st 1867 filed by Ja's C. Wetmore as Ohio State Agent, be settled only with Gen. B. R. Cowen Adjt Gen. of Ohio. The necessity for such direction will be evident to you from the following facts—1st The

State of Ohio has undertaken to collect bounty & back pay claims &c for her volunteer soldiers without charge or expense to the soldier—2d Ja's C. Wetmore, who was an Agent of this State in Washington for the purpose stated, voluntarily resigned such Agency on the 30th June last, & by virtue of the powers vested in me by law, I appointed Gen. Cowen to complete the work of collecting & forwarding to soldiers, at the expense of the State, all claims filed prior to July 1, & remaining uncollected. Gen. Cowen is therefore the *only* person authorized to control said claims so filed by Wetmore when he was State Agent. 3d Wetmore, prior to his resignation, obtained from many Ohio soldiers, powers of Attorney to collect, which he now uses to control those claims, for his own profit, charging fees whilst the State had agreed to do the work *gratis*. Great numbers of letters are daily received from Soldiers, charging that Wetmore obtained such powers of attorney by *fraud*, & by concealment of the fact that the State proposed to collect the claims *gratis* after Wetmore's connection with the Agency should cease. 4th The general rule at all the Departments has been that when a claim was once entrusted to a collector, it should not be transferred to another without the consent of that collector. The State of Ohio is such a collector for her own soldiers, & when they have once entrusted their claims to her I protest against their being controlled by a private claim agent for his own profit. Such a private agent Wetmore now is—He has no official connection with the State whatever. The protection of the Soldiers for whom the *State* has agreed to do this work without charge, makes it necessary for me to request an order that the Pay Department shall recognize no powers of attorney to transfer claims to him *personally* which have heretofore been filed by him as *Agent for this State*, unless in accordance with the rule stated above, *we* consent thereto after inquiry as to whether the soldier has made such transfer with full knowledge of his right to have the collection completed by the State gratis—Knowing that you will unite with me in the desire that the soldier's pittance should not be reduced by the payment of unnecessary fees & commissions, especially when there is any appearance of fraud being used to induce him to transfer the claim from the officers appointed by his own State for the *gratuitous* collection & he is now protesting against such fraud, I feel confident you will not hesitate to make the order required. Requesting advice of your action in the matter, . . ."—LS, DNA, RG 99, Letters Received.

1867, [AUG. *17*].   Thomas J. Durant, Washington, D. C., to USG. "In pursuance of the request made at the close of the letter accompannying this that the views it contains may be laid before you, I beg the favor that you may read it, and return it to me through the Post office that I may compley with the further request of the writer to lay the views also before the Congressional Committee he refers to. The writer of the letter O. B. Hart is one of the oldest, most respectable and most loyal citizens of Florida."— ALS (undated, but received on Aug. 17), DNA, RG 108, Letters Received. Bvt. Brig. Gen. Frederick T. Dent noted on the docket. "Letter of Mr Hart

returned to Mr Durant on 19th of August as requested"—ANS, *ibid.*
According to the docket, the enclosure defended Col. John T. Sprague.

1867, AUG. 17.   Samuel H. Huntington, chief clerk, U.S. Court of Claims,
to USG. "Herewith is enclosed an order of the Court of Claims for evidence
from the War Department, to be used on the hearing of the case of Moses
B. Bramhall vs the United States now pending in said Court."—ALS, DNA,
RG 94, Letters Received, 704C 1867. Huntington enclosed a court order
to USG. "You are hereby requested to furnish to the Court of Claims, that
the same may be used as evidence in the above entitled cause any information in the War Department as to the seizure of certain bales of cotton at
Savannah Georgia, by Lieut. Colo. R. C. Ransom A. Q. M. in the months
of March and April 1865 in the name of Hill Gowdy, as to where they
were stored—by whom seized—how many bales in each place, and what
was done with the same after seizure—also to furnish transcripts of the
books of seizure and shipment of any cotton under the name of said Hill
Gowdy during said months of March and April 1865."—Copy, *ibid.* Additional papers are *ibid.* See *HRC,* 43-1-757.

1867, AUG. 17.   B. H. Jenks, Philadelphia, to USG. "Can you inform me
of the whereabouts of Major Theo. Yates of Milwaukie—"—Telegram
received (at 1:00 P.M.), DNA, RG 107, Telegrams Collected (Bound).

1867, AUG. 17.   Martin R. M. Wallace, Chicago, to USG. "I have the
honor to present herewith recommendations for L. P. Griswold for a Cadetship at West Point—I am sure he is worthy & competent—and if consistent
& proper I respectfully ask your name & influence in his favor—"—ALS,
DNA, RG 94, Correspondence, USMA.

1867, AUG. 18, 7:50 P.M.   To Bvt. Maj. Gen. John Pope, Atlanta. "If
Maj. S. E. St. Onge services can be dispensed with without detrim give
him ninety days leave."—ALS (telegram sent), DNA, RG 107, Telegrams
Collected (Bound); telegram sent, *ibid.*; copies, *ibid.*, RG 108, Telegrams
Sent; DLC-USG, V, 56.

1867, AUG. 19.   Md. AG John S. Berry, Baltimore, to USG. "On the
13th of June I had the honor to make requisition for certain Ordnance and
Ordnance Stores: and failing to receive an answer, I repeated the requisition on the 3rd inst. In answer to which General A. B. Dyer chief of Ordnance U. S. A. writes me on the 5th inst 'that he has referred my letter of
the 3rd inst. to the Secretary of War in connection with my requisition of
the 13th of June last; which has not yet been returned.' I am directed by
the Governor to call your attention to the same and to respectfully ask that
your order for the ~~same~~ issue thereof be made as early as practicable"—
LS (press), Hall of Records, Annapolis, Md.

1867, AUG. 19.   Mary Mitchell, St. Louis, to USG. "I have deemed it to
be my duty to call your attention to the gross abuse and outrageous treatment which I have recd at the hands of an officer of the U. S. Army and I
ask that you will cause an investigation to be made as to the representations
which I make and if you find them supported by proof that you will take
such action in the premises as shall prevent a repetition of like treatment
to others—I will premise my statemet by saying that I am a colored
woman, which fact I have no doubt is the only reason that would Justify
in *his own mind* the conduct of the officer of whom I make this complaint
but I have reason to believe that with you this cannot be offered as an excuse, since the distinction *of caste* thank God, has been done away with in
this country forever—In April 1866 I was employed by Capt & Bvt Lt. Col.
A. M. Powell 31st U. S. Infty who was then stationed at Jefferson Barrack
near this City as a domestic in his family with the understanding that I was
to proceed with his family to Fort Rice Dacota T—which I did—In the
early part of June last Col—Powell was ordered to proceed to Fort Stevenson to which place I declined to accompany himself and family, whereupon
Col—P—theatened to whip & cowhide me for saying that he had used the
cowhide on such as myself before and that he would burst my head but
what he would compel me to accompany him to Fort Bertold (now Fort
Stevenson D. T.), and I was obliged to secrete myself to prevent force
being used to compel obedience to his command—The commanding officer
caused a detail of soldiers to made to search the quarters for me to aid Col
P—to compel me to accompany him—I was fortunate enough to make my
escape—As I was under no obligations to Col P—and was entitled to the
rights and privileges of a free citizen I deem his attempt to coerce me
under the circumstances a gross outrage and an attempt to override the
law of the land—which as an officer of the U. S.—Army he should have
been the first to see enforced,   The fact that this officers comes from an
ex-slave state, and that he has been one of the Lords of my race and used
the cowhide before should not, I think you will admit, protect him—&
moreover he refuses to pay the wages due me amounting $155—which no
doubt grows out of the fact that heretofore such services have not been
remunerated—I enclose certificates as to the truth of statements which I
make—I also refer particularly to Dr B. Knickerbocker Post Surgeon also
to Corporal O. P. Fluke. Sergt Crowley Co. B. Sergt Henry Co. G.—"—L
(signed by mark), DNA, RG 94, Letters Received, 1377M 1867.

1867, AUG. 19.   William Smith, Pittsburgh, to USG. "During the Month
of November 1866, proposals Were issued for furnishing the Goverment,
with Cast Iron Head Blocks for the National Cemeteries, bids were to be
opened on 30th day of that Month, and Contract to be awarded not later
than Jany 1st 1867. In accordance with which I sent in Proposals for the
Whole Number, and at that time it was admitted by the bidders that I was
entitled to, and would undoubtedly receive the Contract. Since that time I
have made large additions to my works expecting to do the Work, but up

to the present time, the Contract remains unawarded. As a matter of simple justice to the other bidders, as well as Myself, and without ~~Casting~~ being desirous of *Casting any reflections on your predecessor*, I most respectfully ask that at your earliest convenience you will give this matter which is so important to me, your careful consideration; feeling confident that had these proposals been in your hands at first, I would have long since been awarded the Contract. . . . P. S. Form of Proposal I herewith annex."— ALS, DNA, RG 94, Letters Received, 827S 1867. The enclosure is *ibid.* On Dec. 19, Bvt. Maj. Gen. Daniel H. Rucker, act. q. m. gen., wrote to USG reporting that Smith had not been the lowest bidder.—LS, *ibid.*, RG 92, Reports to the Secretary of War (Press). On Dec. 30, Rucker wrote to USG. "In connection with my letter of the 19th inst on the subject of permanent marks for soldiers &c. (Par. X,) I have the honor to transmit herewith *five wooden patterns for marble headblocks*, which have been prepared from drawing, marked C. C., (forwarded with the above letter;) and are designed to furnish a lighter and cheaper block than the marble block sent over in a separate letter of that date. Your attention is respectfully invited to the statement of Mr. Edwd Clark, Architect of the Quartermaster Department, (a copy of which is enclosed) that the average cost of blocks of this size, sawed from marble and including lettering, will not exceed $1.50 each."—LS, *ibid.*, RG 107, Letters Received from Bureaus.

1867, AUG. 20. To Secretary of the Treasury Hugh McCulloch. "I have the honor to enclose herewith a statement of the expenditures incurred by the Qr. Mrs. Dept. of the Army, in maintaining and enforcing *Quarantine Regulations* at points along the Southern coast amounting to $58.641 83/100: accompanied by vouchers, and a copy of the letter of the Quarter Master General of the 17th instant, transmitting the same, and to request that you cause the amount stated to be transferred to the credit of the Quartermaster's Department."—Copy, DNA, RG 107, Letters Sent to the President. On Aug. 17, Bvt. Maj. Gen. Daniel H. Rucker, act. q. m. gen., had written to USG. "I have the honor to transmit herewith a statement of the expenditures incurred by the Quartermasters Department in maintaining and enforcing Quarantine Regulations at points along the Southern Coast, amounting to Fifty eight thousand Six hundred and forty one 83/100 Dollars, ($58,641.83) . . ."—LS, *ibid.*, RG 92, Reports to the Secretary of War (Press). On Aug. 23, McCulloch wrote to USG. "I have the honor to acknowledge receipt of your communication 20 instant, covering abstracts and vouchers for expenses incurred in the maintenance of quarantine on the Southern Coast amounting to $58.641.83. As it appears on examination of these vouchers, &c., that a considerable portion of the amount charged is for expenses incurred prior to May 26, 1866, the date of the approval of the Act authorizing the Treasury Department to assist in the enforcement of the Quarantine, and as the said Act does not provide for the payment of expenses incurred prior to its approval, this Department is obliged to return the said accounts, and to request that vouchers for only that portion incurred subsequent to May 26, 1866, and prior to the first Monday in January, be submitted; credit for which expenditures will be at once given the Quartermasters Department."—Copy, *ibid.*, RG 56, Letters Sent. On Oct. 14, Rucker wrote to USG. "I have the honor to return herewith, statement of expenditures incurred by the Quartermasters Department in maintaining Quarantine regulations along the Southern Coast, amounting to Forty nine thousand, nine hundred and ninety seven 32/100 ($49,997 32/100) Dollars. . . ."—LS, *ibid.*, RG 92, Reports to the Secretary of War (Press). On Oct. 18, USG wrote to McCulloch. "I have the honor to return herewith, modified as requested, the abstracts and vouchers for expenses incurred in the maintenance of *Quarantine on the Southern Coast*, which were originally transmitted to the Treas'y. Dept. on the 20th Aug. last & returned for modification on the 23d of the same month, with request that you will direct the transfer of the amount ($49,997.32) to the credit of the Quartermaster's Dept."—Copy, *ibid.*, RG 107, Letters Sent to the President. On Oct. 24, McCulloch wrote to USG. "Your letter 18th inst, with accompanying account and vouchers for disbursements made by the War Department in enforcing the Quarantine and Health laws on the Southern Coast, between the 26th May '66, and the first Monday in January 1867, has been received, and referred to the accounting officers of the Treasury for examination and settlement, with instructions to carry the amount found due to the credit of the Quartermasters Department, as requested in your communication."—LS, *ibid.*, RG 92, Letters Received.

1867, AUG. [*20*].   USG endorsement. "The Adj Gn. will refer copy of this to Sec. of the Treas."—AES (marked as received by the AGO on Aug. 20), DNA, RG 94, Letters Received, 595W 1867. Written on a copy of a telegram of Aug. 19 from George E. Wallace, Evansville, Ind., to USG. "There was several Government boats burned at Johnsonville Tenn during the war.   will pay all Expenses divide with the Gov't for machinery in said boats. Refer to O. P. Morton Gov C B Baker & A. G. Porter Indianapolis Answer"—Telegram received (at 3:25 P.M.), *ibid.*, RG 107, Telegrams Collected (Bound); copy, *ibid.*, RG 94, Letters Received, 595W 1867. On Aug. 26, Andrew Wallace, Indianapolis, wrote to USG. "My son George. E. Wallace of Evansville in one that wishes to get the contract of removing the Machieny out of the goverment Boats burned during the war at Johnsonville Tennesse   you will find him a thorough going man and if any man can acomplish it he will   he was late Major of 79 Ind vol and was first Liutenant Co—A—13 Ind vol at Batle of Rich Mountian and Capton Company A 79 Ind *vol* Battle of Mupheyburrough   hoping he may be successfull . . ."—ALS, *ibid.*, RG 92, Letters Received. On the same day, Act. Governor Conrad Baker of Ind. wrote to USG recommending Wallace.—LS, *ibid.* On Sept. 9, Bvt. Maj. Gen. Daniel H. Rucker, act. q. m. gen., wrote to USG. "I have the honor to return herewith communication of Hon. Conrad Baker Acting Governor of Indiana, dated August 26, 1867: enclosing application of George E. Wallace for the contract for removing the machinery, from the Government steamboats burnt during the war at Johnsonville Tennessee. In reply I would respectfully state that authority has already been given Brevet Major General Thomas Swords Assistant Quartermaster General, at Louisville Kentucky, by this office, to award the contract for removing Government wrecks in the Tennessee River to Mr George Shoecraft, the United States to recieve one third (⅓) of the proceeds realized from the sale of the property recovered."— LS, *ibid.*

1867, AUG. 20.   Bvt. Brig. Gen. Morris S. Miller, deputy q. m. gen., to USG. "In August 1864 a General Court Martial of which I was President, was convened at West Point for the trial of Cadet Petriken. By this Court several Cadets and Soldiers were tried. I would respectfully request, in justice to the Court and to the prisoners tried, that the usual orders promulgating the Proceedings of this Court may now be published."—ALS, DNA, RG 94, Letters Received, 1244M 1864. On Oct. 28, Miller again wrote to USG on this subject.—ALS, *ibid.* The enclosure is *ibid.* On Sept. 24, 1868, Bvt. Maj. Gen. Edward D. Townsend endorsed additional papers. "Respectfully returned to the Secretary of War with the following report: According to my recollection the late Secretary, Hon. E. M. Stanton, restored to the Mily Acady a cadet named Black, who had been summarily dismissed by Genl Tower, the Superintendent. As soon as Cadet Black returned to West Point, Genl Tower ordered him before the Court Martial then in session there, of which Genl M. S. Miller was President, and Lieut. C. C. Parsons, Judge Advocate. The Secretary learning that the trial was going on ordered it to stop & the case to be dismissed. The Court nevertheless decided it to be their duty under their oath to conclude the case which was done and the proceedings were forwarded. The Secretary relieved Genl Tower as Superintendent dissolved the Court, dismissed Lt. Parsons the Judge Advocate, and ordered Genl Miller to duty at New Orleans—This course was supposed to be as a mark of displeasure at the disregard of his orders concerning Cadet Black—The Secretary retained the proceedings and it is not known what became of them. Genl Miller has several times since made a similar application to this, and has been verbally informed that the proceedings cannot be found, and that it was the intention of Mr. Stanton that they should not be published, with which intention Genl Grant when acting Secretary would not interfere. It is not seen how any thing more could or ought to be done in the matter."—AES, *ibid.*

1867, AUG. 20.   Maj. Gen. Philip H. Sheridan, New Orleans, to USG. "I enclose herewith an application for a brevet of Brigadier General in the Regular Army for Lieutenant Colonel Maurice Maloney 16th Infantry. You no doubt recollect him in connection with the 4th Infantry. He is one of the best soldiers I have ever met and is a pure and upright man. It would be a great gratification to him if he could obtain this brevet for his services at the siege of Vicksburg: and especially from your hands. If you can give

him this brevet, you will confer a great favor on your obedient servant"—
LS, DNA, RG 94, ACP, 100 1872. On the same day, Sheridan wrote a
similar letter to the AG.—LS, *ibid.* On Oct. 15, USG endorsed this letter.
"Not approved"—ES, *ibid.*

1867, AUG. 20.   David A. Burr, Washington, D. C., to USG. "I am informed that a Special order has been issued from the War Dept. directing
a Board of Officers to convene in New York City to examine & report upon
the various form of knapsacks & other accoutrements which may be presented, with a view to the adoption of the best for Army use—Please inform
me when this Board will convene & with such information respecting the
same as you may have, relating to the presentation of articles for their
examination—"—ALS, DNA, RG 94, Letters Received, 738B 1867.

1867, AUG. 20.   Frederick L. P. Fogg, Providence, R. I., to USG. "Frederick L. P. Fogg to relieve the Secretary of War from Excessive toil would
be industrious Energetic & trustworthy if ordered to come & assist him as
Clerk—Please. sir. to reply promptly at my Expense."—Telegram received
(at 3:45 P.M.), DNA, RG 107, Telegrams Collected (Bound).

1867, AUG. 20.   M. J. Gross, Cincinnati, to USG. "My husband 1st Lieut
Frank. P. Gross, left last evening for Washington for the purpose of making an effort to obtain an appointment in the Regular Army. Your Father
who is an old and warm friend of my Fathers family gave him a letter of
introduction to you, his acquaintence with my husband being but a slight
one, he well knew my first husband Mr Parrish. Gen'l I know it is not
according to regulations for a wife to interfere in these matters, but I am
anxious for my husbands promotion, and I know he is deserving, he has
ever been a good soldier and an efficient officer. Will you not give my
husband an appointment? It is in your power so to do and I a wife ask this
great favor [a]t yours hands."—ALS, DNA, RG 94, ACP, 397 1873.
Frank P. Gross was appointed 2nd lt., 9th Cav., as of Aug. 9. On Jan. 1,
1872, Gross, Fort McKavett, Tex., wrote to USG. "I humbly approach
your Excellency at this time to solicit the appointment of 'Military Store
Keeper United States Army',   I am actuated in requesting this favor at
your Excellencie's hands by a physical disability under which I labor, and
which seriously interferes with my efficiency as a Cavalry Officer. The
medical certificates accompanying this paper will inform your Excellency
of the nature of my injuries and how received. In view of the above, and
the further fact that in a few months I will have completed ten years of
service, I trust your Excellency may be induced to favorably consider the
claims of your humble petitioner. I present this petition to your Excellency
through General W. H Browne of Washington to whom I would respectfully refer, for a knowledge of my character, as also to accompanying letter
of Colonel Abner Doubleday 24th Infantry, my present Commandg, Officer."—ALS, *ibid.* On Jan. 26, William H. Browne, Washington, D. C.,

wrote to USG recommending Gross.—ALS, *ibid.* On Feb. 8, Louisa Morrow, Augusta, Ky., wrote to USG. "Permit me to ask another favor, your (duly appreciated) kindness in the past, has given me courage to address you in behalf of my Soninlaw Lieut Frank P. Gross, who a few months ago while on a *Scout* Hernia or rupture developed, and is, therefore unfit for *active Cavalry duty*, my wish is, if compatible with your position, and duty, that you appoint him Military Storekeeper   Lieut Gross has been in the service, (and is a sober man) ten years, and nearly five of that time on the frontier, as an Officer, as otherwise his record is an honorable one   having cherish'd for many long years the warmest friendship for your venerable father, and family, I trust this, and the fact of my being the widow, of an honor'd Minister of your own church, will entitle my petition to some consideration; an apology for this, and a prayr that God may bless you, and yours, . . ."—ALS, *ibid.* No appointment followed.

1867, AUG. 20.   William A. Hollingsworth, Philadelphia, to USG. "A splendid chance offers for retrieving yourself—Embrace it.—Resign—"— Telegram received (at 10:40 A.M.), DNA, RG 107, Telegrams Collected (Bound).

1867, AUG. 20.   T. W. Tallmadge, Columbus, Ohio, to USG. "I would respectfully represent that on the 27th Day of Dec. 1865 I forwarded to Hon E. M. Stanton Sec. of War, The claim of John Cavanaugh Priv. Co. "G" 4th Regt. Mich. Vol. Cavalry, for his portion of the reward for the Capture of Jeff Davis—Since which time I have not heard from it. Would respectfully ask that said claim recieve early attention"—ALS, DNA, RG 94, Letters Received, 243T 1867.

1867, AUG. 20.   James W. Webb, Petropolis, Brazil, to USG. "You will doubtless, be surprised at recieving a letter from me, and that too, upon political matters; but when I tell you in advance, that I do not expect or desire any reply to it, but simply wish you to ~~think~~ reflect upon what I write, you will, I am certain, not be annoyed at my addressing you. I entered the ~~Army~~ artillery at 17, and resigned when Adjutant of the old 3d Infantry, in 1827; to aid in electing Genl Jackson to the Presidency,— without one thought upon the fact, that he was the candidate of the Democracy, while I was born a *Federalist*, and always was, am now, and *ever will be*, opposed to ~~Universal~~ unrestricted suffrage. My doctrine has always been, that the true test for the exercise of the suffrage, is *intelligence*; and that no man should be permitted to vote, who cannot read and write; and that all who can,—that is, all freemen, without regard to color, should be permitted to vote. Hence, I always opposed ~~naturalizing Foreign ignorance~~ giving the suffrage to Foreign or Domestic ignorance, while I insisted that our free Negro in New York, should vote if he could read and write; and be excluded from the exercise of the suffrage if he could not,

even if he were worth two hundred & fifty thousand Dollars, instead of
~~$250~~ being entitled to vote if he is worth $250, *without any other qualification.* And hence, in a letter addressed to President Johnson, on the 14th
August 1865, three months after ~~having~~ recieving the intelligence of
~~Presidt~~ the assassination of President Lincoln, I advocated the equality of
all men before the law, without regard to color; and the restriction of the
suffrage to those and those only, who could read and write. I enclose an
extract from that letter. You will at a glance then, understand my past and
present position, and your own good sense must determine of what value
are counsels from such a quarter; even if the writer be sixty five years of
age, and has spent forty years of that period in studying his fellow citizens,
their feelings, their prejudices, their principles and their modes of giving
expression to them   From 1827 to 1861, I was the proprietor and only
responsible editor of the Courier & Enquirer; and from 1832 when I abandoned the support of Gen. Jackson because he ~~supported~~ abandoned me
and the principles to which I was pledged in supporting his election 1828,
I gave notice in future, I was a Party man just so far as Party was *necessary*
to carry out the principles I advocated; and no farther. And in consequence,
in my own state, whenever my party nominated for Governor or Mayor of
New York, a man whose principles were at war with mine, I opposed him
and my party, till they returned to their senses. During this long period of
political life, I was in every sense of the term a *National* Politician; while I
left State & County politics, to such men as *Weed Greeley* & others. I may
safely say that there is no man living to-day, who during the last forty
years, (except those spent here,) has been so intimately connected with all
the men and measures of that period as myself. Consequently if I am not
very much below mediocrity in talent and observation, and if experience be
of any value,—I ought to be as well qualified as most men, to estimate the
present and predict the future. There is another consideration in favour of
my exercising a calm and discriminating judgement upon our National
affairs. Absent from the country since July 1861, with the exception of a
few months in '65, '6, and at the same time thoroughly posted in regard
to passing events, but not mixed up with, or influenced by them, I am like
one standing on a great elevation, calmly observing the fierce battle raging
in the valley at my feet. I am consequently, totally disconnected with each
and every faction of men into which our country is divided; while I can
perceive friends and associates of decided ability and good intentions, in
each and every party and faction. Before the war I opposed the extension
of slavery into free territory; but at the same time, I opposed Abolitionism
all my life, because it was at war with the Constitution which protected
slavery within the slave states, as an institution which belonged solely to,
and was under the exclusive control of, the People of the states where it
existed. But when the Institution of slavery set itself up *against* the Government and the Union which protected and within proper limits defended
it, I said to President Lincoln 'the Constitution was called into being to
preserve the Union, *not* the *Union* to preserve the Constitution. The Con-

stitution was a means to an *end*; and that end, was the perpetuity of the *Union*. If then, at any time, it becomes necessary to trample under foot the Constitution in order to preserve the Union, do so without any hesitation whatever. If one or the other, must go by the board, let it be the *Constitution*; which then, will have failed in its object,—which would viz, to uphold and preserve the Constitution. When our Fathers discovered that the old articles of Confederation, were insufficient to preserve the Union which they had created, they threw them aside as so much waste paper, and adopted our present Constitution. That has accomplished wonders. It is now undergoing a severe trial. God grant it may be equal to the crisis; but if not, that too, must be thrown aside as of no avail. it was made to It was made to to preserve the Union; and by that test it must stand or fall. It is manifest to all, that to preserve the Union, Slavery must be abolished and put down by proclamation. The act is one of *necessity;* and if so, you have no right, and if so you have no right to inquire if it is or is *not* constitutional, to issue such a Proclamation. If one's wife or child is certain to die under the hands of the Family physician and can be saved by calling in a stranger, what sane man hesitates? And in like manner even if in *words*, the Constitution forbade the issuing such a Proclamation as is necessary to do away with Slavery, yet if you deemed such a Proclamation *necessary* to preserve the Union, your paramount duty would be to issue the Proclamation and leave the result to God. But such a Proclamation, in my judgement is not unconstitutional. Slaves are held to be "goods & chattels" and all the "goods and chattels of the *Rebels* have been confiscated by Law. Confiscated to whom? To the United States. All Slaves then, are the property of the United States; and consequently, it is your *Constitutional right* to liberate them by Proclamation, and and thus you can save the Union, and at the same time respect the *Constitution*' When I wrote thus, I was as I am now, *a Conservative Republican*, an old line Whig, who gave to that party its *name*. There is no Radical and no Democratic blood in my veins; and I see far more plainly than those who at home are engaged in the great warfare of reconstruction, the *dangers* which beset the Union at every turn. The approaching Presidential election is to be a great crisis in our affairs; and there is too much reason to fear, *that terminate as it may; it will be full of danger and productive of evil.* There are probably fifty candidates for the Presidency, without any one of them of either Party having a reasonable chance of success. But suppose that one from each party, all were finally agreed upon and selected, what prudent man of ordinary judgement, is prepared to say that the election of either, would not leave the country in as bad a state as it is now? What man of ordinary intelligence does not know, that both candidates would be so trammelled by their surroundings— so hounded on by the Ultra Radicals of both Parties, that the one elected, would enter upon the discharge of his duties so hampered by pledges and promises,—. and so committed by the course of the contest, both in regard to men and measures, that our great Country would be as far from peace as ever, and sound Republican principles lie buried so deep beneath the Radi-

calism and Demagogueism of the day that God only knows, what may be
the future of our Re-United States. I know that our people who are labouring so zealously, each in his way in what he deems a patriotic cause, do not
see what is perfectly transparent to me, a mere looker-on guided by a whole
life-time of political experience. They would hoot at me were I to tell them,
that of all the Candidates named for the Presidency, there is not one who
if elected would ensure the Peace, quiet & prosperity of the Country; and
yet one and all of them would be willing to admit this fact ~~with~~ in regard
to every candidate except his own. With regard to the Presidency, I have
said and published for twenty years past that if it were offered me I would
not accept it. And of all the men in our Country you General are the last,
who guided by considerations of *Self*, can afford to take it. It is at best the
most laborious and most thankless office in our Country; and even in a
pecuniary point of view, as well as socially considered, and bearing in mind
your age and chances of a long life, to accept of the Presidency, would
involve on your part a *sacrifice* such as no man in our Country has ever
been called upon to make. But you General, who have so frequently been
ready to sacrifice your *life* for your country, are not the man to shrink from
a sacrifice of your *time* and comfort, and future quiet to the demands of
that country, if once convinced that your work has only been half finished;
and that to complete it you are to follow in the footsteps of WASHINGTON;
and by accepting the Presidency, consolidate and place on a solid basis, the
Institutions you saved from annihilation. Nobody can doubt that when
WASHINGTON accepted the Presidency, he yearned most sincerely for the
quiet of domestic life. But he recognised the fact that upon him devolved
the duty of preserving in civil life, the liberties he had achieved by his
success in the field. Doubtless there was more or less necessity for his so
thinking and acting; and the great success of our Government and Country,
is fairly attributable to the fact, that he launched the Ship of State and for
eight years, guided her on an unknown sea, and amid shoals and quick-
sands of which there existed no chart. But great as was the necessity for
his thus yielding to the requirements of the hour and the wishes of the
people, the demand upon you to walk in his footsteps and follow his example is a thousand times greater and far more imperative. Our Country has
increased in population ten fold; our wealth a thousand fold; Our flag covers
nearly a Continent, and our boundaries extend from the Atlantic to the
Pacific. A mighty effort has crushed the greatest rebellion known to the
civilized world; but the achievment has cost more than a million of lives,
not less than five thousand millions of treasure and the demoralization in-
separable from a great civil war of more than four years duration. During
the struggle the Ship of State, (as well as the sober judgement of our
People,) has got loose from its moorings and is all afloat; and the first duty
of those who saved her from floundering, is to get her safely re-anchored
in Smooth waters. And precisely this has become the duty of General
Grant. It is 'on this line' he is to perfect his work and none other. I have
not one word of flattery to convey to you. The People very justly attribute

to you the suppression of the Rebellion; and the people in the long run, are always just and always *right*. This is *fact*, not assertion; and the people, regardless of Party and political creeds, and in defiance of political aspirants of the best and worst principles, and of no principles at all, stand ready to make you the President of the *Country* and not of a *Party*; and that too, without stopping to enquire what are your principles?, what your ante-cedents,? and what your probable course in regard to the *isms* of the day? They have confidence in your *Patriotism*, and are grateful for your services in saving the Union by putting down the Rebellion. They required no declaration of principles from WASHINGTON, and they will demand none from *you*. They had confidence in his Patriotism and faith in his talents; and they elected him their President. And what they did by him, they are prepared to do by you, *if* you will let them. Have you a right to thwart them? Look carefully at the state of the country, and ask yourself if you know of any candidate in either party, whose election by that party, would give peace and quiet to our country, and restore to our Institutions stability, by replacing as their base, sound, liberal, Republican, and yet Conservative principles, as distinct from *Democratic Radicalism*, no matter by whom or under what name or garb professed? And if you cannot find any such man and knowing as you do, that you have only to say you will take the Presi-dency, and it will be conferred on you,—is it not your duty, your *imperative* duty from which you may not shrink—to avow your readiness to become the People's Candidate for the Presidency? Once elected you would have the ability and I doubt not the inclination to do what is right and whatever the best interests of the whole country require. I have said my say. To me it appears as if the time for action is near at hand, but how near, you and your friends about you, are best qualified to judge. I have great faith in the principles and political sagacity of your friend *Washburne*; and if you were to show him this letter I think he would agree with me, that it is at least entitled to your candid consideration. I neither expect nor desire you to answer it; but I request you will drop me a single line acknowledging its rects, in order that I may know it has reached its destination."—DfS, CtY.

On Sept. 30, 1868, Webb, Rio de Janeiro, wrote to USG. "If I were not morally certain, that before this can reach ~~you~~ Washington, you will have been elected President of the United States, I certainly should not trouble you to read what I am about to write; and if elected, it would be idle to repeat my well grounded convictions, that the People have vindicated their intelligence, by seelecting for their Chief Magistrate, the only man in our whole country—no matter what his talents or how great his political expediency~~rience~~—whose election, would, of necessity, *heal* the wounds in-flicted by the rebellion, and accommodate the Ship of State to the new order of things, which, by vindicating our Nationality, exhibiting our inexhaust-able resources, and eradicating from our ~~Escutcheon~~ Institutions the only blot upon our Escutcheon, has rendered us at once, the ~~freest~~ freest and the greatest Power on Earth. It was fitting that he who did so much to ~~the~~ ~~achievement of our greatness~~ preserve to us ~~glorious~~ our national *Union*,

and the principles upon which it is based, should be selected by a grateful
People, to consolidate and ~~adapt~~ adapt our Institutions, to the changes they
have undergone, and ~~to~~ restore that love of order and supremacy of the civil
over the Military ~~Power which a~~ authority, which every great Rebellion in
the history of the world, has, of necessity, disturbed. All such disturbances,
~~in times past have however~~, in times past, when put down by the state,
have resulted in increasing the power of the few at the expense of the many.
But not so with the great Rebellion in which you played so conspicuous a
part. The Government and our Institutions, achieved a triumph, ~~never
before~~ rarely witnessed in a struggle of such unparrelled dimensions; and
yet, we emerge from that struggle, with the liberties of the People ~~enlarged~~
greatly enlarged, and better defined and protected, than ever before; with
a Constitution ~~altered and~~ amended and wonderfully improved in the interest of human nature—and at the same time, the authority of the Government strengthed and its efficientcy developed. That this should be ~~possible~~
the result of a great rebellion, is almost incredible; and yet no intelligent
observer of passing events, will pretend to deny, that the principles of
human freedom have been extended,—that the right of every man to par-
ticipate in the Government under which he lives, has been, for the first
time, clearly established,—that the Constitution bequeathed to us by our
fathers, has been materially and wonderfully improved, by amendments
based upon liberty and equality among all men—~~and~~ And, at the same time,
the arm of the General Government has been strengthened, by establishing
the Constitutional rights of the People, speaking through their immediate
Reprentatives, to thrust aside certain crude and extreme notions of 'state
rights' & 'executive supremacy', which for nearly a Century, have hampered the free working of our Institutions, and fostered and protected in
our midst, under the very shadow of the Capital, a cruel mockery of every
line and every sentiment in that admirable Declaration of Independence
under which our fathers marched to liberty for themselves, only to fix more
firmly, the shackels of *Slavery* upon an ignorant & dependent race, ~~whose—~~
A race whose very existance as human beings we ignored, by constituting
them *chattles*, and treating them as beasts of burthen; and then, attempted
to justify our conduct, by pointing to the degradation we had produced &
fostered, as evidence that the character of the Slave, made the institution of
slavery a necessity. But I am wandering from my subject. I perceive that
Senator *Patterson* of Tennessee, has introduced a Bill into congress, for
the establishment of a Diplomatic Corps; and although I have only ~~read~~
seen that feature of it, which classifies the Ministers into different grades
of the same rank, and increases their salaries accordingly, I am convinced,
that want of experiance and ~~the~~ lack of opportunitiesy to study the working
of the system of the great Powers of Europe, have rendered the contemplated changes crude and defective. The subject itself, is one of grave
National importance, and as no one person in the United States, can have
so deep an interest in its successful settlement as yourself, I do not hesitate
to lay before you my experiance. I have always been the advocate of a Dip-

lomatic corps; and from 1827 to 1861, as the sole responsible Editor of the
Courier & Enquirer, ~~I never suffered an opportunity to escape~~ for a period
of thirty four years, I never failed, when opportunity presented, to advocate
the *policy* & *necessity* of such a measure. And if I had never served in a
Diplomatic capacity, and were now editing a leading Public Press, I doubt
not, but Mr *Patterson's* Bill would meet my earnest support, as I perceive
it does the support of the New York *Times,*—whose Editor learned his
Profession in my Office. Unquestionably, Senator *Patterson's* purposes are
patriotic and worthy of all respect and consideration; but a single fact in
the brief synopsis of his Bill that has come under my observation, clearly
demonstrates, that in ignorance of the subject himself, he is but the mouth
piece of selfish and interested parties, who do not look solely to the good
of the service. . . ."—ADfS, *ibid.*

On Feb. 20, 1869, Webb, New York City, wrote to USG. "I sail for
Rio de Janeiro tomorrow; and of course, will not be in the country, when
you enter upon the duties of the Presidency. I have been urged to remain
here, until after the 4th March, but if I were to do so, I could not reach Rio
until *after* my leave of absence had expired,—and I can ask no favours of
those now in authority, my present leave having been refused until my
Physicians certified, that to remain in Brazil during the *Rainy* Season,
would be *fatal.* The simple fact that I will not be here to make known my
wishes *after* your inauguration, will, I presume, be a sufficient apology, for
addressing you at this time. In 1861, it was so well understood that I would
recieve the appointment of Naval Officer of this Port, that I had virtually,
no competitor for it; or at least, none of any consideration,—the Naval office
having always been considered the reward of elderly gentlemen, who had
rendered unquestionable public and Political services, during a long period
of years. *Mrs* Lincoln gave it away to one unknown to all of us; and President Lincoln confirmed the gift, as he told Senator Hamlin and others, in
entire ignorance of the importance of the place. I am now, an applicant for,
and solicit at your hands, the office, which in 1861, my friends supposed I
had fairly won, by *thirty four* years services as the sole responsible Editor
of the Courier & Enquirer in support of the conservative Republicanism of
the day; which, in my judgement, is the *conservatism* of the old Whig
Party, to which I gave its name. An absence of nearly Eight years from
the Country, leaves me without any personal claims upon our present Senators; and I have contented myself with announcing to them my wishes as
a mark of respect. Senator *Conklin,* is, I am informed, long since committed in favour of a member of the House of Reprentatives who does
not reside in this City; and Senator Morgan informs a friend, that he is
pledged to support Mr Conklin's candidate for the Naval office, *whoever
he may be*! To Gov. *Fenton* I am personally, almost unknown; and one of
whom I never heard until now, claims to have the promise of *his* influence.
I therefore, base my pretentions for the place, solely upon your estimate of
my fitness, upon my public services prior to 1861, and upon the faithful
discharge of all my public duties since then,—alike in my visit to the Em-

peror of the French in 1861, at my Post of duty in Brazil, and in negotiating *uninstructed*, the peaceful withdrawal of the French Troops from Mexico; when the present administration had utterly failed to accomplish that vitally important object   At the Chicago Convention in 1860, I was in favour of Mr Seward's nomination to the Presidency. Mr Greely and his friends, were opposed; and Gov. Morgan, then looking to the Senator-Ship, was *neutral*. In the Courier & Enquirer I attributed Seward's defeat to Morgan's neutrali[t]y and it appears he never forgave me, although he was indebted to me for his subsequent nomination and election as Governor;— not from any affection I bore the man, but because the triumph of our principles by the election of *Lincoln*, forbid the punishment of an unfriendly act towards Mr Seward; who was *then*, a Republican. When Mr. Lincoln became President, my Son-in-law, who is a cousin of Senator Morgan, wrote to him on the subject of my appointment to the Naval Office, without my knowledge. His answer, which I enclose, is conclusive, in regard to my position at the time I went to Brazil; and although he had not then forgiven my habit of frankly speaking my thoughts, our social relations have always been kind and agreeable   With referance to the manner in which I have discharged my duties in Brazil, I am content to refer to the archives of the Department of State. I was one of those who urged upon Mr. Lincoln his Proclamation abolishing *Slavery*; to which you will find a reference from in the despatch of Mr Seward, enclosed. And I also enclose another despatch from the Department, in which the President expresses his general approval of my conduct of the affairs of my Legation. And more recent events, familiar to the Public, demonstrate, that I have not ceased to discharge faithfully, all my duties in Brazil. Certain it is, each & every one of my official acts, has been approved. I cannot complain, that in my absence, and in ignorance of my wishes, some prominent Republican friends, should have committed themselves to others; but it is a satisfaction to be assured, as I am, that if relieved from their committals, they should desire my success. I have no right to ask more of them; and Attorney General *Evarts*, Gov. *Fish*, & *Moses* H. *Grinnell*, old & trusted friends, have volunteered their good services, in explaining to His Excellency the President of the U. S. *after* the 4th March, whether or not my appointment to the Naval office, would be acceptable to the People of New York. My continuance in Brazil is simply *impossible*, on account of the climate and its effect on my health. Therefore, earnestly as I desire to stay at home, I venture to request, that if you should not deem it expedient to confer on me the Naval office, you will have me transferred to a European Mission; and on account of my *health*, to *Italy*; or if that may not be, to *Prussia*. In making this request, I do not ask for any gentleman's place, because I hold, that the best interests of the Country demand, that under no circumstances, should any Minister be continued at the same court to exceed one term, & that the present Ministers retained in service by you, should be transferred to other fields of duty, and I arrogate nothing to myself in saying, that during my seven and a half years of Diplomatic service in Brazil, I have done *more duty*, than *all* the gentlemen now filling European Missions, combined,—as the records of the State Dept. will abundantly demonstrate. In conclusion, permit me to add, that under any circumstances, I desire that this letter may be considered *my resignation* of the Brazilian Mission; which, whether Congress does or does not repeal the tenure of office Law, (a species of War measure only,) ~~that place~~ is at your disposal. The Mission is one of great importance to us; and particularly so, in view of our 'Monroe doctrine;' and if any of the gentlemen now in our Diplomatic service in Europe, are to be retained, I would suggest the propriety of sending one of the ablest of them to Brazil. If we are ever to exercise in South America the influence to which we are justly entitled, we must be represented in that region by *Statesmen*, and not by mere *Politicians*."—ALS, DNA, RG 56, Naval Office Appointments. No appointment followed.

1867, AUG. 21. To Secretary of the Interior Orville H. Browning. "I transmit herewith an order of the President designating certain land at Camp Goodwin, Arizona Territory as a Military Reservation. Attention is invited to the President's order endorsed upon the papers that the Reservation be noted in the Land Office"—Copy, DNA, RG 94, Letters Sent. On the same day, USG wrote to Browning. "I transmit herewith an order of the President designating certain lands in San Francisco Bay, called Peninsula Island as a Military Reservation. Attention is invited to the President's order &c (as above)"—Copy, *ibid.* On Oct. 22, Brig. Gen. Andrew A. Humphreys, chief of engineers, wrote to USG. "I have the honor to recommend that the following Islands, near the entrance to San Pabla Bay, California, (shown on the accompanying sketch and indicated by a red line under the name) be reserved for military purposes by the President of the United States, . . ."—Copy, *ibid.*, RG 77, Letters Sent Relating to Land. The enclosure is *ibid.* On Oct. 30, USG wrote to Browning. "I transmit herewith the Presidents order reserving for military purposes certain Islands near the entrance to San Pablo Bay, California. Your attention is invited to this order that the Reservation may be noted in the Land Office."—Copy, *ibid.*, RG 94, Letters Sent. On Nov. 1, Browning wrote to USG. "I have the honor to acknowledge the receipt of your letter of the 30th ultimo, transmitting the President's order for the reservation for military purposes of certain islands near the entrance to San Pablo bay, California. The order and papers and map accompanying it have been transmitted to the Commissioner of the General Land Office for his appropriate action."—LS, *ibid.*, RG 107, Letters Received from Bureaus.

1867, AUG. 21, 2:30 P.M. To Maj. Gen. George G. Meade. "Order Artillery Comp.y from Fort Porter N. Y. to Fort McHenry Md. If a company is necessary at Fort Porter take the one most available from other parts of your command."—ALS (telegram sent), DNA, RG 107, Telegrams Collected (Bound); telegram sent, *ibid.*; telegram received (at 2:40 P.M.), *ibid.*, RG 393, Dept. of the East, Hd. Qrs., Letters Received.

1867, AUG. 21.   Hervie A. Dobson, Washington, D. C., to USG. "I have the honor to make application for the position of Second Lieutenant, in the Veteran Reserve branch of the Regular Army; and to this end I append the following brief personal and military history, which contain my claims to the position: I was born in Owego, Tioga Co., N. Y. in 1842, and am twenty five years of age. I have received a common school and Academic education. At the age of fifteen I lost my left leg, and have worn a wooden one ever since. When twenty one, I made application to President Lincoln to be admitted into the service; (See copy, with endorsements enclosed) President Lincoln personally caused my request to be granted. I served one year as a private soldier, but performing the duties of Commissary Sergeant of my Regt, the 11th, V. R. C., as will be seen by the enclosed order; in this capacity I performed all the duties of an able-bodied man. I served at Elmira, N. Y., at Camp Douglas, Chicago, twice, at Rock Island, and at Washington, D. C. I was discharged August 9th, 1864, by a Special Order from the Secretary of War, thinking I could perform more real service as a clerk than as a private soldier; and I invite your special attention to my discharge. Since my discharge, I have been on duty as clerk in the War Department, Paymaster General's Office. Hoping, sir, that my statement and the enclosed recommendations may be sufficient to procure for me the appointment, . . ."—ALS, DNA, RG 108, Letters Received. On Aug. 22, Dobson again wrote to USG requesting an appointment.—ALS, *ibid.*, RG 94, ACP, 475D CB 1867. USG later noted. "Hervey A Dobson, Discharged from Pay Dept, clerkship, Wishes to be restored. Obtain statement from P. M. Gn. as to his efficiency &c."—AN (undated), *ibid.*, RG 107, Letters Received from Bureaus. On Nov. 1, Bvt. Brig. Gen. Frederick T. Dent wrote to the paymaster gen. about Dobson and, on Nov. 2, Bvt. Brig. Gen. Joseph H. Eaton, act. paymaster gen., endorsed this letter. "Respectfully returned to General Dent. Mr. Dobson is represented to me by those under whose eye he has been serving in this office as having fair abilities as a Clerk but believed by them to be entirely unworthy of confidence   He is reputed as having stated to several clerks in this Office that he had lost a leg at Gettysburg & afterwards made a written Statement acknowledging that he had told a falsehood. This Statement was read in his presence before several gentlemen of the Office."—AES, *ibid.*

1867, AUG. 22.   Judge Advocate Gen. Joseph Holt to USG. "Levant W. Barnhart, 2d Lieut. 4th Cavy, was tried Aug. 6. '67 by General Ct. Martial in Washington, D. C. under the following charges:—1.—Conduct unbecoming an officer and gentleman. In that accused did, at Washington, D. C. May 8. '66, knowingly and with intent to defraud the Government, give to Squier & Alger, claim agents, for collection in his behalf, a false and fictitious claim, to wit: an application for payment for a horse lost in service, to the amount of $201.00. Then and there falsely and perjuriously making oath before N. Callan, J. P. to the truth of said claim, and forging and counterfeiting thereto the signature of G. A. Custer, Brev't. Brig. Gen.

U. S. A.—and knowingly and with intent to defraud, giving to said Alger and Squier the said application, certificate and affidavit; and he did thereupon receive from said agents the sum of $75.50 as an advance on said claim. And having accepted a commission as 2d Lieut. 4th Cavalry on or about May 30th '66, accused, well knowing the premises and still intending to defraud the Governm't, did wholly neglect, omit, and fail, to withdraw from the hands of said Alger & Squier said false claim &c., or to discontinue and prevent the presentation of said claim. . . . The accused previously says: 'At the time he' (Gen. Custer) 'was mustered out of the Volunteer service, he remarked to the officers of his staff that those who had horses lost while serving with him had better prepare their claims then. Some of the officers did so; but as I was coming on to Washington with Gen. Custer, the claim which was embodied in these charges was not prepared until my arrival here. I took it to Gen. Custer's room at the National Hotel, but he not being in I signed his name there to the certificate.' It is shown in evidence that the accused rose by merit from the station of private soldier in the 1st Mich. Cavy. to the rank of Captain and Bvt Major, and was selected for his staff by Gen'l Custer on the urgent advice of Colonel Greene, also a member of the same staff. . . . It is thought that his education while with Gen. Custer may have easily blinded him to the gravity of the offence of which he is convicted, serious as it is; and it is difficult to believe that for the sum of two hundred and one dollars he would have been ready to risk the sacrifice of a military reputation so high as the endorsements quoted above show his to have been. Notwithstanding therefore his plea of guilty under the specifications, which was undoubtedly made without a full appreciation of their force and bearing, it is advised that the sentence of dishonorable dismissal be mitigated to suspension from rank and pay for a certain number of months; the order to distinctly state the ground of such Executive action to be, that irregular & improper as his conduct was, it is believed his unauthorized use of General Custer's name was not so deliberately fraudulent as to call for the severe punishment of expulsion from the army."—Copy, DNA, RG 153, Letters Sent. On Aug. 31, W. S. Huntington, cashier, First National Bank, Washington, D. C., wrote to USG. "I have the honor to submit herewith pay account of L M Barnhart. 2nd Lt. 4th US Cavalry—for June, 1867—$164.34 This account was by me cashed in good faith in advance. of date for Lt Barnharts accomodation, and from some inability said to exist I have not been able to obtain payment of same. If not incompatable with regulations, may I respectfully ask that an order be made for its payment."—LS, *ibid.*, RG 94, Letters Received, 661H 1867. Additional papers are *ibid.*

1867, AUG. 22. Judge Advocate Gen. Joseph Holt to USG. "Edward Houttard, 2d Lieut, 32d Infy, was tried at New York City July 30th last, under the following charges:—1. Conduct unbecoming an officer and a gentleman. 1.—In assigning to one Hans Martens his pay accounts for January, 1867, as security for a lease, when in fact he had already drawn his pay & allowances for that month. 2.—A similar allegation in reference to his pay accounts for February, 1867. . . . 3. Disobedience of orders. In that, having been ordered by Brev't Major Gen. Butterfield to report immediately to Brev't Brig Gen. Wallen, Comm'dg at Fort Columbus, N. Y. harbor, for duty, he did disobey said order and did wholly neglect to report. This May 8th 1867, and thereafter. 4.—Desertion. In deserting the service at N. Y. City, on or about May 16, 1867, and remaining a deserter therefrom until apprehended at said City July 1st following: thirty dollars paid for his arrest and delivery. The accused plead guilty to all the charges except the 4th, and to that not guilty. The Court convict him under the 1st, 2nd, and 3d charges, and their specifications, thereby confirming his pleas; under the 4th charge find him guilty of Absence without leave; and sentence him 'to forfeit to the United States all pay & allowances due, or to become due, and to be dismissed the service.' . . . With reference to the charges of 'disobedience of orders' and 'desertion,' he asserts that at the time he received his instructions to report to Gen. Wallen at Fort Columbus, he was without means; in debt; and most of his baggage seized. After vainly endeavoring to raise money, he wrote to his parents in Europe for aid; and was arrested while waiting the reply to this letter. He declares that he had no intention of deserting, and that mental agitation consequent upon his financial embarrasments was the cause of his failure to report as ordered. It is difficult to believe that this foregoing story is sincerely told. Embarassed as the accused probably was, and agitated and distressed as his mind may in consequence have been, these circumstances afford no excuse for his delaying to obey a positive order of his superior and commanding officer for upwards of two months, or for his preferring to remain in N. Y. City in total neglect of his duties, to reporting himself at Fort Columbus, where he would have been in a great measure relieved from the pressure of his angry creditors. Inasmuch as the accused offers no defence to the charges of swindling and disobedience of orders which have been brought ag'st him, and his misconduct in these particulars has clearly been extremely gross, it is thought that the sentence pronounced by the Court is more lenient than the Prisoner deserved, and its enforcement is advised."—Copy, DNA, RG 153, Letters Sent. See *ibid.*, RG 94, Letters Received, 414B 1867.

1867, Aug. 22. U.S. Senator Henry B. Anthony of R. I., Providence, to USG. "I recommend JOSEPH P. BALCH for the Brevet of Brigadier General of Volunteers. He was one of the first to volunteer, & his military knowledge & influence with young men of military taste were of great value to the gvt. He served as Major of the 1st R. I. Vols. and in the battle of Bull Run was a part of the time in command. He was then placed in the position where he could render greatest service, in raising and training regiments & preparing them for the field. I shall feel personally gratified if you will confer upon him this well merited honor"—ALS, DNA, RG 94, ACP, 1686B CB 1867. USG twice endorsed this letter, first on Aug. 27.

"Disapproved" "Maj. Jos. Balch 1st R. I. Vols. may be breveted Brig. Gn. of Vols. ~~one brevet~~. The intermediate brevets need not be given."—ES and AE (undated and initialed), *ibid.* An unsigned letter of appointment of Nov. 20 from USG to Joseph P. Balch is *ibid.* On Nov. 23, Bvt. Brig. Gen. John C. Kelton, AGO, noted on this letter. "On presenting the papers in this case to the Secy of War, ad interim, action thereon was suspended." —ANS, *ibid.* See *ibid.*, B244 CB 1868.

1867, AUG. 22.   R. S. Brigham, Weston, Mo., to USG. "As a union soldier I take liberty to enclose you a letter by the celebrated P. V: Brady & hope you will heed its contents   It would most sorely grieve the union soldiers of the West to see the bright armor of our revered & illustrious Captain tarnished by the spawn of that base treason policy of A. Johnson, and we trust & hope that those who are earnestly working for humanity & for the welfare of the great American Republic will not be grieved by seeing our brave & noble general the great Captain of the day lending his influence in any manner to aid that basest of traitors A. Johnson Now by accident Pres. of the U, S,"—ALS, USG 3.

1867, AUG. 22.   C. M. Walker, 5th Auditor's Office, Treasury Dept., to USG. "Messrs Talbott, Jones & Co. of Indianapolis, Indiana, sold the War Dept 100 Gatling Guns and have delivered a large number of them, and the 2nd Auditor and 2nd Comptroller have passed upon $12.819.83 July 12th, $25.591.14 July 17th—and $21.327.45 Aug. 3d 1867; and the Head of Ordnance Bureau has allowed $29.004.71 Aug. 15th which has probably now passed the 2nd Comptroller's Office—I am informed by the Acting 2nd Comptroller that the necessary requisitions have not yet been issued by the War Dept for payment of these sums. Messrs Talbott & Co, who are townsmen of mine, request me if possible to expedite their claim— If not improper I would thank you to inform me as to the cause of the delay and whether the necessary Requisitions will be sent to this Department soon—"—ALS, DNA, RG 107, Letters Received, W321 1867.

1867, AUG. 23.   To Cassius M. Clay, U.S. minister. "In compliance with the request contained in your letter of the 25th January last, enclosing memorandum from Colonel Annenhoff, Aide-de-Camp to his Imperial Majesty the Emperor of Russia, asking information concerning the application of Railways to military operations as practiced in the United States during the late war, I have the honor to transmit you herewith a report on the subject prepared by the officer in charge of the U. S. Military Railroad Office; reports of the Quartermaster-General of the Army for the years 1862, 1864, 1865 and 1866, containing tables and information desired; a copy of the report of the late General Manager of the U. S. Military Railroads and a volume of orders relating to the operations of the roads, being all the information on the subject in possession of the Department."—LS, Lincoln Memorial University, Harrogate, Tenn. On Aug. 22, Bvt. Maj.

Gen. Daniel H. Rucker, act. q. m. gen., had written to USG transmitting these documents.—LS, DNA, RG 92, Reports to the Secretary of War (Press). On Sept. 12, Clay, St. Petersburg, wrote to USG. "I have the honor to acknowledge the receipt of your letter of Aut 23d ulto. informing me that you had sent me, for the use of Colo Annenhoff, several documents in reference to our rail-road-system, as a means of war. When the documents come to hand, I shall take care to have them delivered to the proper person. I thank you, General, for the promptness with which you have given the information required: and allow me to avail myself of this occasion to express my admiration for for your brilliant success in the late war, and my gratitude for Your patriotic devotion to our Country."—ALS, *ibid.,* RG 107, Letters Received, S367 1867.

1867, AUG. 23.   Secretary of State William H. Seward to USG. "At the instance of the Acting Consul General of Baden, I have the honor to request information as to whether Baron von Hardenberg held a commission while serving on the staff of General Blencker, in 1861. If so I will thank you to furnish me with the date of his commission and the date of his muster out."—LS, DNA, RG 94, ACP, 1128S CB 1867.

1867, AUG. 23.   Joseph Medill, editor of the *Chicago Tribune,* to USG. "*Private* . . . I think it is only right to state that profound dissatisfaction among Union men exists in the West at Stanton's removal and your 'acceptance' of his place. This feeling is deepened by the removal of the gallant Phil Sheridan who has done his duty so admirably. It is hard to make your warmest friends believe that you could not have averted one or both of those removals   Such articles as the enclosed from the N. Y Tribune are making a profound sensation among Union men. The report now reaches us that Howard, Pope and Sickles are all to be 'put out' within a few days, because they have done their duty and carried out the laws of Congress. A great change has taken place in public feeling respecting impeachment. I think the Union members from the West will vote solid for it. The public exasperation is intense, at Johnson's conduct. We are doing what we can to stem the current runing against you since your acceptance of Stanton's place and official sanction of Sheridan's removal. We are telling your friends to *wait* for the sequel and not form hasty conclusions nor to condemn until they know all the facts. But the best Union men shake their heads, and point to the encomiums contained in the Copperhead papers. General, I have not lost faith, because things are a little foggy but I would feel better if a little sunshine would dispel enough of the mist to enable one to see which way the road leads."—ALS, USG 3.

1867, AUG. 23.   William Steffen, St. John's College, Annapolis, to USG. "The authorities of St John's College are willing to comply with the conditions laid down in Major J. H. Whittlebey's circular to the Colleges of the United States on the subject of Military Education. The Vice-president Mr Nelson D. D. has requested me, in agreement with the board of Supervisors and Trustees to take charge of the Military Department and to take such steps as would facilitate the introduction of military training at once. Before I, however, can consider myself justified in conforming with this request, I should like to know whether it is the opinion of the War-department that none but West-point men are considered able to take charge of the Military education at a College, or whether another person, whose attencedents prove his ability of performing the duties required would be accepted without depriving the College of the advantages held out in the Circular. Requesting you to honor me with a reply at your earliest convenience that I may be able to report to the Faculty and Trustees as soon as possible, I beg to state: that I have been an officer in the Prussian army for 17 years, professor at the Royal military College at Cologne and member of the Board of Examiners for Commissions, that I, later, prepared in England young men for the competitive examinations for Commissions; that I since the beginning of the late war, instructed line and field officers in Boston Mass, before they left with their regiments and that I have been professor of Mathematics &c at this College since its reorganization after the restoration of peace. I am ready to pay my respects, to you, General; at Washington, whenever you shall have indicated the desire to see me to answer such questions as you may think fit to ask."—ALS, DNA, RG 94, Letters Received, 848S 1867. See Bvt. Maj. Gen. Edward D. Townsend to Steffen, Aug. 31.—*Ibid.*, Letters Sent.

1867, AUG. 24. To Secretary of the Treasury Hugh McCulloch. "In reply to your communication of the 15th June to the Quartermaster General relative to some abandoned property, (Engine &c of the U. S. Steamer Alice, destroyed by rebels, on the Neuse river,) I have the honor to request that you will direct the officer of the Treasury Department at Wilmington to turn over the property to General R. O. Tyler, Deputy Quartermaster General, to be disposed of for the benefit of the Quartermaster's Department."—LS, DNA, RG 56, Div. of Captured and Abandoned Property, Letters Received. On Aug. 22, Bvt. Maj. Gen. Daniel H. Rucker, act. q. m. gen., had written to USG. "I have the honor to transmit herewith, copy of a communication from the Assistant Secretary of the Treasury dated June 15, 1867, in relation to some property in North Carolina, belonging to the Quartermasters Department. This property consists of some portions of the machinery of the United States Steamer 'Alice', which was destroyed by the rebels on the Neuse River near Bowens Landing,—during the rebellion. Brevet Major General R. O. Tyler. Chief Quartermaster 2nd Military District, was notified of the existence of this property under date of June 20, 1867. and was instructed to collect the same and have it taken to Charleston, South Carolina to be sold at auction for the benefit of this Department. Upon investigation of the matter, General Tyler ascertained that a Mr

Henry Pearson, temporary Inspector of Customs, had removed this machinery to Wilmington, North Carolina, where it now is. As this property
belongs to the Quartermasters Department, the Acting Quartermaster General respectfully recommends that the Secretary of War request the Secretary of the Treasury to direct the officers of that Department at Wilmington
to turn this property over to General Tyler to be disposed of for the benefit
of the Quartermasters Department. The papers relating to the case are
herewith transmitted."—LS, *ibid.*, RG 92, Reports to the Secretary of War
(Press). On Aug. 31, McCulloch wrote to USG. "Referring to your letter
of the 24th instant, requesting me to 'direct the officer of the Treasury
Department at Wilmington to turn over' the engine and iron of the U. S.
Steamer 'Alice', destroyed by rebels near Bowen's landing on New River,
'to General R. O. Tyler, Deputy Quartermaster General,' I have the honor
to call your attention to the letter addressed to the Quartermaster General
June 15th last, enclosing the report of the Deputy Collector of Internal
Revenue at NewBerne, N. C., from which it appears that such property
was lying at that place uncared for, which he asked leave to collect; that it
is not in his possession, and that, understanding that the steamer belonged
at the time of capture to the Quartermaster's Department, I referred the
whole matter to the Quartermaster General for such action as he might
deem proper. There is no officer of the Treasury Department, whose office
it is now to collect such property. As it rightfully belongs to the Quartermaster's Department, I should suppose there can be no obstacle to its agents
taking immediate possession."—Copy, *ibid.*, RG 56, Letters Sent Relating
to Restricted Commercial Intercourse.

1867, AUG. 24.   To Secretary of the Treasury Hugh McCulloch. "I have
the honor to send herewith papers respecting a claim of Erastus L. Gay,
late of Company G, 1st Massachusetts Cavalry, for commutation of rations,
&c, while on duty in the office of the Solicitor of the Treasury, with a request to be informed, prior to a decision thereon by this Department,
whether it be the design of the Treasury Department to allow him any
compensation for such services."—LS, DNA, RG 56, Letters from Executive Officers. On Oct. 8, McCulloch wrote to USG. "I have the honor herewith to transmit copy of letter from the Solicitor of the Treasury relative
to claim of Erastus L. Gay late of Co G 1st Mass. Cavalry for commutation
of rations &c while on duty in the Solicitor's Office, and in reply to the
inquiry contained in your letter of the 24th Augt to inform you that this
Department concurs in the opinion expressed by the Solicitor—The papers
transmitted with your letter are herewith returned—"—Copy, *ibid.*, Letters
Sent. On Aug. 28, Act. Solicitor of the Treasury Hanson A. Risley wrote
to McCulloch. ". . . There was no agreement for and no expectation on the
part of Mr. Gay, that he would receive any pay from this Department for
his services, but on the 12th June 1865., he was paid ($323.81) Three
hundred, twenty-three Dollars and eighty-one Cents, for expenses incurred
by him while so engaged in detecting counterfeiters. These being the facts,

I am unable to discover any good ground for further payment to him from the Treasury Department or this Office."—LS, *ibid.*, Letters from Executive Officers.

1867, AUG. 24.   To Secretary of the Treasury Hugh McCulloch. "I have the honor to send herewith papers & correspondence respecting the occupancy of the *Marine Hospital at St. Marks, Fla.*, and to request that in accordance with the recommendation of the Qr. Mr. Genl. of the Army, the building be transferred to his Department, for the purpose of quartering U. S. troops, & the sick & the Health officer at that port."—Copy, DNA, RG 107, Letters Sent to the President. On Aug. 17, Bvt. Maj. Gen. Daniel H. Rucker, act. q. m. gen., had written to USG about this matter.—LS, *ibid.*, RG 92, Reports to the Secretary of War (Press).

1867, AUG. 24.   To Secretary of State William H. Seward. "In reply to your letter of the 6th instant, requesting at the instance of *James Phillips*, of Ireland, information concerning his son *James Phillips*, stated to have belonged to the 23d Michigan Cavalry, I have the honor to inform you that there were only eleven regiments of Michigan Cavalry in the service of the U. S. and that the name of the person referred is not borne on the rolls of the 23d Regiment of Michigan Volunteers."—Copy, DNA, RG 107, Letters Sent to the President. While serving as secretary of war *ad interim*, USG (or members of his staff) almost daily sent letters to the State Dept. answering inquiries concerning foreign nationals who had served in the U.S. Army. This correspondence has not been printed in these volumes.

1867, AUG. 24.   To Secretary of State William H. Seward. "Your letter of the 22nd requesting that a *Berdan Rifle* be sent to the Duc de Penthievre was received, and the Chief of Ordnance directed to forward the same through your Department. By his endorsement you will see that the Government have no Berdan Rifles, but can send if you desire it, one of the converted Springfield Muskets."—Copy, DNA, RG 107, Letters Sent to the President.

1867, AUG. 24.   To Attorney Gen. Henry Stanbery. "I have the honor to enclose herewith a communication from the Honorable B. C. Cook, respecting the construction of the Act of Congress approved March 2d 1867, making appropriation for the construction of a bridge at Rock Island, Illinois, and to ask your opinion on the subject."—LS, DNA, RG 60, Letters Received, War Dept. On Sept. 11, Act. Attorney Gen. John M. Binckley reported in the negative to USG concerning the co. proposal.—Copies, *ibid.*, Opinions; *ibid.*, RG 153, Opinions. On Aug. 29, Bvt. Maj. Gen. Alexander B. Dyer, chief of ordnance, wrote to USG.—LS, *ibid.*, RG 156, Letters to the Secretary of War (Press). On Aug. 31, USG wrote to Stanbery. "At the instance of the Chief of Ordnance, U. S. A., I have the honor to send herewith a communication from him of August 29th, enclosing drafts of guarantees to be executed by the Chicago, Rock Island and Pacific Railroad Company for examination; approving his request for the preparation of a bond in the case."—LS, *ibid.*, RG 60, Letters Received, War Dept. On Oct. 4, Stanbery wrote to USG. "I have the honor to return herewith the papers received with your letter of Aug. 31, 1867, concerning the removal of the rail road track across Rock Island and the construction of a bridge across the Mississippi river at that point, and also to transmit the form of a bond prepared in compliance with your request, together with a modification in the form of the agreement submitted by the Chief of Ordnance for carrying out the objects contemplated by the Acts of June 27, 1866, and March 2, 1867; therein cited—Your attention is respectfully directed to the remarks touching these forms contained in the accompanying paper marked "D—" "—Copy, *ibid.*, Letters Sent. On Dec. 11, USG wrote to Stanbery. "I have the honor to send herewith a communication of December 9th from the Chief of Ordnance covering a draft of agreements proposed to be entered into by the Chicago, Rock Island & Pacific Railroad Company with the United States and to request your opinion as to whether they conform to the law on the subject."—LS, *ibid.*, Letters Received, War Dept. On Jan. 7, 1868, Stanbery wrote to USG. "I have considered the two Drafts of agreements proposed to be entered into with the C. R. I. & P. R. R. Co. enclosed to me in your letter of the 11th ultimo, and have the honor to state the conclusions at which I have arrived. . . . Clearly, the Act does not authorize the insertion in the agreement of any provision of the character referred to, calculated to restrain the exercise of any right incident to the ownership of the bridge, or to take away the free control of its future uses by the government, not ~~inconsistent~~ infringing upon, or inconsistent with, the grant of a right of way, and transit to the Company. The clause in the draught here adverte[d] to is therefore open to objection."—Copies, *ibid.*, Letters Sent; *ibid.*, RG 153, Opinions.

1867, AUG. 24. USG endorsement. "Approved for Brevet Major of Vols."—ES, DNA, RG 94, ACP, 295K CB 1867. Written on a letter of July 25 from George W. Griffiths, Louisville, to USG. "I have the honor to present for your kind Consideration the record of a true and faithful Soldier that of Capt. E. D. Kennedy of this City, one who fought gallantly throughout the war, especial attention is Called to that portion stating that he *was not absent* from his Command for a single day during long years of hard and Continuous duty. He is still an unflinching Union Man   His life has been assailed on three different occasions in this City, by rebel sympathizers, shot at by one of these miscreants under the Cover of Night, aiming directly at his heart the ball was only checked in its Career of death by the ring of his watch. The Capt is here in the practice of Law and is daily thrown in Contact with ex Rebel officer Majors, Colonels, an General's. The Capt should at least rank with these traitors   I would earnestly and respectfully ask if you deem it proper to give him a brevet Commission, one that he can always retain as evidence of his devotion to his Country in the trying times of the great rebelion. Memorials from leading loyal men Could be obtained asking that you Confer this great honor upon Capt. K. but it is deemed nescesary—to only Call your attention to his record which is Now Very respectfully submited: — . . ."—ALS, *ibid.*

1867, Aug. 24 and 26.   Bvt. Maj. Gen. Daniel H. Rucker, act. q. m. gen., to USG. "In reply to the letter from the War Department of the 23d inst., I have the honor to report the accounts of the Holladay Overland Mail Company have been adjusted in this office, and referred to Genl Van Vliet at New York, and the Third Auditor Treasury, Washington, D. C., for settlement under decision of the Quartermaster General, deducting there-from 33⅓ per cent, and upon request of the Company, through their Agent, G. K. Otis, for a reconsideration of the decision, the subject was referred to the Hon. Secretary of War for his decision, who returned the papers with the following endorsement: 'Returned to the Quartermaster General with direction to pay so much of this claim as he approves, reserving for further consideration the question of the residue.' The accounts are numerous, and papers in this case voluminous; a more full report will be ~~immediately~~ transmitted to the Hon. Secretary of War as soon as it can be prepared." "In reply to communication from the War Department of the 23d inst, in relation to accounts in favor of M Ben. Holladay, for overland transportation, upon which a reduction of 33⅓ per cent has been made, and to which a brief reply was returned on the 24th inst. I have the honor to make more full report. . . ."—LS, DNA, RG 92, Reports to the Secretary of War (Press). On Sept. 30, Rucker wrote to USG. "In the case of Ben. Holladay for stage transportation, referred to this office from the War Department September 23rd 1867, with directions that the accounts be examined in sufficient detail to ascertain if there have been charges for transportation made against the United States by Mr Holladay of soldiers employed as escorts, or in any capacity to the advantage of Mr Holladay; also the pecuniary value of any services rendered, or materials, forage, &c., furnished Mr Holladay by United States Agents, or employés, I have the honor to report— . . . It appears that the United States has furnished to Mr Holladay for his Stage line, at various times, the services of enlisted men, and other employés of the Government, in building, removing and repairing stations, herding stock, taking care of teams and cooking rations, has furnished teams to transport their forage, and has furnished forage for their teams, and horses to draw their coaches, quarters and rations for their men,—it does not appear that any charge has ever been made, or any consideration received from Mr Holladay for these services, and supplies furnished, and the value thereof is unknown in this office. The papers are herewith respectfully returned."—LS, *ibid.* On Oct. 1, Bvt. Maj. Gen. James A. Hardie, inspector gen., endorsed this letter. "It is the opinion of the Sec'y of War ad int., that there should have been a stipulation arranged by the proper officers of the Quartermaster Department with the proprietors of the Stage line, at the commencem[ent] of the transportation service to be performed, fixing the rates of such transportation. In default of this, and in view of all the facts, it is concluded that justice requires the allowance of the 33⅓ per cent hitherto withheld. The Quarter Master General will accordingly pay that amount. The above decision is to be taken as confined in its scope to this particular case and is not to be interpreted as setting aside the principles upon which the Q. M. Dep't settles accounts for transportation with the transportation lines of the country."—Copies, *ibid.*, Decision Books; *ibid.*, RG 107, Orders and Endorsements.

1867, AUG. 24.   Judge Advocate Gen. Joseph Holt to USG. "Brevet Lieut. Col. F. M. Follett, Capt. 4th U. S. Arty, was tried Aug. 14, by Gen'l. Court Martial in session in Washington, D. C. under the following charges:—1. Drunkenness on duty. . . . The accused concludes his defence by offering his own affidavit, sworn to before a Notary Public, that on the day of Gen. Robert's inspection he 'took several doses of laudanum—between 40 and 50 drops as near as he can estimate—he being unwell at the time.' A Court composed of some of the most respectable and experienced officers in the service has pronounced its opinion against Col. Follett's longer continuance in the army, on the ground of unfitness resulting from habits of private indulgence. In this decision this Bureau fully concurs. It is thought to be clear, that, if the victim of intemperance in liquor, Col. Follett has so far degraded himself by its abuse as to deserve to be made an example of punishment, as he has made himself an example of insubordination. If addicted, as he claims to be, to the use of laudanum as an opiate, the hopelessness of his degradation furnishes an additional reason for enforcing the sentence of the Court. It is respectfully advised that such action be taken by the Executive."—Copy, DNA, RG 153, Letters Sent. Capt. and Bvt. Lt. Col. Frederick M. Follett, USMA 1850, cashiered as of Sept. 3, 1867, reappointed as of Oct. 9, committed suicide shortly after the expiration of that reappointment, unconfirmed by the U.S. Senate.—See *ibid.*, RG 94, Letters Received, 338R 1867; *ibid.*, ACP, F29 CB 1869.

1867, AUG. 24.   Maj. Gen. Winfield S. Hancock, Fort Harker, Kan., to USG. "Capt Armes tenth (10) Cavalry in Command with one (1) Company of his Regiment & two (2) Companies of the Eighteenth (18) Kansas Vols was attacked on the twenty first (21) at noon on the Republic by a large force of Indians reported to be eight hundred or one thousand in number   they were engaged until the night of the twenty second (22)   our troops about one hundred & fifty in number Covering a wide space of Country were finally forced to retire losing three men Killed left on the field & thirty five wounded who were brought in, with a loss of forty (40) horses, Capt Armes reports a large number of Indians Killed & wounded, Lt Price of the Eighteenth Kansas says about one hundred & fifty,   Captain Armes with the rear guard and the wounded encamped three miles from Fort Hays last night   Maj Moore of the Kansas Cavalry from whom I have also had a report informs me that he with the remainder of his Battalion & Maj

Elliott of the seventh Cavalry with about two hundred men of that Regiment would leave this morning for the Indians"—Telegram received (at 10:30 P.M.), DNA, RG 107, Telegrams Collected (Bound); *ibid.*, RG 108, Telegrams Received; copy, DLC-USG, V, 55. On Aug. 27, Hancock, Fort Leavenworth, telegraphed to USG. "Have just returned from the terminus of the Railroad thirty five miles west of Ft Harker & 34 miles East of Ft Hayes My visit was particularly there to Inspect the arrangements made for the protection of the workmen on the RR beyond. The R R. will be finished to Ft Hayes by Oct 15th & from 40 to 60 miles beyond by winter if no very serious injury is done by Indians."—Telegram received (at 1:35 P.M.), DNA, RG 107, Telegrams Collected (Bound); *ibid.*, RG 108, Telegrams Received; copy, DLC-USG, V, 55.

1867, AUG. 24. John F. Callan, Washington, D. C., to USG. "On the 19th March 1864, Mr Stanton then, Secretary of War, issued a public order excluding me from transacting any business in the War Department or its Bureaux. The injustice of this order Mr Stanton has several times acknowledged and has as often promised to revoke it; but it remains operative as against me and against my two sons, altho' President Johnson has told me to disregard it. Knowing, as I do, your unwillingness to punish those who have committed no offence, I beg to appeal to you, in this way, that these orders (above referred to) may be revoked, as publicly as they were made and that I may be allowed to practice, in the War Department and the Bureaux, the profession for which I pay a license to the Government. Independant of Mr Stantons iniquitous treatment to me, he dismissed from Office my two sons, my Brother and nephew SOLELY to gratify his own spitefulness and without any other cause, & they had all been appointed to Office without solicitation on their part."—ALS, DNA, RG 94, Letters Received, 345W 1864. Additional papers are *ibid.* On Sept. 27, Callan wrote to USG. "I am the Compiler of the U. S. Military Laws, of which a copy of the last edition (1864) will be found herewith. It has been the practice of the War Department for many years to subscribe for, from 1000 to 1500 copies of this compilation for distribution to the Officers of the Army, as the best means of knowing the laws by which they are governed. I am now preparing for the press a new edition of this work, embracing all the Military Laws to date, with copious notes & references & with a new and exhaustive index; and, as I cannot publish it without the patronage of the Government, I respectfully ask for a subscription on the part of the War Department, of say 1000 copies. Praying for an early response hereto . . ."—ALS, *ibid.*, 946C 1867. On Nov. 8, Bvt. Maj. Gen. Edward D. Townsend wrote to Callan declining to subscribe.—Copy, *ibid.*, Letters Sent. See *PUSG*, 11, 447.

1867, AUG. 24. C. W. Hildreth, Baltimore, to USG. "Having been a Soldier in your *Brigade* at *Pilot Knob Mo.* and subsequently a clerk at your Head Qrs. at Corinth, though doubtless unremembered by you I have something to ask. I was forced to resign a situation in General Tompkins Office in Washington for expressing radical sentiments. My father who was Chief Clerk (and a good radical) is about to go with Genl Ingalls in New York. I wish to go there too, if I can do so without being compelled to gag myself, will you, ask General Ingalls to employ me? I am aware that my request might be styled *impudent*, but I am not addressing a Halleck, or a Buel or ~~Ruseau~~ Rouseau, by *loyal* Genl. Grant. *Please reply*"—ALS, DNA, RG 107, Letters Received, H323 1867. On Aug. 27, W. H. Hildreth, Washington, D. C., wrote to USG. "Upon the breaking out of the rebellion in 1861, I felt that my experience might be valuable to the Govt having been many years in the Qr Mrs Dept and fully conversant with all the duties of an A. Q. M. and I tendered them to Genl D H Rucker Q M. in this City, who at once (having known me for many years) called upon me to organize the Transportation Office of this Depot in this city and appointed me Chief Clerk, which position I have ever since held. I made an ineffectual effort to obtain a Commission in 186.3. as A. Q. M. but not having much political influence, failed. About two months ago, I applied to the Secretary of War for an appointment to fill the first vacancy as Mily, Store Keeper Q. M. D. and referred therein to Generals Ingalls Rucker, Dana, Tompkins and Swords all of the QrMrs Department. . . . I am about to report in New York to General Ingalls to take charge of his accounts, and I desire to leave this city with some hope and assurance that I may receive the appointment desired should a vacancy occur."—ALS, *ibid.*, RG 94, ACP, H720 CB 1867. On Oct. 18, W. H. Hildreth, New York City, wrote to USG transmitting a letter of the same day from Bvt. Maj. Gen. Rufus Ingalls to USG. "I have the honor to recommend Mr W. H. Hildreth of New York for an appointment as Military Store Keeper of the Quarter Master's Department in the service of the United States. Mr Hildreth has been personally known to me for more than twenty years, and is well and favorably known by a majority of the old Army officers. During the war he was in the employ of Gen'ls. Rucker and Tompkins in Washington, and has received from them most excellent endorsements. The ability, integrity, and fidelity manifested by him in the many responsible positions which he has held clearly indicate that his services would be of great value to the Government. Mr Hildreth is at present on duty in my office, and I shall esteem it a great personal favor, if you will appoint him to the desired position whenever a vacancy occurs."—LS, *ibid.*, RG 108, Letters Received.

1867, AUG. 24. W. Y. Selleck, Baltimore, to USG. "In behalf of the Committee of Arrangements for the dedication of the 'Antietam National Cemetery' (at Sharpsburg, Md.) on the 17th day of September next, I respectfully request (if consistent with the wants of the service) that you will furnish to assist in the ceremonies on that occasion a Battery of light Artillery for the purpose of fireing salutes, a company of Infantry or Cavelry and a Band of Music—The Committee would further ask your indulgence by requesting that Bt. Lt. Col. James M. Moore A. Q. M. whom they have unanamously chosen as marshall for the occasion may be allowed the privelege of accepting and acting—"—ALS, DNA, RG 107, Letters Received, S319 1867. On Aug. 28, James S. Negley, Pittsburgh, wrote to USG. "Arrangements are being mad to dedicate with suitable ceremonies—Antietam Cemetry—on the 17th of September. Artillery will be required—also one or more companies of Infantry—Will it meet your approbation to order these from Washington for the occasion?"—ALS, *ibid.*, RG 94, Letters Received, 147N 1867. On Sept. 14, Negley telegraphed to USG. "Have you consented to order Artillery to Antietam to fire salute on the (17th) seventeenth."—Telegram received (at 9:10 A.M.), *ibid.*, RG 107, Telegrams Collected (Bound); *ibid.*, RG 108, Telegrams Received; copy, DLC-USG, V, 55. At 10:20 A.M., USG telegraphed to Negley. "I do not feel authorized to order troops, and incur expenses to attend celebrations." —ALS (telegram sent), DNA, RG 107, Telegrams Collected (Bound); telegram sent, *ibid.*; copies, *ibid.*, RG 108, Telegrams Sent; DLC-USG, V, 56. On the same day, Selleck telegraphed to USG. "will you please allow the Committee the use of one of the field pieces at Fort McHenry for the Antietam dedication? we will pay all Expenses incurred."—Telegram received (at 2:30 P.M.), DNA, RG 94, Letters Received, 923S 1867; *ibid.*, RG 107, Telegrams Collected (Bound). USG noted at the foot of a telegram received. "Please answer and give the use of Arty. Make any order necessary for that purpose"—AN (initialed), *ibid.*, RG 94, Letters Received, 923S 1867.

1867, Aug. 24. Annie Stokes, New York City, to USG. "Gen Wallen Commander Governors Island refuses to discharge James Stokes because your special order four forty two (442) reads Private James Stokes first U. S. Infantry   as he is only a recruit on the Island and has been most of the time in the Hospital He has not as yet been assigned to any Regiment The error of his being a Private in first US Infy was made through my Parents from the fact that a letter sent by him when in the Hospital stated that he would be assigned to the first US Infy as soon as he was well. Please telegraph to Gen Wallen rectifying the mistake"—Telegram received (at 9:30 P.M.), DNA, RG 107, Telegrams Collected (Bound).

1867, Aug. 24. U.S. Senator Richard Yates of Ill., Jacksonville, to USG. "I congratulate you on having the gallant Sheridan at Fort Leavenworth soon—I want you to watch for a chance as these changes go forward for your own promotion and I will be on hand to help—I want you to set me up with Sheridan which you can well do for I am a great friend of his— *Between you and me* ALONE it may yet turn out best to make him President—Now to the point. I have just received a letter from St Louis saying that some of the leading citizens are going to send me a letter to be at the reception of Sheridan *about three weeks* from now and to make the leading speech—a Campaign speech on General politics—I shall accept the invitation and want you there—and want to refer to you in my speech—Can you comply with this arrangement?—My highest regards to Mrs G—My family & I just returned from trip East for benefit of their health—all much better."—ALS, ICarbS.

1867, AUG. 25. Anonymous, Pittsburgh, to USG. "If you arnt a ruined man, it will be a Strange thing. Your enemies are after you with a determination that you dont Suspect. The Johnsonites in this City boast of having got you just where they want you, where you will be compelled to carry out the Presidents programme of removing all your favorite Generals from the reconstructing Districts. They boast they have already got Sheradan out of the way, Sickles and Pope must Soon follow. The President put you in the War department with a view of making you responsible for these removals, and preparing the way for Johnson & Genl Sherman for the next Presidency   You no doubt are aware of all this, and may be able to check mate the whole thing."—AL, USG 3.

1867, AUG. 26. To Secretary of State William H. Seward. "Immediately on the receipt of yr comn of the 10th inst asking that proper honors sd be paid to the remains of the Hon. Jos A. Wright, expected in NewYork, the requisite instructions were issued. I now enclose a copy of a letter addressed to the Com'g Officer in NewYork harbor by D. Randall, Esqr son-in law of the deceased, from wh. it will be seen that a private funeral having been decided on, the proffer of military honors was declined."—Df, DNA, RG 94, Letters Received, 814S 1867; copy, *ibid.*, RG 107, Letters Sent. On Aug. 10, Seward had written to Secretary of War Edwin M. Stanton. "This Department is unofficially informed that the remains of the Honorable Joseph A. Wright, late United States Minister at Berlin are expected to reach New York in the course of next week. It is desirable and proper that all due honor should be paid to them by the authorities of the UnitedStates there. I will consequently thank you to to instruct those who are subject to the orders of the War Department, as was done in the case of the late Mr Dayton, United States Minister to France, pursuant to the letter of this Department to the Secretary of War of the 27th of December, 1864."—LS, *ibid.*, RG 94, Letters Received, 814S 1867.

1867, AUG. 26. To Attorney Gen. Henry Stanbery. "I have the honor to send herewith papers relative to the payment of bounties which it is claimed are due to certain regiments of U. S. Colored Troops, and to request your opinion as to their rights under the law."—LS, DNA, RG 60, Letters Received, War Dept. On Sept. 9, Act. Attorney Gen. John M. Binckley wrote to USG. "I have examined the papers relating to the distribution of bounties to certain discharged colored regiments, which accompanied your letter to the Attorney General of the 26th ultimo, wherein you request to be advised as to the rights of those troops under the law. These papers do not set forth any distinct question of law for consideration, and from the very general terms in which the subject is presented in your letter, I am unable to extract the real point of difficulty—Accordingly I feel constrained to call upon you for a statement of the particular questions of law connected with this matter on which an opinion from the Attorney General is desired—The papers are herewith returned—"—Copy, *ibid.*, Letters Sent.

On Sept. 14, Judge Advocate Gen. Joseph Holt endorsed papers concerning bounties for colored troops. "Respectfully returned to the Secretary of War. It is recommended that the party raising the within inquiry be furnished with a copy of the enclosed Report of the Paymaster General of the 24th ult., and of the annexed 'Memorandum,' No. 47, from his office of May 26. 1865. From these, considered in connection with the legislation of Congress upon the subject of bounties,—the law, and the practice of the Government, in regard to this complex subject, will, it is believed, be clearly understood; and the supposed unjust discrimination in the matter of the payment of bounties to the colored troops here mentioned, be satisfactorily explained."—Copy, *ibid.*, RG 153, Letters Sent.

1867, AUG. [26]. USG note. "Give Gn. Palmer authority to remain absent from his regt until recruits will be going out to the in Sept. Oct. to the plains he to go there in charge of them."—AN (initialed, undated, docketed as Aug. 26), DNA, RG 94, Letters Received, 539P 1867.

1867, AUG. 26, 10:10 A.M. To Bvt. Maj. Gen. John Pope, Atlanta. "If Give Lt. Coleman 15th Inf.y leave of absence for benefit of his health unless absolutely inconsistent with the interests of the service."—ALS (telegram sent), DNA, RG 107, Telegrams Collected (Bound); telegram sent, *ibid.*; copies, *ibid.*, RG 108, Telegrams Sent; DLC-USG, V, 56.

1867, AUG. 26, 11:23 A.M. To Governor Ambrose E. Burnside of R. I. "Band & escort have been ordered from Fort Adams as requested"—Telegrams sent (2), DNA, RG 107, Telegrams Collected (Bound); copies, *ibid.*, RG 108, Telegrams Sent; DLC-USG, V, 56. On the same day, Burnside, Providence, had telegraphed to USG. "Bvt Maj Wm B. Occleston 33d Inf'y died in this City on Saturday & is to be buried tomorrow. he requested to be buried with military honors. Can an Escort with the band be ordered from Fort adams by telegraph to leave there in first boat tomorrow."—Telegram received (at 9:10 A.M.), DNA, RG 107, Telegrams Collected (Bound); *ibid.*, RG 108, Telegrams Received; copy, DLC-USG, V, 55. At 11:30 A.M., USG telegraphed to the commanding officer, Fort Adams. "Send escort & band to Providence by first boat tomorrow to attend funeral of Bvt. Major Eccleston, 33d Infantry"—Telegrams sent (2), DNA, RG 107, Telegrams Collected (Bound); copies, *ibid.*, RG 108, Telegrams Sent; DLC-USG, V, 56. On Aug. 27, Col. and Bvt. Maj. Gen. Thomas W. Sherman, 3rd Art., Newport, telegraphed to USG. "Telegram received last Evening. Band & One (1) Company sent this morning."—Telegram received (at 11:20 A.M.), DNA, RG 107, Telegrams Collected (Bound); *ibid.*, RG 108, Telegrams Received; copy, DLC-USG, V, 55.

1867, Aug. 26.   Col. Albert J. Myer, chief signal officer, to USG. "I have
the honor to recommend that instruction in the duties of Signal Officers be
made a part of the course of instruction at the Military Academy at West
Point: the course to be as follows: . . ."—Copies (2), DNA, RG 94, Correspondence, USMA; *ibid.*, RG 111, Letters Sent. Printed in full with
enclosures in *HED*, 40-2-1, II, part 1, pp. 618–20. On Aug. 30, Myer
wrote to USG. "I respectfully recommend that the Chief Signal Officer of
the Army be authorized to visit West Point, N. Y. and Such other places as
may be necessary to carry out the instructions in reference to the course of
Signals at the U. S. Military and Naval Academies."—Copy, *ibid.*, RG 111,
Letters Sent.

1867, Aug. 26.   Alexander S. Diven, New York City, to USG. "I am
sued in the Supreme Court of the State of NewYork for the arrest shown to
have been made by the enclosed copies orders &c—I am advised by my
Attornies that the testimony of Col Hardie, Col Foster and Lieut Fitch is
necessary on the trial—Are these officers now in the service? Can they be
ordered to attend as witnesses? The cause is noticed for trial at Elmira, on
2d September—As the act for which I am sued was done in obedience to
orders I presume the War Department will do all in its power to aid in my
defence—An early answer is respectfully solicited"—LS, DNA, RG 94,
Letters Received, 313D 1867. The enclosures are *ibid.*
    On Jan. 6, 1868, Attorney Gen. Henry Stanbery wrote to USG con-
cerning this case.—LS, *ibid.*, RG 107, Letters Received from Bureaus. On
Jan. 10, USG wrote to Stanbery. "In reply to your communication of the
6th instant transmitting a letter from the United States Attorney for the
Southern District of New York, respecting the suit of James A. Creed
against A. S. Diven, formerly Assistant Provost Marshal General, I have
the honor to state that there is no objection to engaging the services of Mr.
Hotchkiss to defend in the case, as recommended by the District Attorney."—LS, *ibid.*, RG 60, Letters Received, War Dept. On Jan. 13, U.S.
Attorney Samuel G. Courtney, New York City, telegraphed to USG. "I
desire immediate instructions as to the case of Creed against Diven   I
understand from the Attorney General that my letter and telegram were
referred to you,   The case is pressed for trial & it is important that Counsel
should be retained at once"—Telegram received (at 1:00 P.M.), *ibid.*, RG
107, Telegrams Collected (Bound).

1867, Aug. 26.   Arthur Rich, Baltimore, to USG. "Having read your
letter—or rather *protest* to the Presidt—I beg leave to express my profound
thaks and admiration for the noble sentiments you utter—It is a perfect
'Multum in Parvo'—so Apropo—The loyal heart throughout the Nation will
feel calm and satisfied until the People representatives in Congress Assembled can convene and render *all necessary succor*—It is to be hoped that
you will remain Secretary of War at all *hazards* until Congress meets—
your letter is statesmanlike, as well as soldierlike and a *text* and a *record*

worthy of a victorious leader of the American Army—and fit at any time
to go before the American people—Whilst in sympathy and unison with a
truly patriotic heart— . . . PS. I should be pleased to be favored with the
Genl. Autograph"—ALS, USG 3.

1867, AUG. 27.   To Secretary of the Treasury Hugh McCulloch. "I have
the honor to transmit herewith, a report of the Quartermaster General and
its accompaniments relative to a deficiency in the money accounts of *Brevet
Major Henry Howland* late Assistant Quartermaster U. S. Vols, for such
action as may be considered proper in the final settlement of his accounts."
—Df, DNA, RG 107, Letters Received from Bureaus; copy, *ibid.*, Letters
Sent to the President.

1867, AUG. 27.   To Secretary of the Treasury Hugh McCulloch. "Referring to your letter of the 20th February last, enclosing a copy of communication from Special Agent H. B. Titus in relation to certain papers
captured with Thomas A. Harris, R. S. McCulloch and others by the
Commanding Officer at Key West, Fla., in 1865, I have the honor to transmit herewith a list of all papers, books and correspondence, taken from
Thomas A. Harris and R. H. McCulloch at the time of their capture, which
are now in the possession of this Department."—LS, DNA, RG 56, Div. of
Captured and Abandoned Property, Letters Received. The enclosed list is
ibid. On Oct. 25, McCulloch wrote to USG. "Referring to your letter of the
27th of August last, transmitting a list of all papers, books and correspondence taken from Thomas A. Harris and R. H. McCulloch at the time
of their capture, which are now in possession of the War Department, I
have now the honor to request that you will cause to be transmitted to this
Department the originals or duly certified copies of all the books or papers
named on the said list which refer to the contract of Mr Harris and others
to furnish ordnance and quartermaster's stores to the late so-styled Confederate States Government, and also those which refer to the cargoes of
any of the vessels named, or to cotton to pay for the same."—LS, *ibid.*, RG
94, Letters Received, W1424 1865. On Nov. 26, USG wrote to McCulloch. "Recurring to your letter of the 25th ultimo, requesting to be furnished with the originals or duly certified copies of all the books and papers
named in the list contained in a previous letter to you, of the 27th August
last, as being taken from Mess. T. A. Harris and R. S. McCulloh at the
time of their capture, and as relating to a contract between the first-named
and the so-called Confederate States, I have the honor to transmit herewith
attested copies of the papers referred to; the originals forming part of a
series which would be rendered incomplete by their detachment from the
records of the Archive Office. Should you further desire it, a list of the
vessels employed in running the blockade, together with a list of many
trading-houses in Europe engaged in furnishing supplies to the rebel government, can be furnished."—LS, *ibid.*, RG 56, Div. of Captured and
Abandoned Property, Letters Received.

On Oct. 2, 1865, Julius A. Pratt, a prisoner captured with Thomas A. Harris *et al.*, wrote from Fort Lafayette, New York Harbor, to Maj. Gen. Joseph Hooker requesting assistance.—ALS, *ibid.*, RG 94, Letters Received, W1424 1865. On Oct. 27, USG endorsed this letter. "Respectfully forwarded to the Secretary of War with the recommendation that *Julius A Pratt* confined at Fort Lafayette N. Y. Harbor be discharged from custody upon his taking the necessary and required oaths, if no charges exist against him for which he should be tried"—ES, *ibid.*

1867, AUG. 27. To Secretary of State William H. Seward. "I have the honor to acknowledge receipt of your letter of the 20th July last, transmitting at the instance of the French Minister, for presentation by the Minister of War of France to the U. S. Military Academy, a copy of the Journal of the *Imperial Polytechnic School*, and to inform you that the same has been transmitted to the Academy."—Df, DNA, RG 107, Letters Received from Bureaus; copy, *ibid.*, Letters Sent to the President.

1867, AUG. 27. To Secretary of State William H. Seward. "I have the honor to transmit herewith, for the proper action of the Department of State, a copy of letter of the Chief of Engineers respecting an appropriation for improving the navigation of the *St. Croix River, Maine*, made by Act of March 2d, 1867."—Df, DNA, RG 77, Explorations and Surveys, Letters Received; copy, *ibid.*, RG 107, Letters Sent to the President. The enclosure is *ibid.*, RG 77, Explorations and Surveys, Letters Received. On Sept. 2, Seward wrote to USG. "I have the honor to acknowledge the receipt of your communication of the 27th ultimo, and of its accompanying copy of a letter from the Chief of Engineers relative to an appropriation for improving the navigation of the St Croix river, Maine, and to state in reply that the attention of the British Minister has been invited to the subject, in accordance with the suggestion of Maj Genl Humphreys."—LS, *ibid.*

1867, AUG. 27. To Attorney Gen. Henry Stanbery. "In conformity with the Joint Resolution approved September 11th, 1841, I have the honor to request your opinion as to the validity of the title, proposed to be vested in the United States, to the land described in the accompanying papers, selected as the site for a National Cemetery at Lebanon, Kentucky."—LS, DNA, RG 60, Letters Received, War Dept. On Oct. 9, Stanbery wrote to USG. "I have the honor to return, herewith, the papers received under cover of your letter of the 27th of August last, wherein you request my opinion respecting the validity of the title to a piece of land described in those papers, containing a little over 2 acres, which has been selected and is now occupied by the government for a *National Cemetery*, near *Lebanon, Ky.* The proposed grantors of this property, James F. and Wm E. McElroy, do not exhibit a documentary title, but they furnish evidence to show that this is now impracticable, from the fact that the land records of the county in which the land lies were all destroyed July 5, 1863 by the rebel forces under Gen'l Morgan, and offer proof of a long and undisputed accessory title in themselves and those under whom they claim. Upon consideration of all the circumstances presented by the papers, I concur in the views of the U States' Attorney for the District of Kentucky, that, by the accompanying conveyance from the parties aforesaid, the United States acquire a valid title to the premises. But as the papers do not disclose whether any search has been made for incumbrances or liens affecting the land, created by mortgages, judgments, unpaid taxes, or otherwise, I would suggest that satisfactory evidence of their non-existence be required before the purchase money is paid."—Copy, *ibid.*, RG 153, Opinions. On Aug. 27, USG wrote to Stanbery. "I have the honor to transmit herewith papers pertaining to the title of land, part of Lebanon Cemetery, Philadelphia, Pa., used and occupied for the burial of deceased soldiers, proposed to be purchased by the United States, and to request, in conformity with Joint Resolution, approved September 11th, 1841, your opinion as to the validity of the title."—LS, *ibid.*, RG 60, Letters Received, War Dept. On Oct. 16, Stanbery wrote to USG. "I have the honor to return, herewith, the papers submitted by you for my examination, on the 27 of August last, respecting the title to fifty six burial lots or pieces of ground, part of section D of 'Lebanon Cemetery of Philadelphia' proposed to be purchased by your Department for the purpose of using the same as burial places for deceased soldiers, and to advise you that in my opinion the accompanying deed from Jacob C. White and wife, executed June 1, 1867, passes to the United States a good and valid title to the premises for the purpose aforesaid"—Copy, *ibid.*, RG 153, Opinions.

On Aug. 27, USG thrice wrote to Stanbery concerning land titles for proposed national cemetery sites at Baton Rouge, Fort Donelson, and Camp Dennison, Ohio.—LS, *ibid.*, RG 60, Letters Received, War Dept. USG also wrote similar letters to Stanbery concerning land titles for cemeteries at Pine Bluff, Ark. (Sept. 4), New Albany, Ind. (Sept. 9), Camden, Ark. (Sept. 13), Richmond (Oct. 7), Fayetteville, Ark. (Oct. 15), Natchez (Nov. 19; Jan. 7, 1868), Frankfort, Ky. (Jan. 2), and Danville, Ky. (Jan. 13).—LS, *ibid.* On Sept. 30, 1867, USG wrote to Stanbery concerning the cemetery at Lexington, Ky., and on Nov. 5 concerning Oakwood Cemetery, Hyde Park, Ill.—Copies, *ibid.*, RG 107, Letters Sent to the President. Also on Nov. 5, USG wrote to Stanbery concerning the cemetery at Knoxville.— LS, Automatic Retailers of America, Philadelphia, Pa.

1867, AUG. 27. Maj. Gen. George G. Meade, Philadelphia, to USG. "I beg leave to recommend to your favorable consideration the application of Mr. West Funk late Col. & Bvt. Brig. Genl. of volunteers for a commission in the regular Army. Genl. Funk was attached to the 121st Rg. Pa. Vol. was under my immediate command at the battle of Fredericksburgh, and subsequently when his regiment, was transferred to the 5th corps, his conduct was frequently brought to my notice by his immediate commanders. Genl. Funk is spoken of specially by Maj. Gen. Warren in his official report of the battle of Five Forks. In fine Genl. Funk is one of those gallant volunteer officers who in the field in the presence of the enemy won a reputation for gallantry & good conduct which has entitled him to the consideration & favor of the Dept. He is willing to take & will be glad to receive a 2d Lieut's. commission, and I earnestly hope it may be in the power of the Department to bestow one on him."—Copy, DNA, RG 59, Letters of Application and Recommendation. Several letters addressed to USG in 1869 and 1870 recommending West Funk for employment are *ibid.* On April 19 and 27, 1875, Funk, Philadelphia, wrote to USG seeking a consular appointment.—ALS, *ibid.* On July 2, Funk wrote to USG requesting the return of his letters.—ALS, *ibid.*

1867, AUG. 27.   Maj. Gen. Philip H. Sheridan, New Orleans, to USG. "About (250) two hundred and fifty Indians made an attack on the Post of Buffalo Springs, Texas, on the 20th of last July and were repulsed; but they had also attacked a small working party about twenty miles from the Post; and were repulsed, but drove off twenty four mules, killing the herder. Yesterday General Griffin notifys me that General Sturgis, at Fort Belknap, reports the Indians collecting in the Wachita mountains, and thinks they may be preparing to come down on the line of the frontier. I have directed General Griffin to collect the whole of the 6th Cavalry at Buffalo Springs and Belknap, and if necessary, to send some Infantry to these points. This looks as though the Indian war may become general."— LS, DNA, RG 108, Letters Received.

1867, AUG. 27.   Edwin Belcher, Bureau of Refugees, Freedmen, and Abandoned Lands, Macon, Ga., to USG. "at the close of the late war for the preservation of the Union I filed my desire at Division Head quarters to remain in the Army &c and since that time I have made three applications to Hon. Edwin M. Stanton for permission or an order to appear before an examining board for examination for a Lieutenantcy in the Army—my application was endorsed by Generals Geary and Hooker and by my former preceptor Prof Fairbanks of Pennsylvania, and several other Officers of less note. I entered the volunteer service in 1861 as a private Soldier and rose to the rank of Captain through my own Conduct in the field. I served from the early part of 1861 untill July 1865. My object now General is to get an order to appear before the board at Louisville Ky or elsewhere for examination—It has been my misfortune to be unable to secure the assistance of Politicians to urge this matter upon the Secty of war as I was too young at the Commencement of the late war to be of any service to such men, being only 16 years of age.   several of my old Comrades who never saw the actual service that I did have secured appointments in the Army and I now ask you to give me an oppertunity—my first application was in Sept 1865 and my second one was in the latter part of December 1865 or the early part of 1866. Hoping that you will favor me with an early reply."— ALS, DNA, RG 94, ACP, 1814B CB 1867. No appointment followed.

On Oct. 19, 1871, U.S. Representative Robert B. Elliott of S. C. and eight others wrote to USG. "The undersigned delegates to the Southern States Convention representing the several Congressional Districts of the Southern States and the District of Columbia would most respectfully pray your Excellency *not* to remove Mr. Edwin Belcher from the Assessorship of the Third Internal Revenue District of Georgia. Mr Belcher was an officer in the Union Army and served with credit through the entire contest for the preservation of the Union and we beleive from a personal Knowledge of him that he has creditably discharged the duties of his present position. Mr Belcher has been conspicuous in every political canvass in his state since the war. Hoping that your Excellency will see fit to retain him in his present position, . . ."—LS, *ibid.*, RG 56, Appointments. On June 15, 1872, Belcher, Augusta, Ga., wrote to USG. "The cordial manner in which you received a part of the Georgia delegation that called on you while en route to Philadelphia inspires me to write to you and submit a matter to you that I deem of more than ordinary importance. I believe that this state can be carried for the Republican party in the Presidential election by a proper effort being made. Let me state a few facts in order to demonstrate the truth of what I claim. 1st There are one hundred thousand colored voters in this state all Republican who would vote for the party at all times if permitted; 2d There are about one hundred and twenty thousand white voters in the state and of that number twenty thousand voted the Republican ticket when Bullock was elected in 1868 and I believe would vote that way again this fall if they could see a reasonable prospect of success. The impediments to casting the entire colored vote for yourself and Mr. Wilson are: 1st A provision in the state constitution requiring the payment of a poll tax for the year as a condition precedent to the exercise of the right to vote which many by reason of our past difficulties in voting have failed to pay but could be induced to do so by proper organization in every county, and 2d The usual intimidation and violence at the polls, a legitimate remedy for which I submitted to Senator Cameron, to which, he informed me, he had called your attention. With a thorough organization and the lukewarm support Greeley will receive from the Democratic party in this state on account of the opposition of Toombs (whose speech recently delivered I enclose) and Alex. H. Stephens, I think I can affirm with perfect safety that there is no necessity for the defeat of the Republican party in this State. I wish to organize the colored voters and for that purpose I am willing to give up my present position for one of a smaller salary, if it is one which will require me to travel over the State and while performing the duties of which I can organize and prepare for the coming campaign. A place either in the Post Office or Treasury Dept. will enable me to do what I desire. As a colored man appreciating the situation thoroughly I cannot afford to see the Democratic party placed in power by Republican inactivity and the election of Mr. Greeley will be virtually a Democratic victory the result of which will be disastrous in its consequences to the colored race. I know the colored people of the South thoroughly and know how to work with them. I ask for a position to enable me to do this work because I am not able to accomplish it without such assistance and desire a position requiring me to travel as the work cannot be done without visiting every section of the state and my present duties as Assessor do not render it incumbent on me to travel at all. Hoping that my application may be favorably considered, . . ."—ALS, *ibid.* See Ruth Currie-McDaniel, *Carpetbagger of Conscience: A Biography of John Emory Bryant* (Athens, Ga., 1987), pp. 122–23.

1867, AUG. 27. J. H. Jordan, Chicago, to USG. "(*Private*) . . . You are right. Stand firm, just where you are! Your letter to the President of the 17th inst. is the best thing of the season—and will do more to place you *high up* in the estimation of the loyal people of the nation—and to *confirm* You there & remove all *doubts* as to your position,—than anything you have yet *said*, if not yet *done*. Continue as you are—and *firm*—and—whether You *wish* it or not—all the powers this side of hell—cant keep you from being our 'next President.' Excuse my intrusion. I cant help it, I feel so good. I believe I have but expressed what *millions* have this morning expressed and *felt*, on reading your late letter (of 17th) to Andy Johnson, the traitor—"—ALS, USG 3.

1867, AUG. 27. C. Macalester, Philadelphia, to USG. "I cannot refrain from expressing to you my gratification upon perusing your noble, Straight forward letter of 17th, in response to an invitation from the President, for an expression of your views upon the expediency of removing Genl Sheridan—The Sentiments expressed are those of a patriot, and your efforts to protect your friend Fellow Soldier, prove you to be a Stedfast friend—I have heard but one opinion expressed upon your letter, and that is in accordance with that which I have given you on the preceding page— . . . P S. No answer expected—none is necessary, & I know the extent of your public duties"—ALS, USG 3.

1867, AUG. 27. U.S. Representative William A. Pile of Mo., St. Louis, to USG. "Some days ago papers were forwarded to Hon. E M. Stanton endorsed by Senator Henderson Gov Fletcher myself & others for the discharge of James Dillon a minor of this City who enlisted in the thirty first U. S. Infantry being the sole dependence of his father it would gratify his friends here if you would order his discharge, The papers are in the War Department"—Telegram received (at 7:00 P.M.), DNA, RG 107, Telegrams Collected (Bound). On Nov. 25, Lt. Gen. William T. Sherman, St. Louis, telegraphed to USG. "I have seen the man Dillon referred to in Special orders four twenty three (423), He is over eighteen (18) years old, If you want him discharged the order must be positive not depending on age for he is over eighteen and is able bodied"—Telegram received (on Nov. 26, 9:00 A.M.), *ibid.*

1867, AUG. 27.   P. B. Templeton, clerk, War Dept., Washington, D. C., to USG. "I read this morning your letter in regard to the removal of General Sheridan and the reply of the President. An experience of nearly forty years on the newspaper press in England and the United States has convinced me that you thoroughly comprehend the situation of affairs. Accept, then, the heartfelt gratitude of one devotedly attached to the Union for the services which saved it in your own person. I am simply a clerk in this Department, have been since Mr. Cameron's administration; have watched operations throaught with intensity of interest, feel that the rebellion is hardly yet suppressed and must have a strong yet gentle hand to put it down. With one exception, I am the oldest stenographer in the United States; have watched the progress of the government for twenty-seven years in the Senate and House of Representatives. Of this, ask Mr. Potts. I desire your acceptance (knowing you to be a smoker) of a genuine meerschaum pipe with its characteristic *claws*, imported by myself, with the complement of a few cigars, which I am sure will not offend your palate. Thanks for your letter to the President."—ALS, USG 3.

1867, AUG. 28.   To Secretary of State William H. Seward. "I have the honor to inform you that your communication to this Department of the 23d July, enclosing a copy of a despatch from the United States consul at Havana concerning an alleged traffic in *Coolies* between that port & New-Orleans, La., was referred to the General of the Army, who has transmitted to this Department a report on the subject from *Major General Sheridan*, a copy of which I send herewith for your information."—Df, DNA, RG 107, Letters Received from Bureaus; copy, *ibid.*, Letters Sent to the President. On Aug. 19, Maj. Gen. Philip H. Sheridan, New Orleans, had written to Maj. George K. Leet. "I am in receipt of a communication from the ~~Treasury~~ State? Department enclosing a letter from the United States Consul-General at Havanna on the subject of Coolies. I will take the necessary precautions to prevent the violation of the laws by the introduction of Coolie slavery: I know of only one small cargo and the case was put into the hands of Mr Torry District Attorney and I furnished him with a Government boat to make the necessary investigation in the matter while the transport on which they were was at quarantine   The allusion that I had promised protection for this system of slavery is without foundation or even the shadow of it."— LS, *ibid.*, Letters Received from Bureaus. On Aug. 24, USG (as gen.) endorsed this letter. "Respectfully forwarded to the Secy of War, for the information of the Secretary of State."—ES, *ibid.* On Sept. 5, Seward wrote to USG. "I have the honor to acknowledge the receipt of your note of the 28th of August inclosing copy of a report from Major General Sheridan on the subject of the 'Coolie traffic' in Louisiana and to express my approbation of the Generals report."—LS, *ibid.*

1867, AUG. 28.   President Andrew Johnson to USG. "The Secretary of War ad interim will please reinstate Mr Winslow M. Watson as a clerk in the Office of the Paymaster General, if General Brice has no objection to urge against Mr Watson."—LS, DNA, RG 99, Letters Received. Bvt. Maj. Gen. Benjamin W. Brice, paymaster gen., endorsed this letter. "Resp.y returned to the Secretary of War. Mr. Watson was dismissed in Consequence of a recommendation to that effect by Col. Luddington Asst Inspr Genl on the charge of neglecting his duties. I am unable to ascertain satisfactorily from inquiry that the charge was sustained, and incline to the impression that injustice may have been done to Mr W. in the order of dismissal. Mr W. is certainly intelligent & very competent, and besides of good moral character & habits. I therefore have no objection to the revocation of the order dismissing him."—AES (misdated Aug. 19), *ibid.* On Oct. 5, Maj. Gen. George H. Thomas, Louisville, wrote to USG. "In the event of any unusual reduction of the clerical force in the Pay Department, I have the honor to request that the services of Mr Winslow M. Watson may be retained, Mr Watson being well known to myself as having held his present position a number of years.—"—LS, *ibid.* On Nov. 20, Winslow M. Watson, Washington, D. C., wrote to USG. "The undersigned, who is by date of commission the senior Clerk of the Pay Dept. was favored by Gen. Geo. H. Thomas, U S A. on the 5th of Oct. last with a letter requesting you as Act. Secy. of War, to retain me in office in the event of any unusual reduction of the clerical force of the Pay Dept. That letter I entrusted to the care of Mr. Hanson, Chief Clerk of the Pay Department, with the request to show it to Gen. Brice, as I was absent on leave at the time of its receipt. This request he omitted to observe, as I am informed by Gen. Brice, and the letter of Gen. Thomas was sent to the War Dept. where I presume it was not presented to your attention, as the request of Gen. Thomas has been disregarded, and my dismissal from office effected. I therefore respectfully request that you will order an investigation into the case herewith presented, that justice may be done both to Gen. Thomas and myself."—ALS, *ibid.*

1867, AUG. 28.   Judge Advocate Gen. Joseph Holt to USG. "The accompanying records of cases tried at New Orleans, La., in the early part of the present month, are respectfully submitted with the following report . . . It is respectfully advised that Sergt. Alfred Gowigs be restored to duty on the ground of a fatal error in the proceedings; that private Williams be released for the same reason; that the sentence against Sergt. Bishop be mitigated to six months imprisonment; that of Corporal Newson to imprisonment for one year; priv't John Williams, the cripple, to one month's confinement; Private Jeffrey, for total failure of proof, to be restored to duty; Private Westley Niggins' sentence to be mitigated to three years imprisonment; and the sentence of Pvt. Leon Joseph, the instigator of the mutiny, be commuted to imprisonment for ten years. Should these suggestions be regarded as inexpedient, it is respectfully advised that prior to any action of the Executive in cases of such grave importance, inquiries be made into the character of Lieut. Warren, the Commanding officer of the Company, and his treatment of the colored soldiers under his command; matters left wholly undeveloped at the hurried trial of the prisoners;—the result of which may be of assistance to the Executive in arriving at a correct conclusion in the premises."—Copy, DNA, RG 153, Letters Sent. On Sept. 3, Holt wrote to USG concerning two additional soldiers involved in the case.—Copy, *ibid.* On Oct. 7, Holt wrote to USG. *"Private Eli Winters Co. A. 39th Infty,* was convicted by a General Court Martial convened at New Orleans, in August last, under the following charges. 1. Violation of the seventh Article of War. In having with other members of his company, and while a member of the guard, excited and joined in a mutiny. This at New Orleans, La., on or about the 14th of July 1867. 2. Violation of the eighth Article of War. In this, that while a member of the guard, and when his company was in a state of mutiny, he failed to exert himself to quell the mutiny, and did remain inactive when the members of his company committed an assault on Lieut. Lucius H. Warren, 39th Infty, the commanding officer of the company. Time and place as above. 3. Violation of the ninth Article of War. In making an assault upon Lieut. Lucius H. Warren his commanding officer, and striking him with a musket, the said Lieut. being in the execution of his office   The court finds the prisoner guilty under all the charges and specifications—except the words in the specification to the third charge, alleging that he struck Lieut Warren, substituting therefor the words 'did lift up a musket against, and did wilfully disobey the lawful command of his superior officer'—and sentence him to be shot to death with musketry, at such time and place as the commanding General may direct, two thirds of the court concurring therein. Genl. Mower approves the findings and sentence, and forwards the record for the action of the President. The conviction in this case rests solely on the testimony of Lieut. Warren, the evidence of the only other witness called for the prosecution—private Henry McGee, being favorable to the prisoner. Lieut. Warren's statement is as follows: 'On the 14th of July 1867 the prisoner was a member of the camp guard, and a mutiny was in existence in the camp. I went out from my tent to stop it. The guard was ordered up to where the mutiny was. I called upon the prisoner as one of the guard to come forward and help me quell the mutiny and assist me in tying up a man named Wilburne; the prisoner positively refused to move, making use at the time of words to the effect that the man Wilburne should not be tied up—that he had been punished enough; or words to that effect. I afterwards called upon every member of the company to come forward and to help put the mutiny down; they all refused, and the prisoner refused with the rest. The mutiny lasted 38 to 40 hours, till the arrival of a company from New Orleans to arrest the mutineers. During this time the prisoner was present with other members of the company who were making use of mutinous language and he was giving assent thereto. One of the expressions was "there is only one white man against all us niggers, Kill him! and all the whisky and money in town belongs to us." Another was "It is a damned shame boys to see men shot down like dogs in this way, and not prevent it, and you are not men if you allow it." I had been in command of the company only two days and with it only thirteen days. During the mutiny I received four bayonet wounds, one of them severe, disabling my arm; and about twelve blows on my right arm and back which left black and blue places from three to eight inches long. The prisoner raised his musket to strike me, but being surrounded closely at the time, and not having known the men long enough at the time to remember faces, I do not know who struck me. I do not know if he did or not.' . . . After a careful study of this unsatisfactory record, this Bureau is of opinion that the testimony adduced does not fully sustain the findings, and it is recommended that they be disapproved."—Copy, *ibid.*

1867, AUG. 28.   Richard M. Corwine, Cincinnati, to USG. "The enclosed resolutions passed unanimously by our County Convention yesterday, may afford you some satisfaction as showing how your Course, in the present trying times, is esteemed. It was the largest and most intelligent Convention ever assembled here, marked by every Characteristic of manhood and patriotism. It fairly represented the Views of the Union population of this part of Ohio."—ALS, USG 3. The enclosure is *ibid.*

1867, AUG. 28.   U.S. Senator Charles D. Drake of Mo., Lanesborough, Mass., to USG. "Permit me to tender you my heartfelt thanks for your letter to the President against the removal of Gen. Sheridan. It gives you another claim to the confidence and gratitude of the loyal people of the country. When, a year ago, I was canvassing the State of Missouri, the Radicals of that State almost everywhere asked me, with much interest, 'What about Gen. Grant?' and I always answered them, 'You can rely upon him to any extent.' I am not surprised that on the first fit opportunity you have vindicated the accuracy of my judgment. It would have been unwise for you to have expressed yourself without such an opportunity: with it, you could not have said less and been true to yourself. Renewedly thanking you, . . ."—ALS, USG 3.

1867, AUG. 28.   U.S. Senator Thomas A. Hendricks of Ind., Indianapolis, to USG. "Genl. Geo C. Thomas, (who commanded the District of Columbia. volunteers during the war), is a clerk in the War Department, in the Bureau of Engineers, and is anxious for an appointment to a better position, and the object of this note is to say that, if you can provide for him a position of better rank & pay I will be specially gratified. He is a very excellent business man, & worthy gentleman."—ALS, DNA, RG 107, Letters Received, T156 1867. On Sept. 2, George C. Thomas, Washington, D. C., wrote to USG. "The accompanying note from Senator Hendricks was prompted by a long personal friendship. I know of no special appointment for which to apply but any position which will increase my present salary ($1600. pr annum) I would gladly fill. My present duties are to me of the most agreeable character but the high price of rent & living render it almost an impossibility to furnish the necessary support for a large family of eight

children and several dependents. I have ten years served of capability &
faithfulness in the War Department to which I can refer in case the Secretary should have the opportunity to better my official position."—ALS,
ibid. See *ibid.*, RG 94, ACP, 470T CB 1867.

1867, AUG. 28. William S. Oliver, Little Rock, to USG. "We the loyal
few of Arkansas have this day received your letter (through the press) to
the President protesting against the removal of Genl Sheridan, and as Vice
Chairman of the 'Ark State Central Republican Committee' thank you in
behalf of the loyal few of this State for thus cheering us when we are
disponding for we are few in number, but not in zeal. God bless you we
all say & may he spare your life long to us is the prayer of the loyal men.
We are and will continue to work for the reconstruction of our State in
accordance with the will of Congress   You will excuse me General for
troubling you with this note but thinking you would not think it impudent
in one of your Old Officers to drop his Genl a line to let him know I am still
in the fight   You will remember me as Col W. S. Oliver of the 7th Mo
Infty to whom you was pleased to give a complimentary Order for running
the Transports by the Batteries of Vicksburg which I now have & prize
highly. I have been living in Ark since the close of the war, and am now
Register (under Reconstruction Act of Congress, for this county. Knowing
that you have not time to drop a line ever to one of your Old Offices who
has always admired you for your patriotism and integrity, it would be folly
to expect an acknowlediment of these few lines. I therefore beg leave to
asure you that your name shall never be forgotten by the loyal men of
Arkansas   Would we had a Sheridan here   I beg leave to subscribe myself One of your old Officers"—ALS, USG 3. See *PUSG*, 8, 125–26; *ibid.*,
9, 591.

1867, AUG. 28. Daniel Ruggles, former C.S.A. brig. gen., Fredericksburg, Va., to USG. "I have the honor to request permission to leave the U.
States for the purpose of visiting relations in Nova Scotia—during a brief
period."—ALS, DNA, RG 94, Letters Received, 397R 1867.

1867, AUG. 28. Hawkins Taylor, Washington, D. C., to USG. "Some
time in last March or 1st April I heard Gen Gordon Granger declare that
'Johnson (the President) should march a file of men up to the capital &
disperse that D—D rump Congress' that they were an illegal body besides
many similar expressions. If such a man is to be put in command the country should know his sentiments at least"—ALS, DNA, RG 108, Letters
Received.

1867, AUG. 29. To Secretary of the Interior Orville H. Browning. "I
have the honor to inform you that your communication of the 23d May, 67,
respecting the claims of certain *Pottawattomie Indians* in Texas, has been
sent to the Treasury Department with a report by the Qr. Mr. Genl., to

whom the subject was referred for investigation."—Copy, DNA, RG 107, Letters Sent to the President. On Sept. 2, Act. Secretary of the Interior William T. Otto wrote to USG. "I have the honor to acknowledge the receipt of your communication of the 29th ult; advising me of the transmission, accompanied by a report of the Quartermaster General, of the letter of the Secretary of the Interior of the 22d May last, relative to the claims of certain Pottawatamie Indians in Texas, to the Treasury Department."—LS, *ibid.*, Letters Received from Bureaus. On Aug. 29, USG wrote to Secretary of the Treasury Hugh McCulloch. "As recommended by the Qr. Mr. General of the Army, I send herewith his report of the 12th June, respecting the claims of certain *Pottawattomie Indians* in the state of *Kansas*, presented in a communication of May 21 /67 from the Department of the Interior which with the accompanying papers is also enclosed herewith."—Df, *ibid.*, RG 92, Letters Received; copy, *ibid.*, RG 107, Letters Sent to the President. On Nov. 21, Bvt. Maj. Gen. Daniel H. Rucker, act. q. m. gen., wrote to USG. "On June 12th, 1867, a report was forwarded to the Secretary of War from this office, recommending that certain Pottowattomie Indians be relieved from the deduction of 50% upon their accounts for tolls, &c., imposed by Genl. Orders No. 6., Q. M. G. O., 1863. It is respectfully requested that this office be informed of the action taken upon that report, with the view of causing proper settlement to be made of similar accounts under adjustment in this office."—LS, *ibid.*, RG 92, Letters Received. Additional papers are *ibid.*

1867, AUG. 29.   To Attorney Gen. Henry Stanbery. "I have the honor to transmit herewith papers in the case of property at Fort Ridgely which is claimed by W H. Randall, and to ask the opinion of the Attorney General as to the validity of his title."—LS, DNA, RG 60, Letters Received, War Dept. See *PUSG*, 16, 160–61, 221.

1867, AUG. 29.   Judge Advocate Gen. Joseph Holt to USG. "J. Lewis Spaulding, 1st Lieut. 1st. U. S. Infantry, was tried Aug. 10th last by General Court Martial at New Orleans, La., under the following charge:— Conduct unbecoming an officer and a gentleman. 1. In that accused, aide-de-camp to Gen. Mower, and a. a. a. G. Dist. of Louisiana, did refuse to approve the vouchers of one Pat. Flannery, amounting to $60—said vouchers being for the arrest & delivery of certain deserters, Howard & Stewart, of the 4th Cavalry; giving as a reason that they would not be paid for a month; and did afterwards purchase said vouchers from said Flannery for the sum of $35,—causing said Flannery to sign the receipt as for the full amount, and obtaining their immediate payment. This June 15. 1867. . . . It is respectfully advised, after a careful study of, and reflection upon, the evidence in this case, that the sentence be enforced. That the accused can have been ignorant of the impropriety of his acts, supposing him to be free from personal venality, can scarcely be believed; and beyond this, he fails to adduce evidence of such a character as to warrant the supposition that his conduct has not been venal. In the conflict of testimony, it is difficult to arrive at a positive judgment upon the question of his deliberate abuse of trust; but the probabilities at least are against the theory of his innocence; and as, with the evidence and the witnesses before them and with a personal knowledge of the accused to guide their judgments, the Court has expressed its opinion that the service will be better for his removal from it, it is thought that it is desirable the sentence should be carried into execution."—Copy, DNA, RG 153, Letters Sent.

1867, AUG. 29.   Brig. Gen. Andrew A. Humphreys, chief of engineers, to USG. "I have the honor to acknowledge the receipt of the letter of the State Department of 28th June, enclosing extract from a dispatch of our Minister to Denmark, presenting interesting professional information respecting the coast defences of Copenhagen; and to say that the information has been communicated from this office to the Board of Engineers for Fortifications at New York; and to request that my thanks may be transmitted to our Minister, Mr. Yeaman, for his consideration in the matter."—LS, DNA, RG 107, Letters Received from Bureaus.

1867, AUG. 29.   Vice Admiral David D. Porter, Annapolis, to USG. "Captain Dominick Lynch of the Navy, an old shipmate and an esteemed friend has applied to me for a letter to enable his son to get into the Army. I take great pleasure in recommending him—I tried to get him appointed on my staff while I commanded the north Atlantic squadron, but for some reason the department did not seem disposed to gratify me, tho I notice that the young man's father had performed valuable services during the time he was under my command.—I would be much gratified to see young Lynch get the appointment he seks, and am sure that he will do credit to the service—"—ALS, DNA, RG 94, ACP, 67 1872. On the same day and on Sept. 20, Dominick Lynch, Jr., Philadelphia, wrote to USG requesting an appointment in the U.S. Army.—ALS, *ibid.* On Sept. 24, Lynch wrote to USG acknowledging receipt of his appointment as 2nd lt., 4th Cav.—ALS, *ibid.*

1867, AUG. 29.   John T. Deweese, Raleigh, N. C., to USG. "I am directed by Gov Holden Chairman of the Republican State Central Commitee of N C to tender to you the thanks and Congratulations of the Union men of this State for your *brave* and *fearless* defence of Major Gen P H Sheridan, and Invite you to be present at the State Convention which meets here on the 4th day September a large number of Deligates will be present representing the Union *Men* of the State, amongst them will be a number of your old Officers and Soldiers of the Western Army"—ALS, USG 3.

1867, AUG. 29.   Thomas O. Edwards, Lancaster, Ohio, to USG. "The recent conduct of President Johnson fills us with astonishment & fear—

When he was 'swinging round the circle'; his acts & speeches mortified & insulted us—now, having no incentive such as was then present—we know not what 'a day may bring forth'—Your character & firmness—your patriotism & intelligence is now our only hope—You have our confidence & love— We trust you—confide in you—without fear—& in you alone in this Emergency—We cannot understand the President—& have no confidence in any promises or acts—of his—Two sons—two sons in law & myself gave our entire time & affection to our country in the past rebellion—Three of us will never be able to fulfill the duties of life from injuries & illnesses received in the war—of that we do not complain—we only want peace & security—This is the sentiment of most who went, as we & you, to the fight, & stayed true—I was a member of 30th Congress & Andrew Johnson was the only member I never spoke to—Let me implore you not to yield one point to this usurper & dangerous man—It is true, he has no party, & is partially divested of his 'main strength'—but there is enough of him in our present party distractions—to make him formidable to our liberty—The Senators who emasculated the House bill, will have a fearful account to settle in the future, & those of both houses who in despite of the Secy. of War's, & your importunities—adjourned; will have against them much popular indignation—But this is not the time for punishment, or fault finding—Conquer the enemy & then have courts-martial—Stand where you are 'Our hearts our hopes are all with thee Are all with thee' May God in whom we confide, & to Whom we can so easily trace our recent escapes from destruction, hold you, in the hollow of his hand, & strengthen & direct you—If you fail we are lost—if you are firm—we are safe—You may not remember me—refer to Genl Ben. Brice paymaster Genl—an old friend"— ALS, USG 3.

1867, AUG. 29.   U.S. Representative J. Lawrence Getz of Pa., Reading, to USG. "Furlough of Henry Ludwig whose case I reported to Dept expires tomorrow   May I be authorized to tell him to remain at house till further orders from your Dept,   Please answer by telegraph"—Telegram received (at 4:00 P.M.), DNA, RG 107, Telegrams Collected (Bound). At 5:30 P.M., Bvt. Maj. Gen. Edward D. Townsend telegraphed to Getz. "Case of Henry Ludwig referred to me—Will examine it and inform you—Meantime please tell him to remain—"—ALS (telegram sent), *ibid.*

1867, AUG. 29.   Oliver Potter, Newport, R. I., to USG. "I Enclose My Business card to show that I am with and among the People, and of course know the Public sentiment in relation to your letter to President Johnson, on the removal of Gen Sheridan.   it meets the hearty approval of a very large Majority of Our Citisens   And although I belong to the Masonic Body Our obligations to Our Country, is always greater and stronger than to an Individual however high His Possittion may be and President. Johnson makes a great mistake if He expects support from the Masons in wrong doing"— ALS, USG 3.

1867, AUG. 29.   A. H. Snyder, Philadelphia, to USG. "I cannot help writing and congratulating you on your truly heroic and manly course— may God bless and direct you—as I believe he always has—and enable you to fight it out successfully, when the line you have marked out is the em- bodiment of right and wisdom, millions of people loved you more now cling to you, your last noble act for your country has everlastingly wrapped you in their unselfish affections, the cry goes up all over the land—as in other dark days—thank *God* that we have Genl. Grant—Remember that the great American people never go backwards—May you—through the assis- tance of the supreme Ruler of the universe—come out of this battle un- scathed and be awarded that eminence among your people which you so justly deserve—Believing that the Country is yet safe, and knowing that you will be backed in any emergency . . ."—ALS, USG 3.

1867, AUG. 30.   To Secretary of the Treasury Hugh McCulloch. "I have the honor to return herewith the letter of the *U. S. Minister at London* enclosed in your communication of the 22d instant, with accompanying Invoice of goods, for the use of the Freedmen of the United States, shipped on the Steamer 'Nebraska' for New York, and to request at the instance of the Commissioner of Freedmen that the *Collector of Customs at that port* be instructed to admit the same free of all duties and charges."—Copy, DNA, RG 107, Letters Sent to the President. On Aug. 22, Asst. Secretary of the Treasury John F. Hartley had written to USG. "I have the honor to transmit herewith a letter from Hon C. F. Adams United States, Minister at London, dated the 9th instant, covering an invoice (No. 519) of goods for the use of the freedmen of the United States—said invoice representing the value of £183-8-4. Before these goods can be admitted to entry free of duty and charges, the usual certification from your Department, that they are for the United States is necessary. The papers are submitted for your action."—Copy, *ibid.*, RG 56, Letters Sent. On Aug. 24, Maj. Gen. Oliver O. Howard endorsed this letter. "Respectfully returned to the Hon. Secty of War, with the request that the usual action may be taken by the Depart- ment, to secure the free entry of the within mentioned goods."—Copy, *ibid.*, RG 105, Endorsements.

    On Nov. 14, Hartley wrote to USG. "I have the honor to transmit here- with a letter from U. S. Minister, C. F. Adams, dated London Nov. 1. 1867, covering an invoice of goods of the value of £272.17.7, for the use of the Freedmen in the United States. Before these goods can be admitted to entry free of duty, the usual certification from your Department, that they are for the use of the United States, is necessary. The papers are sub- mitted for your action."—LS, *ibid.*, Letters Received. On Nov. 19, USG wrote to McCulloch. "Your communication of the 14th instant, transmit- ting letter from the U S Minister at London, covering ian invoice of goods of the value of £272,17.7. for the use of the Freedmen of the United States, whas been received and referred to the Commissioner of the Freedmen's Bureau, at whose instance I have the honor to request that you will instruct the Collector of Customs at the port of New York to deliver the same free of duties and charges. The enclosures to your letter are herewith returned." —Copies, *ibid.*; *ibid.*, RG 107, Letters Sent to the President. On Jan. 6, 1868, Hartley wrote to USG. "I have the honor to transmit herewith a letter from United States Minister Adams dated London 20th ultimo covering an invoice of goods of the value of £177.10.2 intended for the use of the Freedmen in the United States. Before these goods can be admitted to entry free of duty, the usual certification from your Department that they are for the use of the United States is, necessary, The papers are submitted for your action."—Copy, *ibid.*, RG 56, Letters Sent.

1867, AUG. 30. To Attorney Gen. Henry Stanbery. "I have the honor to transmit herewith a communication of the Chief of Ordnance in relation to the title of the Willard Sears estate, authorized to be purchased by the United States by the Army Appropriation Act of March 2d 1867, and to request the the opinion of the Attorney General as to the validity of the title may be given as soon as practicable."—LS, DNA, RG 60, Letters Received, War Dept. On Aug. 28, Bvt. Maj. Gen. Alexander B. Dyer, chief of ordnance, had written to USG. "The abstract of title to the Willard Sears' estate, which was authorized to be purchased by the United States, by the Army appropriation act of March 2d, 1867, was forwarded by the U. S. District Attorney, direct to the Attorney General, at whose office it was received on the first of this month. In order to make the purchase, it is necessary that the opinion of the Attorney General as to the validity of the title should be had; and it is respectfully requested that the Secretary of War will ask that the opinion be given as soon as practicable."—ALS, *ibid.*, RG 156, Letters Received. On Sept. 16, Stanbery wrote to USG. "I have the honor to transmit, herewith, the abstract and other papers relating to the title to the 'Willard Sears estate' which were received here directly from the U. S. Attorney for the District of Massachusetts and to which reference is made in the communication of the Chief of Ordnance inclosed in your letter to this office of the 30th ult. in which you request an opinion as to the validity of said title . . . Before this conveyance is accepted, and payment of the purchase money made, Mr. Sears should be required to relieve the property from the said mortgage and also furnish satisfactory evidence of the non-existence of any tax lien thereon."—Copy, *ibid.*, RG 153, Opinions. On Oct. 12, Judge Advocate Gen. Joseph Holt endorsed papers concerning this case. "Respectfully returned to the Secretary of War. The within account of *Hon. Geo. S. Hilliard*, Dist. Attorney for Mass., amounts to $688 25/100; which is made up of a charge of $600. for examining title and preparing abstract of the Sears Estate in Watertown, Mass., and a further item of $88 25/100 shown to have been incurred for plans and copies of deeds and records. The estate was authorized by Congress to be purchased for the sum of about $50.000. The papers in the case, and especially the elaborate abstract furnished by Mr. Hilliard, sufficiently establish, in the opinion of this Bureau, that his services, in connection with an estate of such value, are estimated by him at a reasonable sum. The title in question is understood to have been finally approved by the Attorney General, and the purchase to have been ordered to be consummated; and as the employment of Mr Hilliard was duly authorized through the Ordnance Department, it is concluded that the account may properly be allowed:—to be paid from the appropriation for 'Arsenals.' "—Copy, *ibid.*, Letters Sent.

1867, AUG. 30. To Bvt. Maj. Gen. Daniel H. Rucker, act. q. m. gen. "You will please take immediate steps to break up *'Lincoln Depot'* (in this city) without delay, and discharge the employees, or such of them as can be spared. Distribute through the country to the nearest depots to where the articles at Lincoln Depot are likely to be wanted such as are serviceable, and dispose of the remainder, or unserviceable portion, to the best advantage for Government."—Copies, DNA, RG 94, Letters Received, 621W 1867; *ibid.*, RG 107, Letters Sent to the President. On Sept. 24, Rucker wrote to USG. "Referring to your instructions of the 30th ult. to take immediate steps to break up the Lincoln Depôt in this City, and to distribute the serviceable stores, now there, through the country to the nearest depôts where the articles are likely to be wanted, and to dispose of the *unserviceable* stores to the best advantage, I have the honor to state that in the list of stores at the Lincoln Depôt there are many which are classed as 'serviceable', which, in the opinion of the Quartermaster General, will not justify the cost of shipment and future care and storage at other depôts. I mention as belonging to this class tin cups, funnels, &c., not worth transportation; horse medicines not included in the standard supply table, and other medicines and stores which may depreciate in value by age, wagons that require considerable expense for repairs before they can be issued; horse and mule shoes of which there is on hand an excess beyond the prospective issue for three years, and many other articles which may be similarly described. I therefore respectfully recommend that, in carrying out the instructions before referred to, the Acting Quartermaster General be authorized to sell such of the stores at the Lincoln Depot as in his opinion it will be more to the interest of the service so to dispose of, than to ship to other depots."—LS, *ibid.*, RG 92, Reports to the Secretary of War (Press).

1867, AUG. 30. Chaplain George W. Pepper, 40th Inf., Wellington, Ohio, to USG. "Can I have ten 10 days Extension Recommended by Gen Sickles. Reason indisposition."—Telegram received (at 1:50 P.M.), DNA, RG 94, Letters Received, 549P 1867; *ibid.*, RG 107, Telegrams Collected (Bound). On the same day, Bvt. Brig. Gen. Frederick T. Dent endorsed this telegram to Bvt. Maj. Gen. Edward D. Townsend. "Gen Grant desires me to say to you to grant this extension"—AES, *ibid.*, RG 94, Letters Received, 549P 1867.

1867, Aug. 30.   R. W. Downman, Washington, D. C., to USG. "The corporation of the town of Fredericksburg Va, has been removing some obstructions & wrecks from the channel of the River, and in so doing, the contractor Mr W. S. Richardson discovered several large iron guns—As these offer obstruction to navigation, and are not included in the contract to remove the wrecks, I am requested to ask, whether the Sect of War will not allow the contractor to sell them to reimburse himself for any expense he may be at in raising them. They will probably bring from $80 to 100 each as old iron, and it would not pay him to take them up unless he could sell them for what they would bring. There are so far as known four iron guns in the river; if he should discover any brass pieces—he will turn them over to the Government and take 50 pr ct. of their value for his services"— ALS, DNA, RG 107, Letters Received, D205 1867.

1867, Aug. 31.   To Secretary of the Interior Orville H. Browning. "Your letter of June 21st enclosing one from the Commissioner of Indian Affairs respecting the *furnishing of rations to the destitute Cherokees*, was referred to the Commissioner of the Bureau of Freedmen &c., who has returned the same with the following report on the subject—'This matter does not appear to come within the operations of the Freedmen's Bureau and in the opinion of the Commissioner there is no authority under the laws regulating the same, for the issue of the rations to the Cherokee Indians   It appears to be entirely within the jurisdiction of the Commissioner of Indian Affairs.' "—Copy, DNA, RG 107, Letters Sent to the President. On Sept. 3, Act. Secretary of the Interior William T. Otto wrote to USG. "I have the honor to acknowledge the receipt of your letter of the 31st ulto., containing the report of the Commissioner of the Bureau of Freedmen. etc., relative to the issue of rations to the destitute Cherokee Indians, in reply to inquiry of this Department of June 21st."—LS, *ibid.*, Letters Received from Bureaus.

1867, Aug. 31.   To Secretary of State William H. Seward. "I have the honor to send herewith a copy of a communication to this Department from the Secretary of the Swiss Consulate General respecting an inspection by U. S. Officers of *arms which are being fabricated for the Swiss Government* & beg to be informed whether it is deemed proper to accede to the request contained in the letter."—Df, DNA, RG 107, Letters Received from Bureaus; copy, *ibid.*, Letters Sent to the President. On Aug. 24, Charles J. Ost, secretary, Swiss Consulate at Washington, D. C., New York City, had written to USG. "During the latter part of May last, the undersigned had the honor to wait upon the Honorable Edwin M Stanton, Secretary of War, introducing Captain de Mechel, of the Swiss Federal Staff, accredited on a special mission to the President of the United States in regard to arms, which the Government of Switzerland desired to obtain from the Government of the United States. The Ordnance Department being unable to furnish the arms at that time, and the war cloud in Europe having passed away for a time, Captain de Mechel contracted with the Peabody Arms Co for a quantity of breech loading guns, to be delivered between the months of September and December proximo. Major General A. B. Dyer, Chief of Ordnance, U. S. Army kindly offered with the consent of the Honorable Secretary (should Captain de Mechel order arms in this Country) to provide Inspector's from the Ordnance Department to inspect and proove the arms made for our Government. The time drawing near, when the Providence Tool Co is prepared to furnish the first instalments of guns, it becomes necessary to employ such inspectors, as the Department will Kindly place at the disposal of Captain de Mechel, and for this reason the undersigned would most respectfully solicit the Department to cause General Dyer to designate such officers or to take such steps as will meet the necessities of the case. Thanking the Department in advance for very Kind attentions, . . ."—ALS, *ibid.*, RG 156, Letters Received. On Sept. 3, Seward wrote to USG. "I have the honor to acknowledge the receipt of your letter of the 31st ultimo, accompanied by a copy of one addressed to you by the Secretary of the Swiss Consul General, asking whether there is any impropriety in acceding to his request for a detail of officers to inspect arms which his government has ordered in this country. In reply, I have the honor to state that this Department is not aware of any objection arising from the foreign relations of the United States, to a compliance with the request."— LS, *ibid.*, RG 107, Letters Received from Bureaus.

1867, AUG. 31.   To Attorney Gen. Henry Stanbery. "I have the honor to send herewith a communication from the Chief of Ordnance, respecting a suit which it is proposed to bring against the United States for the possession of a *tract of land* at *Harpers Ferry*: with a request that the proper defence be made in the case."—Copy, DNA, RG 107, Letters Sent to the President. On Dec. 24, Asst. Attorney Gen. John M. Binckley wrote to USG about lawsuits pertaining to property at Harpers Ferry.—Copy, *ibid.*, RG 60, Letters Sent. On Dec. 28, Bvt. Maj. Gen. Alexander B. Dyer, chief of ordnance, wrote to USG concerning this matter.—LS, *ibid.*, Letters Received, War Dept.

1867, AUG. 31.   To Professor Albert E. Church, USMA. "I am authorized to appoint your Nephew vice Rebhorn if as is understood the latter has not reported or failed in his examination. Woodbridgeuff is appointed vice Reynolds."—ALS (telegram sent), DNA, RG 107, Telegrams Collected (Unbound). See *PUSG*, 16, 475. William S. Church failed to graduate from USMA; Charles Albert Woodruff graduated in 1871.

1867, AUG. 31.   Brig. Gen. Andrew A. Humphreys, chief of engineers, to USG. "I have the honor to recommend that Maj H. M. *Robert*, Corps of Engineers, now at West Point, N. Y. be ordered to report to Maj Gen H. W. Halleck at San Francisco, Cal. for duty on his staff. and that orders be issued by the Adjutant General changing Maj. Robert's station accordingly. If Maj General Halleck's need of an officer be immediate, it is further recommended that Capt *Ernst*, now on duty at San Francisco, as Assistant to Maj and Bt. Col Mendell, Corps of Engineers, be directed to report to Maj Gen Halleck for duty until Maj Robert shall have arrived at San Francisco."—LS, DNA, RG 94, Letters Received, 499P 1867.

1867, AUG. 31.   Moran Brothers, New York City, to USG. "On the 27th april last we wrote to your Department asking authority to remove & take possession of about 366 Tons Rail Road Iron in the old Rebel Fortifications at Galveston Texas, which Iron was confiscated & taken out of the possession of our agents by the Rebel authorities upon the ground that we were alien ennemies. To prove our claim we enclosed *1st.* G. W. Dent Esq U. S. Treasury agent at Galveston certified copy from the Sequestration Record Book of the fact of the Confiscation   *2nd.*—G. W. Dent Esq's certificate that his Department had no claims on said Iron   *3rd.* Printed copy of Genl Wrights special order No 112 authorizing us to take possession of any of our said Iron on the Island of Galveston except such as might be in use in the fortifications—and we particularly asked that if our petition should not be granted the said 3 documents might be returned to us. On the 11th June we received an answer from your department declining to give us an order to take our Iron or to pay us the value thereof; and omitting to return us the documents & altho' we wrote again on the 13 June with the same request we have not yet received them   Please excuse us for again asking that these documents may be returned to us as they are important to us to enable us to prove our claim—"—LS, DNA, RG 107, Letters Received, M472 1867.

1867, AUG. 31.   Alexander H. Stephens, Crawfordville, Ga., to USG. "A youth of fine talents Willie J. Newsom of Green County in this State and which county is in the 5th Congressional District is very desirous of getting the appointment of Cadet at West Point—How those places are now filled from this State or whether filled at all I do not know but I take pleasure in reccommending him as a suitable person for the position in case there be a vacancy from this District and any appointments to the Military Academy are made from this state at present—"—ALS, DNA, RG 94, Correspondence, USMA. On Sept. 2, Willie J. Newsom, Union Point, Ga., wrote to USG. "I take the liberty of addressing to find if you will secure for me an appointment as cadet to the Military Academy at West Point New York   I am very desireous of entering the academy as a Cadet   You will find a letter inclosed from Mr Stephens certifying to my character   I will be eighteen years of age on the fifth of this month and never served in the Confederate army or navy   I do not know whether the appointmets can be made from this state at this time   if they can be made you will favor me very much if you will give me the appointment   If you can not assist me please be so kind as to place my petition before President Johnson as I learn that he can make appointments at large   Hoping to hear from you . . ."— ALS, *ibid.*

[1867, AUG.].   "A friend" to USG. "Private. Splendid Letter. Three cheers for General Grant. Gen Washburn himself could have hardly desired a better letter, or expression of Political views and sentiments. There's nothing like having the heart right, and with it honesty, fidelity, and the utmost cordiality ~~and~~ urbanity and courtesy towards all in the exercise of power. It is a proud record to win on one's merit, worth and integrity—better than a princely fortune and corruption. The whole town is rejoicing to night over the noble protest of the Illinois Favorite General, except some perhaps of those who believe it is just as fair to buy up, a national as they have a state government   The great West however has a voice in this matter, and may it be heard and cry for the right and may Sheridan be kept at N. O. if possible. Please burn"—AL, USG 3.

1867, SEPT. 1.   Thurlow Weed, New York City, to USG. "Public men are responsible for their friends. There is widespread demoralization among Internal Revenue Officers. The combination here is formidable. Among others Col. Hillyer is alledged to be implicated. If, as is represented, he is aiding the effort to remove Mr. Rollins, that fact will confirm suspicion. It is also alledged that Col. Hillyer has paid little to the Government, while his predecessor saved large amounts. There will be Congressional Investigations into these Revenue frauds, and I am unwilling to see damaging exposures in the case of any officer for whose integrity Gen. Grant is responsible. I have no objection that Col Hillyer should see this letter"—Copy, USG 3. On Sept. 4, William S. Hillyer, New York City, wrote to Weed. "Gen. Grant has forwarded to me, without comment, your letter of the 1st inst. addressed to him. The impertinence of the letter would be incomprehensible did it emanate from any other than yourself. The impertinence of your addressing Gen. Grant on any subject, the impertinence of your addressing Gen. Grant about me, the impertinence of you accusing anybody of a political partnership in fraud, is impertinence without parallel. You certainly have lost your reputed shrewdness, or been smitten with unwonted modesty. Don't you suppose that Gen. Grant knows your reputation and my character? I had supposed you gloried in your reputation as 'King of the Lobby and Prince of Jobbers?' . . . Gen. Grant, as you know, is neither responsible for my appointment, nor my integrity. I was appointed at the special request of the President, who told me in Washington that you applied for the appointment for your friend Webster; and the President and Secretary told you the place was promised to me, and that as soon as you heard it; you said it was a most judicious selection. Your suggestion of the appointment of a Congress Committee is what you know that I have announced I would ask for, and what you least desire. I have repeatedly and publicly stated that such a Committee should be appointed, to make a thorough investigation into corruption, and about the revenue system in this city. . . . I have only one more word to say. You state I am said to be implicated in frauds. Your age alone saves you from my denouncing you as a liar. After six months in office I can proudly say what I should not have been able to say had I been controlled by you, that my hands are entirely clean. What prouder record can any officer in New-York, possessing power and patronage, have than the fact that Thurlow Weed was his enemy?"—*New York Tribune*, Sept. 6, 1867.

1867, Sept. 2.   To Secretary of the Interior Orville H. Browning. "I have the honor to send herewith for your consideration, a communication of the 13th Febry. 67, from the Commanding General of the Military Division of the Pacific, concerning a treaty entered into by *Capt Ilges & Col. Lovell* of the 14th U. S. Infantry, with certain tribes of the *Apache Indians*, with a recommendation that it be disavowed."—Df, DNA, RG 94, Letters Received, 163P 1867; copy, *ibid.*, RG 107, Letters Sent to the President. On Sept. 3, Act. Secretary of the Interior William T. Otto wrote to USG acknowledging his letter.—LS, *ibid.*, Letters Received from Bureaus.

1867, Sept. 2.   To Secretary of State William H. Seward. "I beg to enclose herewith a note introducing *Sir Frederick Bruce* to the Supt of the *Military Academy at West Point* as desired in your letter of the 31st ultimo."—Df, DNA, RG 107, Letters Received from Bureaus; copy, *ibid.*, Letters Sent to the President. On the same day, USG wrote to Bvt. Brig. Gen. Thomas G. Pitcher, USMA. *"Sir Frederick Bruce,* her Brittanic Majesty's Minister, near Washington having expressed his intention to visit West Point, I desire to acquaint you thereof & to bespeak for the Minister during his stay at the Post the courtesy due to an Officer of his distinguished position."—Df, *ibid.*, Letters Received from Bureaus; copy, *ibid.*, Letters Sent. On Aug. 31, Seward had written to USG. "Sir Frederick Bruce is going to visit West Point next week. Will you have the goodness to send me a letter introducing him to the Commanding officer there"—LS, *ibid.*, Letters Received from Bureaus.

1867, Sept. 2.   Secretary of the Treasury Hugh McCulloch to USG designating the Atlanta National Bank as a repository for War Dept. funds.—DS, DNA, RG 107, Letters Received from Bureaus.

1867, Sept. 2.   Bvt. Maj. Gen. Alexander B. Dyer, chief of ordnance, to USG. "I have the honor to request authority to visit Fort Monroe for the purpose of examining and seeing tested, two experimental Carriages for 15 inch guns, which I have had prepared with a view to so modifying our Sea Coast Carriages as to enable us to use, with safety, the heavy charges which it has been shown the guns are capable of enduring"—LS, DNA, RG 94, Letters Received, 130O 1867.

1867, Sept. 2.   John Lyon, Petersburg, Va., to USG. "On behalf of an aged widow and her two young daughters, who are remotely connected with me by marriage, without fee or reward, and without their knowledge,

I venture to ask you, is there no way by which they can get possession of their lands on the Coast of South Carolina, at present occupied by freedmen under what is known as 'General Sherman's Order—'? These ladies are quiet modest & pious persons, who have never made themselves disagreeable by any unladylike conduct, in either word or act. They are reduced to absolute poverty, having no property whatever except the lands above mentioned—If they could recover possession of these lands as a basis of credit, either by authority, or by private arrangement with the tenants under the sanction of the authorities, they could borrow money to cultivate the lands, and make them more serviceable to the freedmen than they are or can be now. This is a case of peculiar hardship; and I appeal directly to you General, as the most powerful and most magnanimous, and one of the most gallant of our late enemies—Cannot something be done? I venture to answer, Yes, if you *will* it."—LS, DNA, RG 105, Land Div., Letters Received.

1867, SEPT. 2. William West, Bowling Green, Ky., to USG. "Permit me respectfully to lay before you my case—I was tried by a General Court-Martial on charges preferred against me by (my then) 2nd Lieut. W R Maize April 2nd 67 and to day have received the order that I was sentenced to be cashiered   All I can say is that I was not guilty of drunkenness, Three witnesses swore that I was sober   Three, including the person who preferred the charges swore that I was not,   I was so sure of disproving the charge of drunkenness that I did not employ Council nor seek for more witnesse[s] which I could easily have done. Col Drum, the Judge Advocate of my Court in presence of the President of the Court, said to ~~my~~ me when I was laying sick, (as the Court had to meet at my room) that if I would call no more witnesses he would not prosecute any further   I respectfully beg a copy of the proceedings of the Court as I cannot see, how the Court could find me Guilty if the evidence was correctly taken down   General Permit me to state that I have been in the Army eleven years, six of which I have been an officer, no officer in any regiment has done his duty better— I have never been in arrest nor reproved for misconduct   At the battle of the—wilderness May 5th (while you were commanding the Armies) I commanded three Companys and took one officer 29 men prisoners,   on the 10th May while in Command of my Regiment I drove a large number of Rebels from a log house and orchard, and held the position in advance of the lines until I lost about forty men and four officers including myself—I was among one of the first officers which received Brevet Augt 1 /64   General. I humbly beg that you will have my sentence remitted as I wish to live and die in the service   My health is considerably broken down by long and hard service   I cannot take to any other profession   I have a young family and have no means of present support as I could not save much from my pay   If you would be kind enough to grant me an interview I would proceed to Washington and state or lay before you my case Trusting that for the sake of my long and faithful services, you will accede to my prayers . . ."—ALS, DNA, RG 94, Letters Received, 660W 1867. On Sept. 24, Bvt. Maj. Gen. Edward D. Townsend endorsed this letter. "Respectfully submitted to the Secretary of War with reference to the Military History of Capt. West enclosed herewith. The vacancy occasioned by his being cashiered has not yet been filled. Nearly every officer dismissed presents a strong case for restoration. The discipline of the army cannot be restored unless some examples are made."—ES, *ibid.* On Sept. 27, Bvt. Maj. Gen. Edmund Schriver, inspector gen., endorsed this letter. "The application for restoration is rejected by the Sec of War *ad int*"—AES, *ibid.*

1867, Sept. 3. To Bvt. Maj. Gen. Charles Griffin. "I enclose to you the within papers, pertaining to the claim of *Samuel Norris.* The applicant sets forth certain grievances which he has sustained in the matter of the loss of a large amount of stock, sequestrated by the Confederates in Texas early in the Rebellion; and he asks for certain remedies at the hands of the United States Military Authorities. Upon the presentation of the case to me by his Counsel, I have referred him to the local Courts for the relief sought; and I desire that you will see that the parties representing *Mr. Norris* have every facility for such recourse to the local Courts and such procedure therein as the ends of Justice may require."—Copies, DNA, RG 107, Letters Sent; *ibid.*, Letters Received, D96 1867. Additional papers are *ibid.*

1867, Sept. 3. Absalom H. Markland, Washington, D. C., to USG. "On the 31st day of May, 1865, Samuel Tate, of Memphis, Tenn., was pardoned by the President of the United States and his property ordered to be restored from that date. Some of his property was then in possession of the Quartermaster-General's Department as store-houses. In September, 1865, General John E. Smith, commanding at Memphis, ordered that his property should be returned as per pardon of the President, and that rent should be paid from date of pardon. General R. E. Clary, the chief quartermaster of that department, gave to Mr. Tate vouchers for rent from June 1, 1865, to August 31, 1865, amounting to the sum of $1,000. The Quartermaster-General then declined to pay, upon the ground that the State of Tennessee was one of the States declared in rebellion by the proclamation of President Lincoln. The subsequent action of the Congress of the United States removed that objection, and yet the vouchers remain unpaid. I respectfully ask that the Quartermaster-General may be directed to pay the same. All the papers in the case are on the files of the last-named office."—SRC, 51-1-560. On Sept. 6, Bvt. Maj. Gen. Daniel H. Rucker, act. q. m. gen., wrote to USG. "With reference to the communication of A. H. Markland, relative to the claim of Samuel Tate for rent of a building at Memphis, Tenn., alleged to have been occupied by United States as public offices from June 1st to August 31st, 1865, I have the honor to report: That it appears from the papers in the case that the building in question, alleged to have been owned by Samuel Tates, a rebel, was in the possession of the United

States when Mr. Tates was pardoned by the President, May 31st, 1865, and that it was occupied from that date to the 31st of August following. Under the orders of the War Department, claims for rent of property in States declared to be in rebellion, are not allowed by the Quartermaster's Department.—The date from which rents are allowed in Tennessee is April 2d, 1866, when the President declared by Proclamation: 'That the insurrection which heretofore existed in those States,' (naming Tennessee and nine other States,) 'is at an end.' . . ."—LS, DNA, RG 92, Reports to the Secretary of War (Press).

1867, SEPT. 3.   Oliver G. Richey, Brownsville, Pa., to USG. "I beg leave to apply to you for the position of Chief Engineer on one of the Snag Boats to be employed on the Western Rivers by the Government, and enclose you the recommendation of Vice Admiral D. D. Porter for your favourable consideration"—ALS, DNA, RG 77, Explorations and Surveys, Letters Received. U.S. Representative John Covode of Pa. endorsed to USG a letter of the same day from Oliver P. Baldwin, Brownsville, to Covode requesting that Covode call USG's attention to Richey's application.—ES (undated) and ALS, *ibid.*

1867, SEPT. 3.   John T. Rowan, Louisville, to USG. "Convinced that you look upon the negro Bureau as a merely Radical instrumentality; you will effect much towards its destruction by making its Head a negro instead of a white man. Not only will every honorable man retire from it, but the disgust of every northern man not incurably a Radical become disgusted be secured. The plan is to nausiate the north with Sambo. Yr late removals greatly encourage us in this state. It is yet hoped time enough is left for killing off the disunion party."—ALS, DNA, RG 107, Letters Received, R193½ 1867.

1867, SEPT. 3.   E. W. Schon, Baltimore, to USG. "On yesterday I had the pleasure to see Genl. Dent—Asst. Sec. War. I named to him the fact that I had in my possession an application for funds to repair a church in Clarksg. West. Va. which had been occupied—by U. S. Troops. I forward you the Petition this morning. I sincerely hope you will—if at all consistent—grant the prayer of the Petitioners—The facts are as stated. The estimate is I assure you—very low. Genl. Steadman—who first occupied Clarksg. told me on yesterday—that there was an existing order—to return all churches which had been thus occupied—in same order & repair—as when taken. All the other churches in Clarksg. have recd. remuneration or been repaired. If you can order the $800. paid you will confer on a noble—pious & generous people an act of great kindness. I leave the whole matter in yr. hands."—ALS, DNA, RG 107, Letters Received, S335 1867. The enclosure is *ibid.*

1867, SEPT. 4.   President Andrew Johnson endorsement. "Returned to the Secretary of War ad interim, with instructions to fill the vacancies now existing in the Commission to adjust the claims of Indiana, under the Act approved March 29, 1867, by the appointment of Hon. John Hogan, of St. Louis, Missouri, and William R. Kenney of Louisville, Kentucky."—Copy, DNA, RG 107, Orders and Endorsements. Written on a letter of Aug. 21 from Act. Governor Conrad Baker of Ind.—*Ibid.*, Register of Letters Received. On Sept. 18, James C. Robinson wrote to USG. "Yours of the 5 Inst Is before me. Informing me of the appointments of Hon John Hogan of Mo & William R. Kenney of Ky., as Commisioners for Ind—Under the act of March 29 1867.—and informing me of the time of meeting of the Commision being postponed until June—I will endeavor to meet the other Commisioners at that time"—ALS, *ibid.*, Letters Received, R188 1867. On Oct. 10, Johnson wrote to USG. "The Secretary of War ad interim will please appoint George A. Maguire, of St. Louis Missouri a Commissioner to examine the accounts existing between the United States and the State of Indiana; in place of Willard P. Hall, declined."—Copies (2), DLC-Andrew Johnson.

1867, SEPT. 4.   Caleb S. Benedict, Jr., Washington, D. C., to USG. "On the 17th of August 1867 I received from you an appointment as 2nd Lieutenant in the 9th U. S. Cavalry and the same was accepted by me. In accordance with instructions I reported to Major General David Hunter President of the Examining Board in this City on the 26th and he requested me to report for examination on the 30th which I did, and after a long and tedious examination (of nearly six hours) I was informed that it was unsatisfactory   I have the honor most respectfully to request that another examination be granted me, or that the decision of the board may be recalled, for the following reasons. 1st when I accepted the appointment, I supposed that I would have a military examination, but I find it to be to the contrary. 2nd I have served a long time in the Army and I know that I can perform any duty entrusted to me—"—ALS, DNA, RG 94, ACP, B2181 CB 1867. Bvt. Maj. Gen. David Hunter endorsed this letter. "The President of the Cavalry Examining Board most respectfully reports—that Mr Caleb S. Benedict Jun. is reported by the Examining Surgeon as unfit for the mounted service, having been discharged from the 11th New York Cav. for the same disability now existing. Having also failed in other respects, it is most respectfully recommended that Mr Benedict be not permitted to appear before the Board again."—AES (undated), *ibid.* On Sept. 26, President Andrew Johnson endorsed papers concerning Benedict. "*Respectfully referred to* the Secretary of War who will issue the necessary orders granting a re-examination in the case of C S Benedict"—ES, *ibid.* On Oct. 1, USG endorsed these papers. "Respectfully refered to the Presidet. Shall the appointment be made of a man who was discharged from the Volunteer service because of phyical disability."—AES, *ibid.* USG noted on these papers. "Returned by President to have the Apt. made."—AN (undated), *ibid.* Benedict again failed the reexamination, was appointed 2nd lt., 26th Inf., and once again failed the examination.—*Ibid.*

1867, SEPT. 5.   To Secretary of the Interior Orville H. Browning. "I have the honor to transmit herewith an order of the President, dated September 3rd, 1867, setting apart a tract at *Camp McDermott,* Nevada, as a reservation for military purposes, I will thank you to cause the order to be duly registered, and to inform this Department of your action in the matter."— Copy, DNA, RG 107, Letters Sent to the President. On the same day, USG wrote to Browning an identical letter concerning Camp Douglas, Utah Territory.—Copy, *ibid.* On Sept. 7, Act. Secretary of the Interior William T. Otto twice wrote to USG acknowledging receipt of these letters.—LS, *ibid.,* Letters Received from Bureaus.

1867, SEPT. 5.   To Maj. Gen. Oliver O. Howard. "~~Reply yes to the within.~~ You are authorized to be absent until Wednesday next."—ALS (telegram sent), DNA, RG 107, Telegrams Collected (Bound); telegram sent (dated Sept. 6), *ibid.* Written on the reverse of a telegram of the same day from Howard, Providence, R. I., to USG. "My address before Agricultural society has been postponed till friday   Can I be spared till Wednesday morning next."—Telegram received (at 11:20 A.M.), *ibid.*

1867, SEPT. 5.   Brig. Gen. Andrew A. Humphreys, chief of engineers, to USG. "I beg leave to suggest that the restriction imposed upon the Chief of Engineers on the 12th November 1864, touching the mode of changing the stations of Officers of Engineers, be removed, and I submit herewith a memorandum of the substance of an order or of a letter of instruction to the Chief of Engineers, which, it seems to me, will place the subject on a proper footing. . . ."—LS, DNA, RG 94, Letters Received, 529E 1867. The enclosures are *ibid.*

1867, SEPT. 5.   Brig. Gen. Andrew A. Humphreys, chief of engineers, to USG. "I be leave to submit whether the present classification for allowance of quarters and fuel in which Brigadier Generals and Colonels are placed in the same class, may not properly be amended by placing Brigadier Generals in the class with Major Generals? The existing arrangement was made many years ago when the condition of the service was very different from what it is now"—Copy, DNA, RG 77, Letters and Reports. On Sept. 9, Bvt. Maj. Gen. Daniel H. Rucker, act. q. m. gen., wrote to USG. ". . . the Acting Quartermaster General is of the opinion that the difference between the allowance of rooms for a Major General and a Brigadier General (one) is not greater than the difference between other allowances provided for Officers of these grades, as will be seen by the following, viz: . . . and he cannot therefore recommend that the allowance of quarters and fuel to Brigadier Generals as now established by Regulation, be changed. General Humphreys' communication is herewith respectfully returned"—LS, *ibid.,* RG 92, Reports to the Secretary of War (Press).

1867, SEPT. 5. Bvt. Maj. Gen. Edward O. C. Ord, Vicksburg, to USG. "The last paragraph of Sec. 5th of the law. providing for a Convention and reconstruction, says 'Provided that no person excluded from the privilege of of holding office by said proposed amendment to the Constitution of the United States shall be eligible to election as a member of the Convention to form a Constitution for any of the said rebel states, nor shall any such person vote for member of such Convention—' In no other law since passed, is there any qualification required for members of the Convention I have therefore concluded that all voters for the Convention are qualified to act as members—There is by the 9th Sec. of the last supplementary reconstruction law, an oath required from registrars, and from all persons elected or appointed to office '*Under* any State or Municipal authority' in said Military districts, which I do not believe in consideration of the previous law can be deemed applicable to the members of the Convention—I propose to require the same qualifications from members of the Convention as are now required from voters—I hope this view meets your approval—I can assure you, that if the oath required of Registrars is required from members of the Convention, in many Counties delegates of intelligence cannot be found; a large number of reliable and loyal men, will be excluded, and a great many white voters now in favor of a Convention, would vote against it; these votes the friends of a Convention need, in both this State, and Arkansas—"—ALS, DNA, RG 108, Letters Received.

1867, SEPT. 5. J. G. M. Goss, Jefferson, Ga., to USG. "I beg permission to present to you a matter that I presented to Mr, Stanton, while he was acting as Secretary of War, and to which he did not reply. In the year 1864—Gen Stoneman made a raid through Georgia, and was captured;— a portion of his forces attempted thier escape, but were overtaken in Jackson County Georgia, and Some 17 or 18 left wounded most of them badly, and no Surgeon with them, and they were within the Confederate lines, and they applied to the Physicians in the vicinity, and they refused assistance, Then Major O. J. Smith of the 6th Indiana Cav, called me to attend them, he was badly wounded himself. I obeyed his call promptly. I dressed the wounds of 17 or 18 and Set their factured limbs administered the necessary meds and Continued my attentions, to Some of them, for Six Months, believing that I Should get compensation for my services. When Mr Stanton failed to respond to my address I wrote to a collecting Atny and he informed me that my accounts Should have been directed to the Surgeon General, I then wrote to Mr; Stanton to return my accounts but his clerk replied that the papers could not be returned, but that if just cause could be Shown they could be transfered to the Surgeon General, but did not say what that just cause was. I was unacquainted with diplomacy. I did not know who to refer my claims to, but presumed that it would properly come under the jurisdiction of the Secretary of War, I have not learned what was done with my claims. Please inform me. And will you be so kind as to inform me, whether or not, I can collect my claims? I now have the

affadavits of Major O. J. Smith and Capt Wm Perkins, (both federal officers,) to the facts of my faithful attendance, and of my loyalty. I had nothing to do with the rebelion, and as a Minister of the Gospel I was exempt
from Military duty. The Same forces, the day before, they were overtaken,
captured my horses and I was compelled to walk 12 miles to attend the
wounds until I could get a horse. I was in independant circumstances before
the war, but its ravages have left me poor, and as I have worn down the
vigor of manhood, and now arrived at decripitude, I feel that I need the
proceeds of my honest labour. *Will not the government compensate Such
Services? Now Gen Grant, you have been a Soldier, what would you think
of a Surgeon, professing the religion of Heaven, that would refuse to attend
bleeding, dying Soldiers? And will not* the *government pay* (*my fees?*)
such services? . . . if Gen Grant will direct me how get my dues I will be
very greatful"—ALS, DNA, RG 107, Letters Received, G143 1867. On
Sept. 21, Bvt. Maj. Gen. Joseph K. Barnes, surgeon gen., unfavorably endorsed this letter.—ES, *ibid.*

1867, SEPT. 5. Daniel T. Wainright, Monticello, Mo., to USG. "Near
thirty years sense I traveled West Union and White Oak Circuits, in the
Ohio Conference as a Methodist Minister, dureing this time I often visited
your Fathers house. The kindness shown me by your Father and Mother is
the principal excuse I have for addressing you at this time. I recollect being
at your Fathers at one time when you were on a visit home from West
Point—I desire to address you now in the form of a petition. In order to do
this it will be necessary to state some facts, some pleasant and some unpleasant. Before the church devided I moved to Mo. this threw me in ~~the~~
the Southern wing of the church. I submitted to my situation and tried to do
all the good I could. When the unrightiou Rebellion took place I was located on a farm in this county. I tried to avoid interference in the war so if
posible to keep out of trouble. nearly all my neighbourhood were southern, and it was imposible for me to do any thing without getting into
trouble with them. I stayed at home closely and tried to live in all good
concience with all men, but this did not save me. In the fall of 1862 Maj.
J. B. Rogers under Gen. John McNeal came to our town and I was classed
among the Rebbels. My being a member of the Southern methodist church
he said was enough for him. he ordered me to leave the State in ten days
or he would shoot me. I left and went to Ill. in a few months I was permitted by Gen Schofield to return to my home without any charge being
prefered against me. But while I was gone Maj John B Rogers took from
my farm the property discribed in the claim inclosed. Gen A. B. Eaton in
his reply to my attorney Hon John B. Grey of St. Louis says there is no
record on file in his office of my being called Disloyal. I know nothing of
this evidence and can only say if so, an enemy hath done it. In addition to
the evidence set fourth in my claim, of my loyalty, I could give the evidence
of the best men in this State that the contrary is the fact. I have looked
uppon your earnest strugle through the great strugle we have passed for

National existance with much pride and glad to learn from your letter to the President sustaining Gen Sheridan that you still possess the tru spirit. I send you these papers General, hopeing you will send them to the proper department with your endorsement, and I hope the department will reconcider his desision and order my claim to be paid. I have but small means and have a large family of nine children to support and educate, and it seems hard that I to should be deprived of my means by the government. If such should be the case please have the check sent to me at my address, as above. I could write more but deem it unnecessary. My affidavit will say more than I can say here."—ALS, DNA, RG 107, Letters Received, W349 1867. Additional papers are *ibid.* On Oct. 4, Bvt. Brig. Gen. Orville E. Babcock endorsed this letter. "Rejected—(Evidence of loyalty not satisfactory)"—AES, *ibid.*

1867, SEPT. 5.   U.S. Representative Fernando Wood of N. Y., New York City, to USG. "The father of Cadet John J Casey of New York now at West Point desires his presence here in a law suit as a witness, for some ten or twelve days—I am referred to you as the proper authority to get permission for him to do so"—ALS, DNA, RG 94, Correspondence, USMA.

1867, SEPT. 5.   "Protectior," Cleveland, to USG. "During President Lincoln's administration he was warned by anonymous letters that his life was in danger but for some reason he paid no attention to them either thinking that he knew his own business or paying no attentention to anonymous correspondence.—We all know the result.—I have traveled through Maryland several times during the passed three months, partly to see the country and partly on *other* business. I have learned (and have statements from reliable source to show) that there are now about 27000 armed men (ex rebels) in Maryland   these men are not under arms like soldiers nor all uniformed but are thouroughly organized and at short notice can be brought to gether. By expressing a disire to 'enlist' I became posted   I afterwar[d] enlisted and am now a member of the '23rd Protectiors'   since became a soldier in the 'Protectior' cause I have learned 'our' object   First the existence, object, & controls of 'our' movements is known & rests in a man of *high* position now in Washington   now as in /60 & 61 troops are few in arround and near Washington   27000 Protectiors are within twelve hours march of that city. 'our' General is now in Washington and is holding secrete communications with this 'High Official.' Congress meets this fall but remember that the 'Protectiors' are on the look out. I will conclude by saying you must know my object in joining the 'Protectiors' (simply to inform)   you probably will treat this letter as President Lincoln did those he received but yet it surly do no harm to send it   I have a memoranda of twenty two pages which I have gathered from 'our' officers & through others"—AL, USG 3.

1867, SEPT. 6.   To Secretary of the Treasury Hugh McCulloch. "Adverting to your letter of the 16th April, transmitting the papers in the case of John Devlin, and to your suggestion therein that the monies in question 'having been deposited with the Treasurer by the direction of the War Department and having been placed to the credit of its officers, in whose names the certificates of deposit were issued and still stand, ought not to be delivered to any of the claimants except upon the request, and by the direction of the War Department,' I beg to say that, in view of all the facts of the case, this Department cannot with propriety make any request, upon the Treasury Department in behalf of the claimants."—LS, DNA, RG 56, Letters Received from the War Dept.

1867, SEPT. 6. To Secretary of State William H. Seward. "In reply to your letter of the 26th August enclosing a copy of a communication of the 16th August, from the British Minister, requesting the discharge of *John E. Sheridan*, Co. "H." 2d U. S. Cav'y on the ground of minority—I have the honor to state, that, it appears from the records of this office that John Sheridan who is supposed to be the person referred to, enlisted Dec. 6 /66 at Detroit, Mich., and was assigned to Co. "H." 2d U. S. Cavy., and that he gave his age as 18 yrs and 4 mos. at the time of his enlistment. But that no favorable recommendation can be made in this case, on the ground presented, until the evidence required by the underlined portion of the enclosed circular letter from the Dept. is presented."—Copy, DNA, RG 107, Letters Sent to the President.

1867, SEPT. 6. To Bvt. Brig. Gen. Thomas G. Pitcher, superintendent, USMA, introducing the Chilean minister and his wife.—Charles Hamilton Auction No. 162, March 8, 1984, no. 72.

1867, SEPT. 6. Brig. Gen. Andrew A. Humphreys, chief of engineers, to USG. "Bt. Brg. Genl H. L. Abbot, Major of Engineers, has prepared a very valuable and interesting Memoir upon Siege Artillery in the Campaign against Richmond with notes upon the 15 inch gun, including an Algebraic analysis of the trajectory of a shot in its ricochets upon smooth water   It is very desirable that this memoir should be printed as one of the series of professional papers which have from time to time emanated from the pen of officers of the Corps of Engineers. If printed, the work will contain about 155 pages of letter press, 33 pages of tables and 6 plates. In paper covers, each paper will cost about $2.00—I recommend that authority be given for printing, under my direction, and binding in paper covers, 500 copies of this memoir, the expense to be borne by the appropriation for Contingencies of Fortifications"—Copy, DNA, RG 77, Letters and Reports. See Henry L. Abbot, *Siege Artillery in the Campaigns Against Richmond,* ... (New York, 1868; reprinted, Arendtsville, Pa., 1986).

1867, SEPT. 6. Bvt. Maj. Gen. Edward R. S. Canby, Charleston, to USG. "I find that the statutes at large have not been furnished, and as there is a constant necessity for reference will you please direct a set to be sent to me by Express—Curtiss digest of the decisions of the Supreme Court is also needed   Can that be sent"—Telegram received (at 12:10 P.M.), DNA, RG 107, Telegrams Collected (Bound). On Sept. 7, Canby wrote to USG. "I have the honor to transmit for the information of the General of the Army a slip from the 'Charleston Mercury' of yesterday indicating and suggesting in sufficiently explicit terms the course that may be adopted to obstruct or defeat the execution of the laws of the United States providing for 'the more efficient government of the Rebel States.'—I have not yet made any order in relation to the case of alleged conflict of authority in North Carolina. The questions involved are still more complicated than I supposed them to be when I left Washington. I have no doubt, however, that I will be able to shape the action to be taken so as to preserve intact and unimpaired the jurisdiction conferred by the law of March 2, and the supplementary laws of March 23 & July 19th 1867 and at the same time, avoid all reasonable ground or even pretense for a conflict of authority between the Civil and Military affairs of the Government. If any collisions should occur it must come from an attempt 'to prevent, hinder or delay the execution' of the laws of the United States, 'to provide for the more efficient government of the rebel states', the execution of which has been committed to the Military authority, and not from the acts of the military. I will keep the General fully advised by telegraph and by mail of the condition of affairs in this District and will send the Duplicates of important papers via—New York."—LS, *ibid.*, RG 108, Letters Received; ALS (addressed to Bvt. Maj. Gen. John A. Rawlins), *ibid.* The enclosure is *ibid.*

On Sept. 6, Tod R. Caldwell, Morganton, N. C., wrote to USG. "I have the honor herewith to transmit to you a letter which I wrote to General Sickles on the 8th of August asking in my own name & in the name of others to be relieved from grievances under which we considered ourselves placed by reason of his Genl orders No 10—It appears that Genl Sickles considers that the case made out presents no ground for action—. With all due deference & with the greatest respect, I feel obliged to differ with him in opinion and—hence—knowing not what other course to pursue, have deemed it proper to make an appeal to you—. When my letter was written to Genl Sickles I had not seen his order *prohibiting* the meeting of the General Assembly—."—ALS, *ibid.*, RG 94, Letters Received, 773C 1867. On Sept. 16, Canby endorsed this letter. "Respectfully returned to the Secretary of War   The statute of North Carolina ratified on the 4th day of March 1867 provides 'that in all cases when judgement in actions *ex contractu* have been rendered in any Court of Record in this State previous to May A. D. 1865, the execution in said judgements should be stayed—until the spring term 1868, of the Court in which said judgements were rendered'   Mr. Caldwells statement is not very explicit but as the stay ordered by paragraph 3 of G. O. No 10. expires *by* limitation in one year (April 12 1868) it would appear that he would gain nothing by its abrogation."—AES, *ibid*. See letter to Maj. Gen. Daniel E. Sickles, Aug. 24, 1867.

1867, SEPT. 6. Bvt. Maj. Gen. John Pope, Atlanta, to USG. "I have the honor to request that one of the ambulances, now in the possession of the Depot Quartermaster at this place, may be used at these Head Quarters. The town is very much scattered, and especially during the muddy season of the winter it will be very difficult for the Officers on duty here, and who necessarily live at some distance, to reach these Head Quarters without some conveyance."—LS, DNA, RG 94, Letters Received, 1438M 1867. On Oct. 8, Bvt. Brig. Gen. Horace Porter endorsed this letter unfavorably.—ES, *ibid*.

1867, SEPT. 6. George K. Smith, Coldwater, Mich., to USG. " 'Fight it out on the *"loyal line"* if it takes *150 years*'—I know that your numerous friends everywhere (*& particularly on the Pacific side*) are watching your course with the most *intense interest*, altho' they *know* you will do *your* DUTY, & they will ever pray that you may neutralise the *machinations* of A. Johnson whose *loyalty* is certainly QUESTIONABLE."—ALS, USG 3.

1867, SEPT. 7. To Secretary of the Interior Orville H. Browning. "I have the honor to inform you that the part of the *Fort Randall Milty. Reservation* indicated by the lines M. L. A. Q. in the accompanying map is not wanted for the Military service, and may be relinquished. Please to give the necessary instructions in the case."—Df, DNA, RG 94, Letters Received, T92 1867; copy, *ibid*., RG 107, Letters Sent to the President. On Sept. 12, Act. Secretary of the Interior William T. Otto wrote to USG acknowledging receipt of this letter.—LS, *ibid*., RG 94, Letters Received, T92 1867. Additional papers are *ibid*.

1867, SEPT. 7. To Bvt. Maj. Gen. Edward D. Townsend. "Please at your convenience find the papers relative to the dismissel of Maj. Camp, Vol. PayMaster, in /62, and his subsequent application for restoration and submit them to me."—ALS, MH. Townsend's memorandum concerning this case is in DNA, RG 94, ACP, C1123 CB 1867.

1867, SEPT. 7. Bvt. Brig. Gen. Frederick T. Dent endorsement. "The Sec of War directs that the within Brevets be confered"—AES, DNA, RG 94, ACP, 902W CB 1867. Written on a letter of Sept. 5 from U.S. Representative Elihu B. Washburne, Hallowell, Maine, to USG. "I beg leave to make the following recommendations: 1st. That Col. Adam Badeau, Brevet Brigadier General U. S. Volunteers, be made a brevet Colonel in the United States Army. 2d. That Col. Ely S. Parker, Brevet Brigadier General U. S. Volunteers, be made a brevet Colonel in the United States Army. 3d. That Maj. Geo. K. Leet A. A. G. U. S. A. be made a brevet Lieutenant Colonel

United States Army. 4th. That 2d Lieutenant Amos Webster, Brevet Lt. Col. U. S. Volunteers, be made a brevet Major in the United States Army." —ALS, *ibid.* Probably on Nov. 9, USG noted. "Appoint Cols. Parker and Badeau of Hd Qrs. staff Bvt. Brig. Gens."—AN (initialed), *ibid.,* W1077 CB 1867.

1867, SEPT. 7.   William Claggett, Portsmouth, to USG. "I take the liberty to inclose to you the Portsmouth Journal of this date, as it contains several allusions to you, I caused the acts of Congress to be republished relating to your military authority, and expressed my opinion in respect to the same. On the 2d page 3d column, I moved, at a 'Chowder party' which I attended—three cheers for yourself and was seconded by our Governor— you will notice what followed   In the highly responsible positions you now hold it is not impossible that the future destinies of our glorious Republic may depend upon yourself. History will record your doings, and the noble stand you have taken, in defiance of Executive attempts at usurpation— and be assured that all loyal people in our whole Union will uphold and sustain you. I believe that you are not the man to be swerved from the line of duty by Executive power or threats   I am an aged man, having been in the practice of law more than forty years, and devoted a large portion of my life to our national affairs. Otherwise I would not address you. John L Hayes Esqr., counsellor at Law, and a few others in Washington city, are personally acquainted with me. I acted with the Democratic Party until it deserted truly Democratic Republican principles. As my opinions are freely expressed in the 1st & 2d pages of the Journal, I will not enlarge"—ALS, USG 3.

1867, SEPT. 9.   To Secretary of the Interior Orville H. Browning. "I have the honor to transmit herewith, an order of the President dated Sept. 9th 1867, setting apart a tract at *Camp McGarry,* Nevada, as a reservation for military purposes. I will thank you to cause the order to be duly registered, and to inform this Dept. of your action in the matter."—Copy, DNA, RG 107, Letters Sent to the President. On Sept. 11, Act. Secretary of the Interior William T. Otto wrote to USG acknowledging receipt of this letter. —LS, *ibid.,* Letters Received from Bureaus.

1867, SEPT. 9.   To Secretary of the Treasury Hugh McCulloch. "I have the honor to inform you that your communication of the 5th inst. enclosing a copy of a letter of *Lt. Randolph* (U. S. Revenue service) of the 1st August respecting the *Quarantine Regulations* at *Key West,* has been referred to the Comd'g. Genl. of the 3d Milty. Dist. for such action as he may deem necessary in the case"—Df, DNA, RG 107, Letters Received from Bureaus; copy, *ibid.,* Letters Sent to the President. On Sept. 5, McCulloch had written to USG. "I have the honor to submit herewith for your consideration, copy of letter received from Lieut. Commanding Randolph of the Revenue Cutter 'Resolute' stationed at Key West, wherein it is stated that the present Quarantine Regulations in force at that port, are of such a character, as to render nugatory the duties required of the vessel.—"—LS, *ibid.,* Letters Received from Bureaus. The enclosure is *ibid.* On Nov. 20, USG wrote to McCulloch. "Referring to your letter of the 5th Sept. last enclosing copy of report of *Lt. Wm. B. Randolph* of the Revenue service stationed at Key West, complaining of the interference of the military quarantine regulations with his duties in that harbor, I have the honor to inform you that the same having been referred to the Comdg. Genl 3d Milt'y. Dist., has now been returned with a report from which it appears that the military quarantine was discontinued on the 10th inst. and any further action in the premises is therefore deemed unnecessary."—Copies, *ibid.; ibid.,* Letters Sent to the President. The enclosure is *ibid.,* Letters Received from Bureaus.

1867, SEPT. 9. To Secretary of the Treasury Hugh McCulloch. "I have the honor to send for your consideration copies of papers relating to the vacant portion of the Govt. reservation in *San Francisco* on which the Post Office and Custom House are built, and to say that the views of *Maj. Genl. Halleck* are approved by this Dept."—Copy, DNA, RG 107, Letters Sent to the President. On Sept. 11, McCulloch wrote to USG. "I have to acknowledge the receipt of yours of the 9th instant, transmitting and approving the recommendation of Major General Halleck in regard to the erection of a building for military purposes on a portion of the custom-house lot in San Francisco, and have to say in reply that I do not feel authorized to transfer the custody of the property in question for any permanent purpose without express authority of law. I would, however, suggest that such authority might be embodied in the act making the appropriation, which would avoid any delay or inconvenience."—*HED,* 40-2-39, p. 3. On Sept. 13, USG wrote to McCulloch. "I have the honor to request you to return to this Dept., *Genl. Halleck's* communication respecting the *San Francisco reservation* which was enclosed in my letter to you of the 9th inst."—Copy, DNA, RG 107, Letters Sent to the President. On Sept. 14, McCulloch wrote to USG. "I have the honor to return herewith, as requested in your letter of the 13th instant, the papers relative to the government reservation in San Francisco, which were submitted by you to this department, September 9, 1867."—*HED,* 40-2-39, p. 4. The enclosures are *ibid.,* pp. 5–7. On Sept. 23 and Dec. 5, Bvt. Maj. Gen. Daniel H. Rucker, act. q. m. gen., wrote to USG concerning this matter.—LS, DNA, RG 92, Reports to the Secretary of War (Press). Both are printed in *HED,* 40-2-39. On Dec. 9, USG wrote to Speaker of the House Schuyler Colfax. "I have the honor to send herewith, for the consideration of the proper committee a communication of Dec. 5th '67 from the Quartermaster General with all the plans and papers in the case, respecting an appropriation for a suitable building at *San Francisco* for military offices in that city, and for the transfer of the requisite portion of the public reservation there for a site, as suggested by the Secretary of the Treasury in his communication of the 11th of September 1867"—Copy, DNA, RG 107, Reports to Congress.

1867, SEPT. 9. To Secretary of State William H. Seward. "I have the honor to acknowledge the receipt this morning of your communication dated the 6th inst. transmitting by direction of the *President* a copy of his *Proclamation* of the 3d inst. together with a copy of his instructions in relation thereto."—Df, DNA, RG 94, Letters Received, 908S 1867; *ibid.*, RG 107, Letters Sent to the President. On Sept. 6, Seward had written to USG. "By direction of the President I have the honor to herewith transmit a copy of his Proclamation of the 3d inst. together with a copy of his instructions in relation thereto."—LS, *ibid.*, RG 94, Letters Received, 908S 1867. Seward enclosed a proclamation of Sept. 3 of President Andrew Johnson. ". . . AND WHEREAS impediments and obstructions, serious in their character, have recently been interposed in the States of North Carolina and South Carolina, hindering and preventing for a time a proper enforcement there of the laws of the United States, and of the judgments and decrees of a lawful court thereof, in disregard of the command of the President of the United States; AND WHEREAS reasonable and well-founded apprehensions exist that such ill-advised and unlawful proceedings may be again attempted there or elsewhere; Now, THEREFORE, I, ANDREW JOHNSON, President of the United States, do hereby warn all persons against obstructing or hindering in any manner whatsoever the faithful execution of the Constitution and the laws; and I do solemnly enjoin and command all officers of the Government, civil and military, to render due submission and obedience to said laws, and to the judgments and decrees of the courts of the United States, and to give all the aid in their power necessary to the prompt enforcement and execution of such laws, decrees, judgments, and processes. . . ."—Copy (printed), *ibid.* See letter to Maj. Gen. Daniel E. Sickles, Aug. 24, 1867.

1867, SEPT. 9. President Andrew Johnson to USG. "Please cause the name of Frank Cummings, of Charlotte, Mich, to be entered on the list of applicants for appointments as Cadets to West Point."—LS, DNA, RG 94, Correspondence, USMA.

1867, SEPT. 9. U.S. Representative Samuel Shellabarger of Ohio, Springfield, to USG. "I respectfully and Earnestly request that Stephen A Herriman of South Charleston Clarke Co Ohio late a member of Co K 31st O. V. I in which he served three 3 years be appointed a Captain in the U. S I. army, if consistent assigned to the Eleventh (11th)"—Telegram received (at 11:30 A.M.), DNA, RG 107, Telegrams Collected (Bound).

1867, SEPT. 10. To Secretary of the Interior Orville H. Browning. "I have the honor to transmit herewith accounts of subsistence stores supplied to Indians by various officers of the Subsistence Department of the Army, during the months of May, June and July, 1867, and to request that a transfer warrant be drawn for the amount ($54,165,66) on the appropriation for subsistence of Indians to the credit of the appropriation for subsistence of the Army."—LS, DNA, RG 75, Central Office, Letters Received, Miscellaneous. The enclosure is *ibid.*

1867, SEPT. 10.   To Secretary of the Interior Orville H. Browning. "I have the honor to send herewith a communication from Mr. W. F. M. Arny, U. S. Indian Agent for New Mexico, respecting the Pueblo Indians in that Territory, for such consideration as you may deem proper"—LS, DNA, RG 75, Central Office, Letters Received.

1867, SEPT. 10.   To Secretary of the Interior Orville H. Browning. "I have the honor to enclose herewith a communication from Major C. J. Whiting, 3d U S Cavalry, respecting the construction of a dam on the river Pecos near Fort Sumner, forwarded by Generals Getty and Hancock, which, as its subject pertains to the Indians in charge of the Interior Department, is respectfully referred for your consideration."—LS, DNA, RG 75, Central Office, Letters Received.

1867, SEPT. 10.   To Secretary of the Treasury Hugh McCulloch. "I have the honor to enclose herewith for such action as you may deem proper papers in the case of Miss *S. Ellen Barnes* in which the restoration of her house in Beaufort, S. C. asked and recommended by military officers in the 2d District."—Copy, DNA, RG 107, Letters Sent to the President.

1867, SEPT. 10.   To Secretary of the Treasury Hugh McCulloch. "Referring to your letter of the 7th June, in which is presented a statement of the Claim of H. B. Hawkins, of New York, for one half of the value of certain personal property connected with the Marion County Ironworks in Texas, alleged to have been collected by him; and in which you recommend that Mr Hawkins 'be repaid from the proceeds of the sale of the property, or some like fund in the War Department, the amount actually expended in the collection and preservation of the property and for advertizing the Sales which were ordered by this Department; with a further reasonable sum for his time and services;' I have the honor to enclose to you a copy of a report by the Chief of Ordnance in the premises, from which it would appear that no just grounds are seen for the allowance of the Claim."—LS, DNA, RG 56, Div. of Captured and Abandoned Property, Letters Received. The enclosed letter of July 10 from Bvt. Maj. Gen. Alexander B. Dyer, chief of ordnance, to Secretary of War Edwin M. Stanton is *ibid.*

1867, SEPT. 10.   To Secretary of the Treasury Hugh McCulloch. "At the instance of the Chf. of Engrs. of the U. S. Army, I have the honor to request that the Collector of Customs at N. York, be instructed to deliver free of all duties and charges, the articles specified in the accompanying invoice and bill of lading, imported in the Steamship 'City of Baltimore' and designed for the service of the Eng'r. Dept. in connection with the improvement of the Potomac River."—Copies, DNA, RG 77, Fortifications, Letters Received; *ibid.*, RG 107, Letters Sent to the President. On the same day, Brig. Gen. Andrew A. Humphreys, chief of engineers, had written to USG. "I have the honor to request that application be made to the proper authority for the issue of orders by virtue of which thirty six chains and One Cask of Anchor Shackles, marked S/W and numbered 2549 to 2585 inclusive, as per enclosed invoice and bill of lading: imported by Messrs Lewis L Squire & Sons in the Steamer 'City of Baltimore,' for the United States on the order of Bvt Maj Genl Gillmore—Maj Corps of Engineers—may be admitted free of duty. The articles are for the Potomac river obstructions, and as the vessel is now being unloaded in the port of New York, it is important that the orders be issued without delay."—LS, *ibid.*, RG 77, Fortifications, Letters Received. On Sept. 11, Asst. Secretary of the Treasury John F. Hartley wrote to USG acknowledging his letter.—LS, *ibid.*

On Dec. 6, USG wrote to McCulloch. "At the instance of the Chief of Engineers, I have the honor to request that the *Collector of Customs at New York* be instructed to deliver, free of all duties and charges, one hundred and sixty seven casks of *Asphalt*, marked C. C. Y167 imported on the Ship Almena from Havre, for the use of the United States."—Copy, *ibid.*, RG 107, Letters Sent to the President.

1867, SEPT. 10, 3:50 P.M.   To Adolphus Neir, Union Pacific Railroad Co., St. Louis. "See General Sherman or General Sheridan for escort."—Telegrams sent (2), DNA, RG 107, Telegrams Collected (Bound); copies, *ibid.*, RG 108, Telegrams Sent; DLC-USG, V, 56. On the same day, Neir had telegraphed to USG. "We wrote you on fifth 5 inst relative to Escort for our Engineers & forwarded letter through Gen Shermans HdQrs. Please act upon letter as soon as received—"—Telegram received (at 11:00 A.M.), DNA, RG 107, Telegrams Collected (Bound); *ibid.*, RG 108, Telegrams Received; copy, DLC-USG, V, 55.

1867, SEPT. 10.   Bvt. Maj. Gen. Daniel H. Rucker, act. q. m. gen., to USG. "I have the honor to inform you, that Bvt Brig. Genl J. C. McFerran, Deputy Quartermaster Genl, Washington D. C., to whom instructions had been given to transfer the name of Charles A. Keefer, Telegraph Operator at New-Orleans L'a, now on his Rolls, to the Chief Quartermaster 5th Military District, as approved by the Secretary of War under date of Augt 31. 67—reports in the case as follows: 'Information has reached this office, unofficially, but from a reliable source, that Mr. Keefer, referred to in within letter, has recently died, and that his successor has been appointed, but his name was not given.' "—LS, DNA, RG 107, Letters Received from Bureaus. See telegram to Maj. Gen. Philip H. Sheridan, Aug. 21, 1867.

1867, SEPT. 11.   To Secretary of the Interior Orville H. Browning. "I have the honor to acknowledge receipt of your letter of the 2nd inst., enclosing one from the office of Indian Affairs, calling attention to certain informalities in the vouchers transmitted through this Dept by Lieut. *Mark Walker*, U. S. Army, for payment to an Indian at *Fort Arbuckle* for ransom of *Theodore A. Babb*, a captive white boy, and to inform you that the same has been referred to the officer named for his attention."—Copy, DNA, RG 107, Letters Sent to the President. On Sept. 2, Act. Secretary of the Interior William T. Otto had written to USG. "I have the honor to transmit herewith, a copy of a report from the Acting Commissioner of Indian Affairs of the 23d ult, respecting the claim of Lt Mark Walker U. S. A, for expenses incurred in the ransom of Theodore A. Bobb, from captivity among the Wild Comanche Indians; received from the War Department in letter of the 6th ult."—LS, *ibid.*, RG 94, Letters Received, 986M 1867. The enclosure with additional papers is *ibid.*

1867, SEPT. 11.   USG endorsement. "The within applicant is recommended to fill the vacancy now existing in the Colorado quota."—ES, DNA, RG 94, ACP, T585 CB 1867. Written on a petition from Samuel H. Elbert, secretary, Colorado Territory, *et al.*, to the AG. "We the undersigned, residents of Colorado Territory, being personally acquainted with Second Lieut John E. Tappan, 2d Reg. Colorado Vol, having confidence in his loyalty and integrity—as well in his ability as an officer—desire to obtain for him a Commission as Second Lieuttenant in the Regular Army of the United States. Lieut Tappan has served as an officer with honor to himself and Credit to his profession. No appointment, to our knowledge, has been made to the Regular Army from our Territory, and we do most earnestly desire that Lieut Tappan should obtain the Commission asked for & thereby represent our Territory."—LS (thirteen signatures), *ibid.* On Aug. 26, Bvt. Brig. Gen. John C. Kelton, AGO, had written to USG. "I have the honor to inform you that at present a vacancy exists in the quota of New Mexico and one in the quota of Colorado. I transmit herewith all recommendations for appointment on file from these territories."—ALS, *ibid.* On Nov. 11, John E. Tappan, Junction City, Kan., telegraphed to USG. "I accept my appointment   Letter rec'd through the Adjt Genl. Answer immediately"—Telegram received (on Nov. 12, 8:15 A.M.), *ibid.*; *ibid.*, RG 107, Telegrams Collected (Bound). Appointed 2nd lt., 10th Cav., on Dec. 22, Tappan failed to pass the qualifying examination.—*Ibid.*, RG 94, ACP, T585 CB 1867. On Nov. 4, Tappan, Fort Dodge, Kan., wrote to USG. "I have the honor to transmit herewith an Order rec'd at this post from Hd Qrs Dept of the Mo appointing. R. M. Johnston to the position of post trader & also transmit for your information extracts efrom the proceedings of the post Council ef also letter of transmittal for same. I would state that I have been Sutler at this post since the first day of last November have put up buildings and got large stocks of goods here, I have also given satisfaction to all the officers of this post, (see petition signed and fo-warded May 18th 1867)   I have served during the last War. four years and a half as an officer of the 2nd Colorado Cavalry, was Acting As't Adgt Genl. for Major Genl Jas G. Blunt.—Afterwards was ordinance officer for Maj Gen John B Sanborn   I present my Claims for you to judge between us"—LS, *ibid.*, RG 108, Letters Received. The enclosures are *ibid.*

1867, SEPT. 11.   Col. Adam Badeau to Manning F. Force. "In reply to your letter of Sept. 7th to General Grant, I have the honor to inform you, that no copy of such communication as you speak of is on file at these head quarters. At the same time, General Grant did expect when he started from Culpeper C. House to reach the South side of the James river, and this was his intention during all the movements of what is called the 'Wilderness campaign'; unless some extraordinary emergency or opportunity should arise, calling on him to move by some other line. He called his staff around him at Culpeper, and informed them that he wanted possession of the South side railroad; that when he got that road Richmond would be untenable by the rebels. It took him a year to get that road, but the day that he possessed it, Richmond fell—"—ALS, Force Papers, University of Washington, Seattle, Wash.

1867, SEPT. 11.   U.S. Senator James Dixon of Conn., Hartford, to USG. "I have recd the order transferring my son Lt. Dixon from the cavalry to the 4th Artillery. I find Lt. Cushing with whom Lt. Dixon exchanged em-barrassed by the expense of joining his Regt in NewMexico. Could he not be ordered out with recruits or in some way saved this expense   He seems to be unable to meet it. Unless some such arrangement can be made I shall feel obliged to pay it myself. If not improper to order him to Carlisle Bar-racks I should be very much obliged on his account.—"—ALS, DNA, RG 94, Letters Received, 350D 1867. On Sept. 14, Maj. George K. Leet en-dorsed this letter. "Respectfully referred to the Adjutant General. Lieut. Cushing will be ordered to the Plains with recruits."—ES, *ibid.* On Sept. 6, Maj. Gen. Winfield S. Hancock, Fort Leavenworth, had written to the AG requesting permission to take to New Orleans as staff officers 2nd Lt. James W. Dixon, 3rd Cav., and two others.—LS, *ibid.*, 1257M 1867.

1867, SEPT. 11.   George Gibbs, secretary, British and American Joint Commission, Washington, D. C., to USG. "I take the liberty of suggesting that some apparatus for distilling water be sent to the posts on the plains, as also to the seaboard southern posts. The difficulty of obtaining water not impregnated with organic matter or alkalies throughout the whole extent of country between the Mississippi & the Rocky Mountains is very great, and the expense of furnishing the posts there with the means of purifying it, can be no consideration to the government in comparison with the health of its officers & men—My brother Dr Wolcott Gibbs of Cam-bridge writes me recommending 'Normandy's apparatus' as furnishing

pure water, aërated so as not to be insipid. He states that it is generally
used in the British Navy, and, as he understands, has been introduced into
ours, as also at Fortress Monroe. I regard the subject as of so much consequence that I solicit your speedy attention to it, . . ."—ALS, DNA, RG 108,
Letters Received. On Sept. 18, Bvt. Maj. Gen. Joseph K. Barnes, surgeon
gen., endorsed this letter. "Respectfully returned. It is not of record in this
Department, that the health of troops has been injuriously affected at any
permanent posts, either in the West or on the Seabord, by the character
of the water used. Troops on the march have so suffered, but the introduction of Normandy's apparatus under such circumstances would be impracticable and, under any other, unnecessary."—ES, *ibid.* See *PUSG*, 1,
293–94.

1867, SEPT. 12.   To Secretary of the Interior Orville H. Browning. "I
have the honor to inform you that your com'n of the 9th inst. requesting a
military escort for a surveying party on the boundary line between *Oregon
& Idaho*, has been referred to Maj. Genl. Halleck, Comd'g. the Milty. Div.
of the Pacific with instructions to furnish the escort if the public service
will permit."—Copy, DNA, RG 107, Letters Sent to the President. On
Sept. 9, Act. Secretary of the Interior William T. Otto had written to
USG. "I inclose herewith a copy of a letter of this date addressed to the
Department by the Commissioner of the General Land Office, in relation to
a military escort for a surveying party now engaged in running the boundary line between Oregon and Idaho Territory, and have the honor to request that you will cause the necessary orders to be issued for furnishing
the escort as requested by the Commissioner"—LS, *ibid.*, RG 94, Letters
Received, 84I 1867. The enclosure is *ibid.*

1867, SEPT. 12.   To Secretary of the Interior Orville H. Browning. "I
have the honor to transmit herewith for your information copy of a communication of Brevet Colonel S. B. Hayman, 10th U. S. Infantry, relating
remarks made by Paul Mazarntamanee, an Indian, with reference to annuity, and asking the benefit of competitive trade."—LS, DNA, RG 75,
Fort Berthold. The enclosure is *ibid.*

1867, SEPT. 12.   To Secretary of the Treasury Hugh McCulloch. "Referring to your letter of the 20th May last enclosing copy of a communication addressed on the 17th of same month by *Theodore M. Davis*, of New
York, to the Comptroller of the Currency, concerning the claim of *Alexander M. White* for payment of a voucher issued to him by *Capt. De
Motte*, Asst. Qr. Mr. in payment for supplies alleged to have been furnished by him to the Govmt.,—and asking to be placed in possession of
information touching the same, I have the honor to enclose herewith a certified brief of the case, prepared in the office of the Qr. Mr. General, setting
forth the facts so far as known to the Department and its decision thereupon."—Copy, DNA, RG 107, Letters Sent to the President. On Nov. 2,

McCulloch wrote to USG. "I have the honor to transmit to you a communication referred to the Department by the Comptroller of the Currency relative to a voucher of Capt Mark L. De Mott, late A. Q. M. for twenty five thousand one hundred and seventy six 20/100 dollars ($25,176 20/100) in favor of one A. M. White, which has been assigned to the National Bank of the Metropolis. This Bank is in liquidation, and is indebted to the Government. The Bank, if they can collect the amount of this voucher, will allow the proceeds to be retained by the Government for its benefit, and if the voucher ought properly to be paid, this Department is desirous of facilitating its payment in order to lessen the indebtedness of the Bank to the United States. It appears that a doubt has been raised by the Quarter-Master General as to whether this voucher ought properly to be paid, the suggestion being that the property on account of which it was issued was not properly accounted for by Capt De Mott, and that the voucher was fraudulently issued, and was not received in good faith by Mr White. Will you oblige this Department, on account of the interest which the Government has in the settlement of the question, by directing a full examination at the War Department, of the facts in the case, and inform me whether or not, after this full examination, the War Department, is of opinion that the voucher is not properly due and payable. If it is a legal indebtedness of the Quarter Master's Department, it is for the interests of the Government that it should be promptly paid, the proceeds retained by this Department and credited to the Bank of the Metropolis."—Copy, *ibid.*, RG 56, Letters Sent. On the same day, Judge Advocate Gen. Joseph Holt wrote to USG. "In the matter of certain demands for restitution of money alleged to have been illegally extorted from *Albert A. Wilson* and *others*, by the Government of the United States, the following report is respectfully submitted. . . . it is remarked that the money refunded by them, the restitution of which they now demand, is shown to have been the exact amount out of which they had defrauded the Government. It is advised that none of these claims, or any part of them, be allowed."—Copy, *ibid.*, RG 153, Letters Sent. On Nov. 15, Bvt. Maj. Gen. Daniel H. Rucker, act. q. m. gen., wrote to USG concerning this matter.—LS, *ibid.*, RG 92, Reports to the Secretary of War (Press). On Nov. 16, USG wrote to McCulloch. "In reply to your communication of Nov. 2d relative to a voucher of *Capt. Mark L. De Mott*, late A. Q. M. U. S. Vols. for $25,176.20/100 in favor of *A. M. White*, I have the honor to send herewith a report of the Qr. Mr. Genl dated the 15th inst on the subject."—Copy, *ibid.*, RG 107, Letters Sent to the President. On Dec. 27, McCulloch wrote to USG. "I take the liberty of introducing to you Mr. T. M. Davis, Attorney for the National Bank of the Metropolis, who wishes to confer with you upon the subject of the claim of that bank to certain monies taken from Alex. M. White by the government, and now on special deposit with the Treasurer. Please extend to Mr. Davis your usual courtesy and oblige . . ."—Copy, *ibid.*, RG 56, Letters Sent. On Jan. 9, 1868, USG wrote to President Andrew Johnson. "In the matter of the appl'n. of *Alexr M. White* & others, for the restoration of certain monies, referred to the Sec'y. of War for report on the 21st Dec. last, I have the honor to submit all the papers relating to the case on file in this Dept., especially inviting attention to the reports of the Qr. Mr. Genl. and the J. Adv. Genl. of the Army (particularly that of date Nov. 2d 1867). These reports exhibit what would seem to be overwhelming considerations against entertaining the prayer of the petitioners. In the case of Ferguson it will be observed that the 3d Auditor is of opinion that no money should be paid him, for that he is indebted several hundred thousand dollars to the U. S. on his responsibility as a Qr. Mr. during the war."—Copy, *ibid.*, RG 107, Letters Sent to the President.

1867, SEPT. 12.   President Andrew Johnson to USG. "The Secretary of War ad interim will please appoint Colonel Robert Morrow a Paymaster in the Army of the United States, to date from May 9th 1867,—the Senate having failed to confirm his nomination during the recent session."—LS, DNA, RG 94, ACP, M43 CB 1867.

1867, SEPT. 12.   Edmond Cotterill, Washington, D. C., to USG. "I have the honor to apply for a 2d Lieutenancy in the U. S. A., and present in support thereof the following. . . ."—ALS, DLC-Nathaniel P. Banks.

1867, SEPT. 13.   To Secretary of the Treasury Hugh McCulloch. "Genl. Ketchum, Receiver of the War Dept. has been instructed to *transfer to the Treas'y. Dept.* all the *captured confederate bank-bills*, papers, U. S. bank bills and property of every description in his possession taking proper certificates and Vouchers therefor. The Schedules offered to your Dept. on Feb. 9th 1867 when the property was ready for transfer, have been made to include such property as has been received since that date and are now ready. I have therefore the honor to request you to designate an officer to receive the property and sign receipts therefor."—Df, DNA, RG 94, Letters Received, 774G 1865; copies (2), *ibid.*; *ibid.*, RG 107, Letters Sent to the President. Additional papers are *ibid.*, RG 94, Letters Received, 774G 1865. On Sept. 24, McCulloch wrote to USG. ". . . In reply I have the honor to say that on the delivery at this Department of so much of the property in question as has any actual value, or properly comes within the terms or intent of the laws relating to captured and abandoned property, accompanied by proper invoices and receipts, the latter will be signed by myself, or one of the assistant Secretaries. I deem it inexpedient, however, as stated in my letter of the 16th of February last, to occupy the space or cumber the files of this Department with any property which is not of the character above described."—Copy, *ibid.*, RG 56, Letters Sent Relating to Restricted Commercial Intercourse.

1867, SEPT. 13.   To U.S. District Attorney E. B. Turner. "Your letter of August 28th is received, and in compliance therewith I have the honor to send herewith the following papers, relative to U. S. property seized by the

Rebels at the commencement of the War—Viz. . . . being all on that subject which are on file in the War Department."—Df (list of correspondence omitted), DNA, RG 107, Letters Received, T141 1867; copy, *ibid.*, Letters Sent. On Aug. 28, Turner, Austin, Tex., had written to USG. "As the U. S. Dist Atty I have instituted Two suits against parties the object of which is to recover the value of the public property seized by the Rebels in this state at the commencemet of the war. I am convinced that in many of the cases when truly loyal men had the property in charge they demanded receipts for the property seized by the rebels, and obtained them. these receipts I desire as evidence of the liability of the parties connected with such seizures. I desire also any other original documents relating to the matter. Messrs Maverick Luckett & Divine were Commissioners of the Committee of safety to seize at San Antonio. I am advised by the Qr M Genl that a letter written by said Lucket in regard to the subject was transmitted to your office on the 14th day of May last. It is a matter of much interest & I will be greatly obliged if you will cause any papers relating to the seizures in Texas and especially the Letter of Luckett to be transmitted to this office to be used as evidence on the trial of these causes" —ALS, *ibid.*, Letters Received, T141 1867. On Nov. 18, USG wrote to Attorney Gen. Henry Stanbery. "In compliance with your request I transmit herewith official copies of all the papers in this Department touching the surrender of Government property and stores by Gen. Twiggs in 1861."—LS, *ibid.*, RG 60, Letters Received, War Dept. The enclosures concerning the seizure of U.S. property in Tex. are *ibid.*

1867, SEPT. 13.   USG order. "District Commanders will cooperate with the Commission, and Asst. Commissioners, of the Freedmen's Bureau in reducing the number of employees and volunteers still retained in service by giving details of officers & enlisted men of the Army to take their places when it can be done without manifest detriment to the service."—ADf (issued as AGO General Orders No. 86), DNA, RG 94, Letters Received, 570A 1867.

1867, SEPT. 13.   Secretary of State William H. Seward to USG. "I have the honor to communicate, herewith, for your use, a copy of despatch No. 220, dated the 4th instant, from our Consul at Toronto, together with a letter addressed to that officer by Mrs Mary Benson, formerly Mrs Hudspeth, relative to a claim she presents against the Government for uncompensated services said to have been rendered in November 1864."—LS, DNA, RG 107, Letters Received from Bureaus. The enclosures are *ibid.*

1867, SEPT. 13.   Peter Cooper, New York City, to USG. "Allow me to express to you my heartfelt thanks in behalf of our common country for the wise and patriotic words in which you have replied to the unreasonable requirement of our unfortunate President—He seems determined to encourage and bring into power the rebel element of the south, in preference to those who have labored, and who have suffered all forms of cruelty, to defend our country in the hour of our greatest extremity—He is doing all this after having denounced rebels and their rebellion more severely than any other man in the country—He seems determined to reconstruct the southern states in a way that will leave the blacks in the power of those who held them as slaves, and who are still determined to keep them under a ban, that will depive them of their rights as American citizens—Hoping that you may long live to receive the thanks of all who love and labor for the union and happiness of our whole country, . . ."—ALS, USG 3.

1867, Sept. 14. To Secretary of the Navy Gideon Welles. "In a conversation with Mr. Eads, the proprietor of a gun carriage for large guns, a specimen of which he is willing shall be built by the United States under his direction, and that the same shall become the property of the Government without any charge by him, it was agreed that you be requested to authorize the work to be done at such Navy Yard as you might designate and that the carriage should be for a twenty-inch gun. I beg to communicate this arrangement for your consideration."—LS, DNA, RG 45, Letters Received from the President. On Sept. 3 and 12, Bvt. Maj. Gen. Edmund Schriver, inspector gen., endorsed a letter from James B. Eads. "Disapproved by the Actg Secy of War." "The Secy of War ad int. has reconsidered this subject & he approves this recommendation with the modification of the 'twenty five per cent' feature, wh the projector of the gun carriage will forgo."—Copies, *ibid.*, RG 107, Orders and Endorsements. On Sept. 20, Welles wrote to USG. "I have the honor to acknowledge the receipt of your letter of the 14th inst, in reference to constructing in one of the Navy Yards a gun-carriage upon Mr Ead's plan. Upon your request and the designation of the Navy Yard at which it is desired that the work should be done, the Department will give the necessary order—the actual cost to be refunded to the Naval Appropriations."—LS, *ibid.*, RG 156, Correspondence Concerning Inventions. On Sept. 30, USG wrote to Welles. "I have the honor to acknowledge the receipt of your letter of the 20th instant respecting the construction of a gun-carriage on Mr. Eads' plan, and to request that orders may be given for its fabrication at the Brooklyn Navy Yard. The Chief of Ordnance of the Army will furnish the requisite drawings for the work."—LS, *ibid.*, RG 45, Letters Received from the President. On Oct. 3, Welles wrote to USG. "I have the honor to acknowledge the receipt of your letter of the 30th ulto, and to inform you that Rear Admiral Chas. H. Bell, Commandant of the New York Navy Yard, has been instructed to have constructed, on Mr Eads plan, a gun-carriage when the requisite drawings shall have been furnished by the Chief of Ordnance of the Army."—LS, *ibid.*, RG 156, Correspondence Concerning Inventions.

1867, Sept. 14. Act. Secretary of the Interior William T. Otto to USG. "For your information, I have the honor to transmit a copy of a communication dated the 2d inst; and addressed to the Acting Commissioner of Indian

Affairs by Agent Leavenworth, reporting arrangements for certain Indians to meet the 'Peace Commission' "—LS, DNA, RG 107, Letters Received from Bureaus. The enclosure is *ibid.*

1867, SEPT. 14.   Judge Advocate Gen. Joseph Holt to USG. "The papers relating to the case of Henry Lung, late Private 4th U. S. Artillery, are respectfully returned with the following report. He was tried in August 1864 by a General Court Martial convened at the Head Qrs. Military District of Washington, Washington, D. C. on the following charge & specification:—Murder Specification.—In this that he Privt Henry Lung of Company A. 4th U. S. Arty, did, on or about the 26th day of June 1864, enter into an altercation and come to blows with Priv't Patrick McGovern of the same company and regiment, at or near a grocery store in the vicinity of Fort Totten, D. C., the said Priv't Henry Lung then proceeding to Fort Totten, did procure a knife and returning to the said grocery store, did, then and there stab to death Private Patrick McGovern of the aforesaid company and regiment. All this at or near a grocery store in the vicinity of Fort Totten, D. C. on or about the 26th day of June, 1864. He pleaded not guilty, but presented no testimony in his defence, merely stating that he was drunk on the occasion charged in the specification and knew of nothing that occurred except that he was knocked down by the party whom it was alleged he killed. He was convicted & sentenced 'to be hanged by the neck until dead.' This sentence was commuted by the President to imprisonment at hard labor in the Penitentiary at Albany, N. Y. for life. . . . It is not thought that the three years imprisonment already inflicted upon the prisoner should be accepted as an adequate atonement for his crime, and therefore interference with the enforcement of the sentence, as commuted, cannot be advised."—Copy, DNA, RG 153, Letters Sent. On April 19, 1870, Secretary of War William W. Belknap endorsed papers concerning Henry Lung. "The President directs the pardon of this man."—Copy, *ibid.*, RG 107, Orders and Endorsements.

1867, SEPT. 15.   Eliza V. H. Ellis, New York City, to Julia Dent Grant. "Addressing you dear Madam, I fear is a most unwarrantable libery—but the great anxiety of a Mothers heart overcomes the 'still small voice' within and bids me cast myself upon your patience and Kindness—When the call came to this city for troops to defend our Capital my five sons rallied around our beloved flag—my fourth boy was then a Capt in the 71st S. N. G three of his brothers enlisted as privates in his company the fourth brother *raised* a company in the 79th Highland Regt   they all fought at the first Bull Run battle   after the battle, my second son who was then Brigr Genl of the California Milicia (tho' he fought his battle as private in his brother's company) offered his Brigade to Genl Halleck for he knew his men would follow him—it would have been accepted—but for the distance from the scene of action—my dear Madam *two* of these brave sons, lay, near my dwelling in the *silent grave*—my fourth Capt Julius L Ellis fell mortaly

wounded at Bull Run—my eldest—Augt Van Horne Ellis—Colo of the
124th S. V. (a regt he, himself raised) *fell* at Gett—Do you *now* wonder,
dear Madam—my addressing you—to ask your brave soldier husband for a
SHORT *extention* of leave for my son Bret Lieut Col H. A. Ellis—Capt ~~of~~
in the 35th Infy stationed at San Antonia Texas—he has been in the army
since the Battle of Bull Run—has never been, in that time but seven days
on leave, until last spring—when his health broke down utterly—he applied
for leave—it was granted—that leave expires—on the *15th Octr*—consequently—he will be obliged to leave in the Steamer on Wednesday next
19th Oct,—for Texas where the yellow fever is raging—Once more I ask
you to forgive the liberty I have taken with you—your friends Genl & Mrs
Wallen can vouch for the truth of the above"—ALS, DNA, RG 94, Letters
Received, 362E 1867. On Sept. 17, Bvt. Maj. Gen. Edward D. Townsend
noted on this letter. "Acknowledge receipt of Mrs Ellis' letter to Mrs Grant,
and say that it is much regretted that the interests of the service absolutely
prevent the granting of her request, and that it is believed that no danger
from yellow fever will exist after the 15th of October"—AN (initialed),
ibid.

1867, SEPT. 16.   To secretary of war. "I have the honor to state that the
estimated sum required for expenses of the Commanding General's Office,
for the fiscal year ending June 30th 1869, is Five Thousand dollars
($5000.)."—Copies, DLC-USG, V, 47, 60; DNA, RG 108, Letters Sent.

1867, [SEPT. 16].   USG endorsement. "Respectfully forwarded to the
Secy. of War, with recommendation that Gen. Halleck be directed to revoke his order suspending payment of the vouchers within referred to. By
S O. no. 406, H Q. A., A. G. O., Aug. 10th 67, Bvt. Major Eckerson was
ordered to report with out delay to the Chief Quartermaster Mil. Div. of
the Missouri, for assignment to duty, and it is deemed inexpedient to order
his trial, for the irregularities herein set forth."—ES, DNA, RG 94, ACP,
1239 1871. On Aug. 29, Judge Advocate Gen. Joseph Holt had endorsed
these papers. "Respectfully returned to the Adjutant General. Upon an
examination of the accompanying record and report of the Court of Inquiry,
it is not perceived that it can properly be held that the contractors, in the
inception of the contracts therein referred to, were guilty of such *fraud in
law*, as to constitute a defence to the payment of the vouchers to the bona
fide innocent parties who are within stated to be the present holders of the
same. . . . The Court are of the opinion that the loss to the Government
through the general mismanagement of *Capt. T. J. Eckerson*, as Chief
Quartermaster, and acting Chief Com. of Sub., of the District of Boise—
amounted to at least $100,000 and that his neglects of duty were of a sig-
nal and gross character is a conclusion which must, it is believed, be
arrived at upon a reading of the testimony and report. It does not appear
whether or not he has yet been brought to trial in the Department in which
his malfeasance occurred; if not, it is recommended that the report and

record of the Court be at once returned to Maj. Gen. Halleck, in order that he may cause charges to be preferred and the trial to be proceeded with. . . ."—ES, *ibid.*

On Feb. 26, Maj. Gen. Henry W. Halleck, San Francisco, had telegraphed to Bvt. Maj. Gen. Edward D. Townsend requesting a court of inquiry to investigate Bvt. Maj. Theodore J. Eckerson *et al.*—Telegram received (on Feb. 27), *ibid.*, Letters Received, 122P 1867. On March 5, USG endorsed this telegram. "Respectfully forwarded to the Secretary of War approved."—ES, *ibid.* Probably in Nov., USG noted. "The Adj Gn. will please let Capt. Eckerson see the proceedings of Ct. of Enq. at Ft Boise in /66."—AN (initialed), *ibid.* Additional papers are *ibid.*

On Aug. 1, Eckerson, Portland, Ore., had telegraphed to USG. "I respectfully request to be ordered East and solicit answer by telegraph— Approved. F. STEELE Bvt M. General."—Telegram received (on Aug. 3, 9:05 A.M.), *ibid.*, 280Q 1867; *ibid.*, RG 108, Telegrams Received; copy, DLC-USG, V, 55. On Aug. 7, Bvt. Maj. Gen. Daniel H. Rucker, act. q. m. gen., wrote to USG. "I have the honor to acknowledge the receipt of a copy of a telegram of the 3d inst from Brevet Major T. J. Eckerson Assistant Quartermaster US Army requesting to be ordered East, and to state that I have this day recommended to the Adjutant General that he be ordered to report in person to Brevet Major Genl J. L. Donaldson Asst Quartermaster General, Chief Quartermaster, Military Division of the Missouri, for assignment to duty."—LS, DNA, RG 108, Letters Received.

On Jan. 31, 1868, U.S. Senator George H. Williams of Ore., Washington, D. C., wrote to USG. "Some time Since I asked for the Brevet appointment of Major Eckerson late of Fort Vancouver Wash T.y—Will you allow me once more to call your favorable attention to the subject"— ALS, *ibid.*, RG 94, ACP, 4943 1873.

On April 9, U.S. Senator Henry W. Corbett of Ore. wrote to USG. "Please furnish Mr Cummings with the Amt paid by Majr Eckerson from Boise City to the Interior Posts. Majr E was tried ₤ by Court Marshall for paying such exhorbitant rates for transportation and was acquitted, in that instance it would show the price paid"—ALS, *ibid.*, RG 92, Letters Received from Depts. and Bureaus.

1867, SEPT. 16.   To Attorney Gen. Henry Stanbery. "I have the honor to send herewith papers in the case of the right to bounty of certain Indian Regiments which served the United States during the rebellion and respectfully ask your opinion whether they are entitled to the same."—LS, DNA, RG 60, Letters Received, War Dept. On Sept. 21, Stanbery wrote to USG. ". . . Upon examination of the papers communicated with your letter, the following appears to be a statement of the facts upon which this question arises: Three regiments of Indians numbered as first, second, and third, Indian Regiments were recruited and organized by authority of the War Department in the months of May and August, 1862, according to the provisions of the act of Congress of July 22, 1861; that is, were enlisted as volunteers to serve for three years or during the war. They served as such in Missouri, Kansas, Arkansas, and the Indian Territory, and were honorably discharged from the military service under orders of the Department of May, 1865. As to pay, allowances, and services, they were put in all respects upon the footing of other volunteers. . . . I find, also, that in the treaty made with the Cherokee Nation of Indians, concluded on the 19th of July, 1866, and ratified with amendments on the 27th of July 1866, Article 25, are these words: 'A large number of the Cherokees who served in the army of the United States having died, leaving no heirs entitled to receive *bounties* and arrears of pay on account of such service, it is agreed that all bounties and arrears for service in the regiments of Indian United States *volunteers* which shall remain unclaimed by any person legally entitled to receive the same for two years from the ratification of this treaty, shall be paid,' etc. This is another explicit recognition by the treaty making power of the United States, that these Indian regiments stand upon the footing of United States volunteers in regard to all bounties as well as arrears of pay. Upon the whole, I am clearly of opinion that the soldiers of these regiments are entitled to bounty under the act of July 28, 1866."— LS, *ibid.*, RG 99, Letters Received. On Oct. 7, USG wrote to Stanbery. "For the reasons stated to you verbally, I have the honor to send herewith reports by the Adjt. Genl. and Paymaster Genl. respecting the bounty to Indian regiments, about which you furnished an opinion on 21st Sept."— Copy, *ibid.*, RG 107, Letters Sent to the President. On Oct. 27, 1868, Bvt. Maj. Gen. Benjamin W. Brice, paymaster gen., authorized payment.— *Ibid.*, RG 99, Letters Received.

1867, SEPT. 16. To Solicitor of the Treasury Edward Jordan. "In reply to your letter of May 1st, enclosing one from H. L. Moss, Esq, U. S. District-Attorney for Minnesota, asking that it may be stipulated that $300 00 will be paid for legal services in the case of the United States against William Branch and others, before the conclusion of the trial, I have the honor to inform you that this Department declines to ~~accede to~~ make such proposed stipulation. On the presentation of the account, at the termination of the service, accompanied by evidence of the reasonableness of the items charged, it will be considered and passed upon."—LS, DNA, RG 206, Letters Received from the War Dept. On Sept. 26, Jordan wrote to USG. "I have the honor to transmit herewith a copy of a letter from the U. S. Dist. Attorney for Minnesota, with the papers therein referred to, in relation to the case of the United States vs. William Branch and others,—a suit brought, upon the bond of said Branch to recover the sum of $4.818 51/100 as damages for non-performance of contract to deliver hay at Fort Snelling, in the year 1864. I also transmit the accounts of the District Attorney, and of James Gilfillan, Esq., Associate Counsel for the sums of $300.00, and $200 00 respectively, for services rendered in the preparation and trial of said suit. It appears from the statement of the District Attorney that the trial of this suit resulted in a verdict against the United

States, but this was caused by the unexpected character of the testimony introduced on the part of the defence, and is in no wise attributable to any neglect or lack of ability on the part of the Dist. Attorney or his associate, and I therefore recommend these bills to your favorable consideration. The employment of Mr. Gilfillan is stated to have been under 'authority of letter dated April 26, 1866,' but the records of this Office do not show that any such letter was addressed to him or the District Attorney at any time giving such authority, although such course was recommended by me in a letter to Hon. E. M. Stanton, then Secretary of War under date of April 6. 1866. It is presumed therefore that authority was given by the Secretary, directly, to the Dist Attorney, to employ Mr. Gilfillan. In connection with the account of Mr. Moss, the Dist. Attorney, I beg leave also to refer to your letter to this Office dated 16th inst., in regard thereto. The original papers which were forwarded from the files of the War Department, to be used on the trial of the case, are herewith returned"—Copy, *ibid.*, RG 206, Letters Sent. On Oct. 21, Judge Advocate Gen. Joseph Holt endorsed papers concerning this matter with a recommendation to pay the attorneys.—Copy, *ibid.*, RG 153, Letters Sent. On Oct. 24, USG favorably endorsed these papers.—Copy, *ibid.*, RG 107, Orders and Endorsements.

1867, SEPT. 16.   USG note. "The Adj. Gn. will issue Mr. Harrison the same Military protection throughout the 5 Mil. districts he now has from Gn. Thomas for his command"—AN (initialed), DNA, RG 94, Letters Received, 517A 1867. Written at the foot of protection papers issued on July 13 by Maj. Oliver D. Greene, adjt. for Bvt. Maj. Gen. Edward O. C. Ord, Vicksburg. "The military Commanders throughout this Military District are authorized and instructed to protect the bearer, Mr. Harrison as against arrest by the civil authorities of the state of Georgia on the charge of murder of the rebel officer spoken of in the within letter of His Excellency Gov Brownlow of Tenn. This order to continue in force for 60 days from date or while Mr. Harrison is actually engaged in the search for the murderer of Maj. McGaughey."—Copy, *ibid.* On Sept. 16, Bvt. Maj. Gen. Edward D. Townsend wrote as directed to the five military district commanders.—Copy, *ibid.*, Letters Sent.

1867, SEPT. 16.   Judge Advocate Gen. Joseph Holt to USG. "Capt. Thomas J. Durnin 25th Infantry, was tried in August last by General Court Martial at Louisville, Ky, under the following charge:—Violation of the 45th Article of War. 1.—In that, being on duty as commanding Officer of the Post of Columbus, Ky., and of Co. G. 25th Infy, he was drunk & unfit for duty, and did fall from his horse, in the streets of Columbus. This May 1. 1867   2.—Drunk under the same circumstances when also acting as officer of the day, on the 18th May, 1867. . . . The Court append to the record a paper signed by the Judge Advocate, in which they invite the attention of the Dept. Commander 'to the fact disclosed by the evidence in this case, that two of the witnesses for the Prosecution—Lieut. Baldwin &

Dr. Ferris—both of them belonging to the military service of the U. S., have kept written memoranda of the acts of the accused; evidently with a view to multiply charges against him, which practice is, in the opinion of the Court, unmilitary, against public policy, and deserving the reprobation of the military authorities.' In the judgment of this Bureau, this animadversion upon the two officers in question is uncalled for and unjust; and Gen. Thomas very properly makes no reference to it, in the endorsement of his decision and orders upon the record. It is the inference of the Court that these gentlemen had in view the multiplication of charges against the Accused, but this inference seems to be without adequate foundation. A fairer surmise would appear to be, that these officers, knowing that the accused would surely sooner or later be called to answer for his misconduct, and that they would as surely be summoned as witnesses in the case, fitted themselves for the better performance of that duty by making a memorandum of the occasions on which Capt. Durnin wilfully incapacitated himself for service; an event occurring so frequently, that without some such aid to the memory, there was much reason to fear his escape from punishment through failure of precise proof."—Copy, DNA, RG 153, Letters Sent.

1867, SEPT. 16.   Bvt. Maj. Gen. Rufus Ingalls, New York City, to USG. "Letter was received—was absent. I will see to it at the Earliest moment."— Telegram received (at 12: 10 P.M.), DNA, RG 107, Telegrams Collected (Bound).

1867, SEPT. 17.   USG endorsement. "Respectfully submitted to the President with the recommendation that the sentence awarded to 2d Lt. Bucklin, 34th U. S. Infantry, for a disgraceful offence & approved by Genl Ord com'g 4th Mil. Dist., be approved."—Copy, DNA, RG 107, Orders and Endorsements. On Sept. 18, President Andrew Johnson endorsed this letter approving USG's recommendation.—Copy, *ibid.* Written on a letter of Sept. 12 from Judge Advocate Gen. Joseph Holt to USG. "Second Lieutenant Benjamin F. Bucklin, 34th U. S. Infy, was tried Aug. 16th at Vicksburg, Miss, under the followg charges: 1.—Conduct unbecoming an officer and a gentleman. In that accused did endeavor to procure a room in the Scruggs Hotel at Corinth, Miss., to be jointly occupied by himself and a woman of bad character, and having been refused by the proprietor, did say that 'it made no difference; that if he could'nt get a room one way, he could another'; and did thereupon call for the corporal of the guard and direct him to bring a guard at double-quick; and said guard having reported, he did post a sentinel at each door of the Hotel with instructions to permit no one to enter or leave the house except by his special orders. This at Corinth, July 19. last. 2. In that Accused, having placed a guard as aforesaid, and being asked by Mr. Scruggs, the landlord, whether he was Commandant of the Post of Corinth, did reply that he controlled the house; he was officer of the day; which assertion was false. 2.—Conduct subversive of good order and military discipline. In becoming grossly intoxicated on the 19th July last, and exposing himself in that condition in the streets of Corinth. The Court find accused guilty under charge 1st and its specifications; not guilty under the second charge; and sentence him:— To be dismissed the service. . . . The aggregate proofs in the case, of which the foregoing is a summary, are thought to justify this Bureau in advising some mitigation of sentence. The evidence is probably sufficient to convict the accused of unbecoming and impure *intentions*, for which severe punishment may wisely be inflicted. But in considering his subsequent acts of hasty and transitory anger, and his alleged assumption, for a moment, of a title and authority not his own, something is due to the sensibilities of an officer who, because of the uniform he wears, is subjected to the taunts and insults of the rebellious and disloyal; and still more to the bright & honorable record which he has succeeded in earning for himself. It is suggested that a suspension from rank and pay for one month will be ample atonement for his fault."—Copy, *ibid.*, RG 153, Letters Sent.

1867, SEPT. 17. To Secretary of the Treasury Hugh McCulloch. "I have the honor to send herewith papers relative to certain *copper* ore, said to be sunken in the *James River* by the rebels during the war, the property it is believed being of the class which the law requires the Treasury to take charge of."—Df, DNA, RG 107, Letters Received from Bureaus; copy, *ibid.*, Letters Sent to the President. On Sept. 12, Bvt. Maj. Gen. Daniel H. Rucker, act. q. m. gen., had written to USG concerning this matter.—LS, *ibid.*, RG 92, Reports to the Secretary of War (Press).

1867, SEPT. 17. John J. Good, Hillsborough, Tex., to USG. "I have the honor respectfully to solicit information in reply to the following questions *1st* Can agents of the Freedmans Bureau arrest try and punish citizens for violations of the State law   If so can they do this without the intervention of a jury or in cases where the civil authorities are both able and willing to try and punish for such violations? *2d* Can they take from the custody of the civil authorities before trial prisoners charged with high crimes against the State and set them at liberty? *3d* Can they take up and sell the stock of citizens appropriating the proceeds of such sales to ther own use upon the pretext that such stock is annoying them? *4th* Can they imprison for debt? *5th* Can they refuse legal tender notes in payment of debts adjudicated and fines assessed by them and demand gold and silver coin only? *6th* Can the military authorities invest them with the exercise of powers other than those given such agents by the law of their creation? In seeking this information General I am actuated by patriotic motives an earnest desire to avoid any collision with the United States authorities or even the semblance of impeding the reconstruction of the Southern States   It is desired for my official guidance and coming from you will have weight and authority in my District   You will confer upon me a great favor by replying at your earliest convenience and addressing me at Dallas Dallas County Texas"— ALS, DNA, RG 105, Hd. Qrs., Letters Received. On June 9, 1868, Good,

Dallas, wrote to USG. "Believing injustice done me by Genl Reynolds order of Novr 18th /67 removing me from the Bench of the 5th Judicial District of Texas I respectfully protested against it and sent protest to Maj Genl Hancock New Orleans La   He informed me of its receipt; his want of jurisdiction in the premises and that the same would be forwarded to you for final action   Having heard nothing from it since I respectfully request to know if any and what action was taken upon it."—ALS, *ibid.,* RG 108, Letters Received.

1867, SEPT. 18.   USG note. "This will introduce Gen. Sharpe, late of my staff, to the Hon. Sec. of the Treas. whom the Gen. wishes to see for a few minutes on business."—Kenneth W. Rendell, Inc., Catalogue 84 [1973], p. 12.

1867, SEPT. 18.   Commissioner of Education Henry Barnard to USG. "It is very desirable that the Department of which I am Commissioner should be fully and early informed of the effect produced by the war on the Educational agencies in the late insurgent States, especially as to the amount of funds and endowments misappropriated, the number of schools, academies, and colleges that became extinct, the present conditions of the schools and higher seminaries now in operation, the disposition and ability of the people to provide for primary and public instruction in their several neighborhoods by local taxation. In the Act creating this Department at the close of the last Congress (a copy of which is herewith sent) no allowance or provision was made for contingent expenses in collecting information and statistics; but it has occurred to me, that it might be legitimate for you to authorize the proper military authorities to provide transportation for my Chief Clerk, Mr Neill whom I could send to obtain the information to which I have referred. Will you please therefore to give the subject your consideration and favor me with as early a reply as convenient, . . ."—LS, DNA, RG 107, Letters Received from Bureaus. The enclosure is *ibid.*

1867, SEPT. 18.   W. T. Helm, Nashville, to USG. "Will you please send me copies of the papers in the case of a claim for damages, made out by Vestrymen of the Ch. of the Holy Trinity, Nashville, Tennessee, & allowed in part, by military officers here? The claim was settled a year or two ago." —ALS, DNA, RG 107, Letters Received from Bureaus. On Sept. 28, President Andrew Johnson endorsed this letter. "RESPECTFULLY REFERRED TO the Secretary of War, *ad interim*, who will please grant this request, if it can be done without injury to public interests."—ES, *ibid.* Additional papers are *ibid.*

1867, SEPT. 19.   To President Andrew Johnson. "I have the honor to propose for your consideration the following appointments in the army, and enclose the recommendations in favor of the applicants: Rev E. B. Tuttle, for Chaplain—of Illinois   W. P. Van Ness, for 2d Lieutenant—

of NewYork   L. H. Orleman, for 2d Lieutenant Cavalry—of NewYork
George Taylor, for 2d Lieutenant Cavalry—of Dist. of Columbia   Oliver
Grosvenor, for 2d Lieutenant—of Illinois   There are vacancies to which
these persons may be appointed."—LS, OFH.

On Sept. 10, Edmund B. Tuttle, Chicago, had written to USG. "I beg
respectfully to represent to you, that I served as Post Chaplain in Camp
Douglas, Chicago, Illinois from March 3d 1861, to June 23d 1862, without pay or Compensation of any kind. My position was originated by the
Union Defence Committee of Chicago, who directed me to ~~the~~ take care of
Soldiers families in addition to my duties, as the only Chaplain in the Camp,
excepting the Roman Catholic Chaplain, of Col. Mulligan's Irish Regt. My
services were continuous in the Care of the Sick in Hospitals & other religious duties, until the date of my appointment as U. S. Hospital Chaplain,
by the President, June 23d 1862. I would therefore ask that my claim be
allowed for Said Services for the time specified; and for which you will find
a precedent in the Case of Rev Mr Leonard, who, at the Same time did
partial Service in the Marine Hospital at Chicago, for which the Hon.
Sect'y of War allowed him three years Compensation, as back pay. He was
appointed Hospt. Chaplain Oct. 1864. Date of his Com. Ap. 25./65. Paid
in May '65. I furnished a Hospital Wagon for the use for the Post—there
being no Ambulance at Chicago for one & half years use of the said
Wagon."—ALS, DNA, RG 94, ACP, 3167 1871. On Sept. 21, Tuttle
wrote to USG acknowledging his appointment.—ALS, *ibid.* On Oct. 8,
J. A. Mennicutt, dental surgeon, Chicago, telegraphed to USG. "Rev.
E. B. Tuttle is undergoing a necessary and important Surgical operation
and treatment which makes it absolutely necessary that he should remain
here ten (10) days longer"—Telegram received (at 1:30 P.M.), *ibid.*,
RG 107, Telegrams Collected (Bound). On Oct. 7, 3:00 P.M., USG had
telegraphed to Tuttle. "Ten days extension of time for your departure is
authorized."—ALS (telegram sent), *ibid.*; telegram sent, *ibid.*; copies,
ibid., RG 108, Telegrams Sent; DLC-USG, V, 56. On Dec. 8, 1869, Orvil
L. Grant, Chicago, wrote to USG. "I take pleasure in introducing to you
the Revd E B Tuttle who is Chaplain at Cheyenne. Mr Tuttle has been in
the service for several years and has been constantly exposed to the vicis-
situdes of war and frontier life till his health has become impaired and
now wishes to be removed to some more pleasent place or entirely releived
from duty. He joined our Excursion party at Cheyenne and accompanied us
to California and all of our party (who are prominent business men) join
me in desiring his success for a change"—ALS, DNA, RG 94, ACP, 3167
1871. Other letters addressed to USG recommending Tuttle are *ibid.*

On Sept. 20, 1867, USG wrote to Louis H. Orleman to inform him of
his appointment as 2nd lt., 10th Cav.—James Lowe Autographs, Ltd.,
Catalogue 8 [*1978*], no. 82.

On Aug. 31, William Dennison, Columbus, Ohio, had written to USG
recommending George Tayler for an appointment to the U.S. Army.—
ALS, DNA, RG 94, ACP, T32 CB 1867. On Sept. 2, USG endorsed this

letter. "Refered to Gn. Dent to know if recommendation of Mr. Taylor has been made. If not let his name go on next list of recommendations to the President."—AES, *ibid.* Additional letters addressed to USG are *ibid.* Tayler was appointed 2nd lt., 10th Cav., as of Sept. 20.

On Sept. 10, Thomas W. Grosvenor *et al.*, Chicago, had written to USG recommending Oliver Grosvenor for appointment to the U.S. Army.—LS, *ibid.*, G558 CB 1867. He was appointed 2nd lt., 4th Cav., as of Sept. 20.

1867, SEPT. 19.   To AG. "Relieve Gn. Slemmer from the Board in N. Y. City and appoint Gn. Casey. Take effect Nov. 1st"—AL (initialed), DNA, RG 94, Letters Received, 518A 1867.

1867, SEPT. 19.   Maj. Gen. Oliver O. Howard to USG. "I have the honor to submit the enclosed correspondence relating to the distributi[on] of the National Fund provided for in the treaty with the Creek Indians, dated July 14th 1866, wherein it is claimed that this fund should be distributed proportionately between the Indians of that Nation and the freedmen who were then and are now residing among them. The former Commissioner of Indian Affairs, Mr *Bogy* decided that the freedmen were not entitled to a share of the fund, and upon that decis[ion] it is withheld. The delegates who represented that nation in the Commission which made the treaty, are of the opinion that the freedmen are entitled to a per capita share of the fund and soil donated by the terms of the treaty. I respectfully request that such action be taken as shall secure justice to the freed people who are now by law a part of said nation."—Copy, DNA, RG 105, Letters Sent.

1867, SEPT. 19.   Bvt. Maj. Gen. James H. Wilson, Davenport, Iowa, to USG. "This will be handed to you by Genl Croxton late of my command in Tennessee, Alabama & Georgia. He has been requested by Genl Thomas to make a report in regard to operations in which his command participated, and having sent all of his records to the War Department, as required by regulations, desires authority to consult them. He made the same request of Mr Stanton but was factiously refused, please permit him to examine such documents and records as may be necessary for his purposes. Genl Croxton can give you a full account of affairs in Kentucky."—ALS, DNA, RG 94, Letters Received, 13W 1868.

1867, SEPT. 19.   M. A. Bryson, Cairo, Ill., to USG. "I am today in receipt of a letter from Gen. McAlister, in charge of Improvement of the Mouth of Mississippi River. In said letter he states that the appropriation in the hands of the Department will not enable him now to close the Contract for the dredgeboat to be used in deepening the channel on the Bar. The deficiency is very small, only a few Thousand Dollars. As Chairman of the Committee of the 16 valley states appointed at the Convention held in st Louis, I take the liberty of saying that there is very great anxiety felt in regard to this work of Improvements of Western Rivers. The Gov.s of the valley states to-gether with the Committee will memorialize Congress on the subject at its next session, and the strength of the west will be prompt to sustain it If this assurance will do anything toward ~~enabling~~couraging you to order the construction of this boat I shall in the name of the west be thankfull. Our Com. of one from each state meets on the 9th of October and shall transmitt you our expression. We are confident we have a friend in you."—ALS, DNA, RG 77, Explorations and Surveys, Letters Received.

1867, SEPT. 19. W. B. Chace, Washington, D. C., to USG. "Mr. John P. Kelsey, a native citizen of the United States residing in the city of Camargo, Mexico, under date of June 7th 1865, was ordered by Brig. Genl. E. B. Brown then in command of U. S. forces on the Upper Rio Grande to seize all property belonging to the so called Confederate States, and hold the same subject to the orders of the Commanding General. The accompanying papers will show the manner in which that duty, as well as others which devolved upon Mr. Kelsey in consequence of subsequent orders, was performed; the expenses incurred by him in such performance; the protest for the nonpayment of the draft drawn by General Brown upon Messrs. Burns and Shaeffer of N. Orleans for the payment of such expenses, for the reimbursement of which this and the accompanying papers are now laid before you."—ALS, DNA, RG 107, Letters Received, C509 1867. See *SRC*, 43-1-51.

1867, SEPT. 19. H. P. Dwight, Toronto, to USG. "A homaepathic Physician now practicing here who lived in New Orleans & the South during several Years of Southern Epidemics & had large experience in the treatment of them is willing to go to New Orleans or elsewhere if you require him Expenses & remuneration to be arranged with your Surgeon Genl. Reference if needed, Governo[r] Flanders of New Orleans answer"— Telegram received (at 4:15 P.M.), DNA, RG 107, Telegrams Collected (Bound); *ibid.*, RG 108, Telegrams Received; copies, *ibid.*, Letters Received; DLC-USG, V, 55.

1867, SEPT. 19. F. William E. Lohmann, Richmond, to USG. "While no man can appreciate more highly than myself the multitudinous duties devolving upon any one occupying the high position which you do, and whilst I dislike to add to the burthen of your office, yet I am induced to trespass on your valuable time, from the high estimate in which you are regarded, not only by myself, but by the great majority of Southern citizens. My object in addressing you is for this. Papers, which are now on file in the War office will show that the City property has been occupied for a considerable length of time by U. S. officers. What I wish to know is this whether that property will not be surrendered to the City, or, whether rent should not be paid for the use of it whilst in the occupancy of U. S. officers; of course, expecting that a reasonable rent should be allowed therefor. I am induced to make this application to you from the fact that I, as can be shown by the testimony of U. S. Miliraty officers of high standing, have rendered very essential service to the Government; and if, upon an examination of the records of the War office, you should decide that possession of the property and payment of rent should be made, I would be exceedingly obliged that any order, which may be issued, should pass through my hands, as in that case I should realize something for the trouble taken by me."—ALS, DNA, RG 107, Letters Received, L161 1867. See *PUSG*, 15, 224–25.

1867, SEPT. 20.   USG endorsement. "I am personally cognizant of the application to public uses, viz: the construction of temporary shelter, for officers and men of the U. S. forces at Paducah, of the materials of Mr. Markland's house—referred to in the accompanying papers—and believe the account to be just. It is therefore referred to the Quarter Master General for settlement, and the paying officer will be relieved from the usual property accountability in the case."—Copies, DNA, RG 92, Decision Books; *ibid.*, RG 107, Orders and Endorsements. Written on a claim submitted by Absalom H. Markland "for lumber &c. furnished for barracks at Paducah, Ky., in Nov. 1861, amounting to $2.799.60"—*Ibid.*

1867, SEPT. 20.   To Edward McPherson, clerk, U.S. House of Representatives. "At the instance of the Quartermaster General of the Army, I have the honor to request that you will designate a newspaper in the State of *South Carolina* for the publication of official advertisements"—Copy, DNA, RG 107, Reports to Congress. On Sept. 17, Bvt. Maj. Gen. Daniel H. Rucker, act. q. m. gen., had endorsed papers to USG concerning this matter.—ES, *ibid.*, RG 92, Reports to the Secretary of War (Press). See *ibid.*, RG 94, Letters Received, 1292M 1867.

1867, SEPT. 20.   Bvt. Brig. Gen. Frederick T. Dent endorsement. "Referred to the Adjutant General. The Government will make no further repairs upon the Submarine Teleg'h Cable between Fortress Monroe and Cherrystone Va. Direct the Quarter Master General to dispose of the cable by sale under the most favorable circumstances at once. Notify Thos T. Eckert Supt Western Union Teleg'h Co New York of this action."—ES, DNA, RG 94, Letters Received, 366E 1867. Written on a letter of Sept. 12 from Thomas T. Eckert, Western Union Telegraph Co., New York City, to USG. "In order to retain telegraph connection with Fortress Monroe, and still be relieved of the expense of its maintenance and operation, the line from Wilmington Del to Fortress Monroe which was built by the Government in the early part of the war, was turned over to the American Telegraph Company, by order of the Secretary of War, in consideration of its free use by Government for the transmission of its dispatches, the land line becoming the property of the Telegraph Company and the submarine cable across Chesapeake Bay continuing to be the property of the Government and all expense of its repairs to be borne by the Government. This submarine cable has lately become so injured, that it must be repaired at very considerable expense, before it can be made serviceable—The telegraph company find that the line does not pay the expense of operating it, and in view of the fact that the business from Fort Monroe and Norfolk can now be done via Richmond, as well as via. the cable and eastern shore route, we will make no further outlay upon any portion of this line south of Newtown, Md, unless desired to do so by the Government. Your early attention to this matter is respectfully requested, as, if repairs are to be made to either land line or cable, the work should be commenced without delay."— LS, *ibid.* On Oct. 31, Bvt. Maj. Gen. Charles Thomas, asst. q. m. gen., wrote to USG. "I have the honor to submit for instructions the accompanying papers pertaining to the sub-marine telegraph cable between Fortress Monroe and Cherry Stone, Va., which was directed by the Secretary of War ad interim, on the 21st ultimo, 'to be disposed of at once by sale under the most favorable circumstances,' . . ."—LS, *ibid.*, RG 92, Letters Received.

1867, Sept. [21].   USG endorsement. "The Adj. Gn. will issue the above order."—AE (initialed), DNA, RG 94, Letters Received, 528A 1867. Written on a Sept. 21 draft of AGO General Orders. "The Commissary General of Subsistence will supply posts west of the 96° degree of Longitude liberally with canned fruits, vegetables &c for sales to officers. Commanding officers of Companies are authorized to buy such supplies for their companies at the prices charged to officers. The Com.y Gn. will be authorized to limit the amount of these sales ~~to Companies~~ whenever abuse of the privilege herein given is apprehended"—ADf (last sentence in USG's hand), *ibid.*

1867, Sept. 21, 11:35 a.m.   To Governor Walter Harriman of N. H. "The Fort at Portsmouth is in the hands of the Engineers and workmen for repairs. ~~and~~ tThe troops have been orderd to Boston Harbor to have them out of the way until the work is completed. The order cannot be revoked."— ALS (telegram sent), DNA, RG 107, Telegrams Collected (Bound); telegram sent, *ibid.*; copies, *ibid.*, RG 108, Telegrams Sent; DLC-USG, V, 56. On Sept. 20, Bvt. Maj. Gen. Daniel H. Rucker, act. q. m. gen., had written to USG. "Attention is respectfully invited to the enclosed letter of Bvt. Major Gen'l. G. H. Crosman, Asst. Q. Mr. Gen'l. U. S. A. Chief Q. Mr. Dept. of the East, reporting to this office that the garrison at Fort Constitution Portsmouth N. H. has been ordered to Fort Winthrop Boston Harbor, which renders it necessary to make some disposition of fifty (50) cords of wood and sixty five (65) tons of coal on hand at that fort. It will be observed that the Act'g Asst. Q. Mr. at Fort. Constitution states, that the fuel can be sold at nearly cost prices, and I have the honor to request authority for the sale of the wood and coal at public auction after due advertisement."—LS, DNA, RG 92, Reports to the Secretary of War (Press).

On Oct. 22, U.S. Senator Aaron H. Cragin of N. H., Lebanon, wrote to USG. "About three weeks ago I had an interview with you in relation to retaining the troops at Ft. Constitution, in Portsmouth (N. H.) Harbor, and you refered the matter to Genl Meade. I requested my friend Comr Rollins to see you again, after Genl Meade had reported on the case, and if possible have the troops retained there, as the people of Portsmouth were very anxious for that result. Mr. Rollins wrote me that he had seen you, and that the troops would remain there, at least till after the meeting of Congress. I sent his letter to friends in Portsmouth and all hands were much pleased, and felt that the matter was settled. Yesterday I recd. a dispatch from Portsmouth—of which the following is a copy—'Troops been ordered to Boston Harbor. Can any thing be done'? I replied that I had done all I could do, I suppose it is too late to think of changing this order, and I do not wish to ask it, unless it is perfectly proper. It would be very gratifying to many true men in this state if troops could be kept there."— ALS, *ibid.*, RG 94, Letters Received, 345E 1867. Additional papers are *ibid.* On Oct. 25, 3:00 P.M., USG telegraphed to Maj. Gen. George G. Meade. "If Engineers are not ready to commence work at Portsmouth leave company there untill they are ready."—ALS (telegram sent), *ibid.*, RG 107, Telegrams Collected (Bound); telegram sent, *ibid.*; copies, *ibid.*, RG 108, Telegrams Sent; DLC-USG, V, 56. On Oct. 26, Meade, Philadelphia, telegraphed to USG. "Engineers are not working at Portsmouth and do not expect to work for a long time. Whole matter explained in report dated and sent September thirtieth (30th). The order for transfer of company was issued from A. G. O. Washington. Has been suspended in accordance with your telegram."—Telegram received (at noon), DNA, RG 107, Telegrams Collected (Bound); *ibid.*, RG 108, Telegrams Received; copies, *ibid.*, RG 393, Dept. of the East, Letters Sent; DLC-USG, V, 55.

1867, SEPT. 21.   Judge Advocate Gen. Joseph Holt to USG. *"Capt. I. D. Sailer, 15th U. S. Infantry,* was summarily dismissed the service in December 1863, for having received money ($62.) as an inducement to muster an officer of the volunteer forces (Lieut. Leonard Wightman, 5th Michigan Batty.,) into the service of the United States. This action was taken on a report of Capt. Young, made as the result of an investigation which had been ordered by the Adjutant General. . . . It is recommended that his application for restoration to the service, be denied."—Copy, DNA, RG 153, Letters Sent.

1867, SEPT. 22.   Maj. Gen. Oliver O. Howard to USG. "Allow me to recommend to your favorable consideration Lieut. Hassett late of the 106 Penn—Regt.—for any position as watchman or other place which he is capable of filling & which may be vacant"—ALS (press), Howard Papers, MeB.

1867, SEPT. 22.   U.S. Senator Charles Sumner of Mass., Boston, to USG. "I desire to recommend Brevet Lt. Colonel G. Norman Lieber, Judge Advocate at New Orleans, *for the additional brevet of Colonel.* I have known

Col. Lieber from his childhood & have watched his course during the war. I believe him to be in every respect meritorious, & I am sure that all who have known him would say the same. Genl. Sheridan might be referred to confidently. I trust that I do not take too great a liberty in making this suggestion."—ALS, DNA, RG 94, ACP, 5200 1872. On Dec. 8, Maj. Gen. Philip H. Sheridan wrote to Maj. George K. Leet recommending against the appointment.—LS, *ibid.*

1867, SEPT. 23. USG endorsement. "Respectfully refered to the President with the reccommendation that this appointment be made"—ES, DNA, RG 94, ACP, P571 CB 1867. Written on a letter of Sept. 19 from Robert H. Patterson, Washington, D. C., to USG requesting an appointment in the U.S. Army.—ALS, *ibid.* On Sept. 18, Vice Admiral David D. Porter, Annapolis, had written to USG. "My nephew, Harmon Patterson, is an applicant for the army, and I am in hopes he will succeed in getting the appointment he desires. He is a most correct young man and for the last three years (nearly) has been connected with the Navy. I have known him well from his childhood, and don't hesitate to give him the very best recommendations as to his moral character, and I believe he has sufficient ability to make an excellent officer. I should be pleased to hear that he had received the appointment he seeks."—LS, *ibid.* Patterson was appointed 2nd lt., 1st Art., as of Sept. 23.

1867, SEPT. 23. Erastus O. Haven, president, University of Michigan, Ann Arbor, to USG. "Some time ago I saw it announced in the public prints that the Government proposed to detail a military officer to give instruction in each of the leading Universities of the country. The University of Michigan is very largely attended, is a State University, endowed by a grant of public lands made by Congress. It would be eminently fitting that it should have a Professor, holding office in the Army of the United States. May I ask that some one in the Department give me definite information on this subject, that I may lay it, at an early hour, before our Board of Regents, who meet early in October?"—ALS, DNA, RG 94, Letters Received, 734H 1867.

1867, SEPT. 24. To secretary of war. "I have the honor to recommend the following appointments from volunteers to fill the quotas of the States to which the appointees belong: . . ."—LS, DNA, RG 94, ACP, G572 CB 1867. USG also endorsed the letter. "Appoint the above,"—AES, *ibid.*

1867, SEPT. 24. To Postmaster Gen. Alexander W. Randall. "I have the honor to send herewith for your consideration a petition from the *Mayor of Fayetteville* N. C. and others respecting the mail route from *Carey* N. C. to *Jonesboro* &c"—Df, DNA, RG 107, Letters Received, W475 1867; copy, *ibid.*, Letters Sent to the President.

1867, SEPT. 24. Maj. Gen. George G. Meade, Philadelphia, to USG. "I beg leave to call your attention to the case of 1st Lieut Chas L. Davis 10th Rgt Infty, and to ask that the Brevets of Capt & Major may be conferred on him for his services as a volunteer officer during the war.—Lt. Davis served continuously from the commencement to the close of the war.—My personal knowledge of his services was during the campaigns of 64 & 65, at which time he held a commission in the Signal Corps being during /65 the Chief Signal officer at the Hd Qrs Army of the Potoma[c.] I have therefore to recommend that he be brevetted Captain for the Campaign from the Rapidan to the James in /64—And Major for the Siege of Petersburgh & campaign terminating with Lee's surrender.—"—ALS, DNA, RG 94, ACP, 3552 1875. On Jan. 13, 1866, Meade had written to the AG recommending Charles L. Davis for an appointment in the U.S. Army and USG endorsed this letter. "The recommendation of Gn. Meade for the appointment of Bvt. Maj. Chas. L. Davis in the Regular Army is approved and respectfully forwarded."—AES (undated), *ibid.* Davis was appointed 1st lt., 10th Inf., as of Feb. 23.

1867, SEPT. 24. Maj. Gen. George G. Meade, Philadelphia, to USG. "OnAt my recommendation the Dept was pleased to appoint Mr Edwd Jas Smith a 2d Lieut of Infantry—Mr Smith had served with credit during the war having been promoted from the ranks to a captaincy—At the time of the application, he was in Colorado Territory, where he went at the close of the war—Owing to this fact, he was necessarily late in complying with the order to present himself to the Board for Examination & in consequence went before the Board immediately on his arrival.—The President of the Board has informed him, that his examination was *not* satisfactory, and I have reason to believe from conversation with him, that his failure is due to his not having had a little time to brush up his knowledge & recollection of his studies—Being quite young when the war broke out, and having been engaged in mining since—it is reasonable to presume he would become rusty—but as I have every reason to believe that he is qualified for the duties of an officer, and that with a little time allowed him to study, he will be able to pass a better examination I have to ask the indulgence of the Dept—for an order authorizing his re-examination & allowing him 30 days to prepare himself for the same"—ALS, DNA, RG 94, ACP, S1219 CB 1867. Edward J. Smith was appointed 2nd lt., 22nd Inf., as of Aug. 7.

1867, SEPT. 24. Maj. Gen. George G. Meade, Philadelphia, to USG. "I beg leave to ask your favorable consideration to the application for a commission in the army made by Jas. L. Drum of this state.—Mr Drum was too young to take any active part in the recent war altho he left his college & entered as a volunteer for the emergency when his native state was invaded—Mr Drum is the nephew of the late Capt—Simon—H. Drum who fell in the valley of Mexico, and whose distinguished character & services, it is unnecessary for me to do more than refer to.—He is also the brother of Lt—Col R. C. Drum Asst Adjt Genl—at these Hd Qrs—an officer who has served faithfully & meritoriously since entering the service during the Mexican War.—Mr Drum is in every way qualified for the position he seeks, and in view of the services of his brother & uncle, & particularly of the fact of his uncle's falling in battle, I trust the Department will be able to grant the favor now asked."—ALS, DNA, RG 94, ACP, 541D CB 1867. On Oct. 3 and 5, USG as gen., then as secretary of war *ad interim*, endorsed this letter favorably.—ES, *ibid.*

1867, SEPT. 24.   Maj. Gen. Philip H. Sheridan, Washington, D. C., to USG. "I desire to call the attention of the Government to the claims of Mr. *William Crutchfield* of Chattanooga Tenn for damage done his property and supplies furnished the Army of the Cumberland during the winter of 1863 and 4. He claims for Quartermasters Stores furnished the Army and damages sustained during the occupation of his property about $15.500 and for supplies furnished the Subsistence Department about $7000 more. Both justice and honor demand that these claims be paid in full and promptly   His estimate in my opinion falls short of the actual value of the property taken and destroyed and in less than the amount awarded by a Board of Officers, of which I was a member, convened to assess the value of property taken and destroyed on his estate while occupied by the U. S. forces   The records of said board were never completed and cannot now be found   Every thing that Mr. Crutchfield had was freely placed at the disposal of the Army, and contributed much to its preservation at a critical time and when it was impossible to have given Vouchers for the supplies that as a matter of necessity the army must have. Mr. *Crutchfield* loyalty is beyond question; for over three years he of the war he served as an Aide guide and scout, without any compensation whatever, gladly giving his time and substance and risking his life for his country   I know of no other claim in the country which presents as strong grounds for immediate payment. I endorse the whole claim as eminently just, and Mr. Crutchfields loyalty and devotion to his country is worthy of the highest consideration at the hands of the Government."—Copy, DLC-Philip H. Sheridan. On Nov. 20, Bvt. Maj. Gen. Daniel H. Rucker, act. q. m. gen., wrote to USG. "I have the honor to return herewith two communications of John Jolliffe Esq. relative to the action of Messrs Dodge & McLellan in prosecuting the claim of William Crutchfield and requesting that the War Department do not interfere to deprive them of their rights, . . ."—LS, DNA, RG 92, Reports to the Secretary of War (Press). See *PUSG*, 9, 331.

1867, SEPT. 25, 11:30 A.M.   To U.S. Senator Oliver P. Morton of Ind. "I will"—ALS (telegram sent), DNA, RG 107, Telegrams Collected (Bound); telegram sent, *ibid.* USG wrote his telegram on a telegram from Morton, New York City, to USG. "Will you be in Wash'n tomorrow.   please answer."—Telegrams received (2—at 11:00 A.M.), *ibid.; ibid.*, RG 108, Telegrams Received.

1867, SEPT. 25.   Catherine Brady, Geneva, N. Y., to USG. "I would like to Have you write me at what place William *Baker* formerly Detective, in United States service & now in the *Service* of *the United* States—is on Duty as he is my *son inlaw* & I wish to *write* to him—*please* write to me   He was called Col *Baker* all through the *war*   Have the kindness to write me at *Geneva—Ontario* Co. N. York—"—ALS, DNA, RG 107, Letters Received, B393 1867.

1867, SEPT. 25.   R. C. Link, Philadelphia, to USG. "There is a rumor that my brother first Lieut Henry H. Link 36th U. S. Infantry Fort Sanders Dakotah Territory has been killed or seriously wounded—Please let me know if the Department has any authentic information"—Telegram received (at 11:00 A.M.), DNA, RG 107, Telegrams Collected (Bound). 1st Lt. Henry H. Link was mustered out as of Jan. 1, 1871.

1867, SEPT. 26.   To Secretary of the Treasury Hugh McCulloch. "I have the honor to send herewith a report from the Qr. Mr. Genl. of the Army, dated Sept. 24th, respecting *public property* at *Gloucester*, Miss., concerning which certain papers were referred to this Dept. on 30th August by the Sec'y. of the Treasy. which are now returned."—Copy, DNA, RG 107, Letters Sent to the President.

On Nov. 21, Brig. Gen. Andrew A. Humphreys, chief of engineers, wrote to USG. "I have the honor to return herewith the papers, received from the War Depm't, Nov'r 16th, relative to the claim of *Mr Thomas Niles* for compensation for damages &c, stated to have resulted from the erection during the late war of a field work on his land near Gloucester, Mass. It was recommended from this Office about a year ago that the field works erected during the war for the defence of the minor harbors of Massachusetts (among which Gloucester is included) against predatory incursions, should be retained. Our relations with some foreign powers were not, at that time, considered to be altogether in a permanently friendly condition, and the maintenance of these works involved only a small annual expenditure, as they were well constructed, and, generally, in good condition. It was intended to purchase the sites of these works, if it could be done upon reasonable terms.—It is my opinion, however, after a careful examination of the whole subject, that the purchase of Mr. Niles' farm, or any portion of it, upon the terms proposed by him, should not be made. It is not contemplated at present to erect a permanent work at Gloucester, and the field work at that point may be abandoned, and the site relinquished to the owners. The subject of claims for damages growing out of military occupancy has not yet been provided for by the Legislative branch of the Government."—Copy, *ibid.*, RG 77, Letters Sent Relating to Land. On

Nov. 22, Charles G. Davis, assessor's office, Plymouth, Mass., wrote to USG. "Upon application at the War Office I have been advised that the enclosed applications for payment of damages occasioned to the owners of two farms in the Harbour of Plymouth, by the erection of earthworks or forts by the Military Authorities of the U. States, be presented to you. . . ."—ALS, *ibid.*, RG 107, Letters Received, D245 1867.

1867, Sept. 26.   Thomas Sprague, Washington, D. C., to USG. "Enclosed herewith is a copy of the order issued by Colonel De Witt Clinton, in accordance with your directions, relieving me from further service, as clerk to the Special Claims Commission. I am confident that you were not fully informed as to the total helplessness of my condition, or, surely, you would not have directed the enforcement of that order in my *particular* case, until the very last resort. General, it has been my misfortune to lose the use of both legs in battle, (at the storming of Mission Ridge Chattanooga, Tenn, under the immediate commands of yourself and the gallant Gen'l. Sheridan. I have lost my strength—my independence—and am compelled to resort to the pen for support, and can find no employment outside the several departments of the Government. It was the intention of the Hon. E. M. Stanton to give me permanent employment, as soon as practicable, and for this very reason I was ordered to this city. (See enclosed letter of recommendation from Gen'l. Dunn, approved by the Sec'y of War; and, also, letter of Gen'l. Dunn, to Gen'l. Canby, already forwarded to you through Colonel Clinton.) I can walk by artificial aid, to and from my place of business, and could be of service in one of the many positions, in the several departments, now occupied by able-boddied men, who, perhaps, have never made a sacrifice for the life of the nation. In the absence of the Hon. E. M. Stanton and Generals Dunn and Canby, I am, indeed, destitute of influential friends to intercede in my behalf, and have, respectfully, to appeal to you, personally, for a reconsideration of my case, under the circumstances. Pardon this lengthy letter, General; I would not willingly intrude upon your time and patience, yet, I cannot believe it has become necessary, in order to curtail the expenses of the Government, to take the props from under the country's crippled defenders. Constant employment is necessary to my existence; and when you do take the prop that sustains that existence—you do take my life."—ALS, DNA, RG 107, Letters Received, S261 1867. On Sept. 28, Bvt. Maj. Gen. James A. Hardie, inspector gen., endorsed this letter. "The Secretary of War directs the revocation of the order discharging the applicant"—AES, *ibid.* On Dec. 30, Bvt. Brig. Gen. William M. Dunn, Sr., Washington, D. C., wrote to USG. "Referring to previous communications respecting Mr Thomas Sprague I beg to request that he may be appointed to a permanent clerkship in the War Department. He is now on a temporary clerkship under Col. Clinton, Judge Advocate."—ALS, *ibid.*, Letters Received, 481D 1867. On the same day, USG endorsed this letter. "I would like to have this clerk transfered to the Subsistence or Qr.

Mr. Dept. where he can have permanent employment."—AES, *ibid.* Additional papers are *ibid.*

1867, SEPT. 27.   To Secretary of the Interior Orville H. Browning. "I have the honor to send herewith a communication from the Chief of Engineers recommending that *Bt. Brig. Genl. Simpson*, of the Corps of Engineers, be made available for Engineer duty at the Head-quart[ers] of Lt. Genl. Sherman. As Genl. Simpson is now serving under the orders of your Dept. your assent to the assignment is asked. These new duties will not interfere with the performance of those in which he is now engaged unde[r] your orders."—Df, DNA, RG 77, Explorations and Surveys, Letters Sent; copy, *ibid.*, RG 107, Letters Sent to the President. On Sept. 25, Brig. Gen. Andrew A. Humphreys, chief of engineers, had written to USG. "I would respectfully recommend that Bt. Brig Genl. James H. Simpson, Colonel of Engineers, now on detached service as Commissioner for accepting the finished sections of Pacific Railroad under the orders of the Secretary of the Interior—may, in addition to this duty, be made available for Engineer duty at the Head Quarters of Genl. Sherman. It is beleived there could be no conflict in the performance of the duties both of Commissioner and Engineer—Genl Simpson's presence as Commissioner being required exclusively within the geographical limits of the command of Lieut. General Sherman. Col. Merrill could thus be relieved from duty at those Head Quarters, provided there be no objection on the part of Lieut. General Sherman, and his services be applied elsewhere"—Copy, *ibid.*, RG 77, Letters and Reports.

1867, SEPT. 27.   To Secretary of the Treasury Hugh McCulloch. "I have the honor to inform you that, as requested in your letter of Sept. 11th, authority is hereby given to erect on the military *reservation at Ft. Wilkins*, a dwelling for the keeper of *Copper Harbor Range Lights*, the site to be designated by Genl Raynolds of the Corps of Engineers."—Df, DNA, RG 107, Letters Received from Bureaus; copy, *ibid.*, Letters Sent to the President. On Sept. 11, McCulloch had written to USG. "At the instance of the Light House Board, I have the honor to request, that permission be given the Board to erect upon the Military Reservation at Fort Wilkins, at such point outside of the enclosure of the garrison as may be selected by the Light House Engineer (Genl. W. F. Raynolds) of the District, a dwelling house for the accommodation of the Keeper of Copper Harbor range lights." —LS, *ibid.*, Letters Received from Bureaus.

1867, SEPT. 27.   To Secretary of State William H. Seward. "I have the honor to acknowledge the receipt of your com'n of the 25th inst. covering a translation of two letters addressed to the President and Secretary of State from Monsrs *Brame* French Engr of Bridges & Roads, transmitting a copy of his work on signals for double track railroads. I desire to offer through you to M. Brame my best thanks for his attention and to assure him it would afford me great pleasure to furnish him the information on American R. Rds. which he desires, but there is nothing of the kind which this Dept. can supply the construction of R. Rds. never having been under this Dept. and the management of them only indirectly during the war."—Df, DNA, RG 107, Letters Received from Bureaus; copy, *ibid.*, Letters Sent to the President. On Sept. 25, Seward had written to USG transmitting the letters.—LS, *ibid.*, Letters Received from Bureaus.

1867, Sept. 27.   To Secretary of State William H. Seward. "I have the honor to send herewith a communication from *W. H. Winder*, of 21st Sept. respecting the return of his nephew to this country &c"—Df, DNA, RG 107, Letters Received, W355 1867; copy, *ibid.*, Letters Sent to the President. On Sept. 21, William H. Winder, New York City, had written to USG. "I beg leave to submit, most respectfully, to your consideration the case of Wm S. Winder, Son of the late Genl John H. Winder, Comr of Prisoners in the late Confederacy. Wm. S. Winder was asst. adjt to Gen: Winder, and upon the trial of Wirz and the arrest of Major R. B. Winder Commissary or Quarter master under Genl W. (subsequently released unconditionally) proceeded to Canada to wait until he should be exempt from military jurisdiction, & be subject only to civil Law—Supposing that, since your advent to the Department, this state of affairs might be presumed to exist and that civil Law had resumed its Supremacy, I submit to your consideration the request that you give to W. S. Winder the assurance that he shall not be molested by military power. Mr W. S. Winder was surrendered by Gen: Jos. E. Johnston, gave his parole received his protection, had it indorsed by the Provost marshalls of Raleigh N. C. and of Baltimore, Md. & proceeded openly about his business until the above mentioned trial and arrest—In regard to the treatment of prisoner's, I can assert, with that certainty which a full knowledge of Genl. Winder's character can give, that his purpose towards the prisoners was immaculate; that he was incapable of cruelty towards any one, and most conscientious in the discharge of any duty committed to his charge: that his distress at his defective resources, adequately to provide for the comfort of prisoners, was hardly less a cause of distress to him, than were the unavoidable hardships to the prisoners: So much was this so, that to be relieved from this harrowing condition, with consent of the Richmond authorities, he gave permission to the prisoners to select themselves, from their number a Committee to proceed to Washington to represent the hardships of the prisoners, and the inability of the commander to provide adequately for their comfort; he also urged the paroling of the sick with or without equivalent; and then the paroling of all prisoners, with or without an equivalent, & he sent an aid de camp to Richmond with a written communication to urge this Course as his utmost efforts could not properly provide for the prisoners: Genl. Winder's death, in fact, may be attributed to his anxiety & over exertion to provide for and protect the prisoners, for he had gone to Rome, in person to investigate complaints of prisoners when he fell dead soon after his arrival. I think I may, Safely, assert that all candid men who knew well Gen: Winder, and I may include yourself if you should so have known him, would disbelieve any story representing him as inflicting wanton suffering on anyone A full & fair exposition of all the facts & circumstances, could not fail to secure for Gen. Winder the verdict that the integrity of his intentions was unpimpeachable, & that his exertions to provide properly for the prisoners were eminent, & earnest & unremitting. I have no doubt that Wm S. Winder seconded to the best of his ability his Fathers action in this matters May I ask of you the favor to enclose to me (at the New York Hotel) an assurance for Mr W. S. Winder that he shall not be molested by military authority."—ALS, *ibid.*, Letters Received, W355 1867. See *PUSG*, 15, 633–34.

1867, SEPT. 27.   USG note. "Detail Capt. Atchison, now at Detroit, aid to Gen. Emory."—AN (initialed), DNA, RG 94, Letters Received, 542A 1867. On Dec. 21, 1866, Bvt. Maj. Charles B. Atchison, Detroit, had written to U.S. Representative Elihu B. Washburne. "I have just recd a letter from Genl Ord saying he had applied to Washington for me as his Inspt General, also asking me to write you to have the order issued immediately. You will oblige me by having the order issued as soon as possible assigning me to duty with General Ord as Inspector General of the Department of the Arkansas. Genl Ord had not recd your letter when he wrote, which was on the 8th Inst. Love to Mrs W—"—ALS, *ibid.*, 5A 1867. Washburne endorsed this letter. "Respectfully referred to Genl Grant. I hope the desired order will be made if not incompatible with the good of the service."—AES (undated), *ibid.* On Jan. 2, 1867, Maj. George K. Leet approved this request.—AES, *ibid.* See *PUSG*, 16, 246–53, 298–99.

On June 12, Bvt. Maj. Gen. Edward O. C. Ord, Vicksburg, wrote to Leet. "I have the honor to enclose applications of Bvt. Maj. C. B. Atchison for Brevet appointment approved for Lieut. Colonel; at the same time and for similar reasons I have to apply for the same Brevet Commissions to be conferred on Bvt. Major J. G. Crane, 1st Lieut. Hugh G. Brown, 36th Infantry Bvt Lieut. Col Vols. Lieut. Placidus Ord, 1st Infantry, Bvt. Col. Vols and Major O. D. Greene, A. A. Genl. I believe they all held appointments by Brvt. or otherwise, to those grades during the war, and are all brave, efficient officers and that they distinguished themselves in various Campaigns—I also recommend 1st Lieut. John Tyler, 43d Inft. Bvt. Major Vols. to be brevetted as Major in the Regular Army; he lost his arm after serving in several campaigns and is a first rate officer—"—LS, DNA, RG 94, ACP, O213 CB 1867. On Oct. 28, USG approved this request.—Copy, *ibid.*, RG 108, Register of Letters Received. On April 1, 1868, Leet wrote to Atchison. "You will proceed without delay to the Headquarters Dept. of Dakota, St. Paul, Minn. for the transaction of the business verbally communicated to you, upon the completion of which you will rejoin your proper station."—Copies, DLC-USG, V, 47, 60; DNA, RG 108, Letters Sent. On

June 10, Bvt. Maj. Gen. John Pope, Detroit, telegraphed to USG. "If the services of Col C. B Atchison just relieved from General Emory's staff, are not needed elsewhere. I will be glad to have him ordered here for temporary service, to travel about in collecting the information called for every day by the Adjutant General's Department,"—Telegram received (at 12:40 P.M.), *ibid.*, RG 107, Telegrams Collected (Bound); *ibid.*, RG 108, Telegrams Received; copy, DLC-USG, V, 55.

1867, Sept. 27. Mrs. Gen. Martin Burke, Brooklyn, to USG. "I have the honor to address few lines, to request, the favor if it be possible to grant such an 'order', alluded to, in the tenor of the enclosed Letter, which I have taken the liberty to send for your perusal. where you will learn why? the cause of the request.—Bowed down with grief! I can but make my wish known, with as few words, as possible—I will be thankful for the return of the sad Letter.!! which I refer to for *Dates*! Col. O'Connell, is the *Third* Son! of a Patriotic Family, who has lost their sons, in the service of their Country. The two former Brothers, were killd in Battle which is on record in your Dept at Washington. Mrs O'Connell, *My Daughter* Lost her only Brother, at the storming of Vicksburg—who was a young naval officer, with Admiral Porter's squadron   The Little Orphan Boy! of Four years, mentioned in the Letter, seems to have attached his lone heart to Mr Van Horne and He, in return, gives him the carresses of a Parent—and is desirous to bring his little charge to my arms, if permitted to leave his Post, for ten day, or as long as the voyage, may require. After you have been pleased to give the appeal your reflection, I will be great ful to have a line sent me, that I may know your pleasure in the Case."—ALS, DNA, RG 108, Letters Received. Burke enclosed a letter to her of Sept. 19 from Lucy A. Gregory, Houston. "It becomes my painful duty as a friend of your daughter, Mrs. OConnell, to inform you of the death of Mrs. OConnell, also her husband. They both died of yellow fever. . . . The morning Mrs. OConnell was taken sick she had a Mrs. Delaney, (who had been sewing for her,) take Johnnie to her house, fearing his noise would disturb her. Johnnie was taken down with the fever there but he is now out of danger. The lady is very anxious to keep him until you are heard from, so Lieut. Van Horne, who is now in command, has left him there. Johnnie is much attached to Lieut. Van Horne, and if you could get an order for him to bring Johnnie to you, he would be the best one to take him. . . ."—Copy (ellipses in original), *ibid.* On March 2, 1868, Burke wrote to USG. "I have the honor to address few lines to you this date? Having rec.d instructions from Lt. Genl Sherman to address few lines to the Adj.t General, in regard to the transportation to St. Louis Mo. of the 'Remains'! of the late Col. O'Connell, of the 17th Inf.ty and his Wife's! from Houston, (Texas) where they are in cased in Metalic Coffins in a Vault waiting transportation. I did write, and give the needful address to be placed upon their Coffins and to whom sent to in St. Louis, and forwarded the letter to the Adj.t General without a name, not knowing who had replaced Genl Thomas. Not rec.g no reply! I am fearful my Letter, has been mislaid—and as the season is near past for such duties to the Dead! I again write, to urge the attention, in their behalf. I would dear General be greatful, to recv the late Col.'s (with his wife's) trunks and effects, sent to my address to New York. It being out of my power just now to leave my sick family, to attend those of the Dead. Least my Letter was lost? I will again send directions. And make my appeal direct to 'Fountain Head', where I will be sure of the needful attention, without further delay."—ALS, *ibid.*, RG 94, Letters Received, W37 1868.

1867, SEPT. 27.　John A. Dix, U.S. minister, Paris, to USG. "At the request of the Minister of War, I transmit to you herewith—care of the Department of State—a roll of charts. Will you please cause the receipt, which accompanies the roll, to be Signed by the proper person and return it to His Excellency Marshal Niel, Minister of War?"—LS, DNA, RG 107, Letters Received, D223 1867.

1867, SEPT. 27.　John Jolliffe, Washington, D. C., to USG. "I have the honor to reply to some remarks you made to me in a recent conversation, respecting claims of loyal citizens of States lately in rebellion. I do so in writing, because you can then more carefully examine my remarks, and on my part I can be more accurate. I am the representative of several claimant[s.] Some of the claims are for money taken and deposited to the credit of the United States; others for property taken by Quarter Masters and Commissaries for the United States; and actually used to aid in putting down the rebellion,—duly receipted and properly accounted for by the same officers who took it; others for the rent of buildings for government purposes duly receipted for; others for cotton seized and the proceeds of sales paid over to the Quarter Masters; and others for property *sequestered* by Major General Butler under pledge of prompt restoration upon proof of loyalty. Some of these claims originated in places where the General had issued orders (in the case of Genl. Butler a proclamation.) for the protection of the private property of loyal and neutral persons. Some of these claimants were driven from their homes because of their loyalty and found refuge in the service of the United States as soldiers; others were despoiled of nearly all their property by rebels, and after *they* had left, the United States forces took the residue for public use; others are aliens whose property was plundered by the rebels, and other property taken from them by the United States & payment delayed in violation of solemn pledges both of treaties and of the Constitution of the United States, that they should at all times receive full protection from the government, for person and property. In the conversation to which I have alluded I understood you to say that you considered Mr. Stanton as still Secretary of War. First. If Mr Stanton is Secretary of War, then you are not Secretary of War; as there cannot be two Secretaries of War at the same time. Second. You are Secretary of War *de jure et de facto.* The second section of 'An Act regulating the tenure of certain civil officers' provides 'that, when any officer appointed as aforesaid, excepting judges of the United States Courts shall during a recess of the Senate be shown by evidence *satisfactory* to the *President* to be guilty of misconduct in office, or crime, *or for any reason shall become incapable, or legally disqualified* to perform its duties, in such case and in no other, the President may suspend such officer' &c. This Act makes the President the *exclusive judge* of the nature, kind and degree of evidence that shall *satisfy* him. It may be the evidence of his own senses; ~~the~~ in conversations with the officer; or it may be evidence obtained from the statements of others. When the President *is satisfied* he can act. The Senate may or may not be satisfied from the same evidence. That is a matter for *their* consideration. The inquiry here is only, had the President the power by law to remove.? The expediency of using it is a different question. The President declared he was '*satisfied*' and removed Mr Stanton and appointed you. Therefore, you are Secretary of War, *de jure* by the very words of the Act. Third. But if I am mistaken in this, still it remains that you are Secretary of War *de facto*;—appointed by the President;—in the office,—and discharging its duties. Now if your appointment was made without authority of law, still while you hold the office you can at least have no GREATER power in discharging its duties than you would have, if your appointment had been in all respects regular, and you had been duly confirmed by the Senate. The Secretary of War has no power to discharge *part* of the business of the office and to refuse to discharge the other business thereof. He has no power to pay the officers and clerks in the office and to refuse to pay the officers and soldiers in the field. If he accepts the office he accepts *all* its burdens and duties. But General, you accepted the office of Secretary of War, because you believed it your *duty* so to do; and now you will be controlled only by your *duty*, without fear, favor, or affection. The only inquiry will be what *duty* have you to discharge in the matter in hand according to the Constitution and laws of the United States.? What then are your legal duties in these cases? . . . If you have the right to suspend the payment of any debt for a day, you have the right by the same principle to suspend its payment for a month or a year. Can you do so? If so, the Secretary of the Treasury can do so too. . . . I have thus shown. *First.* That private property taken for public use must be paid for, unless indeed a principle of the Constitution of priceless value, shall be overthrown by influences as malignant and satanic as would pluck the brightest star from Heaven. *Second.* That it is your duty to 'take care' that the laws are *faithfully* executed and the faithful execution of the law necessarily requires that the just claims of loyal citizens and neutral aliens shall be paid. No man who knows you can doubt but that you will discharge these duties with an integrity which never flinched and cannot fail. I have therefore the honor to request your action upon the several claims named in the schedule annexed and that you will order them to be paid."—ALS, DNA, RG 107, Letters Received, J195 1867. The enclosure is *ibid.*

1867, SEPT. 28.   Judge Advocate Gen. Joseph Holt to USG. "This claim, amounting to $1814, for rent for the use and occupation by the Subsistence Department, from 10th Jany '63 to 17th July '65, of a brick house in Murfreesboro', Tenn., owned by *Thomas A. Elliott*, has been rejected by the Quartermaster's Department, . . ."—Copy, DNA, RG 153, Letters Sent.

1867, SEPT. 30.   To Attorney Gen. Henry Stanbery. "I have the honor to inclose, herewith, certain papers pertaining to the case of the steamer 'Leviathan,' from which it will be seen that on the 10th of January last the District Court of the United States, for the District of Louisiana, awarded salvage to the transport 'Crescent' and the naval vessel 'De Soto' to the amount of Seven thousand five hundred dollars ($7.500 00/100) to each; with Proctor's fees and other costs making a judgment of Sixteen thousand seven hundred and fifty dollars ($16.750 00/[100])   These papers are respectfully referred to you with the request that you will instruct the United States District Attorney for the District of Louisiana to institute the proper proceeding for the appeal of the case to the Supreme Court, if, in your judgment, such appeal ought to be made and it be not too late. Should the instructions requested issue from your office, I have further to ask that you will direct the District Attorney to prosecute, the appeal when taken, and to report his action to this Department."—Copies, DNA, RG 107, Letters Received, K92; *ibid.*, Letters Sent to the President.

On Sept. 3, Judge Advocate Gen. Joseph Holt had written to USG. "Respectfully returned to the Secretary of War. The question understood to be herein referred to this Bureau is that of the payment to Mr. C. S. Kellogg, Attorney &c., of the sum of $750, awarded to him by the U. S District Judge at New Orleans as a proctor's fee in the case of the steamer Leviathan. Mr Kellogg represented, in this case, the officers and crew of the U. S. chartered transport 'Cresent' who, in conjunction with those of the U. S. naval vessel 'DeSoto,' libelled the Leviathan for salvage—the two former vessels having recaptured the latter from the rebels in September 1863. The final decree of the District Court in the case is dated on January 10th last. It awarded salvage to the two sets of captors—$7500. to each, fees of $750. to the proctor of each, and other costs to the amount of $250, —making in all a judgment of $16.750. The facts in the case were reported in full from the QuartermasterGeneral's Dept., (to which the Leviathan belonged,) to the Secretary of War on May 11. 1867; and in this report the Q. M. General raises the question 'whether salvage should be paid by the United States to the officers and crews of U. S. vessels for rescuing a vessel belonging to the government;' and he concludes by referring the matter to the Hon Secretary for further instructions. Upon this report it does not appear that any action has been taken. This Bureau indeed would be inclined to hold that salvage was not payable under the circumstances; and if the case had been originally referred to it, would probably have advised that the judgment of the District Judge be appealed from. The law question involved, however, is one for the consideration of the Attorney General rather than of this office, and a reference of the case to that officer, if such reference has not already been made, would be recommended. In regard to the claim of Mr. Kellogg, it can only be said that if it should be determined to acquiesce in the judgment of the District Court, his fee as proctor, having been judicially awarded, might probably well be deemed a reasonable one under the circumstances and therefore proper to be paid. If, on the other hand, it should be decided to appeal from said judgment the disposition of the claim of Mr. Kellogg would of course have to await the final issue of such proceeding."—Copy, *ibid.*, RG 153, Letters Sent. On Oct. 4, C. S. Kellogg, New Orleans, wrote to USG. "Permit me to call your attention to my fee in the case of the U S vs the Str Leviathan on the Intervention of E. Herrick et al Salvers. The case was tried in the U S District Court for this district last spring, and a decree rendered awarding salvage to the salvers and a fee to me of $750.00. The Leviathan was captured from our Navy or rather Q M Department by the Rebels but recaptured from them by Capt Walker (now deceased) in command of the 'Desoto' and E Harrick in command of the 'Crescent' The Leviathan at the time of capture was in the Q M Department to which she belonged and after her re capture was turned over to the same department. I wrote the Hon Stephen J. W Tabor 4th Auditor Treasury Department for my fee. That officer refered me to the Hon Secty of the Navy. I wrote him May 20th 1867. That officer refered me to the Hon Secty of War to whom I wrote June 8. and July 19. 1867. In each letter I inclosed the letter to me from each Department. Copies of the final decree awarding salvage and my fee were sent last spring to the Hon Secty of the Navy and Treasury, and one to the Hon Secty of War. I have not rec'd my fee or any part thereof. As the services were rendered,—the salvage and fee decreed I respectfully submit that I ought to receive my fee. The salvers have not been paid for their gallant services, although the law is clear on the point"—ALS, *ibid.*, RG 107, Letters Received, K141 1867. On Oct. 24, Stanbery wrote to USG. "I have had under consideration your letter of September 30th and the papers enclosed in it relating to the case of the *United States* against the steamer *Leviathan.* The facts appear to be as follows: The steamer *Leviathan,* a public vessel belonging to the Quarter-master's Department of the Army, was captured by a party of Rebels about the twentieth of September, 1863, while she was lying in the Mississippi River. The captors ran out to sea with her hoisting the Confederate flag. She was subsequently recaptured by the United States naval gunboat *De Soto* and the United States chartered armed transport *The Crescent*, and brought into the port of New Orleans for adjudication. I find that the decree of the District Court rendered on the tenth of January, 1867, restored the vessel to the Government, and awarded salvage to each of the recapturing vessels of $7500. You request me to instruct the United States District Attorney for the District of Louisiana 'to institute the proper proceedings for an appeal of the case to the Supreme Court, if, in [my] judgment, such appeal ought to be

made, and it be not too late.' First. The provision of the statute in reference
to appeals in prize causes from the District Court to the Supreme Court is
that the appeal 'shall be made within thirty days of the rendering of the
decree appealed from, unless the court shall previously have extended the
time, for cause shown in the particular case.' As the time for appeal has
long since elapsed and there is nothing in the papers showing an extension
of the time, it is now too late to take an appeal. Second. But upon the merits
of the case, I can see no ground for advising an appeal even if the time had
not elapsed. The question arises upon a doubt suggested by the Acting
Quarter-master General and the Judge-Advocate General, that salvage was
not properly allowable in this case, because the recapture was made by
public vessels of the United States of a public vessel which had been there-
tofore captured by the rebels. It has undoubtedly been held in the English
courts that salvage is not due to a national vessel for the service performed
in recapturing from the enemy another vessel employed in the public service; and this rests upon the ground that the performance of such a service
is in the direct line of duty of national vessels, and has been assimilated to
the service rendered by one ship of war to another in battle. But our legislation upon the subject of prize does not recognize this distinction. In all
cases of capture of vessels that belonged to the United States, the statutes
provide that they shall be restored to the United States, and that there shall
be paid from the Treasury of the United States, the salvage, costs and expenses, ordered by the court. At one time our statutes distinguished as to
the amount of salvage payable to the recaptors of a United States vessel,
giving one moiety as salvage in all cases where the recapture was made by
a private vessel of the United States, and one-fourth of the value when the
recapture was made by a public armed vessel of the United States. But this
distinction is now abolished, and all cases of recapture put upon the same
footing. With the views which I entertain in this case, I should have no
expectation, if an appeal were allowed, that the decree of the District Court
would be reversed, and in a late case the Supreme Court of the United
States admonished counsel that an appeal 'should never be prayed without
some expectation of reversal.' As at present advised, I do not feel authorized to direct this appeal. . . . The papers are herewith returned."—Copies
(brackets in original), *ibid.*, RG 60, Opinions; *ibid.*, RG 153, Opinions.
See *HED*, 40-3-32.

1867, SEPT. 30.   To Secretary of the Navy Gideon Welles. "Your letter
of the 22d August asking that $4000 be deposited with the Assistant
Treasurer at Washington; that being the appraised value of the prize
steamer Governor A. Morton, captured in May, 1862, has been received.
On enquiry it has been ascertained that the papers in the case were referred
for action to the Third Auditor, with whom they remained until called up
by the letter from the Navy Department of the 22d August. This Department is, however, now advised that the subject shall have proper attention
without delay"—LS, DNA, RG 45, Letters Received from the President.

On Aug. 22, Welles had written to USG. "You are respectfully requested to have the sum of $4000, deposited as early as practicable, with the Assistant Treasurer at Washington to the credit of the Judge of the U. S. District Court, District of Columbia, this amount being the appraised value of the prize steamer 'Governor A. Mouton,' which was captured in May 1862, in the Gulf of Mexico, by the U. S. Steamer 'Hatteras,' and turned over to the Quartermasters Department of the Army for the use of the Army. Please advise the Department of the deposit."—Copy, *ibid.*, Letters Sent to the President. On Aug. 26 and Oct. 9, Bvt. Maj. Gen. Daniel H. Rucker, act. q. m. gen., wrote to USG concerning this matter.—Copies (2) and LS (press), *ibid.*, RG 92, Reports to the Secretary of War.

1867, SEPT. 30, 11:10 A.M.   To Governor Arthur I. Boreman of West Va. "Dispatch rec'd, Troops ordered. Telegraph Gn. Thomas for instructions to them."—ALS (telegram sent), DNA, RG 107, Telegrams Collected (Bound); telegram sent, *ibid.*; copies, *ibid.*, RG 108, Telegrams Sent; DLC-USG, V, 56. On Sept. 29, Boreman had telegraphed and written to USG. "I am officially notified by the board of registration of barbour county that they are opposed by violence in the Execution of their duties by rebels and their sympathizers in numbers too formidable to be resisted by the civil authorities   It is important that the registration proceed otherwise the time limited for its completion will have expired & it not finished I do not hesitate to say that the presence of troops is necessary to enforce the law in Barbour County & that they should remain there until after the election on the (24th) twenty fourth of October. I disbanded all the armed forces of the state two 2 years ago at the request of the Sec'y of War, & cannot meet this emergency in proper time & I feel sure that any troops under command of General Thomas cannot be gotten here in time to be of any service   I think the presence of a small body of troops will be sufficient. I therefore request that you send to Phillippi the Court House of Barbour Co a company of troops to aid the civil authorities in the enforcement of the law   They can go by the Balto and Ohio Railroad to Webster within twelve 12 miles of Phillippi   They will be met by a state officer at Grafton I am just officially informed that the board of Registration of Tucker Co which adjoins Barbour has been compelled to decline to act on account of the same sort of opposition & threats of violence   Please answer"— Telegram received (at 4:10 P.M.), DNA, RG 107, Telegrams Collected (Bound); *ibid.*, RG 108, Telegrams Received; copy, DLC-USG, V, 55. "I have just sent you a telegram requesting that troops be sent into Barbour County to aid the civil authorities in enforcing the law. The telegram explains itself pretty fully. But the trouble is not confined to that County alone. In the adjoining County of Tucker the members of the Board of Registration have been threatened with the destruction of their property and the loss of their lives and have been treated with violence until they have declined to attempt to execute the duties of their office and it is now doubtful whether I can find men in the County who can be induced to accept the office at all. In Randolph another adjoining County the condition of things is about the same. This trouble and this violent opposition to the execution of the law is instigated in a great measure by the returned rebels and is participated in by some of them and by their sympathizers who remained on this side of the military lines during the war, but are about as bad as those who took up arms in rebellion. What we are to do with these rebels of both classes God only Knows—I see no hope of enforcing their obedience to the laws, but the most decided and active measures. Kindness and leniency are thrown away on them. Our State has treated them with the utmost magnanimity, except that we do not allow them to vote or to hold office when they have 'voluntarily' participated in or given aid to the rebellion   I write this in explanation of the state of affairs which compelled me to call for troops and if they are sent I will not detain them longer than is absolutely necessary—I think they can be relieved immediately after the election on the 24th of October."—LS, DNA, RG 108, Letters Received.

On Sept. 30, 10:20 A.M., USG telegraphed to Maj. Gen. George H. Thomas, Louisville. "At request of the Governor of West Virginia, one company twelfth Infantry will leave today for Phillippi, Barbour Co., when ~~they~~ it will await your orders. After the coming Election this company will be returned to Dept. of Washington"—Telegrams sent (2), *ibid.*, RG 107, Telegrams Collected (Bound); copies, *ibid.*, RG 108, Telegrams Sent; *ibid.*, RG 393, Dept. of the Cumberland, Telegrams Received; DLC-USG, V, 56. On the same day, Thomas telegraphed to USG. "Your telegram of this date received,   The necessary instructions will be given"—Telegrams received (2—at 4:40 P.M.), DNA, RG 107, Telegrams Collected (Bound); copies, *ibid.*, RG 393, Dept. of the Cumberland, Telegrams Sent; DLC-USG, V, 55. Also on Sept. 30, Bvt. Maj. Gen. William H. Emory, Washington, D. C., was ordered to send one company of the 12th Inf. to Phillippi, West Va.—Copies, *ibid.*, 47, 60; DNA, RG 108, Letters Sent.

On Nov. 6, 1:00 P.M., USG telegraphed to Thomas. "Order to Washington the Comp.y 12th Inf.y now in West. Va."—ALS (telegram sent), *ibid.*, RG 107, Telegrams Collected (Bound); telegram sent, *ibid.*; copies, *ibid.*, RG 108, Telegrams Sent; *ibid.*, RG 393, Dept. of the Cumberland, Telegrams Received; DLC-USG, V, 56. On the same day, Thomas telegraphed to USG. "Orders were issued several days since for the Company of the twelfth Infantry in West Virginia to leave on the tenth (10th) instant. The counting of the Votes cast at the late Election will not be completed much earlier than that"—Telegram received (on Nov. 7, 9:30 A.M.), DNA, RG 107, Telegrams Collected (Bound); *ibid.*, RG 108, Telegrams Received; copies, *ibid.*, RG 393, Dept. of the Cumberland, Telegrams Sent; DLC-USG, V, 55.

1867, SEPT. 30. President Andrew Johnson to USG. "Please appoint D. G. Fenno, Late 1st Lt & Adjt., 62d U. S. C. I., now at Brownsville,

Texas, 2d Lt. of Infy, if there is such a vacancy and the recommendations on file justify belief in the applicant's capacity."—LS, DNA, RG 94, ACP, F95 CB 1868. Darwin G. Fenno was appointed 2nd lt., 17th Inf., as of Sept. 30.

1867, SEPT. Mrs. C. Arthur, Marine Hospital, Vicksburg, to USG. "I appeal to yoᵧu for Justice I enterd service June 61 as a field Nurse assistant surgeon for Dressing wonds fitting up Hospitals on the Lines as the army advance allways keeping sanatary stores an hospital supplies in Ready for any amergency I commence survice at mound citty Hospital from there to the St Charles Hotell in Cairo takeing care of Gen Lawman an his wonded officers after the Battle of Bell Mont. you may Remember the surcumstance of my contending against all the surgeons that Lieutenant Dehuse mite live with the ball in his Lunge you no dout Remember his spedy recovery after being place under my care as he was wone of the twenty seven you gave me transpotation for three weeks after to move them to St Louis Hospital from there on your Expadishion South at fort Henry fort Dolenson Shilow Corenth Iuka from Corenth on your Expadishion to vicksburg Natches New Oleans Mobeil vicksburg careing for the anderson ville prisners then on a Hospital Boat searveing fore years an wone month what I expended for the benafit of the soulgers of my own mony what I have paid for meals on boats when going up with the wonded after Battels an what I have lost by Rebels at Iuka an others places amounts to over seven thousand dollars since I enterd survice an have not Recieve wone dollar yet for my servises ether from private officers or from Goverment—Gen MC ferson ~~MC~~ Gen MC Charther an other have urge me Rapeatedly to take a permit for Cotton suffishunt to make up for my loses an Expenses I preferd waiting an let the goverment settle it all together—Surgeon More of the United States army Gen MC ferson gave me papers to get my pay my papers being taken at Iuka with my cloathing Mager Dickey tuck my papers to present them ~~present~~ for payment at Washington as he soon ecspected to be there he was pay master for the colord Reigment hear since too New Orleans no wone knows his whare abouts he has ben witten to Rapeatedly within the last year an a half by Gen Wood Gen Sheraden to his home in pensylvana an no answer I have ben urge Rapeatedly to write directly to you feeling confidant you wood do somthing amediately to Reilieve my presant sufferings I have to sons who serve over three years in the union army they boath had a hansom property prise orderd it all distroy leaveing them unable to help me I had [twenty acre] hear suffishant to support me but the hye water this spring swept it all away left me sick an destitute I may have some papers or be able to firnish proof to convince you of my writes praying to hear from at wonce I close I can only hold a pen in my hand under a strong influence Morphene"—ALS, DNA, RG 108, Letters Received. On Sept. 28, Bvt. Col. John Moore, surgeon, New York City, endorsed this letter. "Respectfully returned to Surgeon Generals Office. I regret that my personal knowledge of the details of

Mrs. Arthurs services is not sufficiently exact, to assist much in establishing her claims against the Government. When I saw her, as I did often at Vicksburg and other places, she seemed to be acting under the supervision of some branch of the Sanitary Commission, and came and went without reference to the wishes of the Medical Staff.—Mrs Bickerdite was a woman, who will be long and gratefully remembered by the officers and men of the Western Armies for her intelligent and efficient service in the Hospitals; but she never acknowledged herself as regularly employed. Mrs Arthur, I have always understood, was working in the same way, though it is no disparagement to say, that she was not by any means as efficient as Mrs Bickerdite. I have not heard that Mrs Bickerdite has put in any claim for her services. But she deserves a monument."—ES, *ibid.*

Index

All letters written by USG of which the text was available for use in this volume are indexed under the names of the recipients. The dates of these letters are included in the index as an indication of the existence of text. Abbreviations used in the index are explained on pp. xvi–xx. Individual regts. are indexed under the names of the states in which they originated.